THE MOST
TRUSTED NAME
IN **TRAVEL**

Frommer's®

COSTA RICA 2018

11th Edition

by Nicholas Gill

FrommerMedia LLC

Published by
Frommer Media LLC

I ISBN 978-1-62887-338-2 (paper), 978-1-62887-339-9 (e-book)

Editorial Director: Pauline Frommer
Editor: Elizabeth Heath
Production Editor: Kelly Dobbs Henthorne
Cover Designer: Dave Ready
Cartographer: Roberta Stockwell
Photo Editor: Meghan Lamb
For information on our other products or services, see www.frommers.com.

Frommer Media LLC also publishes its books in a variety of electronic formats. Some content that appears in print may not be available in electronic formats.

Manufactured in China

5 4 3 2 1

FROMMER'S STAR RATINGS SYSTEM

Every hotel, restaurant and attraction listed in this guide has been ranked for quality and value. Here's what the stars mean:

★ Recommended
★★ Highly Recommended
★★★ A must! Don't miss!

AN IMPORTANT NOTE

The world is a dynamic place. Hotels change ownership, restaurants hike their prices, museums alter their opening hours, and busses and trains change their routings. And all of this can occur in the several months after our authors have visited, inspected, and written about, these hotels, restaurants, museums and transportation services. Though we have made valiant efforts to keep all our information fresh and up-to-date, some few changes can inevitably occur in the periods before a revised edition of this guidebook is published. So please bear with us if a tiny number of the details in this book have changed. Please also note that we have no responsibility or liability for any inaccuracy or errors or omissions, or for inconvenience, loss, damage, or expenses suffered by anyone as a result of assertions in this guide.

CONTENTS

LIST OF MAPS

ABOUT THE AUTHOR

Writer and photographer **Nicholas Gill** is based in Lima, Peru, and Brooklyn, New York. He is the co-founder of the website *New Worlder*, and his work appears in publications such as the *New York Times, Wall Street Journal, Saveur, New York Magazine*, and *Roads & Kingdoms*.

THE BEST OF COSTA RICA

Costa Rica continues to be one of the hottest vacation and adventure-travel destinations in Latin America, and for good reason. The country is rich in natural wonders and abundant biodiversity. Costa Rica boasts a wealth of unsullied beaches for sunbathing and surfing, lush jungle rivers for rafting and kayaking, and spectacular cloud forests and rainforests with ample opportunities for bird-watching, wildlife viewing, and hiking. In addition to the emblematic eco- and adventure-tourism offerings, you will also find luxury resorts and golf courses, plush spas, and some spectacular boutique hotels and lodges. In this chapter, you'll find the very best of what this unique country has to offer.

COSTA RICA'S best AUTHENTIC EXPERIENCES

o **Taking a Night Tour in a Tropical Forest:** Most neotropical forest dwellers are nocturnal, so nighttime tours are offered at rainforest and cloud-forest destinations throughout the country. Some of the better spots for night tours are **Monteverde** (p 376), **Tortuguero** (p 535), and **Drake Bay** (p 482).

ABOVE: **A spectacular view from Cerro Amigos in Monteverde**
PREVIOUS PAGE: **Surfers at sunset in Tamarindo**

o **Soaking in a Volcanic Hot Spring:** Costa Rica's volcanoes have blessed the country with a host of natural hot springs. From the opulent grandeur of **Tabacón Grand Spa Thermal Resort** (p 354) to the more humble options around **Rincón de la Vieja** (p 218) to the remote hot river pools at **Río Perdido** (p 226), mineral-rich, naturally heated waters are waiting to soothe what ails you.

A nesting sea turtle at Tortuguero National Park

o **Spotting a Resplendent Quetzal:** The iridescent colors and long, flowing tail feathers of this aptly named bird are breathtaking. This rare species can still be regularly sighted in the **Monteverde Cloud Forest Biological Reserve** (p 382) and the **San Gerardo de Dota** region (p 477).

o **Meeting Monkeys:** Costa Rica's rain and cloud forests are home to four species of New World monkeys—howler, capuchin, squirrel, and spider. Your odds of seeing one or more are very good if you visit **Monteverde** (p 376), **Tortuguero** (p 535), **Manuel Antonio** (p 434), or the **Osa Peninsula** (p 481).

o **Help a Hatchling Reach the Sea:** During various months throughout the year, multiple species of sea turtles arrive on beaches on both coasts of Costa Rica to lay their eggs. After hatching, the baby turtles face enormous odds in reaching the sea in places

Relaxing on the hammocks at Monteverde Lodge & Gardens

such as **Las Baulas National Marine** (p 113) and **Ostional National Wildlife Refuge** (p 334), though volunteers around the country help ensure that they do. See chapter 5, "The Best Special-Interest Trips."

o **Visit a Feria:** On Saturdays, a vast network of rural farmers markets comes alive in every part of Costa Rica. There's a brilliant display of colorful fruits and vegetables, local foods, and often live music. Some of the more interesting ferias occur in Puerto Viejo de Talamanca, Guapiles, and San Jose's Feria Verde de Aranjuez.

Climbing trees at Bosque del Cabo

o **Playing in a Pickup Football (Soccer) Game:** You'll find informal, friendly *fútbol* matches all across the country. You can head to **La Sabana Park** (p 136) and find one just about any weekend or afternoon. Or just jump into a game on the beach, with some simple sticks stuck in the sand as goal posts.

o **Touring a Coffee Plantation:** World-renowned and highly coveted, Costa Rican coffee can be enjoyed at the source all across the country. Peek inside the cup with a coffee tour—they're offered around the Central Valley, outside Monteverde, and elsewhere. See chapters 7 and 10.

o **Eating at a Soda:** Costa Rica's traditional, ubiquitous, and relatively cheap *sodas* are simple, family-run restaurants serving local standards. You'll find them just about everywhere. Order *gallo pinto* (rice and beans) for breakfast and try the *casado* (a mixed plate with your choice of meat) or a *gallo* (the Costa Rican version of a taco) for lunch or dinner.

COSTA RICA'S best PLACES TO SEE WILDLIFE

o **Santa Rosa National Park** (northwest of Liberia, in Guanacaste): One of the largest and last remaining stands of tropical dry forest in Costa Rica, Santa Rosa National Park is a great place for all sorts of wildlife viewing, from more than 100 species of bats to three types of monkeys. The sparse foliage, especially during the dry season, makes observation that much easier. See p 228.

○ **Monteverde Cloud Forest Biological Reserve** (in the mountains northwest of San José): There's something both eerie and majestic about walking around in the early-morning mist to the sound of birds calling and lizards skittering through the leaves, completely surrounded by towering trees heavy with bromeliads, orchids, moss, and vines. The reserve has a well-maintained network of trails, and the community is deeply involved in conservation. See p 382.

○ **The Río Sarapiquí Region** (in the country's north center): Protected tropical forests climb from the Caribbean coastal lowlands up into the central mountains, affording you a glimpse of a plethora of life zones and ecosystems. **Braulio Carrillo National Park** borders several private reserves, and here you'll find a variety of ecolodges to suit any budget. See "Puerto Viejo de Sarapiquí" (p 399) in chapter 10.

○ **Manuel Antonio National Park** (on the central Pacific Coast): Here's a spectacular spot for monkeying around. The stunning park is the best place in the country to see a variety of animals, especially monkeys, including the rare squirrel monkey. Keep your backpack snacks away from the nosy white-faced capuchins, who've been known to help themselves to treats. See "Manuel Antonio National Park" (p 434) in chapter 11.

○ **Osa Peninsula** (in southern Costa Rica): This is Costa Rica's most remote and biologically rich region. **Corcovado National Park,** the largest remaining patch of virgin lowland tropical rainforest in Central America, takes up much of the Osa Peninsula. Jaguars, crocodiles, tapirs, and scarlet macaws all call this place home. See chapter 12.

○ **Tortuguero** (on the north Caribbean coast): Tortuguero has been called Costa Rica's Venice because it's laced with canals and transportation is by boat, but you'll feel more like you're floating down the wild, brown Amazon here. Exploring these narrow canals, you'll see a wide variety of aquatic birds, as well as caimans, sloths, and up to three types of monkeys. If you come between June and October, you could be treated to the awe-inspiring spectacle of a green turtle laying her eggs— the beaches here are the largest nesting site in the Western Hemisphere for these endangered giants. See "Exploring the National Park" (p 540) in chapter 13.

Freshly roasted coffee beans at Finca Rosa Blanca

COSTA RICA'S best ECOLODGES & WILDERNESS RESORTS

Ecolodge options in Costa Rica range from tent camps with communal dining and no electricity or hot water to some of the most luxurious accommodations in the country.

- **Arenal Observatory Lodge** (near La Fortuna): Originally a research facility, this lodge now features exquisite gardens and comfortable rooms with impressive views of Arenal Volcano. Excellent trails lead to waterfalls and postcard-pretty vistas, with a great hike to the summit of the dormant Cerro Chato volcano. Toucans frequent the trees near the lodge, raccoon-like coatis roam the grounds, and howler monkeys provide the wake-up calls. See p 361.

- **Hidden Canopy Treehouses** (Monteverde): The individual cabins are on high stilts and nestled into the surrounding cloud-forest canopy. All abound in brightly varnished local hardwoods. The refined yet convivial vibe is palpable in the afternoon over tea or cocktails, when guests enjoy the main lodge's sunset view. See p 391.

- **La Paloma Lodge** (Drake Bay): If your idea of the perfect nature lodge is one where your front porch provides prime-time viewing of flora and fauna, this place is for you. When you've logged enough porch time and are ready to venture out, the Osa Peninsula's lowland rainforests are just outside your door. See p 494.

- **Bosque del Cabo Rainforest Lodge** (Osa Peninsula): Large, unique, and cozy private cabins perched on the edge of a cliff overlooking the Pacific Ocean and surrounded by lush rainforest—this is a spectacular place. See p 508.

- **Lapa Ríos** (Osa Peninsula): This was one of Costa Rica's first luxury ecolodges to gain international acclaim, and it remains one of the best. The attention to detail, personalized service, and in-house tour guides are all top-notch. See p 509.

- **Playa Nicuesa Rainforest Lodge** (Golfo Dulce): Accessible only by boat, this lodge is among the best options on the Golfo Dulce. Set in deep forest, it has individual bungalows

Enjoying a massage at Lapa Rios

with a perfect blend of rusticity and luxury. The guides, service, and surrounding wildlife are all superb. See p 519.

o **Tortuga Lodge** (Tortuguero): This lodge features a beautiful riverfront restaurant and swimming pool. The canals of Tortuguero snake through its maze of lowland primary rainforest. The beaches here are major sea-turtle nesting sites. See p 545.

o **Selva Bananito Lodge** (in the Talamanca Mountains south of Limón): Providing direct access to the southern Caribbean lowland rainforest, this authentic ecolodge combines nature with adventure. You can hike along a riverbed, ride horses through the rainforest, climb 30m (100 ft.) up a ceiba tree, or rappel down a jungle waterfall here. See p 554.

COSTA RICA'S best HOTELS

o **Hotel Grano de Oro** (San José): San José boasts dozens of colonial-era mansions that have been converted into hotels, but few do it like Grano de Oro, with its luxurious accommodations and professional service. All the guest rooms have attractive hardwood furniture, including antique armoires in some rooms. When it's time to relax, you can soak in a hot tub or have a drink in the rooftop lounge while taking in a commanding view of San José. See p 142.

o **Finca Rosa Blanca Coffee Plantation Resort** (Heredia): If the cookie-cutter rooms of international resorts leave you cold, perhaps this unusual inn will be more your style. Square corners seem to have been prohibited here in favor of turrets and curving walls of glass, arched windows, and semicircular built-in couches. It's set into a lush hillside and surrounding organic coffee farm, just 20 minutes from San José. See p 190.

o **Hotel Capitán Suizo** (Tamarindo): With a perfect beachfront setting, spacious rooms, lush gardens and grounds, and a wonderful pool, this is arguably the best option in Tamarindo. See p 275.

The pool set in the lush gardens at Hotel Capitán Suizo in Tamarindo

Florblanca Resort on Playa Santa Teresa

- **Florblanca Resort** (Playa Santa Teresa): The individual luxury villas at this intimate resort feature massive living rooms and private balconies. The service, spa, and food are all outstanding, and the resort is spread over a lushly planted hillside, steps away from Playa Santa Teresa. See p 315.

- **Kura Design Villas** (Uvita): You can watch a migration of humpback whales from the infinity pool of this eco-chic, adults only resort high on a hillside overlooking Marino Ballena National Park. Each of the six minimalist villas features a glass, double rain shower with views of the rainforest canopy. See p 467.

- **Hotel Belmar** (Monteverde): This family-run lodge comes equipped with its own microbrewery, organic farm, and expansive, flower filled grounds. It's one of the oldest hotels in the Monteverde area, yet continual improvements have kept it at the top. See p 392.

- **Arenas del Mar** (Manuel Antonio): The whole resort is surrounded by old-growth rainforest on a hilly piece of land

Bird-watching at Arenas del Mar

abutting two pretty beaches. Try to snag one of the rooms featuring a wrap-around balcony equipped with a sunken hot tub, then marvel at the panoramic coastal view while you soak. Arenas del Mar has a beautiful little spa and the best beach access in Manuel Antonio. See p 446.

o **Harmony Hotel** (Nosara): Founded by a tech entrepreneur who wanted his own piece of paradise, Harmony is Instagram-ready with its mix of kitsch and modern amenities. The low slung rooms and bungalows are hidden within a maze of tropical flowers and tall palm trees, while the wellness program includes everything from yoga and meditation to a juice bar and sushi menu. See p 336.

o **Cariblue Bungalows** (Playa Cocles): Try to book one of the private wooden bungalows here. If you do, you might be so happy and comfortable that you won't want to leave. This small Caribbean-coast resort is surrounded by tall rainforest trees, and just 90m (300 ft.) away are the warm waves of the Caribbean Sea. See p 587.

COSTA RICA'S best RESTAURANTS

o **Maza Bistro** (San José): The country's best breakfast and brunch takes place beside a hostel next to the capital's Parque Nacional. Inside the airy patio you can sip on Bloody Marys with candied bacon while munching on sweet arepas and fried chicken. See p 147.

o **Al Mercat** (San José): After graduating from Le Cordon Bleu in Paris and working for years in France, Chef José Gonzalez returned home to help bring the Costa Rican kitchen into the modern era. He has worked tirelessly to rediscover long lost native ingredients and regional cooking styles, which he reimagines on refined yet casual plates in his Barrio Escalante restaurant. See p 150.

o **Makoko** (Playa Panamá, near Papagayo): The menu of this eclectic restaurant inside the Mangroove Hotel was designed by Argentine chef Sebastian La Rocca, once the right-hand man of England's Jamie Oliver. His fresh take on Costa Rican ingredients makes for an eclectic, international menu where you'll find everything from poke to lamb chops in a miso-anticucho sauce. See p 243.

o **Ginger** (Playa Hermosa, Guanacaste): Serving an eclectic mix of traditional and pan-Asian–influenced tapas, this sophisticated joint is taking this part of Guanacaste by storm. A list of creative cocktails complements the inventive dishes. See p 242.

o **Papaya** (Brasilito): Housed in a simple, unassuming roadside hotel, this lively little restaurant serves fusion cuisine, using the region's

Papaya Restaurant in Brasilito

freshest fish and seafood and other local ingredients, influenced by Asian and Latin American styles. See p 257.

o **Pangas Beach Club** (Tamarindo): Executive chef Jean-Luc Taulere had a long, successful run in Playa Flamingo before moving to this relaxed, elegant restaurant. He combines his Catalan heritage with classical French training; fresh local ingredients; and a mix of local, fusion, and Asian influences. See p 280.

o **Lola's** (Playa Avellanas): With a perfect setting on the sand and excellent hearty fare, Lola's is among the best casual beachfront restaurants in the country. The ocean-loving namesake mascot—a pet pig—adds to the restaurant's quirky charm. See p 285.

o **Playa de los Artistas** (Montezuma): This place has the perfect blend of refined Mediterranean cuisine and beachside funkiness. There are only a few tables, so get here early. Fresh, grilled seafood is served in oversized ceramic bowls and on large wooden slabs lined with banana leaves. See p 311.

Pangas Beach Club, Tamarindo

- **Gingerbread** (Nuevo Arenal): This world fusion restaurant almost qualifies as dinner theater, and participation is encouraged. Chef Eyal is outspoken and outgoing, engaging diners in lively discussions on food, the arts, politics, and current events. Don't come here for a romantic meal in a quiet corner, but do come for some fun and fine dining. See p 375.

- **Graffiti Resto Café & Wine Bar** (Jacó): From the small sushi bar in one corner to the graffiti-painted walls, this place is full of surprises. Pan-Asian cuisine blended with the chef's Alabama roots and New Orleans training results in culinary wonders utilizing local ingredients and spices. See p 429.

- **Celajes** (Monteverde): Overlooking Monteverde's cloud forest not far from the reserve, this creative hotel restaurant sources ingredients from an on-site organic garden and the owner's family farm, which they use in one of Costa Rica's best cocktail lists, aside of their seasonal menus. See p 397.

- **La Pecora Nera** (Cocles, near Puerto Viejo): Surprisingly fine Italian cuisine in a tiny surfer town on the south Caribbean coast. Your best bet here is to allow yourself to be taken on a culinary roller-coaster ride with a mixed feast of the chef's nightly specials and suggestions. See p 590.

COSTA RICA'S best FAMILY DESTINATIONS

- **La Paz Waterfall Gardens** (near Poás Volcano National Park): This multifaceted attraction features paths and suspended walkways set alongside a series of impressive jungle waterfalls. Kids will love the hummingbird, wildcat, and reptile exhibits, and the impressive

Student with toucan at La Paz Waterfall Gardens & Peace Lodge

power of the waterfalls. See p 181.

Poás Volcano National Park in a quieter moment

o **Playa Hermosa:** The protected waters of this Pacific beach make it a family favorite. Just because its waters are calm, however, doesn't mean it's boring. I recommend staying at the beachfront **Bosque del Mar** (p 240) and checking in at **Aqua Sport** (p 236), where you can rent sea kayaks, sailboards, paddleboats, beach umbrellas, and bicycles.

o **Tamarindo:** This surf town has a bit of something for everyone. It's a great spot for kids to learn how to surf or boogie-board, and a host of tours and activities to please the entire family are available. **Hotel Capitán Suizo** (p 275) has an enviable location on a calm section of beach, plus spacious rooms and a great pool for kids and adults alike, with a long, sloping, shallow entrance. See "Playa Tamarindo & Playa Langosta," in chapter 8, p 268.

o **Arenal Volcano:** This adventure hot spot offers a nearly inexhaustible range of activities for all ages. From gentle safari floats to raging whitewater rafting, and from flat, easy hikes over hanging bridges to challenging scrambles over cooled lava flows, you're sure to find something that fits the interests and ability levels of every member of the family. See "Arenal Volcano & La Fortuna" in chapter 10.

o **Monteverde:** This area not only has the country's most famous cloud forest, but also offers a wide variety of attractions and

Playa Tamarindo

Playa Manuel Antonio

activities. After hiking through the reserve, you should be able to keep everyone happy and occupied riding horses; squirming at the serpentarium; or visiting the Monteverde Butterfly Garden, Frog Pond, Bat Jungle, or Orchid Garden. See "Monteverde" in chapter 10, p 376.

o **Jacó:** Jacó's streets are lined with souvenir shops, ice cream stands, and inexpensive eateries. Activity options range from surf lessons to a small-boat cruise among the crocodiles on the Tárcoles River. **Club del Mar** (p 426) is accommodating to families with small children. See "Exploring Jacó," in chapter 11, p 423.

o **Manuel Antonio:** This national park has a bit of everything: miles of idyllic white sand beaches, myriad wildlife (with almost guaranteed monkey sightings), and plenty of tour options. Of the many lodging choices, **Hotel Sí Como No** (p 450)—with its spacious tropical suites, two pools, waterslide, and nightly movies—is a good bet. See "Manuel Antonio National Park" in chapter 11.

COSTA RICA'S best BEACHES

With more than 1,200km (750 miles) of shoreline on its Pacific and Caribbean coasts, Costa Rica offers beachgoers a wealth of options.

o **Santa Rosa National Park:** You'll have to take a four-wheel-drive or hike 13km (8 miles) from the central ranger station to reach these remote beaches, but you'll probably have the place all to yourself. In fact, the only time it gets crowded is in October, when thousands of olive ridley sea turtles nest in one of their yearly *arribadas* (arrivals). See p 228.

o **Las Catalinas:** Take a stand-up paddle boarding lesson at the tranquil public beach in this quickly growing residential community nestled in rolling hills of tropical dry forest. Some of the best diving is near the tiny islets not far from shore where giant manta rays are

13

known to spread their wings. See p 263.

o **Playa Avellanas:** Just south of Tamarindo, this white-sand beach has long been a favorite haunt for surfers, locals, and those in the know. Playa Avellanas stretches for miles, backed by protected mangrove forests. See p 282.

o **Nosara:** Nosara and its beaches have a trendy, New Age vibe with plenty of yoga and juice bars much like Mex-

A surf class in Santa Teresa

ico's Tulum, but without all the crowds. At least for now. Surfers gravitate to Playa Guiones, fishermen head to Playa Garza, and shady Playa Pelada is best for sunsets. See chapter 9.

o **Playa Montezuma:** This tiny beach town at the southern tip of the Nicoya Peninsula retains a funky sense of individuality, with plenty of isolated spots to lay down your towel. It's a favorite of backpackers and fire dancers, but you can also find upscale beachfront lodging and fine dining. Nearby, you'll find two impressive waterfalls, one of them emptying into an oceanfront pool, the other surrounded by thick forest. Farther afield, you can explore the biologically rich **Cabo Blanco** and **Curú** wildlife preserves. See "Playa Montezuma" in chapter 9.

o **Malpaís & Santa Teresa:** With its scattered luxury lodges, surf camps, and assorted hotels and hostels, this is the place to come if you're looking for miles of deserted beaches and great surf. See "Malpaís & Santa Teresa" in chapter 9.

o **Manuel Antonio:** Manuel Antonio National Park was the first beach destination to become popular in Costa Rica, and its beaches are still idyllic. The hills approaching the park offer captivating views

Playa Montezuma

over thick primary rainforest to the Pacific Ocean. See "Manuel Antonio National Park" in chapter 11.

o **Punta Uva & Manzanillo:** These beaches deliver true Caribbean splendor, with turquoise waters, coral reefs, and palm-lined stretches of nearly deserted white-sand beach. Tall coconut palms line the shore, providing shady respite, and the water is usually quite calm and good for swimming. See "Playas Cocles, Chiquita, Manzanillo & South of Puerto Viejo" in chapter 13.

COSTA RICA'S best OUTDOOR ADVENTURES

o **Mountain Biking the Back Roads of Costa Rica:** The rustic back roads bemoaned by drivers are a huge boon for mountain bikers. The country has endless roads and trails to explore on two wheels. The area around La Fortuna and Lake Arenal, with its widely varied terrain, is a top destination. See p 353.

o **Rafting the Pacuare River** (near Turrialba): The best and most beautiful river for rafting in Costa Rica, the class III/IV Pacuare winds through primary and secondary forests, and features one especially breathtaking section that passes through a narrow, steep gorge. For a real treat, take the 2-day Pacuare River trip, which includes an overnight at a lodge or tent camp on the side of the river. See p 112 and 215.

o **Surfing & Four-Wheeling Guanacaste Province:** From Witch's Rock at Playa Naranjo near the Nicaraguan border to Playa Nosara, more than 100km (60 miles) away, you'll find scores of world-class surf spots. In addition to the two mentioned, try a session at Playa Grande, Punta Langosta, and playas Negra, Avellanas, and Junquillal. Or find your own secret spot. See chapter 8.

o **Trying the Adventure Sport of Canyoning:** While every canyoning tour is unique, it usually involves hiking along and through the rivers

Rafting the Pacuare River

and creeks of a steep mountain canyon, with periodic breaks to rappel down the face of a waterfall, jump off a rock into a jungle pool, or float down a small rapid. See chapters 8, 10, and 11.

A canyoning tour

o **Battling a Billfish off the Pacific Coast:** Billfish are plentiful all along Costa Rica's Pacific Coast, and boats operate from Playa del Coco down to the Golfo Dulce. The area is known for world-record catches of both blue marlin and Pacific sailfish. Go to Quepos (just outside Manuel Antonio) for the best après-fish scene, or head down the Osa Peninsula or Golfo Dulce if you want some isolation. See chapters 8, 9, 11, and 12.

o **Windsurfing or Kitesurfing on Lake Arenal:** With steady gale-force winds (at certain times of the year), the stunning northern end of Lake Arenal has become a major international windsurfing and kitesurfing hot spot. See chapter 10.

o **Diving at Isla del Caño** (Drake Bay): This uninhabited island is believed to have been used as a ceremonial burial site by the pre-Columbian residents of the area. Today, the underwater rocks and coral formations here provide arguably the best scuba diving and snorkeling opportunities in the country—aside from the far offshore Isla del Coco. See p 295.

o **Hiking Mount Chirripó** (near San Isidro de El General in the country's central southeast): Hiking to the top of the tallest peak in Costa Rica, Mount Chirripó's 3,724m (12,215-ft.) summit, takes you through a stunning variety of bioregions. Climbers ascend from lowland pastures through cloud forest to an eerie high-altitude *páramo,* a tundra-like landscape with stunted trees and morning frosts. See "San Isidro de El General: A Base for Exploring Chirripó National Park" in chapter 11.

COSTA RICA'S best DAY HIKES & NATURE WALKS

o **Lankester Gardens** (in Cartago, just southeast of San José): If you want a really pleasant but not overly challenging day hike, consider a walk among the hundreds of species of flora on display here. The trails meander from areas of well-tended open garden to shady natural forest, plus there's a highly regarded orchid collection. See p 200.

- **Rincón de la Vieja National Park:** Visit the geysers, mud pots, and fumaroles of "Costa Rica's Yellowstone," or hike down to the Blue Lake and Cangreja Falls, where you'll find a pristine turquoise pool fed by a rushing jungle waterfall. You can also hike up to two craters and a crater lake here, while the Las Pailas loop is ideal for those seeking a less strenuous hike. See p 218.

- **Arenal National Park:** This park has several excellent trails that visit a variety of ecosystems, including primary and secondary rainforest, savanna, and old lava flows. Most of them are on the relatively flat flanks of the volcano, so there's not too much climbing involved. See "Arenal Volcano & La Fortuna," in chapter 10.

- **Monteverde Cloud Forest Biological Reserve:** Take a guided tour in the morning to familiarize yourself with the cloud forest, and then spend the afternoon exploring the reserve on your own. Off the main thoroughfares, Monteverde reveals its rich mysteries with stunning regularity. Even without a guide, you should be able to enjoy sightings of a wide range of unique tropical flora and fauna, and maybe even spot a resplendent quetzal. See p 382.

- **La Selva Biological Station:** La Selva has an extensive and well-marked network of trails. You'll have to reserve in advance and take the guided tour if you aren't a guest at the lodge, but the hikes are led by informed naturalists, so you might not mind the company. See p 403.

- **Corcovado National Park:** The park has a well-designed network of trails, ranger stations, and camping facilities. Most of the lodges in Drake Bay and the Osa Peninsula offer day hikes into the park, but if you've come this far, you should hike in and camp at the Sirena ranger station. See "Puerto Jiménez: Gateway to Corcovado National Park" in chapter 12 (p 496).

- **Cahuita National Park:** Fronted by the Caribbean and an idyllic beach, the park has flat, well-maintained trails through thick lowland forest. They are parallel to the beach, so you can hike out on the trail and back along the beach, or vice versa. White-faced and howler monkeys are common, as are brightly colored land crabs. See p 557.

COSTA RICA'S best BIRD-WATCHING

- **Spotting Hundreds of Marsh & Stream Birds along the Río Tempisque Basin:** A chief breeding ground for gallinules, jacanas, and limpkins, this is a common habitat for many heron and kingfisher species. Options include visits to **Palo Verde National Park** (p 76), **El Viejo Wetlands** (p 256), and **Rancho Humo** (p 326).

o **Looking for 300-Plus Species of Birds in La Selva Biological Station:** With an excellent trail system through a variety of habitats, from dense primary rainforest to open pasturelands and cacao plantations, this is one of the finest places for bird-watching in Costa Rica. With such a variety of habitats, the number of species runs to well over 300. See p 403.

o **Sizing up a Jabiru Stork at Caño Negro National Wildlife Refuge:** Caño Negro Lake and the Río Frío that feeds it are incredibly rich in wildlife and are a major nesting and gathering site for aquatic birds. These massive birds are getting less common in Costa Rica, but this is still one of the best places to spot one. See p 354.

o **Catching a Scarlet Macaw in Flight over Carara National Park:** Macaws are noisy and colorful birds that spend their days in the park but choose to roost in the evenings near the coast. They arrive like clockwork every morning and then head for the coastal mangroves around dusk. These daily migrations give birders a great chance to see these magnificent birds in flight. See p 416.

o **Looking for a Resplendent Quetzal in the Cerro de la Muerte:** Serious bird-watchers won't want to leave Costa Rica without seeing one of these iridescent green wonders. See "Where to See Quetzals in the Wild: Cerro de la Muerte & San Gerardo de Dota" in chapter 11 (p 477).

o **Spotting Hundreds of Species at Wilson Botanical Gardens:** With more than 7,000 species of tropical plants and flowers, this research facility is fabulous for bird-watching. Hummingbirds and tanagers are plentiful, and more than 360 species of birds have been recorded here. See p 515.

o **Taking Advantage of the Caribbean's Best Birding at Aviarios Sloth Sanctuary of Costa Rica:** If it flies along this coast, chances are you'll spot it here; more than 330 species of birds have been seen so far. In the afternoon, large flocks of several heron species nest here. See p 560.

Resplendent quetzal at Mirador de Quetzales

COSTA RICA IN CONTEXT

P

ura vida! (Pure life!) is Costa Rica's unofficial national slogan, and in many ways it defines the country. You'll hear it exclaimed, proclaimed, and simply stated by Ticos from all walks of life, from children to octogenarians. It can be used as a cheer after your favorite soccer team scores a goal, or as a descriptive response when someone asks you, *"¿Cómo estás?"* ("How are you?"). It is symbolic of the easygoing nature of this country's people, politics, and personality.

Costa Rica itself is a mostly rural country with vast areas of protected tropical forests. It is one of the biologically richest places on earth, with a wealth of flora and fauna that attracts and captivates biologists, photographers, ecotourists, and casual visitors alike.

Often called the "Switzerland of Central America," Costa Rica is, and historically has been, a sea of tranquility in a region troubled by turmoil for centuries. For more than 100 years, it has enjoyed a stable democracy and a relatively high standard of living for Latin America. The literacy rate is high, as are medical standards and facilities. Perhaps most significant, at least for proud and peace-loving Costa Ricans, is that this country does not have an army.

COSTA RICA TODAY

Costa Rica has a population of a little more than 5 million people, more than half of whom live in the urban Central Valley. Some 94% of the population is of Spanish or other European descent, and it is not at all unusual to see fair-skinned and blond Costa Ricans. This is largely because the indigenous population that was here when the first Spaniards arrived was small and quickly reduced by war and disease. Some indigenous populations still remain, primarily on reserves around the country; the principal tribes include the Bribri, Cabécar, Boruca, and Guaymí. In addition, on the Caribbean coast there is a substantial population of English-speaking black Creoles who came in the late 19th and early 20th centuries from Jamaica and other Caribbean islands as railroad builders and banana workers. Racial tension isn't palpable, but it exists, perhaps more out of historical ignorance and fear rather than an organized or articulated prejudice.

Costa Ricans are a friendly and outgoing people. When interacting with visitors, Ticos are very open and helpful. But time has a relative meaning here, so don't expect punctuality as a rule.

PREVIOUS PAGE: **Locals in Liberia playing the marimba, a type of large wooden xylophone**

Banana plantation

In a region historically plagued by internal strife and civil wars, Costa Ricans are proud of their peaceful history, political stability, and relatively high level of development. However, this can also translate into arrogance and prejudice toward immigrants from neighboring countries, particularly Nicaraguans, who make up a large percentage of the workforce on many plantations.

Roman Catholicism is the official religion of Costa Rica, although freedom to practice any religion is guaranteed by the country's constitution. More than 70% of the population identifies itself as Roman Catholic, while another 14% are part of a number of evangelical Christian congregations. There is a small Jewish community as well. By and large, many Ticos are religiously observant, if not fervent, though it seems that just as many lead totally secular lives. *Pura vida.*

Costa Rica is the most politically stable nation in Central America, and it has the largest middle class. Even the smallest towns have electricity, the water is mostly safe to drink, and the phone system is relatively good. Still, the gap between rich and poor is wide, and there are glaring infrastructure needs. The roads, hospitals, and school systems have been in a slow but steady state of decay for decades, and improvements are slow in coming.

Here's a quiz. Costa Rica's largest source of foreign income is

1. Coffee
2. Microchips
3. Tourism
4. Bananas

Up until recently, the answer was microchips, thanks to a huge Intel manufacturing facility, though it moved to Asia in early 2014, eliminating 1,500 jobs. The long-term answer is tourism, which according to the Costa Rican Embassy in Washington is the largest source of income and hard currency, exceeding $2.8 billion a year. Costa Rica also makes good money exporting coffee, bananas, pineapples, and palm oil, but it takes in more money from the thousands of spendy tourists who fly into its airports every day.

It's estimated that more than half the working population is employed in the tourism and service industries. Ticos whose fathers and grandfathers were farmers and ranchers find themselves working as hotel owners, tour guides, and waiters. Although most have adapted gracefully and regard the industry as a source of new jobs and opportunities for economic advancement, restaurant and hotel staff can be lackadaisical at times, especially in rural areas. And, unfortunately, an increase in the number of visitors has led to an increase in crime, prostitution, and drug trafficking. Common sense and street savvy are required in San José and in many of the more popular tourist destinations.

The global economic crisis of 2008 hit Costa Rica hard. Tourism took a hit, especially in 2009 to 2010. But it has bounced back nicely. More importantly, perhaps, since credit has historically been so tight, there was never a major mortgage or banking crisis in the country. Today, Costa Rica continues to be a culturally and biologically rich Central American nation struggling to meet the economic and development needs of its population. It seems to be moving in the right direction, even though that movement is sometimes maddeningly slow.

THE MAKING OF COSTA RICA

Early History

Little is known of Costa Rica's history before its colonization by Spanish settlers. The pre-Columbian Indians who made their home in this region of Central America never developed the large cities or advanced culture that appeared farther north in what would become Guatemala, Belize, and Mexico. There are no grand pyramids or large Mayan cities. However, ancient artifacts indicating a strong sense of aesthetics have been unearthed from scattered excavations around the country. Ornate gold and jade jewelry, intricately carved grinding stones, and artistically painted terra-cotta objects point to a small but highly skilled indigenous population. If you love mysteries, Costa Rica's artistic history has an intriguing one. More than 300 polished stone orbs have been uncovered in various sites around the country, some believed to be thousands of years old. No one quite understands why they were made, but the numerous myths about their origins only make them more fascinating.

Spain Settles Costa Rica

In 1502, on his fourth and last voyage to the New World, Christopher Columbus anchored just offshore from present-day Limón. Whether he

Juan Santamaría Memorial Park in Alajuela

actually gave the country its name—"Rich Coast"—is open to debate, but the Spaniards never did find many riches to exploit here.

The earliest Spanish settlers found that, unlike settlements to the north, the native population of Costa Rica was unwilling to submit to slavery. Despite their small numbers, scattered villages, and tribal differences, they fought back against the Spanish until they were overcome by superior firepower and European diseases. When the fighting ended, the European settlers in Costa Rica found that very few Indians were left to force into servitude. The settlers were thus forced to till their own lands, a situation unheard of in other parts of Central America. Few pioneers headed this way because they could settle in Guatemala, with its large native workforce. Costa Rica was nearly forgotten, as the Spanish crown looked elsewhere for riches to plunder and souls to convert.

It didn't take long for Costa Rica's few Spanish settlers to head for the hills, where they found rich volcanic soil and a climate that was less oppressive than in the lowlands. **Cartago,** the colony's first capital, was founded in 1563, but it was not until the 1700s that additional cities were established in this agriculturally rich region. In the late 18th century, the first coffee plants were introduced, and because these plants thrived in the highlands, Costa Rica began to develop its first cash crop. Unfortunately, it was a long and difficult journey transporting the coffee to the Caribbean coast and then onward to Europe, where the demand for coffee was growing.

From Independence to the Present Day

In 1821, Spain granted independence to its colonies in Central America. Costa Rica joined with its neighbors to form the Central American Federation; but in 1838, it withdrew to form a new nation and pursue its own interests. By the mid-1800s, coffee was the country's main export. Free land was given to anyone willing to plant coffee on it, and plantation owners soon grew wealthy and powerful, creating Costa Rica's first elite class—with enough power to elect their own representatives to the presidency.

The stunning interior of Cartago's Basílica de Nuestra Señora de los Ángeles

This was a stormy period in Costa Rican history. In 1856, the country was invaded by mercenaries hired by **William Walker,** a soldier of fortune from Tennessee who was attempting to fulfill his grandiose dreams of presiding over a slave state in Central America (before his invasion of Costa Rica, he had invaded Nicaragua and Baja California). The people of Costa Rica, led by President Juan Rafael Mora, marched against Walker's men and chased them back to Nicaragua. Walker eventually surrendered to a U.S. warship in 1857, but, in 1860, he attacked Honduras, claiming to be the president of that country. The Hondurans, who had had enough of Walker's shenanigans, promptly executed him.

Until 1890, coffee growers had to transport their coffee either by oxcart to the Pacific port of Puntarenas or by boat down the Río Sarapiquí to the Caribbean. In the 1870s, a progressive president proposed a railway from San José to the Caribbean coast to facilitate the transport of coffee to European markets. It took nearly 20 years for this plan to reach

The Little Drummer Boy

Costa Rica's national hero is Juan Santamaría. The legend goes that young Juan enlisted as a drummer boy in the campaign against William Walker. On April 11, 1856, when Costa Rican troops had a band of Walker's men cornered in an inn in Rivas, Nicaragua, Santamaría volunteered for a suicidal mission to set the building on fire. Although he was mortally wounded, Santamaría was successful in torching the building and driving Walker's men out, and they were swiftly routed. April 11 is now a national holiday.

The Last Costa Rican Warrior

"Military victories, by themselves, are not worth much. It's what is built from them that matters."

—José "Pepe" Figueres

fruition, and more than 4,000 workers lost their lives constructing the railway, which passed through dense jungles and rugged mountains on its journey from the Central Valley to the coast.

Partway through the project, as funds were dwindling, the second chief engineer, Minor Keith, proposed an idea that not only enhanced his fortunes but also changed the course of Central American history. Bananas were planted along the railway right of way, partly to feed the workers but also for their export potential. The crop would help to finance the railway, and, in exchange, Keith would get a 99-year lease on 1,976,000 hectares (800,000 acres) of land with a 20-year tax deferment. The Costa Rican government gave its consent, and in 1878 the first bananas were shipped from the country. In 1899, Keith and a partner formed the **United Fruit Company,** a business that eventually became the largest landholder in Central America and caused political disputes and wars throughout the region.

In 1889, Costa Rica held what is considered the first free election in Central American history. The opposition candidate won the election, and the control of the government passed from the hands of one political party to those of another without bloodshed or hostilities. Thus, Costa Rica established itself as the region's only true democracy. In 1948, this democratic process was challenged by **Rafael Angel Calderón,** who had served as the country's president from 1940 to 1944. After losing by a narrow margin, Calderón, who had the backing of the communist labor unions and the Catholic Church, refused to concede the country's leadership to the rightfully elected president, **Otillio Ulate,** and a civil war ensued. Calderón was eventually defeated by **José "Pepe" Figueres.** In the wake of this crisis, a new constitution was drafted; among other changes, it abolished Costa Rica's army.

An international star arose in Costa Rica when **Oscar Arias Sánchez** was elected president in 1986 and won the Nobel Peace Prize in 1987 for his successful mediation of the Sandinista-Contra war in Nicaragua and other regional conflicts. Arias, Costa Rica's best-known native son, served from 1986 to 1990 and again from 2006 to 2010.

In 1994, history seemed to repeat itself—peacefully this time—when **José María Figueres** took the reins of government from the son of his father's adversary, Rafael Angel Calderón. In 2001, Otton Solís and his new Citizen's Action Party (PAC) forced the presidential elections into a second round, opening a crack in a two-party system that had become seemingly entrenched for good. Although Solís finished third and didn't make it to the runoff, his upstart Citizen's Action Party won quite a few deputy slots.

> ### Presidential Welcome
>
> President John F. Kennedy visited Costa Rica in March 1963, just months before his assassination. Upon his arrival, the Irazú Volcano woke up and erupted after more than 2 decades of dormancy. Soot and ash reached as far as San José, where the American leader addressed students and political figures.

The battered traditional two-party system was further threatened in 2004, when major corruption scandals became public. Two former presidents were arrested (Miguel Angel Rodríguez and Rafael Angel Calderón), and another (José María Figueres) fled to Switzerland. All were implicated, as well as a long list of high-level government employees and deputies, in various financial scandals or bribery cases. Both Calderón and Rodríguez were convicted and sentenced to jail time, while charges have been dropped against Figueres.

In 2010, Costa Rica elected its first female president, **Laura Chinchilla,** who was a vice president in the outgoing Arias administration. Then on April 6, 2014, former university professor **Luis Guillermo Solís** of the opposition Citizen's Action Party won a runoff presidential election by a landslide over longtime San José mayor Johnny Araya. So far, Solis's presidency has been a mixed bag. He's had trouble moving legislation forward, and divisions within his own ruling coalition have been a large part of that problem. Longstanding structural issues have hampered attempts at addressing rising public debt and corruption. However, Costa Rica maintains a strong growth rate even while neighboring Central American economies have seen theirs contract.

ART & ARCHITECTURE

For a small country, Costa Rica has vibrant scenes in all the major arts—music, literature, architecture, dance, and even film.

Art

Unlike Guatemala, Mexico, or even Nicaragua, Costa Rica does not have a strong tradition of local or indigenous arts and crafts. The strong suit of Costa Rican art is European and Western-influenced, ranging from neo-classical to modern in style.

Early painters to look out for include **Max Jimenez, Manuel de la Cruz, Teodorico Quiros,** and **Francisco Amighetti.** Of these, Amighetti is the best known, with an extensive body of expressionist-influenced work. Legends of the local modern art world include **Rafa Fernández, Lola Fernández,** and **Cesar Valverde.** Valverde's portraits are characterized by large planes of bold colors. Artists making waves today include **Fernando Carballo, Rodolfo Stanley, Lionel Gonzalez, Manuel Zumbado,** and **Karla Solano.**

Sculpture is perhaps one of the strongest aspects of the Costa Rican art scene, with the large bronze works of **Francisco "Paco" Zuñiga**

Museo de Arte Costarricense

among the best of the genre. Zuñiga's larger-than-life castings include exaggerated human proportions that recall Rodin and Botero. Artists **José Sancho, Edgar Zuñiga,** and **Jiménez Deredia** are all producing internationally acclaimed pieces, many of monumental proportions. You can see examples by all these sculptors around the country, as well as at San José's downtown **Museo de Arte Costarricense ★★** (p 134). I also enjoy the whimsical works of **Leda Astorga,** who sculpts and then paints a pantheon of voluptuous figures in interesting and sometimes compromising poses.

You'll find the country's best and most impressive museums and galleries in San José (p 129), and to a lesser extent in some of the country's larger and more popular tourist destinations, like Manuel Antonio and Monteverde.

Pre-Columbian foundations at Guayabo National Monument

The Basílica de Nuestra Señora de los Ángeles in Cartago

Architecture

Costa Rica lacks the large-scale pre-Columbian ceremonial ruins found throughout much of the rest of Mesoamerica. The only notable early archaeological site is **Guayabo** (p 205). However, only the foundations of a few dwellings, a handful of carved petroglyphs, and some road and water infrastructure are still visible here.

Similarly, Costa Rica doesn't have the same large and well-preserved colonial-era cities found throughout much of the rest of Latin America. The original capital of **Cartago** (p 194) has some old ruins and a few colonial-era buildings, as well as the country's grandest church, the **Basílica de Nuestra Señora de los Angeles (Basilica of Our Lady of the Angels)** ★ (p 197), which was built in honor of the country's patron saint, La Negrita, or the Virgin of Guadalupe. Although legend says the sculpture of the Virgin was discovered here in 1635, the church itself wasn't inaugurated until 1924.

In downtown San José, Barrio Amón and Barrio Otoya are two side-by-side upscale neighborhoods replete with a stately mix of architectural stylings, with everything from colonial-era residential mansions to Art Deco apartment

Colonial-Era Remnant or Crime Deterrent?

Most Costa Rican homes feature steel or iron grating over the doors and windows. Some tour guides will tell you this can be traced back to colonial-era architecture and design, but it seems more likely that this is a relatively modern defense against breaking and entering.

The luxurious Four Seasons Resort at Peninsula Papagayo

buildings and modern high-rise skyscrapers. One of the standout build-ings here is the **Metal School (Escuela Metálica),** which dates to the 1880s, and was shipped over piece-by-piece from Belgium and erected in place.

On much of the Caribbean coast, you will find mostly wooden houses built on raised stilts to rise above the wet ground and occasional flooding. Some of these houses feature ornate gingerbread trim. Much of the rest of the country's architecture is pretty plain. Most residential houses are simple concrete-block affairs, with zinc roofs.

A few modern architects are creating names for themselves. **Ron-ald Zurcher,** who designed the luxurious **Four Seasons Resort** (p 239) and several other large hotel projects, is one of the shining lights of contemporary Costa Rican architecture.

COSTA RICA IN POPULAR CULTURE
Books

Though Costa Rica's literary output is sparsely translated and little known outside the country's borders, there are some notable authors to look for, especially if you can read Spanish.

Some of the books mentioned below might be difficult to track down in U.S. bookstores, but you'll find them all in abundance in Costa Rica. A good place to check for many of these titles is at a well-stocked

The Costa Rica National Library at San José

gift shop, or any branch of **Librería Internacional** (www.libreria internacional.com; ℂ **800/542-7374**), which has storefronts at most major modern malls, and several other stand-alone locations around the country.

GENERAL INTEREST   For a straightforward, albeit somewhat dry, historical overview, there's **"The History of Costa Rica,"** by Ivan Molina and Steven Palmer. For a more readable look into Costa Rican society, pick up **"The Ticos: Culture and Social Change"** by Richard, Karen, and Mavis Biesanz, an examination of the country's politics and culture. Another book worth checking out is **"The Costa Rica Reader: History, Culture, Politics,"** a broad selection of stories, essays, and excerpts edited by Steven Palmer and Ivan Molina.

To learn more about the life and culture of Costa Rica's Talamanca coast, an area populated by Afro-Caribbean people whose ancestors emigrated from Caribbean islands in the early 19th century, look for **"What Happen: A Folk-History of Costa Rica's Talamanca Coast"** by Paula Palmer. This book is a collection of oral histories taken from a wide range of local characters.

FICTION   **"Costa Rica: A Traveler's Literary Companion,"** edited by Barbara Ras and with a foreword by **Oscar Arias Sánchez,** is a broad and varied collection of short stories by Costa Rican writers, organized by region of the country. Entries include works by many of the country's leading literary lights. Availability of Costa Rican fiction in English is very limited, but if you're lucky, you might find a copy of **"Stories of Tatamundo,"** by Fabian Dobles, or **"Lo Peor/The Worst,"** by Fernando Contreras.

Among Costa Rica's most famous novels is **"La isla de los hombres solos,"** or "The Island of the Lonely Men," a semi-autobiographical novel by José León Sánchez based on his years of imprisonment at the ghastly prison island of San Lucas in the Gulf of Nicoya.

Young readers will enjoy Kristin Joy Pratt's **"A Walk in the Rainforest,"** an introduction to the tropical rainforest written by Pratt when she was still in high school. Young children will also like the beautifully illustrated **"The Forest in the Clouds,"** by Sneed Collard and Michael Rothman, and **"The Umbrella"** by Jan Brett. **Pachanga Kids** (www.pachangakids.com) has published several illustrated bilingual children's books with delightful illustrations by Ruth Angulo, including **"Mar Azucarada/Sugar Sea"** by Roberto Boccanera and **"El Coyote y la Luciernaga/The Coyote and the Firefly"** by Yazmin Ross, which includes a musical CD. Another bilingual children's book worth checking out is **"Zari & Marinita: Adventures in a Costa Rican Rainforest,"** the story of the friendship between a morpho butterfly and a tropical frog.

One of the most important pieces in the Costa Rican canon, Carlos Luis Fallas's 1941 tome **"Mamita Yunai"** is a stark look at the impact of banana giant United Fruit on the country. More recently, Fernando Contreras takes up where his predecessor left off in **"Unico Mirando al Mar,"** which describes the conditions of the poor, predominantly children, who scavenge Costa Rica's garbage dumps.

NATURAL HISTORY **"Tropical Nature"** by Adrian Forsyth and Ken Miyata is a wonderfully written and lively collection of tales and adventures by two neotropical biologists who spent quite some time in the forests of Costa Rica.

Mario A. Boza's beautiful **"Costa Rica National Parks"** has been reissued in an elegant coffee-table edition. Other worthwhile coffee-table books include **"Rainforests: Costa Rica and Beyond"** by Adrian Forsyth, with photographs by Michael and Patricia Fogden, **"Costa Rica: A Journey Through Nature"** by Adrian Hepworth, and **"Osa: Where the Rainforest Meets the Sea"** by Roy Toft (photographer) and Trond Larsen (author).

For an introduction to a wide range of Costa Rican fauna, there's **"The Wildlife of Costa Rica: A Field Guide"** by Fiona Reid, Jim Zook, Twan Leenders, and Robert Dean, or **"Costa Rica: Traveller's Wildlife Guides"** by Les Beletsky. Both pack a lot of useful information into a concise package and make great field guides for amateur naturalists and inquisitive tourists.

"A Guide to the Birds of Costa Rica" by F. Gary Stiles and Alexander Skutch is an invaluable guide to identifying the many birds you'll see during your stay. This classic faces competition from the more recent **"Birds of Costa Rica"** by Richard Garrigues and Robert Dean. Birdwatchers might want a copy of **"A Bird-Finding Guide to Costa Rica"** by Barrett Lawson, which details the country's bird-watching bounty by site and region.

Film

Costa Rica has a budding and promising young film industry. Local feature films like Esteban Ramirez's **"Caribe"** (2004), about the confrontation between environmentalists and oil developers on Costa Rica's Caribbean coast, and **"Gestación (Gestation)"** (2009), a tale of teenage love and pregnancy, are both out on subtitled DVD. **"El Camino (The Path)"** by filmmaker Ishtar Yasin Gutiérrez was screened at the Berlin Film Festival, while Paz Fabrega's **"El Viaje"** (2015) was shown to rave reviews at the 2015 Tribeca Film Festival. Released in 2010, Hilda Hidalgo's **"Del Amor y Otros Demonios (Of Love and Other Demons)"** is a compelling treatment of Gabriel García Márquez's novel of the same name. But the film that really took Costa Rica by storm was 2014's **"Maikol Yordan de Viaje Perdido"** ("Maikol Yordan Traveling Lost"), a comedy in which a happy-go-lucky Costa Rican *campesino* goes on a voyage to make money to save his farm. It has been watched by more people in Costa Rica than any movie in history, including Hollywood blockbusters like "Titanic." More recently, 2016's "Entonces Nosotros" ("About Us") tells the tale of a hopeless romantic trying to save his relationship while on a beach vacation.

If you want to see Costa Rica used simply as a backdrop, the major motion picture productions of **"1492: Conquest of Paradise"** (1992) by Ridley Scott, starring Gerard Depardieu and Sigourney Weaver; **"Congo"** (1995), featuring Laura Linney and Ernie Hudson; **"The Blue Butterfly"** (2004) with William Hurt; and **"After Earth"** (2013), a box-office bomb starring Will Smith and directed by M. Night Shyamalan, all feature sets and scenery from around the country. Costa Rica also appears prominently in the seminal surfer flick **"Endless Summer II"** (1994).

Music

Several musical traditions and styles meet and mingle in Costa Rica. The northern Guanacaste region is a hotbed of folk music that is strongly influenced by the *marimba* (wooden xylophone) traditions of Guatemala and Nicaragua, while also featuring guitars, maracas, and the occasional harp. On the Caribbean coast, you can hear traditional calypso sung by descendants of the original black workers brought here to build the railroads and tend the banana plantations. Roving bands play a mix of guitar, banjo, washtub bass, and percussion in the bars and restaurants of Cahuita and Puerto Viejo.

Costa Rica also has a healthy contemporary music scene. The jazz-fusion trio **Editus** has won two Grammy awards for its work with Panamanian salsa giant (and movie star) **Rubén Blades. Malpaís,** the closest thing Costa Rica had to a super-group, suffered the sudden and tragic loss of its lead singer, but still has several excellent albums out.

Marimba player at Hotel Hacienda Guachipelín

You should also seek out **Cantoamérica,** which plays upbeat dance music ranging from salsa to calypso to merengue. Jazz pianist, and former Minister of Culture, **Manuel Obregón** (also a member of Malpaís) has several excellent solo albums, including **"Simbiosis"** (2011), on which he improvises along with the sounds of Costa Rica's wildlife, waterfalls, and weather; as well as his work with the **"Papaya Orchestra,"** a collaboration and gathering of musicians from around Central America.

Local label **Papaya Music ★★★** (www.papayamusic.com) has done an excellent job promoting and producing albums by Costa Rican musicians in a range of styles and genres. Their offerings range from the Guanacasteca folk songs of **Max Goldemberg,** to the boleros of **Ray Tico,** to the original calypso of **Walter "Gavitt" Ferguson.** You can find their CDs at gift shops and record stores around the country.

Classical music lovers will want to head to San José, which has a symphony orchestra, youth symphony, opera company, and choir. The local symphony sometimes features the works of local composers like **Benjamin Guitiérrez** and **Eddie Mora.** On occasion, small-scale music festivals will bring classical offerings to some of the beach and inland tourist destinations around the country.

Bars and discos around the country spin salsa, merengue, and cumbia, as well as more modern grooves that include house, electronic, trip-hop, and reggaeton.

EATING & DRINKING

Although Costa Rican cooking can be fairly simple and plain, creative chefs have livened up the dining scene in San José and at most of the major tourist destinations.

TICO etiquette & CUSTOMS

In general, Costa Ricans are easygoing, friendly, and informal. That said, they tend to be somewhat conservative and try to treat everyone respectfully. Moreover, in conversation, Ticos are relatively formal. When addressing someone, they use the formal *usted* in most instances, reserving the familiar *vos* or *tú* for friends, family, and children or teenagers.

Upon greeting or saying goodbye, both sexes shake hands, although across genders, a light kiss on one cheek is common.

Proud of their neutrality and lack of armed forces, everyday Costa Ricans are uncomfortable with confrontation. What may seem like playful banter or justified outrage to a foreign tourist may be taken very badly by a Tico. Avoid criticizing Costa Rica unless you know exactly whom you're talking to and what you're talking about.

In some cases, especially in the service industry, Ticos may tell you what they think you want to hear, just to avoid a confrontation—even if they know it might not turn out to be true. Sometimes Ticos will give you wrong directions instead of telling you they don't know the way.

Tico men tend to dress conservatively. In San José and other cities in the Central Valley, you will rarely see a Costa Rican man wearing shorts. In many towns and cities, while accepted, tourists will stand out when wearing shorts, sandals, and other typical beach, golf, or vacation wear. Costa Rican women, on the other hand, especially young women, tend to show some skin in everyday, and even business, situations. Still, be respectful in your dress, especially if you plan on visiting churches, small towns, or local families.

Women, no matter how they dress, may find themselves on the receiving end of whistles, honks, hoots, hisses, and catcalls. For more information on this manifestation of Costa Rican machismo, see "Women Travelers," on p 613.

Punctuality is not a Costa Rican strong suit. Ticos often show up anywhere from 15 minutes to an hour or more late to meetings and appointments—this is known as *la hora tica,* or "Tico time." That said, buses and local airlines, tour operators, movie theaters, and most businesses do tend to run on a relatively timely schedule.

Outside of the capital and the major tourist destinations, your options get very limited very fast. In fact, many destinations are so isolated that you have no choice but to eat in the hotel's restaurant. At remote jungle lodges, the food is usually served buffet- or family-style and can range from bland to inspired (depending on who's doing the cooking), and turnover is high.

If you see a restaurant billing itself as a **mirador,** it means it has a view. If you are driving around the country, don't miss an opportunity to dine with a view at some little roadside restaurant. The food might not be all that great, but the view and scenery will be.

At even the more expensive restaurants, it's hard to spend more than $50 per person unless you really splurge on drinks. It gets even cheaper outside the city and high-end hotels. However, if you really want to save money, traditional Costa Rican food, or *comida típica,* is always the cheapest nourishment available. It's primarily served in *sodas,* Costa Rica's equivalent of diners. At a *soda,* you'll have lots of choices: rice and beans with steak, rice and beans with fish, rice and beans with chicken, or, for vegetarians, rice and beans with salad. Additionally, there's usually a list of fresh juices available.

By the way, get used to seeing restaurants proudly advertise their food in English as "typical" (or in the case of one restaurant in La Fortuna, with a big starburst on the front of its menu, "100% Typical!"). The word *típico* in Spanish means traditional or regional, and is a point of pride, but the translation "typical" (meaning ordinary or lackluster) doesn't do it justice.

Restaurant listings throughout this book are separated into three price categories, based on the average cost of a meal per person, including tax and service charge: **Expensive,** more than $30 (roughly C17,000); **Moderate,** $15 to $30 (C8,500–C17,000); and **Inexpensive,** less than $15 (C8,500). (Note that individual items in the listings—entrees, for instance—do not include the sales or service taxes.) Keep in mind that an additional 13% sales tax applies, as well as a 10% service charge. Ticos rarely tip, but that doesn't mean that you shouldn't. If the service was particularly attentive, leave a little extra. And because bars rarely include a service charge, remember to tip your bartender.

Meals & Dining Customs

Rice and beans are the base of every Costa Rican meal—all three of them. At breakfast, they're called *gallo pinto* and come with everything from eggs to steak to seafood. At lunch or dinner, rice and beans are an integral part of the traditional *casado* (which means "married," and is derived from the days when a worker who brought one of these varied meals to work was thought to have a "married man's lunch"). A *casado* usually consists of rice and beans, a cabbage and tomato salad, fried plantains, and chicken, fish, or beef. On the Caribbean coast, rice and beans are called "rice 'n' beans" and are cooked in coconut milk.

Dining hours in Costa Rica are flexible but generally follow North American customs. Some downtown restaurants in San José are open 24 hours; however, expensive restaurants tend to be open for lunch between 11am and 3pm and for dinner between 6 and 10pm.

APPETIZERS Known as *bocas* in Costa Rica, appetizers are served with drinks in most bars. Sometimes the bocas are free, but if not, they're usually inexpensive. Popular bocas include *gallos* (tortillas

ABOVE: **A traditional appetizer of ceviche at The Four Seasons**
BELOW: **Fresh local fish Tacos at Café de Playa in Playa Coco**

Smoothie with fresh papaya at Florblanca Resort

piled with meat, chicken, cheese, or beans), *ceviche* (a marinated seafood salad), *tamales* (stuffed cornmeal patties wrapped and steamed inside banana leaves), *patacones* (fried green plantain chips), and fried yuca.

SANDWICHES & SNACKS   Ticos love to snack, and a large variety of tasty little sandwiches and snacks are available on the street, at snack bars, and in *sodas. Arreglados* are little meat-filled sandwiches, as are *tortas,* which are served on little rolls with a bit of salad tucked into them. Tacos, tamales, *gallos* (see above), and *empanadas* (turnovers) also are quite common.

MEAT   Costa Rica is beef country, having long ago converted much of its rainforest to pastures for raising beef cattle. Consequently, beef is cheap and plentiful, although it might be a bit tougher—and cut and served thinner—than you are used to. One typical local dish is called *olla de carne,* a bowl of beef broth with large chunks of meat, local tubers, and corn. Spit-roasted chicken is also very popular here and is meltingly tender. Lamb is very sparsely used in Costa Rican cooking, although finer restaurants often have a lamb dish or two on the menu.

SEAFOOD   Costa Rica has two coasts, and, as you'd expect, plenty of seafood is available everywhere in the country. *Corvina* (sea bass) is the most commonly served fish and is prepared in many ways, including as *ceviche.* (But be careful: In many cheaper restaurants, particularly in San José, shark meat is often sold as *corvina.*) You should also come across *pargo* (red snapper), *dorado* (mahi-mahi), and tuna on some menus, especially along the coasts. *Trucha* (trout) is also farm raised in some higher altitude regions.

VEGETABLES   On the whole, you'll find vegetables surprisingly lacking in the meals you're served in Costa Rica—usually nothing more than a little pile of shredded cabbage topped with a slice or two of tomato. For a more satisfying and filling salad, order *palmito* (hearts of palm salad).

Chifrijo: King of Costa Rican Bocas

Without a doubt, Costa Rica's most popular and famous *boca* is a bowl of *chifrijo*. The name is a phonetic abbreviation of its two most important ingredients: *chicharrones* (fried pork bellies) and *frijoles* (beans). A proper bowl of *chifrijo* will also have rice, *pico de gallo* (a tomato-based salsa), and a few slices of avocado, accompanied by some tortilla chips to scoop it all up.

The creation was the brainchild of Miguel Cordero, who began serving it in his family bar in Tibas in the early 1980s.

The dish quickly spread like wildfire and can now be found in restaurants and bars around the country. Cordero had the foresight to trademark his dish, and in 2014 he began taking legal action against competitors for trademark infringement. Thanks to Cordero's trademark claims, restaurant and bar owners have had to scramble. In most cases, you can still usually find *chifrijo* on the menu, only it might be called *frichijo*, or *hochifri*, or some other variation on the theme.

A plate of *chifrijo*

The heart (actually one stem of a multi-stemmed palm) is boiled and then chopped into circular pieces and served with other fresh vegetables, with salad dressing on top. If you want something more than this, you'll have to order a side dish such as *picadillo,* a stew or purée of vegetables with a bit of meat in it.

One more vegetable worth mentioning is the *pejibaye,* a peach palm fruit that looks like a miniature orange coconut. Boiled *pejibayes* are frequently sold from carts on the streets of San José. When cut in half, a *pejibaye* reveals a large seed surrounded by soft, fibrous flesh. You can eat it plain, but it's usually topped with a dollop of mayonnaise.

Coconut, Straight Up

Throughout Costa Rica, keep your eye out for roadside stands selling fresh, green coconuts, or *pipas*. Green coconuts have very little meat, but are filled with copious amounts of a slightly sweet, clear liquid that is extremely refreshing. According to local legend, this liquid is pure enough to be used as plasma in an emergency situation. Armed with a machete, the *pipa* seller will grab a cold one, cut out the top, stick in a straw, and ask you for about C500.

FRUITS *Plátanos* (plantains) are giant relatives of bananas that are cooked and served with countless *casados* every day. Green plantains have a very starchy flavor and consistency, but they become as sweet as candy as they ripen, especially when fried. Costa Rica has a wealth of delicious tropical fruits, including mangoes (the season begins in May), papayas, pineapples, melons, and bananas. Other fruits include *marañón*, which is the fruit of the cashew tree and has orange or yellow glossy skin; *granadilla* or *maracuyá* (passion fruit); *mamón chino*, which Asian travelers will immediately recognize as rambutan; and *carambola* (starfruit).

DESSERTS *Queque seco* ("dry cake") is pound cake. *Tres leches* cake, on the other hand, is so moist that you almost need to eat it with a spoon. Flan is a typical custard dessert. It often comes as either *flan de caramelo* (caramel) or *flan de coco* (coconut). Numerous other sweets are available, many of which are made with condensed milk and raw sugar. *Cajetas* are popular handmade candies, made from sugar and various mixes of evaporated, condensed, and powdered milk. They are sold in differing-size bits and chunks at most *pulperías* (small stores) and streetside food stands.

Beverages

Frescos, refrescos, and *jugos naturales* are popular drinks in Costa Rica. They are usually made with fresh fruit and milk or water. Among the

Mixology class using the local liquor, guaro, and local fruits at The Andaz hotel

more common fruits used are mangoes, papayas, blackberries, and pineapples. You'll also come across *maracuyá* (passion fruit) and *carambola* (star fruit). Some of the more unusual frescos are *horchata* (made with rice flour and a lot of cinnamon) and *chan* (made with the seed of a plant found mostly in Guanacaste—definitely an acquired taste). The former is wonderful; the latter requires an open mind (it's reputed to be good for the digestive system). Order *un fresco con leche sin hielo* (a *fresco* with milk but without ice) if you want to avoid untreated water.

Costa Rica is a coffee mecca, but some coffee drinkers might be disappointed here. Most of the best coffee has traditionally been targeted for export, and Ticos tend to prefer theirs weak and sugary. Better hotels and restaurants, catering to foreign tastes, now serve up superior blends. If you want black coffee, ask for *café negro;* if you want it with milk, order *café con leche.*

For something different in the morning, ask for *agua dulce,* a warm drink made from melted sugar cane and served either with milk or lemon, or straight.

WATER Although water in most of Costa Rica is safe to drink, bottled water is readily available and is a good option if you're worried about an upset stomach. *Agua mineral,* or simply soda, is sparkling water in Costa Rica. If you like your water without bubbles, just ask for a *botella de agua.*

BEER, WINE & LIQUOR The German presence in Costa Rica over the years has produced several decent beers, which are fairly inexpensive. Most Costa Rican beers are light pilsners. Almost all mass-produced beers are either produced or imported by one single company, Florida Ice & Farm. The most popular brands are Imperial, Pilsen, and Bavaria.

You can find imported wines at reasonable prices in the better restaurants throughout the country. You can usually save money by ordering a Chilean or Argentine wine over a Californian or European bottle.

Costa Rica distills a wide variety of liquors, and you'll save money by ordering these over imported brands. The national liquor is *guaro,* a

---

Craft Beer Boom

Costa Rica has seen an amazing boom in craft beers and places to drink them in the past few years. **Costa Rica's Craft Brewing Company** (www.beer.cr; ✆ **2249-0919**) has led the way. Their Libertas Golden Ale and Segua Red Ale are available at more and more restaurants and bars around the country, and can be purchased at larger supermarkets. The brewery offers tours and has a small brewpub at its main facility in Ciudad Colón, a western suburb of San José. Other brews and breweries to look for include the lambics and wild ales of Cervecería Calle Cimarrona, Ambar by **Cervecera del Centro** (www.cervecera delcentro.com); Majadera Pale Ale and Japiendin Tropical Ale from **Treinta y Cinco** (www.treintaycinco.com); and Witch's Rock Pale Ale and Gato Malo Dark Ale from Tamarindo's **Volcano Brewing Company** (www.volcano brewingcompany.com).

Outdoor seating at Witch's Rock Volcano Brewing Company

simple cane liquor that's often combined with a soft drink or tonic. When drinking it straight, it's customary to follow a shot with a bite into a fresh lime covered in salt. If you want to try *guaro,* stick to the **Cacique** brand. And don't miss a chance to try a *chile guaro,* which is like a very spicy Bloody Mary in a shot glass.

Several brands and styles of coffee-based liqueurs are produced in Costa Rica. **Café Rica** is similar to Kahlúa, and you can find several types of coffee cream liqueurs. **Café Britt** produces its own line of coffee liqueurs, which are quite good and available in most supermarkets, liquor stores, and tourist shops.

Costa Ricans also drink a lot of rum. The premier Costa Rican rum is **Centenario.**

TIPS ON SHOPPING

Costa Rica is not known as a shopping paradise, as most of what you'll find for sale is pretty run-of-the-mill, mass-produced souvenir fare. So scant are its handicraft offerings that most tourist shops sell Guatemalan clothing, Panamanian appliquéd textiles, Salvadoran painted wood souvenirs, and Nicaraguan rocking chairs. Still, Costa Rica does have a few locally produced arts and handicrafts to look out for, and a couple of towns and villages with well-deserved reputations for their unique works.

Perhaps the most famous of all towns for shopping is **Sarchí ★** (p 191), a Central Valley town filled with handicraft shops. Sarchí is best known as the citadel of the colorfully painted Costa Rican **oxcart,** reproductions of which are manufactured in various scaled-down sizes. These make excellent gifts. (Larger oxcarts can be easily disassembled and shipped to your home.) A lot of furniture is also made in Sarchí.

In Guanacaste, the small town of **Guaitíl** (p 281) is famous for its pottery. A host of small workshops, studios, and storefronts ring the

Beautifully painted art in Sarchí

town's central park (which is actually a soccer field). Many of the low-fired ceramic wares here carry ancient local indigenous motifs, while others get quirky modern treatments. You can find examples of this low-fired simple ceramic work in many gift shops around the country, and at roadside stands all across Guanacaste.

You might also run across **carved masks** ★★★ made by the indigenous **Boruca** people of southern Costa Rica. The small Boruca villages where these masks are carved are off the beaten path, but you will find them for sale at some of the better gift shops around the country. These wooden masks come in a variety of sizes and styles, both painted and unpainted, and run anywhere from $20 to $150, depending on the quality of workmanship. But don't be fooled. You'll see scores of mass-produced wooden masks at souvenir and gift shops around Costa Rica. Many are imported from Mexico, Guatemala, and Indonesia. Real Boruca masks are unique indigenous art works, often signed by their carvers.

Much of the Costa Rican woodwork for sale is mass-produced. A couple of notable exceptions include the work of **Barry Biesanz** ★★ (p 155), whose excellent hardwood creations are sold at better gift shops around the country, and the unique, large-scale sculptures created and sold at the **Original Grand Gallery** (p 365–366) in La Fortuna.

Coffee remains a favorite gift item. It's a great deal, it's readily available, and Costa Rican coffee is some of the best in the world. See the "Joe to Go" box on p 152 for tips on buying **coffee** in Costa Rica.

A few other items worth keeping an eye out for include reproductions of **pre-Columbian gold jewelry** and **carved-stone figurines.** The former are available as either solid gold, silver, or gold-plated. The latter, although interesting, can be extremely heavy.

Caveat Emptor

International laws prohibit trade in endangered wildlife, so don't buy any plants or animals, even if they're readily for sale. Do not buy any kind of sea-turtle products (including jewelry); wild birds; lizards, snakes, or cat skins; corals; or orchids (except those grown commercially). No matter how unique, beautiful, or insignificant it might seem, your purchase will directly contribute to the further hunting of animals and destruction of natural environments.

In addition, be careful when buying wood products, and try to buy sustainably harvested woods. Costa Rica's rainforest hardwoods are a finite and rapidly disappearing resource.

Across the country you'll see **hammocks** for sale, though you may find them crude and unstable. The same vendors usually have single-person hanging chairs, which are strung similarly to the full-size hammocks and are a better bet.

It's especially hard to capture the subtle shades and colors of the rainforests and cloud forests; many a traveler has gone home thinking that his or her digital camera contained the full beauty of the jungle, only to see dozens of bright-green and random blurs when viewing the photos on a larger screen. To avoid this heartache, you might want to pick up a good **coffee-table book** (see p 154) or at least some **postcards** of the sights you want to remember.

Contemporary and **classic Costa Rican art** is another great option, both for discerning collectors and those looking for a unique reminder of their time in the country. San José has the most galleries and shops, but you will find good, well-stocked galleries in some of the more booming tourist destinations, including Liberia, Manuel Antonio, Jacó, and Monteverde.

Finally, one item that you'll see at gift shops around the country is **Cuban cigars.** It's no longer illegal to bring them back to the United States.

WHEN TO GO

Costa Rica's high season for tourism runs from late November to late April, which coincides almost perfectly with the chill of winter in the United States, Canada, and Europe. The high season is also the dry season. If you want some unadulterated time on a tropical beach and a little less rain during your rainforest experience, this is the time to come. During this period (especially during the Christmas holiday and Holy Week before Easter), the tourism industry operates at full tilt—prices are higher, attractions are more crowded, and reservations need to be made in advance.

Local tourism operators often call the tropical rainy season (May through mid-Nov) the "green season," an apt euphemism. At this time of year, even brown and barren Guanacaste province becomes lush and verdant. Many locals will tell you the rainy season is their favorite time of year. It's easy to find or at least negotiate reduced rates, there are far fewer tourists, and the rain is often limited to a few hours each afternoon (although you can occasionally get socked in for a week at a time). One drawback: Some of the country's rugged roads become impassable without four-wheel-drive during the rainy season.

Weather

Costa Rica is a tropical country and has distinct wet and dry seasons. However, some regions are rainy all year, and others are very dry and sunny for most of the year. Temperatures vary primarily with elevations, not with seasons: On the coasts, it's hot all year; in the mountains, it can be cool at night any time of year. Frost is common at the highest elevations (3,000–3,600m/9,840–11,808 ft.).

Average Daytime High Temperatures & Rainfall in San José

	JAN	FEB	MAR	APR	MAY	JUNE	JULY	AUG	SEPT	OCT	NOV	DEC
Temp (°F)	75	76	79	79	80	79	77	78	79	77	77	75
Temp (°C)	24	24	26	26	27	26	25	26	26	25	25	24
Days of rain	1.3	1.5	2.2	4.2	11.5	14.5	13.7	14.5	18.1	17.9	8.6	2.3

Generally, the **rainy season** (or "green season") is from May to mid-November in most of the country, with notable exceptions on the Caribbean coast. Costa Ricans call this wet time of year their winter. The **dry season,** considered summer by Costa Ricans, is from mid-November to April. In Guanacaste, the arid northwestern province, the dry season lasts several weeks longer than in other places. Even in the rainy season, days often start sunny, with rain falling in the afternoon and evening. On the Caribbean coast, especially south of Limón, you can count on rain year-round, although this area gets far less rain in September and October than the rest of the country, making this a great time to visit.

The most popular time of year to visit Costa Rica is in December and January, when everything is still green from the rains, but the sky is clear.

Holidays

Because Costa Rica is a Roman Catholic country, most of its holidays are church-related. The big ones are Christmas, New Year's, and Easter, which are all celebrated for several days. Holy Week (the week preceding Easter) is a huge holiday in Costa Rica, and many families head for the beach. (Controversially, many local governments allow no alcohol sales during Holy Week.) Also, there is no public transportation on Holy Thursday or Good Friday. Government offices and banks are closed on official holidays, transportation services are reduced, and stores and markets might also close.

Official holidays in Costa Rica include **January 1** (New Year's Day), **March 19** (St. Joseph's Day), Thursday and Friday of Holy Week, **April 11** (Juan Santamaría's Day), **May 1** (Labor Day), **June 29** (St. Peter and

St. Paul Day), **July 25** (annexation of the province of Guanacaste), **August 2** (Virgin of Los Angeles's Day), **August 15** (Mother's Day), **September 15** (Independence Day), **October 12** (Discovery of America/Día de la Raza), **December 8** (Immaculate Conception of the Virgin Mary), **December 24** and **25** (Christmas), and **December 31** (New Year's Eve).

Calendar of Events

For information on events with no contact number listed, call the **Costa Rican Tourism Board (ICT)** at ℂ **866/COSTA RICA [26772-7422]** in the U.S. and Canada, or 2223-1733 in Costa Rica, or visit **www.visitcostarica.com**.

JANUARY

Copa del Café (Coffee Cup), San José. Matches for this international event on the junior tennis tour are held at the Costa Rica Country Club (www.copacafe.com; ℂ **2228-9333**). First week in January.

Fiestas of Palmares, Palmares. Perhaps the largest and best organized of the traditional *fiestas*, this includes bullfights, a horseback parade *(tope),* and many concerts, carnival rides, and food booths. First 2 weeks in January.

Fiestas of Santa Cruz, Santa Cruz, Guanacaste. This religious celebration honors the Black Christ of Esquipulas (a famous Guatemalan statue), featuring folk dancing, marimba music, and bullfights. Mid-January.

Fiesta of the Diablitos, Rey Curré village near San Isidro de El General. Boruca Indians wearing wooden devil and bull masks perform dances representative of the Spanish conquest of Central America; there are fireworks displays and an Indian handicrafts market. Late January.

MARCH

Día del Boyero (Oxcart Drivers' Day), San Antonio de Escazú. Colorfully painted oxcarts parade through this suburb of San José, and local priests bless the oxen. Second Sunday in March.

National Orchid Show, San José. Orchid growers throughout the world gather to show their wares, trade tales and secrets, and admire the hundreds of species on display. Contact the Costa Rican Tourist Board for the current year's location and dates. Mid-March.

APRIL

Holy Week. Religious processions are held in cities and towns throughout the country. Week before Easter.

Juan Santamaría Day, Alajuela. Costa Rica's national hero is honored with parades, concerts, and dances. April 11.

MAY

Carrera de San Juan. The country's biggest marathon runs through the mountains, from the outskirts of Cartago to the outskirts of San José. May 17.

JULY

Fiesta of the Virgin of the Sea, Puntarenas. A regatta of colorfully decorated boats carrying a statue of Puntarenas' patron saint marks this festival. A similar event is held at Playa de Coco. Saturday closest to July 16.

Annexation of Guanacaste Day, Liberia. Bullfights, folk dancing, horseback parades, rodeos, concerts, and other events celebrate the day when this region became part of Costa Rica. July 25.

AUGUST

Fiesta of the Virgin of Los Angeles, Cartago. This is the pilgrimage day of the patron saint of Costa Rica. Many walk 24km (15 miles) from San José to the basilica in Cartago. August 2.

Día de San Ramón, San Ramón. More than two dozen statues of saints from various towns are brought to San Ramón, where they are paraded through the streets. August 31.

SEPTEMBER

Costa Rica's Independence Day, celebrated all over the country. One of the most distinctive aspects of this festival is the nighttime marching band parades of children in their school uniforms, playing the national anthem on steel xylophones. September 15.

International Beach Clean-Up Day. Chip in and help clean up the beleaguered shoreline of your favorite beach. Third Saturday in September.

OCTOBER

Fiesta del Maíz, Upala. At this celebration of corn, local beauty queens wear outfits made from corn plants. October 12.

Limón Carnival/Día de la Raza, Limón. A smaller version of Mardi Gras, complete with floats and dancing in the streets, commemorates Columbus's discovery of Costa Rica. Week of October 12.

NOVEMBER

All Souls' Day/Día de los Muertos, celebrated countrywide. Although it is not as elaborate or ritualized as in Mexico, most Costa Ricans take some time this day to remember the dead with flowers and trips to cemeteries. November 2.

DECEMBER

Fiesta de los Negritos, Boruca. Boruca Indians celebrate the feast day of their patron saint, the Virgin of the Immaculate Conception, with costumed dances and traditional music. December 8.

Día de la Pólvora, San Antonio de Belén and Jesús María de San Mateo. Fireworks honor Our Lady of the Immaculate Conception. December 8.

Las Posadas. Countrywide, children and carolers go door-to-door seeking lodging in a reenactment of Joseph and Mary's search for a place to stay. Begins December 15.

El Tope and Carnival, San José. The streets of downtown belong to horses and their riders in a proud recognition of the country's important agricultural heritage. The next day, those same streets are taken over by carnival floats, marching bands, and street dancers. December 26 and 27.

Festejos Populares, San José. Bullfights and a pretty respectable bunch of carnival rides, games of chance, and fast-food stands are set up at the fairgrounds in Zapote. Last week of December.

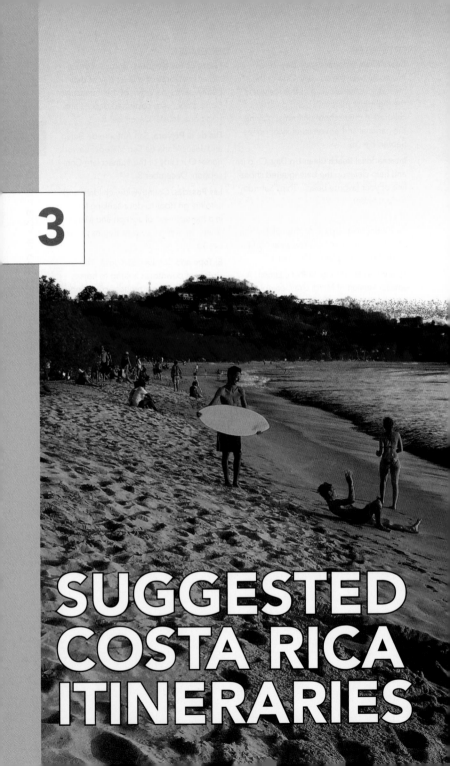

3

SUGGESTED COSTA RICA ITINERARIES

osta Rica is a compact yet unbelievably varied destination with abundant natural attractions and a broad selection of awe-inspiring scenery, adventurous activities, and diverse ecosystems. On a trip to Costa Rica, you can visit rainforests, cloud forests, and active volcanoes, and walk along miles of beautiful beaches on both the Pacific and Caribbean coasts. Adventure hounds will have their fill choosing from an exciting array of activities, and those looking for some rest and relaxation can soak in hot springs, get a volcanic mud wrap and massage, or simply grab a lounge chair and a pair of binoculars. Costa Rica's relatively small size makes visiting several destinations during a single vacation both easy and enjoyable.

The fastest and easiest way to get around the country is by small commuter aircraft. Most major destinations are serviced by regular commuter or charter airline companies. However, this does mean using San José or Liberia as periodic transfer hubs. If your connections don't line up, you may end up having to tack on nights in either of these cities at the start, end, or in the middle of your trip. Luckily, sufficient flights and internal connections make this an infrequent occurrence.

Unless you're traveling on a really tight budget or are unwilling to drive in a foreign country, renting a car is the best way to get around Costa Rica. (But I can't recommend doing much driving in the chaotic capital, unless you have nerves of steel and know where you're going.) Most major destinations are between 2 and 5 hours from San José by car, and many can be linked together in a well-planned and convenient loop. For example, one popular loop links Arenal Volcano, Monteverde, and Manuel Antonio. However, be forewarned that the roads here are often in rough shape, many major roads and intersections are unmarked, Costa Rican drivers can be reckless, and traffic jams can appear out of nowhere. See "By Car" under "Getting Around" in chapter 14 (p 596) for more information on driving in Costa Rica.

The itineraries in this chapter are specific blueprints for fabulous vacations, and you can follow them to the letter. You might also decide to use one or more of them as an outline and then fill in some blanks with other destinations, activities, and attractions that strike your fancy as you explore.

FACING PAGE: **Playa Conchal in the Guanacaste region**

COSTA RICA REGIONS IN BRIEF

Costa Rica is named after one coast but of course has two, the Pacific and the Caribbean. These two coasts are as different from each other as are the East and West coasts of North America.

Costa Rica's **Pacific coast** is the most extensive, and is characterized by a rugged though mostly accessible coastline where forested mountains often meet the sea. It can be divided into four regions: Guanacaste, the Nicoya Peninsula, the Central Coast, and the Southern Coast. There are some spectacular stretches of coastline, and most of the country's top beaches are here, as well as some of the best national parks. This coast varies from the dry, sunny climate of the northwest to the hot, humid rainforests of the south.

The **Caribbean coast** can be divided into two roughly equal stretches. The remote northeast coastline is a vast flat plain laced with rivers and covered with rainforest; it is accessible only by boat or small plane. Farther south, along the stretch of coast accessible by car, are uncrowded beaches and coral reefs.

Bordered by Nicaragua in the north and Panama in the southeast, Costa Rica is only slightly larger than Vermont and New Hampshire combined. Much of the country is mountainous, with three major ranges running northwest to southeast. Among these mountains are several volcanic peaks, some of which are still active. Between the mountain ranges are fertile valleys, the largest and most populated of which is the Central Valley. With the exception of the dry Guanacaste region, much of Costa Rica's coastal area is hot and humid and covered with dense rainforests.

See the following map for a visual of the regions detailed below.

SAN JOSÉ   San José is Costa Rica's capital and its primary business, cultural, and social center—and it sits close to the country's geographical center, in the heart of the Central Valley (see below). It's a sprawling urban area, with a metropolitan population of around two million. Its streets are narrow, in poor repair, poorly marked, and often chock-full of speeding, honking traffic. However, a few notable parks, like the Parque La Sabana and Parque del Este, serve to lessen the urban blight. San José is home to the country's greatest collection of museums, fine restaurants and stores, galleries, and shopping centers.

THE CENTRAL VALLEY   The Central Valley is surrounded by rolling green hills and mountains that rise to heights between 900 and 1,200m (2,952–3,936 ft.) above sea level. The climate here is mild and springlike year-round. The rich volcanic soil of this region makes it Costa Rica's primary agricultural region, with coffee farms making up the majority of landholdings. The country's earliest settlements were in this area, and today the Central Valley (which includes San José) is densely populated, crisscrossed by decent roads, and dotted with small towns. Surrounding the Central Valley are high mountains, among which are four volcanic

peaks. Three of these, **Poás, Irazú,** and **Turrialba,** are still active and have caused extensive damage during cycles of activity in the past 2 centuries. Many of the mountainous regions to the north and to the south of the capital of San José have been declared national parks (Tapantí, Juan Castro Blanco, and Braulio Carrillo) to protect their virgin rainforests against logging.

GUANACASTE   The northwestern corner of the country near the Nicaraguan border is the site of many of Costa Rica's sunniest and most popular **beaches,** including **Playa del Coco, Playa Hermosa, Playa Flamingo, Playa Conchal, Tamarindo,** and the **Papagayo Peninsula.** Scores of beach destinations, towns, and resorts are along this long string of coastline. Because many foreigners have chosen to build beach houses and retirement homes here, Guanacaste has experienced considerable development over the years. You won't find a glut of Cancún-style high-rise hotels, but condos, luxury resorts, and golf courses have sprung up along the coastline here. But you can still find long stretches of deserted sands. However, more and more travelers are using Liberia as their gateway to Costa Rica, bypassing San José and the central and southern parts of the country entirely.

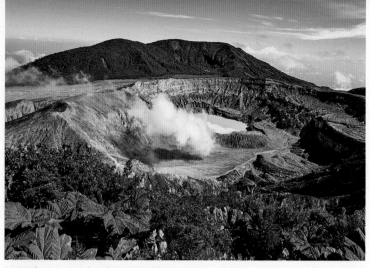

Poás Volcano is now closed to visitors due to recent eruptions.

With about 165cm (65 in.) of rain a year, this region is by far the driest in the country and has been likened to west Texas. Guanacaste province is named after the shady trees that still shelter the herds of cattle roaming the dusty savanna here. In addition to cattle ranches, Guanacaste has semi-active volcanoes, several lakes, and one of the last remnants of tropical dry forest left in Central America. (Dry forest once stretched all the way from Costa Rica up to the Mexican state of Chiapas.)

PUNTARENAS & THE NICOYA PENINSULA   Just south of Guanacaste lies the Nicoya Peninsula. Similar to Guanacaste in many ways, the Nicoya Peninsula is somewhat more inaccessible, and less developed and crowded. However, this is changing. The beaches of **Santa Teresa** and **Malpaís** are perhaps the fastest-growing hot spots anywhere along the Costa Rican coast, while **Nosara** is being hailed as the next Tulum.

As you head south from Guanacaste, the region is similar in terms of geography, climate, and ecosystems, but begins to get more humid and moist, with taller and lusher forests. The Nicoya Peninsula itself juts out to form the Golfo de Nicoya (Nicoya Gulf), a large, protected body of water. **Puntarenas,** a small fishing city, is

Playa del Coco

Playa Flamingo

the main port found inside this gulf, and one of the main commercial ports in all of Costa Rica. Puntarenas is also the departure point for the regular car ferries that connect the Nicoya Peninsula to mainland Costa Rica.

THE NORTHERN ZONE This inland region lies to the north of San José and includes rainforests, cloud forests, hot springs, the famous **Arenal Volcano,** the vast **Braulio Carrillo National Park,** and numerous remote lodges. Because this is one of the few regions of Costa Rica without any beaches, it primarily attracts people interested in nature and active sports. **Lake Arenal** has some of the best windsurfing and kite-surfing in the world, as well as several good mountain-biking trails along

Surfers in Santa Teresa

Hiking through Monteverde Cloud Forest

its shores. The **Monteverde Cloud Forest,** perhaps Costa Rica's most internationally recognized attraction, is another top draw in this region.

THE CENTRAL PACIFIC COAST   Because it's the most easily accessible coastline in Costa Rica, the central Pacific coast has a vast variety of beach resorts and hotels. **Jacó,** a bustling beach town a little over an hour from San José, attracts sunbirds, charter groups, and a mad rush of Costa Rican tourists every weekend. It is also very popular with young surfers, and has a distinct party vibe. **Manuel Antonio,** one of the most emblematic destinations in Costa Rica, is built up around a popular coastal national park, and caters to people looking to blend beach time and fabulous panoramic views with some wildlife viewing and active adventures. South of Manuel Antonio, you'll encounter a wild coastal region where thick rainforests coat steep hillsides that lead down to the undeveloped beaches of Dominical, Matapalo, Uvita, and beyond. This region is also home to the highest peak in Costa Rica—**Mount Chirripó**—a beautiful summit, where frost is common.

THE SOUTHERN ZONE   This hot, humid region is one of Costa Rica's most remote and undeveloped. It is characterized by dense rainforests, large national parks and protected areas, and rugged coastlines. Much of the area is uninhabited and protected in **Corcovado, Piedras Blancas,** and **La Amistad** national parks. A number of wonderful nature lodges are spread around the shores of the **Golfo Dulce** and along the **Osa Peninsula.** There's a lot of solitude to be found here, due in no small part to the fact that it's hard to get here and hard to get around. But if you like your ecotourism authentic and challenging, you'll find the Southern Zone to your liking.

THE CARIBBEAN COAST   Most of the Caribbean coast is a wide, steamy lowland laced with rivers and blanketed with rainforests and banana

plantations. The culture here is predominantly Afro-Caribbean, with many residents speaking an English or Caribbean patois. The northern section of this coast is accessible only by boat or small plane and is the site of **Tortuguero National Park,** which is known for its nesting sea turtles and riverboat trips. The towns of **Cahuita, Puerto Viejo,** and **Manzanillo,** on the southern half of the Caribbean coast, are increasingly popular destinations. The beautiful beaches and coastline here, as yet, have few large hotels. This area can be rainy, especially between December and April.

COSTA RICA HIGHLIGHTS

The timing is tight, but this itinerary packs a lot into a weeklong vacation. This route takes you to a trifecta of Costa Rica's primary tourist attractions: Arenal Volcano, Monteverde, and Manuel Antonio. You can explore and enjoy tropical nature, take in some beach time, and experience a few high-adrenaline adventures.

DAY 1: Arrive & settle into San José

Arrive and get settled in **San José.** If your flight gets in early enough and you have time, head downtown and tour the **Museos del**

53

Banco Central de Costa Rica **(Gold Museum)** ★★ (p 131) or the nearby **Museo de Jade Marco Fidel Tristán (Jade Museum)** ★ (p 133).

☕ Fresh Fruit

As you walk around town, stop at one of the roadside stands or kiosks selling small bags of precut and prepared fruit. Depending on the season, you might find mango, pineapple, or papaya on offer. You might also find *mamón chino*, an odd-looking golf ball-size fruit you might know as *rambutan* or *lychee*.

Head over to the **Teatro Nacional** ★★ (**National Theater;** p 158). If anything is playing that night, buy tickets for the show. For an eye-opening and delicious dinner, try **Al Mercat** ★★★ (p 150), a finca to table restaurant serving elevated Costa Rican cuisine driven by what is growing on their own farm, picked up at farmers markets, or foraged for within the metro area.

DAY 2: Hot stuff ★★

Rent a car and head to the Arenal National Park and the **Arenal Volcano** ★★ area. Hike the **Sendero Coladas (Lava Flow Trail)** ★★, which will take you onto and over a cooled-off lava flow. Spend the evening in the natural hot springs at the **Tabacón Grand Spa Thermal Resort** ★★★ (p 354), working out the kinks from the road and hike. (The volcano may be dormant right now, but the natural hot springs are working just fine.) And you might want to splurge on a massage or spa treatment.

DAY 3: Adventures around Arenal, ending in Monteverde ★★

Spend the morning doing something adventurous around Arenal National Park. Your options include whitewater rafting, mountain

Playa Manuel Antonio in Manuel Antonio National Park

Sunrise on Cerro Chirripó, the highest peak in Costa Rica

biking, horseback riding, and hiking to La Fortuna Waterfall. **Desafío Expeditions ★★** (p 345) offers a great **canyoning** adventure. Allow at least 4 hours of daylight to drive around **Lake Arenal** to **Monteverde.** Stop for a break at the **Lucky Bug Gallery ★★** (p 371), along the road between Tabacón and Nuevo Arenal, an excellent place to shop for gifts, artwork, and souvenirs. Once you get to Monteverde, settle into your hotel and head for a dinner at **Celajes ★★★** paired with beer from their own microbrewery.

DAY 4: Monteverde Cloud Forest Biological Reserve ★★★

Wake up early and take a guided tour of the **Monteverde Cloud Forest Biological Reserve ★★★** (p 382). Spend the afternoon visiting some of the area's other attractions, which might include any combination of the following: the **Butterfly Garden ★**, **Orchid Garden ★★**, **Herpetarium Adventures ★**, **Monteverde Theme Park,** and the **Bat Jungle ★★★** (all on p 388–389).

DAY 5: From the treetops to the coast ★★★

Use the morning to go bird and wildlife watching from a network of paths and suspension bridges at **Sky Walk ★★** (p 385), which puts you up in the cloud forest canopy to peek at flora and fauna you won't see on the ground. Be sure to schedule the visit early enough so that you can hit the road by noon for your drive to **Manuel Antonio National Park.** Settle into your hotel and head for a **sunset drink** at **Agua Azul ★★** (p 454), which offers up spectacular views over the rainforest to the sea.

DAY 6: Manuel Antonio ★★

In the morning, take a boat tour of the **Damas Island estuary** (p 442), and then reward yourself for all the hard touring so far with

55

A sailboat cruise on the Pacific Ocean

an afternoon lazing on one of the beautiful beaches inside **Manuel Antonio National Park ★★** (p 434). If you just can't lie still, hike the loop trail through the rainforest here and around **Cathedral Point ★★**. Make reservations at **Café Milagro ★★★** (p 454) for an intimate and relaxed final dinner in Costa Rica.

DAY 7: Saying *Adiós*

Drive back to **San José** in time to drop off your rental car and connect with your departing flight home.

THE BEST UNDISCOVERED COSTA RICA

Despite Costa Rica's popularity and booming tourism industry, plenty of places are still off the beaten track. And believe me, you'll be richly rewarded for venturing down the road less traveled. Start your trip off with a rental car, which you can turn in after Montezuma. After that, fly to Golfito and then arrange for a boat ride to Playa Zancudo.

Sea turtle in Tortuguero National Park

DAY 1: Rincón de la Vieja National Park

Not nearly as popular as the Arenal Volcano, the **Rincón de la Vieja Volcano,** along with its namesake **national park ★★** (p 218), is an underexplored gem. The park

**The Best
Undiscovered
Costa Rica**

features challenging and rewarding hikes, sulfur hot springs, volcanic mud deposits, and stunning jungle waterfalls. Try the vigorous
2-hour trek to **Blue Lake and La Cangreja Waterfall ★★** (p 220),
which leads to a beautiful forest waterfall emptying into a postcard-
perfect turquoise lake. This is a great spot for a picnic lunch and a
cool dip. If you have time and energy afterward, finish up with the
relatively short and gentle **Las Pailas Loop ★**, which showcases
the volcanic fumaroles and mud pots here.

DAY 2: Horses, high wires & hot springs

You did plenty of hiking yesterday, so start this day off with something a little different. **Hacienda Guachipelín ★★** (p 224) offers
a range of adventure activities, including horseback riding, river tubing, ziplining, and a waterfall rappel canyoning tour (see p 106 for
more about canyoning), in addition to a gorgeous set of natural hot
mineral springs alongside a jungle river.

DAY 3: Going deep down under

Sitting on top of a massive cave system, **Barra Honda National
Park ★** (p 327) is Costa Rica's top spot for spelunking. On a typical
tour here, you'll descend into the depths of the **Terciopelo Cave**

Teatro Nacional in San José

and visit the waterfalls and pools of **La Cascada.** After your visit here, drive to nearby **Nosara,** about an hour away.

🍽 El Chivo Cantina

A short walk from the beach, **El Chivo Cantina** ★★ serves up funky Mexican fare like ceviche tostadas and jalepeño glazed pork belly, alongside 50 or so mostly small batch tequilas and mezcals. See p 338.

DAY 4: Beautiful beaches

The Nicoya Peninsula has many of the same charms and nearly as many miles of beach as Guanacaste, but far fewer crowds. Although the beach at **Nosara** is nice enough, I recommend heading to nearby gems like **Playa Barrigona** ★★ (p 325) or **Playa Carrillo** ★★ (p 325). If you like, sign up for an ultralight flight with the folks at the **Auto Gyro America** (p 326).

DAYS 5 & 6: Montezuma

Montezuma is a great place to mix more beach time with wildlife sightings and visits to some impressive waterfalls. Although you can certainly hike to the foot of the **Montezuma Waterfall** ★★ (p 289), it's even better to visit as part of the **Waterfall Canopy Tour** ★ (p 306). Take a horseback ride to **El Chorro Falls** ★ (p 305), and if you time it right, you can ride home along the beach as the sun sets.

While in Montezuma, visit the **Cabo Blanco Absolute Nature Reserve** ★★ (p 306), the country's first officially protected

Arenal Volcano

area. The main trail inside this park, **Sendero Sueco,** leads to the gorgeous and almost always deserted beach **Playa Balsita.** A trip to Cabo Blanco Nature Reserve can easily be combined with a **kayaking and snorkel tour** to the little cemetery island located just off the village of **Cabuya.**

 Playa de los Artistas

Fresh grilled fish and other Mediterranean fare are the specialty at **Playa de los Artistas ★★★**. If you're limber, slide onto a tatami mat set around one of the low tables closest to the water. See p 311.

DAYS 7, 8 & 9: Playa Zancudo

Finish off this itinerary at one of Costa Rica's most remote and undiscovered beach towns. Playa Zancudo is a sleepy little town on a narrow strip of land between the Golfo Dulce and a saltwater mangrove lagoon. While here, you can go **sportfishing** (p 517), head to nearby **Pavones** (p 525) for a surf session, or take an organized tour with **Zancudo Boat Tours** (p 522).

One of the better day trips heads southward to **Tiskita Jungle Lodge ★★** (p 527), which has a wonderful network of trails through the rainforests and fruit orchards of its private reserve. Any wannabe botanist will also want to allot enough time for a visit to the **Wilson Botanical Gardens ★★★** (p 515), the most impressive botanical garden in the country.

 Sol y Mar

Sol y Mar ★★ is the quintessential beach bar. Stop by for a drink, meal, or friendly game of horseshoes. See p 524.

THE BEST COSTA RICA ADVENTURES

Costa Rica is a major adventure-tourism destination. The following basic itinerary packs a lot of adventure into a single week; if you want to do some surfing, mountain biking, or kayaking, just schedule some more time in. If you're into windsurfing or kiteboarding, you'll definitely want to visit Lake Arenal between December and March.

DAY 1: Starting in San José

You'll probably have a little time to explore and enjoy **San José.** Head first to the **Plaza de la Democracia ★** (p 152), where you'll find the **Museos del Banco Central de Costa Rica ★★** (p 131) and the **Teatro Nacional** (p 158). Take a break for an afternoon beer or kombucha brewed on-site at **Apotecario ★★** (p 161) in Barrio Escalante. For a traditional Costa Rican dinner with a spectacular view of the city lights, head to **Mirador Tiquicia ★** (p 178) in the hills above Escazú.

DAYS 2 & 3: Get wet & wild

Take a 2-day whitewater rafting expedition on the **Pacuare River** with **Ríos Tropicales ★★** (p 215), and spend the night at their remote riverside lodge. When you finish running the Pacuare, they will transport you (as part of the trip package) to **La Fortuna ★★.**

DAY 4: Waterfalls two ways

Go waterfall rappel canyoning with **Desafío Expeditions ★★** (p 345) in the morning, and then hop on a horse or a mountain bike in the afternoon and stop at the **La Fortuna Waterfall ★** (p 352). Take the short hike down to the base of the falls and take a dip in the pool. In the evening, check out the hot springs at **Eco Termales ★★** (p 354).

Hacienda Guachipelin in Rincón de la Vieja

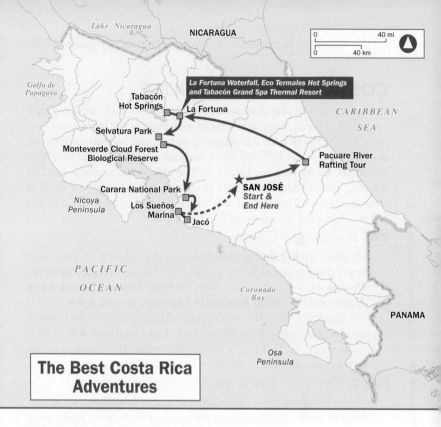

La Fortuna Waterfall, Eco Termales Hot Springs and Tabacón Grand Spa Thermal Resort

NICARAGUA

Lake Nicaragua

Golfo de Papagayo

CARIBBEAN SEA

Tabacón Hot Springs

La Fortuna

Selvatura Park

Monteverde Cloud Forest Biological Reserve

Pacuare River Rafting Tour

Carara National Park

SAN JOSÉ Start & End Here

Nicoya Peninsula

Los Sueños Marina

Jacó

PACIFIC OCEAN

Coronado Bay

PANAMA

Osa Peninsula

0   40 mi
0   40 km

The Best Costa Rica Adventures

DAY 5: Reptiles and surf

Drive south through the rugged jungle hills and towards the Pacific Coast, stopping at the Tárcoles River near **Carara National Park** ★★ (p 408) to spot crocodiles. Get a better look on a 2-hour tour with **Eco Jungle Cruises** ★ (p 415). Continue on to **Jacó** (p 419). Settle in quickly at your hotel, rent a surfboard and head to the beach for one of the country's most consistent breaks. You can also sign up for lessons with **Jacó Surf School** (p 425). In the evening, pick up a few souvenirs and find a bite to eat at the open-air Jacó Walk shopping center (p 431).

DAY 6: Fish for big game ★★★

Wake up early and head to the marina at the **Los Sueños Marriott Resort** ★★ (p 417) and join a sport fishing excursion with **Maverick Sportfishing Tours** (p 416) for a full day out at sea. See if you can reel in Pacific sailfish or 300-pound yellowfin tuna, then transfer back to San José.

DAY 7: Squeeze in a soccer game before splitting

You'll most likely be on an early flight home from **San José,** but if you have a few hours to kill, head for a **hike** or **jog** around Parque

La Sabana or, better yet, try to join a **pickup soccer game** (p 137) here.

COSTA RICA FOR FAMILIES

Costa Rica is a terrific destination for families. If you're traveling with very small children, you might want to stick close to the beaches, or consider a large resort with a children's program and babysitting services. But for slightly older kids and teens, particularly those with an adventurous streak, Costa Rica is a lot of fun. The biggest challenges to families traveling with children are travel distances and the logistical trials of moving around within the country, which is why I suggest flying in and out of Liberia and basing yourself in Guanacaste.

DAY 1: Arrive in Guanacaste

Fly directly into **Liberia.** From here it's a drive of 30 to 45 minutes to any of the area's many beach resorts, especially around the **Papagayo Peninsula.** If you can afford them, the **Four Seasons Resort ★★★** (p 239) and the **Andaz Peninsula Papagayo Resort ★★★** (p 237) are standouts. Both have excellent children's programs and tons of activity and tour options. Alternatively, **Las Catalinas ★★** (p 263) is an entire family-friendly town with condo-style rooms, plus its own beach, multiple pools, and a few restaurants.

DAY 2: Get your bearings & enjoy your resort

Get to know and enjoy the facilities and activities offered up at your hotel or resort. Spend time on the beach or at the pool. Build some sand castles, or get involved in a pickup game of beach volleyball or soccer. In the afternoon, go on a **sail and snorkel cruise** or **stand up paddle boarding.** If you choose a large resort, check out the **children's program** and any scheduled **activities** or **tours** that appeal to your family. Feel free to adapt the following days' suggestions accordingly.

DAY 3: Rafting the Corobicí River

The whole family will enjoy a **rafting tour** on the gentle Corobicí River. **Rios Tropicales ★★** (p 215) offers leisurely trips that are appropriate for all ages, except infants. In addition to the slow float and occasional mellow rapids, there'll be plenty of opportunities to watch birds and other wildlife along the way. If you're here between late September

Montezuma Waterfall

and late February, book a **turtle tour** (p 266) at nearby **Playa Grande** for the evening. The whole family will be awestruck by the amazing spectacle of a giant turtle digging a nest and laying her eggs.

DAY 4: El Viejo Wetlands ★★

About an hour's drive from the Guanacaste beaches, **El Viejo Wildlife Refuge & Wetlands ★★** (p 256) makes a fabulous day trip. Set on a massive old farmstead bordering Palo Verde National Park, this private reserve offers up some of Guanacaste's best wildlife viewing, with boat trips on the Tempisque River and safari-style open-Jeep tours through surrounding wetlands, as well as a host of other cultural and adventure tour options. Lunch is served in a beautiful, century-old farm building.

DAY 5: Hacienda Guachipelín ★

Head for the hills and book a full-day Adventure Pass outing to **Hacienda Guachipelín** (p 224), next to **Rincón de la Vieja National Park.** Older and more adventurous children can go **river tubing,** do a **horseback ride,** or take one of the zipline **canopy tours.** Younger children should get a kick out of visiting the working farm and cattle ranch, butterfly garden, and serpentarium here.

DAY 6: Learn to surf

Head to **Tamarindo ★** (p 268) for the day and arrange for the whole family to take **surf** or **boogie-board lessons.** You can arrange classes and rent equipment at either **Kelly's Surf Shop ★** (p 274) or **Witch's Rock Surf Camp ★** (p 274).

DAY 7: Leaving Liberia

Use any spare time you have before your flight out of **Liberia** to buy last-minute souvenirs and gifts, or just laze on the beach or by the pool. Your best bet for gift shopping is probably **La Gran Nicoya** (p 218). If you want a piece of fine art or a local print, head to **Hidden Garden Art Gallery ★★** (p 218). Both stores are conveniently located on the way to the airport.

THE BEST OF SAN JOSÉ & THE CENTRAL VALLEY

While most tourists opt to get out of San José quickly for greener pastures, Costa Rica's vibrant capital and the surrounding Central Valley offer plenty to see and do. If you have more time, take a whitewater rafting trip on the Pacuare River, tour a coffee farm, or head to Turrialba for a canyoning adventure and a visit to the Guayabo National Monument, Costa Rica's top archaeological site.

DAY 1: Getting to know the city

Start your day on the **Plaza de la Cultura.** Visit the **Museos del Banco Central de Costa Rica ★★** (p 131), and see if you can get tickets for a performance at the **Teatro Nacional ★★** (p 158). From the Plaza de la Cultura, stroll up Avenida Central to the **Museo Nacional de Costa Rica (National Museum) ★★** (p 131).

🔖 Maza Bistro

It's only open for breakfast and lunch, yet Maza Bistro **★★★**, in a funky space beside San José's Parque Nacional, is one of the most sought after tables in town for their market driven approach to comfort foods with dishes like fried chicken with sweet ayote arepas or eggs benedict with green papaya slaw. Don't miss their Bloody Marys, which come with a slice of candied bacon. See p 147.

You can learn to surf and rent equipment at Witch's Rock Surf Camp.

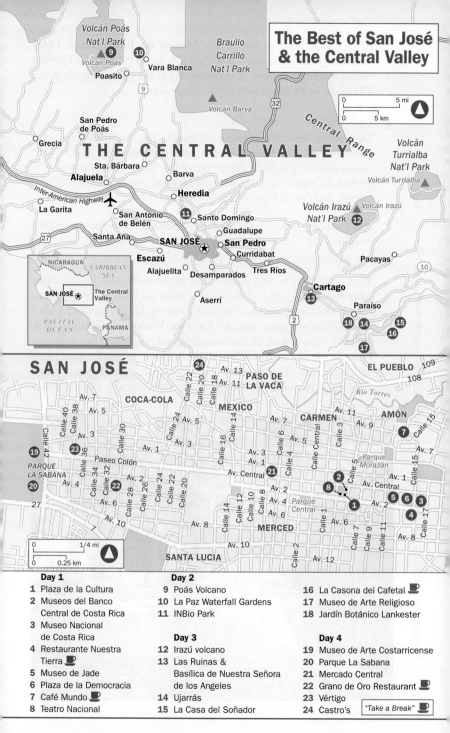

The Best of San José & the Central Valley

THE CENTRAL VALLEY

Volcán Poás Nat'l Park
Volcán Poás
Vara Blanca
Poasito
Braulio Carrillo Nat'l Park
Volcán Barva
Central Range
Volcán Turrialba Nat'l Park
Volcán Turrialba
San Pedro de Poás
Grecia
Sta. Bárbara
Alajuela
Barva
Heredia
Inter-American Highway
La Garita
San Antonio de Belén
Santo Domingo
Volcán Irazú Nat'l Park
Volcán Irazú
Santa Ana
SAN JOSÉ
Guadalupe
San Pedro
Escazú
Curridabat
Pacayas
Alajuelita
Desamparados
Tres Ríos
Cartago
Aserrí
Paraíso
NICARAGUA
CARIBBEAN SEA
SAN JOSÉ
The Central Valley
PACIFIC OCEAN
PANAMA

SAN JOSÉ

PASO DE LA VACA
EL PUEBLO
Río Torres
COCA-COLA
MEXICO
CARMEN
AMÓN
Parque Morazán
Parque La Sabana
Paseo Colón
Av. Central
Parque Central
MERCED
SANTA LUCIA

Day 1	**Day 2**	16 La Casona del Cafetal
1 Plaza de la Cultura	9 Poás Volcano	17 Museo de Arte Religioso
2 Museos del Banco Central de Costa Rica	10 La Paz Waterfall Gardens	18 Jardín Botánico Lankester
3 Museo Nacional de Costa Rica	11 INBio Park	**Day 4**
4 Restaurante Nuestra Tierra	**Day 3**	19 Museo de Arte Costarricense
5 Museo de Jade	12 Irazú volcano	20 Parque La Sabana
6 Plaza de la Democracia	13 Las Ruinas & Basílica de Nuestra Señora de los Angeles	21 Mercado Central
7 Café Mundo	14 Ujarrás	22 Grano de Oro Restaurant
8 Teatro Nacional	15 La Casa del Soñador	23 Vértigo
		24 Castro's *"Take a Break"*

After lunch, head to the nearby **Museo de Jade Marco Fidel Tristán (Jade Museum)** ★★ (p 133). As soon as you're finished taking in all this culture, some shopping at the open-air stalls at the **Plaza de la Democracia** (p 152) is in order.

☕ Café Mundo
Try dinner at Argentine-themed steakhouse La Esquina de Buenos Aires ★★, at Calle 11 and Avenida 4, near the Barrio Chino. This always busy hangout looks straight out of San Telmo and serves classic Porteño dishes like provoleta (baked cheese), mollejas (sweetbreads), and Ojo de Bife (ribe-eye steaks). See p 147.

After dinner, head to the **Teatro Nacional** ★★ for the night's performance.

DAY 2: Alajuela, Heredia & environs

Rent a car for the next 2 days, and get an early start for the **Poás Volcano** ★★ (p 182), before the clouds sock the main crater in. (See p 182 for a note about current closures due to eruptions.) After visiting the volcano, head to **La Paz Waterfall Gardens** ★★ (p 181). Take a walk on the waterfall trail, and enjoy the immense butterfly garden and lively hummingbird garden. This is a good place to have lunch. On your way back to San José, make a loop through the hills of **Heredia** (p 188). Stop at a coffee finca (p 189) for a tour

Streets of San José

The Best of San José & the Central Valley

SUGGESTED COSTA RICA ITINERARIES

and a cuppa, and learn how those precious dark beans make the journey to your morning mug.

DAY 3: Cartago & the Orosi Valley

Start the day taking in the scenery from 3,378m (11,080 ft.) at the top of the **Irazú volcano ★★** (p 198). After admiring the view and hiking the crater trail, head down into the country's first capital city, Cartago, visiting **Las Ruinas ★** (p 196) and the **Basílica de Nuestra Señora de los Angeles ★★★** (p 197), on your way to the Orosi valley. As you drive the loop road around Lake Cachí, stop in **Ujarrás** (p 201) to see the ruins of Costa Rica's oldest church, and to check out the sculpture offerings at **La Casa del Soñador** (p 202).

🍴 La Casona del Cafetal
Set on expansive grounds overlooking Lake Cachí, this place serves good, traditional Costa Rican fare. If the weather's nice, grab an outdoor patio table with a view. See p 203.

After lunch, visit the **Orosi Church & Religious Art Museum ★** (p 203) in the town of **Orosi** (p 201). On your way home, stop at **Lankester Gardens ★★** (p 200), one of the top botanical gardens in the country. Upon returning to San José, you can return the rental car and rely on taxis in the city, as it's much easier and less stressful than dealing with downtown traffic.

Museo Nacional de Costa Rica

DAY 4: More city sights & shopping

Spend this day further exploring the capital. Start by heading out on Paseo Colón to the **Museo de Arte Costarricense (Costa Rican Art Museum)** ★★ (p 134), and spend some time in its wonderful open-air sculpture garden. After visiting the museum, take a stroll around the expansive downtown **Parque La Sabana** (p 136). Intrepid travelers can also do some shopping at the **Mercado Central** ★ (p 156).

Grano de Oro Restaurant

For your final dinner, splurge a bit and head to the elegant **Grano de Oro Restaurant** ★★★, located inside the boutique hotel of the same name (see p 148). Serving up sophisticated contemporary cuisine using the freshest local ingredients, this is arguably one of the best restaurants in the city.

After dinner take a late-night turn on the dance floor at **Vértigo** ★★ (p 159) or **Castro's** ★ (p 159).

COSTA RICA'S
NATURAL
WORLD

4

Costa Rica occupies a central spot in the isthmus that joins North and South America. For millennia, this land bridge served as a migratory thoroughfare and mating ground for species native to the once-separate continents. It was also where the Mesoamerican and Andean pre-Columbian indigenous cultures met.

In any one spot in Costa Rica, temperatures remain relatively constant year-round. However, they vary dramatically according to altitude, from tropically hot and steamy along the coasts to below freezing at the highest elevations. These variations in altitude, temperature, and precipitation give rise to a wide range of ecosystems and habitats, which are described in "Costa Rica's Ecosystems," below.

For its part, the wide variety of ecosystems and habitats has blessed the country with a unique biological bounty. More than 10,000 identified species of plants; 880 species of birds; 9,000 species of butterflies and moths; and 500 species of mammals, reptiles, and amphibians are found here. For detailed info on some of the more common or evocative representatives of Costa Rica's flora and fauna, see p 83.

Thankfully, for both visitors and the local flora and fauna alike, nearly one-quarter of Costa Rica's entire landmass is protected either as part of a national park or private nature reserve. This chapter includes descriptions of the most important national parks and bioreserves in the country.

COSTA RICA'S ECOSYSTEMS
Rainforests

Costa Rica's **rainforests** are classic tropical jungles. Some receive more than 7m (23 ft.) of rainfall a year, and their climate is typically hot and humid, especially in the lowland forests. Trees grow tall and fast, fighting for sunlight in the upper reaches. Life and foliage on the forest floor are surprisingly sparse. The main level of the rainforest is in the canopy, around 30m (100 ft.) high, where the vast majority of animals live, in towering trees festooned with vines and bromeliads.

Among the most interesting of these trees is the parasitic strangler fig, the *matapalo* ("tree killer"), which grows on other trees until it envelopes and suffocates them, and then remains standing as a tree in its own right, with a hollow interior after the original tree rots away.

Mammals that call the Costa Rican rainforests home include the jaguar, three-toed sloth, two-toed sloth, four monkey species, and the

PREVIOUS PAGE: **A red-eyed tree frog**

Baird's tapir. Some of the prettiest birds you are likely to spot are the scarlet macaws and the many-colored toucans.

You can find these lowland rainforests along the southern Pacific coast and Osa Peninsula, as well as along the Caribbean coast. **Corcovado, Cahuita,** and **Manuel Antonio** national parks, as well as the **Gandoca-Manzanillo Wildlife Refuge,** are fine examples of lowland rainforests. Examples of mid-elevation rainforests include the **Braulio Carillo National Park** and the forests around **La Selva** and the **Puerto Viejo de Sarapiquí** region, and those around the **Arenal Volcano** and **Lake Arenal** area.

Tropical Dry Forests

In a few protected areas of Guanacaste (chapter 8), you will still find examples of the otherwise vanishing **tropical dry forest.** During the long and pronounced dry season (late Nov to late Apr), no rain relieves the unabated heat. In an effort to conserve precious water, the trees drop their leaves but bloom in a riot of color: Purple jacaranda, scarlet *poró,* and brilliant orange flame-of-the-forest are just a few examples. During the rainy season, this deciduous forest is transformed into a lush and verdant landscape.

Other common dry forest trees include the *guanacaste,* with its broad shade canopy, and distinctive *pochote,* its trunk covered in thick, broad thorns.

Because the foliage is less dense, dry forests are excellent places to view wildlife. Howler monkeys are commonly seen in the trees, and coatis, pumas, and coyotes roam the ground. Some of Costa Rica's best dry forests are found in **Santa Rosa, Guanacaste, Rincón de la Vieja,** and **Palo Verde** national parks.

Corcovado rainforest

Monteverde Cloud Forest Biological Reserve

Cloud Forests

At higher altitudes, you'll find Costa Rica's famed **cloud forests.** Here the steady flow of moist air meets the mountains and creates a nearly constant mist. Epiphytes—resourceful plants that live cooperatively on the branches and trunks of other trees—grow abundantly in the cloud forests, where they extract moisture and nutrients from the air. Because cloud forests are found in generally steep, mountainous terrain, the canopy here is lower and less uniform than in lowland rainforests, providing better chances for viewing elusive fauna.

The remarkable **resplendent quetzal** is perhaps the most famous and sought-after eye candy in Costa Rica's cloud forests, but there's an immense variety of flora and fauna here, including multiple hummingbird species, wildcats, monkeys, reptiles, amphibians, and bats. **Orchids,** many of them epiphytic, thrive in cloud forests, as do mosses, ferns, and a host of other plants, many of which are exported as houseplants.

Costa Rica's most spectacular cloud forest is the **Monteverde Cloud Forest Biological Reserve** (p 382), followed closely by its neighbor the **Santa Elena Cloud Forest Reserve** (p 385). Much closer to San José, you can also visit the **Los Angeles Cloud Forest Reserve** (p 367).

Mangroves & Wetlands

Along the coasts, primarily where river mouths meet the ocean, you will find extensive **mangrove forests, wetlands,** and **swamps.** Mangroves, in particular, are an immensely important ecological phenomenon. Around the intricate tangle of mangrove roots exists one of the most diverse and rich ecosystems on the planet. All sorts of fish and crustaceans live in the brackish tidal waters. Many larger saltwater and open-ocean fish species begin life in the nutrient-rich and relatively safe environment of a mangrove swamp.

Blue heron in a mangrove

Mangrove swamps are havens for and home to scores of water birds: **cormorants, magnificent frigate birds, pelicans, kingfishers, egrets, ibises,** and **herons.** The larger birds tend to nest up high in the canopy, while the smaller ones nestle in the underbrush. And in the waters, **caimans** and **crocodiles** cruise the maze of rivers and canals.

Mangrove forests, swamps, and wetlands exist all along both of Costa Rica's coasts. Some of the prime areas that can be explored include the areas around the **Sierpe river mouth** and **Diquís delta** near **Drake Bay** (p 482), the **Golfo Dulce** (p 512) in the Southern Zone, **Palo Verde National Park** and the **Tempisque River** basin in Guanacaste (chapter 8), and the **Gandoca-Manzanillo Wildlife Refuge** on the Caribbean coast (chapter 13).

Páramo

At the highest reaches, the cloud forests give way to **elfin forests** and **páramos.** More commonly associated with the South American Andes, a páramo is characterized by tundra-like shrubs and grasses, with a scattering of twisted, windblown trees. Reptiles, rodents, and raptors are the most common residents here, and because the vegetation is so sparse, they're often easier to spot. **Mount Chirripó, Chirripó National Park** (p 471), and the **Cerro de la Muerte** (**Mountain of Death;** p 477) are the principal areas to find páramo in Costa Rica.

Volcanoes

Costa Rica is a land of high volcanic and seismic activity. The country has three major **volcanic mountain ranges,** and many of the volcanoes are still active, allowing visitors to experience the awe-inspiring sight of steaming **fumaroles,** if not sky-lighting **eruptions.** In ecological terms, cooled-off lava flows are fascinating laboratories, where you can watch pioneering lichen and mosses eventually give way to plants, shrubs, trees, and forests.

Arenal Volcano (chapter 10) used to be a top spot for volcanic activity, but it went dark in 2010. One reliable place to view mud pots, fumaroles, and hot springs is **Rincón de la Vieja National Park**

A crater lagoon at Irazú Volcano in Cordillera Central

(p 218). Closer to San José, the **Poás** (temporarily closed; p 182) and **Irazú volcanoes** (p 192) are both currently active. **Turrialba,** meanwhile, has been huffing and puffing so much that it shut down the international airport a few times and forced the closure of Turrialba Volcano National Park until it stops acting up.

COSTA RICA'S TOP NATIONAL PARKS & RESERVES

Costa Rica, which is smaller than West Virginia, has an astonishing 27 national parks, in addition to scores of public and private reserves dedicated to conservation, often funded in part by tourism. Some of these forests are totally inaccessible and even unexplored, notably the vast La Amistad International Park that straddles the Costa Rican–Panamanian border. Others are compact and easily walkable, including the two most popular parks in the country, Manuel Antonio and Poás Volcano.

Most of the national parks charge foreigners around $10 to $15 admission. Costa Ricans and legal residents pay much less. But some parks charge nothing, accept donations, or they charge at one entrance but not at another.

This section is not a complete listing of all of Costa Rica's national parks and protected areas, but rather a selective list of those parks that are of greatest interest and accessibility. You'll find detailed information

Resplendent quetzal

about food and lodging options near some of the individual parks in the regional chapters that follow.

If you're looking for a camping adventure or an extended stay in one of the national parks, I recommend **Corcovado, Santa Rosa, Rincón de la Vieja,** or **Chirripó.** Most of the others are better suited for day trips or guided hikes.

For more information, call the national parks information line at 🕿 **1192,** or the main office at 🕿 **2283-8004.**

The Central Valley

GUAYABO NATIONAL MONUMENT ★   Like historical puzzles? You'll want to visit Guayabo, Costa Rica's top archaeological site. It was once home to a mysterious people whose name has been lost to history and who abandoned the site for reasons unknown before the Spanish arrived. The ruins of homes, roads, and aqueducts, along with petroglyphs and tombs, suggest a complex society led by a *cacique,* a chief, who ruled from this capital over lesser villages. You won't find spectacular ruins like at Chichen Itza or Tikal, but if you read the informative signs and use your imagination, you can picture a fascinating civilization that once thrived here. **Location:** 19km (12 miles) northeast of Turrialba, which is 53km (33 miles) east of San José. See p 205.

IRAZÚ VOLCANO NATIONAL PARK ★   Irazú Volcano is the highest (3,378m/11,080 ft.) of Costa Rica's active volcanoes and a popular day trip from San José. A paved road leads right up to the crater, and the lookout has a view of both the Pacific and the Caribbean on a clear day. The volcano last erupted in March of 1963, on the same day U.S. President John F. Kennedy visited the country. The park has picnic tables, restrooms, an information center, and a parking area. **Location:** 55km (34 miles) east of San José. See p 198.

POÁS VOLCANO NATIONAL PARK ★★   Poás is the other active volcano close to San José. The main crater is more than 1.6km (1 mile) wide, and it is constantly active with fumaroles and hot geysers. Poás is arguably a more inviting trip than Irazú, because it's surrounded by dense cloud forest and has nice, gentle trails to hike. Although the area around the volcano is lush, much of the growth is stunted due to the gases and acid rain. The park has picnic tables, restrooms, and an information center. **Location:** 37km (23 miles) northwest of San José. See p 182. *Note:* A new series of eruptions started in April 2017, and has resulted in the closure of the park, with no date announced for reopening.

Guanacaste & the Nicoya Peninsula

PALO VERDE NATIONAL PARK ★★   A must for bird-watchers, Palo Verde National Park is one of Costa Rica's best-kept secrets. This part of the Tempisque River lowlands supports a population of more than 50,000 waterfowl and forest bird species. Various ecosystems here include mangroves, savanna brush lands, and evergreen forests. The park has camping facilities, an information center, and some rustic, dorm-style accommodations at the Organization for Tropical Studies (OTS) research station here. **Location:** 200km (124 miles) northwest of San José. Be warned that the park entrance is 28km (17 miles) off the highway down a very rugged dirt road; it's another 9km (5½ miles) to the OTS station and campsites. For more information, call the OTS (www.three paths.co.cr; ☎ **2524-0607**). See chapter 8.

RINCÓN DE LA VIEJA NATIONAL PARK ★★   This large tract of parkland experiences high volcanic activity, with numerous fumaroles and geysers, as well as hot springs, cold pools, and mud pots. You'll find excellent hikes to the upper craters and to several waterfalls. Camping is permitted at two sites, each with an information center, a picnic area, and restrooms. **Location:** 266km (165 miles) northwest of San José. See p 218.

SANTA ROSA NATIONAL PARK ★   Occupying a large section of Costa Rica's northwestern Guanacaste province, Santa Rosa has the country's largest area of tropical dry forest, important turtle-nesting sites, and the historically significant La Casona (p 228) monument. The beaches are pristine and have basic camping facilities, and the waves make them quite popular with surfers. An information center, a picnic area, and restrooms are at the main campsite and entrance. Additional campsites are located on the almost-always deserted and entirely undeveloped beaches here. **Location:** 258km (160 miles) northwest of San José. For more information, you can call the park office at © **2666-5051.** See p 228.

BARRA HONDA NATIONAL PARK ★ Costa Rica's only underground national park, Barra Honda features a series of limestone caves that were part of a coral reef some 60 million years ago. Today the caves are home to millions of bats and impressive stalactite and stalagmite formations. Only Terciopelo Cave is open to the public. A camping area, restrooms, and an information center are here, as well as trails through the surrounding tropical dry forest. **Location:** 335km (208 miles) northwest of San José. See p 327.

The Northern Zone

ARENAL NATIONAL PARK ★★ This park, created to protect the ecosystem that surrounds Arenal Volcano, has a couple of good trails and a prominent lookout point that is extremely close to the volcano. The main trail here takes you through a mix of transitional forest, rainforest, and open savanna, before an invigorating scramble over a massive rock field formed by a cooled-off lava flow. **Location:** 129km (80 miles) northwest of San José. See p 348.

CAÑO NEGRO NATIONAL WILDLIFE REFUGE ★ A lowland swamp and drainage basin for several northern rivers, Caño Negro is excellent for bird-watching. A few basic cabins and lodges are in this area, but the most popular way to visit is on a combined van and boat trip from the La Fortuna/Arenal area. **Location:** 20km (12 miles) south of Los Chiles, near the Nicaraguan border. See chapter 10.

MONTEVERDE CLOUD FOREST BIOLOGICAL RESERVE ★★★ This private reserve might be the most famous patch of forest in Costa Rica. It covers some 10,520 hectares (26,000 acres) of primary forest, mostly mid-elevation cloud forest, with a rich variety of flora and fauna. Epiphytes thrive in the cool, misty climate. The most renowned resident is the spectacular resplendent quetzal. The park has a well-maintained trail system, as well as some of the most experienced guides in the country. Nearby you can visit the Santa Elena or other reserves. **Location:** 167km (104 miles) northwest of San José. See p 382.

Central Pacific Coast

CARARA NATIONAL PARK ★★ Located just south of the famous bridge over the Río Tárcoles, where you can always see crocodiles, Carara is a bird-watcher's dream, home to scarlet macaws, toucans, trogons, motmots, woodpeckers, and hummingbirds. Several trails run through the park, including one that is wheelchair-accessible. The park contains various ecosystems, ranging from rainforests to mangroves, and is a

Scarlet macaws in their nest in Carara National Park

transitional zone where the dry forests of Guanacaste turn into the wet forests of the central Pacific. **Location:** 102km (63 miles) west of San José. See p 416.

CHIRRIPÓ NATIONAL PARK ★★ Home to Costa Rica's tallest peak, 3,761m (12,336-ft.) Mount Chirripó, Chirripó National Park is a hike, but on a clear day you can see both the Pacific Ocean and the Caribbean Sea from its summit. In addition to the summit, a number of trails here lead to beautiful rock formations and small lakes—all well above the tree line. **Location:** 151km (94 miles) southeast of San José. See p 471.

MANUEL ANTONIO NATIONAL PARK ★★ Though physically small, Manuel Antonio is the most popular national park in Costa Rica and supports the largest number of hotels and resorts. This lowland rainforest is home to a healthy monkey population, including the endangered squirrel monkey, and the park is known for its splendid beaches. **Location:** 129km (80 miles) south of San José. See p 434.

The Southern Zone

CORCOVADO NATIONAL PARK ★★★ The largest block of virgin lowland rainforest in Central America, Corcovado National Park receives more than 500cm (200 in.) of rain per year. It's remote, but it's easier to get to than you might think, and it's well worth it. Scarlet macaws are abundant here, and it's home to two of the country's largest cats, the jaguar and the puma, as well as Costa Rica's largest land mammal, the Baird's tapir. There are camping facilities at the Sirena ranger station, but you'll have to hire a guide, get a permit, and plan ahead to square away all the logistics. Additionally, there are dozens of ecolodges on the edges of the park that take day hikes to the interior. **Location:** 335km (208 miles) south of San José, on the Osa Peninsula. See p 496.

The Caribbean Coast

CAHUITA NATIONAL PARK ★★   A combination land and marine park, Cahuita National Park protects one of the few remaining living coral reefs in the country. The topography here is lush lowland tropical rainforest. Monkeys, sloths, and birds are common. **Location:** On the Caribbean coast, 42km (26 miles) south of Limón. See p 557.

TORTUGUERO NATIONAL PARK ★★   Tortuguero National Park has been called the Venice of Costa Rica because of its maze of jungle canals, which meander through a dense lowland rainforest. Small boats, launches, and canoes carry visitors through these waterways, where caimans, manatees, and numerous bird and mammal species are common. The extremely endangered great green macaw lives here. Green sea turtles nest on the beaches every year between June and October. The park has a small but helpful information office and some well-marked trails. **Location:** 258km (160 miles) northeast of San José. See p 535.

A boat tour through Tortuguero National Park

HEALTH, SAFETY & ETIQUETTE IN THE WILD

There's a certain amount of risk in any adventure activity, so know your limits. Be prepared for extremes in temperature and rainfall. A sunny morning hike can quickly become a cold and wet ordeal, so it's usually a good idea to carry along some kind of rain gear, or to have a dry change of clothing waiting at the end of the trail. And if you're planning a lot of beach time, don't forget sunscreen. Getting a bad sunburn is one of the easiest ways to ruin a vacation.

Remember that it's a jungle out there, and venomous snakes are abundant. Avoid touching vegetation as you walk, avoid walking on leafy or brushy ground, and don't put your hands or feet anywhere you can't see.

Avoid swimming in rivers unless a guide tells you it's safe. Most mangrove canals and river mouths in Costa Rica support healthy crocodile and caiman populations.

Bug bites will probably be your greatest health concern in the Costa Rican wilderness, but they aren't as big of a problem as you might expect. Coastal visitors will have trouble escaping the bites from the *purruja* sand fleas, especially below the knees. Long pants and sleeves are recommended. Mosquitoes can carry malaria or dengue (see "Staying Healthy," in chapter 14, p 602), but they feed at predictable hours and are easy to guard against with insect repellent. If you are bitten, some cortisone or Benadryl cream will help soothe the itching.

Searching for Wildlife

The best way to see wildlife anywhere is to hire a local guide. Guides have an uncanny ability to spot, smell, hear, or track animals that you would never see otherwise, including sloths, snakes, lizards, spiders, and birds. Guides are also useful for setting up telescopes and taking great pictures using your phone.

A few helpful hints:

- **Listen.** Pay attention to rustling in the leaves; whether it's monkeys up above or coati on the ground, you'll often hear an animal before you see it.

- **Keep quiet.** Noise will scare off animals and prevent you from hearing their movements and calls.

- **Don't try too hard.** Soften your focus and allow your peripheral vision to take over, looking for glimpses of motion all around you.

- **Bring binoculars.** Some birding tours will provide good binoculars, but it's always nice to have your own.

- **Dress appropriately.** Light, long pants and long-sleeved shirts are the best way to protect against insects. Comfortable hiking boots or shoes are also essential, except where heavy rubber boots are necessary.

Avoid loud colors; the better you blend in with your surroundings, the better your chances of spotting wildlife.

- **Be patient.** The jungle isn't on a schedule. However, your best shots at seeing forest fauna are in the very early morning and late afternoon hours.

- **Read up.** Familiarize yourself with what you're most likely to see. Most nature lodges have copies of wildlife field guides, though it's best to bring your own. A good all-around book to use is Carrol Henderson's "Mammals, Amphibians, and Reptiles of Costa Rica: A Field Guide."

RESPONSIBLE TOURISM

Costa Rica is one of the planet's prime ecotourism destinations. Many of the hotels, isolated nature lodges, and tour operators around the country are pioneers and dedicated professionals in the sustainable tourism field. Many other hotels, lodges, and tour operators are earnestly jumping on the bandwagon and improving their practices, while still others are simply "green-washing," using the terms "eco," "green," and "sustainable" in their promo materials, but doing little real good in their daily operations.

In 2016, Costa Rica was ranked 42th globally in the Environmental Performance Index (EPI; http://epi.yale.edu). This is not a particularly impressive feat given the country's image and marketing strategy. Despite its reputation, the substantial amount of good work being done, and ongoing advances being made in the field, Costa Rica is by no means an ecological paradise free from environmental and social threats. Untreated sewage is dumped into rivers, bays, oceans, and watersheds at an alarming rate. Child labor and sexual exploitation are common, and certain sectors of the tourism trade only make these matters worse.

But over the last decade or so, Costa Rica has taken great strides toward protecting its rich biodiversity. Thirty years ago, it was difficult to find a protected area anywhere, but now more than 11% of the country is protected within the national park system. Another 10 to 15% of the land enjoys moderately effective preservation as part of private and public reserves, Indian reserves, and wildlife refuges and corridors. Still, Costa Rica's precious tropical hardwoods continue to be harvested at an alarming rate, often illegally, while other primary forests are clear-cut for short-term agricultural gain.

While you can find hotels and tour operators using sustainable practices all across Costa Rica—even in the San José metropolitan area—a few prime destinations are particular hot spots for sustainable tourism practices. Of note are the remote and wild Osa Peninsula and Golfo Dulce area of southern Costa Rica, the rural Northern Zone that includes both Monteverde and the Arenal Volcano and Lake Arenal attractions, and the underdeveloped Caribbean coast, with the rainforest canals of

Tortuguero, Cahuita National Park, and the Gandoca-Manzanillo Wildlife Refuge.

In addition to focusing on wildlife viewing and adventure activities in the wild, ecolodges in these areas tend to be smaller, often lacking televisions, air-conditioning, and other typical luxury amenities. The more remote lodges usually depend on small solar and hydro plants for their power. That said, some of these hotels and lodges provide levels of comfort and service that are quite luxurious.

In Costa Rica, the government-run tourism institute (ICT) provides a sustainability rating of a host of hotels and tour agencies under its **Certification for Sustainable Tourism (CST)** program. You can look up the ratings at the website www.turismo-sostenible.co.cr.

Bear in mind that this program is relatively new and the list is far from comprehensive. Many hotels and tour operators in the country haven't completed the extensive review and rating process. Moreover, die-hard ecologists find some of these listings and the criteria used suspect. Still, this list and rating system is a good start, and is improving and evolving constantly.

A parallel program, **"The Blue Flag,"** is used to rate specific beaches and communities in terms of their environmental condition and practices. The Blue Flags are reviewed and handed out annually. Current listings of Blue Flag–approved beaches and communities can be found at www.visitcostarica.com.

While sustainable tourism options are widespread in Costa Rica, organic and sustainably grown fruits and vegetables (as well as coffee) are just beginning to become available. Very few restaurants feature organic produce, although that is starting to change. **Cayuga Collection** (www.cayugaonline.com) works with the US based program **Dock to Dish** (https://docktodish.com) to ensure that all of their seafood comes from sustainable sources, and uses only hormone-free poultry and grass-fed beef in their restaurants.

If you're not booking your hotel, tours, and transportation by yourself, you might want to consider using a tour agency that has earned high marks in this area. In Costa Rica, **Horizontes** ★★ (www.horizontes. com; ☏ **888/786-8748** in the U.S. and Canada, or 2222-2022 in Costa Rica) has garnered particularly high marks from several rating agencies and organizations. Other exemplary operators include **Costa Rica Expeditions** ★★ (www.costaricaexpeditions.com; ☏ **2257-0766**) and **Costa Rica Sun Tours** ★ (www.crsuntours.com; ☏ **866/271-6263** in the U.S. and Canada, or 2296-7757 in Costa Rica).

In addition, those looking for a taste of what many think is "the real" Costa Rica should consider booking through **ACTUAR** ★★ (www.actuar costarica.com; ☏ **866/393-5889** in the U.S., or 2290-7514 in Costa Rica). This organization groups together a network of small, rural lodges and tour operators. In many cases, accommodations are quite basic, and bunk beds and thin foam mattresses are common. However, all the hotels, lodges, and tour operators are small-scale and local. In many cases, they are family operations. If you want a true taste of typical, rural Costa Rica, traveling with ACTUAR is a great way to go.

Finally, another great way to make your tourism experience more sustainable is to volunteer. For specific information on volunteer options in Costa Rica, see "Study & Volunteer Programs," in chapter 5, p 114.

Beyond the country's hotels, tour operators, and volunteer options, it's worth noting here that the local commuter airline **Nature Air** (www. natureair.com; © **800/235-9272** in the U.S. and Canada, or 2299-6000) has been a pioneer in the field. In 2004, Nature Air became the first certified carbon-neutral airline on the planet, and it continues to supplement its own sustainable practices with contributions to reforestation and conservation programs.

COSTA RICAN WILDLIFE

For such a small country, Costa Rica is incredibly rich in biodiversity. With just .03% of the earth's landmass, the country is home to some 5% of its biodiversity. Whether you come to Costa Rica to check 100 or more species off your lifetime list, or just to escape from the rat race for a week or so, you'll be surrounded by a rich and varied tableau of flora and fauna.

In many instances, the prime viewing recommendations should be understood within the reality of actual wildlife viewing. Most casual visitors and even many dedicated naturalists will never see a wildcat or kinkajou. However, anyone working with a good guide should be able to see a broad selection of Costa Rica's impressive flora and fauna. The information that follows is a selective introduction to some of what you might see.

Scores of good field guides are available, including **"Costa Rica: Traveller's Wildlife Guides,"** by Les Beletsky. Bird-watchers will want to pick up one or both of the following two books: **"A Guide to the Birds of Costa Rica,"** by F. Gary Stiles and Alexander Skutch, and **"Birds of Costa Rica,"** by Richard Garrigues and Robert Dean. Other specialized guides to mammals, reptiles, insects, flora, and more can be found at Zona Tropical (www.zonatropical.net), which is a Costa Rican–based publishing house that specializes in field guides and wildlife books.

See also "Bugs, Bites & Other Wildlife Concerns" in chapter 14, p 605.

FAUNA
Mammals

Costa Rica has nearly 250 species of mammals. Roughly half of these are bats. While it is very unlikely that you will spot a wildcat, you have good odds of catching a glimpse of a monkey, coati, peccary, or sloth, and any number of bats.

Bird-watching at Bosque del Cabo

Jaguar (Panthera onca) This cat measures from 1 to 1.8m (3½–6 ft.) plus tail and is distinguished by its tan/yellowish fur with black spots. The jaguar is often called simply *tigre* (tiger) in Costa Rica. Jaguars are classified as nocturnal, although some say it would be more accurate to describe them as crepuscular, most active in the periods around dawn and dusk. **Prime Viewing:** Major tracts of primary and secondary forest in Costa Rica, as well as some open savannas; the greatest concentration is in Corcovado National Park (p 496) on the Osa Peninsula. However, jaguars are endangered and extremely hard to see in the wild.

Jaguar

Ocelot (Leopardus pardalis) Known as *manigordo*, or "fat paws," in Costa Rica, the tail of this small cat is longer than its rear leg, which makes for easy identification. Ocelots are mostly nocturnal, and they sleep in trees. **Prime Viewing:** Forests in all regions of Costa Rica, with the greatest concentration found on the Osa Peninsula.

Ocelot

Baird's tapir (Tapirus bairdii) The Baird's Tapir is the largest land mammal in Costa Rica. An endangered species, tapirs are active both day and night, foraging along riverbanks, streams, and forest clearings. It is called *danta* or *macho de monte* in Spanish. **Prime Viewing:** Tapirs can be found in wet forested areas, particularly on the Caribbean and south Pacific slopes.

Baird's tapir

Three-toed sloth (Bradypus variegatus) The larger and more commonly sighted of Costa Rica's two sloth species, the three-toed sloth has long, coarse, brown-to-gray fur and a distinctive eye-band. Each foreleg has three long, sharp claws. These slow-moving creatures spend their whole lives in trees except when they descend to the ground once a week to defecate. **Prime Viewing:** Low- and middle-elevation forests in most of Costa Rica. Although sloths can be found in a wide variety of trees, they are most commonly spotted in the relatively sparsely leaved Cecropia (p 95).

Three-toed sloth

Mantled howler monkey (Alouatta palliate) The highly social mantled howler monkey, or *mono congo*, grows to 56cm (22 in.) in size and often travels in groups of 10 to 30. The loud roar of the male can be heard as far as 1.6km (1 mile) away. **Prime Viewing:** Wet and dry forests across Costa Rica. Almost entirely arboreal, they tend to favor the higher reaches of the canopy.

Mantled howler monkey

Red-backed squirrel monkey (Saimiri oerstedii) The smallest and friskiest of Costa Rica's monkeys, the red-backed squirrel monkey, or *mono titi*, is also its most threatened. Active in the daytime, these monkeys travel in small to midsize groups. Squirrel monkeys do not have a prehensile (grasping) tail. **Prime Viewing:** Manuel Antonio National Park and Corcovado National Park.

Red-backed squirrel monkey

Central American spider monkey (Ateles geoffroyi) Known as both *mono araña* and *mono colorado* in Costa Rica, the spider monkey is one of the more acrobatic monkey species. A large monkey (64cm/25 in.) with brown or silvery fur, it has long thin limbs and a long prehensile tail. It is active both day and night, and travels in small to midsize bands or family groups. **Prime Viewing:** Wet and dry forests across Costa Rica.

Coati (Nasua narica) The raccoonlike coati, often called coatimundi, can adapt to habitat disturbances and is often spotted near hotels and nature lodges. Active both day and night, they are social animals, often found in groups of 10 to 20. Coatimundi are equally comfortable on the ground and in trees. In Costa Rica, the animal is called a *pizote*. **Prime Viewing:** Found in a variety of habitats across Costa Rica, from dry scrub to dense forests, on the mainland as well as the coastal islands.

Coati

Paca (Agouti paca) The paca, known as *tepezquintle* locally, is a nocturnal rodent that feeds on fallen fruit, leaves, and tubers it digs from the ground. It features dark brown to black fur on its back, usually with three to five rows of white spots. Its belly fur tends to be lighter in color. However, because this species is nocturnal, you're more likely to see its cousin, the diurnal agouti or *guatusa*, which in addition to being smaller, is of a lighter brown coloring, with no spots. **Prime Viewing:** Most often found near water throughout many habitats of Costa Rica, from river valleys to swamps to dense tropical forest.

Tayra (Eira Barbara)   This midsize rodent is in the weasel family. Tayras run from dark brown to black, with a brown to tan head and neck. Long and low to the ground, they have a long, bushy tail. It is called *tolumuco* or *gato de monte* in Costa Rica. **Prime Viewing:** Tayras are found across the country, in forests as well as plain areas, and in trees and on the ground.

Collared peccary (Tayassu tajacu)   Called *saino* or *chancho de monte* in Costa Rica, the collared peccary is a black or brown piglike animal that travels in groups and has a strong musk odor. **Prime Viewing:** Low- and middle-elevation forests in most of Costa Rica.

Northern tamandua (Tamandua mexicana)   The Northern tamandua, or collared anteater (*oso hormiguero* in Spanish), grows up to 77cm (30 in.) long, not counting its thick tail, which can be as long as its body. It is active diurnally and nocturnally. **Prime Viewing:** Low- and middle-elevation forests in most of Costa Rica.

White-faced monkey (Cibus capucinus)   Known as both *mono cariblanca* and *mono capuchin* in Costa Rica, the white-faced or capuchin monkey is a midsize species (46cm/18 in.) with distinct white fur around its face, head, and forearms. It can be found in forests all around the country and often travels in large troops or family groups. **Prime Viewing:** Wet and dry forests across Costa Rica.

Birds

Costa Rica has more than 880 identified species of resident and migrant birds. The variety of habitats and compact nature of the country make it a major bird-watching destination.

Jabiru stork (Jabiru mycteria)   One of the largest birds in the world, this stork stands 1.5m (5 ft.) tall and has a wingspan of 2.4m (8 ft.) and a 30cm-long (1-ft.) bill. An endangered species, the jabiru is very rare, with only a dozen or so nesting pairs in Costa Rica. **Prime Viewing:** The wetlands of Palo Verde National Park and Caño Negro Wildlife Reserve are the best places to try to spot the jabiru stork. The birds arrive in Costa Rica from Mexico in November and fly north with the rains in May or June.

Jabiru stork

Keel-billed toucan (Ramphastos sulfuratus)   The rainbow-colored canoe-shape bill and brightly colored feathers make the keel-billed toucan a favorite of bird-watching tours. The toucan can grow to about 51cm (20 in.) in length. Aside from its bill coloration, it is similar in shape and coloring to the chestnut-mandibled toucan. Costa Rica also is home to several smaller toucanet and aracari species. **Prime Viewing:** Lowland forests on the Caribbean and north Pacific slopes, up to 1,200m (4,000 ft.).

Keel-billed toucan

Scarlet macaw (Ara macao) Known as a *lapa* in Costa Rica, the scarlet macaw is a long-tailed member of the parrot family. It can reach 89cm (35 in.) in length, including its long, pointed tail. The bird is considered a threatened species over most of its range, mainly because of habitat loss and the pet trade. Its loud squawk and rainbow-colored feathers are quite distinctive. **Prime Viewing:** Carara National Park, Corcovado National Park, and Piedras Blancas National Park.

Scarlet macaw

Resplendent quetzal (Pharomchrus mocinno) Arguably the most spectacular bird in Central America, this member of the trogon family can grow to 37cm (15 in.). The males are distinctive, with bright red chests, iridescent blue-green coats, yellow bills, and tail feathers that can reach another 76cm (30 in.) in length. The females lack the long tail feathers and have a duller beak and less pronounced red chest. **Prime Viewing:** High-elevation wet and cloud forests, particularly in the Monteverde Cloud Forest Biological Reserve and along the Cerro de la Muerte.

Resplendent quetzal

Magnificent frigate bird (Fregata magnificens) The magnificent frigate bird is a naturally agile flier, and it swoops (unlike other seabirds, it doesn't dive or swim) to pluck food from the water's surface—or more commonly, it steals a catch from the mouths of other birds. **Prime Viewing:** Often seen soaring high overhead, along the shores and coastal islands of both coasts.

Magnificent frigate bird

Montezuma's oropendola (Psarocolius Montezuma) Montezuma's oropendola has a black head, brown body, a yellow-edged tail, a large black bill with an orange tip, and a blue patch under the eye. These birds build long, teardrop-shaped hanging nests, often found in large groups. They have several distinct loud calls, including one that they make while briefly hanging upside down. **Prime Viewing:** Low and middle elevations along the Caribbean slope, and some sections of eastern Guanacaste.

Montezuma's oropendola

Scarlet-rumped tanager (Ramphocelus costaricensis) With a striking scarlet red patch on its backside, this is one of the most commonly sighted tanagers in Costa Rica. It is known locally as *sargento* or *sangre de toro*. **Prime Viewing:** Throughout the country, in lowland and mid-elevation areas.

Scarlet-rumped tanager

Osprey (Pandion haliatus) This large (.6m/2-ft.-tall, with a 1.8m/6-ft. wingspan) brownish bird with a white head is also known as *gavilan pescador,* or "fishing eagle." In flight, the osprey's wings "bend" backward. **Prime Viewing:** Found in lowland coastal areas and wetlands throughout Costa Rica; seen flying or perched in trees near water. A small population is resident year-round, although most are winter migrants, arriving September to October and departing April to May.

Osprey

Violet sabrewing (Campylopterus hemileucurus) The largest hummingbird found in Costa Rica, the violet sabrewing shines a deep purple when the sun strikes it right. Its beak is long, thick, and gently curving. **Prime Viewing:** Mid- and higher-elevation cloud forests and rainforests countrywide.

Violet sabrewing

Roseate spoonbill (Ajaia ajaja) The roseate spoonbill is a large water bird, pink or light red in color, and with a large spoon-shaped bill. Also known as *garza rosada* (pink heron). The species almost became extinct in the United States because its pink wing feathers were used to make fans. **Prime Viewing:** Found in low-lying freshwater and saltwater wetlands nationwide, although rare along the Caribbean coast and plains. Common on the Pacific coast, north-central lowlands, and in the Golfo de Nicoya and Golfo Dulce areas.

Cattle egret (Bubulcus ibis) The cattle egret is a snow-white bird, with a yellow bill and irises and black legs. It changes color for the breeding season: A yellowish buff color appears on the head, chest, and back, and a reddish hue emerges on the bill and legs. **Prime Viewing:** Found near cattle, or following tractors, throughout Costa Rica.

Boat-billed heron (Cochlearius cochlearius) The midsize boat-billed heron (about 51cm/20 in.) has a large black head, a large broad bill, and a rusty brown color. **Prime Viewing:** Throughout the country, near marshes, swamps, rivers, and mangroves.

Laughing falcon (Herpetotheres cachinnans) Also known as the *guaco* in Costa Rica, this falcon gets its name from its loud, piercing call. This largish (56cm/22-in.) bird of prey's wingspan reaches an impressive 94cm (37 in.). It specializes in eating both venomous and nonvenomous snakes but will also hunt lizards and small rodents. **Prime Viewing:** Throughout the country, most commonly in lowland areas, near forest edges, grasslands, and farmlands.

Mealy parrot (Amazona farinosa) Called *loro* or *loro verde,* this large, vocal parrot is common in lowland tropical rainforests on both coasts. Almost entirely green, it has a touch of blue on the top of its head, and small red and blue accents on its wings. *Loro* means parrot, and *verde* means green, so you and locals alike may confuse this parrot with any number of other local species. **Prime Viewing:** Lowland rainforests on the Caribbean and Pacific coasts.

Ferruginous pygmy owl (Glaucidium brasilianum) Unlike most owls, this small (about 38cm/15-in.) grayish-brown or reddish-brown owl is most active during the day. **Prime Viewing:** In wooded areas, forest edges, and farmlands of low and middle elevations along the northern Pacific slope.

Clay-colored robin (Turdus grayi) In a country with such a rich variety of spectacularly plumaged bird species, this plain brown robin is an unlikely choice to be Costa Rica's national bird. However, it is extremely widespread and common, especially in urban areas of the Central Valley, and it has a wide range of pleasant calls and songs. Known locally as the *yigüirro*, it has uniform brown plumage, with a lighter brown belly and yellow bill. **Prime Viewing:** Low and middle elevations nationwide, especially in clearings, secondary forests, and amid human settlements.

Amphibians

Frogs and toads are actually some of the most beguiling, beautiful, and easy-to-spot residents of tropical forests. Of the 175 species of amphibians found in Costa Rica, a solid 85% are frogs.

Marine toad (Bufo marinus) The largest toad in the Americas, the 20cm (8-in.) wart-covered marine toad is also known as the cane toad, or *sapo grande* (giant toad). Females are mottled in color, while males are uniformly brown. These voracious toads have been known to eat small mammals, other toads, lizards, and just about any insect within range. They have a very strong chemical defense mechanism—glands spread across their back and behind their eyes secrete a powerful toxin when threatened.

Marine toad

Prime Viewing: Despite the misleading name, this terrestrial toad is not found in marine environments, but can be found in forests and open areas throughout Costa Rica.

Red-eyed tree frog (Agalychnis callidryas) The colorful 7.6cm (3-in.) red-eyed tree frog usually has a pale or dark green back, sometimes with white or yellow spots, with blue-purple patches and vertical bars on the body, orange hands and feet, and deep red eyes. This nocturnal amphibian is also known as the gaudy leaf frog or red-eyed tree frog. **Prime Viewing:** This arboreal amphibian is most frequently found on the undersides of broad leaves, in low- and middle-elevation wet

Red-eyed tree frog

forests throughout Costa Rica. If you don't find this beautiful, distinctive-looking frog in the wild, you will certainly see its image on T-shirts, postcards, and the covers of guidebooks.

Green and black poison dart frog (Dendrobates auratus) Also called the harlequin poison dart frog, the small green and black poison dart frog ranges between 2.5 and 4cm (1–1½ in.) in length. It has distinctive markings of iridescent green mixed with deep black. **Prime Viewing:** On the ground, around tree roots, and under fallen logs, in low- and middle-elevation wet forests on the Caribbean and southern Pacific slopes.

Green and black poison dart frog

Reptiles

Costa Rica's 225 or so reptile species range from the frightening and justly feared fer-de-lance pit viper and massive American crocodile to a wide variety of less terrifying turtles and lizards. *Note:* Sea turtles are included in the "Sea Life" section below.

Fer-de-lance (Bothrops atrox) Known as *terciopelo* in Costa Rica, the aggressive fer-de-lance can grow to 2.4m (8 ft.) in length. Beige, brown, or black triangles flank either side of the head, while the area under the head is a vivid yellow. These snakes begin life as arboreal creatures but become increasingly terrestrial as they grow older and larger. **Prime Viewing:** Predominantly lower elevation forests, but has spread to almost all regions up to 1,300m (4,265 ft.), including towns and cities in agricultural areas.

Fer-de-lance

Mussurana (Clelia clelia) This bluish-black, brown, or grayish snake grows to 2.4m (8 ft.) in length. While slightly venomous, this snake has rear fangs and is of little danger to humans. In fact, it is prized and protected by locals, because its primary prey happens to be much more venomous pit vipers, like the fer-de-lance. **Prime Viewing:** Open forests, pastures, and farmlands across Costa Rica.

Mussurana

Tropical rattlesnake (Crotalus durissus) Known as *cascabel* in Costa Rica, this pit viper has a triangular head, a pronounced ridge running along the middle of its back, and (of course) a rattling tail. It can reach 1.8m (6 ft.) in length. **Prime Viewing:** Mostly found in low elevation dry forests and open areas of Guanacaste.

Tropical rattlesnake

Basilisk (Basiliscus vittatus) The basilisk lizard can run across the water's surface for short distances on its hind legs, holding its body almost upright; thus its alternate name, "Jesus Christ lizard." **Prime Viewing:** In trees and on rocks located near water in wet forests throughout the country.

Basilisk

American crocodile (Crocodylus acutus) Although it's a threatened species, environmental awareness and protection policies have allowed the massive American crocodile to mount an impressive comeback in recent years. Although these reptiles can reach lengths of 6.4m (21 ft.), most are much smaller, usually less than 4m (13 ft.). **Prime Viewing:** Near swamps, estuaries, large rivers, and coastal lowlands, countrywide. Guaranteed viewing from the bridge over the Tárcoles River, on the coastal highway to Jacó and Manuel Antonio.

American crocodile

Litter skink (Sphenomorphus cherriei) This small, brown lizard has a proportionally large head and neck, and short legs. A black stripe extends off the back of its eyes and down its sides, with a yellowish area below. **Prime Viewing:** Common on the ground and in leaf litter of low- and middle-elevation forests throughout the country.

Litter skink

Boa constrictor (Boa constrictor) Adult boa constrictors (*bécquer* in Costa Rica) average about 1.8 to 3m (6–10 ft.) in length and weigh over 27kg (60 lb.). Their coloration camouflages them. Look for patterns of cream, brown, gray, and black ovals and diamonds. **Prime Viewing:** Low- and middle-elevation wet and dry forests, countrywide. They often live in the rafters and eaves of homes in rural areas.

Green iguana (Iguana iguana) Despite its name, the green iguana comes in a range of coloring. Individuals can vary in color, ranging from bright green to a dull grayish green, with quite a bit of red and orange mixed in. Predominantly arboreal, it often perches on a branch overhanging a river and will plunge into the water when threatened. **Prime Viewing:** All lowland regions of the country, living near rivers and streams, along both coasts.

Slender anole (Anolis [norops] limifrons) This thin, olive-colored lizard can reach 5.1cm (2 in.) in length. There are some 25 related species of *anolis* or *norops* lizards. **Prime Viewing:** Lowland rainforests nationwide.

Sea Life

Boasting over 1,290km (780 miles) of shoreline on both the Pacific and Caribbean coasts, Costa Rica has a rich diversity of underwater flora and fauna.

Whale shark (Rhincodon typus) Although the whale shark grows to lengths of 14m (45 ft.) or more, its gentle nature makes swimming with one a special treat for divers and snorkelers. **Prime Viewing:** Can occasionally be spotted in the Golfo Dulce and off Isla del Caño, and more frequently off Isla del Coco.

Whale shark

4

COSTA RICA'S NATURAL WORLD | Fauna

Green turtle (Chelonia mydas) A large sea turtle, the green turtle has a teardrop-shaped carapace that can range in color from dull green to dark brown. Adults reach some 1.5m (4.9 ft.) and weigh an average of 200kg (440 lb.). **Prime viewing:** Caribbean coast around Tortuguero National Park, from July through mid-October, with August through September being their peak period.

Green turtle

Leatherback sea turtle (Dermochelys coriacea) The world's largest sea turtle (reaching nearly 2.4m/8 ft. in length and weighing more than 544kg/1,200 lb.), the leatherback sea turtle is a threatened species. Unlike most other turtle species, the leatherback's carapace is not a hard shell, but rather a thick, leathery skin. **Prime Viewing:** Playa Grande, near Tamarindo, is a prime nesting site from early October through mid-February; also nests off Tortuguero in much lesser numbers from February through June, peaking during the months of March and April.

Leatherback sea turtle

Olive ridley sea turtle (Lepidochelys olivacea) Also known as *tortuga lora*, the olive ridley sea turtle is the most common of Costa Rica's sea turtles, famous for its massive group nestings, or *arribadas*. **Prime Viewing:** Large *arribadas* occur from July through December, and to a lesser extent from January through June. Playa Nancite in Santa Rosa National Park and Playa Ostional, north of Nosara, are the prime nesting sites.

Olive ridley sea turtle

Humpback whale (Megaptera novaeangliae) The migratory humpback spends the winters in warm southern waters and has been increasingly spotted close to the shores of Costa Rica's southern Pacific coast. These mammals have black backs and whitish throat and chest areas. Females have been known to calve here. **Prime Viewing:** Most common in the waters off Drake Bay and Isla del Caño, from December through April.

Humpback whale

Bottlenose dolphin (Tursiops truncates) A wide tail fin, dark gray back, and light gray sides identify bottlenose dolphins. Dolphins grow to lengths of 3.7m (12 ft.) and weigh up to 635kg (1,400 lb.). **Prime Viewing:** Along both coasts and inside the Golfo Dulce.

Bottlenose dolphin

Moray eel (Gymnothorax mordax) Distinguished by a swaying serpent-head and teeth-filled jaw that continually opens and closes, the moray eel is most commonly seen with only its head appearing from behind rocks. At night, however, it leaves its home along the reef to hunt for small fish, crustaceans, shrimp, and octopus. **Prime Viewing:** Rocky areas and reefs off both coasts.

Manta ray (Manta birostris) The manta is the largest species of ray, with a wingspan that can reach 6m (20 ft.) and a body weight known to exceed 1,360kg (3,000 lb.). Despite its daunting appearance, the manta is quite gentle. If you are snorkeling or diving, watch for one of these extraordinary and graceful creatures. **Prime Viewing:** All along the Pacific coast.

Brain coral (Diploria strigosa) The distinctive brain coral is named for its striking physical similarity to a human brain. **Prime Viewing:** Reefs off both coasts.

Invertebrates

Creepy-crawlies, biting bugs, spiders, and the like give most folks the chills. But this group, which includes moths, butterflies, ants, beetles, bees, and even crabs, features some of the most abundant, fascinating, and easily viewed fauna in Costa Rica. In fact, Costa Rica has over 300,000 recorded species of invertebrates, with more than 9,000 species of butterflies and moths alone.

Blue morpho (Morpho peleides) The large blue morpho butterfly, with a wingspan of up to 15cm (6 in.), has brilliantly iridescent blue wings when opened. Fast and erratic fliers, they are often glimpsed flitting across your peripheral vision in dense forest. **Prime Viewing:** Countrywide, particularly in moist environments.

Blue morpho

Leafcutter ants (Atta cephalotes) You can't miss the miniature rainforest highways formed by these industrious red ants carrying their freshly cut payload. The ants do not actually eat the leaves, but instead feed off a fungus that grows on the decomposing leaves in their massive underground nests. **Prime Viewing:** Can be found in most forests countrywide.

Leafcutter ants

Golden silk orb-weaver (Nephila clavipes) The common Neotropical golden silk spider weaves meticulous webs that can be as much as .5m (2 ft.) across. The adult female of this species can reach 7.6cm (3 in.) in length, including the legs, although the males are tiny. The silk of this spider is extremely strong and is being studied for industrial purposes. **Prime Viewing:** Lowland forests on both coasts.

Golden silk orb-weaver

Mouthless crab (Gecarcinus quadratus) The nocturnal mouthless crab is a distinctively colored land crab with bright orange legs, purple claws, and a deep black shell or carapace. **Prime Viewing:** All along the Pacific coast.

Mouthless crab

Sally lightfoot crab (Grapsus grapsus) Known simply as *cangrego* or "crab," this is the most common crab spotted in Costa Rica. It is a midsize crab with a colorful carapace that can range from dark brown to deep red to bright yellow, with a wide variation in striations and spotting. **Prime Viewing:** On rocky outcroppings near the water's edge all along both coasts.

Sally lightfoot crab

FLORA

Trees

Although it's hard work and easy to be confused, it's often rewarding to be able to identify specific trees within a forest. The following are some of the more prominent and important tree species you are likely to see in Costa Rica.

Ceiba (Ceiba pentandra) Also known as the kapok tree, the ceiba tree is typically emergent (its large umbrella-shaped crown emerges above the forest canopy), reaching as high as 60m (197 ft.); it is among the tallest trees of Costa Rica's tropical forest. The ceiba tree has a thick columnar trunk, often with large buttresses. Sometimes called the silk cotton tree in English, the ceiba's seed pod produces a light, airy fiber that is resilient, buoyant, and insulating. Throughout history this fiber has been used for bedding, and as stuffing for pillows, clothing, and even life jackets. Ceiba trees may flower as infrequently as once every 5 years, especially in wetter forests. **Prime Viewing:** Tropical forests throughout Costa Rica.

Ceiba

Guanacaste (Enterolobium cyclocarpum) The Guanacaste gives its name to Costa Rica's northwesternmost province, and is the country's national tree. With a broad and pronounced crown, the guanacaste can reach heights of over 39m (130 ft.), and its trunk can measure more than 1.8m (6 ft.) in diameter. Guanacaste is prized as a shade tree, and is often planted on pasture lands to provide relief to cattle from the hot tropical sun. **Prime Viewing:** Low elevation forests and plains throughout Costa Rica. Most commonly viewed in the open plains and savannas of Guanacaste.

Guanacaste

Strangler fig (Ficus aurea) This parasitic tree gets
its name from the fact that it envelops and eventually strangles its host tree. The *matapalo* ("tree
killer") begins as an epiphyte, whose seeds are
deposited high in a tree's canopy by bats, birds, or
monkeys. The young strangler then sends long
roots down to the earth. The sap is used to relieve
burns. **Prime Viewing:** Primary and secondary forests countrywide.

Cecropia (Cecropia obtusifolia) Several cecropia (trumpet tree) species are found in Costa
Rica. Most are characterized by large, handlike
clusters of broad leaves, and a hollow, bamboo-
like trunk. They are "gap specialists," fast-growing

Strangler fig

opportunists that can fill in a gap caused by a
tree fall or landslide. Their trunks are usually
home to Aztec ants. **Prime Viewing:** Primary
and secondary forests, rivers, and roadsides,
countrywide.

Gumbo limbo (Bursera simaruba) The bark of
the gumbo limbo is its most distinguishing feature: A paper-thin red outer layer, when peeled off
the tree, reveals a bright green bark. In Costa Rica,
the tree is called *indio desnudo* (naked Indian). In
other countries, it is the "tourist tree." Both names

Cecropia

refer to its reddish, flaking outer bark. The bark is
used as a remedy for gum disease; gumbo limbo–bark tea allegedly alleviates hyper-
tension. **Prime Viewing:** Primary and secondary forests, countrywide.

Flowers & Other Plants

Costa Rica has an amazing wealth of tropical flora, including some 1,200 orchid species, and over 2,000 bromeliad species.

Guaria morada (Cattleya skinneri) The guaria
morada orchid is the national flower of Costa Rica.
Sporting a purple and white flower, this plant is
also called the "Easter orchid," as it tends to
flower between March and April each year. **Prime
Viewing:** Countrywide from sea level to 1,220m
(4,000 ft.). Although usually epiphytic, it also
grows on the ground.

Guaria morada

Heliconia (Heliconia collinsiana) More than 40 of the world's species of tropical heliconia are found in Costa Rica. The flowers of this species are darkish pink in color, and the underside of the plant's large leaves are coated in white wax. **Prime Viewing:** Low to middle elevations countrywide, particularly in moist environments.

Hotlips (Psychotria poeppigiana) Related to coffee, hotlips is a forest flower that boasts thick red "lips" that resemble the Rolling Stones logo. The small white flowers (found inside the red "lips") attract a variety of butterflies and hummingbirds. **Prime Viewing:** In the undergrowth of dense forests countrywide.

Heliconia

Ornamental red ginger (Alpinia purpurata) The red ginger plant has an impressive elongated red bract, often mistaken for the flower. Small white flowers actually emerge out of this bract. Originally a native of Indonesia, it is now quite common in Costa Rica, and is used as both an ornamental plant and cut flower. **Prime Viewing:** Countrywide, particularly in moist environments and gardens.

Poor man's umbrella (Gunnera insignis) The poor man's umbrella, a broad-leaved rainforest ground plant, is a member of the rhubarb family. The massive leaves are often used, as the colloquial name suggests, for protection during rainstorms. **Prime Viewing:** Low- to middle-elevation moist forests countrywide. Commonly seen in Poás National Park and Braulio Carrillo National Park.

Hotlips

Red ginger

Poor man's umbrella

THE BEST SPECIAL-INTEREST TRIPS

5

Active and adventure travelers will have their hands full and hearts pumping in Costa Rica. From scuba diving with whitetip sharks and manta rays off Isla de Caño to kiteboarding over the whitecaps of Lake Arenal, opportunities abound. And Costa Rica is not just for thrill seekers. You can spot a rare green macaw in a Caribbean rainforest, or spend some time with a local family learning Spanish.

This chapter lays out your options, from tour operators who run multi-activity package tours that often include stays at ecolodges, to the best places in Costa Rica to pursue active endeavors. Educational and volunteer travel options are also listed for those who desire to actively contribute to the country's social welfare, or assist Costa Rica in the maintenance and preservation of its natural wonders. For information on Costa Rica's top national parks and private reserves, see p 5.

ORGANIZED ADVENTURE TRIPS

Because many travelers have limited time and resources, organized ecotourism or adventure-travel packages, arranged by tour operators in either Costa Rica or the United States, are a popular way of combining several activities. Bird-watching, horseback riding, rafting, and hiking can be teamed with, say, visits to Monteverde Cloud Forest Biological Reserve and Manuel Antonio National Park.

Traveling with a group has several advantages over traveling independently: Your accommodations and transportation are arranged, and most (if not all) meals are included in the package cost. If your tour operator has a reasonable amount of experience and a decent track record, you should proceed to each of your destinations quickly without snags and long delays. You'll also have the opportunity to meet like-minded souls who are interested in nature and active sports. Of course, you'll pay more for these conveniences.

In the best cases, group size is kept small (10–20 people), and tours are escorted by knowledgeable guides who are either naturalists or biologists. Ask about difficulty levels when you're choosing a tour—most companies offer "soft adventure" packages for those in moderately good shape, while others focus on hardcore activities geared toward seasoned athletes.

PREVIOUS PAGE: **Mountain biking in Heredia**

Costa Rican Tour Agencies

Because many U.S.–based companies subcontract portions of their tours to established Costa Rican companies, smart travelers cut out the middleman and set up their tours directly with these companies. That means these packages are often less expensive than those offered by U.S. companies, but it doesn't mean they're cheap. You're still paying for the convenience of having your arrangements handled for you.

These agencies can arrange everything from whitewater rafting to sightseeing at one of the nearby volcanoes or a visit to a butterfly farm. Although it's generally quite easy to arrange a day trip at the last minute, other tours are offered only on set dates or when enough people are interested. Contact a few companies before you leave home and find out what tours will be offered when you arrive. These local operators tend to be a bit less expensive than their international counterparts, with 10-day tours generally costing in the neighborhood of $1,500 to $4,000 per person, not including airfare to Costa Rica.

ACTUAR ★★ (www.actuarcostarica.com; ✆ **866/393-5889** in the U.S., or 2290-7514 in Costa Rica) is a great option for budget travelers and anyone looking to get a taste of real, rural Costa Rica. ACTUAR manages a network of small, often family-run rural lodges and tour operators, focusing on community interaction and sustainability. It's not luxurious though; bunk beds and thin foam mattresses are common.

Aventuras Tierras Verde ★ (✆ **2249-2354**; www.tierra-verde.com) is a Rainforest Alliance approved, eco-centric tour operator with tour options that range from a 3-day tour of Tortuguero National Park to a 17-day full country tour.

Coast to Coast Adventures ★ (www.ctocadventures.com; ✆ **2280-8054**) has a unique excursion involving no motor vehicles. The company's namesake 12-day trip is a completely human-powered 248km (154 mile) crossing of the country, with participants traveling on rafts, by mountain bike, and on foot. Custom-designed trips (with a minimum of motorized transport) of shorter duration are also available, as well as family-friendly adventures and student tours.

Costa Rica Expeditions ★★ (www.costaricaexpeditions.com; ✆ **2521-6099**) offers everything from 10-day tours covering the entire country to 3-day/2-night and 2-day/1-night tours of Monteverde Cloud Forest Biological Reserve and Tortuguero National Park, where it runs its own lodges. It also offers 1- to 2-day whitewater rafting trips and other excursions. Its tours are some of the most expensive in the country, but it is the most consistently reliable outfitter (and its customer service is excellent). If you want to strike out on your own, Costa Rica Expeditions can supply you with just transportation from place to place.

Costa Rica Sun Tours ★ (www.crsuntours.com; ✆ **866/271-6263** in the U.S. and Canada, or 2296-7757 in Costa Rica) offers a wide range of adventures and specializes in multiday and small group tours that include stays at country lodges.

Horizontes Nature Tours ★★, Calle 32 between Avenidas 3 and 5 (www.horizontes.com; ☏ **888/786-8748** in the U.S. and Canada, or 4052-5850 in Costa Rica), is not a specifically adventure-oriented operator, but it offers a wide range of individual, group, and package tours, including those geared toward active and adventure travelers, as well as families and even honeymooners. The company hires responsible and knowledgeable guides, and it is a local leader in sustainable tourism practices.

International Tour Operators

These agencies and operators are known for well-organized and -coordinated tours. *Be warned:* Most of these operators are not cheap, with 10-day tours generally costing in the neighborhood of $3,000 to $5,000 per person, not including airfare to Costa Rica.

U.S.–BASED TOUR OPERATORS

Abercrombie & Kent ★★ (www.abercrombiekent.com; ☏ **800/554-7016**) offers upscale trips around the globe, including several tours of Costa Rica. It specializes in 10-day highlight tours hitting Monteverde, the Osa Peninsula, and Tortuguero, and also has an excellent 8-day family tour. Service is personalized and the guides are top-notch.

Costa Rica Experts ★ (www.costaricaexperts.com; ☏ **800/827-9046** or 773/935-1009) offers a large menu of a la carte and scheduled departures, as well as day trips and adventure packages, and has decades of experience organizing tours to the country.

Nature Expeditions International ★ (www.naturexp.com; ☏ **800/869-0639**) specializes in educational and "low intensity adventure" trips tailored to independent travelers and small groups.

Overseas Adventure Travel ★★ (www.oattravel.com; ☏ **800/955-1925**) provides natural-history and "soft adventure" itineraries with optional add-on excursions. Tours are limited to a maximum of 16 people and are guided by naturalists. All accommodations are in small hotels, lodges, or tent camps, offering very good bang for your buck.

Southern Explorations ★ (www.southernexplorations.com; ☏ **877/784-5400**) has a range of nature- and adventure-oriented guided excursions—as well as set itinerary self-guided tours—for individuals, groups, and families.

Tauck ★★ (www.tauck.com; ☏ **800/788-7885**) is a soft-adventure company catering to higher-end travelers. It offers an 8-day Costa Rica highlight tour that includes explorations of rainforests and coffee plantations.

In addition to these companies, many environmental organizations, including the **Sierra Club** (www.sierraclub.org; ☏ **415/977-5522**) and the **Smithsonian Institute** (www.smithsonianjourneys.org; ☏ **855/330-1542**), regularly offer organized trips to Costa Rica.

PLANNING A COSTA RICAN wedding

Getting married in Costa Rica is simple and straightforward. You'll have to provide some basic information, including a copy of each passport, your dates of birth, your occupations, your current addresses, and the names and addresses of your parents. Two witnesses are required to be present at the ceremony. If the two of you are traveling alone, your hotel or wedding consultant will provide the required witnesses.

Things are slightly more complicated if one or both partners were previously married. In such a case, the previously married partner must provide an official copy of the divorce decree.

Most travelers who get married in Costa Rica do so in a civil ceremony officiated by a local lawyer. After the ceremony, the lawyer records the marriage with Costa Rica's National Registry, which issues an official marriage certificate. This process generally takes between 4 and 6 weeks. Most lawyers or wedding coordinators then have the document translated and certified by the Costa Rican Foreign Ministry and at the embassy or consulate of your home country before mailing it to you. From here, it's a matter of bringing this document to your local civil or religious authorities, if necessary.

Because Costa Rica is more than 90% Roman Catholic, arranging for a church wedding is usually easy in all but the most isolated and remote locations. To a lesser extent, a variety of denominational Christian churches and priests are often available to perform or host the ceremony. If you're Jewish, Muslim, Buddhist, or a follower of some other religion, bringing your own officiant is a good idea.

Tip: Officially, the lawyer must read all or parts of the Costa Rican civil code on marriage during your ceremony. This is a rather uninspired and somewhat dated legal code that, at some weddings, can take as much as 20 minutes to slog through. Most lawyers and wedding coordinators are quite flexible and can work with you to design a ceremony and text that fits your needs and desires. Insist on this.

Most of the higher-end and romantic hotels in Costa Rica have ample experience in hosting weddings. Many have an in-house wedding planner. Narrowing the list is tough, but the top choices include **Hotel Punta Islita** (p 329), **Villa Caletas** (p 417), **Los Sueños Resort & Marina** (p 417), **Florblanca Resort** (p 315), and the **Four Seasons Resort** (p 239). If you want a remote, yet luxurious, rainforest lodge, try **La Paloma Lodge** (p 494), **Bosque del Cabo Rainforest Lodge** (p 508), **Lapa Ríos** (p 509), or **Iguana Lodge** (p 506).

If you're looking for service beyond what your hotel can offer, or if you want to do it yourself, check out www.weddings.co.cr, www.liquidweddings.com, www.costaricaweddingcelebrations.com, or www.tropicaloccasions.com.

U.K.–BASED TOUR OPERATORS

Imaginative Traveller ★ (www.imaginative-traveller.com; ✆ **44/147-385-2316** outside the U.K.) is a good operator specializing in budget student, group, and family travel. Its offerings in Costa Rica focus on nature and adventure travel, and often include other countries in Central America like Panama or Nicaragua. These trips range in duration from 9 to 18 days.

Journey Latin America ★ (www.journeylatinamerica.co.uk; ℰ **020/ 3553-1554** in the U.K.) is a large British operator specializing in Latin American travel. It offers a range of escorted tours around Latin America, including a few that touch down in Costa Rica. It also designs custom itineraries and often has excellent deals on airfare.

ACTIVITIES A TO Z

Each listing in this section describes the best places to practice a particular sport or activity and lists tour operators and outfitters.

Adventure activities, by their very nature, carry certain risks. Over the years, there have been several deaths and dozens of injuries in activities ranging from mountain biking to whitewater rafting to canopy tours, and drowning in the ocean is also sadly common.

Book with safe, reputable companies, but also know your limits and don't try to exceed them.

Biking

Costa Rica hosts significant regional and international touring races each year, but as a general rule the major roads are dangerous and inhospitable for cyclists. Roads are narrow and without a shoulder, and most drivers show little care or consideration for those on two wheels. The options are much more appealing for mountain bikers and off-track riders. If you plan to do a lot of biking and are very attached to your rig, bring your own. However, several companies in San José and elsewhere rent bikes, and the quality of the equipment is improving all the time. Bike rental shops are listed in each of the regional chapters that follow.

Arguably, **Arenal** has the best mountain biking in Costa Rica. The scenery's great, with primary forests, waterfalls, and plenty of trails. And the hot springs at nearby Tabacón Grand Spa Thermal Resort are a perfect place to unwind after the ride. However, the **Río Perdido** ★★ (www.rioperdido.com; ℰ **888/326-5070** in the U.S. and Canada, 2673-3600) offers many of the same attractions, including incredible hot springs, but also features the country's best specifically designed mountain bike park, with an extensive network of trails and different level circuits. Finally, **Hacienda Guachipelin** ★★ (p 224) also offers a variety of bike trails and some excellent rental bikes. See chapter 8 (p 224) and chapter 10 (p 353) for full details.

Ruta de los Conquistadores

Each year, Costa Rica hosts what many consider to be the most challenging and grueling mountain-bike race on the planet. **La Ruta de los Conquistadores** (The Route of the Conquerors; www.adventurerace.com) retraces the path of the 16th-century Spanish conquistadores from the Pacific Coast to the Caribbean Sea—all in 4 days. The race usually takes place in November, drawing hundreds of competitors from around the world.

TOUR OPERATORS & OUTFITTERS

Bike Arenal ★ (www.bikearenal.com; ✆ **866/465-4114** in the U.S. and Canada, or 2479-9020) is based in La Fortuna and specializes in 1-day and multiday trips around the Arenal area.

Coast to Coast Adventures ★ (www.coasttocoastadventures. com; ✆ **2280-8054**) offers mountain-biking itineraries among its many tour options.

Guanabikers ★ (www.guanabikers.com; ✆ **8817-2971**) has a variety of tours in Guanacaste, including free riding, downhill rides, and dirt jumping on landscapes that include volcanoes, river crossings, and tropical forest paths.

Bird-Watching

With more than 850 species of resident and migrant birds identified throughout the country, Costa Rica abounds with great bird-watching sites. Lodges with the best bird-watching include **Savegre Hotel** in Cerro de la Muerte, off the road to San Isidro de El General (quetzal sightings are almost guaranteed); **La Paloma Lodge** (p 494) in Drake Bay, where you can sit on the porch of your cabin as the avian parade goes by; **Arenal Observatory Lodge** (p 361) on the flanks of Arenal Volcano; **La Selva Biological Station** (p 403) in Puerto Viejo de Sarapiquí; **Aviarios del Caribe** and **Selva Bananito Lodge** (p 554), both north of Cahuita; **Lapa Ríos** and **Bosque del Cabo,** on the Osa Peninsula; **Playa Nicuesa Rainforest Lodge** (p 519) along the Golfo Dulce; **La Laguna del Lagarto Lodge** (p 368) near the Nicaraguan border; and **Tiskita Jungle Lodge** (p 527) near the Panamanian border.

Some of the best parks and preserves for serious birders are **Monteverde Cloud Forest Biological Reserve** (for quetzals and hummingbirds); **Corcovado National Park** (for scarlet macaws); **Caño Negro Wildlife Refuge** (for wading birds, including jabiru storks); **Wilson Botanical Gardens** and **Las Cruces Biological Station,** near San Vito (the thousands of flowering plants here are bird magnets); **Guayabo, Negritos,** and **Pájaros Islands biological reserves** in the Gulf of Nicoya (for magnificent frigate birds and brown boobies); **Palo Verde National Park** (for ibises, jacanas, storks, and roseate spoonbills); **Tortuguero National Park** (for rare green macaws); and **Rincón de la Vieja National Park** (for parakeets and curassows). Rafting trips down the **Corobicí and Bebedero rivers** near Liberia, boat trips to or at **Tortuguero National Park,** and hikes in any cloud forest also provide good bird-watching opportunities.

In San José, your best bets are to head toward the lush grounds and gardens of the **University of Costa Rica,** or to **Parque del Este,** a little farther east in the foothills just outside of town.

COSTA RICAN BIRDING TOURS

Costa Rica Expeditions ★★ (www.costaricaexpeditions.com; ✆ 2221-6099) and **Costa Rica Sun Tours** ★ (www.crsuntours.com; ✆ 866/271-6263 in the U.S. and Canada, or 2296-7757 in Costa Rica) are well-established companies with very competent and experienced guides who offer a variety of tours to some of the better birding spots in Costa Rica.

INTERNATIONAL BIRDING TOURS

Costa Rican Bird Route ★★ (www.costaricanbirdroute.com; ✆ 608/698-3448 in the U.S. and Canada) is a bird-watching and conservation effort that has created several bird-watching-specific itineraries, with guided tours and self-guided adventures.

Field Guides ★ (www.fieldguides.com; ✆ 800/728-4953 in the U.S. and Canada) is a specialty bird-watching travel operator. Its 16-day tour of Costa Rica covers a lot of ground, and group size is limited to 12.

Tropical Birding ★ (www.tropicalbirding.com; ✆ 800/348-5941 in the U.S. and Canada), specializing in birding tours around the world, is based in Ecuador but periodically brings small groups and highly skilled guides to Costa Rica.

WHERE TO SEE THE resplendent quetzal

Revered by pre-Columbian cultures throughout Central America, the resplendent quetzal has been called the most beautiful bird on earth. The ancient Aztecs and Mayans believed the robin-size quetzal protected them in battle. The male of the species has a brilliant red breast, an iridescent emerald head, back, and wing; and white tail feathers complemented by a pair of iridescent green feathers that are more than .5m (1¾ ft.) long.

The belief that these endangered birds live only in the dense cloud forests cloaking the higher slopes of Central America's mountains was instrumental in bringing many areas of cloud forest under protection as quetzal habitats. (Since then, researchers have discovered that the birds do not, in fact, spend their entire lives here.) After nesting between March and July, the quetzals migrate to lower slopes in search of food. These lower slopes have not been preserved in most cases, and now conservationists are trying to salvage enough lower-elevation forests to help the quetzal survive.

Although for many years **Monteverde Cloud Forest** was the premier place to see quetzals, the "crowd forest" that has thronged to visit makes sightings less frequent. Other places where you can see quetzals are in the **Los Angeles Cloud Forest Reserve** near San Ramón, in **Tapantí National Wildlife Refuge,** and in **Chirripó National Park.** Perhaps the best place to spot a quetzal is at one of the specialized lodges located along the **Cerro de la Muerte** between San José and San Isidro de El General.

Victor Emanuel Nature Tours ★★ (www.ventbird.com; ✆ **800/ 328-8368** in the U.S. and Canada) is a well-respected, longstanding, small-group tour operator specializing in bird-watching trips.

WINGS ★ (www.wingsbirds.com; ✆ **866/547-9868** in the U.S. and Canada) is a specialty bird-watching travel operator with more than 30 years of field experience. Group size is usually between 4 and 16.

Bungee-Jumping

Costa Rica's most extreme adventure is on offer at **Monteverde Extremo Park** ★★★ (www.monteverdeextremopark.com; ✆ **2645-6058**). Here you can leap to what looks like certain death from a moving aerial tram 143m (469 ft.) above the ground in one of the most beautiful places you've ever seen. You'll fall 80–100m (260–360 ft.) depending on your body weight before your bungee cord arrests your plunge. This may be the most terrifying thing you've ever done, but for $73, how could you resist?

Camping

Heavy rains, difficult access, and limited facilities make camping a challenge in Costa Rica. Nevertheless, a backpack and tent will get you far from the crowds and into some of the most pristine and undeveloped parts of the country.

Undoubtedly the country's best camping adventure is **Corcovado National Park,** a wild and rugged place teeming with animals, where you can camp at Sirena Ranger Station, pitching a tent on the wooden platforms or on the grass (but watch out for snakes), or you could just rent a cabina. Corcovado is an expensive place to visit because you have to hire a guide, but it's unforgettable.

You could also pitch a tent at **Santa Rosa National Park** and **Ballena Marine National Park.** At both spots you're likely to have miles of unspoiled beach and very few fellow campers around. But in such isolated environments, avoid camping alone, and ask park rangers if there is a risk of being targeted by criminals.

To inquire about organized camping trips, contact **Coast to Coast Adventures** ★ (www.coastocoastadventures.com; ✆ **2280-8054**).

Canopy Tours

Costa Rica has a genuine claim to fame as birthplace of both the jungle canopy zipline (invented by U.S. biology student Donald Perry in 1979 at Finca La Selva) and the jungle canopy zipline *tour* (invented by Canadian entrepreneur Darren Hreniuk in 1997 in Monteverde). From these modest beginnings, ziplining exploded worldwide into one of the most popular forms of extreme adventure there is.

It's a simple concept: String a cable from a high place to a low, clip some weight to it, and watch what happens. You never know what the weather will be like, but you can always count on gravity.

100% Aventura, Monteverde (p 386)

Canopy Safari, Manuel Antonio (p 444)

Cartagena Canopy Tour, Northern beach area, Guanacaste (p 273)

Chiclets Tree Tour, Playa Hermosa (p 423)

Congo Trail Canopy Tour, Northern Guanacaste (p 246)

Hacienda Guachipelín, Rincón de la Vieja (p 224)

Hacienda Pozo Azul, Puerto Viejo de Sarapiquí (p 400)

Mistico Arenal Hanging Bridges, Arenal (p 349)

Monteverdo Extremo Park, Monteverde, (p 386)

Rainforest Aerial Tram Atlantic, en route to Puerto Viejo de Sarapiquí (p 164)

Río Perdido, Bagaces area, near the Miravalles Volcano (p 226)

Selvatura Park, Monteverde (p 387)

Sky Adventures, Arenal (p 350) and Monteverde (p 387)

Vista Los Sueños Canopy Tour, Playa Herradura (p 414)

Sun Trails Waterfall Canopy Tour, Montezuma (p 306)

Witch's Rock Canopy Tour, Papagayo Peninsula, Guanacaste (p 237)

For its size, Costa Rica has a staggering number of canopy tours. The designers of these courses became geniuses at stringing together multiple trees and platforms over broad valleys and rivers, giving guests the heart-fluttering sensation of flying, often at alarming speeds. Many tours include terrifying "Tarzan swings," face-down "Superman flights," controlled rappels, scary suspended bridges, and sometimes rock climbing.

See chapters on your chosen destination for recommendations on canopy tours, and expect to pay somewhere between $40 and $75.

Canyoning Tours

Canyoning means exploring a fast river by rappelling, climbing, swimming, scrambling, and rock-climbing, and it's an exhilarating adventure. The word "rappel" here typically means a fast descent controlled by a guide, while "waterfall rappelling" puts adrenaline junkies in charge of their own ropes. One of Costa Rica's best canyoning operators is **Hacienda Guachipelín ★★** in Rincón de la Vieja, where you rappel into a big river and then grab gigantic staples in the side of a vertical cliff and climb back to safety. After that comes a Tarzan swing in which you're bashed (safely) into a waterfall, but it's all in good fun.

Waterfall rappelling is a perfected art at **Everyday Adventures,** also known as **Psycho Tours ★★★** (p 499), in Matapalo de Osa, where you can rappel down two big waterfalls and also climb a giant *matapalo* strangler fig, all in the same day.

Other canyoning operators in Costa Rica are **Pure Trek Canyoning ★★** (p 351) and **Desafío Expeditions ★★** (p 351), both in La Fortuna, and **Explornatura ★★** (p 205), in Turrialba.

monkey BUSINESS

You should insist on at least one monkey sighting while you're in Costa Rica, and there are four species to choose from.

The most gregarious and commonly spotted is the white-faced or **capuchin monkey** (*mono cara blanca*), said to be among the most intelligent of all monkeys. It's no secret to them that tourists carry food, and like the coati they have learned to beg—or like the raccoon, to steal. Capuchins are agile, medium-size monkeys that make good use of their long, prehensile tails. They inhabit a diverse collection of habitats, ranging from the high-altitude cloud forests of the central region to the lowland mangroves of the Osa Peninsula. It's almost impossible not to spot capuchins at Manuel Antonio (chapter 11), but watch your food, and remember how many times you should feed wild animals in Costa Rica: never.

Howler monkeys (*mono congo*) are sometimes said to have the loudest call in the animal kingdom after the blue whale. Howlers have a unique hyoid bone in their throats that lets them emit alarmingly loud howls, growls, and grunts of warning to other howler troops in the area, advising them to keep their distance. This is remarkably effective at conservation of energy, because the other congo troops answer with the same howls, and the troops stay apart and don't fight. These large monkeys, dark-brown to black, often gaze down tamely from the treetops when in the presence of humans. Howlers are easy to spot in the dry tropical forests of coastal Guanacaste and the Nicoya Peninsula (see chapter 8). If a couple of weeks go by and you never hear one, check and make sure you're in the right country.

The **spider monkey** (*mono araña*), Costa Rica's largest and strongest, is distinguished by the fact that it has four fingers but no thumb—apparently the thumb was selected out by evolution because it only got in the way while swinging through the trees. These long, slender monkeys are dark brown to black and prefer the high canopies of primary rainforests, though you can often see them swinging between lower branches as well. Spider monkeys have good prehensile tails but travel through the canopy with a hand-over-hand motion frequently imitated by their less graceful human cousins on playground monkey bars around the world. Spider monkeys are usually easy to find in Corcovado and Tortuguero.

The rarest and cutest of Costa Rica's monkeys is the little **squirrel monkey** (*mono tití*), with its small brown body, dark eyes with white rings, white ears, white chest, and very long tail. Abundant in and around Manuel Antonio and Corcovado, these fruit-eating acrobats usually travel in large bands, so if you see one, you'll probably see a lot more.

Diving & Snorkeling

Costa Rica is not considered a world-class dive spot except in one extremely remote location, **Isla del Coco,** which Jacques Cousteau called "the most beautiful island in the world." It's famous for big schools of hammerhead sharks and Galapagos-like isolation. But it takes a few thousand dollars and a couple of weeks on a live-aboard boat to get there and back, and you have to be an expert diver.

For the ordinary person certified to dive, the waters off **Isla del Caño,** near Drake Bay, are the prime destination in the country. But other options abound at Pacific dive spots like **Playa del Coco, Islas Murciélagos** (Bat Islands), and the **Catalina Islands,** where you may spot manta rays, moray eels, and white-tipped sharks.

On the Caribbean coast, runoff from banana plantations has destroyed much of the reefs, although **Isla Uvita,** the landing place of Columbus just off the coast of Limón, and **Manzanillo,** near the Pana-manian border, still have good diving.

Visibility varies with season and location. Generally, heavy rainfall tends to swell the rivers and muddy the waters, even well offshore. A two-tank dive should cost around $85, and snorkelers should pay as little as $35.

For snorkelers, the same rain, runoff, and wave conditions that drive scuba divers offshore tend to make coastal and shallow-water conditions less than optimal, but sometimes the weather is calm and the water is clear. Ask around for snorkeling options; there are some good ones at **Manzanillo Beach** on the southern Caribbean coast, especially in the calm months of September and October.

DIVING OUTFITTERS & OPERATORS

In addition to the companies listed below, check the listings at specific beach and port destinations in the regional chapters.

Sirenas Diving Costa Rica ★★ (www.sirenasdivingcostarica. com; © 8721-8055) is perhaps the largest, most professional, and best-established dive operation in the country. Based out of Playa Hermosa, this outfitter is also a local pioneer in Nitrox diving. Based at Playa Oco-tal is **Rocket Frog Divers** ★(© 2670-1589; www.scuba-dive-costa-rica.com), which offers a number of PADI courses and runs dives to popular Pacific Coast sites like the Bat and Catalinas Islands.

Aggressor Fleet ★★ (www.aggressor.com; © 800/348-2628 in the U.S. and Canada) runs the 36m (118-ft.) live-aboard *Okeanos Aggres-sor* on regular trips to Isla del Coco and Isla del Caño. **Undersea Hunter** ★★ (www.underseahunter.com; © 800/203-2120 in the U.S., or 2228-6613 in Costa Rica) offers the *Undersea Hunter* and its sister ship, the *Sea Hunter,* two pioneers of the live-aboard diving excursions to Isla del Coco.

On the Caribbean side of the country, look up **Reef Runner Div-ers** ★ (www.reefrunnerdivers.com; © 2750-0480 or 8796-8898) in Puerto Viejo. On the Pacific, Playa del Coco is a top diving spot, and one of the major outfitters is **Rich Coast Diving** ★ (www.richcoastdiving. com; © 2670-0176 or 2670-0004).

Fishing

Anglers in Costa Rican waters have landed more than 100 world-record catches, including blue marlin, Pacific sailfish, dolphin, wahoo, yellowfin tuna, *guapote,* and snook. Whether you want to head offshore looking for a big sail, wrestle a tarpon near a Caribbean river mouth, or choose a quiet spot on a lake to cast for *guapote*, you'll find it here. You can raise a marlin anywhere along the Pacific coast, while feisty snook can be found in mangrove estuaries along both coasts.

Many of the Pacific port and beach towns—Quepos, Puntarenas, Playa del Coco, Tamarindo, Flamingo, Golfito, Drake Bay, Zancudo— support large charter fleets and have hotels that cater to anglers; see chapters 7 and 9 to 12 for recommended boats, captains, and lodges. Fishing trips usually range between $400 and $2,500 per day (depending on boat size) for the boat, captain, tackle, drinks, and lunch, so the cost per person depends on the size of the group.

Costa Rican law requires all fishermen to purchase a license. The cost ranges from $15 to $50 depending upon the length of the license and whether it covers saltwater or freshwater fishing, or both. All boats, captains, and fishing lodges listed here and throughout the book will help you with the technicalities of buying your license.

Costa Rica Outdoors ★ (www.costaricaoutdoors.com; © **800/308-3394** in the U.S. and Canada or 2231-0306 in Costa Rica) is a well-established operation founded by local fishing legend and outdoor writer Jerry Ruhlow, specializing in booking fishing trips.

Top Fishing Lodges

Aguila de Osa Inn, Drake Bay (p 492)
Crocodile Bay, in Puerto Jiménez (p 501)
Río Colorado Lodge, at the Barra del Colorado National Wildlife Refuge (p 535)
Silver King Lodge, at Barra del Colorado (p 535)
The Zancudo Lodge, in Playa Zancudo (p 523)

Golfing

Costa Rica doesn't have a lot of golf courses, but those it does have offer stunning scenery and almost no crowds. Be aware that strong seasonal winds make playing most of the Guanacaste courses challenging from December through March.

The most spectacular course is at **Four Seasons Resort ★★★** (p 239), designed by Arnold Palmer. Greens fees are $240 for 18-holes and $175 for 9-holes.

Another good option is the **Reserva Conchal ★★** course at the **Westin Playa Conchal Resort & Spa** (p 255) in Guanacaste. Greens fees here are $150, including a cart, for 18-holes, or $95 for 9-holes. With advance notice and depending on available tee times, this course is currently open to guests at other area hotels with advance reservations.

Hacienda Pinilla ★★ (p 273) is an 18-hole links-style course located south of Tamarindo. This might just be the most challenging course in the country, and the facilities, though limited, are top-notch. Currently, the course is open to golfers staying at hotels around the area, with advance reservations. Greens fees run around $150 for 18 holes, including a cart, or $75 for 9-holes.

Another major resort course is **La Iguana** at the **Los Sueños Marriott Ocean & Golf Resort ★★** in Playa Herradura (p 415). Greens fees, including a cart, run around $150 for the general public; guests pay slightly less.

Down the Central Pacific coast south of Dominical, the **San Buenas Golf Resort ★** (www.sbgr.com) has 9 holes. Greens fees, including a cart, run around $55 for 9 holes, or $80 if you play around the course twice.

Currently, the best option for golfers staying in and around San José is **Parque Valle del Sol ★** (www.vallesol.com; ✆ **2282-9222**; p 172), an 18-hole course in the western suburb of Santa Ana. Greens fees are $99, including a cart.

Golfers interested in a deal that includes play on a variety of courses should contact **Costa Rica Golf Adventures ★** (www.golfcr.com; ✆ **888/536-8510** in the U.S. and Canada) or **Tee Times Costa Rica** (www.teetimescostarica.com; ✆ **866/448-3182** in the U.S. and Canada).

Horseback Riding

Costa Rica's rural roots are evident in the continued use of horses for real work and transportation throughout the country. Visitors will find that horses are easily available for riding, whether you want to take a sunset trot along the beach, ride through the cloud forest, or take a multiday trek across the Northern Zone.

Most travelers saddle up for a couple of hours. Rates run between $15 to $30 per hour, depending upon group size and the length of the ride, with full-day rides running around $65 to $120, usually including lunch and refreshments.

In the Jacó area, look up **Discovery Horseback Tours ★** (www.horseridecostarica.com; ✆ **8838-7550**). In Monteverde, try **Horse Trek Monteverde ★** (www.horsetrekmonteverde.com; ✆ **8359-3485**). And in Guanacaste, consider **Hacienda Guachipelin ★★** (www.guachipelin.com; ✆ **2690-2900**), a working horse and cattle ranch.

Paragliding & Ballooning

If you spend much time in Costa Rica, you'll be surprised how often you look up and see someone hanging from a parachute or standing in a balloon. Paragliding is a popular diversion in the cliff areas around Caldera, just south of Puntarenas, as well as other spots along the Central Pacific coast. Check in with **Tandem Paraglide Costa Rica ★** (www.paraglidecostarica.com; ✆ **908/545-3242** in the U.S. and 8950-8676 in Costa Rica). This place caters to paragliders and offers lessons and tandem flights. Lessons cost around $60 per day, including equipment, while a 20-minute tandem flight with an experienced pilot will run you around $95.

Serendipity Adventures ★ (www.serendipityadventures.com; © **888/226-5050** in the U.S. and Canada, or 2556-2222 in Costa Rica) will take you up, up, and away in a hot-air balloon near Arenal Volcano. A basic flight costs around $385 per passenger, with a two-person minimum and a five-person or 800-pound maximum.

Rock Climbing

Although this is a nascent sport in Costa Rica, the possibilities are promising, with several challenging rock formations close to San José and along the Cerro de la Muerte, as well as great climbing opportunities on Mount Chirripó, the Uruca River Canyon, and Aserrí Rock.

Spas & Yoga Retreats

Prices for spa treatments in Costa Rica are generally less expensive than those in the United States or Europe, although some of the fancier options, like the Four Seasons or Tabacón Grand Spa Thermal Resort, rival the services, facilities, and prices found anywhere on the planet.

The **Four Seasons Resort ★★★** (p 239) on the Papagayo Peninsula has ample and luxurious facilities and treatment options, as well as classes in yoga, Pilates, and other disciplines.

Florblanca Resort ★★★ (p 315) in Santa Teresa has some beautiful spa facilities, with two large treatment rooms over a flowing water feature.

In Montezuma on the Nicoya Peninsula, the clifftop **Anamaya Resort ★** (© 2642-1289; www.anamayaresort.com) offers weekly yoga retreats, as well as yoga teacher training. In Nosara, the hip **The Harmony Hotel ★★** (p 336) has an extensive wellness program that includes multiple daily yoga classes, meditation, and frequent workshops.

Luna Lodge ★ (p 510) is a very remote lodge located on a hillside overlooking Playa Carate, on the border of Corcovado National Park. Individual rooms and tents offer views over the rainforests. Luna Lodge offers a fairly full schedule of dedicated yoga and wellness programs and has a good little spa. Nearby, **Blue Osa ★** (www.blueosa.com) offers yoga teacher training.

Pranamar Villas & Yoga Retreat ★★★, Santa Teresa (p 317), is an upscale beachfront resort, with a large Balinese-inspired open air-yoga space and a restaurant focused on delicious spa cuisine. A range of daily classes are offered, and a steady stream of visiting teachers and groups use the spot for longer retreats and seminars.

Samasati ★, Puerto Viejo de Talamanca (p 571), is an intimate yoga retreat set amid dense forest on a hillside overlooking the Caribbean Sea. Accommodations range from budget to rustically luxurious.

Tabacón Grand Spa Thermal Resort ★★★, Tabacón (p 354), is a top-notch spa with spectacular hot springs, lush gardens, and a volcano view. A complete range of spa services and treatments is available at reasonable prices.

Xandari Resort & Spa ★★, Alajuela (p 183), is a luxury boutique hotel with distinctive contemporary architecture, abundant artworks, and its own little "spa village" that offers up top-notch treatments and services. This is a good choice if you're looking for a day or two of pampering, or for day treatments while staying in San José.

Surfing

Significant sections of the movie "Endless Summer II" (1994), the sequel to the all-time surf classic, were filmed in Costa Rica. All along Costa Rica's immense coastline are point and beach breaks that work year-round. **Playas Hermosa, Jacó,** and **Dominical,** on the Central Pacific coast, and **Tamarindo** and **Playa Guiones,** in Guanacaste, are mini surf meccas. **Salsa Brava** in Puerto Viejo is a steep and fast wave that peels off both right and left over shallow coral. It has a habit of breaking boards, but the daredevils keep coming back. Beginners should stick to the mellower sections of **Jacó** and **Tamarindo**—surf lessons are offered at both beaches. Crowds are starting to gather at the more popular breaks, but you can still stumble onto secret spots on the **Osa** and **Nicoya peninsulas** and along the northern **Guanacaste** coast. Costa Rica's signature wave is still at **Pavones,** said to have the second-longest left in the world. Surfers also swear by **Playa Grande, Playa Negra, Guiones**, **Matapalo, Malpaís,** and **Witch's Rock.**

For swell reports, general surf information, live wave-cams, and great links pages, point your browser to **www.surfline.com** or **www. crsurf.com**. Although killer sets are possible at any particular spot at any time of the year—depending upon swell direction, local winds, and distant storms—in broad terms, the northern coast of Guanacaste works best from December to April; the central and southern Pacific coasts from April to November; and the Caribbean coast's short big-wave season is December through March. Surf lessons, usually private or in a small group, will run you anywhere from $20 to $40 per hour, including the board.

Whitewater Rafting, Kayaking & Canoeing

Whether you're a first-time rafter or a world-class kayaker, Costa Rica's got some fast water ready for you. Rivers rise and fall with the rain, but you can get wet here any time of year. Full-day rafting trips run between $75 and $110 per person.

The best whitewater rafting ride in Costa Rica is the **Pacuare River,** which some say is one of the best rafting rivers in the world. It's clean and scenic, and it has heart-jolting Class IV rapids. There is also excellent rafting on the **Savegre** and the **Sarapiquí,** while the **Reventazón** has fallen on hard times because of hydroelectric dams. Some of the most challenging rafting in the country is at the **El Chorro** section of the Naranjo River, where Class V rapids rush through a narrow, steep canyon. Whitewater rafting operators can be found in almost every corner of Costa Rica, and they're worth looking up.

Ríos Tropicales ★★ (www.riostropicales.com; ℭ **866/722-8273** in the U.S. and Canada, or 2233-6455 in Costa Rica), founded in 1985, is perhaps the oldest and most reliable rafting operator in Costa Rica, with tours on most of the country's popular rivers. Accommodation options include a very comfortable lodge on the banks of the Río Pacuare for 2-day trips.

Aventuras Naturales ★★ (ℭ **888/680-9031** in the U.S., or 2224-0505 in Costa Rica) is a major rafting operator with daily trips on the most popular rivers in Costa Rica. Its **Pacuare Lodge ★★★** (p 206) is very plush, and a great place to spend the night on one of its 2-day rafting trips.

Exploradores Outdoors ★ (www.exploradoresoutdoors.com; ℭ **646/205-0828** in the U.S. and Canada, or 2222-6262 in Costa Rica) is another good company run by a longtime and well-respected river guide. They run the Pacuare and Reventazón rivers, and even combine a

IN SEARCH OF turtles

Few places in the world have as many sea-turtle nesting sites as Costa Rica. Along both coasts, five species of these huge marine reptiles come ashore at specific times of the year to dig nests in the sand and lay their eggs. Sea turtles are endangered throughout the world because of hunting, accidental deaths in fishing nets, development on beaches that once served as nesting areas, and the collection and sale of their eggs. International trade in sea-turtle products is prohibited by most countries, but sea-turtle numbers continue to dwindle.

Among the species of sea turtles that nest on Costa Rica's beaches are the **olive ridley** (known for mass egg-laying migrations, or *arribadas*), **leatherback, hawksbill, green,** and **Pacific green turtle.** Excursions to see nesting turtles have become common, and they are fascinating, but please make sure that you do not disturb the turtles. Any light source other than red-tinted flashlights can confuse the turtles and cause them to return to the sea without laying their eggs. As more development takes place on the Costa Rican coast, hotel lighting may cause the number of nesting turtles to drop. Luckily, many of the nesting beaches have been protected as national parks.

Here are the main places to see nesting sea turtles: **Santa Rosa National Park** (near Liberia, olive ridleys nest here from July–Dec, and to a lesser extent from Jan–June), **Las Baulas National Marine Park** (near Tamarindo, leatherbacks nest here early Oct to mid-Feb), **Ostional National Wildlife Refuge** (near Playa Nosara, olive ridleys nest July–Dec, and to a lesser extent Jan–June), and **Tortuguero National Park** (on the northern Caribbean coast, green turtles nest here July to mid-Oct, with Aug–Sept their peak period. In lesser numbers, leatherback turtles nest here Feb–June, peaking Mar–Apr).

1-day river trip with onward transportation to or from the Caribbean coast, or the Arenal Volcano area, for no extra cost.

Canoa Aventura ★ (www.canoa-aventura.com; ✆ **844/479-8200** in the U.S. and Canada, or 2479-8200 in Costa Rica) specializes in canoeing and kayaking. Based in the Arenal area, it offers tours of the Peñas Blancas River, Tres Amigos River, and Lake Arenal, along with other adventures.

Loco's Tropical Tours ★ (www.whiteh2o.com; ✆ **2556-6035**) is a small company based in Turrialba, a good option for hardcore kayakers or small custom group tours.

Windsurfing & Kiteboarding

Windsurfing is not very popular on the high seas here, where winds are fickle and rental options are limited, even at beach hotels. However, **Lake Arenal** is considered one of the top spots in the world for high-wind boardsailing. During the winter months, many of the regulars from Washington's Columbia River Gorge take up residence around the nearby town of Tilarán. Small boards, water starts, and fancy gibes are the norm. The best time for windsurfing on Lake Arenal is between December and March. The same winds that buffet Lake Arenal make their way to **Bahía Salinas** (also known as Bolaños Bay), near La Cruz, Guanacaste, where you can get in some good windsurfing. Both spots also have operations offering lessons and equipment rentals in the high-action sport of kiteboarding. Board rentals run around $55 to $85 per day, while lessons can cost between $50 to $150 for a half-day private lesson. See "La Cruz & Bahía Salinas," in chapter 8, and "Along the Shores of Lake Arenal," in chapter 10, for details.

STUDY & VOLUNTEER PROGRAMS

Language Immersion

As more people travel to Costa Rica with the intention of learning Spanish, the number of options for Spanish immersion vacations increases. You can find courses of varying lengths and degrees of intensiveness, and many that include cultural activities and day excursions. Many of these schools have reciprocal relationships with U.S. universities, so in some cases you can receive college credit.

Most Spanish schools can arrange for home stays with a middle-class local family for a total-immersion experience. Classes are often small, or even one-on-one, and can last anywhere from 2 to 8 hours a day. Listed below are some of the larger and more established Spanish-language schools, with approximate costs. Most are in San José, but there are schools in Monteverde, Manuel Antonio, Playa Flamingo,

Malpaís, Playa Nosara, and Tamarindo. A 1-week class for 4 hours a day, including a home stay, tends to cost between $420 and $630.

Adventure Education Center (AEC) Spanish Institute (www.adventurespanishschool.com; © **800/237-2730** in the U.S. and Canada, or 2787-0023 in Costa Rica) has branches in Arenal, Dominical, and Turrialba, and specializes in combining language learning with adventure activities. Nursing, Medical, and Agricultural focuses are also offered.

Centro Panamericano de Idiomas (CPI) (www.cpi-edu.com; © **877/373-3116** in the U.S., or 2265-6306) has three campuses: one in the quiet suburban town of Heredia, another in Monteverde, and one at the beach in Playa Flamingo.

Costa Rican Language Academy in San José (www.spanishandmore.com; © **866/230-6361** in the U.S., or 2280-1685 in Costa Rica) has intensive programs with classes held Monday to Thursday to give students a chance for longer weekend excursions. The academy also integrates Latin dance and Costa Rican cooking classes into the program.

Escuela D'Amore (www.academiadamore.com; © **877/434-7290** in the U.S. and Canada, or 2777-0233 in Costa Rica) is situated in the lush surroundings of Manuel Antonio.

Wayra Instituto de Español (www.spanish-wayra.co.cr; © **2653-0359**) is a longstanding operation located in the beach town of Tamarindo.

Alternative Educational Travel

Adventures Under the Sun ★★ (www.adventuresunderthesun.com; © **866/897-5578** in the U.S. and Canada, or 2289-0404 in Costa Rica) is a Costa Rican–based outfit specializing in adventure and volunteer-focused teen travel. Its strong suit is organizing custom group itineraries.

Outward Bound Costa Rica ★★ (www.crrobs.org; © **800/676-2018** in the U.S., or 2278-6058 in Costa Rica) is the local branch of this international adventure-based outdoor-education organization. Courses range from 2 weeks to a full semester, and offerings include surfing, kayaking, tree climbing, and learning Spanish.

Eco Teach ★ (www.ecoteach.com; © **800/626-8992** in the U.S. and Canada) works primarily to facilitate educational trips for high school and college student groups. Trips focus on Costa Rican ecology and culture. Costs run around $1,695 to $2,285 per person for 8- to 10-day trips, including lodging, meals, classes, and travel within the country (airfare to Costa Rica extra).

The **Institute for Central American Development Studies** ★ (www.icads.org; © **2225-0508**) offers internship and research opportunities in the fields of environment, agriculture, human rights, and women's studies. An intensive Spanish-language program can be combined with work-study or volunteer opportunities.

The **Organization for Tropical Studies ★★** (http://tropical studies.org; ℰ **919/684-5774** in the U.S., or 2524-0607 in Costa Rica) represents several Costa Rican and U.S. universities. This organization's mission is to promote research, education, and the wise use of natural resources in the tropics. Research facilities include the La Selva, Las Cruces, and Palo Verde Biological Stations. The wide variety of programs range from full-semester undergraduate programs to specific graduate courses to tourist programs. (These are generally sponsored/run by established operators such as Costa Rica Expeditions or Elderhostel.) Programs range in duration from 3 to 10 days, and costs vary greatly. Entrance requirements and competition for some of these courses can be demanding.

Sustainable Volunteer Projects

Below are some institutions and organizations that are working on ecology and sustainable development projects in Costa Rica.

APREFLOFAS (Association for the Preservation of the Wild Flora and Fauna; www.apreflofas.or.cr; ℰ **2240-6087**) is a pioneering local conservation organization that accepts volunteers and runs environmentally sound educational tours around the country.

Asociación de Voluntarios para el Servicio en las Areas Protegidas (**ASVO;** www.asvocr.org; ℰ **2258-4430**) organizes volunteers to work in Costa Rican national parks. A 2-week minimum commitment is required, as is an ability to adapt to rustic conditions and remote locations and gain a basic ability to converse in Spanish. Housing is provided at a basic ranger station; a $245 weekly fee covers lodging, logistics, and food.

Sea Turtle Conservancy (www.cccturtle.org; ℰ **800/678-7853** in the U.S. and Canada, or 2278-6058 in Costa Rica) is a nonprofit organization dedicated to sea-turtle research, protection, and advocacy. Formerly known as the **Caribbean Conservation Corporation,** its main operation in Costa Rica is headquartered in Tortuguero, where volunteers can aid in various scientific studies, as well as nightly patrols of the beach during nesting seasons to prevent poaching.

Global Volunteers (www.globalvolunteers.org; ℰ **800/487-1074** in the U.S. and Canada) is a U.S.–based organization that offers a unique opportunity to travelers who've always wanted a Peace Corps–like experience but can't make a 2-year commitment. For 2 to 3 weeks, you can join one of its working vacations in Costa Rica. A certain set of skills, such as engineering or agricultural knowledge, is helpful but by no means necessary. Each trip is undertaken at a particular community's request, to complete a specific project. However, *be warned:* These "volunteer" experiences do not come cheap. You must pay for your transportation as well as a hefty program fee, around $2,700 for a 2-week program.

Habitat for Humanity International (www.habitat.org; © 2296-3436) has offices in Costa Rica and sometimes runs organized Global Village programs here.

Vida (www.vida.org; © 2221-8367) is a local nongovernmental organization working on sustainable development and conservation issues; it can often place volunteers.

WWOOF Costa Rica (www.wwoofcostarica.org) is the national branch of a global organization of organic farms that accepts volunteers that can stay and work for one week to months at a time.

MEDICAL & DENTAL TOURISM

Costa Rica is an increasingly popular destination for dental and medical tourists. Facilities and care are excellent, and prices are quite low compared to the United States and other private care options in the developed world. Travelers are coming for everything from a simple dental checkup and cleaning to elective cosmetic surgery or a triple heart bypass operation. In virtually every case, visitors can save money on the overall cost of care. In some cases, the savings are quite substantial.

The country's two top hospitals have modern facilities and equipment, as well as excellent doctor and nursing corps, many of whom speak English. **Clínica Bíblica,** Avenida 14 between Calles Central and 1 (www.clinicabiblica.com; © 2522-1000), is conveniently close to downtown; the **Hospital CIMA** (www.hospitalcima.com; © 2208-1000) is in Escazú on the Próspero Fernández Highway, which connects San José and the western suburb of Santa Ana. The latter has the most modern facilities in the country. There is also an annex of the Hospital CIMA on the outskirts of Liberia, close to the beaches of Guanacaste.

6

SAN JOSÉ

Although most tourists enter Costa Rica through the international airport just outside this city, San José is not a place where most travelers linger. Costa Rica's bustling capital and population center is not a bad place to hang out for a few days, or to get things done that can't be done elsewhere, but it isn't a major tourist destination. Still, San José is the country's biggest urban center, with varied and active restaurant and nightlife scenes, several museums and galleries worth visiting, and a steady stream of theater, concerts, and other cultural events that you won't find elsewhere in the country.

San José can come across as little more than a chaotic jumble of cars, buses, buildings, and people. The central downtown section of the city exists in a near-constant state of gridlock. Antiquated buses spewing diesel fumes and a lack of emission controls have created a brown cloud over the city's sky. Sidewalks are poorly maintained, narrow, and overcrowded, and street crime is a perennial problem.

Founded in 1737, San José was a forgotten backwater of the Spanish empire until the late 19th century, when it boomed with the coffee business. At 1,125m (3,690 ft.) above sea level, San José enjoys springlike temperatures year-round, and its location in the Central Valley—the lush Talamanca Mountains rise to the south, the Poás, Barva, and Irazú volcanoes to the north and east—makes it a convenient base of exploration.

THE best SAN JOSÉ EXPERIENCES

- **Taking In the Riches at the Gold Museum:** With more than 2,000 pieces spread over three floors, the Gold Museum provides a fascinating look into the pre-Columbian artistry that inspired colonial-era quests, conquests, and excesses. See p 131.

- **Catching a Show at the National Theater:** Completed in 1897, and fronting the downtown Plaza de la Cultura, the National Theater is beautiful and well-preserved. It features a stunning marble entryway, a series of marble sculptures, and intricate paintings and murals throughout. It also hosts concerts, theater performances, and special events. See p 158.

FACING PAGE: **National Theater of Costa Rica in San José**

Artifacts at the Gold Museum

- **Basking in Tropical Opulence at a Boutique Hotel:** Throughout the late 18th and early 19th centuries, newly rich coffee barons built beautiful mansions around downtown San José. Today, many of these have been converted into charming boutique hotels. See "Where to Stay," p 139.

- **Visiting the Costa Rican Art Museum and La Sabana Park:** Inhabiting the country's first airport terminal building, the Costa Rican Art Museum houses the country's greatest art collection—from colonial times to the present. Just outside its doors lies La Sabana Park, where you can spend the afternoon relaxing in the grass or practicing any number of sports and activities, alongside some newly made Tico friends. See p 134 and 136.

- **Getting Out on the Dance Floor:** San José is teeming with dance clubs, and most nights the city's dance floors are packed to overflowing. Choose between an old-school salsa dance hall with a live band or a more contemporary club blasting the latest electronica. See p 158.

ORIENTATION

Arriving

BY PLANE

Juan Santamaría International Airport (www.fly2sanjose.com; ℂ **2437-2626** for 24-hr. airport information; airport code SJO) is near the city of Alajuela, about 20 minutes from downtown San José. A taxi or Uber into town costs between C10,000 and C25,000, and a bus is only

C540. The Alajuela–San José buses run frequently and will drop you off anywhere along Paseo Colón or at a station near the Parque de la Merced (downtown, btw. calles 12 and 14 and avs. 2 and 4). There are two lines: **Tuasa** (✆ **2442-6900**) buses are red; **Station Wagon** (✆ **2442-3226**) buses are yellow/orange. At the airport, the bus stop is directly in front of the main terminal, beyond the parking structure. Be sure to ask whether the bus is going to San José, or you'll end up in Alajuela. If you have a lot of luggage, you probably should take a cab.

Most car-rental agencies have desks and offices at the airport, but if you're planning to spend a few days in San José itself, I think a car is a liability. (If you're heading off immediately to the beach, though, it's much easier to pick up your car here than at a downtown office.)

Tip: Chaos and confusion greet arriving passengers the second they step out of the terminal. You face a gauntlet of aggressive taxi drivers, shuttle drivers waving signs, and people offering to carry your bags. Fortunately, the official airport taxi service (see below) has a booth inside the calm area just before the terminal exit. Keep a very watchful eye on your bags: Thieves have historically preyed on newly arrived passengers and their luggage. You should tip porters about C200 to C300 per bag.

In terms of taxis, you should stick with the official airport taxi service, **Taxis Unidos Aeropuerto** (www.taxiaeropuerto.com; ✆ **2221-6865**), which operates a fleet of orange vans and sedans. This service has a kiosk in the no man's land just outside the exit door for arriving passengers. Here they will assign you a cab. These taxis use meters, and fares to most downtown hotels should run between C15,000 and C30,000. Despite the fact that Taxis Unidos has an official monopoly at the airport, you will usually find a handful of regular cabs (in traditional red sedans) and "pirate" cabs, driven by freelancers using their own vehicles. You certainly could use either of these latter options ("pirate" cabs tend to charge a dollar or two less), but I highly recommend using the official service for safety and standardized prices. Ordering a car with the smart phone app Uber is another option, and rates are often significantly less than official taxis.

You have several options for **exchanging money** when you arrive at the airport—but you'll get the best rate if you exchange your money at a bank, and until then you'll find that almost all businesses accept dollars. An ATM in the baggage claim area is connected to both the PLUS and Cirrus networks. A **Global Exchange** (www.globalexchange.co.cr; ✆ **2431-0686**) money exchange booth is just as you clear Customs and Immigration. It's open whenever flights arrive; however, it exchanges at more than 10% below the official rate. A branch of **Banco de San José** is inside the main terminal, on the second floor across from the airline check-in counters, as well as a couple more ATMs up there. Most taxis and all rental-car agencies accept U.S. dollars. See "Money & Costs" in chapter 14 (p 608) for more details.

Tip: There's really no pressing need to exchange money the minute you arrive. Taxis Unidos accepts dollars. You can wait until after you settle into your hotel, and see if the hotel will give you a good rate of exchange, or use one of the many downtown banks or ATMs.

If you arrive in San José via small commuter or charter airline, you might find yourself at the **Tobías Bolaños International Airport** in Pavas (© **2232-2820;** airport code SYQ). This small airport is on the western side of downtown San José, about 10 minutes by car from the center. The airport has no car-rental desks, so unless you have a car or a driver waiting for you here, you will have to take a cab into town, which should cost between C10,000 and C20,000.

BY BUS

If you're coming to San José by bus, where you disembark depends on where you're coming from. (The different bus companies have their offices, and thus their drop-off points, all over downtown San José. When you buy your ticket, ask where you'll be let off.) Buses arriving from Panama pass first through Cartago and San Pedro before letting passengers off in downtown San José; buses arriving from Nicaragua generally enter the city on the west end of town, on Paseo Colón. If you're staying here, you can ask to be let off before the final stop.

Additionally, many long-distance buses heading to Guanacaste, the Pacific Coast, and Nicaragua depart from the **Terminal 7-10** (www. terminal7-10.com; © **2519-9740**) at Ave. 7 and Calle 10 in Barrio Mexico, across from the old Líbano movie theater.

BY CAR

If arriving by car, you'll probably enter San José via the Inter-American Highway. If you arrive from Nicaragua and the north, the highway brings you first past the airport and the city of Alajuela, to the western edge of downtown, right at the end of Paseo Colón, where it hits Parque La Sabana. The area is well marked with large road signs that direct you either to downtown (centro) or to the western suburbs of Rohrmoser, Pavas, and Escazú. If you're heading toward downtown, follow the flow of traffic and turn left on Paseo Colón.

If entering from Panama and the south, things get a little more complicated. The Inter-American Highway first passes through the city of Cartago and then through the San José suburbs of Curridabat and San Pedro before reaching downtown. This route is relatively well marked, and if you stick with the major flow of traffic, you should find San José without any problem.

Visitor Information

The **Costa Rican National Tourism Chamber** (**CANATUR;** www. canatur.org; © **2234-6222**) has a desk at the Juan Santamaría International Airport, in the baggage claims area, just before Customs. You can

SEARCHING FOR addresses

This is one of the most confusing aspects of visiting Costa Rica in general, and San José in particular. Although downtown San José often has street addresses and building numbers for locations, they are almost never used. Addresses are given as a set of coordinates such as "Calle 3 between avenidas Central and 1." It's then up to you to locate the building within that block, keeping in mind that the building could be on either side of the street. Many addresses include additional information, such as the number of meters from a specified intersection or some other well-known landmark. (These "meter measurements" are not precise but are a good way to give directions to a taxi driver. In basic terms, 100m=1 block, 200m=2 blocks, and so on.) These landmarks are what become truly confusing for visitors to the city because they are often simply restaurants, bars, and shops that would be familiar only to locals.

Things get even more confusing when the landmark in question no longer exists. The classic example of this is "the Coca-Cola," one of the most common landmarks used in addresses in the blocks surrounding San José's main market. The trouble is, the Coca-Cola bottling plant that it refers to is no longer there; the edifice is long gone, and one of the principal downtown bus depots stands in its place. Old habits die hard, though, and the address description remains. You might also try to find someplace near the *antiguo higuerón* ("old fig tree") in San Pedro. This tree was felled over a decade ago. In outlying neighborhoods, addresses can become long directions, such as "50m (½ block) south of the old church, then 100m (1 block) east, then 20m (two buildings) south." Luckily for visitors, most downtown addresses are more straightforward.

Oh, and if you're wondering how letter carriers manage, well, welcome to the club. Some folks actually get their mail delivered this way, but most people and businesses in San José use a post office box. This is called an *apartado* and is abbreviated "Apdo." or "A.P." in mailing addresses.

pick up maps and brochures, and they might even lend you a phone to make or confirm a reservation. It's usually open for all arriving flights.

City Layout

Downtown San José is laid out on a grid. *Avenidas* (avenues) run east and west, while *calles* (streets) run north and south. The center of the city is at **Avenida Central** and **Calle Central.** To the north of Avenida Central, the avenidas have odd numbers beginning with Avenida 1; to the south, they have even numbers beginning with Avenida 2. Likewise, calles to the east of Calle Central have odd numbers, and those to the west have even numbers. The main downtown artery is **Avenida 2,** which merges with Avenida Central on either side of downtown. West of downtown, Avenida Central becomes **Paseo Colón,** which ends at Parque La Sabana and feeds into the highway to Alajuela, the airport, Guanacaste, and the Pacific coast. East of downtown, Avenida Central leads to San Pedro and then to Cartago and the Inter-American Highway heading south. **Calle 3** takes you out of town to the north, onto the Guápiles Highway that leads to the Caribbean coast.

The Neighborhoods in Brief

San José is divided into dozens of neighborhoods, known as *barrios*. Most of the listings in this chapter fall within the main downtown area, but you'll need to know about a few outlying neighborhoods. In addition, the nearby suburbs of Escazú and Santa Ana are so close that they could almost be considered part of San José. For more information on these towns, see chapter 7.

DOWNTOWN   In San José's busy downtown, you'll find most of the city's museums, a handful of urban parks and open-air plazas, and the city's main cathedral. Many tour companies, restaurants, and hotels are located here. Unfortunately, traffic noise and exhaust fumes make this one of the least pleasant parts of the city. Streets and avenues are usually bustling and crowded with pedestrians and vehicular traffic, and street crime is most rampant here. Still, the sections of Avenida Central between calles 6 and 7, as well as Avenida 4 between calles 9 and 14, have been converted into pedestrian malls, greatly improving things on these stretches.

BARRIO AMÓN/BARRIO OTOYA   These two picturesque neighborhoods, just north and east of downtown, are the site of the greatest concentration of historic buildings in San José. Some of these have been renovated and turned into boutique hotels and atmospheric restaurants. If you're looking for character and don't mind the noise and exhaust fumes from passing cars and buses, this neighborhood makes a good base for exploring the city.

BARRIO ESCALANTE   This former residential district to the northeast of downtown has quickly emerged as one of the city's primary restaurant

A typical commercial street in San José

and nightlife zones. Many of the old mansions have been converted into craft beer bars and hipster coffeehouses, while others are being torn down to make way for modern apartment buildings.

LA SABANA/PASEO COLÓN Paseo Colón, a wide boulevard west of downtown, is an extension of Avenida Central and ends at Parque La Sabana. It has several good, small hotels and numerous restaurants. This is also where several of the city's car-rental agencies have their in-town offices. Once the site of the city's main airport, the Parque La Sabana (La Sabana Park) is San José's largest public park, with ample green areas, sports and recreation facilities, the National Stadium, and the Museo de Arte Costarricense (Costa Rican Art Museum). The neighborhoods north and south of the park are known as Sabana Norte and Sabana Sur.

SAN PEDRO/LOS YOSES Located east of downtown San José, Los Yoses is an upper-middle-class neighborhood that is home to many diplomatic missions and embassies. San Pedro is a little farther east and is the site of the University of Costa Rica. Numerous college-type bars and restaurants are all around the edge of the campus, while more upscale and refined restaurants and boutique hotels can be found in the residential sections of both neighborhoods.

GETTING AROUND
By Bus

Bus transportation around San José is cheap—the fare is usually somewhere around C200 to C500—although the Alajuela/San José buses that run in from the airport cost C540. The most important buses are those running east along Avenida 2 and west along Avenida 3. The **Sabana/Cementerio** bus runs from Parque La Sabana to downtown and is one of the most convenient buses to use. You'll find a bus stop for the outbound Sabana/Cementerio bus near the main post office on Avenida 3 near the corner of Calle 2, and another one on Calle 11 between avenidas Central and 1. This bus also has stops all along Avenida 2. **San Pedro** buses leave from the end of the pedestrian walkway on Avenida Central between calles 9 and 11, and take you out of downtown heading east.

Sculpture in the National Theater

You pay as you board the bus. The city's bus drivers can make change, although they don't like to receive large bills. Be especially mindful of your wallet, purse, or other valuables, because pickpockets often work the crowded buses.

By Taxi

Although taxis in San José have meters (*marías*), the drivers sometimes refuse to use them, particularly with foreigners, so you'll occasionally have to negotiate the price. Always try to get them to use the meter first (say "*Ponga la maría, por favor*"). The official rate is C640 per kilometer (½ mile). If you have a rough idea of how far it is to your destination, you can estimate how much it should cost from this figure. Wait time is charged at C3,650 per hour, and is pro-rated for smaller increments.

Depending on your location, the time of day, and the weather (rain places taxis at a premium), it's relatively easy to hail a cab downtown. You'll always find taxis in front of the Teatro Nacional (albeit at high prices) and around the Parque Central at Avenida Central and Calle Central. Taxis in front of hotels and the El Pueblo tourist complex usually charge more than others, though this is technically illegal. Most hotels will gladly call you a cab, either for a downtown excursion or for a trip back out to the airport. You can also get a cab by calling **Coopetaxi** (✆ **2235-9966**), **Coopeirazu** (✆ **2254-3211**), or **Coopetico** (✆ **2224-7979**). **Cinco Estrellas Taxi** (✆ **2228-3159**) is based in Escazú but services the entire metropolitan area and airport, and claims to always have an English-speaking operator on call. **Uber** (www.uber.com) tends to be considerably cheaper than most taxis. However, the service is still in a legal gray area in San José, therefore there are not nearly as many cars as other cities.

On Foot

Downtown San José is very compact. Nearly every place you might want to go is within a 15×4-block area. Because of traffic congestion, you'll often find it faster to walk than to take a bus or taxi. Be careful when walking the streets any time of day or night. Flashy jewelry, loosely held handbags or backpacks, and expensive camera equipment tend to attract thieves. **Avenida Central** is a pedestrian-only street from calles 6 to 7, and has been redone with interesting paving stones and the occasional fountain

Avenida Central

in an attempt to create a comfortable pedestrian mall. A similar pedestrian-only walkway runs along **Avenida 4,** between calles 9 and 14.

By Train

San José has sporadic and minimal urban commuter train service, and it is geared almost exclusively to commuters. There are three major lines. One line connecting the western neighborhood of Pavas with the eastern suburb of San Pedro passes right through downtown, with prominent stops at, or near, the U.S. Embassy, Parque La Sabana, the downtown court area, and the Universidad de Costa Rica (University of Costa Rica) and Universidad Latina (Latin University). This train runs commuter hours roughly every hour between 5 and 8:30am and 4 and 7:30pm.

Another line runs between downtown San José and Heredia. This train runs roughly every 30 minutes between 5:30 and 8am, and 3:30 and 7:30pm.

And a third line runs between downtown San José and Cartago. This train runs roughly every 30 minutes between 6:30 and 8am, and between 3:30 and 7:30pm. This later route is potentially useful for tourists, but again, the train is predominantly for local commuters, and not geared toward tourists. You cannot purchase tickets in advance, and trains often fill up, leaving you waiting 30 minutes or more for the next train.

Fares range from C420 to C550, depending on the length of your ride.

By Car

It will cost you between $25 and $100 per day to rent a car in Costa Rica (the higher prices are for 4WD vehicles). Many car-rental agencies have offices at the airport. If not, they will usually either pick you up or deliver the car to any San José hotel. If you decide to pick up your rental car in downtown San José, be prepared for some very congested streets.

The following companies have desks at Juan Santamaría International Airport, as well as offices downtown: **Adobe Rent A Car** (www.adobecar. com; ℂ 2542-4800), **Avis** (www.avis.com; ℂ 800/633-3469 in the U.S. and 800/879-2847 in Canada, or 2293-2222 central reservation number in Costa Rica), **Budget** (www.budget.co.cr; ℂ 800/472-3325 in the U.S. and Canada, or 2436-2007 in San José), **Dollar** (www.dollar.com; ℂ 800/800-6000 in the U.S. and Canada, or 2257-1585 in San José), **Hertz** (www.hertz.com; ℂ 800/654-3131 in the U.S. and Canada, or 2221-1818 in San José), **National Car Rental** (www.nationalcar.com; ℂ 877/222-9058 in the

> ### Car-Rental Advice
>
> If you plan to rent a car, it's best to reserve it in advance from home. All the major international agencies and many local companies have toll-free numbers and websites. Sometimes you can even save a bit on the cost by reserving in advance. Costa Rica's car-rental fleet is not sufficient to meet demand during the high season, when rental rates run at a premium. Sometimes this allows agencies here to gouge last-minute shoppers.

U.S. and Canada, 2221-4700 in San José), and **Payless Rent A Car** (www.paylesscr.com; ☎ 800/497-3659 in the U.S. and Canada, or 2432-4747 in Costa Rica).

Dozens of other smaller, local car-rental agencies are in San José, and most will arrange for airport or hotel pickup or delivery. Some of the more dependable local agencies are **Toyota Rent A Car** (www.toyota rent.com; ☎ **2105-3400**); and **Vamos Rent A Car** ★★ (www.vamos rentacar.com; ☎ **800/950-8426** in the U.S. and Canada, or 4000-0557 in Costa Rica). Vamos gets especially high marks for customer service and transparency.

For more advice on renting cars, see "Getting Around: By Car," in chapter 14 (p 596).

[FastFACTS] SAN JOSÉ

ATMs/Banks You'll find an extensive network of banks and ATMs around San José. Banks are usually open Monday through Friday from 9am to 4pm, although many have begun to offer extended hours. Post offices are generally open Monday through Friday from 8am to 5:30pm, and Saturday from 7:30am to noon. To protect against crime, some banks have taken to disabling their ATM networks at night.

Dentists Call your embassy, which will have a list of recommended dentists. Because treatments are so inexpensive in Costa Rica, dental tourism has become a popular option for people needing extensive work.

Doctors Contact your embassy for information on doctors in San José, or see "Hospitals," below.

Drugstores San José has countless pharmacies and drugstores. Many of

them deliver at little or no extra cost. The pharmacy at the **Hospital Clínica Bíblica,** Avenida 14 between calles Central and 1 (☎ **2522-1000**), is open daily 24 hours, as is the **Hospital CIMA** pharmacy (☎ **2208-1080**) in Escazú. **Farmacia Fischel** (www.fischel.co.cr; ☎ **800/347-2435** toll-free in Costa Rica) has scores of branches around the metropolitan area.

Embassies & Consulates See chapter 14.

Emergencies In case of any emergency, dial ☎ **911** (which should have an English-speaking operator); for an ambulance, call ☎ **1028;** and to report a fire, call ☎ **1118.**

Hospitals **Clínica Bíblica,** Avenida 14 between calles Central and 1 (www. clinicabiblica.com; ☎ **2522-1000**), is conveniently close to downtown and has several English-speaking doctors. The **Hospital CIMA** (www.hospitalcima.com;

☎ **2208-1000**), located in Escazú on the Próspero Fernández Highway, which connects San José and the western suburb of Santa Ana, has the most modern facilities in the country.

Internet Access Internet cafes were once ubiquitous in San José but are now a rarity, with free Wi-Fi widely available in hotels and restaurants.

Maps The information desks at the airport are usually stocked with decent maps of both Costa Rica and San José. Also try **Librería Lehmann,** Avenida Central between calles 1 and 3 (☎ **2522-4848**; www. librerialehmann.com); and **Librería Universal,** Avenida Central and calles Central and 1 (☎ **2222-2222**). Perhaps the best map to have is the waterproof country map of Costa Rica put out by **Toucan Maps** (www. mapcr.com), which can be ordered directly from its website or any major online bookseller.

Police Dial ℂ **911** or 2295-3272 for the police. They should have someone available who speaks English.

Post Office The main post office (correo) is on Calle 2 between avenidas 1 and 3 (www.correos.go.cr; ℂ **2223-9766**). See "Mail," on p 607, for more information.

Restrooms Public restrooms are rare to nonexistent, but most big hotels and restaurants will let you use their restrooms. Downtown, you can find public restrooms at the entrance to the Museos del Banco Central de Costa Rica (p 131).

Safety Pickpockets and purse snatchers are rife in San José, especially on public buses, in the markets, on crowded sidewalks, near hospitals, and lurking outside bank offices and ATMs. Leave most of your money and other valuables in your hotel safe, and carry only as much as you need when you go out. If you do carry anything valuable with you, keep it in a money belt or special passport bag around your neck. Day packs are a prime target of brazen pickpockets throughout the city. One common scam involves someone dousing you or your pack with mustard or ice cream. Another scamster (or two) will then quickly come to your aid, but they are usually much more interested in cleaning you out than cleaning you up.

Stay away from the red-light district northwest of the Central Market. Also be advised that the Parque Nacional is not a safe place for a late-night stroll. Other precautions include walking around corner vendors, not between the vendor and the building. The tight space between the vendor and the building is a favorite spot for pickpockets. Avoid parking your car on the street, and never leave anything of value in a car, even if it's in a guarded parking lot. With these precautions in mind, you should have a safe visit to San José. Also, see "Safety," in chapter 14 (p 610).

Time Zone San José is on Central Standard Time (same as Chicago and St. Louis), 6 hours behind Greenwich Mean Time. For the exact time (in Spanish), call ℂ **1112.**

Useful Telephone Numbers For directory assistance, call ℂ **1113;** for international directory assistance, call ℂ **1024.**

Weather The weather in San José (including the Central Valley) is usually temperate, never getting extremely hot or cold. May through November is the rainy season, although the rain usually falls only in the afternoon and evening.

EXPLORING SAN JOSÉ

San José has some of the best and most modern museums in Central America, with a wealth of fascinating pre-Columbian artifacts. Standouts include the Museo de Jade (Jade Museum) and the Museo de Arte Costarricense (Costa Rican Art Museum), featuring a fine collection of Costa Rican art, and a large and varied, open-air sculpture garden.

Just outside San José in the Central Valley are also several great things to see and do. With day trips out of the city, you can spend quite a few days in this region. See chapter 7 for additional touring ideas.

The Top Attractions
DOWNTOWN SAN JOSÉ

Catedral Metropolitana (Metropolitan Cathedral) ★ CATHEDRAL   San José's principal Catholic cathedral was built in 1871. Though rather plain from the outside, the large neoclassical church features a mix of stained-glass works, and assorted sculptures and bas-reliefs. It

A bus stop in San José

also has a wonderfully restored 19th-century pipe organ. A well-tended little garden surrounds the church and features a massive marble statue of Pope Juan Paul II carved by celebrated Costa Rican sculptor Jorge Jiménez Deredia, who also has a work at the Vatican. The cathedral is just across from the downtown Parque Central (Central Park).

Av. 2 and Calle Central. © **2221-3820.** Free admission. Mon–Sat 6:30am–6:30pm; Sun 6:30am–9pm.

Centro Nacional de Arte y Cultura (National Center of Art and Culture) ★ CULTURAL COMPLEX Housed in what was formerly the National Liquor Factory (FANAL), this complex of museums and performance spaces is also home to the Ministry of Culture. The

"Tico" sculptures in San José

best museum here is the Museum of Contemporary Art and Design (MADC), which has several very large exhibition spaces and features rotating shows of predominantly local and regional artists, with the occasional exhibition from the rest of the world. The theaters, as well as the central courtyard amphitheater, host a wide range of cutting-edge Costa Rican drama, dance, and musical performances. The complex takes up a full city block between the Parque España and Parque Nacional, and just a half-block away from the Jade Museum (p 133).

Calle 13, btw. avs. 3 and 5. © **2257-7202.** www.madc.cr. Admission $3. Tue–Sat 9:30am–4:45pm.

Museo Nacional de Costa Rica (National Museum) ★★ MUSEUM

Sitting atop the Plaza de la Democracia, the Museo Nacional provides a solid, all-around sampling of the archaeological, historical, and natural wonders of Costa Rica from pre-Columbian times to the present. That means pre-Columbian art and artifacts, including musical instruments, recreated tombs, pottery, and pieces in jade and gold. In the area devoted to the colonial period and onward, you'll find recreated interiors, paintings, furniture, and dioramas, with lots of explanations in English. Housed in a large, former army barracks, the building features turrets and outside walls that still bear the bullet marks from fighting in the 1948 civil war. In addition to all the historical exhibits, this place also has a large butterfly garden with more than 25 species fluttering about. Plan on around 2 hours to get a good feel for this museum.

Calle 17, btw. avs. Central and 2, on Plaza de la Democracia. www.museocostarica. go.cr. © **2257-1433.** Admission $9 adults, $4 students; children 12 and under free. Tues–Sat 8:30am–4:30pm; Sun 9am–4:30pm. Closed on national holidays.

Museos del Banco Central de Costa Rica (Gold Museum) ★★

MUSEUM   A trove of some 1,600 gold pieces dating from 500 B.C. to

Stone spheres in the National Museum

San José

PASO DE LA VACA

COCA-COLA

MEXICO

Av. 17
Av. 15
Av. 13
Av. 11
Av. 7
Av. 7
Av. 5
Av. 5
Av. 3
Av. 3
Av. 3
Av. 1
Av. 1
Av. 7
Av. Central
Av. 2
Av. 2
Av. 4
Av. 4
Av. 6
Av. 6
Av. 8
Av. 10
Av. 10

Calle 42
Calle 40
Calle 38
Calle 36
Calle 34
Calle 32
Calle 30
Calle 28
Calle 26
Calle 24
Calle 22
Calle 20
Calle 18
Calle 16
Calle 14
Calle 12
Calle 10
Calle 8
Calle 6
Calle 4
Calle 2

PARQUE LA SABANA

Paseo Colón

Coca-Cola Bus Terminal

MERCED

0   1/4 mi
0   0.25 km

1500 A.D., is the primary lure here; visitors are usually bowled over by the intricate workmanship on the small gold items. Interestingly, gold was used in many forms, from cast animal figurines to jewelry to functional pieces. But the museum goes beyond the shiny, yellow stuff with a smartly curated survey of pre-Columbian culture, including exhibits on history, metalworking, and customs. The Gold Museum is directly underneath the downtown Plaza de la Cultura, and the same complex contains the Museo Numismático, a coin museum. Admission is free every Wednesday.

Calle 5, btw. avs. Central and 2, underneath the Plaza de la Cultura. www.museosdel bancocentral.org. © **2243-4202.** Admission $11 adults, $8 students, free for children 11 and under. Free admission Wed. Daily 9:15am–5pm.

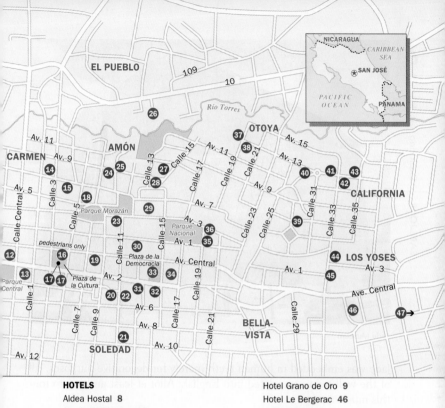

BARRIO AMÓN/BARRIO OTOYA

Museo de Jade (Jade Museum) ★ MUSEUM   No commodity was more valuable among the pre-Columbian cultures of Central America and Mexico than jade; it was worth more than gold. Set on the western edge of the Plaza de la Democracia, this five-story building has more than 7,000 sq. m (75,000 sq. ft.) of exhibition space, which is able to display an impressive 7,000-piece collection. The museum also houses an extensive collection of pre-Columbian polychrome terra-cotta bowls, vases, and figurines, some of which are startlingly modern in design (and exhibit a surprisingly advanced technique). Particularly intriguing is a vase that incorporates actual human teeth, and a display that shows how

Jade Museum

jade was embedded in human teeth merely for decorative purposes. All of the wall text is translated into English. Allot at least an hour to tour this museum.

Calle 13, btw. avenidas 2 and Central. © **2521-6610.** www.museodeljadeins.com. Admission $15 adults; $5 students with valid ID, $2 for children 12 and under. Daily 10am–5pm.

LA SABANA/PASEO COLÓN

Museo de Arte Costarricense (Costa Rican Art Museum) ★★ ART MUSEUM   Originally the main terminal and control tower of San José's first international airport, this museum houses the largest and most important collection of works by Costa Rican artists from the colonial time to the present. The museum's permanent collection has over 6,000 pieces, including works by big names like Juan Manuel Sánchez, Max Jiménez, Francisco Amighetti, Lola Fernández, and more. There's a sizeable collection of Amighetti's stark and minimalistic lithographs, and 19th-century oil paintings of classic rural country scene's like "El Portón Rojo (The Red Door)" by Teodorico Quiros. On the back patio—which used to lead to the tarmac—is a sculpture garden. This museum is free, and anchors the eastern edge of La Sabana city park, making it easy to combine a visit here with a stroll through the park.

Calle 42 and Paseo Colón, Parque La Sabana Este. www.musarco.go.cr. © **2256-1281.** Free admission. Tues–Sun 9am–4pm.

ON THE OUTSKIRTS OF DOWNTOWN

Spirogyra Butterfly Garden ★ ZOO   Smaller and less elaborate than the Butterfly Farm, Spirogyra still provides a good introduction to the life cycle of butterflies. First watch the 18-minute video (it runs continuously), then grab the provided butterfly booklet and take a self-guided tour. It's a calm and quiet oasis in a noisy and crowded city, just a short taxi ride to downtown (it's near El Pueblo).

100m (1 block) east and 150m (1½ blocks) south of El Pueblo Shopping Center. www. butterflygardencr.com. *(f)* **2222-2937.** Admission $7 adults and students, and $5 children 12 and under. Mon–Fri 9am–2pm, Sat–Sun 9am–3pm.

Especially for Kids

Museo de Los Niños (Children's Museum) ★ MUSEUM   A massive attraction that's both fun and informative, the Museo de Los Niños features interactive exhibits and educational displays describing everything from the rainforest to pre-Columbian village life to the interior of a spaceship (in honor of Costa Rican astronaut Franklin Chang). The simulated earthquake exhibit is always a favorite. It's housed in a former prison, so if anyone in your family is acting out, you can actually lock them in an old prison cell to set them straight. The museum is also home to the National Auditorium, and often features temporary exhibitions of contemporary art. You can easily spend 2 to 3 hours here but you'll want to take a taxi for transportation, because the museum borders a rather seedy section of the city's red-light district.

Calle 4 and Av. 9. www.museocr.org. *(f)* **2258-4929.** Admission $4 adults, $3.50 for children 15 and under. Tues–Fri 8am–4:30pm Sat–Sun 9:30am–5pm.

A butterfly at the Spirogyra Butterfly Garden

Museo de los Niños

Outdoor Activities & Spectator Sports

Because of the chaos and pollution, you'll probably want to get out of the city before undertaking anything too strenuous. But if you want to brave the elements, San José does have a few outdoor activities to enjoy. For information on horseback riding, hiking, and whitewater rafting trips from San José, see "Day Trips from San José," p 163 in this chapter.

Parque La Sabana ★★ (La Sabana Park, at the western end of Paseo Colón), formerly San José's international airport, is the city's center for active sports and recreation. Here you'll find jogging trails, a banked bicycle track, soccer fields, a roller-rink, a few public tennis courts, and the huge National Stadium. Aside from events at the stadium, all the facilities are free and open to the public. On weekends, you'll usually find free aerobic, yoga, or dancercise classes taking place. Families gather for picnics, people fly kites, pony rides are available for

Fountain in La Sabana Park

the kids, and everyone strolls through the outdoor sculpture garden. If you really want to experience the local culture, try getting into a pickup soccer game. However, be careful in this park, especially at dusk or after dark, when it becomes a favorite haunt for youth gangs and muggers.

BIRD-WATCHING   Serious birders will want to head out of San José, but it is still possible to see quite a few species in the metropolitan area. Two of the best spots for urban bird-watching are the campus at the **University of Costa Rica,** in the eastern suburb of San Pedro, and **Parque del Este ★,** located a little farther east on the road to San Ramón de Tres Ríos. You'll see a mix of urban species, and if you're lucky, you might spy a couple of hummingbirds or even a blue-crowned motmot. To get to the university campus, take any San Pedro bus from Avenida Central between calles 9 and 11. To get to Parque del Este, take the San Ramón/Parque del Este bus from Calle 9 between avenidas Central and 1.

BULLFIGHTING   While traditional bullfighting is a blood-and-gore/life-and-death confrontation, Ticos just like to tease the bull. **Las Corridas a la Tica (Costa Rican bullfighting)** is a popular and frequently comic stadium event. In a typical *corrida* (bullfight), anywhere from 50 to 150 *toreadores improvisados* (literally, "improvised bullfighters") stand in the ring waiting for the bull. What follows is a slapstick scramble to safety whenever the bull heads toward a crowd of bullfighters. The braver bullfighters try to slap the bull's backside as the beast chases down one of his buddies.

You can see a bullfight during the various Festejos Populares (City Fairs) around the country. The country's largest Festejos Populares are in Zapote, a suburb east of San José, during Christmas week and the first week in January. Admission is C5,000 to C10,000. This is a purely seasonal activity and occurs in San José only during the Festejos. However, nearly every little town around the country has yearly *festejos*. These are spread out throughout the year. Ask at your hotel; if your timing's right, you might be able to take in one of these.

JOGGING   Try **Parque La Sabana** (see above), or **Parque del Este,** east of town in the foothills above San Pedro. Take the San Ramón/Parque del Este bus from Calle 9 between avenidas Central and 1. It's never a good

A Costa Rican bullfight

Saprissa fans at a *fútbol* match

idea to jog at night, on busy streets, or alone, particularly if you're a woman. And remember, Tico drivers are not accustomed to joggers on residential streets, so don't expect drivers to give you a wide berth.

SOCCER (FÚTBOL)   Ticos take their *fútbol* seriously. Costa Rican professional soccer is some of the best in Central America, and the national team, or *Sele (selección nacional),* qualified for the World Cup in 2002 and 2006. Although they failed to qualify for the 2010 World Cup in South Africa, they did qualify for the 2014 in Brazil—and did quite well, considering the odds, losing to the Netherlands on penalty kicks in the quarterfinals.

The local professional soccer season runs from August through June, with a break for Christmas and New Year's, and separate championship playoffs every December and July. The main San José team is Saprissa (affectionately called El Monstruo, or "The Monster"). **Saprissa's stadium** is in Tibás (www.saprissa.com; © **2240-4034;** take any Tibás bus from Calle 2 and Av. 5). Games are often held on Sunday at 11am, but occasionally are scheduled for Saturday afternoon or Wednesday evening. Check the local newspapers for game times and locations.

International and other important matches are held in the **National Stadium** on the northeastern corner of Parque La Sabana.

Aside from major international matches at the National Stadium, you don't need to buy tickets in advance. Tickets generally run between C1,500 and C10,000. It's worth paying a little extra for *sombra numerado* (reserved seats in the shade). This will protect you from both the sun and the more rowdy aficionados. Periodic outbursts of violence, both inside and outside the stadiums, have marred the sport here, so be careful.

National Stadium

Other options include *sombra* (general admission in the shade), *palco* and *palco numerado* (general admission and reserved mezzanine), and *sol general* (general admission in full sun).

It is possible to buy tickets to most sporting events in advance from **E-Ticket** (www.eticket.cr), but the site is entirely in Spanish.

WHERE TO STAY

San José offers up a wide range of hotel choices, from plush boutique hotels to budget *pensiones* and backpacker hangouts. Many downtown hotels and small inns are housed in beautifully converted and restored old mansions. The vast majority of accommodations—and the best deals— are in the moderate range, where you can find everything from elegant little inns to contemporary business-class chains. Staying in San José puts you in the center of the action, and close to all of the city's museums, restaurants, and nightlife venues. However, it also exposes you to many urban pitfalls, including noise, traffic, pollution, and street crime.

Downtown San José/Barrio Amón

The urban center of San José is the city's heart and soul, with a wide range of hotels and restaurants and easy access to museums and attractions. It has several popular public parks and plazas, and the atmospheric Barrio Amón, a charming neighborhood that is home to the city's greatest concentration of colonial-era architecture. The neighborhood's biggest drawbacks are the street noise, bus fumes, gridlocked traffic, and petty crime.

Barrio Amón, San José

MODERATE

The **Sleep Inn** ★, Av. 3, between calles 9 and 11 (www.sleepinnsanjose. com; ✆ **2521-6500**), is a modern, American-style chain hotel in the heart of downtown. **Hotel Colonial** ★, Calle 11, between avenidas 4 and 6 (www.hotelcolonialcr.com; ✆ **2223-0109**) is another solid boutique option.

Aurola Holiday Inn ★   At 17 stories tall, the Aurola Holiday Inn's gleaming glass facade towers over the Parque Morazán and surrounding Barrio Amón neighborhood. This central location provides easy walking access to a host of restaurants, bars, and several of the city's better museums. Despite being one of the older downtown hotels, the rooms and common areas have received regular updating and feel contemporary, with furnishings made from varnished local hardwoods, and firm orthopedic mattresses. The hotel has a small indoor pool and hot tub beneath atrium skylights, just off its well-equipped gym.

Av. 5 and Calle 5, San José. www.ihg.com. ✆ **888/465-4329** in the U.S. and Canada, or 2523-1000. 195 units. $112 double; $165 suites. Free parking. **Amenities:** Restaurant; bar; poolside snack bar; exercise room; pool; room service; free Wi-Fi.

Hotel Presidente ★★   The Presidente's setting on a bustling, pedestrian-only street is both its greatest asset and its curse. Shops and restaurants are just steps away for guests, but some rooms can get noisy (try for one higher up if you're a light sleeper). That said, the rooms are quite attractive: spacious, with white duvets, marble bathrooms, and wire art on the walls that gives a taste of local flair. If you fancy spoiling yourself, the spa suites come with a private Jacuzzi for two.

Av. Central and Calle 7, San José. www.hotel-presidente.com. ✆ **877/540-1790** in the U.S. and Canada, or 2010-0000 in Costa Rica. 90 units. $89–$149 double; $166 suite, includes breakfast buffet. Free parking. **Amenities:** Restaurant; bar; casino; small gym; spa; room service; free Wi-Fi.

INEXPENSIVE

Kap's Place ★ (www.kapsplace.com; ☏ **2221-1169**), across from the Hotel Aranjuez on Calle 19 between avenidas 11 and 13, is a good choice for budget travelers, as is **Hostel Pangea** ★ (www.hostelpangea.com; ☏ **2221-1992**), on Avenida 7 and Calle 3; **Hostal Casa del Parque** ★ (http://www.hostelcasadelparque.com; ☏ **2223-3437**), on Calle 19 avenidas 1 and 3; and **Pension de la Cuesta** (www.pensiondelacuesta. com; ☏ **2256-7946**), on Avenida 1 between calles 11 and 15.

Hemingway Inn ★   This rambling old house built for a coffee baron in the 1920s is just across the street from the more expensive Hotel Don Carlos. The rooms are worn and vary in size and shape, though they are full of character, some adding balconies, wood-beamed ceilings, or four poster beds. There's a buffet breakfast offered each morning on the tropical patio, while there's always free coffee and tea out for guests. Wi-Fi can be spotty in parts of the hotel.

Av. 9 at Calle 9. www.hotelsantotomas.com. ☏ **2257-8630**. 17 units. $36-$44 double, includes breakfast. **Amenities:** Free Wi-Fi.

Hotel Aranjuez ★★   On a quiet side street in the Barrio Amón neighborhood, five adjacent wooden homes have been joined in an intricate maze of hallways and courtyards to create one of the best budget hotels in the country. The courtyards and hallways overflow with mature trees, tropical flowers and potted ferns. These lead to quiet nooks for

reading and a half-dozen or so common areas where guests gather to trade travel tales and play board games. Rooms vary greatly in size but most feature high ceilings and handsome antique wood or tile floors. A massive buffet breakfast is served each morning and the staff couldn't be more accommodating and helpful. The only downside: Some of the nearly century-old walls in these homes are fairly thin, so noise can be a problem.

Calle 19, btw. avs. 11 and 13. www.hotel aranjuez.com. ☏ **2256-1825**. 35 units, 6 with shared bathroom. $42 double w/ shared bathroom; $52–$70 double w/ private bathroom; $75 superior, includes breakfast buffet. Limited free parking. **Amenities:** Free Wi-Fi.

Patio of Hotel Aranjuez

Hotel Don Carlos ★★   Brimming with colonial-era charm and an unmistakably Costa Rican ambience, this converted downtown home once belonged to a former Costa Rican president. The rooms and hallways are decorated with local art and crafts—large stone sculptures, painted oxcart wheels, wall-mounted mosaics, antique oil paintings, and vivid stained glass works, as well as lush potted plants and flowing fountains. Rooms can vary tremendously in size, so ask what you're getting before you book. The restaurant serves local cuisine and has a lovely covered patio. The hotel's Boutique Annemarie gift shop (p 155) is one of the best stocked in Costa Rica, plus they have their own car rental service.

779 Calle 9, btw. avs. 7 and 9, San José. www.doncarloshotel.com. 🕿 **866/675-9259** in the U.S. and Canada, or 2221-6707 in Costa Rica. 30 units. $80-$90 double, $100 family room for up to 5 guests, includes breakfast. Free parking. **Amenities:** Restaurant; bar; room service; tour desk; free Wi-Fi.

Hotel Santo Tomás ★★   Built by a coffee baron more than 100 years ago, the house has been lovingly renovated by its owner, Thomas Douglas. Throughout the property you'll enjoy the dark tones of well-aged wood, and various open-air terraces, courtyards and garden nooks. Rooms vary in size, but most are spacious enough to have a small table and chairs. A newer annex adds even more spacious rooms with balconies. A small outdoor pool with a Jacuzzi is attached to the property; both are solar-heated and connected by a tiny water slide. The staff and management are wonderfully gracious, and the restaurant here is top-notch.

Av. 7, btw. calles 3 and 5. www.hotelsantotomas.com. 🕿 **2255-0448.** 30 units. $62-$82 double, $88 suite, includes breakfast. **Amenities:** Restaurant; bar; lounge; exercise room; Jacuzzi; small outdoor pool; free Wi-Fi.

La Sabana/Paseo Colón

Located on the western edge of downtown, La Sabana Park is San José's largest city park, and Paseo Colón is a broad commercial avenue heading straight into the heart of the city. Stay in this neighborhood if you're looking for fast, easy access to the highways heading to Escazú, Santa Ana, the Pacific coast, and the airport and Northern Zone. Because it's on the edge of town, the area can be pretty dead at night.

EXPENSIVE

Hotel Grano de Oro ★★★   This is the standard-bearer for luxury boutique hotels in San José. A combination of restoration and expansion has transformed this grand colonial-era mansion into a refined refuge in the center of a busy city and immaculate maintenance ensures it stays that way. For those who can afford to splurge, the signature suite is elegantly decorated to evoke a bygone era, with wood-paneled walls, a carved antique bed, and a private Jacuzzi with views of the city skyline through massive picture windows. But if that's beyond your budget, there are appealing standard rooms too, with such niceties as wrought-iron bed frames, shiny wood floors, and plush bedding. The restaurant is one of the best in the city (p 148,) and the chic rooftop patio with its two large Jacuzzi spas will almost make you forget you are in bustling San José. A

Hotel Grano de Oro

final reason to visit: Your money will help do good work. Owners Eldon and Lori Cook support a range of social and environmental causes.

Calle 30, no. 251, btw. avs. 2 and 4, 150m (1½ blocks) south of Paseo Colón. www. hotelgranodeoro.com. © **2255-3322.** 40 units. $150–$234 double; $305-$395 suite. Free parking. **Amenities:** Restaurant; bar; lounge; 2 rooftop Jacuzzis; room service; spa services; free Wi-Fi.

MODERATE

Tryp Sabana by Wyndham ★ (www.tryphotels.com; © **800/4683-261** in the U.S. and Canada, or 2547-2323 in Costa Rica), inside the Centro Colón building on Avenida 3, between calles 38 and 40, is a well-located business class hotel, with a very good tapas restaurant.

Crowne Plaza Corobicí ★   On the northeastern corner of La Sabana Park, this 11-story hotel has an odd architectural style that makes it look like a cross between a pyramid, an air-traffic control tower and a Soviet-era housing block. But it's quite handsome inside, with a huge lobby and oversized and very comfortable guest rooms. A remodel has given most of the rooms happy tangerine-colored walls, fine dark wood furnishings, 37-inch flatscreen TVs and luxurious bedding. There are several OK dining options, plus a casino, conference center, and well-equipped gym and spa.

Autopista General Cañas, Sabana Norte, San José. www.ihg.com. © **877/227-6963** in the U.S. and Canada, or 2543-6000 in Costa Rica. 213 units. $110 double; $126–$230 suite; $390 presidential suite. Free parking. **Amenities:** 2 restaurants; bar; lounge; casino; extensive health club and spa; Jacuzzi; midsize outdoor pool; room service; sauna; babysitting; free Wi-Fi.

INEXPENSIVE

Aldea Hostal ★ (www.aldeahostelcostarica.com; ☎ **2233-6365**) is a solid budget hostel option, with a popular little pizza restaurant attached.

Hotel Cacts ★ This budget hotel is housed in a converted family home on a side street about 2 blocks in from the busy Paseo Colón. There's a hostel-like vibe, a friendly staff, a small pool, and a Jacuzzi. The open-air rooftop patio has chairs and chaise lounges and offers a spectacular view of the city and surrounding mountains.

Av. 3 bis, no. 2845, btw. calles 28 and 30, San José. ☎ **2221-2928** or 2221-6546. 25 units. $66 double, includes taxes and breakfast buffet. Free parking. **Amenities:** Lounge; Jacuzzi; small outdoor pool; free Wi-Fi.

San Pedro/Los Yoses

Located just east of downtown, Los Yoses is home to numerous foreign embassies and consulates, and was one of the city's early upper-class outposts, while San Pedro is home to the University of Costa Rica, and offers up a distinct college town vibe. Staying here, you'll be close to much of the city's action but still enjoy some peace and quiet. If you've rented a car, be sure your hotel provides secure parking or you'll have to find (and pay for) a nearby lot.

MODERATE

Hôtel Le Bergerac ★ On a residential side street off the busy Avenida Central, about midway between downtown and the university district of San Pedro, the Hôtel Le Bergerac is a delightful boutique hotel with the air of an intimate French inn and an understated elegance. Three contiguous houses have been joined to create this hotel. Rooms are spacious and bright, most with varnished wood floors, and some with French doors opening onto a balcony or patio among the tropical gardens.

Calle 35, avenida 0 y 8, San José. www.bergerachotel.com. ☎ **2234-7850**. 28 units. $81–$150 double, includes full breakfast. Free parking. **Amenities:** Restaurant; lounge; free Wi-Fi.

INEXPENSIVE

Hotel Milvia ★ Housed in a converted old wooden plantation home, this boutique hotel is the handiwork of Steve Longrigg and Florencia Urbina. Steve has spent decades in the hospitality industry in Costa Rica, and Florencia is one of the country's more prominent artists and the former director of the Costa Rican Art Museum (p 134). Rooms, hallways and common areas feature a varied and striking collection of contemporary Costa Rican art by Florencia and her friends. Guest rooms are also blessed with plenty of natural light, and most lead out onto a veranda with mountain vistas or common courtyard sitting area. All of these common areas overflow with tropical plants and flowers and

Alternative Accommodations

If you plan to be in town for a while or are traveling with family or several friends, you might want to consider staying in an *apartotel,* a cross between an apartment complex and a hotel. You can rent by the day, week, or month, and you get a furnished apartment with a full kitchen, plus housekeeping. Options include **Apartotel El Sesteo** ★ (www.

sesteo.com; ℰ **2296-1805**) and **Aparto-tel La Sabana** ★ (www.apartotel-la sabana.com; ℰ **877/722-2621** in the U.S. and Canada, or 2220-2422). Additionally, check out Airbnb.com, which has hundreds of room and apartment listings in the San José, often for a fraction of the price of a hotel room.

striking artworks. This hotel is close to the Universidad Latina and one of the city's few train lines, so street noise can be a problem at times.

1 block north and 2 blocks east of the Muñoz y Nanne Supermarket, San Pedro. www.hotelmilvia.com. ℰ **2225-4543.** 9 units. $69 double, includes continental breakfast. **Amenities:** Free Wi-Fi.

WHERE TO EAT

San José has a variety of restaurants serving cuisines from all over the world. You can find superb French, Italian, and contemporary fusion restaurants around the city, as well as Peruvian, Japanese, Swiss, and Spanish spots. The greatest concentration and variety of restaurants is in the downtown area, as well as in the nearby suburbs of Escazú and Santa Ana. If you're looking for cheap eats, you'll find them all across the city in little restaurants known as *sodas,* which are the equivalent of diners in the United States.

Fruit vendors stake out spots on almost every street corner in downtown San José. If you're in town between April and June, you can sample more varieties of mangoes than you ever knew existed. Be sure to try a green mango with salt and chili peppers—it's guaranteed to wake up your taste buds. Another common street food is *pejibaye,* a bright orange palm nut about the size of a plum. They're boiled in big pots on carts; you eat them in much the same way you eat an avocado, and they taste a bit like squash.

Downtown San José

EXPENSIVE

La Esquina de Buenos Aires ★★ ARGENTINE/STEAKHOUSE Frankly, the Argentines do steak much better than the Ticos, and this Argentine-themed steakhouse is one of the best restaurants in the city. The decor and ambience are pure Porteño, and the extensive menu features a long list of grilled meats, including bife de chorizo (strip), ojo de bife (rib eye), and mollejas (sweatbreads), as well as some very good

La Esquina Restaurant

pastas and various seafood and poultry offerings. The place is festive and almost always filled to brimming, so you'll need reservations.

Calle 11 and Av. 4. © **2223-1909** or 2257-9741. www.laesquinadebuenosaires.net. Main courses C5,500–C18,800. Mon–Fri 11:30am–3pm and 6–10:30pm; Sat 12:30pm–11pm; Sun noon–10pm.

MODERATE

Restaurante Nuestra Tierra ★ COSTA RICAN   Almost a cross between a TGI Fridays and an old Costa Rican homestead kitchen, Nuestra Tierra has waitstaff in traditional garb serving traditional Costa Rica fare to crowds sitting at heavy wooden tables on bench seating. Bunches of bananas and onions and scores of painted enamel coffee mugs hang from wooden columns and beams. Hefty portions are served on banana leaves draped over large plates. The prices are a bit high for what you get, but service is prompt and pleasant.

Av. 2 and Calle 15. © **2258-6500.** Main courses C6,000–C15,000. Daily 24 hr.

Sapore Trattoria ★ ITALIAN This traditional trattoria is well located just off the Plaza de la Democracia, a stone's throw from the Jade Museum. The long, narrow dining room features wooden

Dining room of Sapore Trattoria

floors and some exposed brick and stone work. Start things off with a mixed antipasto plate, or some thin-sliced beef *carpaccio,* followed by above average pasta or the porcini and truffle risotto. For something more filling, try the *osso buco* (veal stew). There's a good selection of Italian wines and beers, and sometimes live music in the evenings.

Calle 13 and Avenida 2. ℭ **2222-8906.** http://saporetrattoria.com. Main courses C6,000–C12,000. Mon–Sat 11:30am–2:30pm and 6–10pm (Sat until 11pm); Sun 11:30am–6pm.

INEXPENSIVE

Alma de Café ★ CAFE/COFFEEHOUSE   Housed in an anteroom off the main lobby of the neo-baroque National Theater (Teatro Nacional), what should be just a simple coffee shop and restaurant is elevated by its setting—marble tables and floors, as well as elaborate painted ceiling murals, and regularly rotating exhibits of contemporary local artists. The menu features healthful salads, a selection of crepes, sandwiches, and lasagna. Alma de Cafe often stays open late on theater performance nights.

In the Teatro Nacional, Av. 2, btw. calles 3 and 5. ℭ **2010-1119.** Sandwiches C3,000–C5,5890; main courses C4,000–C5,000. Mon–Sat 9am–7pm; Sun 9am–6pm.

Coconut ★ CHINESE   Most guidebooks list the overly-touristy, Pan-Asian Tien Jo for Chinese food in San José, but locals in the know head to this unassuming spot a few blocks away. There are no golden dragons or patches of bamboo here, just a straightforward dining room backed by an open kitchen that slings out authentic Cantonese dishes made from scratch. Order the dumplings, which they call empanaditas, plus the wonton soup and their unbelievable BBQ pork. Dishes often sell out.

Calle 11 between Av. 10 and 12. ℭ **2223-8869.** Main courses C2,500–C6,000. Mon–Sat noon–10pm; Sun 12:30pm–5pm.

Barrio Amón/Barrio California

MODERATE

Café Mundo ★ INTERNATIONAL   A popular spot with a lively atmosphere and artsy ambience, this restaurant is housed in a remodeled old mansion, with tables and chairs spread through several rooms, hallways, outdoor patios, and terraces. The largest dining room here features floor-to-ceiling flowers painted by Costa Rican artist Miguel Casafont. Other rooms feature antique wallpaper and painted tile floors. Serving continental cuisine and thick crust pizzas, it's a reliable spot for a pleasant weekday lunch or evening out with a glass of wine or sangria.

Calle 15 and Av. 9, 200m (2 blocks) east and 100m (1 block) north of the INS Building. ℭ **2222-6190.** Main courses C4,500–C18,000. Mon–Thurs 11am–10:30pm; Fri 11am–11:30pm; Sat 5–11:30pm.

Maza Bistro ★★ CAFE/BISTRO   Costa Rica's best brunch, which lasts all day long for six days a week, is in this quirky café beside the Parque Nacional. Costa Rican ingredients and dishes are transformed into tasty plates like sweet arepas with fried chicken or French toast topped with muddled wild blackberries and gooseberries. There's also one of the city's best burgers. The cocktails here are not to be missed, maybe the best in the city, especially the Bloody Mary with candied bacon.

Calle 19 at Parque Nacional. © **2248-4824.** Main courses C3,800–C7,500. Tue-Sun 9am–6pm.

Olio ★ MEDITERRANEAN   This dimly lit, intimate restaurant has a romantic vibe, with several small rooms and quiet nooks located off the main dining area. A laundry list of classic Greek, Italian, and Spanish dishes is served in tapas-size portions, alongside more hearty pasta and main-course options. The wine list ventures far and wide to include offerings from Chile, Argentina, and even Bulgaria.

Calle 33 at Avenida 3, Barrio California. © **2281-0541.** Reservations recommended. Main courses C4,950–C13,750. Mon–Wed 11:45am–11pm; Thurs–Fri 11:45am–midnight; Sat 5:30pm–midnight.

La Sabana/Paseo Colón

EXPENSIVE

Grano de Oro Restaurant ★★ INTERNATIONAL   It's no accident that the city's most elegant boutique hotel (p 142) also has one of its most revered fine dining restaurants. The owners wooed and won French-born Francis Canal, a classically trained chef who has never stopped evolving, combining classic techniques from his homeland with local ingredients, tropical flavors, and contemporary fusion elements. That means a meal here might include an appetizer of Costa Rican snails in puff pastry, followed by local pork with tamarind sauce or seabass crusted with macadamia nuts. The 200-plus bottle wine list features offerings from four continents, and nearly a dozen choices by the glass. Leave room for dessert; the namesake pie is a silky layering of coffee and

Restaurant at Hotel Grano de Oro

mocha mousse on a rich cookie crust. The main dining room, a white linen and fine china affair, rings an open-air central courtyard, with a flowing fountain, tall potted trees and large stained-glass features.

Calle 30, no. 251, btw. avs. 2 and 4, 150m (1½ blocks) south of Paseo Colón. www. hotelgranodeoro.com. ℂ **2255-3322.** Reservations recommended. Main courses C8,500–C30,000. Daily 7am–10pm.

Park Café ★★ FUSION   While the Grano de Oro thrives on elegance and consistency, this place has a more off the cuff vibe. But the payoff from British chef Richard Neat, who ran a two-star Michelin restaurant in London before moving to Costa Rica, can also be substantial. The menu changes seasonally, but always features creative, contemporary dishes with sometimes dazzling presentations, often in tapas-sized portions to encourage broad samplings. Options include pargo (snapper) cooked in a salt pastry with asparagus and cauliflower cream, and caramelized veal tongue. Dining is spread throughout the courtyard and garden of a stately old home that functions as an antiques and decorative arts shop by day.

Sabana Norte, 1 block north of Rostipollos. www.parkcafecostarica.blogspot.com. ℂ **2290-6324.** Reservations recommended. Main courses C10,900–C15,800. Tues–Sat 5:30pm–9pm.

MODERATE

Machu Picchu ★ PERUVIAN/INTERNATIONAL   This longstanding local institution serves up excellent and traditional Peruvian cuisine in a converted old home (exposed brick walls and red tile floors), just off of Paseo Colón. The menu is extensive, with a wide range of ceviches and other cold and hot appetizers. The *parihuela* (a delicious seafood soup almost big and rich enough for a full meal) is a specialty. The house drink is the classic Peruvian pisco sour, made in a blender with pisco, lime juice, and an egg white.

Calle 32, btw. avs. 1 and 3, 150m (1½ blocks) north of the KFC on Paseo Colón. ℂ **2222-7384.** Reservations recommended. Main courses C7,000–C12,000. Mon–Sat 11am–10pm; Sun 11am–6pm.

INEXPENSIVE

Soda Tapia ★ COSTA RICAN   Dine with the locals at this prototypical Tico *soda* in a retro 1950s-style American diner, complete with bright lights and Formica tables. The food is solid and the service speedy. Its extended hours make it a good choice for a late-night bite. The main branch is just across from the popular La Sabana Park and Museo de Arte Costarricense (p 134). Other branches are around the Central Valley, including ones in Santa Ana (Centro Comercial Vistana Oeste, across from MATRA; ℂ **2203-7175**) and Alajuela (Centro Comercial Plaza Real Alajuela; ℂ **2441-6033**).

Calle 42 and Av. 2, across from the Museo de Arte Costarricense. ℂ **2222-6734.** Sandwiches C4,000–C4,400; main dishes C3,000–C5,000. Mon–Thurs 6am–2am; Fri–Sun 24 hrs.

Barrio Escalante/San Pedro

Vegetarians swear by the little **Comida Para Sentir Restaurante Vegetariano** ★ (© 2224-1163), located 125m (1¼ blocks) north of the San Pedro Church. Despite the massive size and popularity of the nearby **Il Pomodoro** ★ (© 2224-0966), **Pane E Vino** ★ (www.paneevino.co.cr; © 2280-2869), is an excellent pasta-and-pizza joint on the eastern edge of San Pedro. If you're hankering for sushi, try **Matsuri** ★ (www.restaurantematsuri.com; © 2280-5522), which has multiple storefronts around town.

MODERATE

Al Mercat ★★★ FARM TO TABLE   Without a doubt the best restaurant in Costa Rica. After graduating from Le Cordon Bleu in Paris and working around France, chef José González returned home to open Al Mercat in 2014. In just a few years he has managed to redefine what Tico cuisine can be with his ingredient driven dishes srouced from his parent's finca and regional farmer markets that explore Costa Rica's biodiversity. The split-level restaurant is relaxed and unpretentious, serving approachable dishes like gallos (Costa Rican tacos), a hot shrimp ceviche, and sweet potato gnocchi with a Caribbean style sauce. Additionally, González hosts food tours and lunches at his family's farm on the outskirts of San José.

200 meters north of Iglesia Santa Teresita, Barrio Escalante. © **2221-0783.** www.almercat.com. Main courses C4,100–C17,200. Mon–Thurs 11am–10:30pm; Fri 11am–11:30pm; Sat 5–11:30pm.

Kalú ★★ CAFE/BISTRO   Costa Rican–born chef Camille Ratton trained at Le Cordon Bleu and has created a wonderfully casual little bistro restaurant and gallery in a converted 1950s-era Art Deco home in a quiet neighborhood. The menu features an eclectic mix of sophisticated global cuisine like ceviche, soba noodles, pork and rabbit terrine, and even a burger topped with raclette. Don't miss out on the desserts, Camille's specialty—especially the Tarta Cahuita, an individual tartlet with a caramelized banana filling, grated lime peel, and chocolate ganache. Kalú serves brunch on the weekends and is renowned for its coffee, serving 34 different preparations of java. The attached **Kiosco** ★★ (p 156) is one of San José's more creative gift shops.

Calle 31 and Av. 5. www.kalu.co.cr. © **2253-8426.** Main courses 7,200–C15,000. Tues–Fri noon–10pm; Sat 9am–10pm; Sun 9am-4pm.

Whapin ★★ COSTA RICAN/CARIBBEAN   It's hard to find authentic Costa Rican Caribbean cooking away from the coast, but this humble place does a good job with a wide range of specialties more commonly served up in Cahuita and Puerto Viejo. They've always got the seafood and root vegetable stew *rondon* on the menu (see "That Run-Down Feeling," on p 577), as well as rice and beans cooked in coconut milk and served with your choice of chicken, meat, or fish. Other specialties: the jerk chicken and the whole fried red snapper. Most dishes come with a side of *patacones* (fried plantains). The decor is Caribbean, too: rustic clapboard wooden walls painted the emblematic reggae colors of red, yellow, and green surround rough-hewn tables and chairs.

Barrio Escalante, 200m (2 blocks) east of El Farolito. ✆ **2283-1480.** Main courses C5,900–C15,900. Mon–Fri 11am–3pm and 6–10pm, Sat 11am–10pm.

INEXPENSIVE

Jardin de la Abuela ★ CAFE   This no-frills café serves homey Costa Rican dishes made with lot of love. Come for a hearty Tico breakfast or lunchtime *casado,* as well as a piece of lasagna or a good cup of local coffee. They're only open during weekdays.

Calle 33 and Av. 13, Barrio Escalante. ✆ **2234-2129.** Main courses C4,500–C20,000. Mon–Fri 8am–4pm.

Mantras Veggie Café and Tea House ★ VEGETARIAN   This is among the best vegetarian restaurants in the city, with garden seating under bright red canvas umbrellas. The menu features a broad mix of soups, salads, wraps, sandwiches, and main dishes in both vegan and raw states. Signature dishes here include the raw zucchini "pasta" with pesto and the pad Thai. A broad selection of herbal teas is sold here, many grown on-site or purchased at local organic markets.

2 blocks east and ¼ block west of El Farolito, in Barrio Escalante. ✆ **2253-6715.** Main courses C3,850–C3,800. Mon–Sat 8:30am–5pm.

Raw To Go★ VEGAN   With the amount of yogis and surfers in Costa Rica, it's no wonder raw and health food restaurants are popping up all over San José. This fast-casual Barrio Escalante eatery offers cold pressed juices, a few bowls (açaí, granola), and a variety of whole grain toasts and wraps. They also make their own probiotic yogurt from cashews and nut butters.

Av 7 between Calle 33 and Calle 35, in Barrio Escalante. ✆ **2234-5235.** www.rawcocr.com. Main courses C3,500–C6,000. Mon–Fri 8am–7pm; Sat 9am–5pm.

SHOPPING

Serious shoppers may be disappointed in San José, because aside from oxcarts and indigenous masks, there isn't much that's distinctly Costa Rican. To compensate for its relative lack of goods, Costa Rica does a brisk business in selling crafts and clothes imported from Guatemala, Panama, and Ecuador.

San José's central shopping corridor is bounded by avenidas 1 and 2, from about Calle 14 in the west to Calle 13 in the east. For several blocks west of the Plaza de la Cultura, **Avenida Central** is a pedestrian-only street mall where you'll find store after store of inexpensive clothes for men, women, and children. Depending on the mood of the police that

joe **TO GO**

Two words of advice: Buy coffee.

Coffee is the best shopping deal in all of Costa Rica. Although the best Costa Rican coffee is allegedly shipped off to North American and European markets, it's hard to beat the coffee that's roasted right in front of you here. Best of all is the price: One pound of coffee sells for around $4 to $7. It makes a great gift and truly is a local product.

Café Britt is the big commercial name in Costa Rican coffee. It has the largest export business in the country, and, although high-priced, its blends are very dependable. Café Britt is widely available at gift shops around the country, and at both international airports. Also good are the coffees roasted and packaged in Manuel Antonio and Monteverde, by **Café Milagro** and **Café Monteverde,** respectively. If you visit either of these places, definitely pick up their beans.

In general, the best place to buy coffee is in any supermarket. Why pay more at a gift or specialty shop? If you buy prepackaged coffee in a supermarket in Costa Rica, the whole beans will be marked either *grano* (grain) or *grano entero* (whole bean). If you opt for ground varieties *(molido),* be sure the package is marked *puro;* otherwise, it may be mixed with a good amount of sugar, the way Ticos like it.

One good coffee-related gift to bring home is a coffee sock and stand. This is the most common mechanism for brewing coffee beans in Costa Rica. It consists of a simple circular stand, made out of wood or wire, which holds a "sock." Put the ground beans in the sock, place a pot or cup below it, and pour boiling water through. You can find the socks and stands at most supermarkets and in the Mercado Central. In fancier crafts shops, you'll find them made out of ceramic. A stand will cost you between $1.50 and $15; socks run around 30¢, so buy a few spares.

day, you might find a lot of street vendors as well. Most shops in the downtown district are open Monday through Saturday from about 8am to 6pm. Some shops close for lunch, while others remain open. You'll be happy to find that sales and import taxes have already been figured into display prices.

Markets

Several markets are near downtown, but by far the largest is the **Mercado Central ★** (p 156), located between avenidas Central and 1 and calles 6 and 8.

Plaza de la Democracia ★★   Two long rows of outdoor stalls sell t-shirts, Guatemalan and Ecuadorian handicrafts and clothing, small ceramic *ocarinas* (a small musical wind instrument), and handmade jewelry. The atmosphere here is much more open than at the Mercado Central, which can be a bit claustrophobic. You might be able to bargain prices down a bit, but bargaining is not a traditional part of the culture here, so you'll have to work hard to save a few bucks. On the west side of the Plaza de la Democracia, Calle 13 bis, btw. avs. Central and 2. No phone.

Modern Malls

With globalization taking hold in Costa Rica, much of the local shopping scene has shifted to large megamalls, modern multilevel affairs with cineplexes, food courts, and international brand-name stores. The biggest and most modern of these malls include the **Mall San Pedro, Multiplaza** (one each in Escazú and the eastern suburb of Zapote), and **Terra Mall** (on the outskirts of downtown on the road to Cartago). Although they lack the charm of small shops found around San José, they are a reasonable option for one-stop shopping; most contain at least one or two local galleries and crafts shops, along with a large supermarket, which is always the best place to stock up on local coffee, hot sauces, liquors, and other nonperishable foodstuffs.

Shopping A to Z
ART GALLERIES

Galería Kandinsky ★   Owned by the daughter of one of Costa Rica's most prominent modern painters, Rafa Fernández, this small gallery usu-

Artwork in Galería Valanti

ally has a good selection of high-end contemporary Costa Rican paintings, be it the house collection or a specific temporary exhibit. Centro Comercial Calle Real, San Pedro. © **2234-0478.**

Galería Valanti ★★   This is a well-lit and expertly curated gallery. The collection here is ever-evolving, but always includes a good mix of contemporary and classic Costa Rican and Latin American artists. Av. 11 #3395, btw. calles 33 and 35, Barrio Escalante. www.galeriavalanti.com. © **2253-1659.**

TEOR/éTica ★★   This small downtown gallery was founded by one of the more internationally respected collectors and curators in Costa Rica, the late Virginia Pérez-Ratton. It's still one of the best galleries in the country, bringing in guest curators from around the world, and you'll usually find cutting-edge exhibitions and installations here, with everything from sound and light sculptures to contemporary comics on offer. Calle 7, btw. avs. 9 and 11. www.teoretica.org. © **2233-4881.**

Admiring the art at TEOR/éTica

BOOKS

Librería Internacional ★ This is the closest Costa Rica has to a major book retailer. Most of the books here are in Spanish, but there is a small-to-modest selection of English-language contemporary fiction, nonfiction, and natural history texts. Librería Internacional has various outlets around San José, including in most of the major modern malls. Av. Central, ¾ block west of the Plaza de la Cultura. www.libreriainternacional.com. ℭ **2257-2563.**

Librería Internacional

Beautifully crafted chocolates from Sibú Chocolate

CHOCOLATE

Sibú Chocolate ★★ Chocolate lovers will definitely want to visit this gourmet organic chocolate maker, which features a small cafe, gift shop, and tours of its production facility in Escazú. The tour includes an informative presentation about the history and techniques of chocolate making, as well as several tempting tastings. Plaza Itskatzú #124, Escazú. www.sibuchocolate.com. © **2289-9010.** Tasting tours $27 (Tues–Sat at 10am; reservations essential). Gift shop and production facility Tues–Sat 8am–5pm.

HANDICRAFTS

The range and quality of craftworks for sale here has improved greatly in recent years. In addition to the places listed below, you might want to check out the works of Lil Mena, a local artist who specializes in painting on handmade papers and rough fibers, and **Cecilia "Pefi" Figueres ★★**, who specializes in brightly colored abstract and figurative ceramic bowls, pitchers, coffee mugs, and more. Both Mena and Figueres are sold at some of the better gift shops around the city. Another artist to look out for is **Barry Biesanz ★★**, whose bowls and boxes are works of art. Biesanz's works are also carried at fine gift shops around San José, as well as in his workshop and gallery in the hills above Escazú (p 170). Vendors at the Plaza de la Democracia market (p 152) also sell handicrafts.

Boutique Annemarie ★★ Occupying two floors at the Hotel Don Carlos (p 141), this shop has an amazing array of wood products, leather goods, papier-mâché figurines, paintings, books, cards, posters, and jewelry. You'll see most of this merchandise at the city's other shops, but not in such quantities or in such a relaxed and pressure-free environment. At the Hotel Don Carlos, Calle 9, btw. avs. 7 and 9. © **2233-5343.**

Chietón Morén ★★★ *Chietón Morén* means "fair deal" in the Boruca language. This place features arts and craft works from a dozen or so different Costa Rican indigenous communities displayed in a space that is part museum and part showroom and market. It operates as a nonprofit and is certified "fair trade," and all profits are given directly back to the artisans and their communities. Offerings include a wide range of textiles, carved masks, prints, and jewelry. Calle 1, btw. avs. 10 and 12. www.chietonmoren.org. ✆ **2221-0145.**

Galería Namu ★★★ Galería Namu has some very high-quality arts and crafts, specializing in truly high-end indigenous works, including excellent Boruca and Huetar carved masks and "primitive" paintings. It also carries a good selection of more modern arts and craft pieces, including the ceramic work of Cecilia "Pefi" Figueres. This place organizes tours to visit various indigenous tribes and artisans as well. Av. 7, btw. calles 5 and 7. www.galerianamu.com. ✆ **2256-3412.**

Mercado Central ★ Although this tight maze of stalls is primarily a food market, vendors also sell souvenirs, leather goods, musical instruments, and many other items. Be especially careful with your wallet, purse, and prominent jewelry, as skilled pickpockets frequent the area. All the streets around the Mercado Central are jammed with produce vendors selling from small carts or loading and unloading trucks. It's always a hive of activity, with crowds of people jostling for space on the streets. Your best bet is to visit on Sunday or a weekday; Saturday is particularly busy. Btw. avs. Central and 1 and calles 6 and 8, San José. No phone.

JEWELRY

Kiosco ★★ Attached to the restaurant Kalú (p 150), this place features a range of original and one-off pieces of functional, wearable, and practical jewelry made by contemporary Costa Rican and regional artists and designers. While the offerings are regularly changing, you'll usually find a selection of jewelry, handbags, shoes, dolls, furniture, and knickknacks. Often the pieces are made with recycled or sustainable materials. Calle 31 and Av. 5, Barrio Escalante. http://kalu.co.cr/boutique-kiosco-sjo. ✆ **2253-8367.**

Duo ★★ The outgrowth of a jewelry-making school and studio, this shop has some excellent handcrafted jewelry in a range of styles, using everything from 18-karat white and yellow gold and pure silver, to some less exotic and expensive alloys. Some works integrate gemstones, while many others focus on the metalwork. 6½ blocks east of the Iglesia Santa Teresita, Barrio Escalante. www.duo.co.cr. ✆ **2281-3207** or 2281-3207.

LEATHER GOODS

Del Río ★ This local leather goods manufacturer has several storefronts around the city, and in most of the country's modern malls. Works are high-quality and fairly priced, and range from wallets and belts to briefcases, boots, and fancy leather jackets and pants. Del Río also has outlets in several of the modern malls around the city. Av. Central, btw. calles 3 and 5, fronting the Plaza de la Cultura. www.delrio.cr. ✆ **2262-1415.**

LIQUOR

Some of the best prices on liquor are at the city's large supermarkets, such as **Automercado** and **Más x Menos.** A Más x Menos store is on Paseo Colón and Calle 26, and another is on Avenida Central at the east end of town, just below the Museo Nacional.

ENTERTAINMENT & NIGHTLIFE

Catering to a mix of tourists, college students, and party-loving Ticos, San José has a host of options to meet the nocturnal needs of visitors and residents alike. You'll find plenty of interesting clubs and bars, a wide range of theaters, and some very lively discos and dance salons.

To find out what's going on in San José while you're in town, go to **www.ticotimes.net**, or pick up *La Nación* (Spanish; www.nacion.com). The former is a good place to find out where local expats are hanging out; the latter's "Viva" and "Tiempo Libre" sections have extensive listings of discos, movie theaters, and live music.

Tip: Several very popular nightlife venues are in the upscale suburbs of Escazú and Santa Ana, as well as in Heredia (a college town) and Alajuela. See "The Central Valley" (p 168) more info on nightlife in these areas.

The Performing Arts

Visiting artists stop in Costa Rica on a regular basis. Recent concerts have featured hard rockers Aerosmith, Red Hot Chili Peppers, and

Orquesta Sinfónica Nacional de Costa Rica

Metallica; Mexican crooner Lila Downs; pop legend Elton John; Colombian sensation Shakira; and Latin heartthrob Marc Anthony. These performances take place at one of San José's performing arts theaters or one of the city's large sporting stadiums.

The **National Symphony Orchestra** (📞 **2240-0333**) is respectable by regional standards, although its repertoire tends to be rather conservative. Symphony season runs March through November, with concerts roughly every other weekend at the Teatro Nacional. Tickets cost between C4,000 and C7,000 and can be purchased at the box office.

Costa Rica's cultural panorama changes drastically every March when the country hosts large arts festivals. One of these is El Festival Nacional de las Artes, featuring purely local talent. **El Festival Internacional de las Artes** (FIA) is a month-long party with a nightly smorgasbord of dance, theater, and music from around the world. For dates and details, visit the festival's Facebook page (www.facebook.com/festivaldelasartescr), although information is in Spanish.

It is possible to buy tickets to many cultural events and concerts in advance from **E-Ticket** (www.eticket.cr), though the site is entirely in Spanish.

Auditorio Nacional ★   Housed inside the Museo de Los Niños (p 135), this is the city's most modern performing arts theater, with the best seats and sound system. However, it gets much less use than the more classic Teatro Nacional and Teatro Melico Salazar. Calle 4 and Av. 9. 📞 **2222-7647.**

Teatro Melico Salazar ★   Built in 1928, this 1,180-seat baroque theater is owned by the Costa Rican Ministry of Culture and houses the National Theater Company and National Dance Company. A regular slate of concerts and dance and theater performances is offered, ranging from productions by in-house companies, to concerts by visiting Latin American pop crooners, to full-scale productions of Broadway shows. Av. 2 btw. calles Central and 2. www.teatromelico.go.cr. 📞 **2295-6032.**

Teatro Nacional (National Theater) ★★   Costa Rica's most elegant and elaborate theater, the Teatro Nacional opened in 1897. Funded with a special tax on coffee, and modeled on the Paris Opera House, this neo-baroque theater features marble floors and columns; numerous sculptures, including busts of Beethoven and Chopin; and a painted fresco on the main auditorium's ceiling meant to suggest the majesty of the Sistine chapel. It is home base for the National Symphony Orchestra, and site of numerous other cultural events. Av. 2 btw. calles 3 and 5. www.teatronacional.go.cr. 📞 **2010-1129.**

The Club, Music & Dance Scene

You'll find plenty of places to hit the dance floor in San José. Salsa and merengue are the main beats that move people here, and many of the city's dance clubs, discos, and salons feature live music on the weekends.

Teatro Nacional

You'll find a pretty limited selection, though, if you're looking to catch some small-club jazz, rock, or blues performances.

The daily "Viva" and Friday's "Tiempo Libre" sections of *La Nación* newspaper have weekly performance schedules. Some dance bands to watch for are Gaviota, Chocolate, Son de Tikizia, Taboga Band, and La Orquestra Son Mayor. While Ghandi, Foffo Goddy, Kadeho, and Akasha are popular local rock and pop groups, Marfil is a good cover band, and the Blues Devils, Chepe Blues, and the Las Tortugas are outfits that play American-style hard rock and blues. If you're looking for jazz, check out Editus, El Sexteto de Jazz Latino, or pianist and former Minister of Culture Manuel Obregón. Finally, for a taste of something eclectic, look for Santos y Zurdo, Sonámbulo Psicotrópical, or Cocofunka.

Most of the places listed below charge a nominal cover charge; sometimes it includes a drink or two.

Castro's ★ This is a classic Costa Rican dance club. The music varies throughout the night, from salsa and merengue to reggaeton and occasionally electronic trance. It's open daily from noon to anytime between 3 and 6am. Av. 13 and Calle 22, Barrio Mexico. ✆ **2256-8789.**

Vértigo ★★ Tucked inside a nondescript office building and commercial center on Paseo Colón, this club remains one of the more popular places for rave-style late-night dancing and partying. The dance floor

159

Jazz Café in San Pedro

is huge and the ceilings are high, and electronic music rules the roost. It's open Friday and Saturday from 10pm until 6am. Edificio Colón, Paseo Colón. www.vertigocr.com. ☏ **2257-8424.**

The Bar Scene

San José has something for every taste. Lounge lizards will be happy in most hotel bars downtown, while students and the young at heart will have no problem mixing at the livelier spots around town. Sports fans have plenty of places to catch the most important games, and a couple of brewpubs are drastically improving the quality and selection of local suds.

    The best part of the varied bar scene in San José is something called a *boca,* the equivalent of a tapa in Spain: a little dish of snacks that arrives at your table when you order a drink. Although this is a somewhat dying tradition, especially in the younger, hipper bars, you will still find *bocas* alive and well in the older, more traditional San José drinking establishments. The most traditional of these are known locally as *cantinas.* In most, the *bocas* are free, but in some, where the dishes are more sophisticated, you'll have to pay for the treats. You'll find drinks reasonably priced, with beer costing around $3 to $4 a bottle, and mixed drinks costing $4 to $10.

Apotecario ★★ BREWPUB   Barrio Escalante has become a hotbed of craft beer in recent years and the best brewers can be found at Apotecario. Nicknamed the "house of fermentation," the brewpub produces wild ales under the label Cervecería Calle Cimarrona, including a long list of lambics and other small batch beers. Additionally, they make their own kombucha and have a varied pub menu with burgers and tapas. Calle 31 and Av. 9. © **4034-6485.** Tue–Sat 11:30am–10pm.

El Cuartel de la Boca del Monte ★★   This popular bar, one of San José's best, began life as an artist-and-bohemian hangout, and has evolved into a massive melting pot, attracting everyone from the city's young hipsters to foreign exchange students. Live music is usually Monday, Wednesday, and Friday nights, when the place is packed shoulder to shoulder. From Monday to Friday, it's open for lunch and again in the evenings; on weekends it opens at 6pm. On most nights it's open until about 1am, although the revelry might continue until about 3am on Friday or Saturday. Av. 1, btw. calles 21 and 23 (50m/½ block west of the Cine Magaly). © **2221-0327.**

El Lobo Estepario ★★   Named after Herman Hesse's classic novel, "Steppenwolf," this popular bohemian hangout is a top place to come for alternative music, poetry or theater, or to just have a few drinks with friends. There's a dedicated performance space upstairs, and the main room features walls made of blackboard material, with chalk provided for doodles, and tables made from old 55-gallon drums. The simple bar menu features some healthy and vegetarian options. Av. 2 and Calle 13. © **2256-3934.**

El Observatorio ★★   It's easy to miss the narrow alley that leads to the main entrance to this hot spot across from the Cine Magaly. Owned by a local filmmaker, the Observatorio's decor includes a heavy dose of cinema motifs. The main bar and performing space is large, with high ceilings and exposed brick walls on one side. Mondays tend to be for salsa dancing, while Wednesdays often feature stand-up comedy. There's occasional live music and movie screenings, and a decent menu of tapas and assorted appetizers and main dishes drawn from various world cuisines. It's open Monday through Saturday, 6pm to 2am. Calle 23, btw. avs. Central and 1. www.elobservatorio.tv. © **2223-0725.**

El Sótano ★★★   "El Sótano" means "the basement," and that's just where you'll find this tiny bar and performance space. Most nights, some of the city's best jazz and blues players hold down the scene, and on Tuesdays they host an open jam session. There's a small menu of bar food and sandwiches. When there's no live band, music is entirely played from vinyl. Upstairs from El Sótano is a separate bar and lounge space, El Solar. It's open until 2am daily. Calle 3, btw. av 11. © **2221-2302.**

Mercado La California ★ FOOD HALL   This extremely popular night market less than two blocks from Estación El Atlantico has a handful of food and drink stalls selling things like American style BBQ, tacos, craft beer, and cocktails. The later it gets, the more cool hipsters cram into the open courtyard. Calle 21 between Av. 1 and 2. No phone. Snacks C3,000–C8,000. Tue 9pm-3:30pm, Thur-Sat 6pm-3:30am, Sun 1pm-3:30am.

HANGING OUT IN SAN PEDRO

The funky 2-block stretch of **San Pedro** ★★ just south of the University of Costa Rica has been dubbed La Calle de Amargura, or the "Street of Bitterness," and it's the heart and soul of this eastern suburb and college town. Bars and cafes are mixed in with bookstores and copy shops. After dark, the streets are packed with teens, students, and professors barhopping and just hanging around. You can walk the strip until someplace strikes your fancy—or you can try one of the places listed below. *Note:* La Calle de Amargura attracts a certain unsavory element. Use caution here. Try to visit with a group, and avoid carrying large amounts of cash or wearing flashy jewelry.

You can get here by heading east on Avenida 2 and following the flow of traffic. You will first pass through the neighborhood of Los Yoses before you reach a large traffic circle with a big fountain in the center (La Fuente de la Hispanidad). The Mall San Pedro is located on this traffic circle. Heading straight through the circle, you'll come to the Church of San Pedro, about 4 blocks east of the circle. The church is the major landmark in San Pedro. You can also take a bus here from downtown.

Jazz Café ★   The intimate Jazz Café is one of the more happening spots in San Pedro. Jazz buffs will want to test their knowledge by trying to identify the various artists depicted in large sculpted busts behind the main stage. Most nights feature live music. It's open daily until about 2am. Sister club **Jazz Café Escazú** (℗ **2288-4740**) is on the western end of town. Next to the Banco Popular on Av. Central. www.jazzcafecostarica.com. ℗ **2253-8933**.

Mundoloco ★   This bar and pizzeria is the brainchild of DJ, radio host, and musician Bernal Monestel. The performance space in the back hosts live music or DJs most nights—usually with a slight cover charge. Bands tend to be eclectic, with a tendency toward electronic and world music, in addition to the homegrown rock and reggae outfits that are popular with the university crowd this place tends to attract. Southeast corner of the Banco Popular on Av. Central. www.facebook.com/Mundoloco ElChante. ℗ **2253-4125**.

Terra U ★   Set on a busy corner in the heart of the university district, this is one of the most "go-to" bars in the area. Part of this is due to the inviting open-air street-front patio area and inexpensive drink specials.

Although not officially a "sports bar," it has flatscreen televisions all around, and crowds are attentive whenever there's a big game or prize-fight on. It's open daily until 2am. 200m (2 blocks) east and 150m (1½ blocks) north of the church in San Pedro. ✆ **2225-4261.**

The Gay & Lesbian Scene

Because Costa Rica is such a conservative Catholic country, the gay and lesbian communities here are rather discreet. Homosexuality is not generally under attack, but many gay and lesbian organizations guard their privacy, and the club scene is changeable and not well publicized.

The most established and happening gay and lesbian bar and dance club in San José is **La Avispa** ★, Calle 1 between avenidas 8 and 10 (www.laavispa.com; ✆ **2223-5343**). It is popular with both men and women, although it sometimes sets aside certain nights for specific persuasions. There's also **Pucho's Men's Club** ★ (✆ **2256-1147**), on Calle 11 between Avenida 8 and 10; **El 13** (www.el13cafebar.com; ✆ **2221-3947**) on Calle 9, btw. avs. 12 and 14; and **El Bochinche** ★ (✆ **2221-0500**), on Calle 11 between avenidas 10 and 12.

Casinos

Gambling is legal in Costa Rica, and there are casinos at many major hotels. However, as with Tico bullfighting, some idiosyncrasies are involved in gambling *a la Tica.* If blackjack is your game, you'll want to play "rummy." The rules are almost identical, except that the house doesn't pay 1½ times on blackjack—instead, it pays double on any three of a kind or three-card straight flush. If you're looking for roulette, what you'll find here is a bingo-like spinning cage of numbered balls. The betting is the same, but some of the glamour is lost.

You'll also find a version of five-card-draw poker, but the rule differences are so complex that I advise you to sit down and watch for a while and then ask questions before joining in. That's about all you'll find. There are no craps tables or baccarat.

There's some controversy over slot machines, but you will be able to play electronic slots and poker games. Most casinos here are casual and small by international standards. You may have to dress up slightly at some of the fancier hotels, but most are accustomed to tropical vacation attire.

DAY TRIPS FROM SAN JOSÉ

San José makes an excellent base for exploring the lovely Central Valley. For first-time visitors, the best way to make the most of these excursions is usually to take a guided tour, but if you rent a car, you'll have greater independence. Some day trips also can be done by public bus.

Guided Tours & Adventures

A number of companies offer a wide variety of primarily nature-related day tours out of San José. The most reputable include **Costa Rica Sun Tours** ★ (www.crsuntours.com; ✆ 866/271-6263 in the U.S. and Canada, or 2296-7757 in Costa Rica), **Horizontes Nature Tours** ★★ (www.horizontes.com; ✆ **888/786-8748** in the U.S. and Canada, or 2222-2022), and **Swiss Travel Service** ★ (www.swisstravelcr.com; ✆ **2282-4898**). Prices range from around $35 to $75 for a half-day trip, and from $75 to $180 for a full-day trip.

> **Tip**
>
> Virtually every attraction, tour, and activity described in "The Central Valley" (chapter 7) makes for an easy day trip out of San José.

Before signing on for a tour of any sort, find out how many fellow travelers will be accompanying you, how much time will be spent in transit and eating lunch, and how much time will actually be spent doing the primary activity. I've had complaints about tours that were rushed, that spent too much time in a bus or on secondary activities, or that had a cattle-car, assembly-line feel to them. You'll find many tours that combine two or three different activities or destinations.

In addition to the tours and attractions offered around the Central Valley, a few others just a bit farther afield are convenient for day trips from San José. These include the following.

CANOPY TOURS & AERIAL TRAMS

Getting up into the treetops is a defining theme in Costa Rican tourism, and there are dozens of companies doing it.

The most popular day trip destination from San José is **Rainforest Adventures** ★ (www.rainforest adventure.com; ✆ **866/759-8726** in the U.S. and Canada, or 2257-5961 in Costa Rica), built on a private reserve bordering Braulio Carrillo National Park. It boasts a pioneering aerial tram built by rainforest researcher Donald Perry,

The aerial tram at Rainforest Adventures

whose cable-car system through the forest canopy at Rara Avis helped establish him as an early expert on rainforest canopies. On the 90-minute tram ride through the treetops, visitors have the chance to glimpse the complex web of life that makes these forests unique. Additional attractions include a butterfly garden, serpentarium, and frog collection. There's also a zipline tour, and the grounds feature well-groomed trails through the rainforest and a restaurant. With all this on offer, a trip here can easily take up a full day. If you want to spend the night, 10 simple but clean and comfortable bungalows cost $110 per person per day (double occupancy), including three meals, a guided hike, taxes, the tram ride, and use of the rest of the facilities.

The cost for a full-day tour, including both the aerial tram and canopy tour, as well as all the park's other attractions, is $99 for adults; students and anyone under 18 pay $65. Packages, including round-trip transportation and lunch, are also available. Alternatively, you can drive or take one of the frequent Guápiles buses—they leave every half-hour throughout the day and cost C1,450—from the Caribbean bus terminal (Gran Terminal del Caribe) on Calle Central and Avenida 15. Ask the driver to let you off in front of the teleférico. If you're driving, head out on the Guápiles Highway as if driving to the Caribbean coast. Watch for the tram's roadside welcome center—it's hard to miss. This is a popular tour for groups, so get an advance reservation in the high season and, if possible, a ticket; otherwise you could wait a long time for your tram ride or even be shut out. The tram handles about 80 passengers per hour, so scheduling is tight.

DAY CRUISES Several companies offer cruises to the white-sand beaches of the remote and uninhabited Tortuga Island in the Gulf of Nicoya. These full-day tours generally entail an early departure for the 1½-hour chartered bus ride to Puntarenas, where you board your vessel for a 1½-hour cruise to Tortuga Island. Then you get several hours on the uninhabited island, where you can swim, lie on the beach, play volleyball, or try a canopy tour, followed by the return journey.

The original and most dependable company running these trips is **Calypso Tours ★** (www.calypsocruises.com; © **855/855-1975** in the U.S. and Canada, or 2256-2727 in Costa Rica). The tour costs $145 per person and includes round-trip transportation from San José, Jacó, Manuel Antonio or Monteverde, a buffet breakfast before embarking on the boat, all drinks on the cruise, and a buffet lunch on the beach at the island. The Calypso Tours main vessel is a huge motor-powered catamaran. The company also runs a tour to a private nature reserve at **Punta Coral ★**. The beach is much nicer at Tortuga Island, but the tour to Punta Coral is more intimate, and the restaurant, hiking, and kayaking are all superior. Daily pickups are from San José, Manuel Antonio, Jacó,

The beach at Tortuga Island

and Monteverde, and you can use the day trip on the boat as your transfer or transportation option between any of these towns and destinations.

FOOD TOURS   Chef José González, of the restaurant Al Mercat (see p 150), runs frequent tours ★★ to his family's finca 10km outside of town, which includes tastings of native fruits and produce for $35. He'll also set up urban foraging trips to learn about the edible produce on the streets of San José, to explore the city's markets, and to taste authentic Costa Rican food at some of the city's hidden Sodas.

HIKING   Most of the tour agencies listed above offer 1-day guided hikes to a variety of destinations. In general, I recommend taking guided hikes to really see and learn about the local flora and fauna.

RAFTING, KAYAKING & RIVER TRIPS   Cascading down Costa Rica's mountain ranges are dozens of tumultuous rivers, several of which are very popular for whitewater rafting and kayaking. If I had to choose just one day trip out of San José, it would be whitewater rafting. For $100 or less, you can spend a day rafting a beautiful river through lush tropical forests, and multi-day trips are also available. Some of the most reliable rafting companies are **Tour Costa Rica** ★★ (www.tourcostarica.com; ✆ **888/680-9031** in the U.S.), **Exploradores Outdoors** ★ (www. exploradoresoutdoors.com; ✆ **646/205-0828** in the U.S. and Canada, or 2222-6262 in Costa Rica), and **Ríos Tropicales** ★★ (www.rios tropicales.com; ✆ **866/722-8273** in the U.S. and Canada, or 2233-6455 in Costa Rica). These companies all ply a number of rivers of varying difficulties, including the popular Pacuare River. For details, see "Whitewater Rafting, Kayaking & Canoeing" in chapter 5, p 112.

VOLCANO VISITS   The **Poás, Irazú** (see chapter 7 for more details), and **Arenal** volcanoes are three of Costa Rica's most popular destinations, and the first two are easy day trips from San José. Although numerous companies offer day trips to Arenal, travel time is at least 3½ hours in each direction. For more information on Arenal Volcano, see chapter 10.

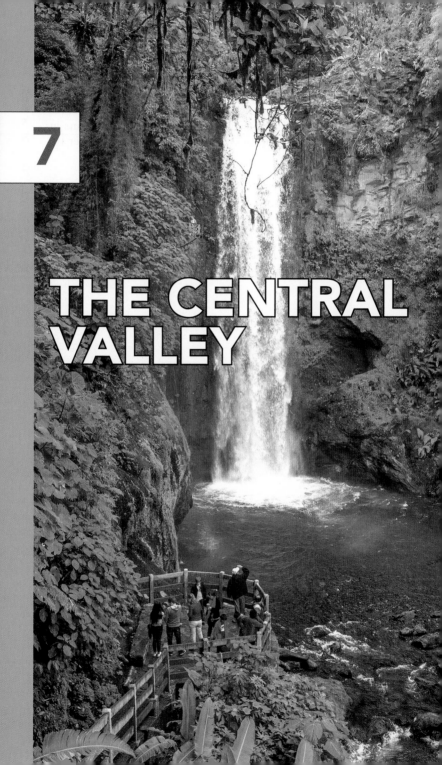

7

THE CENTRAL VALLEY

K
nown locally as La Meseta Central or El Valle Central, the long, thin, doglegging Central Valley is Costa Rica's most densely populated region. In addition to San José, it is home to Alajuela and Heredia; numerous smaller cities, suburbs, and towns; and the country's principal international airport. Most visitors start and end their vacations here.

The hills, mountains, and volcanoes that ring the Central Valley are an agricultural wonderland, with farms, fields, and plantations growing a wide range of crops, most prominently coffee. These towns, cities, hillsides, and volcanoes are home to a wide range of compelling attractions, from volcanic national parks and La Paz Waterfall Gardens, to pre-Colombian ruins and colonial-era churches. This is a perfect place to tour a working coffee farm. Although technically one valley over, the colonial-era capital city of Cartago is included in this chapter, because of its general geographic location and proximity to San José. With its ornate and locally revered basilica, earthquake-damaged Central Park ruins, and the neighboring Orosi Valley, this is an area well worth exploring.

THE best CENTRAL VALLEY EXPERIENCES

- **Dining at a *Mirador*:** Grab a window seat at a *mirador,* and enjoy your meal with the lights of San José at your feet. You'll find these restaurants with a view set up on most of the foothills surrounding the Central Valley. See "Dining Under the Stars," p 178.

- **Visiting a Volcano:** Several of Costa Rica's most impressive and accessible volcanoes are found in the mountains that define the Central Valley. These include Poás, Irazú, and Turrialba, all active volcanoes with their own namesake national parks. See p 182, 198, and 204.

- **Visiting La Paz Waterfall Gardens:** This place is akin to a Costa Rican tropical theme park. Consider combining a visit here with a stay in the luxurious on-site Peace Lodge (p 183). Its multiple attractions also make this a great day-trip option. See p 181.

- **Touring the Orosi Valley:** Among the most picturesque drives in Costa Rica, a trip around the Orosi Valley offers stunning vistas, ancient ruins, charming small towns, and top-notch attractions. See p 201.

- **Getting Wet & Wild in Turrialba:** This small, rural city is Costa Rica's main base for whitewater rafting and kayaking, especially on the nearby Pacuare River. You'll also find a thrilling canyoning operation and plenty of opportunities for other adventure activities. See p 204.

ESCAZÚ & SANTA ANA

Escazú: 5.5km (3½ miles) W of San José; Santa Ana: 13km (8 miles) W of San José

Located just west of San José, these affluent suburbs, once almost entirely farmlands and vacation estates, have boomed as the metropolitan area continues to expand. The two largest cities in this area, Escazú and Santa Ana, are popular with the Costa Rican professional class, as well as North American expatriates. Quite a few hotels have sprung up to cater to their needs. Both have large modern malls, endless little strip malls, and important business parks. It's easy to commute between Escazú or Santa Ana and downtown San José via car, bus, or taxi. And the area is about the same distance from the airport as downtown San José.

Essentials

GETTING THERE & DEPARTING   By Car: Head west out of San José along Paseo Colón. Turn left when you hit La Sabana Park, and turn right a few blocks later, at the start of the Próspero Fernández Highway (CR27). You will see well-marked exits for both Escazú and Santa Ana.

By Bus: Escazú- and **Santa Ana–bound** buses leave from the Coca-Cola bus station, as well as from Avenida 1 between calles 24 and 28. Or you can pick up both the Escazú and Santa Ana buses from a busy bus stop at the start of the Próspero Fernández Highway (CR27) on the southeast corner of the Parque La Sabana, next to the Gimnasio Nacional. Buses leave roughly every 5 to 10 minutes from 5am until 8pm, and less frequently during off hours. A bus costs between C300 and C400.

By Taxi: Taxi fare should run around C4,000 to C8,000, each way between San José and Escazú, and another C5,000 to C7,500 or so between Escazú and Santa Ana.

ORIENTATION   Both Escazú and Santa Ana are former farming towns that have been swallowed up by metro San José's urban sprawl. Each has a small downtown core built around an old church, with ever-expanding rings of residential and commercial development radiating off this core. Both also have numerous little satellite towns, such as San Antonio de Escazú, San Rafael de Escazú, and Pozos de Santa Ana.

FAST FACTS   You'll find banks and ATMs all over Escazú and Santa Ana, especially in the many malls.

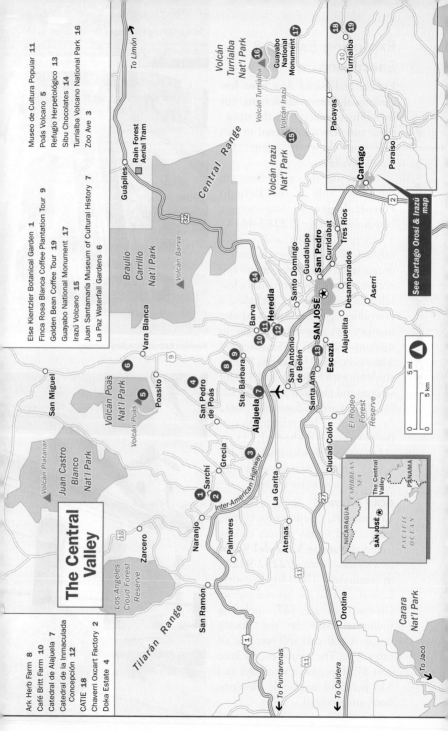

The Central Valley

Ark Herb Farm 8
Café Britt Farm 10
Catedral de Alajuela 7
Catedral de la Inmaculada Concepción 12
CATIE 18
Chaverri Oxcart Factory 2
Doka Estate 4

Else Kientzler Botanical Garden 1
Finca Rosa Blanca Coffee Plantation Tour 9
Golden Bean Coffee Tour 19
Guayabo National Monument 17
Irazú Volcano 15
Juan Santamaría Museum of Cultural History 7
La Paz Waterfall Gardens 6

Museo de Cultura Popular 11
Poás Volcano 5
Refugio Herpetológico 13
Sibú Chocolates 14
Turrialba Volcano National Park 16
Zoo Ave 3

See Cartago Orosi & Irazú map

Exploring Escazú & Santa Ana

Escazú and Santa Ana have few traditional tourism attractions, but both offer easy access to the attractions and activities offered in San José and elsewhere around the Central Valley.

One of the exceptions to the above rule is the **Refugio Herpetológico** ★ (http://refugio herpetologico.com; ✆ **2282-4614**), a family-run reptile and wildlife exhibition. In addition to a few dozen snakes, both venomous and nonvenomous, the center has a few rehabilitating animals, including a crocodile, iguanas, and a spider monkey. It's open from 9am to 4:30pm, Tuesday to Sunday, and admission is $20 for adults; $10 for students with valid ID; and $10 for seniors and children 3 through 12.

Avenida Escazu shopping complex

If you are in downtown Santa Ana, do take a few minutes to visit the town's main **cathedral,** a lovely old stone church, with thick wooden beams, colorful stained-glass windows, and a red-clay tile roof.

GOLF & TENNIS Some of the best Central Valley facilities for visiting golfers and tennis players can be found at **Parque Valle del Sol** ★ (www.vallesol.com; ✆ **2282-9222**), in Santa Ana. The 18-hole course here is open to the general public. Greens fees are $67, including unlimited balls on the driving range. A golf cart will run you an extra $32. The tennis courts here cost $7.50 per hour weekdays and $13 per hour weekends. Reservations are essential.

Santa Ana's cathedral

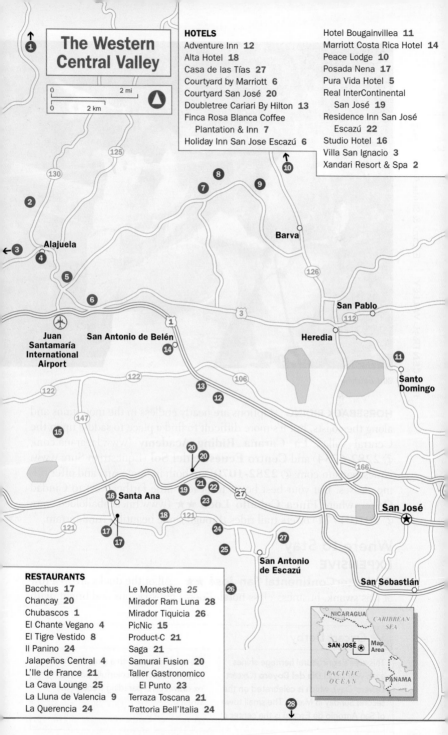

The Western Central Valley

0 — 2 mi

0 — 2 km

1

↑

HOTELS

Adventure Inn **12**
Alta Hotel **18**
Casa de las Tías **27**
Courtyard by Marriott **6**
Courtyard San José **20**
Doubletree Cariari By Hilton **13**
Finca Rosa Blanca Coffee
  Plantation & Inn **7**
Holiday Inn San Jose Escazú **6**

Hotel Bougainvillea **11**
Marriott Costa Rica Hotel **14**
Peace Lodge **10**
Posada Nena **17**
Pura Vida Hotel **5**
Real InterContinental
  San José **19**
Residence Inn San José
  Escazú **22**
Studio Hotel **16**
Villa San Ignacio **3**
Xandari Resort & Spa **2**

Barva

Alajuela

Juan
Santamaría
International
Airport

San Antonio de Belén

Heredia

San Pablo

**Santo
Domingo**

Santa Ana

San José

**San Antonio
de Escazú**

San Sebastián

RESTAURANTS

Bacchus **17**
Chancay **20**
Chubascos **1**
El Chante Vegano **4**
El Tigre Vestido **8**
Il Panino **24**
Jalapeños Central **4**
L'Ile de France **21**
La Cava Lounge **25**
La Lluna de Valencia **9**
La Querencia **24**

Le Monestère **25**
Mirador Ram Luna **28**
Mirador Tiquicia **26**
PicNic **15**
Product-C **21**
Saga **21**
Samurai Fusion **20**
Taller Gastronomico
  El Punto **23**
Terraza Toscana **21**
Trattoria Bell'Italia **24**

NICARAGUA

CARIBBEAN
SEA

SAN JOSÉ ✪ Map
Area

PACIFIC
OCEAN

PANAMA

Bird-watching

HORSEBACK RIDING　Options are nearly endless in the mountains and along the coasts, but it's more difficult to find a place to saddle up in the Central Valley. **La Caraña Riding Academy** (www.lacarana.com; ☎ 2282-6754) and **Centro Ecuestre del Sol** (Equestrian Sun; www.equestriansun.com; ☎ 2282-1070) are both in Santa Ana and offer riding classes. But your best bet is to head a little farther west to Ciudad Colón, where **Finca Caballo Loco** ★★ (www.fincacaballoloco.com; ☎ 7010-1771) offers trail rides through some beautiful rural terrain.

Where to Stay
EXPENSIVE
Real InterContinental San José ★★　All of the ducks are in a row at this swank, business-class hotel. Rooms are spacious and bright, with

Oxcart Derby

This area's agricultural heritage shines each year on **El Día del Boyero** (Oxcart Drivers' Day), which is celebrated on the second Sunday in March. The small town of San Antonio de Escazú is the center of the celebrations, with a street fair and a large collection of colorfully painted ox-drawn carts parading through the streets.

the type of cushy mattresses, soothing color palette, and solid furnishings you'd expect from any InterContinental. The palm-fringed swimming pools are lovely and large enough that they never feel crowded. The spa and fitness center are state-of-the-art. Guests also like the five on-site restaurants and a location that's right across the street from a large mall with a multiplex cinema.

Autopista Próspero Fernández, across from the Multiplaza mall, Escazú. www.ichotels group.com. © **800/496-7621** U.S./Canada, or 2208-2100 in Costa Rica. 372 units. $196–$265 double; $523 suite, includes taxes. **Amenities:** 5 restaurants; 2 bars; concierge; health club; spa; Jacuzzi; pools; room service; tennis; free Wi-Fi.

MODERATE

In addition to the hotels below, the **Courtyard San José** ★ (www. marriott.com; © **888/236-2427** in the U.S. and Canada, or 2208-3000), **Residence Inn San José Escazú** ★ (www.marriott.com; © **888/236-2427** in the U.S. and Canada, or 2588-4300), and **Holiday Inn San José Escazú** ★ (www.ihg.com; © **877/407-2373** in the U.S. and Canada, or 2506-5000 in Costa Rica) are all modern business-class hotels a few miles from each other, right on the western Próspero Fernández Highway connecting Santa Ana and Escazú with San José.

Alta Hotel ★★ This boutique hotel is blessed with old-world charm. High arches and curves abound. The top touch is the winding interior alleyway that snakes down from the reception through the hotel. Most of the rooms have superb views of the Central Valley from private balconies; the others have pleasant garden patios. All are up to modern resort standards (although some have cramped bathrooms), and are minimalist in style, with white-washed walls and black-and-white photos from the 1920s. The suites are far larger, each with a separate sitting room and big Jacuzzi-style tubs in spacious bathrooms. The hotel's La Luz restaurant is a winner, serving up organic Mediterranean fare.

Alto de las Palomas, old road to Santa Ana. www.thealtahotel.com. © **800/242-0500** in the U.S. and Canada, or 2282-4160. 23 units. $140 double; $245-305 suite, taxes and continental breakfast included. Free parking. **Amenities:** Restaurant; bar; concierge; small gym; Jacuzzi; pool; room service; sauna; free Wi-Fi.

Casa de las Tías ★★ The Escazú and Santa Ana areas are awash in modern, business-class chain hotels and upscale boutique options, but this converted wooden home offers something special for those seeking a real Costa Rican experience at a good price. The charming, detached house features a yellow-and-blue exterior and offers cozy rooms and a Costa Rican breakfast. Owners Xavier and Pilar live on site and are very hands-on hosts. The hotel is close to the bustling Escazú intersection, yet feels a world apart with its large garden and quiet, secure grounds.

San Rafael de Escazú. www.casadelastias.com. © **2289-5517.** 5 units. $100–$110 double, includes breakfast. **Amenities:** Free Wi-Fi.

Studio Hotel ★ Art lovers will feel right at home in this small contemporary hotel. The lobby, common areas and rooms all feature a wealth of original works by major contemporary and historical Costa Rican artists, including Rafa Fernandez, Isidor Con Wong, and Edgar Zuñiga. The stylish Katowa restaurant here serves up fab Costa Rican fusion cuisine. However, the piece de resistance is the third-floor rooftop pool and lounge area under a soaring white canvas tent structure, with mountain and city views. The hotel sits on a busy intersection at the entrance to Santa Ana, with many restaurants and bars a short walk away.

Santa Ana. www.costaricastudiohotel.com. Ⓒ **866/978-8123** in the U.S. and Canada, or 2282-0505 in Costa Rica. 82 units. $95-$114 double; $134 suite, taxes and breakfast included. **Amenities:** Restaurant; small gym; rooftop pool; free Wi-Fi.

INEXPENSIVE

Posada Nena ★   Friendly and helpful service is what sets the Posada Nena apart. Its German owners live on the property and make sure that guests are happy and all of the cheerful, bright rooms are kept ship-shape. Rooms surround a breeze-blessed courtyard garden (with sunken Jacuzzi), shaded by a bamboo canopy. Also on-site is a tiny, rustic restaurant. Posada Nena is booked, often with repeat guests, by folks with friends or family in Santa Ana. Previously called Casa Alegre, the compact residential area hotel is just 2 blocks from the pretty stone church and central park of this once quiet farming town.

Santa Ana. www.posadanena.com. Ⓒ **2282-1173.** 9 units. $72-$84 double, taxes and breakfast included. **Amenities:** Restaurant; bar; Jacuzzi; free Wi-Fi.

Where to Eat

These two suburbs have the most vibrant restaurant scenes in San José. In addition to the places listed below, **Trattoria Bell'Italia** ★ (Ⓒ **2588-2833**) is primo for Italian cuisine, as is **Il Panino** ★ (www.ilpanino.net; Ⓒ **2228-3126**), an upscale sandwich shop and cafe. Both are located in the Centro Comercial La Paco.

Good restaurants are also clustered at **Plaza Itskatzú** (just off the highway and sharing a parking lot with the Courtyard San José), and **Avenida Escazú** (which is anchored by the Marriott Residence Inn and is next to the CIMA Hospital). Good options at Plaza Itskatzú include **Chancay** ★ (www.chancay.info; Ⓒ **2588-2327**), which serves Peruvian cuisine; and **Samurai Fusion** ★ (Ⓒ **2288-2240**), a fine sushi and teppanyaki joint. On Avenida Escazú, try **Saga** ★ (www.sagarestaurant.com; Ⓒ **2289-6615**), with a casual bistro menu; **Terraza Toscana** ★ (www.terrazzatoscanacr.com; Ⓒ **4000-2220**) an excellent and elegant Italian restaurant; or **L'Ile de France** ★ (http://enjoyrestaurants.net; Ⓒ **2289-7533**), for high-end French fare.

EXPENSIVE

Bacchus ★★ ITALIAN   This elegant restaurant, inside an adobe home built in 1870, is one of the best Italian options in the city, if not the country. Thin-crust pizzas come out of the wood-burning oven from the open kitchen. Pastas and ravioli are homemade and all are scrumptious, particularly the pappardelle with white wine, arugula, carrots, and crabmeat. From the selection of creative desserts, the banana and apple croquettes (topped with Grand Marnier sauce) reign supreme. Changing art exhibits adorn the walls, and there's an ample covered patio.

Downtown Santa Ana. http://enjoyrestaurants.net/bacchus. © **4001-5418.** Reservations required. Main courses C6,500–C14,700. Mon–Fri noon–3pm and 6–10pm; Sat noon–10pm; Sun noon–8pm.

Taller Gastronomico El Punto ★ FUSION   Set within a pretty contemporary house on a busy road, this edgy restaurant with high tech kitchen equipment and modernist plates has its sights set high. While the restaurant attracts a well-heeled crowd, the food can be hit or miss. Main courses are mostly just a piece of protein and a vegetable, which might say as much about the clientele than the chef's cooking abilities. The appetizers are far more interesting, with fun plates like lobster rolls, *cochinita pibil* tacos, and ossobuco croquettes.

800 mts north of CC La Paco, Escazú. www.tgelpunto.com. © **2215-0381.** Main courses C13,800–C15,700. Mon 7-10pm; Tue-Fri noon–10pm; Sat 1–10pm.

MODERATE

La Querencia ★ ARGENTINEAN   This upscale Escazú restaurant and market specializes in foods cooked in a wood fired oven and house made pastas, which are available to eat in or take out. There is a long list of Argentine baked goods, like empanadas or *media lunas* (croissants), as well as grilled meats and sausages. Prices are a bit higher than the standard carry out spot or deli, but when you see the amount of work and quality of the ingredients through the open kitchen you immediately understand why.

Centro Comercial Paco 3, Escazú. © **2289-5955.** Main courses C4,500–C18,500. Mon, Wed–Fri 10am–9:30pm; Sat-Sun 9am–9:30pm.

Product-C ★ SEAFOOD   Although San José is inland, this fish market and restaurant prides itself on daily predawn runs to Puntarenas and other coastal supply points to get the freshest catch possible. It even set up the first oyster farm in Costa Rica, producing small yet very tasty oysters. The daily chalkboard menu features a range of specials. Feel free to check out the display case and choose whatever fish or seafood strikes your fancy, and have it cooked to order in any number of styles.

Av. Escazú.. © **2288-5570.** Reservations recommended. Main courses C6,500–C14,500. Mon–Sat noon–11pm; Sun noon–6pm.

INEXPENSIVE

PicNic ★★ DELI   In a strip of youngm casual eateries with indoor and outdoor seating, this organic deli, decorated in white subway tiles and industrial furnishings, stands out. Everything revolves around the bakery, which produces the bread for the sandwiches (roast beef, Caprese,

DINING under the stars

One of the best Costa Rican experiences is dining on the side of a volcano with the lights of San José shimmering below. These hanging restaurants, called *miradores*, are a resourceful response to the city's topography. Because San José is in a broad valley surrounded on all sides by volcanic mountains, people who live in these mountainous areas have no place to go but up—so they do, building roadside cafes up the sides of the volcanoes.

The food at most of these establishments is not spectacular, but the views often are, particularly at night, when the wide valley sparkles in a wash of lights. The town of **Aserrí,** 10km (6¼ miles) south of downtown San José, is the king of *miradores*, and **Mirador Ram Luna ★** (www.restauranteramluna.com; ☏ **2230-3022**), open since 1967, is the king of Aserrí. Grab a window seat and, if you've got the fortitude, order a plate of *chicharrones* (fried pork rinds). There's often live music. You can hire a cab for around C15,000 or take the Aserrí bus at Avenida 6 between calles Central and 2. Just ask the driver where to get off.

Miradores are also in the hills above Escazú and in San Ramón de Tres Ríos and Heredia. The most popular is **Le Monestère ★** (www.monastere-restaurant.com; ☏ **2228-8515;** closed Sun), an elegant converted church serving somewhat overrated French and Belgian cuisine in a spectacular setting above the hills of Escazú. I recommend coming here for the less formal **La Cava Lounge ★**. There's also **Mirador Tiquicia ★** (☏ **2289-7330**), which occupies several rooms in a sprawling old Costa Rican home and has live folkloric dance shows on Thursdays.

Cubano), the pancakes, tarts, cakes, and other goodies. There is a long list of juices and coffee drinks too.
Plaza Futura #2 (beside Hotel Indigo), Santa Ana. www.picniccr.com. ☏ **4033-4111.** Main courses C3,000–C6,500. Tue–Fri 7am–7pm; Sat 8am–5pm.

Shopping

One of the country's best and largest megamalls, **Multiplaza Escazú,** is located along the Próspero Fernández Highway (CR27), just west of downtown Escazú. In the same general area, you'll find two other smaller malls, **Avenida Escazú** and **Plaza Itskatzú,** each of which has an attractive mix of high-end shops, boutiques, restaurants, and art galleries.

Biesanz Woodworks ★★   Biesanz makes a wide range of high-quality wood items, including bowls, jewelry boxes, humidors, and some wonderful sets of chopsticks. The company is actively involved in local reforestation. Bello Horizonte, Escazú. www.biesanz.com. ☏ **2289-4337.**

Galería 11–12 ★★★   This outstanding gallery handles high-end Costa Rican art, from neoclassical painters such as Teodorico Quirós to modern masters such as Francisco Amighetti and Paco Zuñiga, as well as current stars such as Rafa Fernández, Rodolfo Stanley, Fernando

Carballo, and Fabio Herrera. Plaza Itzkatzú, off the Próspero Fernández Hwy., Escazú. ℂ **2288-1975.**

Entertainment & Nightlife

Escazú has a handful of popular bars and clubs, many frequented by the Central Valley's well-heeled urban youth. The most popular is the **Jazz Café Escazú ★★** (Próspero Fernández Hwy.; www.jazzcafecostarica. com; ℂ **2288-4740**), a top spot for live music. If a high-level act is visiting from the United States, Europe, or South America, they will certainly play here.

ALAJUELA, POÁS ★★ & THE AIRPORT AREA

Airport: 15km (9¼ miles) NW of San José; Alajuela: 18½ km (11½ miles) NW of San José; Poás Volcano: 37km (23 miles) northwest of San José

Most people visiting Costa Rica land at the Juan Santamaría International Airport in Alajuela. The downtown area of Costa Rica's second largest city is just a mile or so north of the airport. The city itself is of little interest to most tourists, although it is the gateway to the Poás Volcano and other top Central Valley attractions.

A crater lake at Poás Volcano

Essentials

GETTING THERE & DEPARTING
By Car: Head northwest out of San José on the Inter-American Highway (CR1).

By Bus: Two separate lines make the run between San José and Alajuela: **Tuasa** (ℂ **2442-6900**) buses are red; **Station Wagon** (ℂ **2441-1181**) buses are beige/yellow. Buses leave roughly every 10 minutes between 5am and 11pm, less frequently in off hours (fare C555).

By Train: A commuter train runs between downtown San José and Heredia. This train runs roughly every 10 minutes between 5:30 and 9:00am, and again between 3:30 and 8:30pm. Fares range from C420 to C550, depending on the length of your ride.

Catedral de Alajuela

ORIENTATION Downtown Alajuela is a tight jumble of one-way streets, often choked to a standstill with gridlocked traffic. Most people will be heading up into the hills from downtown. The best way to find the route out of town is usually to follow signs for the Poás Volcano or some other well-known attraction.

FAST FACTS You'll find banks and ATMs all over Alajuela, especially in the central downtown area, and nearby malls and shopping centers. The **Hospital San Rafael de Alajuela** (© **2436-1001**) is large, modern, and well-equipped. If you need a taxi, call **COOTAXA** (© **2443-3030**) or **Taxi Radio Liga** (© **2441-1212**). The Uber app also works.

Exploring Alajuela

Alajuela's main church, the **Catedral de Alajuela** (**Alajuela Cathedral;** © **2441-4665**) is a large, relatively ornate Catholic church, with a striking white-washed exterior, ceiling frescos, and a gold-leaf painted interior dome. Mass is held Monday to Friday at 9am and 5pm; Saturday at 9am and 7pm; and Sunday at 9 and 11am and 5 and 7pm.

The **Museo Historico Cultural Juan Santamaría (Juan Santamaría Museum of Cultural History)** ★, Avenida 3 between calles Central and 2 (www.museojuansantamaria.go.cr; © **2441-4775**), commemorates Costa Rica's national hero, Juan Santamaría, who gave his life defending the country against a mercenary army led by William Walker, a U.S. citizen who invaded Costa Rica in 1856, attempting to set up a slave state. Housed in a sprawling two-story downtown building with a large central courtyard, the museum features permanent exhibits about Santamaría and Walker's filibuster exploits, as well as temporary expositions, and evening concerts and theater performances. The museum is open Tues through Sun from 10am to 5:30pm; admission is free.

NEARBY ATTRACTIONS

Doka Estate ★ FARM   This large and long-standing coffee estate/farm in Alajuela offers a tour that takes you from "seed to cup." Along the way, you'll get the rundown of the processes involved in the growing, harvesting, curing, packing, and brewing of award-winning coffee. This tour is similar to that offered at **Café Britt Farm** ★★ (p 189), but has a little more down-home feel. Also on site: a butterfly garden, Bonsai tree garden, and orchid exhibit. Allow about 2½ hours.

Sabanilla de Alajuela. www.dokaestate.com. ℭ **888/946-3652** in the U.S. and Canada or 2449-5152 in Costa Rica. Admission $20 adults, $16 students, $10 children 6–12, free for children 5 and under. Packages including transportation and meals available. Tours daily at 9, 10, and 11am; 1:30 and 2:30pm. Reservations required.

La Paz Waterfall Gardens ★★ NATURAL ATTRACTION   The original attraction here consists of a series of trails through primary and

secondary forests alongside La Paz River, with lookouts over a series of powerful falls, including the namesake La Paz Fall. In addition to the orchid garden and a hummingbird garden, you must visit the huge butterfly garden. A small serpentarium, featuring a mix of venomous and nonvenomous native snakes, several terrariums containing frogs and lizards, and a section of wildcats and local monkey species in large enclosures are added attractions. Although the admission fee is a little steep, everything is well done, especially the trails and waterfalls. That said, some find the whole operation a little artificial in feel. Yet it's a good place to get a broad experience in one compact package, especially for families with young children. This is also a nice stop after a morning visit to the Poás Volcano.

Touring the coffee plantation at Doka Estate

Plan to spend 3 to 4 hours here. The hotel rooms here at **Peace Lodge** (p 183) are some of the nicest in the country.

6km (3¾ miles) north of Varablanca on the road to San Miguel. www.waterfall gardens.com. ☏ **2482-2720.** Admission $40 adults, $26 children 3–12, free for children 2 and under. Daily 8am–5pm. No easy or regular bus service here; you will need to come in a rental car or taxi, or arrange with the gardens for transport.

A coffee tree at Café Britt

Poás Volcano ★★★ NATURAL ATTRACTION **(CURRENTLY CLOSED; see note below.)** From San José, narrow roads wind through a landscape of fertile farms and dark forests to this active volcano. A paved road leads right to the top, although you'll have to hike in about 1km (½ mile) to reach the crater. The volcano stands 2,640m (8,659 ft.) tall and is located within a national park, which preserves not only the volcano but also dense stands of virgin forest. The Poás crater, one of the largest in the world, is more than a 1.6km (1 mile) across. Geysers in the crater sometimes spew steam and muddy water 180m (590 ft.) into the air.

The information center has a slideshow about the volcano, and well-groomed hiking trails through the cloud forest ring the crater. About 15 minutes from the parking area, along a forest trail, is an overlook onto beautiful Botos Lake, formed in one of the volcano's extinct craters.

Be prepared when you come to Poás: This volcano is often enveloped in dense clouds. If you want to see the crater, it's best to come early and during the dry season. You can also call ahead and ask the staff whether the crater is clear. Moreover, it can get cool up here, especially when the sun isn't shining, so dress appropriately. **Note**: Due to increased and unpredictable volcanic activity the park was closed as press time, so be sure to call the park office for updated status before visiting.

Poás de Alajuela. 37km (23 miles) from San José. ☏ **2482-1228.** Admission $15. Daily 8:30am–3:30pm.

Zoo Ave ★★ ZOO Dozens of scarlet macaws, reclusive owls, majestic raptors, several different species of toucans, and a host of brilliantly colored birds from Costa Rica and around the world make this one exciting place to visit. In total, over 115 species of birds are on display, including some 80 species found in Costa Rica. Bird-watching enthusiasts will be able to get a closer look at birds they might have seen in the wild. Other critters to observe include iguana, deer, tapir, ocelot, puma, and monkey—and look out for the 3.6m (12-ft.) crocodile. Zoo Ave houses only injured, donated, or confiscated animals. It takes about 2 hours to walk the paths and visit all the exhibits here.

La Garita, Alajuela. www.rescateanimalzooave.org. ✆ **2433-8989.** Admission $20, $15 students. Daily 9am–5pm.

Where to Stay in & Around Alajuela

Of the following hotels, the Doubletree Cariari by Hilton, Holiday Inn Express, Marriott Costa Rica Hotel, Courtyard by Marriott Alajuela, and Pura Vida Hotel are the closest to the airport.

EXPENSIVE

Marriott Costa Rica Hotel ★★　Designed to resemble a colonial-era mansion, the Marriott is close enough to the airport to be considered an "airport hotel," yet still feels like a country retreat, featuring a massive central courtyard meant to mimic Havana's Plaza de Armas. The elegant, traditional-style rooms are large and have views of the surrounding hillsides, suburbs, and coffee fields. There are several distinct dining choices, and the Casa de Café coffee house and restaurant actually fronts a small working coffee field. With tennis courts, a golf driving range, pools, and a top spa, guests rarely run out of amusements here.

San Antonio de Belén. www.marriott.com. ✆ **2298-0000.** 299 units. $234-$293 double; suites $356–$979. Valet parking. **Amenities:** 3 restaurants; 2 bars; concierge; golf range; spa; Jacuzzi; 2 pools; room service; sauna; 2 tennis courts; free Wi-Fi.

Peace Lodge ★★★　Part of the popular **La Paz Waterfall Gardens** (p 181), Peace Lodge is about 45 minutes from the airport, near the Poás Volcano. The rooms and villas are huge and feature faux rustic decor, including massive four-poster log beds and river stone fireplaces. All come private balconies with Jacuzzis, while the deluxe rooms also feature an immense bathroom with a second indoor Jacuzzi backed by a full wall of orchids, flowers, and bromeliads, with a working waterfall. Nightly rates can be steep, but remember: They get you not only these fanciful rooms but also unlimited access to the Waterfall Gardens.

6km (3¾ miles) north of Varablanca on the road to San Miguel. www.waterfall gardens.com. ✆ **954/727-3997** in the U.S., or 2482-2720 in Costa Rica. 17 units. $430–$510 double; $710–$940 villa, includes entrance to La Paz Waterfall Gardens. **Amenities:** Restaurant; bar; Jacuzzi; 2 pools; free Wi-Fi; hiking trails; butterfly exhibits; disc golf.

Xandari Resort & Spa ★★　Located on a hilltop above the city of Alajuela just 20-minutes from the airport, Xandari commands magnificent views of nearby coffee farms and the Central Valley below. Owners

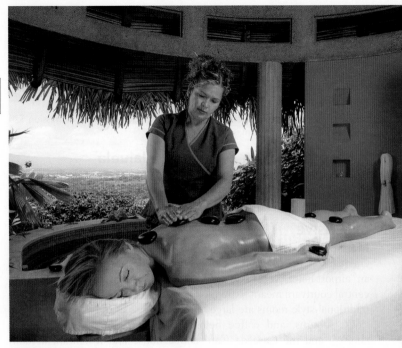

Hot stone massage at Xandari Spa

Sherrill and Charlene Broudy are artists, and their original works and inventive design touches abound. The villas are huge private affairs with stained-glass windows, high ceilings, living rooms with rattan chairs and sofas, and small kitchenettes. All come with an outdoor patio with a view and a private covered palapa, as well as an interior terrace with seating. The adjacent spa has a series of private thatched-roof treatment rooms; a wide range of fitness classes are offered, too. The grounds contain several miles of trails that pass by jungle waterfalls, orchards, and gardens. The restaurant serves decent Tico-Mediterranean cuisine.

Alajuela. www.xandari.com. ℂ **866/363-3212** in the U.S., or 2443-2020. 24 villas. $215–$485 villa for 2, includes continental breakfast. $25 for extra person. **Amenities:** Restaurant; bar; lounge; several Jacuzzis; 3 pools; full-service spa; free Wi-Fi.

MODERATE

If you want a classic airport hotel with shuttle service, both the **Courtyard by Marriott** ★ (www.marriott.com; ℂ **888/236-2427** U.S./Canada or 2429-2700 in Costa Rica) and **Holiday Inn Express** ★ (www.hiexpress.com; ℂ **800/439-4745** U.S./Canada, or 2443-0043 in Costa Rica) are solid chain hotels located right across from the airport.

Adventure Inn ★ A popular option located right along the main highway between the airport and downtown (on the same stretch as the

Guest room at Peace Lodge and La Paz Waterfall Gardens

Doubletree Cariari, below), the Adventure Inn offers friendly service and good value. Rooms here can feel a bit sparse, but that's because most of them are quite large; many have murals or painted accents on the wall to brighten them up, plus Jacuzzis in a few. The common areas are cheery

Marriott Costa Rica Hotel

and often filled with fellow travelers, and there's a large central courtyard area with a good-sized pool. The management here runs a full-service tour operation and generally goes out of its way to help guests with onward plans and arrangements.

Guest room at Adventure Inn

Autopista General Cañas, Ciudad Cariari, San José. www.adventure-inn.com. ☎ **866/258-4740** in the U.S. and Canada, or 2239-2633 in Costa Rica. 34 units. $104–$120 double, includes taxes, breakfast and airport transfers. **Amenities:** Restaurant; bar; pool; Jacuzzi; small gym; free Wi-Fi and international calls.

Doubletree Cariari By Hilton ★★ With its open-air lobby, stone walls, and lush garden, the Cariari has a warm, tropical feel. The rooms, which feature shiny tile floors and a neutral color scheme enlivened by pops of color, are roomy enough for a king-size bed or two double beds, although most of the bathrooms are a bit small. The suites are similarly appointed, but are even more spacious and have larger bathrooms. The hotel has a small casino as well as several restaurants, and it's just in front of a small mall with more good dining options.

Autopista General Cañas, Ciudad Cariari, San José. www.cariarisanjose.doubletree. com. ☎ **800/222-8733** in the U.S. and Canada, or 2239-0022. 222 units. $119–$149 double; $179–$259 suites. **Amenities:** 2 restaurants; 1 bar; casino; concierge; gym; pool; Jacuzzi; room service; free Wi-Fi.

Pura Vida Hotel ★★ Located just 10 minutes from the airport, this homey little inn is run by the genial couple Bernie Jubb and Nhi Chu. Rooms and private *casitas* (little houses) are spread around a spacious compound and lush gardens of vine-covered arbors, fruit trees, and exotic flowers. The two-bedroom *casitas* are perfect for families. Nhi is an expert chef specializing in Asian cuisine. Three-course fixed-menu meals are served around long communal tables and need to be booked in advance. The hotel is located just a kilometer or two north of downtown Alajuela.

Tuetal de Alajuela. www.puravidahotel.com. ☎ **2430-2929** or 8878-3899. 6 units. $99–$165 double, includes breakfast and one-way airport transfer. **Amenities:** Restaurant; free Wi-Fi.

INEXPENSIVE

Villa San Ignacio ★★ This boutique hotel is only 10 minutes or so from the airport, on the road that leads to the summit of the Poás Volcano. It's a quietly elegant option, with soft colors, plush appointments, and minimalistic decor, all at an amazing price. The hotel sits on 22 acres of land with tall native trees on a sloping hillside and is great for

Villa San Ignacio

bird-watching. There's a refreshing mid-size pool off the main lobby, with low-lying Balinese-style chaise lounges. The Pandora restaurant serves excellent creative concoctions rooted in locally grown ingredients, and sometimes has live music on weekends. This hotel can be a bit hard to find, so be sure you're armed with good directions or a GPS. *Note:* Street noise can be a problem in some rooms.

Poás de Alajuela. www.villasanignacio.com. *𝒞* **2433-6316.** 22 units. $95-140 double; $195 suite, includes breakfast. **Amenities:** Restaurant; bar; pool; free Wi-Fi.

Where to Eat

Vegetarians should definitely head to **El Chante Vegano** ★ (www.elchantevegano.com; *𝒞* **8911-4787**), a tasty and thoughtful vegan restaurant in the heart of downtown, a half-block south of the post office.

A longtime favorite up toward the Poás Volcano is **Chubascos** ★ (www.chubascos.co.cr; *𝒞* **2482-2280**), which serves excellent versions of Costa Rican classics in a cozy mountain setting. In addition, the restaurants at **Pura Vida Hotel** and **Marriott Costa Rica Hotel** are both excellent.

Jalapeños Central ★ MEXICAN/TEX MEX   Also known as "Norman's Jalapeño," this downtown favorite was opened more than 10 years ago by Norman Flores, a U.S. expat and world traveler. Burritos and chimichangas are the most popular dishes on the menu, but another good option is the tasty *sopa Azteca,* or tortilla soup. Vegetarians have a number of choices. Jalapeños has a strong local following, so it's sometimes hard to get a table in this tiny little spot.

½ block south of the Post Office, downtown Alajuela. © **2430-4027.** Main courses C3,400–C4,500. Mon–Sat 11:30am–9pm; Sun 11:30am–8pm.

HEREDIA

8.8km (5½ miles) north of San José

Founded in 1706 on the flanks of the impressive Barva Volcano, Heredia is known as "Ciudad de las Flores," City of Flowers, though that's reportedly because of the large number of people here with the name Flores. It's also said to represent the beauty of women from Heredia. Of all the cities in the Central Valley, Heredia has the most colonial feel—you'll still see adobe buildings with Spanish tile roofs along narrow streets. Heredia is also the site of the **National University,** and you'll find some nice coffee shops and bookstores near the school.

Surrounding Heredia is an intricate maze of picturesque villages and towns, including Santa Bárbara, Santo Domingo, Barva, and San Joaquín de Flores. The hills and fields surrounding these towns contain some of the best and most fertile coffee plantations in Costa Rica.

Essentials

GETTING THERE & DEPARTING   By Car: The road to Heredia turns north off the Inter-American Highway (CR1) between San José and the airport.

By Bus: Buses (© **2261-0506**) leave for Heredia every 10 minutes between 5am and 11pm from Calle 1 between avenidas 7 and 9, or from Avenida 2 between calles 12 and 14. Bus fare is C445.

CITY LAYOUT   Coming from San José, the most common route passes first through Santo Domingo de Heredia, although another popular route leads into downtown Heredia from San Joaquín de los Flores. The **Universidad Nacional Autonoma (National Autonomous University)** sits on the eastern edge of the city.

Exploring Heredia

The colonial **Catedral de la Inmaculada Concepción ★** (Church of the Immaculate Conception; © **2237-0779**), inaugurated in 1763, stands guard over Heredia's central park—and the stone facade leaves no questions as to the age of the church. The altar inside is decorated with neon stars and a crescent moon surrounding a statue of the Virgin Mary.

In the middle of the palm-shaded central park is a large gazebo, **El Templo de la Música (The Music Temple) ★**, where live music is often performed. Across the street, beside several municipal buildings with red tile roofs, is **El Fortín ★**, the tower of an old Spanish fort.

Anyone with an interest in medicinal herbs should visit the **Ark Herb Farm** ★★ (www.arkherbfarm.com; ✆ **6253-7655** or 2269-9683). It offers guided tours of its gardens, which feature more than 300 types of medicinal plants, as well as a beekeeping operation. The tour costs $40 per person and includes light refreshments. Reservations are required.

Chocolate lovers will want to visit **Sibu Chocolates** ★★★ (www.sibuchocolate.com; ✆ **2268-1335**). This gourmet organic chocolate maker has a small cafe and gift shop, and it offers tours of its production facility, open Tuesday through Saturday from 8am to 5pm. The tasting tours are offered on these days at 10:30am. Reservations are essential, and the tour costs $26. The tour includes an informative presentation about the history and techniques of chocolate making, as well as several tempting tastings.

While on the road to Barva, you'll find the small **Museo de Cultura Popular** ★ (www.museo.una.ac.cr; ✆ **2260-1619**), which is open Sunday from 10am to 5pm; admission is C500.

TOP ATTRACTIONS

Café Britt Farm ★★ FARM   Café Britt is one of the largest coffee producers in Costa Rica, and the company has put together an interesting and professional tour at its farm, which is 20 minutes outside of San José. Here you'll see how coffee is grown, and you'll visit the roasting and processing plant to learn how a coffee "cherry" is turned into a delicious roasted bean. Tasting sessions are offered for visitors to experience the different qualities of coffee. The farm also has a restaurant and a store where you can buy coffee and coffee-related gift items. The entire tour, including transportation, takes about 3 to 4 hours. Allow some extra time and an extra $10 for a visit to the nearby working plantation and mill. You can even strap on a basket and go out coffee picking during harvest time. North of Heredia on the road to Barva. www.coffeetour.com. ✆ **2277-1600.** Admission $25 adults, $20 children 6–11; $43 adults and $38 children, including transportation from downtown San José. Add $14 for a buffet lunch. Tours daily at 9:30 and 11am and at 1:15 and 3:15pm. Store and restaurant daily 8am–5pm.

Finca Rosa Blanca Coffee Plantation Tour ★★ FARM   This boutique hotel (below) in Heredia also has its own organic coffee plantation, with some 12 hectares (30 acres) of shade-grown arabica under cultivation. The hotel offers daily, 2.5 hour coffee tours at 9am or 1pm, led by a very knowledgeable guide. Consider combining the coffee tour with lunch at the open-air restaurant here; sitting under the shady gazebo, you'll enjoy a wonderful view of the Central Valley along with some fine healthy dining. The good in-house spa offers several treatments featuring homemade, coffee-based products. Santa Bárbara de Heredia. www.fincarosablanca.com. ✆ **2269-9392.** Admission $35 adults, free for children 10 and under. Reservations required.

Where to Stay

While I don't recommend any hotels right in the city center, the small towns and agricultural villages surrounding Heredia are home to one of the country's finest boutique inns.

EXPENSIVE

Finca Rosa Blanca Coffee Plantation & Inn ★★★ Finca Rosa Blanca is an eccentric architectural gem surrounded by the green, lush hillsides of a coffee plantation. A turret tops the main building, and arched windows, walls of glass, and curves instead of corners are at almost every turn. Throughout, the glow of polished hardwood blends with white stucco walls and brightly colored murals. If breathtaking bathrooms are your idea of luxury, splurge on the Rosa Blanca suite, which has a stone waterfall that cascades into a tub in front of a huge picture window, and a spiral staircase that leads to the top of the turret. All the suites and villas have the same sense of creative luxury, with beautiful tile work, fab views, and other design touches. The restaurant and spa here are top-notch, and the owners have a real dedication to sustainable practices. The in-house coffee tour (see above) is terrific.

Santa Bárbara de Heredia. www.fincarosablanca.com. ✆ **305/395-3042** in the U.S., or 2269-9392 in Costa Rica. 15 units. $280–$450 double, includes breakfast. **Amenities:** Restaurant; bar; lounge; concierge; pool; room service; spa; free Wi-Fi.

MODERATE

Hotel Bougainvillea ★★ Tennis courts, a large pool, a bar and a business center—for those hankering for a real resort experience, this three-story property is the ticket. It's not fancy by any means, with endless corridors and spacious but faceless rooms. But the lovely landscaping of the grounds, the unusually attentive service, and the fact that there's a very good restaurant here make up for a lot. Every room has a balcony; ask for one overlooking the gardens, as they're much quieter and have nicer views.

In Santo Tomás de Santo Domingo de Heredia, 100m (1 block) west of the Escuela de Santo Tomás, San José. www.hb.co.cr. ✆ **866/880-5441** in the U.S. and Canada, or 2244-1414 in Costa Rica. 81 units. $128-$138 double; $145-$155 suites, includes breakfast buffet. **Amenities:** Restaurant; bar; pool; 2 lighted tennis courts; free Wi-Fi.

Where to Eat

It's worth making the winding drive to San Pedro de Barva de Heredia to stop in at **La Lluna de Valencia ★** (www.lallunadevalencia.com; ✆ **2269-6665**), a delightful rustic Spanish restaurant with amazing paella and sangria, and a very colorful and amiable host.

El Tigre Vestido ★★ INTERNATIONAL/VEGETARIAN "The Dressed Tiger" is the in-house restaurant for the artsy Finca Rosa Blanca Coffee Plantation & Inn (see above). Owners Glenn and Teri Jampol are hardcore foodies and environmentalists, meaning much of the produce used is grown on site (you'll also find their homegrown coffee making its way into rubs, sauces, and desserts). The menu here seeks to jazz up traditional Costa Rican classics and to create new dishes out of local ingredients. The best seats are on the deck, which is under tall trees overlooking the city lights of the Central Valley.

At Finca Rosa Blanca, Santa Bárbara de Heredia. www.eltigrevestido.com. © **305/ 395-3042** in the U.S., or © **2269-9392** in Costa Rica. Main courses C8,640–C13,230. Daily 7am–10pm.

Entertainment & Nightlife

Home to the National Autonomous University, the center of Heredia is chock-full of bars and clubs frequented by college kids. Some of the best are **Bulevar Relax** (© 2237-1832), **Katta Pub** (© 4200-3131), and **La Choza** (© 2238-3495), all right near each other on Avenida Central, with lively, fun-loving crowds.

GRECIA, SARCHÍ & ZARCERO ★

All these towns are northwest of San José and can be visited in a long day trip if you have a car, perhaps in conjunction with a visit to Poás Volcano (when it reopens) and/or the Waterfall Gardens. The scenery here is rich and verdant, and the small towns and scattered farming communities are truly representative of Costa Rica's agricultural heartland and *campesino* (rural farmer) tradition. This is a great area to explore on your own in a rental car, if you don't mind getting lost a bit (roads are narrow, winding, and poorly marked). If you're relying on buses, you'll be able to visit any of the towns listed below, but probably just one or two per day.

Grecia

9km (12 miles) NW of Alajuela; 37km (23 miles) NW of San José

The picturesque little town of Grecia is noteworthy for its unusual **metal church**—painted a deep red with white gingerbread trim—just off the town's central park. A famed serpentarium, the **World of Snakes**, once a major attraction here, is now closed.

GETTING THERE   By Car: Grecia is located just off the Inter-American Highway (CR1), on the way from San José to Puntarenas.

By Bus: Tuan (© **2494-2139**) buses leave San José half-hour for Grecia from Calle 18 between avenidas 3 and 5 (on the east side of the Abonos Agros building). The fare is C1,125.

Sarchí

7km (4 miles) NW of Grecia; 44km (27 miles) NW of San José

Sarchí is Costa Rica's main artisan town. The colorfully painted miniature **oxcarts** that you see all over the country are made here. Oxcarts such as these were once used to haul coffee beans to market. Today, although you might occasionally see oxcarts in use, most are purely decorative. However, they remain a well-known symbol of Costa Rica. In addition to miniature oxcarts, many carved wooden souvenirs are made here with rare hardwoods from the nation's forests. The town has dozens of shops, and all have similar prices. Perhaps your best one-stop shop in Sarchí is the large and long-standing **Chaverri Oxcart Factory ★★** (✆ **2454-4411**), which is right in the center of things, but it never hurts to shop around and visit several of the stores. The **Fabrica de Carretas Eloy Alfaro ★** (www.souvenirscostarica.com; ✆ **2454-4131**) is another good option, offering a factory tour and meals at a cafeteria-style restaurant.

Built between 1950 and 1958, the town's main **church ★** is painted pink with aquamarine trim and looks strangely like a child's birthday cake. It's definitely worth a quick visit.

GETTING THERE **By Car:** If you're going to Sarchí from San José, head north on the Inter-American Highway (CR1), and take the exit for Grecia. From Grecia, the road to Sarchí heads off to the left as you face the main church, but because of all the one-way streets, you'll have to drive around the church. Rural roads connect Sarchí to Naranjo, San Ramón, and Zarcero.

Room at Finca Rosa Blanca

The Chaverri Oxcart Factory in Sarchí

By Bus: Tuan (© **2494-2139**) buses leave San José for Grecia, with connections to Sarchí from Calle 18 between avenidas 3 and 5. Fare is C1,000. Or you can take one of the Alajuela-Sarchí buses, leaving every 30 minutes from Calle 8 between avenidas Central and 1 in Alajuela.

Else Kientzler Botanical Garden ★★ GARDEN

Located on the grounds of an ornamental flower farm on the outskirts of Sarchí, these are extensive, impressive, and lovingly laid-out botanical gardens. Over 2.5km (1½ miles) of trails run through a collection of more than 2,000 species of flora. All the plants are labeled with their Latin names, with some further explanations around the grounds in both English and Spanish. On the grounds are a topiary labyrinth, as well as a variety of lookouts, gazebos, and shady benches. A children's play area features some water games, jungle gym setups,

Detail of a typical Costa Rican oxcart

Coffee tasting room at Finca Rosa Blanca Coffee Plantation

and a child-friendly little zipline tour. Over 40% of the gardens are wheelchair-accessible.

About 6 blocks north of the central soccer stadium in the town of Sarchí, Alajuela. www.elsegarden.com. © **2454-2070.** Admission $14 adults, $10 students and children 5–12, includes a guided tour. Reservations recommended. Daily 8am–4pm.

WHERE TO STAY & EAT

Very few people stay in Sarchí itself, and there are few noteworthy options.

El Silencio Lodge & Spa ★★★   This isolated luxury lodge, a member of the swank Relais & Châteaux, features large bungalows scattered over a forested hillside with idyllic views over primary rainforests. The bungalow suites each offer a king bed (with regal bedding), a sitting area with built-in couches that convert to two twin beds, a spacious balcony and an outdoor Jacuzzi, with privacy provided by bamboo screening. The two-bedroom family suites are the only units here that come with TVs. There are trails around the grounds and private reserve, as well as a top-notch spa and open-air yoga studio; classes and hikes are often included in nightly costs. El Silencio also runs its own waterfall rappel canyoning and zipline canopy tour operations. On-site organic gardens supply the kitchen, which specializes in spa cuisine. El Silencio has earned "5 Leaves" in the CST Certification for Sustainable Tourism program, the highest rating. To get here, you must first drive to Sarchí. From the Palí supermarket in the center of town, head north and follow the signs. El Silencio is 22km (13 miles) outside of Sarchí.

Bajos del Toro, Alajuela. www.elsilenciolodge.com. © **2231-6122** reservations office in San José, or 2476-0303 at the hotel. 20 units. $243–$550 suites, includes breakfast. **Amenities:** Restaurant; bar; small spa; free Wi-Fi.

Zarcero

60km (38 miles) NW of San José

Beyond Sarchí, on picturesque roads lined with cedar trees, is the town of Zarcero. In a small park in the middle of town is a **menagerie of sculpted shrubs** that includes a monkey on a motorcycle, people and animals dancing, an ox pulling a cart, a man in a top hat, and an elephant. Behind all the topiary is a wonderful rural **church.** It's not worth the drive just to see this park, but it's a good idea to take a break in Zarcero to walk the gardens if you're on the way to La Fortuna and Arenal.

GETTING THERE   By Car: Zarcero is located along the popular route from San José to La Fortuna. Take the Inter-American Highway (CR1) north to Naranjo, and follow signs to Ciudad Quesada and Zarcero.

By Bus: Daily buses (© **2255-0567**) for Zarcero leave from San José hourly from the Atlántico del Norte bus station at Calle 12, Avenidas 14 and 18. This is actually the Ciudad Quesada–San Carlos bus. Just tell the driver that you want to get off in Zarcero, and keep an eye out for the topiary. The ride takes around 1½ hours, and the fare is C1,900.

CARTAGO ★

24km (15 miles) SE of San José

Cartago is the original capital of Costa Rica. Founded in 1563, it was Costa Rica's first city—and was, in fact, the *only* city for almost 150 years. Irazú Volcano rises up from the edge of town, and although it's quiet these days, it has not always been so peaceful. Earthquakes have damaged Cartago repeatedly over the years, so today few of the old colonial buildings remain. In the center of the city, a public park winds through the ruins of a large church destroyed in a 1910 earthquake, before it could be finished.

Essentials

GETTING THERE & DEPARTING   By Car: Head east out of San José on Avenida 2, toward the suburbs of Los Yoses and San Pedro, continuing on through Curridabat. As you exit Curridabat, you will see signs to Cartago, putting you on the Inter-American Highway (CR2) to Cartago. This section of the highway is also known locally as the Florencio del Castillo Highway. There's a C80 toll charged in one direction, as you leave Curridabat heading toward Cartago.

By Bus: Lumaca buses (© **2537-2320**) for Cartago leave San José every 3 to 5 minutes between 4:30am and 9pm, with slightly less frequent service until midnight, from Avenida 5, between Calle 4 and 6. You can also catch one en route at any of the little covered bus stops along Avenida Central in Los Yoses and San Pedro. The length of the trip is 45 minutes; the fare is C570.

By Train: San José's scenic but sporadic main train line **INCOFER** (www.incofer.go.cr; *C* **2542-5800**) runs all the way from downtown San José to downtown Cartago, with no stops. The train runs during commuter hours roughly every ½ hour between 5:30 and 9:30am and again between 3:30 and 8pm. One-way fare is C550.

ORIENTATION   The main route into town from the highway, Avenida 2, enters downtown Cartago from the west and leads to the center of town, with the central park and church ruins. The Basilica is 6 blocks farther east, near where you pick up the road to Paraíso and the Orosi Valley.

Exploring Cartago

Cartago is a quiet city, with little of interest to tourists aside from the Basilica (p 197). If you spend time in the city, head to the **Parque Central** (Central Park), also known as **Las Ruinas (the Ruins)** ★. This is the site of the city's ill-fated original cathedral. Begun in 1575, the church was devastated by a series of earthquakes. Despite several attempts, construction was abandoned after the massive 1910 quake, and today the stone and mortar ruins sit at the heart of a lovely park, with quiet paths and plenty of benches. The ruins themselves are closed off.

You might want to stop in at the **Museo Municipal de Cartago** ★ (Cartago Municipal Museum; *C* **2591-1050**), on Avenida 6 between calles 2 and 4. Located in a former military barracks that has been wonderfully restored, the museum houses a series of local historical displays, as well as a range of changing exhibits, including some featuring local artists. The museum is open Tuesday to Saturday, 9am to 4pm, and Sunday until 3pm; admission is free.

Cartago (and the Orosi Valley) is also a good stop along the way to visit one of the quetzal-viewing lodges in the Dota and Cerro de la Muerte region (p 477).

If you're looking to stay at a nice hotel in this region, I suggest leaving Cartago and heading for the Orosi Valley or Turrialba. But if you're hungry, a couple of restaurants in the Cartago area are worth a visit: **Nila Restaurante** (*C* **2552-4398**), serving an extensive menu of steak, seafood, pasta, soups, and appetizers, just east of Cartago; and **Restaurante Malanga** (*C* **2551-0750**), offering Caribbean fusion, tapas, salads, and vegetarian options, on the road from San José to Irazú.

Basílica de Nuestra Señora de los Angeles ★★★ CHURCH
Dedicated to the patron saint of Costa Rica, the impressive Basilica of Our Lady of the Angels anchors the east side of the city. Within the walls of this Byzantine-style church is a shrine containing the tiny carved figure of **La Negrita,** the Black Virgin, nearly lost amid its ornate altar. The walls of the shrine are covered with a fascinating array of tiny silver images left in thanks for cures affected by La Negrita. Amid the plethora of diminutive silver arms and legs are also hands, feet, hearts, lungs,

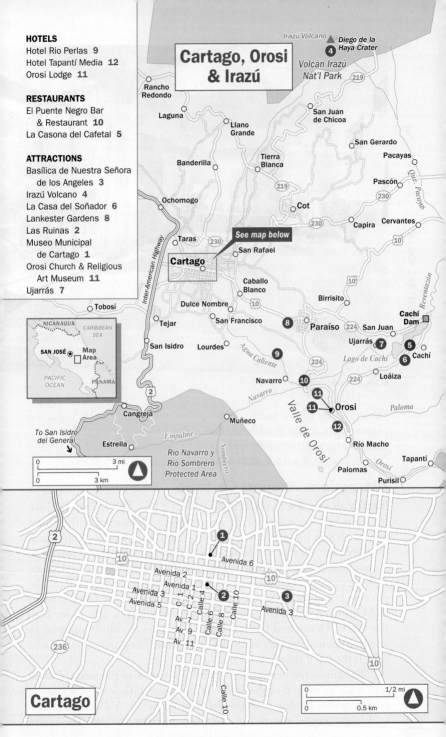

HOTELS
Hotel Rio Perlas **9**
Hotel Tapantí Media **12**
Orosi Lodge **11**

RESTAURANTS
El Puente Negro Bar
& Restaurant **10**
La Casona del Cafetal **5**

ATTRACTIONS
Basílica de Nuestra Señora
de los Angeles **3**
Irazú Volcano **4**
La Casa del Soñador **6**
Lankester Gardens **8**
Las Ruinas **2**
Museo Municipal
de Cartago **1**
Orosi Church & Religious
Art Museum **11**
Ujarrás **7**

Cartago, Orosi
& Irazú

El Silencio Lodge and Spa

kidneys, eyes, torsos, breasts, and—peculiarly—guns, trucks, beds, and planes. Outside the church, vendors sell a wide selection of these trinkets, as well as little candle replicas of La Negrita.

Calle 16, btw. avs. 2 and 4. © **2551-0465.** Free admission. Daily 5:30am–6:30pm.

Attractions Around Cartago

Irazú Volcano ★★ NATURAL ATTRACTION   The 3,378m (11,080-ft.) Irazú Volcano is historically one of Costa Rica's more active volcanoes, although it's relatively quiet these days. It last erupted on March 19, 1963, the day that President John F. Kennedy arrived in Costa Rica. A good paved road leads right to the rim of the crater, where a desolate expanse of gray sand nurtures few plants and the air smells of sulfur. The drive up from Cartago has magnificent views of the fertile Central Valley and Orosi Valley, and if you're very lucky, you might be able to see both the Pacific Ocean and the Caribbean Sea. Clouds usually descend by noon, so get here as early in the day as possible. Dress in layers; it can be cold at the top if the sun's not out.

The landscape here is often compared to that of the moon. A short trail leads to the rim of the volcano's two craters, their walls a maze of eroded gullies feeding onto the flat floor far below. A 2km (1.25-mile) trail loops around the rim of the Playa Hermosa Crater. The visitor

La Negrita

Legend has it that while gathering wood, a girl named Juana Pereira stumbled upon the statue of La Negrita sitting atop a rock. Juana took it home, but the next morning it was gone. She went back to the rock, and there it was again. This was repeated three times, until Juana took her find to a local priest. The priest took the statue to his church for safe-keeping, but the next morning it was gone, only to be found sitting upon the same rock later that day. The priest eventually decided that the strange occurrences were a sign that the Virgin wanted a temple or shrine built to her upon the spot. And so work was begun on what would eventually become today's impressive basilica.

Miraculous healing powers have been attributed to La Negrita, and, over the years, parades of pilgrims have come to the shrine seeking cures for their illnesses and difficulties. August 2 is her patron saint's day. Each year on this date, tens of thousands of Costa Ricans and foreign pilgrims spend hours walking to Cartago from San José and elsewhere out of devotion to La Negrita.

center up here has info on the volcano and natural history. The park restaurant, at an elevation of 3,022m (9,912 ft.), with walls of windows looking out over the valley below, claims to be the highest restaurant in Central America.

Irazú de Cartago, 52km (32 miles) east of San José. ⓒ **2200-4422** or 2220-2025. Admission $15 adults, $5 children. Daily 8am–3:30pm.

The topiary gardens in Zarcero

The Irazú Volcano is an active volcano.

Lankester Gardens ★★ GARDEN   Costa Rica has more than 1,400 varieties of orchids, and almost 800 species are cultivated and on display at this botanical garden. Created in the 1940s by English naturalist Charles Lankester, the gardens are now administered by the University

of Costa Rica, with the goal to pre-serve the local flora, with an emphasis on orchids and bromeli-ads. Paved, well-marked trails meander from open, sunny gardens into shady forests. In each environ-ment, different species of orchids are in bloom. An information cen-ter and a gift shop are also on site. Plan to spend between 1 and 3 hours here if you're interested in flowers and gardening. You can easily combine a visit here with a tour at Cartago and/or the Orosi Valley and Irazú Volcano.

1km (½ mile) east of Cartago, on the road to Paraíso de Cartago. www.jbl.ucr. ac.cr. 🕿 **2511-7949.** Admission $10 adults, $7.50 students and children 6–16. Daily 8:30am–4:30pm.

An orchid in bloom at Lankester Gardens

THE OROSI VALLEY ★★

The Orosi Valley, southeast of Cartago, is generally considered one of the most beautiful valleys in Costa Rica. The Reventazón River meanders through this steep-sided valley until it collects in the lake formed by the Cachí Dam. A well-paved road winds a near-perfect loop around the lake, allowing for easy access to all the attractions listed below. Scenic overlooks are near the town of Orosi, at the head of the valley, and above Ujarrás. This is primarily an agricultural area, but the valley comes alive on weekends as picnickers and bicyclists fill the roads and restaurants.

GETTING THERE & DEPARTING If you're driving, take the road to Paraíso from Cartago, head toward Orosi, and continue around the lake counterclockwise, passing through Cachí and Ujarrás and back to Paraíso. It is difficult to explore this whole area by public bus because connections are often infrequent or unreliable. Regular buses do run from Cartago to Orosi, Cachí, and Ujarrás, but they do not make the entire loop. These buses run roughly every half-hour and leave the main bus terminal in Cartago. The trip takes 30 minutes, and the fare runs between C250 to C500, depending on where you get off the bus.

Exploring the Orosi Valley

Along the main road around the valley, especially near the town of Orosi, are several **scenic overlooks;** take the time to pull over and admire the

The Orosi Valley

views and snap a photo or two. In the town of **Orosi** itself is a **colonial church** (see below) and convent worth visiting.

Near **Ujarrás** are the ruins of Costa Rica's oldest church, built in 1693. Little remains beyond the worn brick and adobe facade of the church, but the gardens are a great place to sit and gaze at the surrounding mountains.

From the Orosi Valley, it's a quick shot to the entrance to the **Tapantí National Park** ★ (✆ **2571-1781** or 2206-5615), where you can find both gentle and strenuous hiking trails, as well as riverside picnic areas. The park is open daily from 8am to 4pm; admission is $10.

TOP ATTRACTIONS

Casa del Soñador ★ COMMERCIAL ART GALLERY   The "House of the Dreamer" is the home and gallery of the late sculptor Macedonio Quesada. Quesada earned fame with his primitive sculptures of La Negrita (see "La Negrita," p 199) and other religious and secular characters carved on coffee tree roots and trunks. You can see some of Macedonio's original work here, including his version of "The Last Supper" carved onto one of the walls of the main building. Today, his sons carry on the family tradition, making small sculptures, carved religious icons, and ornate walking sticks.

1km (½ mile) south of Cachí. ✆ **8955-7779**. Daily 9am–6pm.

Sculptures at La Casa del Soñador

Iglesia de San José de Orosi

Orosi Church & Religious Art Museum ★ CHURCH/ART MUSEUM

The beautiful Orosi river valley is home to Costa Rica's oldest still-functioning church. Built by Franciscan monks in the mid–18th century, the church features well-maintained adobe walls that have endured for centuries and survived several major earthquakes. Off to the side you'll find a small museum with a collection of religious paintings and artifacts, as well as original furniture and period clothing exhibits.

West side of the soccer field, Orosi. © **2533-3051.** Admission C500 adults, C250 children. Daily 9am–noon; 1-5pm.

Where to Stay & Eat

Consider the splendid **Hotel Rio Perlas Spa Resort ★★** (www. rio-perlas.com; © **2533-3341**), the valley's only luxury resort, spa, and casino. It's 2km (1¼ miles) west of Puente Negro in Orosi, on the road following the river. The charming **Orosi Lodge ★** (www.orosilodge. com; © **2533-3578**) is on the south side of Orosi, next to some simple hot-spring pools. It offers wonderful breakfasts that are served in the frying pan. The **Hotel Tapantí Media ★** (© **2533-9090**) offers modest rooms and has a restaurant serving excellent pizza and other Italian fare. It's just south of Orosi on the Rte. 224 loop. For dining, the **Restaurante Tradiciones Don Jose** (© 2533-1414) in Palomo is a rustic steakhouse with outdoor dining and a full bar.

El Puente Negro Bar & Restaurant ★★ AMERICAN This popular American-style roadhouse is worth a stop just to gawk at the pictures of dead rock stars, gold records, musical instruments, license plates, and other kitsch on the walls and ceilings. The expat hosts throw a lively party, with satellite TVs, reasonably priced fare, and karaoke or live music most Saturday nights. The chicken wings are delicious and appear to come from gigantic chickens.

Between Paraíso and Orosi, just past the bridge over the Agua Caliente River. www. blackbridgebar.com. © **2533-2269.** Main courses C3,300–C4,950. Wed–Thurs 5pm–midnight; Fri–Sun 11am–midnight.

La Casona del Cafetal ★ COSTA RICAN A popular lunch stop, primarily because of its views, this long-standing institution is located on expansive grounds overlooking Lake Cachí. Tables are spread around patios and verandas designed to take in the view, and the restaurant serves traditional Costa Rican cuisine. There's also an all-you-can-eat Sunday buffet for C12,900, including tax and tip.

Cachí. www.lacasonadelcafetal.com. © **2577-1414.** Main courses C6,500–C15,500, taxes included. Daily 11am–4pm.

TURRIALBA ★

53km (33 miles) E of San José

This attractive town is best known as the starting point for whitewater rafting trips. But the city's increasingly active namesake volcano has brought it another kind of fame in recent years. In 2015, a series of ash eruptions briefly closed the Juan Santamaría International Airport. Despite current volcanic activity, Turrialba is considered safe, as the eruption patterns head away from the town.

Turrialba is situated in the heart of a rich agricultural region where coffee and sugar cane are the principal crops. Along with rafters, many come to explore the area's pre-Columbian history and tropical botany.

The area is lower in elevation than San José and much of the rest of the Central Valley, and for visitors (and the happy crops) this translates into generally higher temperatures. See "The Central Valley" map on p 171.

Turrialba sits on the old transit route between San José and the Caribbean port city Limón. This makes Turrialba an excellent stop en route to the Caribbean coast or back.

Essentials

GETTING THERE & DEPARTING   By Car: Follow the directions to Cartago (p 196), and then take the well-marked road from Cartago to Paraíso, through Juan Viñas, and on to Turrialba. Alternatively, you can head toward the small town of Cot, on the road to Irazú Volcano, and then through the town of Pacayas on to Turrialba, another well-marked route.)

By Bus: Transtusa buses (www.transtusacr.com; © **2222-4464** or 2557-5050; fare C1,455) leave San José at least once every hour for Turrialba between 5:15am and 10pm from Calle 13 between avenidas 6 and 8. Around three buses also head to the ruins at Guayabo National Monument daily from the main bus terminal in Turrialba (fare C545).

CITY LAYOUT   Turrialba itself is a bit of a jumble, and you may have to ask for directions to get to locations in, around, and outside of town. Guayabo is about 20km (12 miles) beyond Turrialba on a road that is paved the entire way except for the last 3km (1¾ miles).

Exploring Turrialba

Most of the whitewater rafting companies in Costa Rica have an operational base in Turrialba, and the put-in points for several of the more popular river trips are nearby. See p 112 for more info on rafting.

In addition to rafting and kayaking, **Explornatura** ★★ (www. explornatura.com; © **866/571-2443** in the U.S. and Canada, or 2556-0111 in Costa Rica) is an excellent local adventure tour operator that offers a range of activities, including canopy and canyoning tours, horseback riding, hiking, and mountain biking. The **canyoning tour** ★★ is a wet adventure that includes several rappels down the face of rainforest waterfalls.

Guayabo National Monument ★ (© **2559-1220**) is Costa Rica's premier pre-Columbian archaeological site. It's 19km (12 miles) northeast of Turrialba and preserves a town site that dates from between 1000 B.C. and A.D. 1400. Archaeologists believe that Guayabo might have supported a population of as many as 10,000 people, but no clues yet explain why the city was abandoned shortly before the Spanish arrived in the New World. Excavated ruins consist of paved roads, aqueducts, stone bridges, and house and temple foundations. The site also has gravesites and petroglyphs. The monument is open daily from 8am to 3:30pm. This is a national park, and admission is $6.

Hovering over the town, the **Turrialba Volcano National Park** ★★ holds nearly 1,600 hectares (3,950 acres) of lush rainforest, as well as its namesake 3,340m (10,955-ft.) volcano. *NOTE:* Recent volcanic activity has closed the park to the public. When it's open, it is possible to hike to the volcano's summit, which offers fantastic views. It's best to visit as part of a tour, as the final 8km (5 miles) to the park entrance is on a rough road.

Botanists and gardeners will want to pay a visit to the **Center for Agronomy Research and Development** ★ (**CATIE;** www.catie.ac.cr; © **2556-2700**), which is located 5km (3 miles) southeast of Turrialba on the road to Siquirres. This center is one of the world's foremost facilities for research into tropical agriculture. Among the plants on CATIE's 810 hectares (2,000 acres) are hundreds of varieties of cacao and thousands of varieties of coffee. The plants here have been collected from all over the world. In addition to trees used for food and other purposes, other plants grown here are strictly for ornamental purposes. CATIE is open Monday through Friday from 7am to 3pm. Guided tours are available with advance notice for $15 per person.

If you're a java junkie, you'll want to take the **Golden Bean Coffee Tour** ★ (www.goldenbean.net; © **2251-0853** or 8701-2637; $22/person), a comprehensive and informative tour of a working coffee plantation. The mill and processing facilities here have been in operation for almost a century. The tour takes around 2 hours, and operates daily at 9am and 2pm.

Where to Stay & Eat

In addition to the places listed below, check out **Turrialtico** ★ (www. turrialtico.com; © **2538-1111**), a simple hotel with an open-air restaurant on a hill overlooking the Turrialba Valley. The view here is one of the finest in the area, with volcanoes in the distance. The Costa Rican food is good and reasonably priced, and a double room in the rambling old wooden building will cost $64 to $75, including breakfast and taxes. Turrialtico is popular with rafting companies that bring groups for meals and overnights before, during, and after multiday rafting trips.

Casa Turire ★★   This lakefront boutique hotel was built to resemble a majestic old plantation home, complete with a long driveway lined with tall royal palms. Large rooms have painted tiles or varnished wood floors and colonial-style furnishings that evoke a bygone era. Casa Turire was actually built before the nearby hydroelectric dam created Lake Angostura, which now laps gently just below the hotel's well-tended gardens.

1.5km (1 mile) from the Cruce de Atirro, Turrialba. www.hotelcasaturire.com. ✆ **2531-1111** in Costa Rica. 16 units. $168–$185 double; $288–$452 suite, includes taxes and breakfast. **Amenities:** Restaurant; bar; Jacuzzi; pool; small spa; free Wi-Fi.

Pacuare Lodge ★★★   Built on the edge of the roaring Pacuare River, this luxurious raft in–raft out jungle lodge is a marvel, owned and operated by Aventuras Naturales (p 113). The bungalows and private suites are some of the plushest nature lodge digs you'll find anywhere in the country. A few even have private plunge pools. Of these, the remote honeymoon suite is the real star, reached by a long private suspension bridge. For a really unique experience, reserve El Nido, "The Nest," which is 40 feet or so above the ground on a treetop platform reached by zipline. The Pacuare Lodge has received the highest "5 Leaves" rating from the CST Certification for Sustainable Tourism program.

On the banks of the Pacuare River. www.pacuarelodge.com. ✆ **800/963-1195** in the U.S. and Canada, or 2225-3939 in Costa Rica. 19 units. Rates begin at $223 per person for a 2-day/1-night package, including 3 meals, transportation to and from San José and 2 days on the river. **Amenities:** Restaurant; bar; pool; spa; free Wi-Fi.

GUANACASTE: THE GOLD COAST

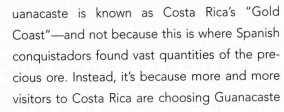

Guanacaste is known as Costa Rica's "Gold Coast"—and not because this is where Spanish conquistadors found vast quantities of the precious ore. Instead, it's because more and more visitors to Costa Rica are choosing Guanacaste as their first—and often only—stop. Beautiful beaches abound along this coastline. Several are packed with a mix of hotels and resorts, some are still pristine and deserted, and others are backed by small fishing villages. Choices range from long, broad sections of sand stretching for miles, to tiny pocket coves bordered by rocky headlands. There are several famous surf breaks and beaches, and protected spots perfect for a mellow swim or snorkel.

Guanacaste is Costa Rica's most popular vacation destination and its most developed tourist target. The international airport in Liberia receives daily direct flights from a host of major U.S. and Canadian hub cities, allowing tourists to visit some of Costa Rica's prime destinations without having to go through San José.

Here in Costa Rica's driest region, the rainy season starts later and ends earlier, and overall it's more dependably sunny here than in other parts of the country. Combine this climate with a coastline that stretches south for hundreds of miles, from the Nicaraguan border all the way to the Nicoya Peninsula, and you have an equation for beach bliss.

One caveat: During the dry season (mid-Nov to Apr), when sunshine is most reliable, the hillsides in Guanacaste turn browner than the Texas plains. Dust from dirt roads blankets the trees in many areas, and the vistas are far from tropical. You might think you're at Burning Man at times. Driving these dirt roads without a/c and with the windows rolled up tight can be extremely unpleasant, and walking along them can be awful.

On the other hand, if you happen to visit this area in the rainy season (particularly from May–Aug), the hillsides are a beautiful, rich green, and the sun usually shines all morning, giving way to an afternoon shower—just in time for a nice siesta.

Inland from the beaches, Guanacaste remains Costa Rica's "Wild West," a land of dry plains populated with cattle ranches and cowboys,

PREVIOUS PAGE: **Beach in Tamarindo**

Andaz Hotel in Peninsula Papagayo in Guanacaste

who are known here as *sabaneros,* a name that derives from the Spanish word for "savanna" or "grassland."

Guanacaste is home to several active volcanoes and some beautiful national parks, including **Santa Rosa National Park ★**, which is famous for both sea-turtle nests and a major battle for independence; **Rincón de la Vieja National Park ★★**, which features hot springs, pristine waterfalls, and an active volcanic crater; and **Palo Verde National Park ★**, a beautiful expanse of mangroves, wetlands, and savanna.

THE best GUANACASTE EXPERIENCES

- **Barefoot Dining with Your Feet in the Sand:** Beachfront dining options range from the grilled octopus with cavatelli at **Makoko ★★★** (p 243) to the just-grilled daily catch at a simple Costa Rican *soda.* See the "Where to Eat" sections of the various destinations below.

- **Catching Your First Wave:** All up and down the Guanacaste coast are excellent breaks, and many are perfect for beginners. See the "Exploring" sections of the various destinations below for surf school recommendations.

- **Taking a Sailboat Cruise:** Most of the beach towns and destinations in Guanacaste boast a small fleet of charter boats and sunset cruises, often with an open bar. Cruises usually include lunch and snorkeling.

Some boats stop at deserted beaches, or linger at sea for the sunset. See the "Exploring" sections below.

o **Having Some Me Time:** Wellness programs have infiltrated the hotel scene in places like Nosara, where juice bars and Vinyasa yoga are as common as howler monkeys.

o **Exploring Rincón de la Vieja:** This volcano-powered national park, dubbed Costa Rica's Yellowstone for its geysers and mud pots, is well worth a visit for its hot springs, waterfalls, and adventure tours. See "Rincón de la Vieja National Park," p 218.

LIBERIA ★

217km (135 miles) NW of San José; 132km (82 miles) NW of Puntarenas

Founded in 1769, Liberia is the capital of Guanacaste province, which Costa Rica snatched away from Nicaragua by popular vote in 1824. Most visitors become acquainted with Liberia because of its relatively new international airport, which allows visitors to Guanacaste to avoid flying into San José and taking a long drive to the beach.

Although Liberia is one of the biggest cities in Costa Rica, few visitors would opt to stay here, but it's a good place to fill your tank, visit a bank, stock up on groceries, or stay at a comfortable hotel for the night. Liberia is a business center that feeds the coastal boom, and it serves as a housing hub for the many workers serving the tourist hotspots along the coast.

Yet Liberia offers up more colonial atmosphere than almost any other city in the country. Its streets are lined with charming old adobe homes, many of which have ornate stone accents on their facades, carved wooden doors, and aged red-tile roofs above shuttered windows opening onto narrow streets. The central plaza, which occupies 2 square blocks in front of the church, remains the city's social hub and principal gathering spot.

A white-headed capuchin monkey in a mangrove in Santa Rosa National Park

Essentials

GETTING THERE & DEPARTING By Plane: The **Daniel Oduber Quirós International Airport** (airport code LIR) in Liberia receives a

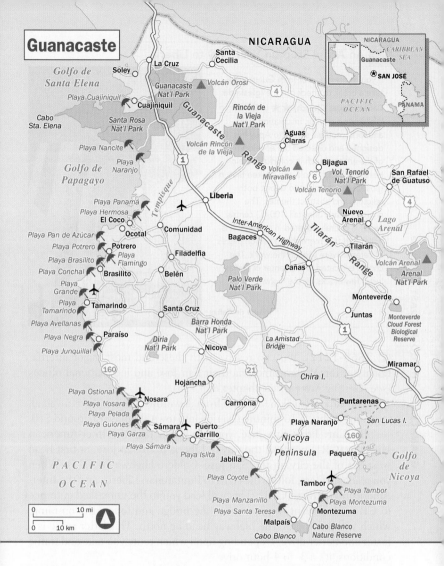

steady stream of commercial and charter flights throughout the year. Major North American airlines have direct links to Liberia; check p 593. In addition, numerous commercial charter flights from various North American cities fly in throughout the high season. **Nature Air** (www.natureair.com; © **800/235-9272** in the U.S. and Canada, or 2668-1106 in Liberia) and **Sansa** (www.flysansa.com; © **877/767-2672** in the U.S. and Canada, or 2290-4100 in Costa Rica) both have several flights daily to Liberia. Fares run between $74 and $148 each way. Flight duration is around 50 minutes.

Along with the multinational chains, the following local companies rent cars from the airport: **Adobe** (© **2667-0608**) and **Toyota**

An Artful Stop on Your Way to Liberia

If you're driving to or from Guanacaste, take a break to check out the **Iglesia de Cañas (Cañas Church)** ★★ in Cañas. Well-known painter, installation artist, and local prodigal son Otto Apuy has designed and directed the envelopment of the entire church in colorful mosaic. Here you'll find whole and broken tiles in glossy, vibrant colors to depict both religious and abstract themes. The church's nearly 30m-tall (100-ft.) central tower is entirely covered in mosaics. It is estimated that more than a million pieces of ceramic were used in the work. The church is located in the center of Cañas, just a few blocks off the highway.

Iglesia de Cañas

(📞 **2668-1212**). You can reserve with these and most major international car rental companies via their San José and international offices (see "Getting Around," in chapter 6, p 125).

The airport is 13km (8 miles) from downtown Liberia. Taxis await all incoming flights; a 10-minute taxi ride into town should cost around $10.

By Car: From San José, you can either take the Inter-American Highway (CR1) north all the way to Liberia from San José, or first head west out of the city on the San José–Caldera Highway (CR27). When you reach Caldera, follow the signs to Puntarenas, Liberia, and the Inter-American Highway (CR1). This will lead you to the unmarked entrance to CR1. You'll want to pass under the bridge and follow the on-ramp, which will put you on the highway heading north. This latter route is a faster and flatter drive. Depending upon which route you take and traffic conditions, it's a 3- to 4-hour drive.

By Bus: Pulmitan express buses (📞 **2222-1650** in San José, or 2666-0458 in Liberia) leave San José roughly every hour between 6am and 8pm from Calle 24 between avenidas 5 and 7. The ride to Liberia takes around 4 hours, and a one-way fare costs around ₡4,000. Also, check with **Terminal 7-10** (www.terminal7-10.com; 📞 **2519-9740**) in San José for itineraries and prices. It's located at Ave. 7 and Calle 10 in Barrio Mexico. Tell the taxi driver "diagonal al antiguo Cine Líbano" (diagonal to the old Líbano movie theater).

Both **Gray Line** (www.graylinecostarica.com; 📞 **800/719-3905** in the U.S. and Canada, or 2220-2126 in Costa Rica) and **Interbus** (www.interbusonline.com; 📞 **4100-0888**) have two daily buses leaving San

José for Liberia and all beaches in this area, one in the morning and one in the afternoon. The fare is around $50. The morning buses make connections to Rincón de la Vieja and Santa Rosa national parks. Both companies will pick you up at most San José-area hotels, and provide connections to and from most destinations in Costa Rica. Express buses for San José leave roughly every hour between 3am and 8pm.

CITY LAYOUT   Liberia's small city center lies just to the east of the main intersection of the Inter-American Highway and the road to the beaches. On the southern outskirts of the city is a modern shopping mall, the place to come for a food court fix or to catch a semi-late-run movie. Smaller, contemporary strip malls and shopping centers can be found near the airport, and at the major intersection near the entrance to town.

FAST FACTS   Several bank offices are clustered in downtown Liberia, as well as a branch of the **Banco de Costa Rica** inside the airport. The local **police** number is © **2690-0129**, and the **Liberia Hospital** number is © **2690-2300**. If you need a taxi, dial © **2666-3330**.

Exploring the Town

The central plaza in Liberia is a great place to people-watch, especially in the early evenings and on weekends. Grab a seat on one of the many

Liberia's Central Park

Coconut vendor in Liberia

concrete benches, or join families and young lovers as they stroll around.

Just off the northwest corner of the main central plaza, the **Museo de Guanacaste** (Guanacaste Museum; © **2665-7114**) occupies the city's former military barracks and prison. Amassing a permanent collection is a work in progress, but the space is often used for traveling exhibits and cultural events, including concerts, lectures, and recitals. Inaugurated in 1940, the building is known as the Comandancia de Plaza de Liberia.

If you venture for a few blocks down **Calle Real ★**, you'll see fine examples of classic Spanish colonial adobe buildings with ornate wooden doors, heavy beams, central courtyards, and faded, sagging, red-tile roofs.

Although the Catholic church that anchors the central plaza is unspectacular, if you head several blocks east of the plaza, you will come to **Iglesia La Ermita de la Agonía ★** (© **2666-0518**). Built in 1865, this whitewashed stone church is in surprisingly good shape. Inside it is plain and bare, but it is the only remaining colonial-era church to be found in Guanacaste. The visiting hours are seriously limited (daily 2:30–3:30pm), though local tour agencies can sometimes arrange visits during off hours. Even if you can't enter, you'll still get a good feel for the place by checking out its whitewashed stucco exterior.

Outdoor Adventures near Liberia

In addition to the activities listed below, Liberia is a major jumping-off point for Rincón de la Vieja National Park (p 218).

LLANOS DE CORTÉS WATERFALL ★★

Located about 25km (16 miles) south of Liberia, the **Llanos de Cortés Waterfall ★★** is one of the most beautiful falls in Costa Rica, with an excellent pool at the base for cooling off and swimming. At roughly 12m (40 ft.) wide, the falls are actually slightly wider than they are tall. This is a good spot for a picnic. Because of construction on the highway, the turnoff for the dirt road to the falls is poorly marked, but it's about 3km (1¾ miles) north of the crossroads for Bagaces. From the turnoff, you must drive a rough dirt road to the parking area and then hike down a

Llanos de Cortés Waterfall

short steep trail to the falls. A donation of C1,000 is suggested to support the local school. Even though guards are on duty, be careful about leaving anything of value in your car.

BIRDING

The **Río Tempisque Basin** ★, southwest of town, is one of the best places in the country to spot marsh and stream birds by the hundreds. This area is an important breeding ground for gallinules, jacanas, and limpkins, as well as numerous heron and kingfisher species and the roseate spoonbill. Several tour operators offer excursions to the region. **Swiss Travel Services** (www.swisstravelcr.com; ✆ **2282-4898**) is the largest and most reliable of the major operators here.

One of the most popular tours is a boat tour down the Bebedero River to **Palo Verde National Park** ★, which is south of Cañas and is best known for its migratory bird populations. Some of the best bird-watching requires little more than walking around the park's biological station.

You can get a similar taste of these waterways and bird-watching opportunities at **El Viejo Wetlands** (p 256) and **Rancho Humo** (p 326).

RAFTING TRIPS

Trips on the Upper Tenorio River are offered by **Ríos Tropicales** ★★ (www.riostropicales.com; ✆ **2233-6455**), about 40km (25 miles) south

---

Shady Business

This province gets its name from the abundant guanacaste (*Enterolobium cyclocarpum*), Costa Rica's national tree. This distinctive tree is known for its broad, full crown, which provides welcome shade on the Guanacaste's hot plains and savannas. The guanacaste is also known as the elephant-ear tree because of the distinctive shape of its large seedpods. Its fragrant white flowers bloom between February and April.

of Liberia. Its day long ($105) excursions explore 8-miles along this challenging river with mostly Class III-IV rapids, not to mention a Class V, 12-foot drop. Along the way you may see many of the area's more exotic fauna: howler monkeys, iguanas, coatis, toucans, parrots, motmots, trogons, and many other species of birds. Aside from your binoculars and camera, a swimsuit and sunscreen are the only things you'll need. Ríos Tropicales is based out of the Restaurant Rincón Corobicí, right on the Inter-American Highway in Cañas (CR1). Additionally, **Hacienda Guachipelín** (see p 224) offers exhilarating whitewater tubing trips on the narrow Río Colorado.

ESPECIALLY FOR KIDS

Believe it or not, antelopes, zebras, giraffes, and elands roam the grassy plains of Guanacaste. **Ponderosa Adventure Park** ★ (www.ponderosa adventurepark.com; ℂ **2288-1000**) offers a variety of adventure tours and a safari-style open-jeep tours through its 100-hectare (247-acre) private reserve, populated with a wide range of native and non-native (predominantly African) species. Kayaking trips, zip-lining, horseback riding, and waterfall tours are also offered. There is no charge for admission, but each activity has a fee. Ponderosa Adventure Park is located just off the Inter-American Highway, 8km (5 miles) south of Liberia. The park is open daily from 8am to 5pm.

Where to Stay

MODERATE

Hilton Garden Inn Liberia Airport ★   Located directly across the two-lane Highway 21 from the Daniel Oduber Quirós International Airport (LIR), this five-story contemporary chain hotel is a good choice for folks with late arrivals or early departures. Still, with drive times of between 30 minutes to an hour to most nearby beach hotels, it is debatable how useful staying this close to the airport really is. But should your needs dictate an airport stay, you'll get everything that you'd expect from a Hilton Garden Inn, with a free airport shuttle, as well as a small shopping mall adjacent to the hotel with a few restaurant options.

Across from the Liberia airport. www.hilton.com/Garden_Inn/Liberia. ℂ **800/445-7444** in the U.S. and Canada, or 2690-8888 in Costa Rica. 169 units. $119 double; $149–$169 suite, includes taxes. **Amenities:** Restaurant; bar; gym; Jacuzzi; pool; room service; free Wi-Fi.

INEXPENSIVE

Hotel Liberia ★   A colonial-style adobe home on Calle Real, the Hotel Liberia features ornate painted tile floors in the lobby and main dining room. Open since 1918, the hotel has been declared a historic structure. All of the rooms are spacious and kept meticulously clean, with locally built hardwood beds and crisp linens. Especially nice are the

Restaurant at Hotel Liberia

La Casona rooms off the main central hallway, which open onto a broad, shady, shared veranda. The restaurant here serves up fairly priced local cuisine, with both indoor and outdoor seating, and they have an airport shuttle for $25 (up to 4 people).

Calle Real, 75m south of the old Gobernación building, Liberia. www.hotelliberiacr. com. © **2666-0161.** 18 units. $15 per person, dorm room; $52–$60 double, includes taxes. **Amenities:** Restaurant; bar; free Wi-Fi.

Where to Eat

Liberia has plenty of dining choices. For local flavor, choose one of the *sodas* around the central park. Another option for Costa Rican cuisine is **La Choza de Laurel** (www.lachozadelaurel.com; © **2668-1019**), located along the main highway, about 800m (2,624 ft.) east of the Liberia airport entrance. It serves good, authentic Costa Rican food, but has a more touristy feel than the simple places you'll find in town. For a slightly more upscale option, head along Avenida Central a block beyond the central park to **Toro Negro Steakhouse ★** (© **2666-2456**), which offers thick-cut steaks, wood-oven fired pizzas, and sushi. Another popular alternative is **Pizzería Pronto** (© **2666-2098**), for wood-oven pizzas and assorted pasta dishes in a restored colonial home.

For food with a good bar scene, try **Liberia Social Club** (www. liberiasocialclub.com; © **2665-0741**), which sometimes features live music and dancing at night, and is in the Centro Comercial Santa Rosa, at the main highway crossroads.

INEXPENSIVE

El Café Liberia ★ INTERNATIONAL/COSTA RICAN   Set in an atmospheric colonial-era home, with a sagging clay tile roof that shows its age, El Café Liberia is *the* place to eat in Liberia. Helmed by a French chef who has made the cuisine of the Americas his own, the restaurant's specialties are superb ceviche, chicken *casado,* a rich spinach dip, grilled steaks, and all kinds of fresh seafood. All are served on large, white plates, with colorful patterns made from sauces and reductions. Dessert lovers will want to save room for the decadent "lava flow" molten chocolate cake.

Calle Real. 1⅕ blocks south of the Central Plaza. ℂ **2665-1660.** Main courses C3,000–C7,500. Mon 3–9pm and Tues–Sat 9am–9pm.

Shopping

On the road to the beaches, just west of the airport, are several large souvenir shops. The best of the bunch for a one-stop shop is **La Gran Nicoya** (ℂ 2667-0062). However, you might find better selections and prices, especially for Guaitíl pottery, at some of the makeshift roadside kiosks that line the road between Liberia and the Guanacaste beaches.

For something different, check out the **Hidden Garden Art Gallery** ★★ (www.hiddengardenart.com; ℂ 8386-6872), a contemporary gallery with a large stable of prominent Costa Rican and expatriate artists and regularly changing special exhibitions. It's located 5km (3 miles) west of the Liberia airport, on the road to the beaches.

RINCÓN DE LA VIEJA NATIONAL PARK ★★

242km (151 miles) NW of San José; 25km (16 miles) NE of Liberia

This sprawling national park begins on the flanks of the Rincón de la Vieja Volcano and includes this volcano's namesake active crater. Down lower is an area of geothermal activity similar to that of Yellowstone National Park in the United States. Fumaroles, geysers, and hot pools cover this small area, creating a bizarre, otherworldly landscape. In addition to hot springs and mud pots, you can explore waterfalls, a lake, and volcanic craters. Bird-watching here is rewarding, as the sparse foliage of

---

What's in a Name?

Rincón de la Vieja literally means "the old lady's corner." In this case, "la vieja" has the connotation of a witch or hag, while "rincón" is better interpreted as "lair." The name is derived from a legend that a woman's father threw her lover into the smoking, belching volcanic crater, and she moved onto the mountain and became a hermit. It was said she had healing powers.

Rincón de la Vieja National Park mud pots

the dry forest makes spotting easier, and from the high volcanic slopes here you can enjoy sweeping views all the way to the ocean.

Essentials

GETTING THERE   By Car: Follow the directions to Liberia (p 210). When you reach Liberia, head straight through the major intersection, following signs to Peñas Blancas and the Nicaraguan border.

To reach the **Las Pailas (Las Espuelas) entrance,** drive about 5km (3 miles) north of Liberia and turn right on the dirt road to the park. The turnoff is well marked. In about 12km (7½ miles), you'll pass through the small village of Curubandé. Continue on this road for another 6km (3¾ miles) until you reach Hacienda Guachipelín. The lodge is private property, and the owners charge a small toll to pass through their gate and continue on to the park. Pass through the gate and continue for another 4km (2½ miles) until you reach the park entrance.

Two routes lead to the **Santa María entrance.** The principal route heads out of the northeastern end of Liberia toward the small village of San Jorge. This route is about 25km (16 miles) long and takes about 45 minutes. A four-wheel-drive vehicle is required. Alternatively, you can reach the entrance on a turnoff from the Inter-American Highway at

Bagaces. From here, head north through Guayabo, Aguas Claras, and Colonia Blanca. Although the road is paved up to Colonia Blanca, four-wheel-drive is required for the final, very rough 10km (6¼ miles) of gravel road.

Exploring Rincón de la Vieja National Park

Rincón de la Vieja National Park has several excellent trails. The easiest hiking is the gentle **Las Pailas loop ★**. This 3km (1.75-mile) trail is just off the Las Espuelas park entrance and passes by several bubbling mud pots and steaming fumaroles. Don't get too close, or you could get scalded. Happily, the strong sulfur smell given off by these formations works well as a natural deterrent. This gentle trail crosses a river, so you'll have to either take off your shoes or get them wet. The whole loop takes around 2 hours at a leisurely pace.

A more grueling hike here is to the **Blue Lake** and **La Cangreja Waterfall ★★**. Along this well-marked 9.6km (6-mile) round-trip trail, you'll pass through several ecosystems, including tropical dry forest, transitional moist forest, and open savanna. You are likely to spot a variety of birds and mammals and have a good chance of coming across a group of the raccoon-like coati. Although it does not require any great climbs or descents, the hike is nonetheless long and arduous (some say too arduous for what you see). At the end of your 2-hour hike in, you'll come to the aptly named Blue Lake, where a 30m (98-ft.) waterfall empties into a small, crystal-blue pond. This is a great spot for a swim. Pack a lunch and have a picnic before hiking back out.

La Cangreja Waterfall

Because of volcanic activity and the extreme nature of the hike, the summit trail has been closed to visitors since 2013 and will likely remain that way for the foreseeable future. If it reopens, energetic hikers can tackle the **summit ★** and explore the craters and beautiful lakes up here. The trail is 16.6km (10.3 miles) round-trip and takes about 7 hours (the trail head is at the ranger station). It heads pretty much straight up the volcano and

Blue and gold macaw

is steep in places. Along the way, you pass through different ecosystems, including sections of tropical moist and tropical cloud forests, while climbing some 1,000m (3,280 ft.) in altitude. After about 6km (3.7 miles), the trail splits. Take the right-hand fork to the Cráter Activo ("Active Crater"). Filled with rainwater, this crater is 700m (2,300 ft.) in diameter and still active. Off to the side is the massive Laguna Jigueros.

The park entrance fee is $15 per person per day, and the park is open Tuesday to Sunday from 8am to 4pm.

Camping will cost you an extra $2 per person per day. There are actually two entrances and camping areas here: **Santa María** and **Las Pailas** (also called Las Espuelas; ℂ **2666-5051**) ranger stations. Las Pailas is by far the more popular and accessible, and it's closer to the action. These small camping areas are near each other. For those seeking a less rugged tour of the park, there are several lodges around the park that offer guided hikes and horseback rides into it.

Other Adventures Around Rincón de la Vieja

ONE-STOP ADVENTURE SHOP

Hacienda Guachipelín (p 224) offers up a range of adventure tour options, including horseback riding, whitewater tubing, ziplining, canyoning, rappelling, hot springs, and mud baths. If all of this sounds good to you, buy the **1-Day Adventure pass ★★**, where you can do all of the above any day (except the canyoning and rappelling, which are offered only a couple of times a week) at a published price of $90, including lunch. For a daylong multi-adventure package, this is one of the best bargains anywhere in Costa Rica. Almost all Guanacaste beach hotels and resorts offer day trips here, or you can book directly with the lodge. *Be forewarned:* During high season, the operation has a cattle-car feel, with busloads of day-trippers coming in from the beach.

HOT SPRINGS & MUD BATHS

The active Rincón de la Vieja Volcano has blessed this area with several fine hot springs and mud baths. Even if you're not staying at the **Hacienda Guachipelín** (p 224) or the **Hotel Borinquen Mountain**

Hot springs at Hotel Hacienda Guachipelín

Resort (p 223), you can take advantage of their hot spring pools and hot mud baths. Both have on-site spas offering massages, facials, and other treatments.

Up the road from its lodge, Hacienda Guachipelín has opened the **Río Negro Hot Springs ★★** (© **2666-8075**). Admission is included in the 1-Day Adventure or Nature pass, otherwise there is a $20 entrance fee that gets you access to the pools and an application of the hot volcanic mud. For $55 you can do a horseback ride from the main lodge to the springs. A wide range of massages, mud wraps, facials, and other treatments are available at reasonable prices.

At the **Hotel Borinquen Mountain Resort,** a $25 entrance fee allows you access to a range of **hot spring–fed pools ★**, which vary from tepid to very hot, as well as the fresh volcanic mud bath area and large freshwater pool, though various other adventure packages can be combined too.

Finally, **Vandara Hotsprings ★★** (www.vandarahotsprings.com; © **4000-0660**) is an excellent spa and adventure center run by the staff of Buena Vista Lodge, with a pretty artificial pool fed by natural hot springs. Unlike many of the pools mentioned above, this one has no sulfuric smell. Admission is $30, but various packages, with a canopy tour, horseback ride, waterslide, hanging bridges, and other activities, are also available. Meals and spa treatments are also offered.

Where to Stay & Eat Around Rincón de la Vieja National Park

Around Aguas Claras, **La Anita Rainforest Ranch** ★★ (www.laanita rainforestranch.com; ☎ **8388-1775** or 2466-0228) is a remote and rustic yet very cozy lodge, with a series of wooden cabins set on a working farm, on the edge of lush rain- and cloud forests. The area around the lodge is home to several hot springs, and this area also provides easy access to the seldom-used Santa María sector of Rincón de la Vieja National Park.

EXPENSIVE

Hotel Borinquen Mountain Resort ★★   This is the swankiest resort in the Rincón de la Vieja area. Individual and duplex bungalows are set on a hillside above the main lodge, restaurants, and hot springs. Rooms feature heavy wooden beds and armoires, high ceilings, and plush decor. All include a spacious wooden deck with a view over the valley and surrounding forests. At the foot of the valley are a natural sauna, several hot springs of varying temperatures, and an area for full-body mud baths with hot volcanic mud. The hotel also boasts a lovely, free-form outdoor pool and full-service spa, set beside a rushing creek in the middle of dense forest. Packages that include hiking and horseback riding trails, ATV adventures, ziplining, and nice waterfalls nearby add to the fun, and golf carts are available to shuttle you around.

Cañas Dulces. www.borinquenresort.com. ☎ **2690-1900.** 39 units. $167 double villa; $189–$249 double bungalow; $281 junior suite, includes breakfast and unlimited use of the hot springs, sauna, and mud baths. Drive 12km (7½ miles) north of Liberia along the Inter-American Hwy (CR1), take the turnoff toward Cañas Dulces, and follow the signs. The hotel is about 21km (13 miles) from the highway, along a mostly rugged dirt road. **Amenities:** 2 restaurants; bar; large outdoor pool; small spa; free Wi-Fi.

MODERATE

Blue River Resort ★★   Blue River offers one thing truly unique to Central America: dinosaurs. Dino Park, the brainchild of Israeli owner Daniel Apelboim, is a one-of-a-kind exhibit that opened in 2016 with 26 life-size, animatronic foam dinosaurs that move their bodies, gnash their teeth, and roar at visitors. They're incredibly lifelike and well worth a visit, whether you're staying at the resort or not. Blue River also has beautiful botanical gardens, four hot springs, a swimming pool with a waterslide, plus volcanic mud baths, butterfly and frog exhibits, and a koi pond. The resort offers its own canopy tour, whitewater tubing, rafting, and horseback riding. Rooms are huge, with either two queen beds or one king bed, high ceilings, walk-in closets and bathrooms so spacious you could fit another bed in them. Rooms also come with large porches, widescreen TVs, air-conditioning, ceiling fans, and mini-fridges.

North of Rincón de la Vieja, near Dos Ríos de Upala. www.blueriverresort.com. ℂ **800/840-5071** in the U.S. and Canada or 7298-3200 in Costa Rica. 25 units. $150–$166 for 2 adults and 2 children under 10, includes taxes and breakfast. **Amenities:** Dinosaur park; 3 hot springs; 2 swimming pools; gardens; mud bath; spa; gym; free Wi-Fi.

Hacienda Guachipelín ★★ A first-rate hotel, working horse and cattle ranch, and huge adventure center: What's not to like? If you're coming here anyway for one or more of the many activities, save yourself the drive back and spend the night in a well-appointed room on immaculate grounds for a surprising price. With some 60 to 80 horses available at any time, overseen by 20 *sabanero* cowboys, horseback riding here is almost a must. ("Don't worry," says the head cowboy, "the horses all speak English!") The whitewater tubing is superb, as are the ziplining, the canyoning, and the mud bath at the hot springs. Rooms are laid out in a large horseshoe around an ample garden area a short walk from the main lodge and restaurants. Rooms are spacious, airy, and pretty, with heavy wood and iron-framed beds and lots of natural light. The hotel operates a free shuttle several times a day to the national park, as well as to its own riverside hot springs (free for guests) in the middle of a pristine forest.

Rincón de la Vieja (23km/14 miles northeast of Liberia). www.guachipelin.com. ℂ **888/730-3840** in the U.S. and Canada, or 2690-2900 for reservations in Costa Rica. 77 units. $130 double; $153 superior double; $223 suite, includes taxes and breakfast. Rates higher during peak periods. **Amenities:** Restaurant; pool; small spa; free Wi-Fi.

INEXPENSIVE

Cañon de la Vieja Lodge ★★ This place offers pretty much everything other area lodges offer except the long drive. Just 8km from Liberia on the paved road to Curubandé, Cañon de la Vieja (owned by the same family that has the more remote Buena Vista Lodge; see below) offers whitewater rafting and tubing on the Río Colorado, ziplining, rappelling, rock climbing, horseback riding, hot springs, and a mud bath. When you're done, relax at the swim-up bar in the pool, set amid attractive gardens with lots of trees. Rooms are in duplexes along a U-shaped road around the pool and have a/c but no TV or Internet, though there's Wi-Fi in common areas.

8km from Liberia on the road to Curubandé and the Pailas sector of Rincón de la Vieja National Park. www.thecanyonlodge.com. ℂ **2665-3161.** 50 units. $111 double, includes taxes and breakfast. **Amenities:** Restaurant; bar; pool; spa; free Wi-Fi.

Hotel Buena Vista Lodge ★ Just up the road from Borinquen, the Buena Vista is a former working cattle farm that started offering lodging 25 years ago, when that was a novel idea here. The Ocampo family sold 12 milk cows to build five rustic cabinas with a restaurant in the middle, but as soon as they opened, the fierce winds here blew off all the roofs. Undaunted, they got a loan from the bank and planted trees to block the wind. Today the lodge has 82 rooms, five restaurants, a canopy tour, a big hot springs complex with mud baths, a thrilling 450-meter waterslide, and horseback riding. Rooms are basic but adequate and vary widely in style; some are a bit dark.

Just west of Rincón de la Vieja National Park at the end of the Cañas Dulces road. www.buenavistalodgecr.com. © **2690-1400.** 82 units. $80–$92 double, includes taxes and breakfast. **Amenities:** 5 restaurants; 6 bars; outdoor pool; regular and "extreme" canopy tours; hanging bridges; waterslide; hot springs; horseback riding; free Wi-Fi.

Río Celeste & Tenorio Volcano ★★★

One of Costa Rica's best-kept secrets is the **Río Celeste ★★★**, the stunning, sky-blue river that is the centerpiece of Tenorio Volcano National Park. The unique color of the Celeste is caused by aluminosilicate particles suspended in the water that reflect sunlight only in the blue spectrum, and the effect is glorious. The Río Celeste Waterfall, with its cool blue pool at the bottom, is arguably the most beautiful in the country. Río Celeste is inside the **Parque Nacional Volcán Tenorio** (Tenorio Volcano National Park; © **2206-5369;** daily 8am–4pm; admission $12). An easy trail follows the river and its prime attractions—the Blue Lagoon, the Borbollones (where the water bubbles because of venting gas), and the Teñidores ("dyer's shop"), where you can see two colorless rivers collide and turn blue. The hike is one-way in, one-way out, and could be jogged in 1 hour or strolled for 3 or 4. Be aware that rainstorms can turn the water muddy and brown, so check with the rangers at the entrance on the current state of the water and the weather outlook. *Tip:* Once you've seen Río Celeste, you've seen the best of Tenorio Volcano National Mark, so this makes a great day trip from Arenal, Monteverde, and elsewhere.

If you do want to overnight here, look up the humble yet delightful **La Carolina Lodge ★** (www.lacarolinalodge.com; © **843/343-4201** in the U.S. and Canada, or 2466-6393), which is on a working farm, next to a clear flowing river. Another solid option is the **Celeste Mountain Lodge ★** (www.celestemountainlodge.com; © **2278-6628**), a handsome property boasting swell views of the surrounding volcanoes.

Getting There: Tenorio National Park is located near the small town of Bijagua. The road to Bijagua (CR6) heads north off the Inter-American Highway about 5km (3 miles) northwest of Cañas. From here, it's another 30km (18½ miles) to Bijagua, and another 12km (7½ miles) to the park entrance. The last part is on rough dirt roads, and even though it's a short distance as the crow flies, it can often take 30 to 40 minutes. There are also other ways to access the area if coming from La Fortuna.

Río Celeste Hideaway ★★   This remote lodge is located in a patch of dense tropical rainforest alongside the area's namesake river. The lodge is one of the closest to the national park, and also has its own well-kept trail system along the Rio Celeste. All the lodgings are individual *casitas* (little houses), with varnished wood floors, high peaked ceilings made from locally cut cane and either four-poster king bed or two queens, with hand-carved headboards. All of the *casitas* are virtually identical in size and layout, though the suites have forest-view balconies and hot tubs. Off season rates are often 50 percent lower.

Rio Celeste. www.riocelestehideaway.com. ✆ **800/320-3541** in the U.S. and Canada, or 2206-5114 in Costa Rica. 26 units. $199 double Casita Forest; $279-$329 double Casita Suite, includes breakfast. Follow the directions/signs to Rio Celeste and Tenorio National Park. **Amenities:** Restaurant; outdoor pool; Jacuzzi; small spa; free Wi-Fi.

Near the Miravalles Volcano

Part of a string of active volcanoes running down the spine of the country, the **Miravalles Volcano** is a major energy supplier for the country's electric grid, but a rather undiscovered area for tourism. **Río Perdido ★★** (www.rioperdido.com; ✆ **888/326-5070** in the U.S. and Canada, or 2673-3600) aims to change all that. With a setting among rolling hills and

A footbridge across Río Celeste

striking rock formations, this hotel, spa, and adventure center features lovely rooms and a gorgeous hot-spring complex. The hot springs here range from a modern pool fed by warm mineral waters up near the main lodge, to a natural river with pools of clear water and varied temperatures. The lodge also has a zipline canyon tour, an extensive mountain bike park, and whitewater tubing.

LA CRUZ & BAHÍA SALINAS ★

277km (172 miles) NW of San José; 59km (37 miles) NW of Liberia; 20km (12 miles) S of Peñas Blancas

Near the Nicaraguan border, La Cruz is a tiny hilltop town that has little to offer beyond a fabulous view of Bahía Salinas (Salinas Bay), but it does serve as a gateway to the nearly deserted kite-surfing beaches below, a few mountain lodges bordering the nearby Santa Rosa and Guanacaste national parks, and the Nicaraguan border crossing at Peñas Blancas.

Essentials

GETTING THERE & DEPARTING **By Plane:** The nearest airport with regular service is in Liberia (see "Liberia," earlier in this chapter).

By Car: Follow the directions for driving to Liberia (p 210). When you reach Liberia, head straight through the major intersection, following signs to Peñas Blancas and the Nicaraguan border. Allow about 5 hours to get from San José to La Cruz.

By Bus: Transportes Deldú buses (© **2256-9072** in San José, or 2679-9323 in La Cruz) leave San José roughly every 2 hours (more frequently during the middle of the day) between 3:30am and 7pm for **Peñas Blancas** from Calle 10 and 12, Avenida 9. These buses stop in La Cruz and will also let you off at the entrance to Santa Rosa National Park if you ask. The ride to La Cruz takes 5½ hours; a one-way fare costs between C4,565 and C5,000. Additional buses are often added on weekends and holidays.

Grupo Transbasa (© **2666-0517**) leaves Liberia for Peñas Blancas throughout the day. The ride to La Cruz takes about 1 hour and costs

On to Nicaragua

Guanacaste is a popular starting point for trips into Nicaragua. The main border point is at Peñas Blancas, Costa Rica. Several tour agencies and hotel desks arrange day trips to Nicaragua from resorts and hotels around Guanacaste.

Be forewarned that this border crossing is among the most difficult in Central America, as it is strict, slow, and hot

(except when it's pouring rain). If you've never done this before, you'll be completely mystified about what to do first and where to go next unless you hire a *tramitador*, a border fixer. These smooth operators can be very helpful if you're in a bind, but if you're not careful they can also fleece you blind.

C1,670. Buses depart for San José from Peñas Blancas daily between 3:30am and 5:30pm, passing through La Cruz about 20 minutes later. Daily buses leave Liberia for San José roughly every hour between 3am and 8pm.

CITY LAYOUT The highway passes slightly to the east of town. You'll pass the turnoffs to Santa Rosa National Park and Playa Cuajiniquil before you reach town. For the Bahía Salinas beaches, head into La Cruz and take the road that runs along the north side of the small central park and then follow the signs down to the water.

Exploring Santa Rosa National Park

Known for its remote, pristine beaches (reached by several kilometers of hiking trails or 4WD vehicle), **Santa Rosa National Park ★** (www. acguanacaste.ac.cr; ✆ **2666-5051;** entrance $15; day visits 8am–3:30pm) is an isolated place to camp on the beach, surf, bird-watch, or maybe even see sea turtles. Located 30km (19 miles) north of Liberia and 21km (13 miles) south of La Cruz on the Inter-American Highway, Costa Rica's first national park blankets the Santa Elena Peninsula. Unlike other national parks, it was founded to protect a building, **Museo Histórico La Casona ★★**, where Costa Rica fought its most important battle on its own soil. In March 1856, days after the mercenary army of U.S. adventurer William Walker invaded Costa Rica on foot, Costa

Hiking in Santa Rosa National Park

Santa Rosa National Park

Rican forces surprised, shocked, and routed the foreigners in this very place, killing 26 and capturing 19. Costa Rican–led forces went on to defeat Walker's men on Nicaraguan soil in the Second Battle of Rivas, setting the stage for Walker's removal from office and eventual execution. La Casona was destroyed by arson in 2001, but it has been completely rebuilt with exquisite attention to period detail, and it's among the very best museums dedicated to a single historical event that you'll find anywhere.

If all this learning has put you in the mood for hiking, try the **Indio Desnudo (Naked Indian) trail,** a 2.6km (1.5-mile) loop that might take you about 45 minutes. It cuts through a small patch of tropical dry forest and into overgrown former pastureland that is a habitat for white-tailed deer, coatis, and howler and white-faced monkeys.

Camping is allowed at several sites in the park for around $20 per person per day. Camping is near the entrance, the principal ranger station, La Casona, and by playas Naranjo and Nancite.

THE BEACHES ★★   Eight kilometers (5 miles) west of La Casona, down a rugged road that's impassable during the rainy season and rough on 4WD vehicles even in the dry season, is **Playa Naranjo.** Four kilometers (2½ miles) north of Naranjo, along a hiking trail that follows the beach, you'll find **Playa Nancite. Playa Blanca** is 21km (13 miles) down a dirt road from Cuajiniquil, which is 20km (12 miles) north of the park entrance. None of these three beaches has shower or restroom facilities except Playa Nancite, where the facilities are in a reservation-only camping area. Bring your own water, food, and anything else you'll need, and expect to find things relatively quiet and deserted.

Playa Nancite is known for its *arribadas* ("arrivals," or mass egg-layings) of olive ridley sea turtles, which come ashore to nest by the tens of thousands each year in October. Playa Naranjo is legendary among surfers who have come by boat from Playa del Coco or Tamarindo to ride the towering waves at **Witch's Rock**.

On the northern side of the peninsula is **Playa Blanca,** a remote, calm, white-sand beach. It's accessible during the dry season by way of the small village of Cuajiniquil.

If you head north from Cuajiniquil on a rugged dirt road for a few kilometers, you'll come to a small annex of the national park system at **Playa Junquillal ★ (© 2666-5051)**, not to be confused with the more-developed beach of the same name farther south in Guanacaste. This is a handsome little beach that is also often good for swimming. You'll have to pay the park entrance fee ($10) to use the beach, and $2 more to camp here. There are basic restroom and shower facilities.

La Casona at Santa Rosa National Park

Junior suite at Dreams Las Mareas

Fun on the Waves

The waters of Bahía Salinas are buffeted by serious winds from mid-November through mid-May, making this a prime spot for windsurfing and kiteboarding. **Ecoplaya Beach Resort** ★ (p 232) has a good equipment rentals. For kiteboarding, inquire at the **Kitesurfing Center,** which operates out of the **Blue Dream Hotel** (www.bluedreamhotel. com; ✆ **8826-5221** or 2676-1042) in Playa Copal.

Beach lovers should head to the far western tip of Bahía Salinas, where they'll find **Playa Rajada** ★★, a beautiful little white-sand beach, with gentle surf and plenty of shade trees.

Where to Stay & Eat Near La Cruz

To get to either of these hotels from La Cruz, take the dirt road that heads toward Bahía Salinas and Soley, and then follow signs to the hotels. This is a very rough, washboard dirt road most of the year.

In addition to the places listed below, the **Dreams Las Mareas** (www.dreamsresorts.com/las-mareas; ✆ **866/2DREAMS [2-373267]** in the U.S. and Canada, or 2690-2400 in Costa Rica) is a 447-room luxury all-inclusive resort on remote Playa Jobo.

Enjoying a beach at Papagayo

EXPENSIVE

Recreo ★   More a pool of vacation rentals than a true resort, Recreo is popular for family vacations, yoga retreats, and basically anyone else looking for a one- to five-bedroom villa with cooking facilities and private plunge pools. The houses are part of a remote gated development spread over rolling hills. The property lacks a restaurant, but you could arrange to have a private chef cook for you in your villa. The resort is not right on the water, but just a few minutes away from the gorgeous and semi-deserted Playa Rajada. A car is a necessity here.

El Jobo Beach, Salinas Bay. www.recreocostarica.com. ℂ **877/268-2911** in the U.S. and Canada, or 2676-1230 in Costa Rica. 5 units. $395–$960 villa; $50 per person resort fee. **Amenities:** Bar; small, well-equipped gym; pools; tennis court; free Wi-Fi.

MODERATE

Ecoplaya Beach Resort ★   Ecoplaya primarily caters to windsurf-ers, especially between December and March, when the winds really howl, and is happy to arrange lessons or rentals for beginners. The hotel itself features two sections: standard hotel rooms in a two-story concrete building with floor-to-ceiling glass walls and sliding doors that open onto private balconies, and a variety of even better villas with more spacious front porches.

La Coyotera Beach, Salinas Bay. www.ecoplaya.com. ℂ **2676-1010.** 44 units. $95–$160 double; $125–$200 villa, includes taxes. **Amenities:** Restaurant; bar; hot tubs; pool; kayak rental; free Wi-Fi.

PLAYA HERMOSA, PLAYA PANAMÁ & PAPAGAYO ★★

258km (160 miles) NW of San José; 40km (25 miles) SW of Liberia

This area is one of Costa Rica's standouts, with the Papagayo Peninsula sheltering a large gulf, small bays, and beautiful beaches, not to mention some of the country's most exclusive accommodations. While much of the coast in this vicinity is coveted by surfers, the waters here tend to be protected and calm, making them good destinations for families. **Playa Hermosa ★** means "beautiful beach," an apt moniker for this pretty crescent of sand. Surrounded by steep, forested hills, this curving gray beach is long and wide, and the surf is usually quite gentle. Fringing the beach is a swath of trees that stay surprisingly green even during the dry season. The shade provided by these trees, along with the calm waters, make this site very appealing. Rocky headlands jut out into the surf at both ends of the beach, where there are fun-to-explore tide pools.

Beyond Playa Hermosa lies **Playa Panamá ★** and the calm **Bahía Culebra ★**, a large protected bay dotted with small, private patches of beach and ringed with mostly intact dry forest. On the northwestern reaches of Bahía Culebra is the **Papagayo Peninsula ★**, home to two large resorts and a championship golf course. This peninsula has a half-dozen or so small- to mid-size beaches, the nicest of which might just be **Playa Nacascolo ★★★**, which is inside the domain of the Four Seasons Resort here—but all beaches in Costa Rica are public, so you can still visit, albeit after parking at the public parking lot and passing through security.

Essentials

GETTING THERE & DEPARTING   By Plane: The nearest airport with regularly scheduled service is in Liberia (p 210). From there, a taxi ride takes about 25 minutes and should cost $50 to $60.

By Car: Follow the directions for getting to Liberia (p 210). When you reach the main intersection in Liberia, take a left onto CR21, which heads toward Santa Cruz and the beaches of Guanacaste. The turnoff for the Papagayo Peninsula is prominently marked 8km (5 miles) south of the Liberia airport. At the corner here, you'll see a massive Do It Center hardware store and lumberyard.

If you are going to a hotel along the Papagayo Peninsula, turn at the Do It Center and follow the paved road out and around the peninsula. If you are going to Playa Panamá or Playa Hermosa, you should also turn here and take the access road shortcut that leads from a turnoff on the Papagayo Peninsula road, just beyond the Do It Center, directly to Playa Panamá. When you reach Playa Panamá, turn left for Playa Hermosa.

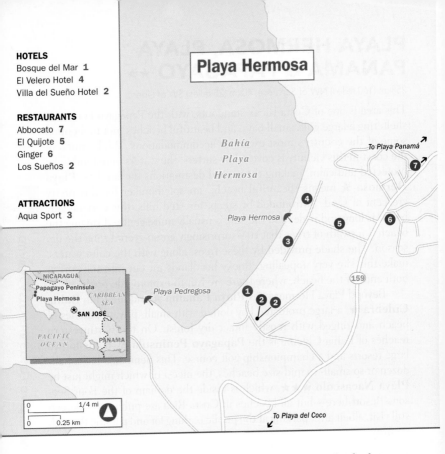

HOTELS
Bosque del Mar **1**
El Velero Hotel **4**
Villa del Sueño Hotel **2**

RESTAURANTS
Abbocato **7**
El Quijote **5**
Ginger **6**
Los Sueños **2**

ATTRACTIONS
Aqua Sport **3**

Playa Hermosa

Bahía Playa Hermosa

To Playa Panamá

Playa Hermosa

Playa Pedregosa

NICARAGUA
Papagayo Peninsula
Playa Hermosa
CARIBBEAN SEA
SAN JOSÉ
PACIFIC OCEAN
PANAMA

159

To Playa del Coco

0   1/4 mi
0   0.25 km

To get to Playa Hermosa, you can also continue on a bit farther west on CR21, and, just past the village of Comunidad, turn right. In about 11km (6¾ miles) you'll come to a fork in the road; take the right fork.

These roads are all relatively well marked, and a host of prominent hotel billboards should make it easy enough to find the beach or resort you're looking for. The drive takes about 4 to 4½ hours from San José.

By Bus: A **Tralapa** express bus (② **2221-7202**) leaves San José daily at 3:30pm from Calle 20 and Avenida 3, stopping at Playa Hermosa and Playa Panamá, 3km (1¾ miles) farther north. One-way fare for the 5-hour trip is around C5,800.

Both **Gray Line** (www.graylinecostarica.com; ② **800/719-3105** in the U.S. and Canada, or 2220-2126 in Costa Rica) and **Interbus** (www.interbusonline.com; ② **4100-0888**) have two daily buses leaving San José for all beaches in this area, one in the morning and one in the afternoon. The fare is $54. They will pick you up at most San José-area hotels, and offer connections to most other major tourist destinations.

You can take a bus from San José to Liberia (see "Essentials," earlier in this chapter), and then take a bus from Liberia to Playa Hermosa and

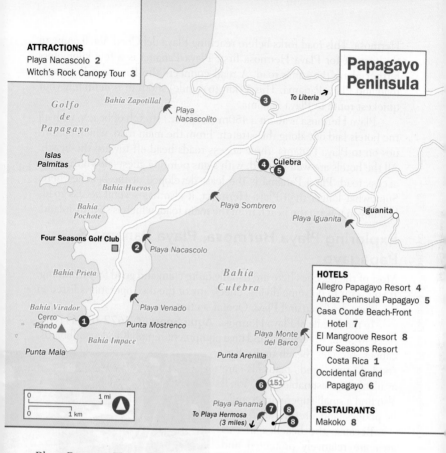

To Liberia →

Papagayo Peninsula

ATTRACTIONS
Playa Nacascolo **2**
Witch's Rock Canopy Tour **3**

Golfo de Papagayo

Bahía Zapotillal
Playa Nacascolito

3

Islas Palmitas

Culebra **4** **5**

Bahía Huevos

Bahía Pochote

Playa Sombrero

Playa Iguanita

Iguanita

Four Seasons Golf Club

2 Playa Nacascolo

Bahía Prieta

Bahía Culebra

Bahía Virador
Cerro Pando **1**

Playa Venado

Bahía Impace

Punta Mostrenco

Playa Monte del Barco

Punta Mala

Punta Arenilla

0 — 1 mi
0 — 1 km

6 151

Playa Panamá **7** **8**
To Playa Hermosa **8**
(3 miles) ↓

HOTELS
Allegro Papagayo Resort **4**
Andaz Peninsula Papagayo **5**
Casa Conde Beach-Front
  Hotel **7**
El Mangroove Resort **8**
Four Seasons Resort
  Costa Rica **1**
Occidental Grand
  Papagayo **6**

RESTAURANTS
Makoko **8**

Playa Panamá. **Transportes La Pampa** buses (② **2665-7530**) leave Liberia for Playa Hermosa and Playa Panamá at least a half-dozen times daily between 4:30am and 5:30pm. The trip lasts 40 minutes because the bus stops frequently to drop off and pick up passengers. The one-way fare costs C750. These bus schedules change from time to time, so it's best to check in advance. During the high season and on weekends, extra buses from Liberia are sometimes added. You can also take a bus to Playa del Coco, from which playas Hermosa and Panamá are a relatively quick taxi ride away. Taxi fare should run C9,000–C12,000.

One direct bus departs for San José daily at 5am from Playa Panamá, with a stop in Playa Hermosa along the way. Buses to Liberia leave Playa Panamá regularly between 6am and 7pm, stopping in Playa Hermosa. Ask at your hotel about current schedules and where to catch the bus.

AREA LAYOUT   From the well-marked turnoff for the Papagayo Peninsula, a paved road leads around to the Allegro Papagayo and Four Seasons resorts. If you are heading to the beaches a little farther south, continue on to the well-marked turnoff for Playa del Coco and Playa

Hermosa. This road forks before reaching Playa del Coco. You'll come to the turnoff for Playa Hermosa first. Playa Panamá is a few kilometers farther along the same road. A road connects the Papagayo Peninsula road and Playa Panamá. This 11km (6¾-mile) shortcut is definitely your quickest route to Playa Panamá.

Playa Hermosa is about a 450m (1,476-ft.) stretch of beach, with all the hotels laid out along this stretch. From the main road, which continues on to Playa Panamá, three access roads head off toward the beach. All the hotels are well marked, with signs pointing guests down the right access road. Playa Panamá is the least developed of the beaches here. Somewhat longer than Playa Hermosa, it also has several access roads heading in toward the beach from the main road, which is slightly inland.

Exploring Playa Hermosa, Playa Panamá & Papagayo

Most of the beaches here are usually quite calm and good for swimming. If you want to do some diving, check any of the dive operations listed in the Playa del Coco and Playa Ocotal section.

In the middle of Playa Hermosa, **Aqua Sport** (℗ **2672-0151**) is the place to go for watersports and dive equipment rental. Kayaks, sailboards, canoes, bicycles, beach umbrellas, snorkel gear, and parasails are available at reasonable rates. You'll also find a small supermarket, public phones, and a restaurant.

Because the beaches in this area are relatively protected and generally flat, surfers should look into boat trips to nearby **Witch's Rock** ★★ and **Ollie's Point** ★ (p 248).

The waters here are prime sportfishing grounds, and the Papagayo Marina (https://marina papagayo.com; ℗ **2690-3600**) is near the Four Seasons and Andaz resorts. Aside from that there are a host of boats anchored off both Playa Hermosa and nearby Playa del Coco. Try www.getmyboat.com for discounted charters.

If you're interested in a surf trip or some sportfishing, ask at your hotel or check at the listings

Ziplining through the trees on a canopy tour

below for "Surfing" and "Sportfishing" in Playa del Coco and Playa Ocotal.

Sailboat enthusiasts need look no further than **El Velero Hotel ★** (p 240) or any of the other sailboat options listed in the Playa del Coco and Playa Ocotal section (p 243). All offer a range of full- and half-day tours, with snorkel stops, as well as sunset cruises.

Other Options

Charlie's Adventures ★ (www.charliesadventure.com; ✆ **2672-0317**) offers a wide range of activities and tours, including trips to Santa Rosa or Rincón de la Vieja national parks, and rafting on the Corobicí River.

The best zipline canopy tour in this area is the **Witch's Rock Canopy Tour ★** (www.witchsrockcanopy.com; ✆ **2696-7101**), near the Allegro Papagayo Resort. The 1½-hour tour covers 3km (1¾ miles) of cables, touching down on 24 platforms and crossing three suspension bridges. The tour costs $75.

Finally, the Arnold Palmer–designed course at the Four Seasons Resort (p 239) is hands-down the most scenic and challenging **golf course** in the country.

Where to Stay

EXPENSIVE

Andaz Peninsula Papagayo Resort ★★   Sharing the Papagayo Peninsula with the Four Seasons, this Hyatt resort offers similar luxury and service at a nicer price. Rooms are a blend of modern design and Costa Rican aesthetics, with woven textiles, bamboo, and carved artifacts. Balconies (and showers!) look out on the serene Culebra Bay. The 11,000-square-foot spa is quite impressive, and there are three themed restaurants: the Río Bhongo, which mimics a river island; the elegant Ostra seafood restaurant; and the fun Chao Pescao, where the drink menu runs multiple pages. There are two beaches and two swimming pools, one for families and one for adults only. Smaller dogs are allowed, and there's a kids' club.

Papagayo Peninsula. http://papagayo.andaz.hyatt.com. ✆ **800/233-1234** from U.S. and Canada, 2690-1234 in Costa Rica. 153 units. $489–$559 for standard rooms; $789-$1,114 suites, plus taxes and 10% resort fee. Small dogs allowed. **Amenities:** 3 restaurants; 1 bar; 2 pools; 2 beaches; spa; free transportation on the peninsula; free kayaking, stand-up paddling, and snorkeling; kids' club; free Wi-Fi.

Casa Conde Beach-Front Hotel ★★   This all-inclusive resort (which allows children, unlike the Occidental [below]), is located on a large property abounding in beautiful palm, ceiba and guanacaste trees, right on Playa Panamá. It has two big swimming pools, one freshwater and one saltwater, both with swim-up bars. The air-conditioned rooms have 43-inch TVs and minibars, and some have fully equipped kitchens, living and dining room areas, and hot tubs. Standard rooms have high

Pool at El Mangroove

wooden ceilings with skylights, attractive wooden furniture, and nice linens. Pets are allowed for a fee. The hotel has two restaurants, the buffet-style Vista del Golfo and the seafood restaurant Mare Calmo.

Playa Panamá, Papagayo Gulf. www.grupocasaconde.com. (℅ **2586-7300** or 2227-4232. 48 units. Standard rooms $324-$365 per person, double occupancy; superior suites, $390–$521 per person, double occupancy, includes taxes, meals, and drinks. **Amenities:** 2 restaurants; 4 bars; 2 outdoor pools; kayaking; snorkeling; free Wi-Fi.

El Mangroove ★★★ In your room at El Mangroove, you may forget you're in Costa Rica and feel like a Wall Street executive in a penthouse suite in Manhattan—except for the hammock in the living room. The king-size bed is plush, the TV is huge, the minibar is stocked, the furniture is modern, the art is chic, the Internet is high-speed, and everything is new. There's even a walk-in closet, connecting to the shower. This luxury hotel has a 24-hour gym, a full service spa, an adventure center, a kids' club, and a long, narrow pool perfect for swimming laps. Next to the pool are cabanas with comfy couches, TVs, and minibars, and just beyond is a serene beach with waves gentle enough for a toddler and a stunning view of the serene Papagayo Gulf. The 5-star resort, designed by the celebrated architect Ronald Zurcher, has been awarded "5 Leaves" in the Certification for Sustainable Tourism program. Matiss and Makoko restaurants, overseen by culinary director Sebastian La Rocca, who was once Jamie Oliver's right hand man, are outstanding. And if you're in the mood for a midnight snack, indulge in the 24-hour room service.

Playa Panamá, Papagayo Gulf. www.elmangroove.net. (℅ **855/219-9371** from the U.S. and Canada, 2105-7575 in Costa Rica. 85 suites. Standard rooms $253–$286, master suites $307–$482, plus tax and $20 resort fee. Free valet parking. **Amenities:** 2 restaurants; 2 bars; spa; gym; kids zone; tour operator; car rental; pool; free Wi-Fi.

One of the beaches at the Four Seasons

Four Seasons Resort Costa Rica ★★★ Ideally located on the neck of a stunning peninsula with pristine white-sand beaches on either side, the Four Seasons is hands-down the premier luxury resort hotel in Costa Rica, if not in all of Central America. Its unique look, designed by industrious Ronald Zurcher, features roof lines and building shapes meant to evoke turtles and armadillos. Rooms are large, plush, and

The pools at the Four Seasons

239

graced with colorful throw pillows and rattan and fine wood furnishings. Suites and villas are dazzling, with multiple rooms, full kitchens, and private infinity pools. Four restaurants offer up the top-notch dining experience you'd expect from the Four Seasons—and the hotel's famed service remains peerless. The Arnold Palmer–designed golf course has ocean views from the tees, greens, and fairways of 15 of its 18 holes. After a closing for several months in 2017 for renovations, the resort is better than ever.

Papagayo Peninsula. www.fourseasons.com/costarica. © **800/332-3442** in the U.S., or 2696-0000. 182 units. $550–$975 double; suites and villas $875 and up. Children stay free in parent's room. **Amenities:** 4 restaurants; 2 bars; babysitting; children's programs; championship 18-hole golf course; 3 outdoor pools; room service; spa; 5 tennis courts; watersports equipment; free Wi-Fi.

Occidental Grand Papagayo ★ This sprawling, adults-only all-inclusive is located on a hilly point of land overlooking the beautiful Papagayo Gulf. Rooms feature red or white tile floors, bright white linens, a private balcony or porch, large flatscreen TVs, air-conditioning, cappuccino makers, and minibars. Wildlife abounds in the trees around the property, so you might see monkeys, raccoons, or skunks. At the base of the hotel's property you'll find a beach that is broad and calm at low tide, but recedes up to the treeline at high tide.

Playa Buena, just north of Playa Hermosa. www.barcelo.com/grandpapagayo. © **2690-8000.** 163 units. $232–$256 per person standard room; suites $450–$590 per person, includes meals, drinks, a range of activities, and taxes. **Amenities:** 5 restaurants; 4 bars; disco; large health club and spa; large outdoor pool; hot tub; lighted tennis court; gym; watersports equipment; free Wi-Fi.

MODERATE

Bosque del Mar ★ One of the prettiest hotels in the area, Bosque del Mar is distinguished by beautiful wooden latticework throughout the rooms and their exteriors, and by tall, V-shaped roofs. Suites are spread around a free-form pool amid the shade of tall, lovingly preserved old-growth trees (which are inhabited by iguanas and troops of monkeys). These gorgeous trees are everywhere, popping up through decks and roofs in the main lobby and even jutting through the center of a balcony of one of the junior suites. Steps away from the sand on the quiet southern end of Playa Hermosa, this is among the best beachfront boutique hotels in the area. All rooms have two queen beds, as well as air-conditioning, TV, a mini-fridge, and a safe. The oceanfront suites are colorful and comfortable, with hot tubs on private balconies where guests can soak in the sunset.

Playa Hermosa. www.bosquedelmar.com. © **2672-0046.** 35 units. $210–$310 double. **Amenities:** Restaurant; bar; outdoor pool; spa services; free Wi-Fi.

INEXPENSIVE

El Velero Hotel ★ This longstanding hotel is a solid option just steps from the sand on Playa Hermosa. The motif here is Mediterranean, with whitewashed walls, tile floors, and interior archways. Artwork of tropical animals on the walls looks like silk-screen prints, but are actually women's beach sarongs, framed. Rooms are spacious and air-conditioned, with recently replaced linens, towels, orthopedic mattresses, headboards, mirrors, and 32-inch flatscreen TVs. Rooms on the second floor have higher ceilings and are somewhat preferable. There's a small plunge pool and a popular restaurant and bar, but the place shuts down around 10pm and is not a big party spot. The beach in front is beautiful (with masseuses doing a brisk business) and the ocean is highly swimmable, with no undertow or riptides—but woe to the surfers who mistake this for Playa Hermosa de Jacó, which has happened. Canadian owner Mike Tesluk, who lives on-site, is very helpful and fun to talk to. El Velero means "the sailboat" and there is, in fact, a sailboat available for charter. Playa Hermosa, Guanacaste. www.costaricahotel.net. © **2672-1017.** 22 units. $99 double. **Amenities:** Restaurant; bar; small outdoor pool; free Wi-Fi.

Villa del Sueño Hotel ★★   Tall trees and mature gardens give this sprawling complex of hotel rooms and condo units a cool and refreshing feel, even on the hottest of Guanacaste's summer days. A thatched-roof tiki bar just off the main pool also helps beat the heat. The eye-pleasing Mediterranean architecture features lots of big arches and red-tile roofs. Of the two swimming pools, one has a little island sporting three palm trees, and the beach is just a 3-minute walk away. Red tile floors and bright tropical paintings and wall hangings give the rooms a cheery feel, and those on the second floor enjoy higher ceilings. Standard hotel rooms and privately owned suites are divided by a little road, and there is Wi-Fi only on the side closest to the beach. The in-house restaurant is one of the best in town, and offers live music three times a week in the high season.

Playa Hermosa, Guanacaste. www.villadelsueno.com. © **800/378-8599** in the U.S., or 2672-0026 in Costa Rica. 46 units. $99–$159 double; $175–$305 suites. **Amenities:** Restaurant; bar; room service; 2 outdoor pools; free Wi-Fi.

Where to Eat

In addition to the places listed below, you'll find good restaurants at both the **El Velero Hotel** (p 240) and the **Bosque del Mar** (p 240). There's also fresh seafood and sushi, and a relaxed yet lively ambience at **El Quijote** (© **2672-0176**), located along the second entrance road toward the beach (see map p 234).

Abbocato ★★ FUSION/BISTRO   Husband-wife chefs Andrea and Paola create two distinct nightly tasting menus. One typically features Asian-inspired flavors and preparations, and the other is Mediterranean in style. It's anybody's guess which of the two is behind any one dish, but no matter—everything is sublime. On the Asian side, you might get home-smoked fresh tuna in a light ginger dressing with homemade pickles; on the Mediterranean side, it could be mushroom sausage in a phyllo

Outdoor dining at Ginger

quiche with pesto and Fontina cheese. As for the ambience: The dining room features travertine tile floors, heavy wooden tables, walls of glass, and high peaked ceilings with exposed wood beams. It opens onto a broad patio that overlooks the Pacific Ocean and provides great sunset views. An excellent wine list completes the experience. Open for lunch and tapas.

Inside Hacienda del Mar, 1km (½ mile) inland from Playa Panamá. www.abbocatocr. com. (✆) **2672-0073** or 8820-2576. Reservations necessary for dinner. Main courses $12–$35. 4-course prix-fixe dinner $45. Tues–Sat noon–9pm.

Ginger ★★ FUSION/TAPAS   With a design by famed Costa Rican architect Víctor Cañas, creative cocktails, and a wide-ranging tapas menu, this is easily the hippest place to drink and dine in the Papagayo area. The entire restaurant is open air, on a raised deck under tall trees, with angled steel supports and slanted rooflines. The menu spans the globe from Thailand to Spain to Italy. The firecracker shrimp and the shredded pork lettuce wraps in a mango-tamarind sauce are especially good. And there are more than a dozen specialty martinis, margaritas, and mojitos.

On the main road, Playa Hermosa. www.gingercostarica.com. (✆) **2672-0041.** Tapas $5–$13. Tues–Sun 5–10pm.

Los Sueños ★ INTERNATIONAL   You get dinner and a show at the restaurant of the Villa del Sueño Hotel and condo complex (p 241). Throughout the high season, a house band, which features one of the owners, usually plays (Celine Dion reportedly once joined in). But even if there's no music, this open-air restaurant is wonderfully pleasant with a dimly lit, covered dining room, and outdoor tables and chairs spread around the lush gardens. The kitchen serves up local ingredients used in contemporary Continental recipes like steak with pepper sauce, or fresh red snapper topped with locally caught shrimp in a cream sauce.

At the Villa del Sueño Hotel. © **2672-0026.** Main courses $18–$28. Daily 7am–9:30pm.

Makoko ★★★ FUSION/BISTRO   Beneath a wooden spaceship like, open-air structure near the pool inside the Mangroove Hotel, Argentine chef Sebastian La Rocca oversees one of the most exciting menus in Costa Rica. Here he infuses local ingredients, from 30-day aged Costa Rican beef to mahi mahi, into elegant meals that wouldn't be out of place in a top restaurant in any North American city. Start your meal with red snapper crudo before moving to mouthwatering main courses like seed crusted snook or glazed short ribs with apple-jalapeño purée.

Playa Panamá, Papagayo Gulf. www.elmangroove.net. © **855/219-9371** from the U.S. and Canada, 2105-7575 in Costa Rica. Reservations necessary. Main courses $17–$34. Daily 6–10pm.

Entertainment & Nightlife

Most of the large resorts have bars, and a few feature nightly entertainment revues or live bands. In general, Playa Hermosa, Playa Panama, and the Papagayo peninsula are very laid back and fairly spread out. For a mellow cocktail on an open-air deck, head for **Ginger** ★★ or **Los Sueños** ★ restaurant (see above) on a night the band is playing (ask). For a livelier bar and club scene, many visitors head to Playa del Coco (see below).

PLAYA DEL COCO & PLAYA OCOTAL ★

253km (157 miles) NW of San José; 35km (22 miles) W of Liberia

Playa del Coco is one of Costa Rica's busiest and most developed beach destinations. A large modern mall and shopping center anchor the eastern edge of town. You'll pass through a tight jumble of restaurants, hotels, and souvenir shops for several blocks before you hit the sand and sea; homes, condos, and hotels are strung along the access roads that parallel the beach in either direction. This has long been a popular destination for middle-class Ticos and weekend revelers from San José. It's also a prime base for some of Costa Rica's best scuba diving. The beach,

Café del Playa on Playa del Coco

which has grayish-brown sand and gentle surf, is quite wide at low tide and almost nonexistent at high tide. The crowds that come here like their music loud and late, so if you're in search of a quiet retreat, stay away from the center of town. Still, if you're looking for a beach with a wide range of hotels, lively nightlife, and plenty of cheap food and beer, you'll enjoy Playa del Coco. (And by the way, it's often called Playas del Coco, presumably because there's more than one beach in the area.)

Also worth checking out is **Playa Ocotal ★**, a few miles to the south. This tiny pocket cove features a small salt-and-pepper beach bordered by high bluffs, and it's quite beautiful. When it's calm, there's good snorkeling around rocky islands close to shore.

Essentials

GETTING THERE & DEPARTING   By Plane: The nearest airport with regularly scheduled flights is in Liberia (p 210). From there, you can arrange for a taxi to take you to Playa del Coco or Playa Ocotal, which is about a 25-minute drive, for $40 to $65.

By Car: From Liberia, head west on CR21 toward Santa Cruz. Just past the village of Comunidad, turn right. In about 11km (6¾ miles), you'll come to a fork in the road. Take the left fork. The right fork goes to Playa Hermosa. The drive takes about 4 hours from San José.

By Bus: Pulmitan express buses (© **2222-1650** in San José, or 2670-0095 in Playa del Coco) leave San José for Playa del Coco at 8am and 2 and 4pm daily from Calle 24 between avenidas 5 and 7. Allow 5 hours for the trip. A one-way ticket is about C4,500. From Liberia, buses

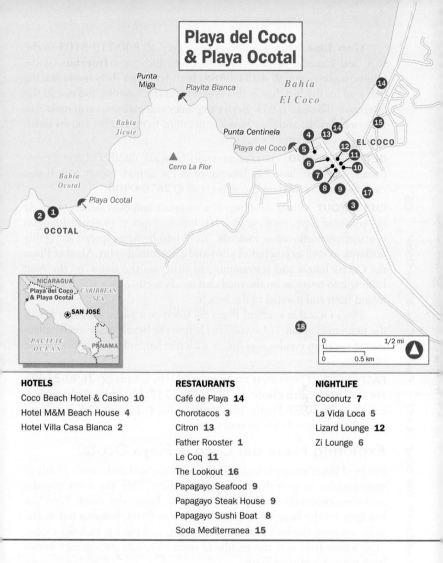

Playa del Coco & Playa Ocotal

Punta Miga

Playita Blanca

Bahía El Coco

Bahía Jicote

Punta Centinela

Playa del Coco

Cerro La Flor

EL COCO

Bahía Ocotal

Playa Ocotal

OCOTAL

NICARAGUA

Playa del Coco & Playa Ocotal

CARIBBEAN SEA

SAN JOSÉ

PACIFIC OCEAN

PANAMA

| 0 | 1/2 mi |
| 0 | 0.5 km |

HOTELS

Coco Beach Hotel & Casino **10**
Hotel M&M Beach House **4**
Hotel Villa Casa Blanca **2**

RESTAURANTS

Café de Playa **14**
Chorotacos **3**
Citron **13**
Father Rooster **1**
Le Coq **11**
The Lookout **16**
Papagayo Seafood **9**
Papagayo Steak House **9**
Papagayo Sushi Boat **8**
Soda Mediterranea **15**

NIGHTLIFE

Coconutz **7**
La Vida Loca **5**
Lizard Lounge **12**
Zi Lounge **6**

(© **2666-0458**) to Playa del Coco leave regularly throughout the day between 5am and 7pm. A one-way ticket for the 40-minute trip costs around C850. These bus schedules change frequently, so it's always best to check in advance. During high season and on weekends, extra buses from Liberia are sometimes added. The bus for San José leaves Playa del Coco daily at 4 and 8am and 2pm. Buses for Liberia leave daily between 5am and 7pm.

Depending on demand, the Playa del Coco buses sometimes go as far as Playa Ocotal; it's worth checking beforehand. Otherwise, a taxi should cost around C3,500 to C5,000.

Gray Line (www.graylinecostarica.com; ✆ **800/719-3105** in the U.S. and Canada, or 2220-2126 in Costa Rica) and **Interbus** (www.interbusonline.com; ✆ **4031-0888**) both have two daily buses leaving San José for the beaches in this area, one in the morning and one in the afternoon. The fare is $54. Both companies will pick you up at most San José–area hotels, and they have connections to most other tourist destinations around Costa Rica.

GETTING AROUND   You can rent cars from any number of rental companies. Most are based in Liberia, or at the airport. See p 210. If you can't flag down a **taxi** on the street, call ✆ **2670-0408.**

CITY LAYOUT   Playa del Coco is a compact and busy beach town. At the center of town, running for a few hundred meters in either direction is a seafront walkway, or *malecón.* You'll find benches spread along this walkway, as well as patches of grass and a basketball court. Most of Playa del Coco's hotels and restaurants are either on the water, on the road leading into town; or on the road that heads north, about 100m (328 ft.) inland from and parallel to the beach.

Playa Ocotal is south of Playa del Coco on a paved road that leaves the main road about 183m (600 ft.) before the beach. It's a small collection of vacation condos and hotels with one bar and a restaurant on the beach.

FAST FACTS   The nearest major hospital is in Liberia (✆ **2690-2300**). For the local **health clinic,** call ✆ **2670-1717;** for the local **pharmacy,** call ✆ **2670-2050.** For the local **police,** dial ✆ **2670-0258.** You'll find several banks and ATMs around town.

Exploring Playa del Coco & Playa Ocotal

Plenty of boats are anchored at Playa del Coco, and that means plenty of opportunities to go fishing, diving, or sailing. Still, the most popular activities, especially among the hordes of Ticos who come here, are lounging on the beach, walking along the *malecón,* hanging out in the *sodas,* cruising the bars and discos at night, and playing pick-up soccer. (The soccer field is in the middle of town.) You can also arrange horseback rides; ask at your hotel.

CANOPY TOUR   The **Congo Trail Canopy Tour** ★ (www.congocanopy.com; ✆ **2666-4422** or 2697-1801) is set in a stand of thick, tropical dry forest on the outskirts of Playa del Coco, along a dirt road that leads to Playa Pan de Azúcar. In addition to a zipline, there's a small butterfly farm and a few zoo enclosures, with monkeys and reptiles. The tour runs every day from 8am to 5pm, and costs $35 for the canopy tour, plus $10 to see the animals.

GOLF   Located about 10km (6¼ miles) outside Playa del Coco, the **Vista Ridge Golf & Country Club** ★ (www.vistaridgecr.com; ✆ **2697-0169**) is an 18-hole course with a pro shop, driving range, and rental equipment. The $100 greens fees include a cart and access to the pool area. Reservations are necessary on weekends. It's closed on Mondays.

HORSEBACK RIDING   You can't ride on the beaches here, but the folks at **Haras del Mar** (harashorses@gmail.com; ✆ **8823-5522**) offer great trail and country riding on well-tended, trained horses about 20 minutes outside of Playa del Coco.

SAILING   Several cruising sailboats and longtime local salts offer daily sailing excursions. The 47-foot ketch-rigged *Kuna Vela* (www.kunavela.com; ✆ **8301-3030**) and the 45-foot ketch *Seabird* (www.seabird-sailingexcursions.com; ✆ **8880-6393**) both ply the waters off Playa del Coco. They also offer half- and full-day and sunset sailing options, with snorkel stops and an open bar.

SCUBA DIVING   Scuba diving is the most popular watersport in the area, and dive shops abound. **Sirenas Diving Costa Rica ★★** (www.sirenas divingcostarica.com; ✆ **8721-8055**), **Summer Salt ★** (www.summer-salt.com; ✆ **2670-0308**), and **Rich Coast Diving ★★** (www.rich coastdiving.com; ✆ **2670-0176**) are the most established and offer equipment rentals and dive trips. A two-tank dive, with equipment, should cost between $85 and $150 per person, depending on the distance to the dive site. The more distant dive sites visited include the Catalina Islands and Bat Island. All shops also offer PADI certification courses.

SPORTFISHING   Full- and half-day sportfishing excursions can be arranged through any of the hotel tour desks, or with **Dream On Sport-fishing ★★** (www.dreamonsportfishing.com; ✆ **8735-3121**) or **North Pacific Tours ★** (www.northpacifictours.com; ✆ **8398-8129**). A half-day of fishing, including the boat, captain, food, and tackle, should cost $400 to $1,150 for two to four passengers; a full day, $600 to $1,200.

SURFING   Playa del Coco has no surfing to speak of, but is a popular jumping-off point for daily boat trips to Witch's Rock and Ollie's Point in Santa Rosa National Park (p 228). Most of the above-mentioned sport-fishing and dive operations also ferry surfers to these isolated surf breaks. A boat that carries five surfers for a full day, including lunch and beer, should run $350 to $600. *Note:* Both Witch's Rock and Ollie's Point are technically within Santa Rosa National Park. Permits are required, and boats without permits are sometimes turned away. If you decide to go, be sure your boat captain is licensed and has cleared access to the park. You will also have to pay the park's $15 per person fee. **Single Fin Surf Charters** (www.singlefinsurfcharters.com; ✆ **8935-2519**) offers a plush trip out to these surf spots at $1330 for up to 10 passengers for a full-day trip. But if you ask around town, you should be able to find one of the local skippers, who tend to offer trips for up to six surfers for much less. Alternatively, check the website www.getmyboat.com.

   Pacific Coast Stand Up Paddle & Surf Trips (www.pacific coastsuptours.com; ✆ **8359-8115**) offer lessons and guided outings for

Ollie's Point is named after Oliver North, the former lieutenant colonel at the center of the Iran-Contra scandal. A secret airstrip near the point was used covertly by the CIA to fly in supplies for the

Nicaraguan Contra rebels during the guerrilla war in the 1980s. One of the biggest surf breaks in Costa Rica, Ollie's Point can be reached by boat from Playa del Coco or Tamarindo.

both traditional surfing, and for those looking to try out stand-up paddling (which can be done without traveling to another beach).

Where to Stay

MODERATE

Coco Beach Hotel & Casino ★   If you want to be in the center of the action, this is the place for you. Set right in the heart of Playa del Coco's busiest restaurant, bar and commercial strip, the hotel offers clean if fairly bland rooms that are brightened by colorful paintings based on indigenous designs. The staff is friendly and helpful. Thatched-roof structures ring the pool area and separate rooms from the street, helping to block the blazing Guanacaste sun and street noise. The beach is 2 blocks away.

Playa del Coco, Guanacaste. www.cocobeachcr.com. ℭ **4000-0600.** 32 units. $103–$119 double, includes full breakfast. **Amenities:** Restaurant; bar; small casino; small outdoor pool; free Wi-Fi.

INEXPENSIVE

Hotel M&M Beach House ★   With a perfect location on the beach, the M&M also comes with a price that's nice. The two-story building is rectangular and open-air in the middle, with lounging areas upstairs and down facing the beach. There's no restaurant or bar, but breakfast is included, and there's a shared kitchen. Rooms have TVs and fans but no a/c or hot water—though you may find that in this heat you prefer a cold shower anyway. Pets are welcome for $10 extra, and guests can use the swimming pool at the M&M Garden House, a 5-minute walk away.

150m west of the police station on the beach, Playa del Coco. www.hotelmym.com. ℭ **2670-1212.** 17 units. $47–$54 double, includes taxes and breakfast. **Amenities:** Shared kitchen; free Wi-Fi.

Hotel Villa Casa Blanca ★   A friendly staff, a serene setting slightly uphill from Playa Ocotal, and a nice pool area are all good reasons to pick the Casa Blanca, along with the reasonable nightly rate. But this is not the place for those who hanker for swank, or even new, furnishings (it doesn't get more basic than this, and some of the bathrooms are in lousy shape, with chipped and stained tiles).

Playa Ocotal, Guanacaste. ℭ **2670-0448.** 11 units. $55-$84 double; $131 family suite, includes taxes and breakfast. **Amenities:** Lounge and bar; Jacuzzi; pool; free Wi-Fi.

Where to Eat

A clutch of basic open-air *sodas* is at the traffic circle in the center of El Coco village, serving Tico standards, with an emphasis on fried fish. Prices are quite low—though the quality is good, for the most part.

You can get excellent Italian food, however, at **Soda Mediterránea ★** (℡ **8742-6553**), in the little El Pueblito strip mall on the road running north and parallel to the beach, and decent tacos with fillings like jerk chicken or beer braised pork at the **Chorotacos ★** (℡ **8341-0413**), a taco cart run by a Canadian couple in front of SuperLuperon. For a quick or light meal, try **Le Coq ★** (℡ **2670-0608**), an open-air Lebanese restaurant on the main drag in the center of town.

Right on the main strip, you'll also find the various Papagayo operations. Building on the success of their seafood restaurant, **Papagayo Seafood ★** (℡ **2670-0298**), **Papagayo Steak House ★** (℡ **2670-0605**), and **Papagayo Sushi Boat ★** (℡ **2670-0298**) attempt to cover all bases.

Café de Playa ★ FUSION/INTERNATIONAL   Eat, drink, swim, repeat. That's the appeal of this laid back beachfront cafe, where many guests spend the entire day lounging, drinking well-mixed cocktails, and dipping in both the ocean and the pool. Meals (breakfast, lunch, and dinner) are served on heavy teak tables and chairs spread on a large, open-air wooden deck and out onto the grassy lawn. Food ranges from burgers and fish and chips to more upscale fare like Thai beef salad or fresh sea bass in a coconut-milk sauce.

On the beach, Playa del Coco. www.cafedeplaya.com. ℡ **2670-1621.** Reservations recommended. Main courses C6,500–C20,000. Sun–Fri 8am–9:30; 8am–10:00pm

Citron ★★ FUSION/INTERNATIONAL   Even though it's in a small strip mall, this is easily the town's most elegant and creative restaurant. The service is top-notch, the setting romantic (local cane ceiling, soft lighting, neutral colors) and the food is leaps and bounds better than what you'll get elsewhere in the area. Citron does particularly well by sea bass, usually served with orzo and a Catalan sauce or stir fried in a wok. Other star dishes include the tenderloin and Portobello risotto in red-wine reduction, and the vanilla crème brûlée, which is made with local organic vanilla. There's outdoor seating on a broad, open deck, but the daytime heat and nighttime bugs often make this a less-than-ideal option.

In the Pacífico mall, on the main road into town. Playa del Coco. www.citroncoco. com. ℡ **2670-0942.** Main courses C7,200–C11,900. Mon–Sat 5:30–10pm.

Father Rooster ★ SEAFOOD/BAR   A casual, open-air beachfront bar, Father Rooster is just steps from the water on tiny Playa Ocotal. Burgers, tacos, beer-battered fish or shrimp, nachos, and other bar fare are on offer. The building itself is a rustic wood affair painted in haphazard primary colors, with a pool table in one room. Most people try to get seats at the tables on the sand; all are shaded by canvas umbrellas and a tall mango tree. On the weekends, you'll sometimes catch a live band here.

On the beach, Playa Ocotal. www.fatherrooster.com. ✆ **2670-1246.** Main courses C6,500–C11,000. Daily 11:30am–9:30pm.

The Lookout ★★ SEAFOOD/BAR   It's worth the short drive or taxi ride to this rooftop bar/restaurant on the outskirts of Playa del Coco for the outstanding sunsets and upscale pub food. Menu standouts include the tuna poke nachos and the lobster grilled cheese, both created from locally sourced seafood. A wide-ranging selection of Costa Rican craft beers is on offer, as well as fresh, locally farmed oysters.

On the outskirts of Playa del Coco, inside the Hotel Chantel. www.thelookoutcoco. com. ✆ **8548-8679.** Main courses C3,500–C9,500. Tues–Sun 3pm–10pm.

En Route: Between Playa del Coco & Playa Flamingo

Hotel Sugar Beach ★★   Spread over a gently curved, forested hillside that cradles Playa Pan de Azúcar, this isolated hotel's lovely grounds are rich in wildlife. It's not uncommon to find troops of howler monkeys in the trees here, so be prepared for some unrequested early wake-up calls. While there are no private beaches in Costa Rica, for all intents and purposes the beach here is the exclusive playground of the hotel guests. (Playa Pan de Azúcar means "Sugarloaf Beach," but the loaf was dropped in translation, and it's known in English simply as "Sugar Beach.") The rocky outcroppings just off and around this beach are very good for snorkeling. Rooms are all spacious, spotless, and comfortable, some with romantic four-poster beds.

Playa Pan de Azúcar. www.sugar-beach.com. ✆ **2654-4242.** 27 units. $169–$209 double; $277–$290 suite; 667 3-bedroom villa, includes breakfast and taxes. **Amenities:** Restaurant; bar; small pool; free Wi-Fi.

RIU Guanacaste, RIU Palace Costa Rica ★   With more than 1,200 rooms, a half-dozen swimming pools, and almost a dozen bars, these massive side-by-side all-inclusive resorts might remind you of spring break in Cabo or Cancún. In the high season the bars, buffets, and pools are brimming with sunburned revelers looking to max out on the free-flowing booze, food, and myriad activities. Rooms are large and well-equipped, with private balconies, and at the more upscale RIU Palace they are truly sumptuous. Activities are non-stop, the food is palatable, and the casino is always bustling with optimists. The two resorts have the wide, crescent-shaped Playa Matapalo all to themselves.

Playa Matapalo, south of Playa del Coco. www.riu.com. ✆ **800/748-4990** in the U.S. and Canada, or 2681-2300 at the hotel. 701 units at RIU Guanacaste, 538 at the RIU Palace. $400-$539 RIU Guanacaste; $463–$589 per person at RIU Palace, includes all meals, drinks, taxes, a wide range of activities, and use of non-motorized land and watersports equipment; 3-night minimum stay. **Amenities:** At the two resorts, 10 restaurants; 11 bars; casino; disco; babysitting; free bike usage; kids' programs; gym;

spa; multiple swimming pools; tennis court; free snorkeling and canoeing; free Wi-Fi.

Entertainment & Nightlife

Playa del Coco is one of Costa Rica's liveliest beach towns after dark. Most of the action is centered along a 2-block section of the main road into town, just before you hit the beach. Here you'll find the **Lizard Lounge ★** (© **2670-0307**), which has a raucous party vibe. Just across the street is the large, open-air **Zi Lounge ★★** (www.zilounge.com; © **2670-1978**). For a gringo-influenced sports bar try **Coconutz ★** (www.coconutz-costarica.com; © **2670-1982**), with frequent live bands, DJs, and movie nights. On the south end of the beach, reached via a rickety footbridge over the estuary, you'll find **La Vida Loca ★** (© **2670-0181**), a beachfront bar with a pool table, Ping-Pong table, foosball table, and live bands.

PLAYAS CONCHAL & BRASILITO ★★

280km (174 miles) NW of San José; 67km (42 miles) SW of Liberia

Playa Conchal ★★ is the first in a string of beaches stretching north along this coast. It's almost entirely backed by the massive Westin Playa Conchal resort and Reserva Conchal condominium complex. The unique

Watching the sunset on Playa Conchal

beach here was once made up primarily of soft crushed shells—a shell-collectors' heaven. Unfortunately, as Conchal's popularity spread, unscrupulous builders brought in dump trucks to haul away the name-sake seashells for landscaping and construction, and the impact is, sadly, quite noticeable. The beach is still primarily comprised of crushed bits of polished sea shells, but it's become increasingly hard to find larger pieces or complete shells.

Just beyond Playa Conchal to the north, you'll come to **Playa Brasilito,** a tiny beach town and one of the few real villages in the area. The soccer field is the center of the village, and around its edges are a couple of little *pulperías* (general stores). The long stretch of gray sand beach has a quiet, undiscovered feel to it.

Essentials

GETTING THERE & DEPARTING   By Plane: The nearest airport with regular flights is in Tamarindo (p 268) although it is also possible to fly into Liberia (p 210). From either place, you can arrange for a taxi to drive you to any of these beaches. Playas Brasilito and Conchal are about 25 minutes from Tamarindo and 40 minutes from Liberia. A taxi from Tamarindo should cost around $35 to $50, and between $50 and $70 from Liberia.

Vendors on Playa Conchal beach

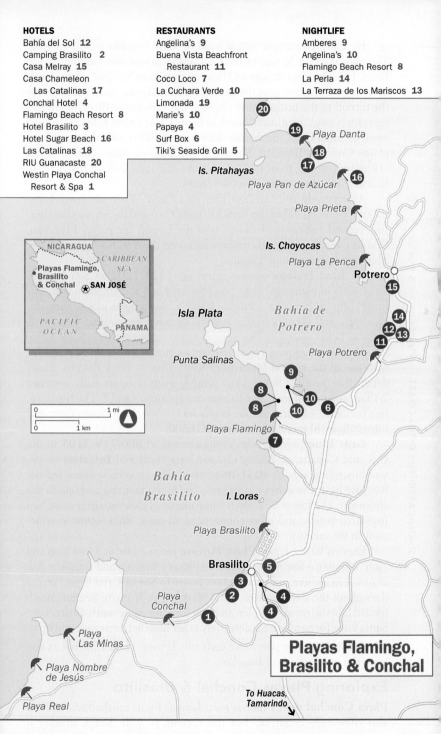

HOTELS

Bahía del Sol **12**
Camping Brasilito **2**
Casa Melray **15**
Casa Chameleon
  Las Catalinas **17**
Conchal Hotel **4**
Flamingo Beach Resort **8**
Hotel Brasilito **3**
Hotel Sugar Beach **16**
Las Catalinas **18**
RIU Guanacaste **20**
Westin Playa Conchal
  Resort & Spa **1**

RESTAURANTS

Angelina's **9**
Buena Vista Beachfront
  Restaurant **11**
Coco Loco **7**
La Cuchara Verde **10**
Limonada **19**
Marie's **10**
Papaya **4**
Surf Box **6**
Tiki's Seaside Grill **5**

NIGHTLIFE

Amberes **9**
Angelina's **10**
Flamingo Beach Resort **8**
La Perla **14**
La Terraza de los Mariscos **13**

20

19 *Playa Danta*

18

17 **16**

Is. Pitahayas

Playa Pan de Azúcar

Playa Prieta

Is. Choyocas

Playa La Penca

Potrero ○

15

NICARAGUA

CARIBBEAN SEA

Playas Flamingo,
Brasilito
& Conchal   ★ SAN JOSÉ

PACIFIC
OCEAN   PANAMA

Isla Plata

*Bahía de
Potrero*

14

12 **13**

11

Punta Salinas

Playa Potrero

9

0 ___ 1 mi
0 ___ 1 km

8

8 **10** **6**

Playa Flamingo

7

*Bahía
Brasilito*

I. Loras

Playa Brasilito

Brasilito ○ **5**

3

2   **4**

*Playa
Conchal*   **4**

1

*Playa
Las Minas*

*Playa Nombre
de Jesús*

Playa Real

Playas Flamingo,
Brasilito & Conchal

*To Huacas,
Tamarindo*

By Car: Two major routes head to these beaches from San José. The most direct is by way of the La Amistad Bridge over the Tempisque River. Take the Inter-American Highway west from San José. Forty-seven kilometers (29 miles) past the turnoff for Puntarenas, you'll see signs for the turnoff to the bridge. After crossing the Tempisque River, follow the signs for Nicoya, continuing north to Santa Cruz. About 16km (10 miles) north of Santa Cruz, just before the village of Belén, take the turnoff for playas Conchal, Brasilito, Flamingo, and Potrero. After another 20km (12 miles), at the town of Huacas, take the right fork to reach these beaches. The drive takes about 4½ hours.

Alternatively, you can drive here via Liberia. When you reach Liberia, turn west and follow the signs for Santa Cruz and the various beaches. Just beyond the town of Belén, take the turnoff for playas Flamingo, Brasilito, and Potrero, and continue following the directions given above. This route takes around 5 hours.

By Bus: **Tralapa** express buses (© **2221-7202** in San José, or 2654-4203 in Flamingo) leave San José daily at 8 and 10:30am and 3pm from Calle 20 between avenidas 3 and 5, stopping at playas Brasilito, Flamingo, and Potrero, in that order. The ride takes around 5 hours. A one-way ticket costs C6,350.

The same company's buses to Santa Cruz (© **2680-0392**) connect with one of the several buses from Santa Cruz to Playa Potrero. Buses depart San José for Santa Cruz roughly every 2 hours daily between 7:15am and 6pm from Calle 20 between avenidas 3 and 5. The trip duration is around 4 hours; the fare is around C5,500. From Santa Cruz, the ride is about 90 minutes; the fare is C1,500.

Gray Line (www.graylinecostarica.com; © **800/719-3105** in the U.S. and Canada, or 2220-2126 in Costa Rica) and **Interbus** (www.interbusonline.com; © **4031-0888**) both have two daily buses leaving San José for the beaches in this area, one in the morning and one in the afternoon. The fare is $54. Both companies will pick you up at most San José–area hotels, and offer connections to most other tourist destinations in the country.

Express buses depart **Playa Potrero** for San José at 3 and 9am and 2pm, stopping a few minutes later in playas Flamingo and Brasilito. Ask at your hotel where to catch the bus. Buses to **Santa Cruz** leave Potrero throughout the day and take about 90 minutes. If you're heading north toward Liberia, get off at Belén and wait for a bus going north. Buses leave Santa Cruz for San José roughly every other hour between 6am and 6pm.

ORIENTATION The pavement ends just beyond Playa Conchal as you leave the small village of Brasilito.

Exploring Playas Conchal & Brasilito

Playa Conchal ★★, which is most famous for its crushed seashells, is also stunningly beautiful, but the dropoff is quite steep, making it

Guest room at The Westin Playa Conchal Resort & Spa

notorious for strong riptides. The water at **Playa Brasilito** is often fairly calm, which makes it a good swimming choice. This is also a great base for visiting other nearby and less popular beaches, like **Playa La Penca ★★** and **Playa Pan de Azúcar ★★**, both of which are north of here.

All the hotels have tour desks offering a range of activity options, including those available in the Flamingo and Potrero area (p 258).

Tip: All beaches in Costa Rica are public property. But the land behind the beaches is not, and the Westin hotel and Reserva Conchal condo development own almost all of it in Playa Conchal, so the only public access is along the soft-sand road that follows the beach south from Brasilito. Before the road reaches Conchal, you'll have to ford a small river and then climb a steep, rocky hill, so four-wheel-drive is recommended.

GOLF   The **Westin Playa Conchal Resort & Spa ★★** (© 2654-4123) is home to the excellent **Reserva Conchal Golf Course.** Robert Trent Jones II designed the course, which features broad open fairways, fast greens, and a few wonderful views of the ocean. It costs $150 in greens fees for 18 holes and $95 for 9 holes. If you tee off after 1pm, you'll be charged $95 for all the rounds you can squeeze in.

WATERSPORTS   You can rent jet skis and Wave Runners on the beach in Playa Conchal from **Conchal Tours** (httwww.conchalfun.com; © 8557-2776). This operation also offers guided snorkel tours to the Catalina

A Day Trip Destination: El Viejo Wetlands

Located a bit inland from the Guanacaste agricultural town of Filadelfia and bordering the Palo Verde National Park, **El Viejo Wildlife Refuge & Wetlands ★★** (www.elviejowetlands.com; ✆ **2296-0966**) is a unique and intriguing option for a day tour. The principal attraction here is the wildlife, which is abundant, and can be viewed from both open-air safari-style vehicles and small boats on the Tempisque River. You'll see scores of water birds and probably a crocodile or two. The main hacienda-style building at the heart of this operation dates to 1870, and is where excellent Costa Rican lunches are served. Additional tour options here include a zipline canopy tour, as well as a tour of the on-site organic farm and sugar cane processing mill, or *trapiche*. Rates run from $63 to $155, depending upon how many activities or tours you take, and whether or not you want lunch.

Islands, as well as wet and wild banana boat rides, where your group gets pulled behind a speedboat on a giant, inflatable, banana-shaped boat, plus nearly every other type of adventure activity in the region.

Where to Stay

EXPENSIVE

Westin Playa Conchal Resort & Spa ★★★   This is among the most appealing large-scale, all-inclusive resorts anywhere in Costa Rica. Not only does it sit on one of the country's prettiest beaches, but its massive, amoeba-like free-form swimming pool is a marvel, meant to mimic a tropical lagoon. (Parents might want to tag their kids with GPS chips so as not to lose them in the many interconnected sections of water.) There are more than a dozen first-rate eating options, with choices for kids, incorporating superfoods into your diet, and candlelight dinners in the sand. Every handsome rooms here is rightly considered a suite and comes with either one king-size or two double beds. All have either a private patio or balcony in front of the sliding-door entrance. For golfers there's a wide, resort-style course with trees and water features that attract a range of local wildlife. One of the lakes is even home to a resident caiman. And golf is just one of the many activities guests can take part in each day.

Playa Conchal. www.westinplayaconchal.com. ✆ **800/937-8461** in the U.S., or 2654-3442. 406 units. $429-$609 and up double; $894-$1,060 suite double; children 3–12 add $90–$185 per child per day; kids 13 and up charged as adults; kids under 3 free. Includes all meals, drinks, taxes, a wide range of activities, and use of non-motorized watersports equipment. Golf and spa services extra. **Amenities:** 11 restaurants; 5 bars; casino; babysitting; bike rental; kids' programs; golf course; exercise facilities and spa; 2 massive pools w/several Jacuzzis; 4 lighted tennis courts; room service; free Wi-Fi.

INEXPENSIVE

A string of inexpensive *cabinas* line the main road leading into Brasilito, just before you hit the beach. It's also possible to camp on playas Potrero and Brasilito. At the former, contact **Camping Mayra** (© **2654-4213**); at the latter, try **Camping Brasilito** (© **2654-4452**). Both of these places offer some budget rooms as well. Each charges around C5,000 per person to make camp and use the basic restroom facilities, or around C15,000 to C30,000 per person to stay in a rustic room.

Conchal Hotel ★★ Burned to the ground in early 2013, the Conchal was quickly rebuilt and is better than ever. Rooms are spacious and feature sturdy steel bed frames, white linens, and whitewashed walls offset with bright primary accents. Superior rooms come with large flatscreen televisions and more space. Most rooms open onto a private or shared balcony or veranda fronting the small central pool and gardens. Despite its name, this hotel really should be considered part of Playa Brasilito, which is about 2 blocks away. Owners Simon and Hilda are delightful and very hands-on. The hotel's tropical fusion **Papaya** ★★ restaurant (p 257) is one of the best in the area.

Playa Brasilito. www.conchalcr.com. © **2654-9125.** 13 units. $105-$140 double; $140 family suite, includes continental breakfast and taxes. Seriously reduced rates available in the off-season. **Amenities:** Restaurant; bar; pool; free Wi-Fi.

Hotel Brasilito ★ This longstanding hotel offers clean, well-kept rooms with wood or tile floors in a pair of two-story wood buildings just a stone's throw from the water. Snag a room with a balcony and you'll be in budget heaven. The owners offer an excellent in-house tour operation. The open-air restaurant, El Oasis, is equally recommendable.

Playa Brasilito. www.brasilito.com. © **2654-4237.** 18 units. $35–$79 double. **Amenities:** Restaurant; free Wi-Fi.

Where to Eat

Tiki's Seaside Grill ★ SEAFOOD A prototypical tropical grill on the main corner in Brasilito, Tiki's is a good all day option with simple yet reliable menu of pub foods like burgers, tacos, and fried coconut shrimp. Additionally, there are the obligatory neon beach cocktails and a dozen local craft beers on tap, plus live music on most Saturdays.

Playa Brasilito. www.tikiscr.com. © **2654-9028.** Reservations recommended in high season. Main courses C5,000–C17,000. Daily 8am–10pm.

Papaya ★★ INTERNATIONAL/SEAFOOD Easily the finest restaurant in the Brasilito/Conchal area, Papaya specializes in Pacific Rim and Nuevo Latino fare. Occupying a large, open-air space overlooking the pool and gardens of the Conchal Hotel, it's also date-night central thanks to its dim lighting and candlelit tables. Either go with a special from the chalkboard or try the fresh mahi-mahi in a coconut crust and local lobster tails seasoned with Chinese five spice. A winner!

Playa Brasilito. © **2654-9125.** Main courses C3,400–C11,400. Thurs–Tues 7am–8:30pm.

Entertainment & Nightlife

Pretty much all the nightlife in Playa Conchal happens at the large Westin resort (p 256), which has a range of bars, nightly entertainment, and a casino. In Brasilito, there might be live music or sporting events on the TVs at **Tiki's Seaside Grille** (℡ **2654-9028**).

PLAYAS FLAMINGO ★★ & POTRERO

285km (176 miles) NW of San José; 71km (44 miles) SW of Liberia

Playa Flamingo ★★ is one of the prettiest beaches in the region. A long, broad stretch of pinkish white sand, it is on a long spit of land that forms part of Potrero Bay. At the northern end of the beach is a high rock outcropping upon which most of Playa Flamingo's hotels and vacation homes are built. This rocky hill has great views.

If you continue along the road from Brasilito without taking the turn for Playa Flamingo, you'll come to **Playa Potrero,** located in a broadly curving bay, protected by the Flamingo headlands. The sand here is a brownish gray, but the beach is long, clean, deserted, and very calm for swimming. You can see the hotels of Playa Flamingo across the bay. Drive

Pool and restaurant at Flamingo Beach Resort.

a little farther north and you'll find the still-underdeveloped beaches of **Playa Prieta ★**, **Playa La Penca ★**, and **Playa Pan de Azúcar ★★**.

Essentials

GETTING THERE & DEPARTING   By Plane: The nearest airport with regular flights is in Tamarindo (p 268), although it is also possible to fly into Liberia (p 210). From either, you can arrange for a taxi to drive you to any of these beaches. Playas Flamingo and Potrero are about 30 minutes from Tamarindo and 45 minutes from Liberia. A taxi from Tamarindo should cost around $40 to $55, and between $60 and $80 from Liberia.

By Bus: For info on reaching these beaches by bus, see p 270.

By Car: See the information for driving to Playas Conchal and Brasilito, p 252. Playa Flamingo is the first beach you'll come to beyond Playa Brasilito. Two prominent turnoffs on your left will take you to the beach, whereas if you continue straight, and follow signs bearing right, you'll soon come to Playa Potrero.

GETTING AROUND   Economy Rent A Car (www.economyrentacar.com; ✆ **2654-4152**) has an office in Playa Flamingo.

Exploring Playas Flamingo & Potrero

Playa Flamingo ★★ is a long and beautiful stretch of soft white sand, although the surf can sometimes get a bit rough. The beach doesn't have much shade, so be sure to use plenty of sunscreen and bring an umbrella if you can. If you're not staying here, parking spots are available all along the beach road—just don't leave anything of value in the car. **Playa Potrero** has much gentler surf and is the better swimming beach. However, the beach is made up of hard-packed dark sand that is much less appealing than that of Playa Flamingo.

A BEACH CLUB   If your hotel doesn't have a pool or beach access, you can always head to **El Coconut Beach Club** (www.elcoconut-tamarindo.com; ✆ **2654-4300**), which has both. It's located right on Playa Potrero. You can enjoy the facilities, as long as you eat and drink at the excellent **Buena Vista Beach Restaurant.**

HORSEBACK RIDING   You can arrange a horseback ride with **Casagua Horses** (www.paintedponyguestranch.com; ✆ **2653-8041**). Depending on the size of your group, it should cost between $25 and $50 per person per hour.

LANGUAGE LEARNING   The **Centro Panamericano de Idiomas** (www.cpi-edu.com; ✆ **2265-6306**), which has schools in San José and Monteverde, has a branch in Flamingo, across from the Flamingo Marina, facing Potrero Bay. A 1-week program in a small group with 4 hours of class per day costs $460, with private tutoring at $30 per hour.

SCUBA DIVING   Scuba diving is quite popular here. **Costa Rica Diving** (www.costarica-diving.com; ☎ **2654-4148**) has a shop in Flamingo and offers trips to the Catalina Island for around $85. You can also check with the **Flamingo Beach Resort ★** (p 262).

SPORTFISHING & SAILBOAT CHARTERS   There are plenty of sportfishing and sailboat charter options here. Jim McKee manages a fleet of boats through his company, **Oso Viejo** (www.flamingobeachcr.com; ☎ **8827-5533** or 2653-8437). A full-day fishing excursion costs between $375 and $2,200, depending on the size and quality of the boat, and the distance traveled. Half-day trips cost between $275 and $700.

If you're looking for a full- or half-day sail or sunset cruise, check in with Oso Viejo to see what boats are available, or ask about the 52-foot cutter *Shannon.* Prices range from around $50 to $120 per person, depending on the length of the cruise. Multiday trips are also available.

Another option is to head down the beach at Playa Potrero to the **Costa Rica Sailing Center** (www.costaricasailing.com; ☎ **8699-7289**), which offers sailing lessons and rentals, with a wide range of small sailcraft to choose from. The center also rents out stand-up paddle boards, kayaks, fishing gear, and snorkel equipment.

WATERSPORTS   You can rent jet skis, boogie boards, skim boards, and stand-up paddle boards on Playa Flamingo from **Playa Vida** (☎ **2654-4444**). This company is on the south side of the Flamingo Beach resort (p 262) and offers guided snorkel tours to the Catalina Islands.

A sailboat cruise near Tamarindo

Live music at the beach bar at Witch's Rock Surf Camp in Tamarindo

If you're interested in stand-up paddling, surfing, or surf lessons, check in at **Point Break Surf School** (www.pointbreaksurf.com; ✆ 8866-4148).

Where to Stay

Along with the places mentioned below, **Casa Melray** ★ (www.casa melray.com; ✆ 2654-4316) is a swank, beachfront B&B (house rental) in Playa Potrero. If you plan to be here for a while or are coming down with friends or a large family, there are numerous condos or houses available for rent in the area. For info and reservations, contact **ETS Costa Rica** (www.etscr.net; ✆ **888/215-3657** in U.S. and Canada, or 2653-7444 in Costa Rica).

MODERATE

Bahía del Sol ★   Mother Nature rules at this small resort, a place beloved by both humans and other critters for its handsome, lush landscaping, in particular the flowering ginger that overflows in the tropical gardens. The hotel is located on a grassy patch of land just in from the center of Playa Potrero, a calm and protected beach with hard-packed, dark gray sand. The interior isn't quite as spectacular: Rooms are simple, with high ceilings and beds that can be too hard. That said, the house-keeping staff is diligent and rooms are fairly priced, particularly the studio apartments with kitchenettes, which are good for families or for longer stays. A very good restaurant is also on the property, as is a small spa. Daily yoga and Pilates classes are included in the rate. This hotel has received "4 Leaves" in the Certification of Sustainable Tourism program.

Playa Potrero. www.bahiadelsolhotel.com. © **866/223-2463** in the U.S. and Canada, or 2654-4671 in Costa Rica. 28 units. $120–$225 double; $240–$410 suite, includes breakfast. **Amenities:** Restaurant; bar; Jacuzzi; pool; room service; spa; free Wi-Fi.

Flamingo Beach Resort ★ This is the only true beachfront hotel in Playa Flamingo. And what it lacks in style and pizzazz, it makes up for in location. You can enjoy sunsets from the second-floor beachfront restaurant and split the day between body-surfing sessions off Playa Flamingo and lounging in the large resort pool. The oceanfront rooms here are the best, though all are large, with tile floors, modern furnishings, and a splash of color provided by locally produced paintings. Some of the suites and family rooms come with kitchenettes, although these are some of the more dated units in the resort. The resort also offers an all-inclusive option, but it's not your best bet.

Playa Flamingo. www.resortflamingobeach.com. © **877/856-5519** in the U.S. and Canada, or 2654-4444 in Costa Rica. 120 units. $145–$255 double; $205–$415 suite. **Amenities:** Restaurant; 2 bars; casino; exercise room; large outdoor pool; room service; small spa; lighted tennis court; watersports equipment rental; free Wi-Fi.

Where to Eat

In addition to the spots below, you also can't go wrong with the rabbit pappardelle or pizza cooked in a wood fired oven at **Angelina's ★★** (www.angelinasplayaflamingo.com; © **2654-4839**), on the second floor of La Plaza shopping center, or at **Buena Vista Beachfront Restaurant ★** (www.elcoconut-tamarindo.com; © **2654-4300;** see "A Beach Club," p 259). For something light and healthy, there's the vegan and organic **La Cuchara Verde ★** (© **2573-0096**), beside the Super Automarket, with veggie burgers, grain bowls, and smoothies.

Coco Loco ★★ COSTA RICAN/SEAFOOD Chef Jean-Luc Taulere, who owned the much beloved but now closed Mar y Sol restaurant, has opened up this casual beachfront bar and restaurant. It has a lovely setting, with teak tables under white canvas umbrellas spread out on the sand at the far southern end of Playa Flamingo. The menu features such items as blackened swordfish wraps, fresh yellowfin tuna tacos, and slow-cooked pork ribs in a pineapple barbeque sauce. Some dishes are served inside a hollowed-out half-coconut, including the fresh ceviche; homemade coconut ice cream; and house specialty Loco Coco, a coconut rice dish featuring mussels, octopus, and fresh-caught snapper, with a Thai-inspired basil, ginger, and lime sauce. Come for a frozen tamarind mojito at sunset (there's an extensive cocktail menu) and stay through the evening; there's often live music after sundown.

South end of Playa Flamingo. www.cocolococostarica.com. © **2654-6242.** Main courses C4,000–C11,900. Daily 11am–9pm.

Marie's ★★ COSTA RICAN/SEAFOOD   Marie has been serving fresh, fairly priced food here for decades, and her restaurant is justifiably popular. She's still running the show, which means the menu thankfully hasn't changed from burritos and quesadillas, plus simply grilled fish or slow cooked baby-back ribs. The large, open-air restaurant features extremely high thatched roofs with slow-turning ceiling fans.

Playa Flamingo. http://mariesrestaurantcostarica.com. © **2654-4136.** Main courses C5,000–C12,000. Daily 6:30am–9:30pm.

Surf Box ★★ CAFÉ   Cute and colorful, this Instagram-friendly breakfast and brunch spot run by an expat couple is like an updated Jewish deli, but redesigned for the tropics. Start with the fresh fruit smoothies before moving to the açai bowls, shakshuka, Montreal style bagel sandwiches, or Challah French toast. There are some of the best coffee drinks in Guanacaste, including matcha lattes and cold brews. There's both air-conditioned indoor and shaded outdoor seating available.

Playa Flamingo. www.mariesrestaurantincostarica.com. © **8437-7128.** Main courses C4,500–C7,000. Mon-Fri 7:30am–3:30pm; Sat-Sun 8am-1pm.

Entertainment & Nightlife

With both a disco and casino, **Amberes** (http://amberescostarica.com; © **2654-4001**), slightly up the hill at the north end of town, is the undisputed hot spot in this area; however, **Flamingo Beach Resort** ★ (p 262) also has a casino. You'll find a mellower bar and lounge scene at the bar of **Angelina's** ★ (p 262), or on the beach at **Coco Loco** (see above).

In Potrero, there is **Perlas** ★★ (http://perlas.pub; © **2654-4500**), a simple concrete slab building with a corrugated zinc roof and mostly open walls that has been nicely decorated. Located on a dusty corner, this is a very typical Costa Rican–style cantina, but it draws a good mixed crowd of locals, expats, and tourists alike.

LAS CATALINAS ★

259km (161 miles) NW of San José; 52km (32 miles) SW of Liberia

Still a few years from completion, Las Catalinas is an entire posh beach town being designed by a group of developers. The core of the city—an almost Mediterranean-like grid of winding, cobblestone streets lined with clay-tile topped townhouses—is intact and a beach club, a few restaurants, and the first of two planned hotels are up and running. Up in the hills more houses and residential developments are being built, as well as a school. Sustainability is a key feature here and the development includes a major reforestation project and wastewater management.

Essentials

GETTING THERE & DEPARTING   By Plane: The nearest airport to Las Catalinas is in Tamarindo (p 268), although it is also possible to fly into

Liberia (p 210). From either of these places, you can arrange for a taxi to drive you to Las Catalinas. Playa Grande is about 15 minutes from Tamarindo and 45 minutes from Liberia. A taxi from Tamarindo should cost $40 to $55; between $60 and $80 from Liberia.

By Car: The most direct route to Las Catalinas is by heading north for 4 km on Camino las Catalinas from CR911 at Playa Portrero.

Exploring Las Catalinas

Playa Danta and Playa Dantita ★ The wide Playa Danta extends for the length of Las Catalinas town and is quite calm, though there's some boogie boarding going on at high tide. Playa Dantita, to the north, is more secluded.

HIKING Las Catalinas is surrounded by hills through a patch of rare tropical dry forest, which is conveniently marked with 25 km of hiking, biking, and horseback riding trails. Contact **Pura Vida Ride** (✆ 2654-6137; www.puravidaride.com) for tour information or equipment rental.

WATER SPORTS Las Catalinas is the home base of **Connect Ocean** (http://connectocean.com), an international marine awareness, research, and education organization. They are very active in the community here and frequently hold events around town. For adventure sports, **Pura Vida Ride** ★★ (✆ 2654-6137; www.puravidaride.com) on the waterfront can arrange kayaking, stand-up paddleboarding, surf lessons, sailing lessons, and snorkeling. Just off shore are the Las Catalinas islands, which are one of Costa Rica's most renowned diving sites, to where they also run trips.

Where to Stay

Casa Chameleon Las Catalinas ★★ Perched on the hilltop on the southern end of Las Catalinas, Casa Chameleon offers up stunning views of one of Costa Rica's prettiest stretches of shoreline. The minimalist villas are decorated with eclectic furnishings and decked out with smart electronics. Each room has a mini bar stocked with Costa Rican products, a private salt water plunge pool, and a balcony with endless views that make it truly hard to leave. The hotel's restaurant, Sentido Norte ★, focuses on healthy, ingredient driven dishes. While there is no formal spa, yoga and massage treatments can de organized in each villa. Las Catalinas. www.casachameleonhotels.com. ✆ **800/808-4605** in the U.S. and Canada, or 2653-1636 in Costa Rica. 21 units. $299–$475 villas. **Amenities:** Restaurant; bar; outdoor pool; free Wi-Fi.

Las Catalinas ★★★ Studios to seven bedroom townhouses, not to mention the occasional shop or restaurant, line the cobblestone streets that form the town center of La Catalinas. Complete with a concierge staff, the houses are individually decorated—though all rather extravagant—and have full kitchens, patios, and some even have small pools (though there are larger ones at the beach club). Rates are discounted for longer stays.

Playa Danta. www.lascatalinascr.com. © **866/-357-3872** or 4020-1075 in Costa Rica. 38 units. From $250 and up studios; $350 and up houses. **Amenities:** Restaurant; bar; beach club access; pools in some; free Wi-Fi.

Where to Eat

Aside of the restaurant below, there is a casual restaurant beside the beach club and **Sentido Norte** ★, the restaurant at Casa Chameleon, is a great place for a sunset dinner or cocktail.

Limonada ★ INTERNATIONAL This bustling, two-level sidewalk bar and grill, with picnic tables spilling out into the sand and illuminated by strings of lights, is the first restaurant to open in the expanding Las Catalinas project. The food is simple yet hearty and well prepared, with whole fried red snapper, burgers and fish tacos. It has a juice and cocktail bar as well, with a long list of creations that utilize local fruits and herbs. Also, if you catch a fish out at sea, they'll cook it for you.

Playa Danta. © **2654-6150.** Main courses C4,500–C14,500. Daily 7:30am–8:30pm.

PLAYA GRANDE ★★

295km (183 miles) NW of San José; 70km (43 miles) SW of Liberia

Playa Grande is one of the principal nesting sites for the giant leatherback turtle, the largest turtle in the world. The beach is a long, straight stretch of soft, golden sand that boasts a well-formed and consistent beach break with surfable waves along its entire length. When the surf is up, the beach can be a bit rough for casual swimming. Playa Grande is relatively undeveloped, but the steady influx of tourists is severely threatening its status as a turtle nesting site. For help locating the following hotels, restaurants, and attractions, see the map "Around Tamarindo" on p 271.

Essentials

GETTING THERE & DEPARTING   By Plane: The nearest airport with regularly scheduled flights is in Tamarindo (p 268), although it is also possible to fly into Liberia (p 210). From either of these places, you can arrange for a taxi to drive you to Playa Grande. Playa Grande is about 15 minutes from Tamarindo and 45 minutes from Liberia. A taxi from Tamarindo should cost $35 to $45; between $60 and $80 from Liberia.

By Car: See the information for driving to Tamarindo on p 270. The dirt and gravel entrance roads to Playa Grande are located along CR155 between Tamarindo and Huacas.

Exploring Playa Grande

Leatherback sea turtles nest on Playa Grande between early October and mid-February. The turtles come ashore to lay their eggs only at night.

Fishermen in Playa Grande

During the nesting season, you'll be inundated with opportunities to sign up for nightly tours, which usually cost $35 to $60 per person. No flash photography or flashlights are allowed because any sort of light can confuse the turtles and prevent them from laying their eggs; guides must use red-tinted flashlights.

Note: Turtle nesting is a natural, unpredictable, and increasingly rare event. Sadly, things have gotten worse here over the years. All indications are that excessive building and lighting close to the beach are the culprits. With a limited nesting season, the annual numbers of nesting turtles fluctuate wildly year to year. Even during heavy nesting years, you sometimes have to wait your turn for hours, hike quite a way, and accept the possibility that no nesting mothers may be spotted that evening.

If your hotel can't set a tour up for you, you'll see signs all over town offering tours. Make sure you go with someone licensed and reputable. Do-it-yourselfers can drive over to Playa Grande and book a $30 tour directly with the **National Parks Service** (© **2653-0470**). The Parks Service operates out of a small shack just before the beach, across from the Hotel Las Tortugas (below). It opens each evening at around 6pm to begin taking reservations. The phone is sometimes answered during the day, but it's best to make a reservation in advance because only a limited number of people are allowed on the beach at one time. Spots fill up fast, and if you don't have a reservation, you may have to wait until really late, or you may not be able to go out on the beach at all.

Where to Stay

In addition to the places listed below, **Hotel Bula Bula** ★ (www.hotel bulabula.com; ☎ 877/658-2880 in the U.S. and Canada, or 2653-0975 in Costa Rica) is an excellent inland option, while the **Playa Grande Surf Camp** (www.playagrandesurfcamp.com; ☎ 2653-1074) is geared toward surfers and budget travelers.

Hotel Las Tortugas ★   Owner and local surf legend Louis Wilson came to Costa Rica decades ago for the waves. He's stayed and still surfs, but has also been a leading figure in creating a protected habitat for the nesting sea turtles. The hotel sits right at the center of Playa Grande, near some of the best breaks, and is quite popular with surfers. Some guests complain about the lack of ocean view at this beachfront hotel; however, a natural barrier of trees and shrubs is a deliberate measure to block artificial light from reaching the beach, as it confuses and scares off turtles. Rooms vary greatly in size and comfort level. All have a/c, and the main lodge rooms boast cool, smooth, local-stone floors and interesting accents like clear glass blocks used in walls. Economy rancho rooms, on the other hand, feel a little small and dormlike, with bunk beds and limited natural light. The hotel also rents and manages fully equipped apartments and condos.

Playa Grande. www.lastortugashotel.com. ☎ 2653-0423 or 2653-0458. 11 units. $50 economy room; $90 double; $120 suite. **Amenities:** Restaurant; bar; Jacuzzi; small outdoor pool; free Wi-Fi.

Rip Jack Inn ★   These are some of the most comfortable and best-equipped rooms in Playa Grande, particularly the deluxe rooms and suites, with their wall-mounted air-conditioning units; hardwood beds; and wall hangings from Bali, Indonesia, and India. The hotel itself is about a block from the beach. Daily yoga and Pilates classes are offered in a large space here. There's a refreshing but very small pool, and the hotel's second-floor restaurant is one of the best in town, serving healthy fare and sushi.

Playa Grande. www.ripjackinn.com. ☎ 800/808-4605 in the U.S. and Canada, or 2653-1636 in Costa Rica. 21 units. $100–$150 double; $250 suite. **Amenities:** Restaurant; bar; lap pool; free Wi-Fi.

Where to Eat

Dining options are pretty limited in Playa Grande, but it's worth trying **Upstairs** ★, the restaurant at the Rip Jack Inn (see above); or the **Great Waltini's** ★, at the Hotel Bula Bula (above). Both serve fresh seafood and prime meats, cooked with care. You might also try the **Taco Star** (no phone) a simple open-air beachfront joint serving up fresh fish tacos and other Mexican favorites. For breakfast, head to **Mamasa** (www.mamasa restaurant.com; ☎ 8445-1797) for its eggs Benedict with a jalapeño hollandaise, filling breakfast burritos, and homemade bagels.

PLAYA TAMARINDO ★ & PLAYA LANGOSTA ★★

295km (183 miles) NW of San José; 73km (45 miles) SW of Liberia

Tamarindo is the biggest boomtown in Guanacaste, and many say the boom has gone too far, too fast. The main road into Tamarindo, sometimes featuring bumper-to-bumper traffic, is a helter-skelter jumble of strip malls, surf shops, hotels, and restaurants. Ongoing development is spreading up the hills inland from the beach and south to Playa Langosta. None of it is regulated or particularly well planned out.

Still, abundant accommodations and restaurants, and active nightlife, along with very dependable surf, have established Tamarindo as one of the most popular beaches on this coast. The beautiful beach here is a long, wide swath of white sand that curves from one rocky headland to another. Fishing boats bob at their moorings and brown pelicans skim the water's surface just beyond the breakers. Tamarindo is very popular with surfers, who ply the break here or use the town as a jumping-off place for beach and point breaks at playas Grande, Langosta, Avellanas, and Negra.

Essentials

GETTING THERE & DEPARTING   By Plane: Both **Nature Air** (www. natureair.com; ✆ **800/235-9272** in the U.S. and Canada, or 2299-6000)

Playa Tamarindo

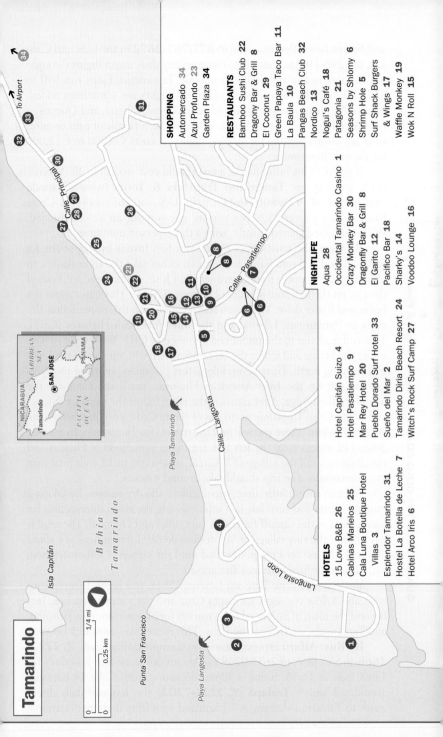

Tamarindo

Isla Capitán

Bahía Tamarindo

PACIFIC OCEAN

Punta San Francisco

Playa Tamarindo

Playa Langosta

To Airport

NICARAGUA
CARIBBEAN SEA
★ SAN JOSÉ
Tamarindo
PACIFIC OCEAN
PANAMA

Calle Principal
Calle Pasatiempo
Calle Langosta
Langosta Loop

0   1/4 mi
0   0.25 km

HOTELS

15 Love B&B **26**
Cabinas Marielos **25**
Cala Luna Boutique Hotel
Villas **3**
Esplendor Tamarindo **31**
Hostel La Botella de Leche **7**
Hotel Arco Iris **6**
Hotel Capitán Suizo **4**
Hotel Pasatiempo **9**
Mar Rey Hotel **20**
Pueblo Dorado Surf Hotel **33**
Sueño del Mar **2**
Tamarindo Diria Beach Resort **24**
Witch's Rock Surf Camp **27**

SHOPPING

Automercado **34**
Azul Profundo **23**
Garden Plaza **34**

RESTAURANTS

Bamboo Sushi Club **22**
Dragony Bar & Grill **8**
El Coconut **29**
Green Papaya Taco Bar **11**
La Baula **10**
Pangas Beach Club **32**
Nordico **13**
Nogui's Café **18**
Patagonia **21**
Seasons by Shlomy **6**
Shrimp Hole **5**
Surf Shack Burgers
& Wings **17**
Waffle Monkey **19**
Wok N Roll **15**

NIGHTLIFE

Aqua **28**
Occidental Tamarindo Casino **1**
Crazy Monkey Bar **30**
Dragonfly Bar & Grill **8**
El Garito **12**
Pacifico Bar **18**
Sharky's **14**
Voodoo Lounge **16**

and **Sansa** (www.flysansa.com; ☏ **877/767-2672** in the U.S. and Canada, or 2290-4100 in Costa Rica) have several daily direct flights throughout the day to the small airstrip outside Tamarindo. Fares run $90 to $155. During the high season, additional flights are sometimes added. Nature Air also connects Tamarindo and Arenal, Liberia, and Quepos.

Whether you arrive on Sansa or Nature Air, a couple of cabs or minivans are always waiting for arriving flights. It costs C9,000 to C12,000 for the ride into town.

If you're flying into Liberia, a taxi should cost around $120. Alternatively, you can use **Tamarindo Transfers & Tours** (www.tamarindo shuttle.com; ☏ **929/800-4621** in the U.S., or 2653-4444 in Costa Rica), which charges $20 per person, one-way for an air-conditioned, Wi-Fi equipped shared shuttle, with a three-person minimum.

By Car: The most direct route from San José is by way of the La Amistad bridge. From San José, you can either take the Inter-American Highway (CR1) north from downtown San José, or first head west out of the city on the San José–Caldera Highway (CR27). This latter route is a faster and flatter drive. When you reach Caldera on this route, follow the signs to Puntarenas, Liberia, and the Inter-American Highway (CR1). This will lead you to the unmarked entrance to CR1. You'll want to pass under the bridge and follow the on-ramp, which will put you on the highway heading north. Forty-seven kilometers (29 miles) north of the Puntarenas exit on the Inter-American Highway, you'll see signs for the turnoff to the bridge. After crossing the river, follow the signs for Nicoya and Santa Cruz. Continue north out of Santa Cruz, until just before the village of Belén, where you will find the turnoff for Tamarindo. In another 20km (12 miles), take the left fork for Playa Tamarindo at Huacas and continue on until the village of Villareal, where you make your final turn into Tamarindo. The trip should take around 4 hours.

You can save a little time, especially in the dry season, by taking a rougher route: You turn left just after passing the main intersection for Santa Cruz at the turnoff for playas Junquillal and Ostional. The road is paved until the tiny village of Veintesiete de Abril. From here, it's about 20km (12 miles) on a rough dirt road until the village of Villareal, where you make your final turn into Tamarindo.

You can also drive here via Liberia. When you reach Liberia, turn west and follow the signs for Santa Cruz and the various beaches. Just beyond the town of Belén, take the turnoff for playas Flamingo, Brasilito, and Tamarindo, and follow the signs. This route takes around 5 hours.

By Bus: Alfaro express buses (www.empresaalfaro.com; ☏ **2222-2666** in San José, or 2653-0268 in Tamarindo) leave San José daily for Tamarindo at 11:30am and 3:30pm, departing from Calle 14 between avenidas 3 and 5. **Tralapa** (☏ **2221-7202**) also has two daily direct buses to Tamarindo leaving at 7:15am and 4pm from their main terminal

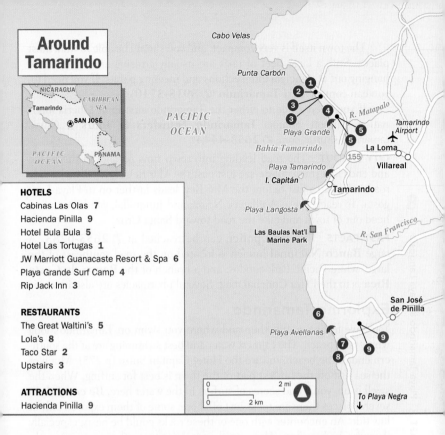

Around Tamarindo

HOTELS
Cabinas Las Olas **7**
Hacienda Pinilla **9**
Hotel Bula Bula **5**
Hotel Las Tortugas **1**
JW Marriott Guanacaste Resort & Spa **6**
Playa Grande Surf Camp **4**
Rip Jack Inn **3**

RESTAURANTS
The Great Waltini's **5**
Lola's **8**
Taco Star **2**
Upstairs **3**

ATTRACTIONS
Hacienda Pinilla **9**

at Calle 20 between avenidas 3 and 5. The trip takes around 5 hours, and the one-way fare is around C5,800.

You can also catch a bus to Santa Cruz from either of the above bus companies. Buses leave both stations for Santa Cruz roughly every 2 hours between 6am and 6pm. The 4-hour, one-way trip is around C5,800. Buses leave Santa Cruz for Tamarindo roughly every 1½ hours between 5:45am and 10pm; the one-way fare is around C700.

Gray Line (www.graylinecostarica.com; ✆ **800/719-3105** in the U.S. and Canada, or 2220-2126 in Costa Rica) and **Interbus** (www. interbusonline.com; ✆ **4031-0888**) have two daily buses leaving San José for Tamarindo (one in the morning, one in the afternoon); the fare is $54. Both companies will pick you up at most San José-area hotels, and offer connections to other major tourist destinations in Costa Rica.

Direct buses leave Tamarindo for San José daily at 3:30 and 5:30am (except on Sun) and 2 and 4pm. Buses to Santa Cruz leave roughly every 2 hours between 4:30am and 8:30pm. In Santa Cruz, you can transfer to one of the frequent San José buses.

GETTING AROUND Adobe (✆ **2542-4800**) and all the multinational chains have rental car offices in Tamarindo.

The town itself is very compact, and you should be able to walk most places. Still, a large fleet of taxis are usually cruising around town, or hanging out at principal intersections and meeting points. If you need to, you can contact **Taxi Tamarindo** (✆ **8918-3710**).

If you need a ride to either the Tamarindo airstrip or Liberia international airport, contact **Tamarindo Transfers & Tours ★** (www. tamarindoshuttle.com; ✆ **2653-4444**).

CITY LAYOUT   The road leading into town runs parallel to the beach and ends in a small cul-de-sac just past the Mar Rey Hotel. A major side road, a left turn just before the Mar Rey, leads farther on to Playa Langosta. To reach playas Avellanas, Negra, and Junquillal, you have to first head out of town and take the road toward Santa Cruz.

FAST FACTS   The local **police** can be reached at ✆ **2653-0283**. A large **Banco Nacional** branch is located on the road southeast of the large, white Pacific Park condos, and a branch of the **Banco de Costa Rica** is in the Plaza Conchal mall. Several pharmacies are also in town.

Exploring Tamarindo

You have to be careful when and where you swim on Tamarindo's long white-sand beach. The calmest water and best swimming are at the southern end of the beach, toward the Hotel Capitán Suizo (p 275). Much of the sea just off the busiest part of the town is best for surfing. When the swell is up, you'll find scores of surfers in the water here. *Be careful:* In several places there are rocks just offshore, some of them exposed only at low tide. An encounter with one of these rocks could be nasty, especially if you're bodysurfing. Also, avoid swimming near the estuary mouth, where there are two dangers: strong currents and crocodiles.

Tamarindo has a host of good tour operators. The best are **Xplore CR ★** (www.xplorecostarica.com; ✆ **844/278-6877** in U.S. and Canada; 2653-4130 in Costa Rica), **Tamarindo Transfers & Tours ★** (www. tamarindoshuttle.com; ✆ **2653-4444**), and **Iguana Surf** (www.iguana surf.net; ✆ **2653-0613**). All offer a range of half- and full-day trips, including outboard or kayak tours through the nearby estuary and mangroves, excursions to Santa Cruz and Guaitíl, raft floats on the Corobicí River, and tours of Palo Verde and Rincón de la Vieja national parks. Rates run between $50 and $200, varying by the length of the tour and group size. All the hotel desks and tour operators here offer **turtle nesting tours ★★★** to Playa Grande (p 265), in season, or you can contact **ACOTAM** (✆ **2653-1687**), a specialized local operator.

Yo Quiero Hablar Español

If you want to try an intensive immersion program or just brush up on your rusty high school Spanish, check in with the folks at **Wayra Instituto de Español** (www.spanish-wayra.co.cr; ✆ **2653-0359**). The school is located up a side street from the dirt road that connects Tamarindo to Playa Langosta.

Guest room and guanacaste tree at Hotel Capitán Suizo in Tamarindo

CANOPY TOURS   No canopy tour is available right in Tamarindo, but the **Monkey Jungle Canopy Tour** (www.canopymonkeyjungle.com; ℂ 2653-1172) and **Cartagena Canopy Tour ★** (ℂ 2675-0801) are nearby. Both charge $50 per person and include transportation from Tamarindo. Of these two, the Monkey Jungle operation is much closer, but the Cartagena tour has a much more lush forest setting. But your best bet in this region is to take a day trip to Hacienda Guachipelín (p 224) and do the zipline and canyoning tours there.

FOUR-WHEELING   **Arenas Adventure Tours ★** (www.tamarindo aventuras.com; ℂ 2653-0108) offers a variety of guided ATV tours from 1 to 3 hours and from $45 to $140 per person. The company also rents dirt bikes, snorkel equipment, surf and boogie boards, and jet skis, and offers a full menu of other guided tours around the region.

GOLF   **Hacienda Pinilla ★★** (www.haciendapinilla.com; ℂ 2681-4500) is an eye-candy 18-hole course located south of Tamarindo. Greens fees run around $150 for 18 holes, including a cart, with discounts for guests staying at Hacienda Pinilla or the JW Marriott resort. Many people staying in Tamarindo also play at the **Westin Playa Conchal Resort & Spa ★★**, an excellent resort course (p 256).

HORSEBACK RIDING Look up **Casagua Horses** ★ (www.painted ponyguestranch.com; ✆ **2653-8041** or 8871-9266). Rates for horse rental, with a guide, are around $25 and $40 per hour.

SAILBOAT CHARTERS Several boats offer cruises from Tamarindo, many of them with an open bar. Catch a ride on the 80-foot schooner *Antares,* built in 1947 (www.tamarindosailing.net; ✆ 8587-3095), or try the 40-foot catamaran **Blue Dolphin** ★ (www.bluedolphinsailing.com; ✆ **855/842-3204** in the U.S., or 8842-3204 in Costa Rica) or 66-foot catamaran **Marlin del Rey** (www.marlindelrey.com; ✆ **877/827-8275** in the U.S., or 2653-1212 in Costa Rica). A half-day snorkel or shorter sunset cruise should cost $75 to $85 per person, and a full day should run between $100 and $150. This usually includes an open bar and snacks on the half-day and sunset cruises, and all of that plus lunch on the full-day trip.

SCUBA DIVING For scuba diving or snorkeling, check with **Agua Rica Diving Center** ★ (www.aguarica.net; ✆ **2653-0094**), the best and longest-running operator in Tamarindo. This is a full-service shop offering day trips, multiday dive cruises, and resort- and full-certification courses.

SPORTFISHING A host of captains offer anglers a chance to go after the "big ones" that abound in the offshore waters. From the Tamarindo estuary, it takes only 20 minutes to reach the edge of the continental shelf, where the waters are filled with mostly marlin and sailfish. Although fishing is good all year, the peak season for billfish is between mid-April and August. Contact **Tamarindo Sportfishing** (www.tamarindosportfishing. com; ✆ **2653-0090**), **Capullo Sportfishing** ★ (www.capullo.com; ✆ **2653-0048**), or **Osprey Sportfishing** (www.osprey-sportfishing. com; ✆ **8754-9292**).

WATERSPORTS If you want to try snorkeling, surfing, or sea kayaking in Tamarindo, **Agua Rica Diving Center, Iguana Surf,** and **Arenas Adventure Tours** (p 273) rent all the necessary equipment. They have half-day and hourly rates for many of these items.

Tamarindo has a host of surf shops and surf schools, if you want to learn to catch a wave while in town. Tamarindo's got a great wave to learn on, although it can get very crowded at the popular beginners' breaks. For gear and lessons, try **Tamarindo Surf School** (www.tamarindosurf school.com; ✆ **2653-0923**), **Kelly's Surf Shop** ★ (www.kellyssurf shop.com; ✆ **2653-1355**), or **Witch's Rock Surf Camp** ★ (www. witchsrocksurfcamp.com; ✆ **888/318-7873** in the U.S. and Canada, or 2653-1238 in Costa Rica).

WELLNESS CENTERS Most of the higher-end hotels have their own spas, and most hotels can call you a massage therapist. But if you're looking for a local day spa experience, try **Cocó Beauty Spa** (www.coco beautyspa.com; ✆ **2653-2562**), which has a wide range of treatments and packages, from facials and pedicures to hot stone massages. Alternately, you can head about 15 to 20 minutes inland to boutique hotel and spa **Los Altos de Eros** ★ (www.losaltosdeeros.com; ✆ **800/391-1944** in the U.S. and Canada or 8850-4222 in Costa Rica) for one of its signature, full-day experiences.

For a good yoga session, contact **Ser Om Shanti Yoga Studio** (www.seryogastudio.com; ✆ **8951-6236**).

Especially For Kids

Bolas Locas Mini Golf (www.bolaslocas.com; ✆ **2653-1178;** daily 9am–11pm), located next to Dragonfly Bar & Grill (p 280), is a nice change from the beach and pool. This 18-hole course features a wave wall, a waterfall, and a traditional Costa Rican oxcart as obstacles. A round of golf costs $8 for adults, $6 for children under 10.

Where to Stay

In addition to the hotels listed below, Tamarindo, Playa Langosta, and Playa Grande have a wide range of beach houses and condos for rent by the night, the week, or the month. For more information on this option, check out **RE/MAX Tamarindo** (www.remax-oceansurf-cr.com; ✆ **866/976-8898** in the U.S. and Canada, or 2653-0073 in Costa Rica) or **RPM Vacation Rentals** ★ (www.rpmvacationrentals.com; ✆ **2653-0738**). You'll also find many options on VRBO.com and Airbnb.com.

EXPENSIVE

Aside of those mentioned below, the area's largest all-inclusive resort is the 198-room Occidental Tamarindo (www.barcelo.com; ✆ **2653-0363**), previously called the Barceló Langosta Beach.

Cala Luna Boutique Hotel & Villas ★★ By far the most luxurious option in Tamarindo, Cala Luna offers beautiful guest rooms done in warm tones with a stone-wash effect on the walls. Sawed-off tree trunks are used as nightstands, and sea shells and driftwood are incorporated into the decor. However, the real draws here are the two- and three-bedroom villas, each with its own private kidney-shaped swimming pool, a large and fully equipped kitchen, ample living and dining areas, and a washer and dryer. Playa Langosta is reached via a short private path across a dirt road, and Tamarindo is a short taxi ride or a 15-minute walk away. The hotel's grounds and gardens are lushly landscaped, and it's not uncommon to spot howler monkeys in the trees.

Playa Langosta. www.calaluna.com. ✆ **800/774-7729** in the U.S. and Canada, or 2653-0214 in Costa Rica. 20 units, 16 villas. $208–$431 double; $402–$766 villa. Rates for rooms, but not villas, include breakfast. **Amenities:** 2 restaurants; bar; babysitting; pool w/poolside bar; room service; watersports equipment rental; free Wi-Fi.

Hotel Capitán Suizo ★★★ Built in 1995 and owned by Ursula Schmid of Switzerland, this luxury hotel on the quieter southern end of

Tamarindo Beach has top-notch service, and the rooms are large, well-kept, and thoroughly inviting. Most feature colonial-style terra cotta floors and four-poster canopy beds. Private balconies and patios open onto exuberant tropical gardens, where monkeys are common visitors. The hotel's zero-entry, free-form pool is one of the largest and best in town, with a rope swing for a touch of playfulness, and a large children's section. This hotel is great for families and honeymooners alike. Rooms don't have TVs, if that matters, but all have air-conditioning. The restaurant is excellent, the gardens are large and lush, and the beach in front is beautiful.

On the road between Tamarindo and Playa Langosta. www.hotelcapitansuizo.com. ☏ **2653-0075** or 2653-0075. 28 units and 6 bungalows. $275 double; $430 bungalow; $430–$665 suite, includes taxes and breakfast buffet. **Amenities:** Restaurant; bar; outdoor pool and children's pool; spa; free Wi-Fi.

Tamarindo Diria Beach Resort ★

This resort may be a victim of its own success, having grown just a bit too big, and service and upkeep can suffer at times. Many of the beds are too hard, the Wi-Fi is spotty, and some of the rooms need updating. Still, the Diria has arguably the best location of any hotel in Tamarindo, a short walk to all of the town's restaurants and shops in one direction, a hop to the beach in the other. The landscaping is still lovely, with tall sea grape trees and coconut palms providing shade and the thatched roofs over the restaurant and bar areas giving the resort a tropical feel. The original hotel rooms are beachfront, just steps away from the waves, and the third-floor sunset rooms offer up sensational ocean and sunset views from their private balconies.

Tamarindo beachfront. www.tamarindodiria.com. ☏ **866/603-4742** in the U.S. and Canada, or 4032-0032 in Costa Rica. 250 units. $155–$225 double; $350 suite, includes breakfast buffet. **Amenities:** 6 restaurants; 3 bars; 4 swimming pools; free Wi-Fi.

MODERATE

In addition to the places listed here, tennis lovers (or just lovers) should check out the **15 Love Bed & Breakfast ★** (www.15lovebedandbreakfast. com; ☏ **2653-0898**.

Esplendor Tamarindo ★★

This cushy Wyndham resort gets its wow factor from the spectacular view of Tamarindo Bay from the infinity pool, though the distance from town and the beach can be a downside. It has three towers with five floors each, and all 104 rooms have an ocean view. Great place for sunset cocktails.

Tamarindo, from the Banco Nacional 200m east and 800m north. www.esplendor tamarindo.com. ☏ **4700-4747**. 104 units. $132–$260 double, includes breakfast. Pet-friendly, depending on size. **Amenities:** Restaurant; bar; infinity pool; ocean view; free Wi-Fi.

Hotel Arco Iris ★★

The charm quotient is high at this little complex of rooms and bungalows located about a 5-minute walk from the beach.

Much of that has to do with the attentiveness of Richard Resnick, the U.S. owner and his staff, who make all the guests feel like VIPs. The rooms are immaculate, featuring white travertine tile floors and pure white linens and bedcovers on beds with hardwood and woven bamboo headboards (and in-room minibars). There's a small pool, and the restaurant here, **Seasons By Shlomy** (p 281), is excellent.

Tamarindo, 50m east and 100m south of the Banco Nacional. www.hotelarcoiris. com. ℂ **2653-0330**. 13 units. $129–$165 double, includes breakfast. **Amenities:** Restaurant; bar; small outdoor pool; free Wi-Fi.

Sueño del Mar ★★   This intimate bed-and-breakfast, in a quiet setting on Playa Langosta, has a loyal following that comes back year after year for the personalized service, gorgeous sunsets, and spectacular breakfasts. It's a great spot for a once-in-a-lifetime romantic occasion like a wedding or honeymoon. The Luna Suite is the prime room in the house and is worth the splurge if it's available—it's a second-floor unit with wrap-around windows facing the sea and an open-air shower that also shares the view. The standard rooms also have cute open-air showers with small gardens and plantings providing privacy. Hammocks are strung under shade trees, and wooden chairs in the sand facing the waves are where guests gather every evening to toast the sunset.

Playa Langosta. www.sueno-del-mar.com. ℂ **2653-0284**. 4 units, 2 casitas. $205 double; $230–$310 suite or casita, includes breakfast. Children 13 and over only. **Amenities:** Small pool; free use of snorkel equipment and boogie boards; free Wi-Fi.

INEXPENSIVE

Cabinas Marielos ★   This longstanding, family-run budget hotel is located right across from the beach near the entrance to town. Owner Maria de los Angeles ("Marielos") Gonzalez and her children run a tight ship, meaning rooms are neat as a pin. They come either with fans or air-conditioning, and a few even have kitchenettes. The best rooms here are the second-floor units with private balconies. Although right near the center of all the action and just steps from the sand, the gardens and grounds here create a quiet oasis amid all the tumult of Tamarindo.

On the left as you enter Tamarindo from the north. www.cabinasmarieloscr.com. ℂ **2653-0141**. 24 units. $55–$80 double, includes taxes. **Amenities:** Surfboard and boogies rentals; free Wi-Fi.

Hostel La Botella de Leche★★   This cool hostel is back on the map, with a renewed emphasis on customer service. Manuel Fontana of Argentina, who bought the quaint blue hostel in 2015, says there are three pillars essential to running a hostel: hardware (air-conditioning and bathrooms in all the rooms, though no hot water); soul (decoration, lighting, music); and service (24/7 reception, very attentive management). And in case you're wondering, the hostel, established in 2000, was named after the Milk Bottle Motel in the 1996 John Travolta movie "Michael." It occasionally hosts surf or cross fit camps.

50m east of the Banco Nacional. www.labotelladeleche.com. © **2653-0189.** 12 units, 6 more planned. $50–$60 for private rooms for 2, dorms $15–$20, depending on season. **Amenities:** Swimming pool, concierge service, free Wi-Fi.

Hotel Pasatiempo ★★ This small resort, located a few blocks inland from the water, offers rooms that are spacious and well maintained, with cool tile floors and a relaxed, tropical decor. Each room is named after a local beach, and they all come with a hammock, chaise lounge, or wooden Adirondack chairs on a private patio. The large central pool is quite inviting, with a broad natural-stone and wooden deck area encircling it and tall shade trees all around. The hotel's poolside bar and restaurant is one of the livelier spots in town (with frequent live music and open-mic nights), so this is not the best spot to come for peace and quiet.

Tamarindo. www.hotelpasatiempo.com. © **2653-0096.** 22 units. $86–$95 double; $105 suite, includes breakfast. **Amenities:** Restaurant; bar; pool; free Wi-Fi.

Mar Rey Hotel ★ For more than 40 years, the Martinez and Reyes families have run this budget favorite under the name Zullymar, but they recently decided on a rebranding that combines the two family names. The name has changed, but the ambience hasn't. The two-story building is still painted a blinding white and features heavy concrete arches, balcony railings, and bannisters. The rooms continue with the all-white theme, getting their only splash of color from vibrant print bedspreads. The carved hardwood doors, featuring native animal motifs, are perhaps the most striking design element here. It's worth the small splurge for a room with air-conditioning and television. You can enjoy a small, free-form pool for cooling off, but the beach is just across the street. Be forewarned, this hotel is located on the busiest corner in Tamarindo.

Central Tamarindo, just south of Subway. © **2653-0028.** 22 units. $56–$99 double. **Amenities:** Swimming pool; small spa; free Wi-Fi.

Pueblo Dorado Surf Hotel ★ This two-story, 29-room hotel with a swimming pool, one of the oldest lodging options in town, had fallen into some disrepair before being acquired in 2015 by Joe Walsh (not the rock star) of Witch's Rock Surf Camp, about 300m to the south. It's now being used to house overflow customers of the popular 18-room surf camp, as well as ordinary travelers. The new management plans to replace many aging elements, so expect improvements, though current annoyances are few and rooms have air-conditioning, hot water, and cable TV.

Entering Tamarindo from the north, it's the first hotel on your left after you see the ocean. www.pueblodorado.com. © **2653-0008**. 29 units. $85 double, includes breakfast at nearby Witch's Rock. **Amenities:** Pool; parking; free Wi-Fi.

Witch's Rock Surf Camp hotel in Tamarindo

Tamarindo Backpackers Hostel ★   A few blocks from the beach, this hostel is secluded enough to be quiet at night but close enough to walk to a party. The pretty little hostel has a swimming pool and a shared kitchen, with two dorms and four private rooms with a/c and cable TV.

300m south of the Kahiki Restaurant on the Tamarindo-Langosta Road. www.tama backpackers.com. © **2653-1720.** 2 dorms, 4 private units. Dorms are $10–$15, private rooms $30 for 2 to $80 for 4. **Amenities:** Swimming pool, 24/7 reception, free Wi-Fi.

Witch's Rock Surf Camp ★   While you don't have to be a surfer to stay here, you most likely are. This beachfront surf resort caters mostly to young, budget-minded surfers interested in a weeklong surf camp, surf lessons, or just hanging out and catching Guanacaste's best waves. The rooms are comfortable yet rather bland. There's a surf bar, surf restaurant, surf radio show, and a microbrewery all on the same property. The same owners offer more rooms at their sister hotel, Pueblo Dorado (see above).

Waterfront, beside Economy Car Rental. http://witchsrocksurfcamp.com. © **888/ 318-7873** in the U.S. and Canada, or 2653-1262 in Costa Rica. 18 units. $980-$1505 per person, includes a week long surf camp, equipment, and breakfast. **Amenities:** 2 restaurants; bar; outdoor pool; board rentals; free Wi-Fi.

Where to Eat

Tamarindo has a glut of good restaurants. **El Coconut ★** (www.el coconut-tamarindo.com; © **2653-0086**), right on the main road, is an institution with a European flair, specializing in fresh seafood. **Nogui's Bar ★** (www.noguistamarindo.com; © **2653-0029**), open since 1974, is one of the more popular places in town, and rightly so. This simple open-air cafe just off the beach on the small traffic circle serves hearty breakfasts and well-prepared salads, sandwiches, burgers, and casual meals. And it has a few tables and chairs right on the beach.

Wok N Roll ★ (www.woknrolltamarindo.com; © **2653-0156**), a half-block inland from the Mar Rey along the road to Playa Langosta, is a lively, open-air affair, with a big menu of Asian cuisine. For pizzas, there's **La Baula ★** (© **2653-1450**), another open-air place, on the road to Dragonfly (see below). For Mexican fare and breakfast burritos, try **Green Papaya Taco Bar** (© **2653-0863**), just across the street, while there's seafood street food like poke, ceviche, and shrimp burgers at **Shrimp Hole** (www.shrimphole.com; © **8726-0359**), beside the Super 2001 Supermarket. Coffee and Belgian waffles can be found at **Waffle Monkey** (© **8515-3960**), near the rotunda, or just coffee at **Nordico** (© **4700-9521**), at Plaza Tamarindo. And, for hearty steaks and Argentine fare, try **Patagonia** (© **2653-0612**), right across from the Tamarindo Diria Hotel.

Finally, if you're staying in a condo, or just too lazy to head out for a meal, **Tico To Go** (www.ticotogo.com; © **800/8426-8646**) offers up delivery service from a wide range of local restaurants.

Dragonfly Bar & Grill ★★ INTERNATIONAL/FUSION   The menu here features spices and flavors from around the world, with prominent influences from the Pacific Rim and southwestern United States. So you might find yourself dining on thick-cut pork loin crusted in panko and served with a brandy-Dijon cream sauce or a similarly creative fish dish. Portions are large, so don't be afraid to share. The look of the place is as fun as the food: A zinc roof is held high by columns made from locally farmed tree trunks, and finished underneath with woven mats and thin bamboo. The bar serves up fab cocktails and local craft beer, sometimes to live music.

Down a dirt road behind the Hotel Pasatiempo. www.dragonflybarandgrill.com. © **2653-1506.** Reservations recommended. Main courses C6,000–C11,500. Mon–Sat 5:30–10pm. Closed on Tuesdays during low season.

Pangas Beach Club ★★★ SEAFOOD/INTERNATIONAL   Located on the main road in a residential complex near the northern end of town, this restaurant opens onto the beach, right about where the ocean meets the estuary, a scenic spot. Heavy wooden tables are spread under tall coconut trees, which are strung with rope lighting and bare bulbs, giving this place a rustically romantic feel by night. While fresh seafood is the specialty, the steak tenderloin cooked at the table on a hot volcanic stone is the sleeper hit here. Breakfast and lunch are also served.

On the waterfront, north end of Tamarindo. http://pangasbeachclubcr.com. ☏ **2653-0024.** Reservations recommended. Main courses C9,500–C24,000. Mon–Thurs noon–10pm and Sun 9am–10pm.

Seasons by Shlomy ★★ INTERNATIONAL   Le Cordon Bleu Paris-trained chef and owner Shlomy Koren began his time in Tamarindo at Pachanga. Since 2008 he's been serving up his tasty Mediterranean-inspired cuisine with an Asian twist out of a small kitchen at the Hotel Arco Iris (p 276). Good menu choices include seared tuna in a honey chili marinade; red snapper with spinach, artichoke and cherry tomatoes; jumbo shrimp with coconut milk and sweet chilis; and beef tenderloin in a rosemary sauce. Don't get too attached to any item, because the menu changes regularly, with daily specials and seasonal variations.

At the Hotel Arco Iris. www.seasonstamarindo.com. ☏ **8368-6983.** Reservations recommended in season. Main courses $15–$20. No credit cards. Mon–Sat 5:30–10pm.

Surf Shack Burgers & Wings ★ AMERICAN   In 2010, Brian Gough of Seattle started the popular Longboards barbecue place just up the street, then he sold that and opened the Surf Shack in 2014. His philosophy: "Make good food, make it fast, and give it to people at a good price." If you're from the U.S. and craving some comfort food, this place will make you feel right at home with a pound of hot buffalo wings, a Blue Ribbon Blue Cheese Burger or a Hang 10 hot dog with bacon, cheese, jalapeños, pineapple relish, tomato, onion, and dill pickle.

Just off the *rotonda* downtown, near Nogui's. ☏ **2653-2346.** Main courses $7–$10. Fri–Wed 11am–9pm.

Shopping

Tamarindo's main boulevard is awash in souvenir stands, art galleries, jewelry stores, and clothing boutiques. For original beachwear and jewelry, try **Azul Profundo** ★ (☏ **2653-0395**), in the Plaza Tamarindo shopping center. The modern **Garden Plaza** shopping center, near the

Pretty Pots

The lack of any longstanding local arts and crafts tradition across Costa Rica is often lamented. One of the outstanding exceptions to this rule is the small village of Guaitíl, located on the outskirts of the regional capital of Santa Cruz. Its small central plaza—actually a soccer field—is ringed with craft shops and artisan stands selling a wide range of ceramic wares. Most are low-fired, relatively soft clay pieces with traditional Chorotega indigenous design motifs. All the local tour agencies offer day trips to Guaitíl, or you can drive there yourself, by heading first to Santa Cruz, and then taking the turnoff for Guaitíl, just south of the city, on the road to Nicoya.

entrance to town, has several high-end shops, as well as a massive **Auto-mercado** (supermarket).

Entertainment & Nightlife

As a popular surfer destination, Tamarindo has a raging nightlife scene. The most happening bars in town are **El Garito ★★** (© 2653-2017), located about a block inland, on the road to Playa Langosta, and **Aqua ★** (© 8934-2896), on the main road through town. Other popular spots throughout the week include the **Crazy Monkey Bar** at the Best Western Tamarindo Vista Villas (© 2653-0114), **Pacifico Bar** (© 8705-4762) near the rotunda, and the **Dragonfly Bar & Grill** (p 280). For a chill-out dance party, try the **Voodoo Lounge** (© 2653-0100); those looking for a rocking sports bar can head to **Sharky's ★★** (© 8918-4968). These latter two places are just across from each other, a little up the road that heads to Playa Langosta. The best casino in town is at the **Occidental Tamarindo** resort (© 2653-0363) in Playa Langosta.

En Route South: Playa Avellanas & Playa Negra ★

Heading south from Tamarindo are several as-yet-undeveloped beaches, most of which are quite popular with surfers. Beyond Tamarindo and Playa Langosta are **Playa Avellanas** and **Playa Negra,** both with a few

Playa Avellanas

The Hacienda Pinilla golf course

basic surfer cabinas and little else. To locate the hotels and restaurants listed below, see the map "Around Tamarindo," on p 271.

WHERE TO STAY

About a 15- to 20-minute drive inland is **Los Altos de Eros ★** (www.losaltosdeeros.com; © **8850-4222**), a small, adults-only, luxury hotel and spa.

In addition to the JW Marriott (see below), the large golf, residential, and vacation resort complex of **Hacienda Pinilla** (www.haciendapinilla.com; © **2681-4318**) features small hotels and condo rental units.

Expensive

JW Marriott Guanacaste Resort & Spa ★★★ This handsome resort is built around a massive pool (said to be the largest in Central America) and fronts a gorgeous but small patch of soft, white-sand beach. The rooms are ample and well-equipped, with fine dark-wood furnishings and red tile floors in a herringbone pattern. The bathrobes are some of the plushest you'll ever fondle. Every room has a large balcony or patio, though some patios open onto heavily trafficked walkways (potted plants, palms, and bamboo have been placed to try to provide some privacy). The best rooms have ocean and sunset views. The various dining options include a semi-formal steakhouse and a contemporary

Pool at JW Marriott Guanacaste

Asian fusion restaurant. The hotel runs a regular shuttle to nearby Playa Langosta, where guests have access to a small beach club with a pool, showers, bathrooms, restaurant, and bar, as well as boogie- and surfboard rental.

Hacienda Pinilla. www.marriott.com. © **888/236-2427** in the U.S. and Canada, or 2681-2000. 310 units. $407–$495 double; $535 and up suite. **Amenities:** 7 restaurants; 1 bar; babysitting; kids' programs; 18-hole golf course nearby; large health club and spa; massive pool; room service; tennis courts nearby; watersports equipment; paid Wi-Fi.

Moderate

In addition to the places listed below, **Villa Deevena** (www.villadeevena.com; © **2653-2328**) offers up six cool, comfortable, and well-appointed rooms in a quiet setting, a few hundred yards from Playa Negra.

Cabinas Las Olas ★
This is the only hotel in Playa Avellanas with direct beach access, making it a favorite with surfers, as a range of gnarly breaks stretch up and down the white-sand beach in each direction. The hotel's five duplex buildings are located 100 yards or so inland under tall trees, and reached via a raised walkway through a mangrove reserve. The rooms are fairly plain, but they are very spacious, and feature private little verandas with hammocks that are perfect for an afternoon siesta.

Playa Avellanas. www.cabinaslasolas.co.cr. © **2652-9315.** 10 units. $100 double, includes taxes and breakfast. **Amenities:** Restaurant; bar; bike rentals; limited watersports equipment rentals; free Wi-Fi.

Hotel Playa Negra ★
This small collection of hexagonal thatched-roof concrete bungalows is just steps away from Playa Negra, a legendary

right point break that was made famous in the surf film classic "Endless Summer II." Hotel Playa Negra caters to families as well as surfers, and the bungalow suites have large wooden decks, air-conditioning, small fridges, and hammocks. Most of the beds are built-in concrete affairs, although the mattresses are comfortable. Tables at the simple seafood and Costa Rican–style restaurant and bar have prime views of the wave action.

Playa Negra. www.playanegra.com. © **2652-9134.** 17 units. $111 bungalow; $180 bungalow suite. Rates higher during peak periods. **Amenities:** Restaurant; bar; midsize outdoor pool; free Wi-Fi.

WHERE TO EAT

In addition to those listed below, the restaurants inside the **JW Marriott** resort (p 283) are excellent, and open to the general public, while the restaurant at **Villa Deevena** (p 284), in Playa Negra, is also first rate.

Lola's ★★★ INTERNATIONAL/SEAFOOD Named for the owner's pet pig (who sometimes frolics in the waves as diners watch), this quintessential beach bar and restaurant sits on a patch of land and sand fronting the quiet and underdeveloped Playa Avellanas beach. The Belgian and U.S. owners serve up hearty, fresh food (like seared tuna atop salad with an Asian dressing) on homemade wooden tables and chairs under the shade of palm trees and large linen umbrellas. Lola's is extremely popular, especially on weekends, so be prepared to wait occasionally for food or a table (sorry, no reservations). When you're finished, you might snag a siesta in one of the hammocks strung between the many coconut palms.

On the beach, Playa Avellanas. © **2652-9097.** Main courses $12–$22. Tues–Sun 11am–sunset.

PLAYA JUNQUILLAL ★

30km (19 miles) W of Santa Cruz; 20km (12 miles) S of Tamarindo

A long, windswept beach that, for most of its length, is backed by grasslands, Playa Junquillal remains mostly undiscovered on an increasingly crowded coast. With no village to speak of here and a rough road, this is a good place to get away from it all and enjoy some unfettered time on a nearly deserted beach. The long stretch of white sand is great for strolling, and the sunsets are superb. When the waves are big, this beach is great for surfing, but can be a little dangerous for swimming. When it's calm, jump right in.

Essentials

GETTING THERE & DEPARTING **By Plane:** The nearest airport with regularly scheduled flights is in Tamarindo (p 268). You can arrange a taxi from the airport to Playa Junquillal. The ride should take around 40 minutes and cost about $50 to $70.

By Car: From San José, you can either take the Inter-American Highway (CR1) north from downtown San José, or first head west out of the city on the San José–Caldera Highway (CR27). This latter route is a faster and flatter drive. When you reach Caldera on this route, follow the signs to Puntarenas, Liberia, and the Inter-American Highway (CR1). This will lead you to the unmarked entrance to CR1. You'll want to pass under the bridge and follow the on-ramp, which will put you on the highway heading north. Forty-seven kilometers (29 miles) past the Puntarenas on-ramp, you'll see signs and the turnoff for the La Amistad Bridge. After crossing the river, follow the signs for Nicoya and Santa Cruz. Just after leaving

Playa Junquillal

the main intersection for Santa Cruz, you'll see a marked turnoff for Playa Junquillal, Ostional, and Tamarindo. The road is paved for 14km (8½ miles), until the tiny village of Veintesiete de Abril. From here, it's another rough 18km (11 miles) to Playa Junquillal.

From Liberia, head south to Santa Cruz on the main road to all the beach towns, passing through Filadelfia and Belén. Then follow the directions above from Santa Cruz.

By Bus: To get here by bus, you must first head to Santa Cruz and, from there, take another bus to Playa Junquillal. Buses depart San José for Santa Cruz roughly every 2 hours between 7:15am and 6pm from the **Tralapa** bus station (☎ **2221-7202**) at Calle 20 between avenidas 3 and 5, and from the **Alfaro** bus station (www.empresaalfaro.com; ☎ **2222-2666**) at Calle 14 between avenidas 3 and 5. The 4-hour trip is around C5,500.

Buses leave Santa Cruz for Junquillal about 6 times daily, roughly every 2 hours between 5am and 6pm from the town's central plaza. The ride takes about an hour, and the one-way fare is C1,200. Buses depart Playa Junquillal for Santa Cruz daily pretty much just after they arrive.

Always check with your hotel in advance as the schedule of buses between Junquillal and Santa Cruz is notoriously fickle. If you miss the connection, or there's no bus running, you can hire a taxi for the trip to Junquillal for $90 to $100. From Tamarindo, a taxi should cost $55 to $75.

Exploring Playa Junquillal

Other than walking on the beach, surfing, swimming when the surf isn't too strong, and exploring tide pools, there isn't much to do here—which you might like just fine. This beach is ideal for anyone who wants to relax without any distractions. Bring a few good books. If you have a car, you can explore the coastline just north and south of here.

Junquillal is a nesting site for both olive ridley and leatherback turtles, although conservation efforts and organized turtle-watching tours are both in their infancy here.

For surfers, the Junquillal beach break is often pretty good. I've also heard that if you look hard enough, there are a few hidden reef and point breaks around. However, be careful here, as the beach and rip currents are often a bit rough for casual swimming.

Several sportfishing boats operate out of Playa Junquillal. Inquire at your hotel. To rent a mountain bike, you can also check in at the Iguanazul.

Where to Stay & Eat

In addition to the two hotels mentioned below, **Hotel & Pizzería Tatanka** (www.hoteltatanka.com; ☎ **2658-8426**) offers well-designed rooms at very reasonable rates, as well as excellent wood-oven pizzas and fresh seafood. It's near the Iguanazul Hotel on your left as you come into Junquillal, and also has good ocean and sunset views.

Hotel Hibiscus ★ This long-established, German-owned hotel is located just a few hundred feet or so from the beach at Playa Junquillal. The shady grounds, tropical gardens, and cozy rooms are all immaculately maintained. The rooms themselves feature bright white walls and polished red-tile floors. They all have air-conditioning, but it will cost you an extra $10 daily to use it. The hotel serves breakfast, also for $10, and, although it doesn't have a full-service restaurant, it will prepare dinners with 24 hours' notice, specializing in German and Swiss food.

Playa Junquillal. www.hibiscus-info.com. ☎ **2658-8437.** 4 units and 1 small "backpacker room." $50 double, includes taxes. **Amenities:** Free Wi-Fi.

PUNTARENAS & THE NICOYA PENINSULA

9

The beaches of the Nicoya Peninsula don't get nearly as much attention or traffic as those to the north in Guanacaste. However, they are just as stunning, varied, and rewarding. Montezuma, with its jungle waterfalls and gentle surf, was the first beach destination out this way to capture any attention. It's since been eclipsed by increasingly trendy Malpaís and Santa Teresa.

Farther up the peninsula lie the beaches of Playa Sámara and Playa Nosara. With easy access via paved roads and the time-saving La Amistad Bridge, Playa Sámara is one of the coastline's more popular destinations, especially with Ticos looking for an easy weekend getaway. Just north of Sámara, Nosara and its neighboring beaches, despite the horrendous dirt road that separates these distinctly different destinations, is rapidly turning into the next Tulum. Aside of being one of the country's top surf spots, with a host of different beach and point breaks from which to choose, it's quickly becoming the New Age center of the region.

Nearby Puntarenas was once Costa Rica's principal Pacific port. The town bustled and hummed with commerce, fishermen, coffee brokers, and a weekend rush of urban dwellers enjoying some sun and fun at one of the closest beaches to San José. Today, Puntarenas is a run-down shell of its former self. Still, it remains a major fishing port, and the main gateway to the isolated and coveted beaches of the Nicoya Peninsula.

THE best PUNTARENAS & NICOYA PENINSULA TRAVEL EXPERIENCES

o **Taking a Dip in the Pool at the Foot of Montezuma Waterfall:** Nestled in thick forest, the **Montezuma waterfall** features a large, deep, and cool pool at its base—perfect for swimming. The hike in is pretty awesome as well. Take the zipline tour above it and do some cliff-jumping, if you dare. See p 304.

o **Getting Your Yoga On:** The Nicoya Peninsula is home to several of the country's top yoga retreat centers. **Harmony Hotel** (p 336) in Nosara, **Pranamar Villas & Yoga Retreat** (p 317) in Santa Teresa, **Anamaya Resort** (p 308) in Montezuma, and the **Nosara Yoga Institute** (p 335) are all good choices.

FACING PAGE: **Cathedral in Puntarenas**

- **Having Playa Barrigona (Almost) to Yourself:** Access is a bit rough, especially in the rainy season, but if you're feeling adventurous, head to Playa Barrigona, a largely undiscovered gem of white sand and clear waters. You'll probably need local help to find the unmarked entrance, but it's worth it. See p 325.

- **Going Deep (Underground) at Barra Honda:** Strap on a headlamp and some climbing gear and descend into the underworld at **Barra Honda National Park.** After exploring the nooks and crannies of Terciopelo Cave, take a refreshing dip in La Cascada. See p 327.

- **Mingling with the Hip & Famous in Malpaís & Santa Teresa:** Arguably the most happening of Costa Rica's beach hot spots, **Santa Teresa and Malpaís** are among the country's top destinations for both surf bums and celebrities. Even if you don't bump into Leonardo DiCaprio, Flea, or Tom Brady and Gisele Bündchen, you can wander miles of nearly deserted beaches and enjoy beautiful sunsets. See p 312.

PUNTARENAS

115km (71 miles) W of San José; 191km (118 miles) S of Liberia; 75km (47 miles) N of Playa de Jacó

Puntarenas is best-known to tourists for its gigantic ferry—the easiest way to get from central Costa Rica to the southern Nicoya Peninsula if

Playa Sámara

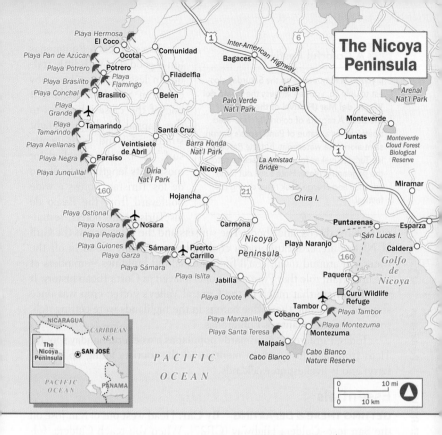

you have a rental car. If you want to drive to Montezuma and Santa Teresa, this is the way to go; if you're headed to Sámara, Nosara, or Tamarindo, consider the Costa Rican–Taiwan Friendship Bridge at the northern end of the Nicoya Gulf. If headed north of Tamarindo to places like Papagayo, the quickest way is probably to take the Inter-American Highway to Liberia.

Puntarenas has never taken off as a major tourism destination, though some Ticos in the Central Valley swear by it as a great weekend getaway. Despite serious investment and the steady influx of cruise ship passengers, Puntarenas retains its image as a rough-and-tumble, perennially run-down port town. Although the seafront **Paseo de los Turistas (Tourist Walk)** has a string of restaurants and souvenir stands, this town has little to interest visitors, and the beach here pales in comparison to most others.

A 16km (10-mile) spit of land jutting into the Gulf of Nicoya, Puntarenas was once Costa Rica's busiest port, but that changed drastically when the government inaugurated nearby Puerto Caldera, a modern container port facility. After losing its shipping business, the city has survived primarily on commercial fishing.

You can reach Puntarenas (on a good day, with little traffic) in less than two hours by car from San José, making it one of the closest beaches to the capital. A long, straight stretch of sand with gentle surf, the beach is backed for most of its length by the Paseo de los Turistas. Across a wide boulevard from the Paseo de los Turistas are hotels, restaurants, bars, discos, and shops. The sunsets and the views across the Gulf of Nicoya are beautiful, and a cooling breeze usually blows in off the water. All around town, you'll find unusual old buildings, reminders of the important role that Puntarenas once played in Costa Rican history. It was from here that much of the Central Valley's coffee crop was once shipped, and while the coffee barons in the highlands were getting rich, so were the merchants of Puntarenas.

Today, Puntarenas is primarily popular as a weekend holiday spot for Ticos from San José (not to mention all the tourists lining up for the ferry) and is liveliest on weekends.

Essentials

GETTING THERE & DEPARTING   By Car: Head west out of San José on the San José–Caldera Highway (CR27). When you reach Caldera, follow the signs to Puntarenas. The drive is supposed to take a little over an hour, but plan on 2 hours. To reach Puntarenas from Liberia, just take the Inter-American Highway south until the exit for Puntarenas.

By Bus: Empresarios de Unidos Puntarenas express buses (© **2222-0064** or 2261-3138) leave San José daily every hour between 6am and 7pm from Calle 16 and Avenida 12. The trip is 2 hours; the fare is around C2,800. Buses to San José leave the main station daily every hour between 6am and 7pm.

The Puntarenas bus station is diagonally opposite from the main pier on the Paseo de los Turistas. Buses to Quepos and Manuel Antonio leave the main station daily at 5, 7, 9, and 10:30am and 1, 2:30, and 4:30pm. The trip's about an hour; the fare is around C2,500. There are also about three daily buses between Puntarenas and Monteverde and Santa Elena.

By Ferry: See "Playa Tambor" (p 297) or "Playa Montezuma" (p 302), for information on crossing to and returning from Puntarenas from Paquera or Naranjo on the Nicoya Peninsula.

GETTING AROUND   If you need a taxi, call **Coopetico** (© **2663-2020**).

CITY LAYOUT   Puntarenas is built on a long, narrow sand spit that stretches 16km (10 miles) out into the Gulf of Nicoya and is only five streets wide at its widest. The north side of town faces an estuary, and the south side faces the gulf. The Paseo de los Turistas, on the south side of town, begins at the pier and extends out to the point. The ferry docks for the Nicoya Peninsula are near the far end of town, as are the bus station and market.

FAST FACTS   Several banks and general markets are all within a 2-block radius of the town's small church and central park. The town's main post office can be found here as well. The **Hospital Monseñor Sanabria** (© **2663-0033**), on the outskirts of downtown, is the largest and best-equipped hospital in the region.

Exploring Puntarenas

Don't be spooked by Puntarenas' image as a rough and dangerous port town. The average tourist might find that the stifling midday heat is the city's biggest challenge. If you've gotten over that, take a walk along the ocean-facing **Paseo de los Turistas,** which feels a bit like a Florida beach town from the 1950s. The hotels here range in style from converted old wooden homes with bright gingerbread trim to modern concrete monstrosities to tasteful Art Deco relics that need a new coat of paint.

If you venture into the center of the city, check out the **central plaza around the Catholic Church.** The large, stone church is interesting because it has portholes for windows, reflecting the city's maritime tradition. In addition, it's one of the few churches in the country with a front entry facing east (most face west). Here you'll also find the city's cultural center, **La Casa de la Cultura** (© **2661-1394**). In addition to rotating exhibits and the occasional theater performance, this place houses the **Museo Histórico** (© **2661-1394**), a small museum on the city's history, especially its maritime history, with exhibits in both English and Spanish. Admission is free, and it's open Monday to Saturday from 8am to 4pm. If you're looking for a shady spot to relax, there are some inviting benches in a little park just north of the church.

If you want to go swimming, the gulf waters in front of Puntarenas are perfectly safe, although the beach is not very attractive. Some folks choose to head a few kilometers south of town, to **Playa Doña Aña,** a popular local beach with picnic tables, roadside vendors, and a couple of *sodas*. A little farther south, you will come to **Playa Tivives,** which is virtually unvisited by tourists, but quite popular with Ticos, many of whom have beach houses up and down this long, brown-sand beach. Surfers should check out the beach break here or head to the mouth of the Barranca River, which boasts an amazingly long left break. But be careful, because crocodiles live in both the Barranca and Tivives river mouths, and a lot of pollution empties out of the rivers here.

If you don't want to swim in the gulf and your hotel doesn't have a pool, try the **San Lucas Beach Club** (www.sanlucasbeachclub.com; ☎ **2661-3881**; Tue-Sun 9am–5pm; C3,000). This misleadingly named attraction is actually a landlocked recreation complex with a large free-form pool and small snack bar. It's at the end of the peninsula, with a view of the gulf. It tends to fill up when a cruise ship is at port.

Puntarenas isn't known as one of Costa Rica's prime sportfishing ports, but a few charter boats are usually available. Head to the docks and ask around or go to www.getmyboat.com. Rates (for up to six) are between $450 and $650 for a half-day and between $800 and $1,800 for a full day.

You can also take a yacht cruise through the tiny, uninhabited islands of the Guayabo, Negritos, and Pájaros Islands Biological Reserve. These cruises include a lunch buffet and a relaxing stop on the beautiful **Tortuga Island ★**, where you can swim, snorkel, and sunbathe. The water is clear blue, and the sand is bright white. However, this trip has surged in popularity, and many cruises have a cattle-car feel.

Calypso Tours ★ (www.calypsocruises.com; ☎ **855/855-1975** in the U.S. and Canada, or 2256-2727 in Costa Rica) is the most reputable company that cruises out of Puntarenas. In addition to **Tortuga Island** trips, Calypso Tours takes guests to its own private nature reserve at **Punta Coral** or on a sunset dinner cruise. Either cruise can run $145 per person. The company provides daily pickups from San José, Manuel Antonio, Jacó, and Monteverde, and you can use the day trip on the boat as your transfer option between any of these towns and destinations.

Where to Stay

In addition to the places mentioned below, the **DoubleTree Resort by Hilton Central Pacific** (www.puntarenas.doubletree.com; ☎ **800/445-8667** in the U.S. and Canada, or 2660-1600 in Costa Rica) is an all-inclusive resort located on an unspectacular patch of sand.

MODERATE

Apartotel Alamar ★★ If you need to spend a night or more in Puntarenas, this should be your top choice. The staff is friendly and helpful, the property is extremely well-maintained and, along with the standard hotel rooms (modest-looking, but spotless and comfortable), are one- and two-bedroom condo-style units with full kitchens. The hotel is located right on the Paseo de los Turistas, toward the western end of the peninsula, directly across the street from the beach, and walking distance to several good restaurants. It boasts a small, rectangular pool and Jacuzzi.

Paseo de los Turistas, Puntarenas. www.alamarcr.com. ☎ **2661-4343.** 34 units. $119–$139 double; $249 family room, includes breakfast and taxes. **Amenities:** Restaurant; bar; Jacuzzi; small outdoor pool; free Wi-Fi.

DIVING TRIPS TO isla del coco

This little island in the middle of the ocean, located some 480km (300 miles) off the Pacific coast, was a prime pirate hideout and refueling station in the old days. Robert Louis Stevenson was said to have modeled "Treasure Island" on Isla del Coco, and it was also the inspiration for Isla Nublar, the setting of "Jurassic Park." Jacques Cousteau called it the most beautiful island in the world. Sir Francis Drake, Captain Edward Davis, William Dampier, and Mary Welch are just some of the famous corsairs who dropped anchor in the calm harbors of this Pacific pearl. Some visitors reportedly left troves of buried loot, although scores of treasure hunters over several centuries have failed to unearth more than a smattering of the purported bounty. The Costa Rican flag was first raised here on September 15, 1869. Throughout its history, Isla del Coco has provided anchorage and fresh water to hundreds of ships and has entertained divers and dignitaries. (Franklin Delano Roosevelt visited it three times.) In 1978 it was declared a national park and protected area.

The clear, warm waters around Isla del Coco are widely regarded as one of the most rewarding **dive destinations** ★★★ on the planet. This is a prime place to see schooling herds of hammerhead sharks. Other denizens of these waters include white- and silver-tipped reef sharks; marbled, manta, eagle, and mobula rays; moray and spotted eels; octopi; spiny and slipper lobsters; hawksbill turtles; plus squirrel fish, trigger fish, angelfish, surgeon fish, trumpet fish, grouper, grunts, snapper, jack, tangs, and more. Two of the more spectacular underwater residents here are the red-lipped batfish and the frogfish.

Most diving at Cocos is relatively deep (26–35m/85–115 ft.), often with strong currents and choppy swells to deal with—not to mention all those sharks. This is not a trip for novice divers.

The perimeter of Isla del Coco is ringed by steep, forested cliffs punctuated by dozens of majestic waterfalls cascading down in stages or steady streams for hundreds of feet. The island itself has a series of trails that climb its steep hills and wind through its rainforest interior. Several endemic bird, reptile, and plant species here include the ubiquitous Cocos finch, and the wild Isla del Coco pig.

With just a small ranger station housing a handful of national park guards, Isla del Coco is essentially uninhabited. Visitors come on a variety of boats. It's a long trip: Most vessels take 30 to 36 hours to reach Cocos.

Both **Aggressor Fleet Limited** (www.aggressor.com; © **800/348-2628**) and **Undersea Hunter** (www.underseahunter.com; © **800/203-2120** in the U.S., or 2228-6613 in Costa Rica) regularly run 10-day dive trips to Isla del Coco from Puntarenas, beginning at $5,299 per person.

Hotel Las Brisas ★ There's a touch of a Greek theme to some of the design elements and menu items here, thanks to the charming owner's mix of American and Greek heritage. The rooms are simple, but very spacious and clean, plus many have ocean views. The hotel has plenty of secure parking, if you're waiting for the next day's ferry, as well as a refreshing small pool.

Paseo de los Turistas, Puntarenas. www.lasbrisashotelcr.com. © **2661-4040.** 30 units. $109-$144 double, includes taxes and breakfast. **Amenities:** Restaurant; bar; small outdoor pool; free Wi-Fi.

INEXPENSIVE

Hotel La Punta ★   Another good budget option, Hotel La Punta is one of the closest hotels to the ferry docks (on the downside, that means it's on the estuary side of the peninsula, so has no sea views and is a longer walk to the beach). Rooms feature wooden beds and red tile floors, giving them a hint of colonial-era charm. A small kidney-shaped pool with a broad surrounding deck and tall palm trees for shade offers some respite from the midday heat.

Puntarenas (½ block south of the ferry terminal). www.hotellapunta.net. ✆ **2661-0696.** 8 units. $65–$75 double. **Amenities:** Small outdoor pool; free Wi-Fi.

Where to Eat

You're in a seaport, so try some of the local catch. Corvina (sea bass) is the most popular offering, and it's served in various preparations. It's hard to go wrong with the *ceviche*, served almost everywhere.

The most economical option is to pull up a table at one of the many open-air *sodas* along the Paseo de los Turistas (sandwiches for around $2, a fish filet with rice and beans for about $5, plus ice cream, snacks, and more). If you want seafood in a slightly more formal atmosphere, try the **Jardín Cervecero, Capitán Moreno, Casa de los Mariscos,** or the open-air **Delicias del Puerto,** all located on the Paseo de los Turistas.

Casa Almendro ★★   STEAK/SEAFOOD   Occupying the former home of La Yunta (see below), this converted residence has been given a major makeover. Today, you'll climb wide varnished wood entrance steps and grab a table along the railing fronting the beach to enjoy excellent views of the water with your meal. It's all quite nice, as is the food: *arroz con mariscos* (rice with seafood) loaded with fresh local catch; *pulpo a la parrilla* (grilled octopus); or the *filete al diablo* (devil's fish filet), a boneless fillet of *corvina* in a well-seasoned tomato sauce, with jalapeños for kick. There are also excellent grilled steak and chicken options, as well as a small children's menu.

Corner of Avenida 4 and Calle 21, Paseo de los Turistas. ✆ **2661-0901.** Main courses C4,300–C11,000. Daily noon–10pm.

A Frosty Churchill

No one should leave Puntarenas without trying a "Churchill." Sold by scores of vendors out of makeshift carts, food trucks, and kiosks all along the Paseo de los Turistas, these concoctions are made from freshly shaved ice smothered with a wide range of toppings—usually sweet syrup, condensed milk, or fruit salad. Some also come with ice cream and some sort of sweet cookie or cracker. Most of the sellers serve them in plastic cups, but if you look around, you might find them in large soda-fountain-style glasses. Dating to at least the 1940s, the local legend claims that the original creator of these refreshing sweet treats bore a striking resemblance to the wartime prime minister of Great Britain, Winston Churchill.

Yoga circle at Anamaya Resort

El Shrimp Shack ★ SEAFOOD   Shrimp burger, shrimp scampi, fried shrimp, buffalo shrimp, shrimp ceviche, coconut shrimp, Thai shrimp…this little restaurant run by the staff of Calypso Tours, on the water on the mangrove side of the peninsula has a lot of shrimp. The simple restaurant is based on a roadside eatery in Hawaii.

350 m east of Mercado Central. www.elshrimpshack.com. ℂ **2661-0585.** Main courses C4,300–C11,000. Daily 11am–5:30pm.

PLAYA TAMBOR

150–168km (93–104 miles) W of San José (not including ferry ride); 20km (12 miles) S of Paquera; 38km (24 miles) S of Naranjo

Playa Tambor was the site of Costa Rica's first large-scale all-inclusive resort, the Barceló Tambor. Despite big plans, the resort and surrounding area have never really taken off. Today, Tambor has a forgotten, isolated feel to it. Part of the blame lies with the beach itself. Playa Tambor is a long, gently curving stretch of beach protected on either end by rocky headlands (making this a good beach for swimming). However, the sand is an unattractive, dull gray-brown color, and often receives large amounts of flotsam and jetsam from the sea. Playa Tambor pales in comparison to the beaches located farther south along the Nicoya Peninsula.

That said, Tambor is the site of the only major commuter airport on the southern Nicoya Peninsula, and you'll be arriving and departing here if you choose to visit Montezuma, Malpaís, or Santa Teresa by air.

Essentials

GETTING THERE & DEPARTING **By Plane: Sansa** (www.flysansa.com; (C) 877/767-2672 in the U.S. and Canada, or 2290-4100 in Costa Rica) and **Nature Air** (www.natureair.com; (C) 800/235-9272 in the U.S. and Canada, or 2299-6000 in Costa Rica) both have several flights daily to a small airstrip in **Tambor airport** (airport code: TMU). The flight is about 30 minutes, and fares range from $84 to $124, one-way.

By Car: The traditional route here is to drive to Puntarenas and catch the ferry to either Naranjo or Paquera. Tambor is about 30 minutes south of Paquera and about an hour and 20 minutes south of Naranjo. The road from Paquera to Tambor is paved, and taking the Paquera ferry will save you time and some rough, dusty driving. The road from Naranjo to Paquera is all dirt and gravel and often in very bad shape. For directions on driving to Puntarenas, see p 303.

Naviera Tambor (www.navieratambor.com; (C) 2661-2084) car ferries to Paquera leave Puntarenas at 5, 9 and 11am and 2, 5, and 8:30pm. The trip takes 1½ hours. The fare is C11,400 per car, including the driver; C810 for each additional adult, and C485 for children. Arrive early during the peak season and on weekends because lines can be long; if you miss the ferry, you'll have to wait 2 hours or more for the next one. The ferry schedule changes frequently, with fewer ferries during the low season, and the occasional extra ferry added during the high season to meet demand. It's always best to check in advance.

The car ferry from Paquera to Puntarenas leaves at 5:30, 9 and 11am and 2, 5, and 8pm. **Note:** If you have to wait for the ferry, avoid leaving your car unattended, as break-ins are common.

The **Naranjo ferry** (www.coonatramar.com; (C) 2661-1069) leaves daily at 6:30 and 10am and 2:30 and 7:30pm. The trip takes 1½ hours. Return ferries leave Naranjo for Puntarenas daily at 8am and 12:30, 5:30, and 9pm. The fare is C9,000 per car, including the driver; C1,050 for each additional adult; and C600 for children.

Another option is to drive via La Amistad Bridge over the Tempisque River. I recommend this route only when the ferries are on the fritz, or when the wait for the next car ferry is over 3 hours. (When the lines are long, you may not find room on the next departing ferry.) Although heading farther north and crossing the bridge is more circuitous, you'll be driving the whole time, which beats waiting around in the midday heat. To go this route, take the Inter-American Highway west from San José. Forty-seven kilometers (29 miles) past the turnoff for Puntarenas, turn left for La Amistad Bridge. After you cross the Tempisque River, head to

Quebrada Honda and then south to Route 21, following signs for San Pablo, Jicaral, Lepanto, Playa Naranjo, and Paquera.

To drive to Tambor from Liberia, head out of town on the main road to the Guanacaste beaches, passing through Filadelfia, Santa Cruz, and Nicoya on your way toward the turnoff for La Amistad Bridge. Continue straight at this turnoff, and follow the directions as listed above.

By Bus & Ferry: Transportes Cóbano (© 2642-1112) runs two daily direct buses between San José and Cóbano, dropping passengers off in Tambor en route. The buses leave from the Coca-Cola bus terminal at Calle 12 and Avenida 5 at 6am and 2pm. The fare is C7,000, including the ferry ride, and the trip takes a little over 4 hours.

Alternatively, it takes two buses and a ferry to get to Tambor. **Empresarios Unidos de Puntarenas** express buses (© 222-8321) leave San José daily every hour between 6am and 7pm from Calle 16 and Avenida 12. Trip duration is 2 hours; the fare is C2,750. From Puntarenas, take the car ferry to Paquera mentioned above. A bus south to Montezuma (this will drop you off in Tambor) will be waiting to meet the ferry when it arrives in Paquera. The bus ride takes about 40 minutes; the fare is C1,200. Be careful not to take the Naranjo ferry because it does not meet with regular onward bus transportation to Tambor.

When you're ready to head back, buses originating in Montezuma, Cóbano, or Malpaís pass through Tambor roughly every 2 hours between 6am and 4:30pm. Theoretically, these should connect with a waiting ferry in Paquera. Total trip duration is 3½ hours. Buses to San José leave Puntarenas daily every hour between 5am and 8pm.

ORIENTATION   Although there's a tiny village of Tambor, through which the main road passes, the hotels themselves are scattered along several kilometers, with Tango Mar (p 302) definitively outside Tambor proper. You'll see signs for all these hotels as the road passes through and beyond Playa Tambor. If you need a bank, pharmacy, or post office, you'll have to head to nearby Cóbano.

Exploring Tambor

Curú Wildlife Refuge ★★ (www.curuwildliferefuge.com; © 2641-0100; $10/person per day admission), 16km (10 miles) north of Tambor, is a private reserve of pretty, secluded beaches, as well as forests and mangrove swamps. This area is extremely rich in wildlife. Howler and white-faced monkeys are often spotted here, and quite a few species of birds, including scarlet macaws (the refuge is actively involved in a macaw protection and repopulation effort). Horses are available to rent for $15 per hour. Typically you'll ride with a guide for about an hour to a lovely beach, hang out on the sand for another hour, and then ride back. You only get charged for the time you're actually on horseback, so trips run about $20-$25. Some very rustic cabins are available with advance notice for $30 per person per day. Meals are $10. If you don't have a car,

Catholic church in Puntarenas

you should arrange pickup with the staff who manage this refuge. Or you can contact **Turismo Curú** (www.curutourism.com; ✆ **2641-0004**), which specializes in guided tours to the refuge, as well as kayaking trips and other adventures.

Both the hotels listed below offer horseback riding and various tours around this part of the peninsula and can arrange fishing and dive trips.

Where to Stay & Eat

Aside from the hotels listed here, a few inexpensive *cabinas* are available near the town of Tambor, at the southern end of the beach. Most are very basic, and charge around $15 per person.

Paddle After Dark

The waters off the Curú Wildlife Refuge are ripe with **bioluminescent dinoflagellates,** a plankton that emits light when moved or agitated. This creates an effect commonly known as bioluminescence. The phenomenon exists year-round here, although it varies in intensity. The best timing for a visit is around a new moon in the dry season. Strong moonlight and muddy waters from runoff both diminish the effect. If interested in doing a nighttime kayak or stand-up paddleboard tour here, contact **Bahía Rica Tours** (www.bahiarica.com; ✆ **2641-8111**). The tour costs $50 per person, or $45 per person for groups of four or more.

Soccer match on the beach at Puntarenas

The **Barceló Tambor** was Costa Rica's first all-inclusive resort, but its beach is mediocre and the hotel had some flood damage in late 2016.

Tambor Tropical ★   This is easily one of the better beach hotels in Playa Tambor, although there's really not much competition. Lodgings are in individual and two-story bungalows, which are huge, octagonal affairs with walls, floors, ceilings, and furnishings of brightly varnished local hardwoods. They also come with full kitchens. Second-floor rooms are best, with big wrap-around verandas facing the sea and offering

Tambor ferry

inspiring views. A small free-form pool lies under tall coconut palms, and the beach is just a stone's throw away. The restaurant and bar, housed under a soaring thatched roof, serve excellent seafood, continental cuisine, and cocktails.

Tambor. www.tambortropical.com. © **866/890-2537** in the U.S., or 2683-0011 in Costa Rica. 14 units. $245–$270 double; $400 villa, includes breakfast. No children under 17. **Amenities:** Restaurant; bar; room service, small pool, Jacuzzi; small spa; free Wi-Fi.

Tango Mar Resort ★★ Very popular with honeymooners, Tango Mar fronts a beautiful white-sand beach, and is a short hike from a jungle waterfall that empties into a pool formed by a rock formation adjacent to the sea. Because of its extremely isolated location, the beach feels like the private domain of the resort. Of the several pools here, one particularly gorgeous one is just a few steps away from the surf. Colorful and well-appointed rooms and suites are located in various buildings around the sprawling grounds. Deluxe beachfront rooms have private ocean-view balconies, but for panoramic views, you can't beat the Tropical Suites, which are built on a high bluff and come with Jacuzzi tubs. The resort also has a 9-hole golf course (greens fee $20) a few kilometers away and two tennis courts. Villas around the grounds are also for rent.

Tambor. www.tangomar.com. © **800/297-4420** in the U.S., or 2683-0001 in Costa Rica. 45 units. 17 tropical suites, 6 deluxe, 5 bungalows, and 2 villas. $230–$260 double; $305 suite, includes breakfast. **Amenities:** 2 Restaurants; 2 bars; bike rental; 4 pools; room service; small spa; 2 lighted tennis courts; free Wi-Fi.

PLAYA MONTEZUMA ★★

166–184km (103–114 miles) W of San José (not including the ferry ride); 36km (22 miles) SE of Paquera; 54km (33 miles) S of Naranjo

For decades, this remote village and its surrounding beaches, forests, and waterfalls have enjoyed near-legendary status among backpackers, UFO seekers, hippie expatriates, natural healers, and European budget travelers. Although it maintains its alternative vibe, Montezuma is a great destination for all manner of travelers looking for a beach retreat surrounded by some stunning scenery and lush forests. Active pursuits abound, from hiking in the Cabo Blanco Absolute Nature Reserve to horseback riding to visiting a beachside waterfall. The natural beauty, miles of almost abandoned beaches, rich wildlife, and jungle waterfalls here are what first made Montezuma famous, and they continue to make this one of my favorite beach towns in Costa Rica.

Essentials

GETTING THERE & DEPARTING **By Plane:** The nearest airport is in Tambor, 17km (11 miles) away (p 297). Some of the hotels listed below might pick you up in Tambor for a reasonable fee. If not, you'll have to hire a taxi, which could cost $40 to $60. **Taxis** are generally waiting to

Male violet sabrewing in Puntarenas

meet regularly scheduled planes, but if they aren't, call **Gilberto Rodrí-guez** (ⓒ **8826-9055;** gilbertotaxi@gmail.com).

By Car: The traditional route here is to drive to Puntarenas and catch the ferry to either Naranjo or Paquera. Montezuma is about 30 minutes south of Tambor, 1 hour south of Paquera, and 2 hours south of Naranjo. The road from Paquera to Tambor is paved, and taking the Paquera ferry will save you time and some rough, dusty driving. The road from Naranjo to Paquera is all dirt and gravel and often in bad shape. For info on car ferries, see p 299. For driving directions to Puntarenas, see p 292.

To drive to Montezuma from Liberia, head out of town on the main road to the Guanacaste beaches, passing through Filadelfia, Santa Cruz, and Nicoya on your way toward the turnoff for La Amistad Bridge. Continue straight at this turnoff, and follow the directions for this route as listed above.

By Bus & Ferry: Transportes Cóbano (ⓒ **2642-1112**) runs two daily direct buses between San José and Montezuma. The buses leave from the Coca-Cola bus terminal at Calle 12 and Avenida 5 at 6am and 2pm. Fare is C7,500, including the ferry. The trip takes a bit over 5 hours.

A Time-Saving Route

The fastest route is the daily speedboat shuttle between Montezuma and Jacó (actually Playa Herradura). This 1-hour shuttle departs Montezuma for Playa Herradura at 9:30am and makes the return trip from Playa Herradura to Montezuma at 11am. **Zuma Tours** (www. zumatours.net; ⓒ **2642-0024**) can book this, including connecting shuttle service to or from San José, Manuel Antonio, Malpaís, and other destinations. The boat shuttle itself is $40 per person, one-way.

Alternatively, it takes two buses and a ferry ride to get to Montezuma. **Empresarios Unidos de Puntarenas** express buses (© **2222-0064**) to Puntarenas leave San José daily every hour between 6am and 7pm from Calle 16 and Avenida 12. The trip takes 2 hours; the fare is C2,640. From Puntarenas, you can take the ferry to Paquera, mentioned on p 299. A bus south to Montezuma will be waiting to meet the ferry when it arrives in Paquera. The bus ride takes about 1½ hours; the fare is C1,850. Be careful not to take the Naranjo ferry because it does not meet with regular onward bus transportation to Montezuma.

Buses are met by hordes of locals trying to corral you to one of the many budget hotels. Remember, they are getting a commission, so their information is biased. Not only that, they are often flat-out lying when they tell you the hotel you want to stay in is full.

When you're ready to head back, direct buses leave Montezuma daily at 6:30am and 2:30pm. Regular local buses to Paquera leave Cóbano roughly every 2 hours during the day starting around 4am. Buses to San José leave Puntarenas daily, hourly between 6am and 7pm. Buses from Montezuma to Paquera leave about every 2 hours between 5:30am and 5pm.

CITY LAYOUT   As the winding mountain road that descends into Montezuma bottoms out, you turn left onto a small dirt road that defines the village proper. On this 1-block road, you will find El Sano Banano Village Cafe and, across from it, a small shaded park with plenty of tall trees, as well as a basketball court and children's playground. The bus stops at the end of this road. From here, hotels are scattered up and down the beach and around the village's few sand streets. Around the center of town are several tour agencies among the restaurants and souvenir stores.

Exploring Montezuma

The ocean here is a gorgeous royal blue, and idyllic beaches stretch out along the coast on either side of town. Be careful, though: The waves can occasionally be too rough for casual swimming. Be sure you know where the rocks are and what the tides are before going bodysurfing. Given the prevailing currents and winds here, Montezuma also has experienced several severe and long-lasting red tide episodes at different times over the years. During these periods of massive algae bloom, the ocean is reddish-brown in color and not recommended for swimming. The best places to swim are a couple of hundred meters north of town in front of **El Rincón de los Monos,** or several kilometers farther north at Playa Grande.

Don't miss the **Montezuma waterfall ★★** just outside town—it's one of those tropical fantasies where water comes pouring down into a deep pool. It's a popular spot, and it's a fairly easy hike from town up the stream. Along this stream are a couple of waterfalls, but the upper falls are by far the most spectacular. You'll find the trail to the falls just over

Kayaking through the mangroves

the bridge south of the village (on your right just past Las Cascadas restaurant). At the first major outcropping of rocks, the trail disappears and you have to scramble up the rocks and river for a bit. A trail occasionally reappears for short stretches. Just stick close to the stream and you'll eventually hit the falls. **Note:** Be very careful when climbing close to the rushing water, and also if you plan on taking any dives into the pools below. The rocks are quite slippery, and several people each year get very scraped up, break bones, and otherwise hurt themselves here.

Another popular local waterfall is **El Chorro** ★, located 8km (5 miles) north of Montezuma. It cascades down into a tide pool at the edge of the ocean, making it a delightful mix of fresh- and seawater. You can bathe while gazing out over the sea and rocky coastline. When the water is clear and calm, this is one of my favorite swimming holes in all of Costa Rica. The pool here is dependent upon the tides—it disappears entirely at very high tide. It's about a 2-hour hike along the beach to reach El Chorro. You can take a horseback tour here offered by any of the tour operators in town.

> **Buy the Book . . . or Just Borrow It**
>
> If you came unprepared or ran out of reading material, check in at **Librería Topsy** (ⓒ 2642-1187), which, in addition to selling books, runs a lending library and serves as the local post office. It also has a branch in Cabuya.

BUTTERFLY GARDEN For an intimate look at the life cycle and acrobatic flights-of-fancy of butterflies, head to the **Mariposario Montezuma Gardens** ★ (www.montezumagardens.com; ⓒ 2642-1317 or

8888-4200; daily 8am–4pm; $8 entry). This has perhaps the wildest and most natural feel of all the butterfly gardens in Costa Rica. Wooden walkways wind through thick vegetation under black screen meshing. Most of the butterflies in the enclosure are self-reproducing. You can also see butterflies and other wildlife on trails through open forested areas outside the enclosure. It's along the dirt road heading up the hill just beyond the entrance to the waterfall trail. These folks also rent out a few pretty rooms and have a microbrewery.

A UNIQUE CANOPY TOUR The **Waterfall Canopy Tour ★** (www.montezumatraveladventures.com; ℰ **2642-0808**; daily at 9am, 1pm and 3pm; $45) is built right alongside Montezuma's famous falls. The tour, which features nine cables connecting 13 platforms, includes a swim at the foot of the falls.

HORSEBACK RIDING Several people around the village rent horses for around $15 to $20 an hour, although most people choose to do a guided 4-hour horseback tour for $30 to $50. Any of the hotels or tour agencies in town can arrange this.

OTHER ACTIVITIES Some shops in the center of the village rent bicycles by the hour or day, as well as boogie boards and snorkeling equipment (although the water must be very calm for snorkeling).

A range of guided tour and adventure options is available in Montezuma **Zuma Tours** (www.zumatours.net; ℰ **2642-0024**) and **Sun Trails** (www.montezumatraveladventures.com; ℰ **2642-0808**) can both arrange horseback riding, boat excursions, scuba-dive and snorkel tours, ATV outings, and rafting trips; car and motorcycle rentals; airport transfers; and currency exchange.

An Excursion to Cabo Blanco Absolute Nature Reserve ★★

As beautiful as the beaches around Montezuma are, the beaches at **Cabo Blanco Absolute Nature Reserve ★★** (ℰ **2642-0093**), 11km (6¾ miles) south of the village, are even more stunning. At the southernmost tip of the Nicoya Peninsula, Cabo Blanco is a national park that preserves a nesting site for brown pelicans, magnificent frigate birds, and brown boobies. The beaches are backed by a lush tropical forest that is home to howler monkeys. The main trail here, Sendero Sueco (Swedish Trail), is a rugged and sometimes steep hike through thick rainforest. The trail leads to the beautiful Playa Balsita and Playa Cabo Blanco, two white-sand stretches that straddle either side of the Cabo Blanco point. The beaches are connected by a short trail. It's 4km (2.5 miles) to Playa Balsita. Alternately, you can take a shorter 2km (1.25-mile) loop trail through the primary forest here. This is Costa Rica's oldest official bioreserve and was set up thanks to the pioneering efforts of conservationists

Karen Mogensen and Nicholas Wessberg. Admission is $10; the reserve is open Wednesday through Sunday from 8am to 4pm.

On your way out to Cabo Blanco, you'll pass through the tiny village of **Cabuya.** There are a couple of private patches of beach to discover in this area, off deserted dirt roads. A small offshore island serves as the town's picturesque cemetery; snorkel and kayak trips to this island are offered out of Montezuma.

> ### Backroads Exploring & Beach Hopping
>
> This is a great area to explore by 4×4 or ATV. A single coastal road heads up the coast to Cabuya and Cabo Blanco, with a half-dozen or more spots to pull over for a swim at a semi-private beach. Moreover, several dirt roads head into the hills here connecting Montezuma with Cabuya, Delicias, Malpaís, and Santa Teresa.

Shuttle buses head from Montezuma to Cabo Blanco roughly every 2 hours beginning at 8am, and then turn around and bring folks from Cabo Blanco to Montezuma; the last one leaves Cabo Blanco around 5pm. The fare is $3 each way. These shuttles often don't run during the off-season. You can also share a taxi: The fare is around $15 to $20 per taxi, which can hold four or five passengers. Taxis tend to hang around Montezuma center. One dependable *taxista* is **Gilberto Rodríguez** (© **8826-9055;** gilbertotaxi@gmail.com).

Sunset at Playa Montezuma

Where to Stay

EXPENSIVE

In addition to the places mentioned below, the **Anamaya Resort ★** (www.anamayaresort.com; ☎ **866/412-5350** in the U.S. or 2642-1289 in Costa Rica) is a lovely and luxe option on a high hillside above Montezuma. Anamaya specializes in yoga and wellness retreats.

Ylang Ylang Beach Resort ★★★   This pioneering rainforest resort does an excellent job of blending tropical fantasy with hints of luxury. The complex is just off the beach in a dense patch of forest and flowering gardens. Lodging options range from glamping-style tent cabins (slat wood floors, private porches, indoor plumbing, batik window coverings) to individual bungalows and geodesic domes. All are comfortable and quite pretty. The on-site restaurant serves some of the tastiest fare on this stretch of coastline. There is no regular vehicular access to the resort, so check-in is at **El Sano Banano Village** hotel and restaurant (p 311) in town; you and your bags are shuttled in via Jeep or dune buggy. The owners, Lenny and Patricia, have been here for decades and have done much to promote and protect the area.

Montezuma. www.ylangylangbeachresort.com. ☎ **888/795-8494** in the U.S. and Canada, or 2642-0636 in Costa Rica. 22 units. $220–$325 double; $135 tent cabins, includes breakfast and dinner. **Amenities:** Restaurant; bar; pool; spa; free Wi-Fi.

MODERATE

Amor de Mar ★★★   A little slice of paradise, Amor de Mar is a large house perched on a high spot of land that runs down to a rocky outcropping hiding a small natural swimming pool carved into the coral stones. Between this pool and the rooms is a broad lawn and a small grove of mango trees and coconut palms strung with hammocks. The rooms themselves are comfortable and pretty, awash in varnished hardwoods, with large windows (though they vary greatly in size and location; the prized choices are those on the second floor, especially those with ocean-view balconies). Beside and behind the main hotel building lie Casa Luna and Casa Sol, two separate two-story, fully equipped villas perfect for families and small groups. The trailhead to Montezuma's famous waterfall is directly across the dirt street from Amor de Mar, and it's a short walk into town. The in-house restaurant is open only for breakfast and lunch.

Montezuma. www.amordemar.com. ☎ **2642-0262.** 11 units. $90–$120 double; $250–$270 villa. **Amenities:** Restaurant; free Wi-Fi.

INEXPENSIVE

El Pargo Feliz (☎ **2642-0064**) and **Cabinas Mar y Cielo** (☎ **2642-0261**) are two recommended budget options right in the center of town. The owners of Ylang Ylang (p 308) also run the in-town **El Sano Banano B&B** (www.elbanano.com; ☎ **866/795-8494** in the U.S. and Canada, or 2642-0636 in Costa Rica). Double rooms are $75, including breakfast.

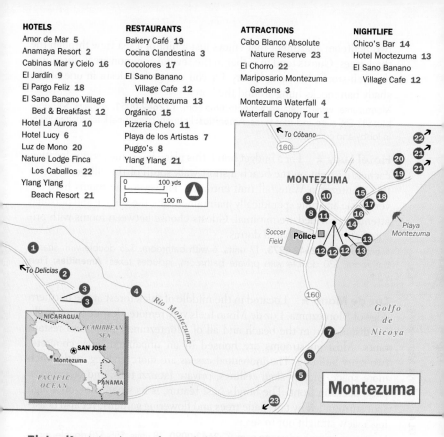

HOTELS		RESTAURANTS	
Amor de Mar	**5**	Bakery Café	**19**
Anamaya Resort	**2**	Cocina Clandestina	**3**
Cabinas Mar y Cielo	**16**	Cocolores	**17**
El Jardín	**9**	El Sano Banano	
El Pargo Feliz	**18**	Village Cafe	**12**
El Sano Banano Village		Hotel Moctezuma	**13**
Bed & Breakfast	**12**	Orgánico	**15**
Hotel La Aurora	**10**	Pizzeria Chelo	**11**
Hotel Lucy	**6**	Playa de los Artistas	**7**
Luz de Mono	**20**	Puggo's	**8**
Nature Lodge Finca		Ylang Ylang	**21**
Los Caballos	**22**		
Ylang Ylang			
Beach Resort	**21**		

ATTRACTIONS		NIGHTLIFE	
Cabo Blanco Absolute		Chico's Bar	**14**
Nature Reserve	**23**	Hotel Moctezuma	**13**
El Chorro	**22**	El Sano Banano	
Mariposario Montezuma		Village Cafe	**12**
Gardens	**3**		
Montezuma Waterfall	**4**		
Waterfall Canopy Tour	**1**		

El Jardín ★★ As you descend the steep hill that leads into Montezuma, you'll find this place on your right, just before the main crossroads of the village. Rooms here are clean and tidy, and feature Guatemalan woven bedspreads and either varnished wood or cool concrete block walls. A couple of the rooms have smooth, local river stones integrated into the masonry. Buildings are spread up the hillside, and some offer excellent views over town and out to the ocean. Rooms farthest from the road and reception require a bit of a steep hike, but the higher vantage point and better views are worth it. The hotel's pool and Jacuzzi area is its best feature, built in two distinct tiers connected by a sculpted waterfall. The location provides easy access to town, yet still feels removed. Montezuma. www.hoteleljardin.com. ⓒ **2642-0074.** 16 units. $85–$95 double; $130 villa, includes taxes. **Amenities:** Jacuzzi; small outdoor pool; free Wi-Fi.

Hotel La Aurora ★ You'll see the stone columns and yellow archway entrance to this intimate budget option on your left as soon as you hit the town's main crossroad. Spread over three floors, the rooms are not as comfortable as they could be, with low wooden beds and rather thin mattresses. Still, rooms and common areas (including a much-used communal kitchen for the guests) are immaculate. On the top floor, you'll find a two-bedroom apartment that enjoys just a hint of a sea view through the thick trees. Guests tend to gather in the several common areas, including the well-stocked lending library. Or you can grab a siesta in one of the shady hammocks hung around the hotel.

Montezuma. www.hotelaurora-montezuma.com. © **2642-0051.** 20 units. $40 double; $45-$50 suite, includes taxes. **Amenities:** Lounge; communal kitchen; free Wi-Fi in lobby and common areas.

Hotel Lucy ★ For a budget hotel, this place has some serious location cachet; it's right on the beach a short walk south of the village, close to the Montezuma Waterfall trail entrance. However, the rooms here are very basic and only sporadically maintained, and the service and personal attention provided are minimal. Guests choose between rooms with private bathrooms or shared dorms.

Montezuma. © **2642-0273.** 17 units, 6 with bathroom. $25 double with shared bathroom; $30 double with private bathroom, includes taxes. **Amenities:** Free Wi-Fi.

Luz de Mono ★ Located in the middle of thick forest at the northern edge of Montezuma, Luz de Mono feels very remote, despite being walking distance from the beach and all of Montezuma's shops and restaurants. Most guestrooms are housed in an unpainted, gray concrete, two-story building. The individual *casitas* are more inviting, with much more space, high peaked ceilings, private Jacuzzi tubs, and ocean-view patio decks in front. The hotel's best feature is its small pool, on a high spot surrounded by tall shade trees and flowering gardens, yet also boasting a view straight out to sea.

Montezuma. www.luzdemono.com. © **2642-0090.** 18 units. $55-$70 double, includes breakfast and taxes. **Amenities:** Restaurant; bar, free Wi-Fi.

Nature Lodge ★★ An oasis of serenity in the heart of the forest (you'll need a car if you stay here), Nature Lodge was originally a ranch. Today it's delighting tourists with better-than-usual food, excellent service, and rooms that are on the verge of being stylish (white walls with an occasional splash of color from a painting or wall hanging, low-lying beds made of varnished bamboo or local hardwoods). Some have ocean views; most look out into the jungle or garden.

3km (1¾ miles) outside Montezuma, on the way to Cóbano. www.naturelodge.net. © **2642-0124.** 12 units. $86-$146 double, includes breakfast buffet. **Amenities:** Restaurant; small outdoor pool; spa; free Wi-Fi.

Where to Eat

You'll find several basic *sodas* and casual restaurants right in the village. The best is **Soda Típica Las Palmeras** (© **2642-0269**), about 1km south of town. **Chelo's** (© **2642-1430**), at the crossroads into town, serves Argentinean fare and thin-crust pizzas, calzones, and pastas. You might also want to check out the Spanish cuisine and fabulous setting at the downtown **Hotel Moctezuma** (✆ 2642-0058), or the varied international fare at **Cocolores** (✆ 2642-0348). Just outside of downtown proper, the Israeli-owned **Puggo's** ★ (✆ 2642-0325) serves up an eclectic menu that ranges from falafel to *ceviche* to focaccia and beyond.

For breakfast, coffee, and light meals, **Orgánico** ★ (✆ 2642-1322) is the pick, with a range of healthy sandwiches, daily specials, and fresh baked goods. The **Bakery Café** (✆ 2642-0458) is another option, serving everything from gourmet coffee drinks to full meals.

Cocina Clandestina ★★ LATIN AMERICAN
Hidden between a butterfly garden and a monkey jungle, this Latin street food restaurant serves fresh, casual dishes like tacos, ceviche, and arepas using the best ingredients. It's a bit of an uphill hike from town, but there are cold beers waiting, which they brew themselves. There are plenty of options for vegans and vegetarians.

Near the Mariposario, Montezuma. ✆ **8315-8003.** Main courses C4,000–C10,000. Tues Sat–3pm, 5-9pm.

El Sano Banano Village Cafe ★★ INTERNATIONAL/ VEGETARIAN
El Sano Banano has always been the heart and soul and social center of Montezuma. It doesn't hurt that it's also located at the rough geographic center of town, just across from the small central park. The menu is focused on vegetarian and market-fresh cooking, with a long list of vegan, gluten-free, and raw food choices. The salads are huge and plentiful and the sandwiches are served on home-baked whole-wheat bread and buns. No red meat is offered, but seafood and free range poultry make their way into a range of dishes, from Thai-style spring rolls to enchiladas to pasta arrabiata. Every evening at 7:30pm, recent releases and classic movies are shown on a large screen. *Tip:* There are lots of seating options, but the prized tables are located in the back patio garden, under the tall shade trees.

Montezuma. http://elsanobanano.com. ✆ **2642-0944.** Main courses C3,500–C8,500. Daily 7am–9pm.

Playa de los Artistas ★★★ ITALIAN/MEDITERRANEAN
This is the place to go for a special occasion or a date night. Dim lighting, soft electronic music, and large wooden tables spread around the covered patio and open garden area (just a few steps from the ocean) make this a wonderfully romantic place to dine. And the food is superb. It arrives from two distinct places: a small kitchen in the owners' home behind the dining area, and a large outdoor grill and wood-burning oven. The menu is handwritten every day and adapts to what's fresh and available. You might find some fresh-caught octopus grilled and served over crostini, or slow-cooked pork ribs in a rum-and-honey glaze. Seafood is the main draw here, and the whole grilled fresh catch of the day is hard to top.

Across from Hotel Los Mangos, Montezuma. ✆ **2642-0920.** Reservations recommended. No credit cards. Main courses C6,000–C10,000. Mon–Fri 5pm–9:30pm, Sat noon–9:30. **Note:** Lunch is sometimes served on weekdays during the high season.

Ylang Ylang ★ INTERNATIONAL/VEGETARIAN The main restaurant at the wonderful **Ylang Ylang Beach Resort** ★★★ (see p 308) tries to please all its guests, and usually succeeds, by offering quite a few vegan, gluten-free, and raw options, as well as sushi and a range of Asian-inspired dishes. Presentations are artistic, and there are also plenty of meat, chicken, and seafood dishes. The setting is also pleasing: an open-air but covered patio, where you'll be able to see the beach and the ocean beyond.

Ylang Ylang Beach Resort, Montezuma. ℂ **2642-0402.** Reservations recommended. Main courses $14–$28, including tax and tip. Daily 7am–9pm.

Entertainment & Nightlife

Montezuma has had a tough time coming to terms with its nightlife. For years, local businesses banded together to force most of the loud, late-night activity out of town. This has eased somewhat, allowing for quite an active nightlife in Montezuma proper. The local action seems to base itself either at **Chico's Bar** ★ or at the bar at the **Hotel Moctezuma** (ℂ **2642-0058**). Both are located on the main strip in town facing the water. If your evening tastes are mellower, **El Sano Banano Village Cafe** ★★ (p 311) serves as the local cinema, with nightly late-run features projected on a large screen.

MALPAÍS & SANTA TERESA ★★

150km (93 miles) W of San José; 12km (7½ miles) S of Cóbano

Malpaís (or Mal País) means "badlands," but that's hardly descriptive of this booming beach area today. Malpaís is a term sometimes used to refer to a string of neighboring beaches, including Malpaís, Playa Carmen, Santa Teresa, Playa Hermosa, and Playa Manzanillo—though the region is increasingly referred to as Santa Teresa. These beaches are long, wide expanses of light sand dotted with rocky outcroppings. This is one of Costa Rica's hottest spots, and development rages on at a dizzying pace, especially in Santa Teresa. Still, it will take some time before this place is anything like more developed destinations Tamarindo or Manuel Antonio. In Malpaís and Santa Teresa today, you'll find a mix of beach hotels and resorts, restaurants, shops, and private houses, as well as miles of often deserted beach, and easy access to some nice jungle and the nearby **Cabo Blanco Absolute Nature Reserve** ★★ (p 306).

Essentials

GETTING THERE & DEPARTING By Plane: The nearest airport is in Tambor (p 297), about 22km (14 miles) from Malpaís; the ride takes around 20 to 25 minutes. Some of the hotels listed below might be willing to pick you up in Tambor for a reasonable fee. If not, you'll have to hire a taxi, which could cost $60 to $70. **Taxis** are generally waiting to

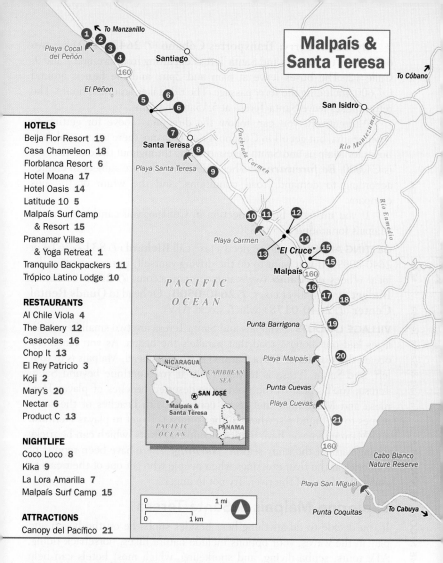

Malpaís & Santa Teresa

To Manzanillo

Playa Cocal del Peñón

Santiago

El Peñón

To Cóbano

San Isidro

Río Montezuma

Santa Teresa

Quebrada Carmen

Playa Santa Teresa

Río Enmedio

Playa Carmen

"El Cruce"

Malpaís

PACIFIC OCEAN

Punta Barrigona

Playa Malpaís

Punta Cuevas

Playa Cuevas

NICARAGUA

CARIBBEAN SEA

SAN JOSÉ

Malpaís & Santa Teresa

PANAMA

PACIFIC OCEAN

Cabo Blanco Nature Reserve

Playa San Miguel

Punta Coquitas

To Cabuya

0 — 1 mi
0 — 1 km

HOTELS
Beija Flor Resort **19**
Casa Chameleon **18**
Florblanca Resort **6**
Hotel Moana **17**
Hotel Oasis **14**
Latitude 10 **5**
Malpaís Surf Camp
  & Resort **15**
Pranamar Villas
  & Yoga Retreat **1**
Tranquilo Backpackers **11**
Trópico Latino Lodge **10**

RESTAURANTS
Al Chile Viola **4**
The Bakery **12**
Casacolas **16**
Chop It **13**
El Rey Patricio **3**
Koji **2**
Mary's **20**
Nectar **6**
Product C **13**

NIGHTLIFE
Coco Loco **8**
Kika **9**
La Lora Amarilla **7**
Malpaís Surf Camp **15**

ATTRACTIONS
Canopy del Pacífico **21**

meet most regularly scheduled planes, but if they aren't, you can call **Richard** (© **8360-8166** or 2640-0099) for a cab.

By Car: Follow the directions to Montezuma (see "Playa Montezuma," p 302). At Cóbano, follow the signs to Malpaís and Playa Santa Teresa. It's another 12km (7½ miles) down a rough dirt road that requires four-wheel-drive much of the year, especially during the rainy season.

To drive from Liberia, head out of town on the main road to the Guanacaste beaches, passing through Filadelfia, Santa Cruz, and Nicoya on your way toward the turn for La Amistad Bridge. Continue straight at this turnoff, and follow the directions for this route as listed above.

By Bus & Ferry: Transportes Cóbano (© 2642-1112) has two daily buses to Malpaís and Santa Teresa departing from Avenida 7 and 9, Calle 12. The buses leave at 6am and 2pm, and the fare is around C7,600, including the ferry passage. The ride takes around 6 hours. The return buses leave Santa Teresa at 5:15am and 2pm.

Alternatively, you can follow the directions above for getting to Montezuma, but get off in Cóbano. From Cóbano, there are several daily buses for Malpaís and Santa Teresa running throughout the day. The fare is C1,000. **Be forewarned:** These bus schedules are subject to change according to demand, road conditions, and the whim of the bus company.

If you miss the bus connection in Cóbano, you can hire a cab to Malpaís for around $25 to $30.

GETTING AROUND   If you need a taxi, call **Richard** (© 8317-7614 or 2640-0099). If you want to do the driving yourself, you can contact the local offices of **Alamo** (www.alamocostarica.com; © 2640-0526) or **Budget** (www.budget.co.cr; © 2640-0500). Or head to **Quads Rental Center** (© 2640-0178), which stocks ATVs.

VILLAGE LAYOUTS   Malpaís and Santa Teresa are two small beach villages laid out along a road that parallels the beach. As you reach the ocean, the road forks; Playa Carmen is straight ahead, Malpaís is to your left, and Santa Teresa is to your right. If you continue beyond Santa Teresa, you'll come to the even-more-deserted beaches of playas Hermosa and Manzanillo (not to be confused with beaches of the same names to be found elsewhere in the country). To get to playas Hermosa and Manzanillo, you have to ford a couple of rivers, which can be tricky during parts of the rainy season. **Warning:** There have been reports of robberies at the river crossings when people who get out of their cars to check the depth of the river. Try not to linger.

Exploring Malpaís & Santa Teresa

If you decide to do anything here besides sunbathe on the beach and play in the waves, your options include nature hikes, horseback riding, ATV tours, scuba diving, and snorkeling, which most hotels can help arrange. Surfing is a major draw, with miles of beach breaks and a few points to boot. If you want to rent a board or take a lesson, try **Costa Rica Surf & SUP** (www.costaricasurfandsup.com; © 2640-0328), **Surfing Costa Rica Pura Vida** (www.surfingcostaricapuravida.com; © 8333-7825), or **Del Soul Surf School** (www.surfvacationcostarica. com; © 8878-0880).

If you've gotten beat up by the waves, or are sore from paddling out, you'll find several excellent spas in town. The best and most extensive (and expensive) is at the **Florblanca Resort** (p 315). But you might also check in with the **Pranamar Villas & Yoga Retreat** (p 317), located on

Surfing in Santa Teresa

the beach, at the northern end of Santa Teresa.

For zipline adventures, head to **Canopy del Pacífico** (www.canopymalpais.com; ℂ **2640-0360;** $50), which is toward the southern end of Malpaís and just slightly inland. A 2-hour tour over the nearly 2km (1.2 miles) of cables touches down on 11 plat-forms, features two rappels, and offers good views of both the forest and the ocean below. Round-trip transportation from an area hotel is $10 per person.

For fishing, wildlife viewing and bird-watching, there's the highly recommend **Sapoa Adventures ★★** (www.sapoaadventures.com; ℂ **8996-9000**).

Where to Stay

EXPENSIVE

Casa Chameleon ★★   Don't let the steep narrow driveway scare you off. Once you make it to the top, you'll find a collection of refined bun-galows at this couples-only retreat from this growing brand with chic hotels popping up around the country. Every bungalow is different, but all feature airy layouts, large kitchenettes or full kitchens, and French doors that open onto a private plunge pool with panoramic ocean and jungle views. Antique dressers and nightstands, four-poster beds, and Balinese lamps are all part of the swank decor. The bungalows are spread over a steep hillside, and those farthest from the main lodge and restau-rant are a bit of a hike. The food here is standout, with a set menu con-sisting of a few unique options every night, usually involving the fusion of local ingredients with recipes from around the globe.

Malpaís. www.hotelcasachameleon.com. ℂ **888/705-0274** in the U.S. and Canada, or 2288-2879 in Costa Rica. 6 units. $455 double, includes breakfast and taxes. No children allowed. **Amenities:** Restaurant; bar; pool; free Wi-Fi. Minimum 2-night stay.

Florblanca Resort ★★★   This is the premier boutique luxury beach resort in this area in a region full of boutique luxury beach resorts. Flor-ablanca consists of a collection of massive, elegant private villas spread around exuberant gardens. The foliage is so thick and abundant that you may get lost on the stone walkways that weave through the resort. About half the villas are designed for couples, and the rest feature a separate

Guest room at Florblanca Resort

upstairs bedroom with two twins perfect for families—although no children under 6 are allowed. All feature a humongous living room that opens to an equally spacious private patio area, as well as large, open-air bathrooms with outdoor rain showers and separate free-standing tubs in a small private garden. Enjoy a morning Pilates or Ashtanga yoga class in the ocean-view open-air dojo, and follow it up with a cool dip in the large two-tiered pool. The spa is superb and the on-site restaurant **Nectar ★★★** (see p 320) is one of the best in the area.

Playa Santa Teresa. www.florblanca.com. 📞 **800/683-1031** in the U.S. and Canada, or 2640-0232 in Costa Rica. 11 units. $400 double; $675 2-bedroom villa, includes breakfast and taxes. No children under 6. **Amenities:** Restaurant; bar; small gym; outdoor pool; room service; spa; watersports equipment rental; free Wi-Fi.

Latitude 10 ★★ If you're looking for an intimate and exclusive beachfront getaway, it's hard to beat this fine-looking little resort. With only five independent bungalows and one main lodge room, it never gets crowded, and often is rented out entirely by a family or group. The bungalows are built from local hardwoods and show heavy Indonesian and Balinese influences in the design and decor. With sliding wooden doors and slatted windows, they are designed to be entirely open (there's no air-conditioning or locks on the doors), especially during the day. The resort sits on the far northern end of Santa Teresa beach, with just a pool, a patch of well-manicured lawn and a string of coconut palms separating it from the sand and sea.

Santa Teresa. www.latitude10resort.com. © **4001-0667.** 6 units. $290–$410 double; includes breakfast and taxes. **Amenities:** Restaurant, bar; outdoor pool; free Wi-Fi.

Pranamar Villas & Yoga Retreat ★★   Pranamar feels like a small village, with tight paths overflowing with tropical foliage weaving between thatched-roof buildings, with wood and bamboo walls. As is common on this coast, there's a heavy dose of Balinese, Thai, and Indonesian artwork, crafts, and furnishings, but it's mixed in with elements from Mexico, Guatemala, and Ecuador. As the name suggests, yoga is an integral part of the program here, with regular daily classes, a steady stream of visiting workshops, and a large and pretty yoga studio. The hotel's Buddha Eyes restaurant specializes in healthy and vegetarian cuisine, without skimping on flavor. This hotel is located on the far northern edge of Santa Teresa, right where it becomes Playa Hermosa.

Santa Teresa. www.pranamarvillas.com. © **2640-0852.** 10 units. $275–$405 double; $375-$510 villa, includes breakfast, daily yoga class, and taxes. **Amenities:** Restaurant; bar; saltwater pool; spa treatments; free Wi-Fi.

Pranamar Villas & Yoga Retreat

MODERATE

Indigo Yoga Surf Resort ★ (http://indigoyogaresort.com; ☎ **2640-1007**) is a cozy little resort with an excellent restaurant in Malpaís. Look at it if the ones below are full.

Hotel Moana ★ Spread over a steep mountainside toward the northern end of Malpaís, just a little inland from the beach, the Hotel Moana has an African theme, which makes for a fun change. Many of the rooms are decorated with tribal masks, shields, spears, and even a zebra skin hung on the walls. The best rooms and the hotel's restaurant are on the highest points of the property. And though it requires a bit of energy to climb the steps, it's definitely worth the effort to soak in the unobstructed views of the Pacific Ocean and rugged coastline. Hotel Moana also rents out a spectacular five-bedroom independent house, Casa Moana, located above the hotel, perfect for larger groups or families.

Malpaís. www.moanacostarica.com. ☎ **888/865-8032** in the U.S. and Canada, or 2640-0230 in Costa Rica. 10 units. $105–$145 double; $245-$280 suite, includes breakfast and taxes. Closed Sept–Oct. **Amenities:** Restaurant, bar; Jacuzzi; pool; free Wi-Fi.

Trópico Latino Lodge ★★ This small beachfront resort is set on a large, mostly forested piece of land fronting a prime patch of sand in the center of Santa Teresa. You can opt for the older, spacious, and economical garden units, or splurge for a newer beachfront room or bungalow. These latter bungalows feature roughhewn wood planks for walls and peaked wood ceilings; it's a handsome look. The expansive grounds here are covered with tall pochote trees that are often frequented by roaming bands of howler monkeys. The hotel has a small pool, a yoga studio and a spa, all with ocean views, and the Shambala restaurant is excellent. Some of the most coveted surf spots in Santa Teresa are directly in front of this resort.

Santa Teresa. www.hoteltropicolatino.com. ☎ **800/724-1235** in the U.S. and Canada, or 2640-0062 in Costa Rica. 21 units. $150–$301 double, includes breakfast and taxes. **Amenities:** Restaurant; bar; Jacuzzi; pool; small spa; free Wi-Fi.

INEXPENSIVE

Hardcore budget travelers should check out **Tranquilo Backpackers** ★ (www.tranquilobackpackers.com; ☎ **2640-0589**), a bit inland off the road to Santa Teresa. It has a mix of dorm-style and private rooms.

Hotel Oasis ★★ This hotel is aptly named. Individual bungalows and studio apartments are spread around shady grounds, just a short walk from the beach and some of Malpaís's most popular surf breaks. The rooms are quite sparse in decor but are well-maintained and very fairly priced. Most feature exposed beam ceilings and varnished wood lattice work over the windows. All have a basic kitchenette; and those in the studios are outdoors. The bungalows are fab for families, with separate master and kids' rooms. However, only the two studios have air-conditioning. There's a small pool, and the owners are very hands-on and attentive.

Malpaís. www.oasis.cr. ✆ **2640-0259.** 8 units. $105-$140 double. **Amenities:** Small outdoor pool; free Wi-Fi.

Malpaís Surf Camp & Resort ★   This multifaceted, budget-conscious resort offers a wide range of rooms and prices. You can opt for everything from bunk-bed rooms with shared bathrooms to private poolside villas. You can even pitch a tent here. Budget-conscious surfers tend to fill the garden ranchos, which have crushed-stone floors and tree-trunk columns supporting corrugated plastic roofs. This same green roofing material is used as half-walls to divide up the ranchos into separate sleeping areas. On the other end of the spectrum, there are fully equipped villas with air-conditioning and contemporary appointments. A good-size, free-form pool sits at the center of the complex, which itself is about a 5-minute walk from the waves.

Malpaís. http://malpaissurfcamp.com. ✆ **2640-0031.** 16 units, 8 with shared bathroom. $15 per person, camping; $45 double w/shared bathroom; $75 double w/ private bathroom; $95 villa. **Amenities:** Restaurant; bar; gym; pool; board rental; free Wi-Fi.

Where to Eat

Mary's (www.maryscostarica.com; ✆ 2640-0153) is a very popular open-air joint that features wood-oven baked pizzas and fresh seafood. It's toward the northern end of Malpaís. At the Playa Carmen Commercial Center, at the crossroads at the entrance to town, you'll find a small food court with a wide range of options, including the bistro-style **Chop It** ★★ (✆ 2640-0000). Open just for lunch, it serves a range of salads, wraps, and justifiably popular burgers. Gluten-free buns are even offered. Another good option here is **Product C** ★★ (✆ 2640-1026), a seafood retail outlet that also cooks up the daily catch, makes fresh *ceviche,* and serves fresh, farm-grown, local oysters. Just across the street you'll find **The Bakery** ★★ (✆ 2640-0560), which serves an amazing array of fresh pastries and baked goods, along with sandwiches and pizzas. For sushi and Asian fusion, there's **Katana** (✆ 2640-0920), north of the crossroads.

On the far northern end of Playa Santa Teresa, **El Rey Patricio** ★★ (www.elreypatricio.com; ✆ 2640-0248) has tasty tapas, drinks, and a sunset view, and **Al Chile Viola** ★ (✆ 2640-0433) is a good Italian restaurant in town. Even farther, near the start of Playa Hermosa, **Koji** ★★ (✆ 2640-0815) another popular sushi joint.

Nectar restaurant at Florblanca Resort

EXPENSIVE

Nectar ★★★ FUSION The flagship restaurant at **Florblanca Resort** ★★★ (p 315) is consistently one of the top fine-dining experiences in the country. Chef Norman Roqhuett Mata has built upon a long tradition of fine chefs at the helm of the kitchen here. Start things off with a ceviche tasting or a rock octopus salad. Main courses run the gamut from a fresh-caught togarashi spiced seared tuna to perfectly grilled grass-fed beef tenderloin. Those looking for lighter fare can peruse the sushi and tapas menus. Meals are served at heavy teak tables in an elegant open-air dining area overlooking the pool and beach. At night, dim lighting and candles create a romantic vibe.

Florblanca Resort, Santa Teresa. © **2640-0232.** Reservations recommended. Main courses $24–$30. Daily 7am–9pm.

INEXPENSIVE

Las Caracolas ★★ SEAFOOD/COSTA RICAN/MEXICAN This place would win major points for the view and ambience alone, but the food is super fresh and tasty, and it's a great value. The ceviche here is made daily with locally caught fish and seafood, and you can't go wrong with a grilled filet of dorado in garlic sauce. The fish tacos are really good; they're served in a crispy fried flour tortilla, more like a *flauta*. As for the ambience, patrons dine at large communal tables under trees close to the water, or in a series of more intimate pop-up shade structures and rustic thatched-roof *palapas* spread around the sloping grounds. When you're finished with your meal, feel free to stretch out in one of the hammocks hung between the coconut palms. Caracolas is also a perfect choice for sunset cocktails and appetizers.

On the beach, about 1km south of the main crossroads in Malpaís. ✆ **2291-1470.** Main courses C4,950–C9,500. Daily 11:30am–8:30pm.

Entertainment & Nightlife

The most popular bar in the area is **Coco Loco ★** (✆ **6097-2557**), right on the beach in Malpaís. It features a mix of live bands and DJs, with weekly reggae and Latin nights, as well as a monthly full moon party. Thursday nights in Santa Teresa belong to the punk-ska-reggae band that holds forth at **Kika** (✆ **2640-0408**). Also in Santa Teresa, **La Lora Amarilla** (✆ **2640-0134**) is a classic local nightspot that heats up on Saturday night, when the locals come to dance salsa and merengue.

A Truly Remote Beach: Undiscovered, for Now

The Nicoya Peninsula coastline between Santa Teresa and Playa Sámara is perhaps the last undeveloped stretch of Costa Rican coastline. The following hotel is roughly midway between Santa Teresa and Playa Sámara. It can be reached year round by rough, mostly unmarked dirt roads, so it's best to coordinate your transportation with the hotel.

Cristal Azul ★ You'll need a four-wheel-drive vehicle to reach this isolated hilltop hotel and its four individual cabins. They are simple, almost to the point of austere, but all offer 180-degree views over a patch of flat farmland and out to the sea. At the beach, Playa San Miguel is a virtually undiscovered piece of Pacific coast sand. The hotel operates a small beachfront bar and restaurant during the day. Hosts Zene and Henner Morales are very personable and attentive and pretty much always on-site.

Playa San Miguel. www.cristalazul.com. ✆ **888/822-7369** in the U.S. and Canada, or 2655-8135 in Costa Rica. 4 units. $225 double, includes breakfast and taxes. **Amenities:** Restaurant; bar; pool; free Wi-Fi.

PLAYA SÁMARA ★

35km (22 miles) S of Nicoya; 245km (152 miles) W of San José

Playa Sámara is a long, broad beach on a gently curved horseshoe-shaped bay. Unlike most of the other beaches along this stretch of the Pacific coast, the water here is usually relatively calm and safe for swimming

Horseback riding by Florblanca Resort

because an offshore island and rocky headlands break up most of the surf. That said, there are often gentle rollers, and you'll find plenty of surf schools and lessons perfect for beginners. Playa Sámara is popular both with Tico families seeking a quick getaway and with young Ticos looking to do some serious beach partying. On weekends, in particular, it can get rowdy. Still, the calm waters and steep cliffs on the far side of the bay make this a very attractive spot, and the beach is so long that the crowds are usually well dispersed. Moreover, if you drive along the rugged coastal road in either direction, you'll discover some truly spectacular and isolated beaches.

Essentials

GETTING THERE & DEPARTING   By Car: Head west from San José on the San José–Caldera Highway (CR27). When you reach Caldera, follow the signs to Puntarenas and the Inter-American Highway (CR1). You will actually follow signs for Liberia and San José, which are, in fact, leading you to the unmarked entrance to CR1. This road (CR23) ends when it hits the Inter-American Highway. Pass under the bridge and follow the on-ramp, which will put you on the highway heading north. Forty-seven kilometers (29 miles) after you get on the Inter-American Highway heading north, you'll see signs and the turnoff for La Amistad Bridge (CR18). After crossing the bridge, continue on CR18 until it hits CR21. Take this road north to Nicoya. Turn into the town of Nicoya, and head more or less straight through town until you see signs for Playa Sámara. From here, it's a well-marked and paved road (CR150) all the way to the beach.

To drive to Sámara from Liberia, head out of town on the main road to the Guanacaste beaches, passing through Filadelfia, Santa Cruz, and Nicoya. Once you reach Nicoya, follow the directions outlined above.

By Bus: Alfaro express buses (www.empresaalfaro.com; © **2222-2666**) leave San José daily at noon and 5pm from Avenida 5 between calles 14 and 16. The trip lasts 5 hours; the one-way fare is C4,265. Extra buses are sometimes added on weekends and during peak periods.

Alternatively, you can take a bus from this same station to Nicoya and then catch a second bus from Nicoya to Sámara. **Alfaro** buses leave San José nearly every hour between 5:30am and 5pm. The fare is C4,250.

The trip can take between 4 and 5½ hours, depending if the bus goes via Liberia or La Amistad Bridge. The latter route is much faster and much more frequent. **Empresa Rojas Castro** (© **2685-5032**) buses leave Nicoya for Sámara and Carrillo regularly throughout the day, between 5am and 9pm. The trip's duration is 1½ hours. The fare to Sámara is C3,730; the fare to Carrillo is C3,500.

Express buses to San José leave daily at 10am and noon. Buses for Nicoya leave throughout the day between 5am and 6pm. Buses leave Nicoya for San José nearly every hour between 3am and 5pm.

Interbus (www.interbusonline.com; © **4100-0888**) has a daily bus that leaves San José for

Playa Sámara

Cabo Blanco Absolute Nature Reserve

Playa Sámara at 8am. The fare is $54, and the bus will pick you up at most San José-area hotels.

GETTING AROUND   If you need a ride around Sámara, or to one of the nearby beaches, have your hotel call you a taxi. Rides in town should cost $3 to $5; rides to nearby beaches might run $10 to $25.

CITY LAYOUT   Sámara is a busy little town at the bottom of a steep hill. The main road heads straight into town, passing the soccer field before coming to an end at the beach. Just before the beach is a road to the left that leads to most of the hotels listed below. This road also leads to Playa Carrillo (below) and the **Hotel Punta Islita** (p 329). If you turn right 3 blocks before hitting the beach, you'll hit the coastal road that goes to playas Buena Vista, Barrigona, and eventually Nosara.

FAST FACTS   To reach the local police, dial ℂ **2656-0436.** Sámara has a small **medical clinic** (ℂ **2656-0166**). A branch of **Banco Nacional** (ℂ **2656-0089**) is on the road to Playa Buena Vista, just as you head out of town. For full-service laundry, head to **Green Life Laundry** (ℂ **2656-1051**), about 3 blocks west of the Banco Nacional.

Exploring Playa Sámara

Playa Sámara is a somewhat quiet and underdeveloped beach town, and most folks are content to simply hang on the beach and swim in the gentle waves. If you're looking for something more, there's horseback riding either on the beach or through the bordering pastures and forests. There's also sea kayaking in the calm waters off Playa Sámara, sportfishing, snorkeling, scuba diving, boat tours, mountain biking, and tours to Playa Ostional to see the nesting of olive ridley sea turtles. You can book any of these tours at your hotel or through **Carrillo Adventures** (www.carrilloadventures.com; ✆ **2656-0606**), an excellent all-around local tour company.

You'll find that the beach is nicer and cleaner down at the south end. Better yet, head about 8km (5 miles) south to **Playa Carrillo ★★**, a long crescent of soft, white sand. With almost no development here, the beach is nearly always deserted. Loads of palm trees provide shade. If you've got a good four-wheel-drive vehicle, ask for directions at your hotel and set off in search of the hidden gems of **Playa Buena Vista** and **Playa Barrigona ★★**, which are north of Sámara, less than a half-hour drive.

Scuba diving near Playa Samara

CANOPY TOURS **Wingnuts Canopy Tours** (www.wingnutscanopy. com; ✆ **2656-0153**) offers zipline canopy tours. The 2-hour outing costs $60 per person or $45 for those under 12. If you want to repeat the adventure, Wingnuts offers a 25% discount on your second tour. The office is by the giant strangler fig tree, or *matapalo,* toward the southern end of the beach.

SPORTFISHING Almost every hotel in the area can arrange sportfishing trips, or you can contact **Kingfisher** ★ (www.costaricabillfishing.com; ✆ **800/783-3817** in U.S or 8358-9561 in Costa Rica). Rates run from $900 for a half day to $1,250 for a full day.

SURFING The waves hitting Playa Sámara are somewhat muffled by an offshore reef and headlands on each side. For some this makes it a great wave to learn on. For lessons or to rent a board, check in with **C&C Surf Shop and School** (www.cncsurfschool.com; ✆ **5006-0369**) or **Choco's Surf School** (www.chocossurfschool.com; ✆ **8937-5246**). Surfboard rentals run around $15 per day. Private lessons cost $30 to $50 per hour.

ULTRALIGHT FLYING For a bird's-eye view of the area, go to the **Auto Gyro America**★★ (http://autogyroamerica.com; ✆ **8330-3923**) in Playa Buena Vista. It offers flights in a two-seat (one for you, one for the pilot) Gyrocopter, the ultralight equivalent of a helicopter. Although it might feel like little more than a modified tricycle with a nylon wing and lawnmower motor, these winged wonders are very safe. A 20-minute flight runs $110, while an hour-long tour costs $230.

WILDLIFE VIEWING Located near Barra Honda National Park (p 327), **Rancho Humo** ★★ (www.ranchohumo.com; ✆ **2233-2233**) is a private wildlife reserve that offers fabulous bird-watching and wildlife viewing opportunities along the Tempisque River basin and surrounding wetlands. The area is rich in waterbird species, shore lizards, and crocodiles. A full-day tour ($99) includes a river boat trip, a tour of the reeds and lowland forest in a motorized safari-style vehicle, a tour of nearby cattle ranching operations, as well as lunch. Transportation can be provided, and you can choose a half-day tour that combines some elements of the full-day tour.

Learn the Language

Intercultura Costa Rica (www.interculturacostarica.com; ✆ **2656-3000** in Sámara) offers a range of programs and private lessons and can arrange for a home stay with a local family. The facility even features classes with ocean views, although that might be a detriment to your language learning.

Going Down Under

Barra Honda National Park ★ (℃ **2659-1551;** daily 8am–4pm; $17 admission) is an extensive system of caves with a long history. Here human remains have been found that are thought to be 2,000 years old, believed to be Chorotega nobles. In 1967, spelunkers discovered 42 caves here, though only 19 were ever explored and only one, **Caverna Terciopelo**, is open to the public. To go inside, you'll need to hire a guide, which should cost around $30 per person, depending on the size of your group and your bargaining abilities. You begin the tour by getting harnessed and roped and then descending a scary vertical aluminum ladder that is 17m (56 ft.) long, about the height of a five-story building. Inside you'll see an impressive array of stalactites and stalagmites, many of them named after something they resemble (like a hen and her chicks, and papaya, and fried eggs). Cave tours are conducted from 8am to 1pm daily, and the park is open for hiking until 4pm, though the park is closed during the rainy season (May to Mid-Nov). Headlamps and helmets are provided. Do not wear flip-flops; you will be turned away for wearing them. Even if you don't enter the cave, the trails around Barra Honda and its prominent limestone plateau are great for hiking and bird-watching. Be sure to stop at **La Cascada,** a gentle waterfall that fills and passes through a series of calcium and limestone pools, some of them large enough to bathe in.

Getting there: Head 62km (38 miles) northeast of Playa Sámara on the road to La Amistad Bridge and follow the signs to Barra Honda. If you don't have a car, your best bet is to get to Nicoya, which is about a half-hour away by bus, and then take a taxi to the park, which should cost around $25-$30.

Where to Stay

MODERATE

Fenix Hotel ★   These beachfront studio apartments are a real value. They have a primo location in the middle of Playa Sámara—just a short walk from most of the restaurants, clubs, and downtown hubbub, and yet are quiet and slightly removed. Rooms are set around the hotel's small pool, each unit featuring tropical rattan furnishings and a fully equipped kitchen. Boogie boards are offered free for guest use, and there are hammocks strung from coconut palms perfectly positioned right between the pool and sea. The owners are very hands-on, friendly, and helpful.

Playa Sámara. www.fenixhotel.com. ℃ **2656-0158.** 6 units. $115–$145 double, includes breakfast and taxes; children 17 and under stay free in parents' room. **Amenities:** Small outdoor pool; free Wi-Fi.

The Hideaway Hotel ★★ This two-story boutique hotel has the feel of a converted home, due in no small part to the warm welcome owner Martina and her staff give the guests. Rooms are oversized, with really handsome blue, green, and white comforters and curtains. The color theme continues outside, where bright blue chairs and lounges ring a crescent-shaped pool. The hotel is about a block or so inland from the far southern end of Playa Sámara, so a rental car is helpful to get to and from the many restaurants, bars, and shops in town.

Playa Sámara. www.thehideawayplayasamara.com. ℂ **2656-1145.** 12 units. $119–$139 double, includes breakfast and taxes. **Amenities:** Restaurant; bar; pool; free Wi-Fi.

Hotel Guanamar ★ Guests spend a lot of time in and around the pool here. It's right next to the restaurant and bar; has a broad wooden deck on all sides; and boasts captivating views of Carillo Bay, offshore islands, and shimmering seas. Rooms tend to be spare-looking, but those that are set into the hillside have those same spectacular views from their balconies, so you likely won't mind much. The Bay Front rooms are located on the lowest point of the property, so you'll be getting a workout trekking to and from meals, though you are also much closer to the beach. As at The Hideaway Hotel (above), it helps to have a rental car here.

Puerto Carrillo. www.hotelguanamar.com. ℂ **2282-8700.** 37 units. $150–$170 double, includes breakfast and taxes. **Amenities:** Restaurant; bar; pool; room service; free Wi-Fi.

INEXPENSIVE

Tico Adventure Lodge ★ (www.ticoadventurelodge.com; ℂ **2656-0628**), with a spa and surf school, is a good budget option about 2 blocks from the beach, in the heart of town. A slew of very inexpensive places to stay are along the road into town and around the soccer field, but many of them are not very appealing.

Casa del Mar ★★ You enter under a shower of flowering bougainvillea and immediately are enveloped by the calm, cool, and relaxed atmosphere that pervades the Casa del Mar. Rooms are spacious, clean, and comfortable, and most come with air-conditioning and private bathrooms (a few of the cheapest ones have neither). The beach is just a few steps away, across the street. The pool is just a bit bigger and no deeper than a fountain, but it will cool you off on a hot day.

Playa Sámara. www.hotelcasadelmarsamara.com. ℂ **2656-0264.** 17 units, 11 w/ private bathroom. $55 double w/shared bathroom; $90–$100 double w/private bathroom and A/C, includes taxes. Breakfast included in most rates. **Amenities:** Pool; Jacuzzi; free Wi-Fi.

Hotel Belvedere ★ German emigrants Manfred and Michaela Landwehr opened the Belvedere more than 2 decades ago. It's grown over the years, but always kept to its mission of providing clean, cozy rooms at a reasonable price. In the newer rooms in the annex a bit uphill from the original hotel, you'll find a larger pool and more exuberant gardens. In fact, these gardens join wild forest and are occasionally visited by troops of howler and spider monkeys. No matter the location, rooms are well-kept and many feature a yellow hand-painted wash effect that serves as wainscoting. Large, filling breakfasts are served at the main lodge, where you'll also find a second, smaller pool. It's just a 1-block walk into the heart of town, and 2 blocks to the beach.

Playa Sámara. www.belvederesamara.net. ⓒ **2656-0213.** 24 units. $85–$110 double, includes breakfast and taxes. **Amenities:** Lounge; Jacuzzi; 2 pools; free Wi-Fi.

Sámara Tree House Inn ★★ It's not possible to find a room closer to the waves in Playa Sámara. While not true treehouses, four raised-stilt wooden cabins are supported by columns made from whole tree trunks in a tight line facing the ocean. They have prized ocean views from the elevated perch of their large sitting rooms, although the bedrooms feel a bit small and spartan, and there's no air-conditioning. However, every unit here comes with a kitchenette, as well as a large space underneath the living area equipped with a varnished-wood table and chairs and a couple of woven hammocks. There's a tiny pool at the center of the complex, and a few chaise lounges on a patch of well-tended grass facing the beach.

Playa Sámara. www.samaratreehouse.com. ⓒ **2656-0733.** 6 units. $110–$155 double, includes breakfast. **Amenities:** Jacuzzi; pool; free Wi-Fi.

A NEARBY LUXURY HOTEL

Hotel Punta Islita ★★★ This exclusive and remote luxury resort, part of Marriott's exclusive Autograph Collection, sits on a hilltop above the beach. Most of the rooms are private bungalows or villas, adorned with terracotta floor tiles and both thatched and antique-clay-tile roofs. White muslin is hung from the driftwood log used to fashion the four-poster beds—very romantic! And many come with either a private Jacuzzi or plunge pool. The larger villas are great for families and small groups. The beach is 10 minutes or so away on foot, but the hotel runs regular shuttle services and has a canopy tour that ends at the beach (the last is the most fun way to get to the sand). The resort's fab infinity pool is up on the hillside; another pool and bar and grill are down by the beach. Punta Islita actively supports a range of local social, artistic, and conservation projects.

Playa Islita. www.hotelpuntaislita.com. ⓒ **866/446-4053** in the U.S. and Canada, or 2231-6122 in Costa Rica. 58 units, 10 villas. $285–$355 double; $495-$545 suite, includes breakfast. **Amenities:** 2 restaurants; 2 bars; 9-hole golf course and driving range; small gym and spa; Jacuzzi; 2 pools; room service; 2 tennis courts; free Wi-Fi.

9

PUNTARENAS & THE NICOYA PENINSULA

Playa Sámara

Hotel Punta Islita

Where to Eat

Sámara has numerous inexpensive *sodas,* and most of the hotels have their own restaurants. **El Ancla** (www.isamara.co/ancla.htm; © **2656-0716**), located a bit south of downtown, serves up good, simple meals, with an excellent view of the beach and waves.

El Lagarto ★ STEAK/GRILL   Here's the macho way to dine! A massive fire churns out a stream of hot wood-burning coals to feed the large, long barbeque grill stations at this restaurant and bar. Tables are made from massive heavy planks and the food is served on huge, crosscut blocks of wood, which adds to the rustic vibe. Grilled grass-fed and aged meats, seafood, and organic veggies are the heart of the long menu here. North end of Playa Sámara. www.ellagartobbq.com. © **2656-0750.** Reservations recommended. Main courses $8–$32. Daily 3–11pm.

Gusto Beach ★★ ITALIAN/BISTRO   This simple, Italian-run restaurant is basically a beachfront trattoria—and then some. It's also a beach club, where people rent chaise longues to hang for the day, playing volleyball, and catching rays. Food choices range from pastas, panini, and thin-crust pizzas to sushi, sashimi, and curries. Presentations can be creative, like the crisp pan-fried potatoes served in the cooking pan, or the fresh gelato made and served in a mason jar and topped with shaved chocolate. At night, this becomes nightlife central, with live music or DJs.

On the beach, north end of Playa Sámara. © **2656-0252.** Reservations recommended. Main courses C4,900–C14,000. Daily 9am–11pm.

Entertainment & Nightlife

After dark the most happening place in town is **Bar Arriba ★**, a second-floor affair with a contemporary vibe a couple of blocks inland from the beach on the main road into town. Nearby, there's **Microbar Samara ★** (© **8784-7467**) a cutesy pub with craft beer. You might also check out what's going on at **Gusto Beach ★** (see above), **La Vela Latina** (© **2656-2286**), or **Tabanuco** (© **2656-1056**), all on the beach or fronting the water, right near the center of the action, on the main road running parallel to the beach off the center of town.

PLAYA NOSARA ★★

55km (34 miles) SW of Nicoya; 266km (165 miles) W of San José

Playa Nosara is an umbrella term used to refer to several neighboring beaches, spread along an isolated stretch of coast. **Playa Guiones, Playa Pelada, Playa Garza,** and (sometimes) **Playa Ostional** are also lumped into this area. In fact, the village of Nosara itself is several kilometers inland from the beach.

Playa Guiones is one of Costa Rica's most dependable beach breaks, and surfers come here in good numbers throughout the year. Happily, the waves are much less crowded than in Tamarindo.

The best way to get to Nosara is to fly, but with everything so spread out, that makes getting around difficult after you've arrived. The roads to, in, and around Nosara are almost always in very rough shape, with little sign that this will improve anytime soon.

Essentials

GETTING THERE & DEPARTING   By Plane: Nature Air (www.nature air.com; © **800/235-9272** in the U.S. and Canada, or 2299-6000 in Costa Rica) has several flights daily to **Nosara airport** (airport code: NOB). Fares run between $94 and $144 each way.

It's usually about a 5- to 10-minute drive from the airport to most hotels. Taxis wait for every arrival, and fares range between C3,500 and C6,000 to most hotels in Nosara.

By Car: Follow the directions for getting to Playa Sámara (p 322), but watch for a well-marked fork in the road a few kilometers before you reach that beach. The right-hand fork leads to Nosara over another 22km (14 miles) of rough dirt road.

Surfers on Playa Nosara

By Bus: An **Alfaro** express bus (www.empresaalfaro.com; ⓒ **2222-2666** in San José, or 2682-0064 in Nosara) leaves San José daily at 5:30am from Avenida 5 between calles 14 and 16. The trip's duration is 5½ hours; the one-way fare is around C4,800.

You can also take an Alfaro bus from San José to Nicoya and then catch a second bus from Nicoya to Nosara. **Alfaro** buses leave San José nearly every hour between 7:30am and 5pm. The fare is C3,950. The trip can take between 4 and 5½ hours, depending on whether the bus goes via Liberia or La Amistad Bridge. The latter route is much faster and much more frequent. **Empresa Rojas** buses (ⓒ **2685-5352**) leave Nicoya for Nosara daily at 4:45 and 10am, 12:30pm, and 3:30 and 5:30pm. The trip is about 2 hours, and the one-way fare is C1,870. Return buses leave Nosara for Nicoya at 5, 6, and 7am, noon and 3:30pm. A direct Alfaro bus from Nosara to San José leaves daily at 12:30pm. Buses to Nicoya leave Nosara daily at 4:45 and 10am, noon, and 3 and 5:30pm. Buses leave Nicoya for San José nearly every hour 3am to 5pm.

GETTING AROUND **Economy** (www.economyrentacar.com; ⓒ **877/326-7368** in the U.S. and Canada, or 2582-1246 in Costa Rica) and **National** (www.natcar.com; ⓒ **2242-7878**) have offices here. Because demand often outstrips supply, I recommend you reserve a car in advance. You could also rent an ATV from several operators around town, including **Iguana Expeditions** and **Boca Nosara Tours** (p 334). If you need a taxi, call **Taxi Freddy** (☏ 8662-6080) or **Gypsy Cab Company** (www.gypsycabnosara.com; ☏ 8302-1903).

VILLAGE LAYOUT The village of Nosara is about 5km (3 miles) inland from the beach. The small airstrip runs pretty much through the center of town; however, most hotels listed here are on or near the beach itself.

This area was originally conceived and zoned as a primarily residential community. The maze of dirt roads and lack of any single defining thoroughfare can be confusing for first-time visitors. Luckily, a host of hotel and restaurant signs spread around the area help point lost travelers in the direction of their final destination.

FAST FACTS You'll find the post office and police station (☏ 2682-1130) right at the end of the airstrip. An EBAIS medical clinic (☏ 2682-0266) and a couple of pharmacies are in the village as well. Both Banco Popular and Banco de Costa Rica have offices in Nosara with ATMs. There's even a tiny strip mall at the crossroads to Playa Guiones.

Exploring Playa Nosara

Among the several beaches at Nosara are the long, curving **Playa Guiones** ★★, **Playa Nosara** ★, and the diminutive **Playa Pelada** ★. Because the village of Nosara is several miles inland, these beaches tend to be clean, secluded, and quiet. Surfing and bodysurfing are good here, particularly at Playa Guiones, which is garnering quite a reputation as a consistent and rideable beach break. Pelada is a short white-sand beach with three deep scallops, backed by sea grasses and mangroves. There isn't too much sand at high tide, so you'll want to hit the beach when the tide's out. At either end of the beach, rocky outcroppings reveal tide pools at low tide.

When the seas are calm, you can do some decent snorkeling around the rocks and reefs just offshore. Masks, snorkels, and fins can be rented at **Café de Paris** (p 337) or **Coconut Harry's** (p 334). Bird-watchers should explore the mangrove swamps around the estuary mouth of the Río Nosara. Just walk north from Playa Pelada and follow the riverbank; then take the paths into the mangroves. In addition to numerous seabird species, you may spot hawks and other raptors, as well as toucans and parrots.

FISHING All the hotels in the area can arrange fishing charters for $250 to $500 for a half-day, or $450 to $1,200 for a full day. These rates are for one to four people and vary according to boat size and accouterments.

HIKING & WILDLIFE VIEWING Located on land surrounding the Nosara river mouth, the **Nosara Biological Reserve** (www.lagarta.com/reserva.htm; ☏ 2682-0035) features a network of trails and raised walkways through tropical transitional forests and mangrove swamps. More than

270 species of birds have been spotted here. This private reserve is owned and managed by Lagarta Lodge (p 336), and the trails start right at the hotel. Admission is $6. Guided tours and guided boat tours are also available.

HORSEBACK RIDING & QUAD TOURS   The folks at **Boca Nosara Tours** (www.bocanosaratours.com; *©* **2682-0280**) have a large stable of well-cared-for horses and a range of beach, jungle, and waterfall rides to choose from. They also run similar tours on motorized off-road quads. Rates run between $80 and $140 per person, depending on the size of your group and the length of the tour. Another good option for ATV tours and rentals is **iQuad** (www.iquadnosara.com; *©* **8629-8349**).

SEA TURTLE–WATCHING   If you time your trip right, you can do a night tour to nearby **Playa Ostional** to watch nesting olive ridley sea turtles. These turtles come ashore by the thousands in a mass egg-laying phenomenon known as an *arribada*. The *arribadas* are so difficult to predict that no one runs regularly scheduled turtle-viewing trips, but when the *arribada* is in full swing, several local guides and agencies offer tours. These *arribadas* take place 4 to 10 times between July and December; each occurrence lasts between 3 and 10 days. Consider yourself very lucky if you happen to be around during one of these fascinating natural phenomena. Your best bet is to ask the staff at your hotel or check in with the **Associación de Guias de Ostional** ★ (Ostional Local Guide Association; *©* **2682-0428;** asoc.guiasostional@hotmail.com). Tours are generally run at night, but because the turtles come ashore in such numbers, you can sometimes catch them in the early morning light as well. Even if it's not turtle-nesting season, you might want to look into visiting Playa Ostional just to have a long, wide expanse of beach to yourself. However, be careful swimming here because the surf and riptides can be formidable. During the dry season (mid-Nov to Apr), you can usually get here in a regular car, but during the rainy season you'll need four-wheel-drive. This beach is part of **Ostional National Wildlife Refuge** (*©* **2682-0428**). At the northwest end of the refuge is **India Point,** which is known for its tide pools and rocky outcrops.

SURFING   With miles of excellent beach breaks and relatively few crowds, this is a great place to surf or to learn how. If you want to try to stand up for your first time, check in with **Coconut Harry's Surf Shop** (www.coconutharrys.com; *©* **2682-0574**) or **Del Mar Surf Camp** (www.delmarsurfcamp.com; *©* **855/833-5627** in the U.S. and Canada, 2682-1433 in Costa Rica). Both offer solo or group

Yo Quiero Hablar Español
You can brush up on or start up your Spanish at the **Rey de Nosara Language School** (www.reydenosara.itgo.com; *©* **2682-0215**). It offers group and private lessons according to demand, and can coordinate week or multi-week packages.

Yoga class at Nosara Yoga Institute

lessons, multiday packages with accommodations and meals included, and board rental.

YOGA & MORE **Nosara Yoga Institute** ★★ (www.nosarayoga.com; ☏ 866/439-4704 in the U.S. and Canada, 2682-0071 in Costa Rica) offers daily yoga classes, and a host of custom-designed "retreat" options. This is an internationally recognized institute. Its daily 90-minute classes are open to the public and cost just $15, with a mat provided.

There are also regular yoga classes throughout the day, as well as the occasional meditation session, offered up at the Harmony Hotel & Spa (see below).

Where to Stay

The **Nosara Beach House** ★ (www.thenosarabeachhouse.com; ☏ 2682-0019), on Playa Guiones, has clean, comfortable rooms and a swimming pool—and it's right on the beach. For an intimate option that's also a very good deal, check out the **Nosara B&B Retreat** ★ (www.nosararetreat.com; ☏ 2682-0209).

EXPENSIVE

Bodhi Tree Yoga Resort ★ One of a number of new yoga themed resorts in Nosara, Bodhi Tree, a 5-minute walk to the beach, has an all-around wellness vibe that encourages clean, green living. Imagine waking up a yoga session on a platform surrounded by rainforest to the chants of howler monkeys, followed by a green drink at the juice bar, then maybe a surf lesson or spa treatment. Rooms range from simple, cozy cabins with shared bathrooms to the 2-bedroom Bodhi House with its own pool.

Playa Guiones. https://bodhitreeyogaresort.com. © **2682-0256.** 26 units. $205–$359 double; $600 Bodhi House, includes breakfast and one daily yoga class. **Amenities:** Restaurant; bar; pool; spa; gym; free Wi-Fi.

The Harmony Hotel & Spa ★★★

With an enviable setting right on Playa Guiones, this is by far the best hotel option in Nosara. Well-heeled surfers and yogis flock here, and it's often hard to get a room, though it's not over the top luxurious by any means. The entry-level "Coco" rooms are quite spacious, with high peaked wood-paneled ceilings; queen-size beds; and a private, enclosed garden deck area featuring an outdoor shower with massive rainwater-style shower head. The bungalows are even larger, with king-size beds, and there are two-bedroom suites for families or small groups of friends. A short path through thick foliage leads to the waves, and the hotel has a shower and fresh towels waiting for guests where the property lets out onto the beach. There's an excellent on-site spa and yoga facility, which includes meditation and regular workshops. The restaurant serves top-notch locally sourced cuisine and sushi, and there's a juice and coffee bar too. This hotel was awarded the maximum "5 Leaves" by the CST Certification for Sustainable Tourism program, thanks to a comprehensive commitment to environmental protection.

Playa Guiones. www.harmonynosara.com. © **2682-4114.** 25 units. $240–$370 double; $300–$400 bungalow; $600 2-bedroom suite, includes breakfast and 1 yoga class. **Amenities:** Restaurant; bar; loaner bikes; pool; spa; surfboard rental; free Wi-Fi.

Harbor Reef Surf Resort ★

This mini-resort features a mix of rooms and suites at excellent prices, and is quite popular with the surf crowd. All of the rooms are spacious and clean, although a bit bare, with very few decorative touches. Some of the suites come with full kitchens; the staff also rents out several fully equipped houses. The grounds feature tall trees, pretty gardens, and two swimming pools—one with a swim-up bar and the other with a stone waterfall that forms a small private grotto-like area underneath. The beach and popular surf break at Playa Guiones is about a 3-minute walk away. Attached to the resort is a well-stocked convenience store that rents bicycles, ATVs, and golf carts.

Playa Guiones. www.harborreef.com. © **2682-5049.** 23 units. $225 double; $250 suite, includes continental breakfast. **Amenities:** Restaurant; bar; 2 pools; free Wi-Fi.

Lagarta Lodge ★★

Set on a jungle-covered hill on a private nature reserve at the southern end of Playa Nosara, Lagarta Lodge is helping usher in a new era in this rapidly growing beach town. More ecolodge than beach resort with the lush green jungle all around it, Lagarta is still quite refined, with comfortable rooms equipped with a/c and high-end Billerbeck bedding, plus private verandas with views over the treetops to the sand. Eco and social initiatives include wastewater recycling and regular Nicoya dance performance, while their art gallery is filled with Maleku artifacts. While the beach is just a short walk away, there are still good opportunities for spotting motmots and monkeys via electric boat or kayak along the mangroves that line the adjacent Nosara and Montaña rivers.

Playa Nosara. www.lagartalodge.com. © **2682-0035.** 26 units. $285-$400 double, includes breakfast. **Amenities:** Restaurant; bar; 2 pools; Jacuzzi; spa; free Wi-Fi.

INEXPENSIVE

In addition to the place mentioned below, **Kaya Sol ★** (www.nosarahotelkayasol.com; © **2682-1459**) is a popular budget option and surfer hangout.

The Gilded Iguana ★ Located in the heart of Playa Guiones, about 200m (600 ft.) inland from the beach, the Iguana features a mix of rooms, a midsize pool, and one of the best restaurant and bar scenes in the area (p 338). The downside to the restaurant and bar's popularity is that it can be noisy here, especially when there's a live band or major sporting event going on. At press time, the hotel was closed for a major renovation that will add additional rooms, and should re-open sometime in 2018.

Playa Guiones. www.thegildediguana.com. © **2682-0450.** 30 units. $80–$105 double; $120–$150 suite. **Amenities:** Restaurant; bar; pool; free Wi-Fi.

Where to Eat

In addition to the places mentioned below, **Marlin Bill's** (© **2682-0458**) is a popular and massive open-air haunt on the hillside on the main road, just across from **Café de París** (p 337). You can expect to get good, fresh seafood and American classics here. **La Dolce Vita ★★** (© **2682-0107**), on the outskirts of town on the road to Playa Sámara, serves up Italian fare nightly. **Robin's Ice Cream ★** (www.robins icecream.com; © **2682-0617**) makes homemade ice cream and also serves breakfast, lunch, and dinner. Finally, **Go Juice ★** (© **8682-4692**) is a semi-permanent "food truck" dishing out fresh juices, iced coffee drinks, and tuna *poke* bowls. Their signature frozen banana coffee drink has won over more than a few skeptics. For local flavor, **Doña Olga's** is a simple Costa Rican *soda* right on the beach in Playa Pelada. For sushi or just a good cocktail, there's the restaurant at the **Harmony Hotel & Spa** (© 2682-4114).

Café de Paris ★ BAKERY/BISTRO You can stop here for a freshly baked croissant and cup of coffee or a full breakfast. It's also worthwhile for lunch (think burgers, nachos, or wraps) or dinner—both the steak au poivre and fish curry are excellent. A pool, minigolf course, and children's playset just off the main dining area make this a good choice for families with young kids. Café de Paris is located right at the main crossroads for access to Playa Guiones.

On the main road into Nosara. www.cafedeparis.net. ✆ **2682-1036.** Main courses C6,500–C9,900. Daily 7am–5pm.

El Chivo ★ MEXICAN/GRILL The goat, a quirky, thatched roof Mexican dive has the region's best list of tequila and mescal, though the food can be hit or miss. Burritos, quesadillas, and tacos come with a choice of fillings, which include Baja-style fish, jerk chicken, and crispy pork belly, though there is also roasted chicken and Tex-Mex poutine. It gets crowded on Thursday and Friday nights when there is live music (7-10pm).

Playa Pelada. www.elchivo.co. ✆ **2682-0887.** Main courses C4,500–C9,900. Daily 7am–10pm.

The Gilded Iguana ★ SEAFOOD/GRILL The fare here is bar-food-plus, with all the staples you'd expect—burgers, nachos, quesadillas, fajitas, and wings—as well as more substantial (chicken Parmesan) or eclectic (Thai shrimp) fare. The menu also features vegetarian, gluten-free, and low-calorie options. Try the fresh-fish dishes, which are provided daily by Chiqui, the owner's husband, a Nosara-born fisherman and tour guide. Along with the hotel, the restaurant is undergoing a major renovation and should re-open sometime in 2018.

About 90m (295 ft.) inland from the beach at Playa Guiones. www.thegildediguana. com. ✆ **2682-0259.** Main courses C4,000–C9,000. Daily 7am–10pm.

La Luna ★★ INTERNATIONAL This funky, oceanfront bistro enjoys the best setting of any restaurant in Nosara. From its sand and grass perch right above Playa Pelada, you can watch surfers just below from one of the outdoor tables or long couches with overstuffed pillows. This is also a great place to catch the sunset. As darkness sets in, candlelight and strings of bare bulbs running between the trees and main building are lit to create a romantic atmosphere. Wood oven–fired pizzas and Mediterranean fare are the specialties here, but nightly chalkboard specials might feature anything from pad Thai to chicken curry. For lunch, consider the fish tacos. Service can be slow and a bit gruff.

Playa Pelada. ✆ **2682-0122.** Main courses C6,700–C12,500. Daily noon–9pm.

Entertainment & Nightlife

When evening rolls around, don't expect a major party scene. **Kaya Sol** (✆ **2682-1459**) has a lounge that's popular with surfers, and El VChivo has live music on Thursdays and Fridatys. In "downtown" Nosara, you'll probably want to check out either the **Tropicana** (✆ **2682-0140**), the town's long-standing local disco; or **Legends Bar** (© **2682-0184**), an American-style bar with big-screen TVs and pool and foosball tables.

North of Nosara

Just north of Nosara lies Playa Ostional, famous for its massive nestings of olive ridley sea turtles (p 334). This is a very underdeveloped beach village with only a few hotels, the best of which is **Hotel Luna Azul ★** (www.hotellunaazul.com; © **2682-1400**), which features nice individual bungalows and a great view of the ocean—although the beach is a good distance away. If you come to Ostional to surf, try the **Ostional Turtle Lodge** (www.surfingostional.com; © **2682-0131**), a basic hostel right on the beach near the center of the village.

THE NORTHERN ZONE: MOUNTAIN LAKES, CLOUD FORESTS & A VOLCANO

C osta Rica's Northern Zone is a fabulous destination for all manner of adventurers, naturalists, and down-to-earth travelers. The region is home to several prime ecotourism destinations, including the majestic **Arenal Volcano ★★** and the misty **Monteverde Cloud Forest Biological Reserve ★★★**. Changes in elevation create unique microclimates and ecosystems throughout the region. You'll find rainforests and cloud forests, jungle rivers and waterfalls, mountain lakes, lowland marshes, and an unbelievable wealth of birds and other wildlife. In addition to these natural wonders, this region also provides an intimate glimpse into the rural heart and soul of Costa Rica. Small, isolated lodges flourish, and the region's many towns and villages remain predominantly small agricultural communities.

This area is also a must for adventure travelers. The Northern Zone has one of the best windsurfing spots in the world, on **Lake Arenal ★**, as well as excellent opportunities for mountain biking, hiking, canyoning, and river rafting. Zipline canopy tours and suspended forest bridges abound. And after you partake of these adventure activities, you'll find soothing natural hot springs in the area where you can soak your tired muscles. Most travelers would do well to include some time spent in the Northern Zone on any trip to Costa Rica.

THE best NORTHERN ZONE TRAVEL EXPERIENCES

- **Soaking in a Hot Spring at the Foot of Arenal Volcano:** Although the eruptions have stopped, Arenal Volcano remains the source of several natural hot springs, ranging from the over-the-top splendor of Tabacón Grand Spa Thermal Resort, to the simple forest enshrouded pools at the family-run Eco Termales. See p 354.

- **Rappelling Down the Face of a Rainforest Waterfall:** Canyoning is a wet and wild adventure sport that is thriving in the Northern Zone. A mix of hiking, river wading, and rappelling, these tours are offered in La Fortuna and Monteverde. See p 342 and 376.

o **Hiking the Trails of a Cloud Forest:** The well-groomed network of trails at the Monteverde Cloud Forest Biological Reserve reveals its rich mysteries with stunning regularity. Walk through gray mist and peer up at the dense tangle of epiphytes and vines, looking for exotic birds and troops of monkeys. See p 382.

o **Climbing Over Cooled-Off Lava at Arenal National Park:** This area has tons of great hiking, which includes scrambling over the volcano's old lava flows. Most trails are on the relatively flat flanks of the volcano, so there's not too much climbing involved. See p 348.

o **Riding a Horse or Mountain Bike Along a Rural Back Road:** The dirt roads and ox-trails of this rural zone provide a wealth of great opportunities for mountain biking and horseback riding. See the "Exploring" sections of individual destinations throughout this chapter.

ARENAL VOLCANO & LA FORTUNA ★★

140km (87 miles) NW of San José; 61km (38 miles) E of Tilarán

In July 1968, Arenal Volcano, which had lain dormant for hundreds of years, surprised everybody by erupting with sudden violence. The nearby

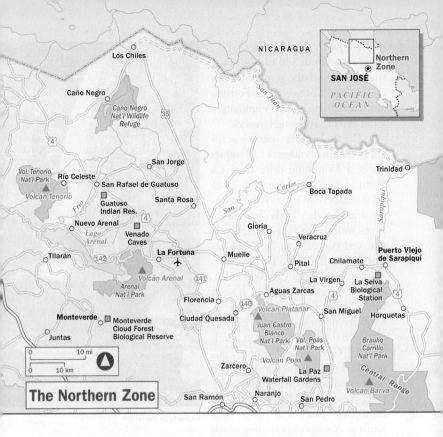

village of Tabacón was destroyed, and nearly 80 of its inhabitants were killed. At 1,607m (5,271 ft.) high, Arenal was for many decades afterward one of the world's most regularly active volcanoes. Sometime around December 2010, it entered into a relatively quiet phase. No one knows how long this will last. Still, rising to a near-perfect cone, the volcano itself remains majestic to gaze upon. And the area offers up a rich variety of primary rainforests, rushing jungle rivers and waterfalls, lush natural hot springs, and a wide range of adventure activities.

Lying at the eastern foot of this natural spectacle is the town of **La Fortuna.** Once a humble little farming village, La Fortuna has become a magnet for travelers from around the world.

Essentials

GETTING THERE & DEPARTING Nature Air (www.natureair.com; *②* **800/235-9272** in the U.S. and Canada, or 2299-6000 in Costa Rica) and **Sansa** (www.flysansa.com; *②* **877/767-2672** in the U.S. and Canada, or 2290-4100 in Costa Rica) each have one daily flight to Arenal/La Fortuna (airport code: FOR) from Juan Santamaría International Airport in San José (airport code: SJO). Fares range from $80 to $110 one-way. Nature Air also sometimes has direct flights between La Fortuna and Tortuguero, which eliminate a lot of driving and long layovers.

The La Fortuna airstrip is actually in the small village of El Tanque, about a 15-minute drive from La Fortuna, and anywhere from 20 to 40 minutes from most of the popular area hotels. **Taxis** are sometimes waiting for arriving flights. If not, you can call one at © **2479-9605.** The fare to La Fortuna runs around C8,500 to C16,000. Also, Nature Air can arrange to have a van waiting for you, for $65 to $130 for up to six people depending upon the location of your hotel.

By Car: Several routes connect La Fortuna and San José. The most popular is to head west on the Inter-American Highway (CR1) from San José, and then turn north at Naranjo, continuing north

La Fortuna Waterfall

through Zarcero to Ciudad Quesada on CR141. From Ciudad Quesada, CR141 passes through Florencia, Jabillos, and Tanque on its way to La Fortuna. This route offers fab views of the San Carlos valley as you come down from Ciudad Quesada; Zarcero, with its topiary gardens and quaint church, is a good place to stop and snap a few photos (see chapter 7).

You can also stay on the Inter-American Highway (CR1) until San Ramón (west of Naranjo) and then head north through La Tigra on CR142. This route is very scenic and passes the Villa Blanca Cloud Forest & Spa (p 367). The travel time on any of the above routes is roughly 3 to 3½ hours.

By Bus: Buses (© **2255-0567** or 2255-4318) leave San José for La Fortuna at 6:30, 8:40, and 12:30am from the **Atlántico del Norte** bus station at Avenida 7 and 9 and Calle 12. The trip lasts 4 hours; the fare is C2,600. The bus you take might be labeled tilarán. Make sure it passes through Ciudad Quesada (also known as San Carlos). If so, it passes through La Fortuna; if not, you'll end up in Tilarán via the Inter-American Highway, passing through the Guanacaste town of Cañas, a long way from La Fortuna.

You can also take a bus from the same station to Ciudad Quesada (San Carlos) and transfer there to another bus to La Fortuna. These buses depart roughly every 40 minutes between 5am and 7:30pm. The fare for the 3 hours trip is C1,900. Local buses between Ciudad Quesada and La Fortuna run regularly through the day, although the schedule changes frequently, depending on demand. The trip lasts an hour; the fare is C1,500.

Buses depart **Monteverde/Santa Elena** for Tilarán every day at 7am. This is a journey of only 35km (22 miles), but the trip lasts 2½ hours because the road is in rough shape. People with bad backs should think twice about making the trip, especially by bus. The return bus from Tilarán to Santa Elena leaves at 12:30pm. The fare is C1,300. Buses from Tilarán to La Fortuna depart daily at 7am and 12:20 and 4:30pm, and make the return trip at 8am and 12:15 and 5:30pm. The trip is 2 to 3 hours; the fare is C1,600.

Buses depart La Fortuna for San José roughly every 2 hours between 5am and 6pm; in most instances, you will have to transfer in Ciudad Quesada to one of the frequent buses to San José.

Gray Line (www.graylinecostarica.com; © **800/719-3105** in the U.S. and Canada, or 2220-2126 in Costa Rica) and **Interbus** (www.interbusonline.com; © **4031-0888**) have two buses daily leaving San José for La Fortuna. The fare is around $54. Both will pick you up at most San José-area hotels. And both companies also run routes from La Fortuna with connections to most other major destinations in Costa Rica.

CITY LAYOUT As you enter La Fortuna from the east, you'll see the massive volcano directly in front of you. The main road into town, CR142, passes through the center of La Fortuna and then out toward Tabacón and the volcano. La Fortuna is only a few streets wide, with almost all the hotels, restaurants, and shops clustered along the main street and around the small central park.

VISITOR INFORMATION **Desafío Expeditions ★★** (www.desafiocostarica.com; © **855/818-0020** in the U.S. and Canada, or 2479-0020 in Costa Rica), **Jacamar Tours** (www.arenaltours.com; © **888/719-6377** in the U.S. and Canada, or **2479-9767**), and **Pure Trek Canyoning ★★** (www.puretrek.com; © **866/569-5723** in the U.S. and Canada, or 2479-1313 in Costa Rica) are the main tour operators in the area. All these companies offer most of the tours listed in this section, as well as fishing and sightseeing excursions on the lake, and transfers to and from other destinations around Costa Rica.

GETTING AROUND If you don't have a car, you'll need to either take a cab or go on an organized tour if you want to visit the hot springs or view the volcano. La Fortuna has tons of taxis (you can flag one down

boats, **HORSES & TAXIS**

You can travel between La Fortuna and Monteverde by boat and taxi, or on a combination of boat, horseback, and taxi. A 10- to 20-minute boat ride across Lake Arenal cuts out hours of driving around its shores. From La Fortuna to the put-in point is about a 25-minute taxi ride. It's about a 1½-hour four-wheel-drive taxi ride between the Río Chiquito dock on the other side of Lake Arenal and Santa Elena. Trips can be arranged in either direction for between $30 and $60 per person.

You can also add on a horseback ride on the Santa Elena/Monteverde side of the lake. Several routes and rides are on offer. The steepest heads up the mountains and through the forest to the town of San Gerardo, only a 30-minute car ride from Santa Elena. Other routes throw in shorter sections of horseback riding along the lakeside lowlands. With the horseback ride, this trip runs around $85 per person.

Warning: The riding is often rainy, muddy, and steep. Many find it much more arduous than awe-inspiring. Moreover, there have been complaints about the condition of the trails and the treatment of the horses, so do your research before signing on. Find out what route you'll be taking, as well as the condition of the horses. **Desafío Expeditions ★★** (www.desafiocostarica.com; ✆ **855/818-0020** in the U.S. and Canada, or 2479-0020 in Costa Rica) is one of the more reputable operators. It will even drive

your car around for you while you take the scenic route.

If you're looking to make the ride just by taxi and boat, check in with **Jeep Boat Jeep** (www.jeepboatjeep.com; ✆ **8305-0113**), which has daily fixed departures in each direction at 8am and 2pm for $25 per person. **Note:** This is a very popular service and it is booked by almost all of the hotels and tour operators in town. However, it's also very rugged adventure. Travelers often have to carry their own luggage from the van or jeep to the boat (or vice versa), sometimes over rough, muddy terrain, and there's often confusion during the transitions between boat and van or jeep. **Desafío Expeditions** has begun its own **Monteverde Express** van-boat-van shuttle between Arenal and Monteverde. It's a little more expensive, but much better in terms of service and ease of use. Moreover, it can also be combined with a stop at the Don Juan Coffee Farm (p 389) and lunch.

practically anywhere, or dial ✆ **2479-9605**), and a line of them is always ready and waiting along the main road beside the central park. Another alternative is to rent a car when you get here. **Alamo** (www.alamocostarica.com; ✆ **2479-9090**) has an office in downtown La Fortuna.

SPECIAL EVENTS   Each year, starting around February 1, La Fortuna pulls out all the stops for a 2-week celebration of the town's *Fiestas Cívicas,* or Civic Celebrations. There are horse parades, bullfights, mechanical rides, food stands, and concerts.

FAST FACTS   You'll find several information and tour-booking offices, as well as a couple of pharmacies, general stores, ATMs, and laundry facilities within a few blocks of the town's central park and church. If you need assistance, call the Tourist Police at ✆ **2479-7257.**

Exploring Arenal Volcano & La Fortuna

It's worth a quick visit to tour the town's **Catholic Church,** a contemporary church designed by famous Costa Rican artist Teodorico Quirós. It features a soaring concrete front steeple and clock tower.

EXPERIENCING THE VOLCANO ★★★

As mentioned above, the Arenal Volcano has been quiet since December 2010, with no loud eruptions or pyroclastic blasts. Still, the actual volcano remains a stunning sight, and the natural park and surrounding trails and activities make this a fabulous destination. That said, Arenal is surrounded by cloud forests and rainforests, and the volcano's cone is often socked in by clouds and fog. Many people come to Arenal and never see the exposed cone. **Note:** Although it's counterintuitive, the rainy season is often a better time to see the exposed cone of Arenal Volcano. For some reason, during the dry season the volcano can often be shrouded for days at a time. The bottom line is that catching a glimpse of the volcano's cone is never a sure thing.

Despite its current state of dormancy, climbing Arenal Volcano remains illegal. Over the years, many daredevil climbers have lost their lives, and others have been severely injured. This is still a very "alive" volcano, with steam vents and a molten core.

Arenal Volcano looms over La Fortuna church.

ARENAL NATIONAL PARK ★★

Arenal National Park ★★ (© 2461-8499; daily 8am–3pm; $15/person) constitutes an area of more than 2,880 hectares (7,114 acres), which includes the viewing and parking areas closest to the volcano. The trails through forest and over old lava flows inside the park are gorgeous and fun. (Be careful climbing on those volcanic boulders, though.)

The principal trail inside the park, **Sendero Coladas (Lava Flow Trail)** ★★, is just under 2km (1.25 miles) long and passes through secondary forest and open savanna. At the end of the trail, a short natural stairway takes you to a broad, open lava field left in the wake of a massive 1992 eruption. Scrambling over the cooled lava is a real treat, but be careful—the rocks can be sharp in places. Many spots throughout the park offer great views of the volcano, but the closest view can be found at **El Mirador (The Lookout)** ★. From the parking lot near the trail head for the Lava Flow Trail, you have the option of hiking or driving the 1km (.6 mile) to El Mirador.

NEARBY ATTRACTIONS

BUTTERFLY GARDEN   Located 2km (a little over a mile) beyond the Arenal dam out beyond the Mistico Arenal Hanging Bridges Park, the **Mot Mot Jungle** ★ (© 2479-1170; daily 7:30am–4pm; $10 admission) has a large enclosure where a wide variety of local butterfly species are bred and displayed. The attraction also has gentle paths planted with local flowers that attract a number of free-flying butterflies and hummingbirds. A tour here includes an exhibit on the insect's life cycle.

COOKING CLASSES   Tropical Cooking Class ★ (www.costarica cooking.com; © 2479-1569; $125/person; advance reservations required), offered by the Lava Lounge, is a 3½-hour class on Costa Rican cuisine. It's held at a beautiful lookout and open-air kitchen near the **Río Fortuna waterfall.** They can also set up tours to area farms.

ESPECIALLY FOR KIDS

Located a couple of miles outside La Fortuna, the **Ecocentro Danaus** ★ (www.ecocentrodanaus.com; © 8588-9314; daily 8am–4pm; admission $17 with tour, $12 for self-guided visit) is a private biological reserve and sustainable tourism project, which offers educational and engaging tours. Among the attractions here are a butterfly garden and reproduction center, botanical and medicinal plant gardens, and a small museum honoring the local Maleku indigenous culture. Night tours ($37) are offered by reservation. Children 5 to 10 get a 50% discount, and children 4 and under are free.

Those looking for close and intimate animal encounters might want to head to **Proyecto Asis** ★ (www.institutoasis.com; © 2475-9121), a wildlife rescue center and volunteer project. The staff offers two types of daily tours twice daily (once in the morning and once in the afternoon). The standard tour is informative and comprehensive and takes you through the facility and introduces you to their charges and mission. This tour lasts 1½ hours and costs $31 for adult and $18 for children 4 through 9. However, if you sign up for the "volunteering" addition, you get to stay on for another 2 hours and help around the center, nursing injured animals or cleaning cages. This option costs $54 for adults and $31 for children 4 through 9. Longer-term volunteer residencies and language classes are also available. Proyecto Asis is located about 30 to 40 minutes outside La Fortuna on the way to Ciudad Quesada.

Along the banks of the Arenal River, **Club Río ★★** (www.thesprings costarica.com; *C* **954/727-8333** in the U.S., or 2401-3313 in Costa Rica; 2-day pass $65 adults, $45 for kids 12 and under) is a wonderful playground for parents and kids alike. You can go tubing on the river, ride a horse through the forest trails, visit the midsize zoo, and take a shot at the three-story climbing wall. There's also a series of naturally fed hot springs sculpted alongside the river, as well as a restaurant. It's part of the **Springs Resort & Spa** (p 359), but you don't have to stay at the resort to enjoy the activities and facilities here. The pass gets you access to the facilities and two of the above-mentioned adventure activities, as well as a full lunch and free run of all the pools and waterslides at the resort itself.

Finally, the newest attraction on the block is the **Kalambu Hot Springs & Water Park ★** (www.kalambu.com; *C* **2479-0170**; daily 9am–10pm; $32 adults, $25 children). While most of the other hot springs in the area might have a waterslide or two, this place is a true water park, with several large waterslides and a massive and very entertaining children's play area and pools. The latter includes a giant bucket that is constantly filled and then dumped on everyone below. There are also a few quieter pool and hot spring areas.

OUTDOOR ACTIVITIES

ATV Best of the area's operators is **Original Arenal ATV** (www.original arenalatv.com; *C* **2479-7522**), which offers a 2½-hour ATV tour along the area around the lake and national park. The cost is $99 per person, or $130 for two people riding tandem. Another option is **La Pradera** (www.lapraderadelarenal.com; *C* **2479-9597**), which offers a 3-hour adventure through the forests and farmlands around La Fortuna. The cost is $95 per ATV.

CANOPY TOURS & HANGING BRIDGES You have numerous ways to get up into the forest canopy here. Perhaps the simplest is to hike the trails and bridges of **Mistico Arenal Hanging Bridges ★** (www.mistico park.com; *C* **2479-1170**; daily 7:30am–4pm; $26 adults, $16 ages 11-18, free ages 10 and under). Located just over the Lake Arenal dam,

Rock climbing at Club Rio Outdoor Center

this attraction is a complex of gentle trails and suspension bridges through a beautiful tract of primary forest. Additionally, night tours depart at 6pm every evening ($49 adults, $39 ages 11-18, $23 ages 10 and under).

Another option is the **Sky Tram ★★** (www.skyadventures.travel; ℭ **844/468-6759** in the U.S., or 2479-4100), an open gondola-style ride that begins near the shores of Lake Arenal and rises up, providing excellent views of the lake and volcano. From here, you hike a series of trails and suspended bridges. In the end, you can hike down, take the gondola, or strap on a harness and ride the zipline down to the bottom. The zipline tour, called Sky Trek, features several very long and very fast sections, with impressive views of the lake and volcano. The cost is $81 for the combined tram ride up, a guided hike to the trails and hanging bridges, and the zipline tour back down. It's $46 to ride the tram round-trip. The tram runs daily from 7:30am to 3pm. Sky Tram also has a butterfly and orchid garden. The same company also runs similar tours in Monteverde.

Ecoglide ★ (www.arenalecoglide.com; ℭ **2479-7120**) and **Arenal Canopy Tour** (www.arenalcanopy.com; ℭ **2479-8712**) are two other good zipline operations close to La Fortuna.

CANYONING   This adventure sport is a mix of hiking through and alongside a jungle river, punctuated with periodic rappels through and alongside the faces of rushing waterfalls. **Pure Trek Canyoning** ★★★ (www.puretrek.com; ℂ **866/569-5723** in the U.S. and Canada, or 2479-1313 in Costa Rica; $101/person) and **Desafío Adventure Company** ★★★ (www.desafiocostarica.com; ℂ **855/818-0020** in the U.S. and Canada, or 2479-0020 in Costa Rica; $99/person) are the primary operators in this area. Pure Trek's trip is probably better for first-timers and families with kids, while Desafío's tour is just a bit more rugged and adventurous. Both companies offer various combination full-day excursions, mixing canyoning with other adventures, and tend to have two to three daily departures.

Desafío also has a more extreme canyoning option: **Gravity Falls** ★★★. Although it features only one major rappel, this tour consists of a series of leaps from high rocks into river pools below. The cost is $125.

FISHING   With Lake Arenal just around the corner, fishing is a popular activity here. The big fish to catch is *guapote,* a Central American species of rainbow bass. However, you can also book fishing trips to Caño Negro, where snook, tarpon, and other game fish can be stalked. Most hotels and adventure-tour companies can arrange fishing excursions, or you can try **Captain Ron** (http://arenalfishing.com; ℂ 2694-4678), who runs a variety of fishing tours on the lake. Or try www.getmyboat.com. Costs run around $150 to $250 per boat, and a full day goes for around $250 to $500.

HIKING & HORSEBACK RIDING   Horseback riding is a popular activity in this area, with scores of good rides on dirt backroads and through open fields and dense rainforest. Volcano and lake views come with the terrain on most rides. Horseback trips to the Río Fortuna waterfall are perhaps the most popular, but the horse will get you only to the entrance; from there, you'll have to hike a bit. A horseback ride to the falls should cost between $30 and $45, including the entrance fee. You can also book with **Grupo Rio del Arenal** ★ (www.gruposriosdelarenal.com; ℂ **2479-1912**), which runs a 2½-hour tour on its private land—a mix of farmland and forest, with terrific views of the volcano. Two tours leave daily at 8:30am and 1:30pm; cost is $65 per person. Alternative tours are offered at nights and during full moons.

El Silencio Mirador y Senderos ★ (www.miradorelsilencio.com; ℂ **2479-9900;** daily 7am–7pm; $8) is a great place for hiking outside the national park. This private reserve has four well-marked and well-groomed trails, one of which takes you to a patch of the 1968 lava flow. There's a pretty pond and excellent views of the volcano.

For a more strenuous hike, climb **Cerro Chato** ★★, a dormant volcanic cone on the flank of Arenal with a beautiful little crater lake.

Horseback riding in the Arenal area

Desafío Adventures Company ★★ (www.desafiocostarica.com; ℂ **855/ 818-0020** in the U.S. and Canada, or 2479-0020 in Costa Rica) leads a 5- to 6-hour hike for $85, including lunch, though you can do it on your own from either La Fortuna Waterfall or the Arenal Observatory Lodge.

LA FORTUNA FALLS   Leading the list of side attractions in the area is the impressive **Río Fortuna Waterfall** ★★ (www.arenaladifort.com; ℂ **2479-8338;** daily 8am–5pm; $11 entrance), about 5.5km (3½ miles) outside of town in a dense jungle setting. A sign in town points the way to the road out to the falls. You can drive or hike to just within viewing distance. It's another 15- to 20-minute hike down a steep and often muddy path to the pool formed by the waterfall. The hike back up will take slightly longer. You can swim, but stay away from the turbulent water at the base of the falls—several people have drowned here. Instead, check out and enjoy the calm pool just around the bend, or join the locals at the popular swimming hole under the bridge on the paved road, just after the turnoff for the road up to the falls.

It's also possible to reach the falls by horseback. Most tour operators in town, as well as the waterfall folks themselves, offer this option for around $45. The tour generally lasts around 3 to 4 hours.

MOUNTAIN BIKING   This region is very well suited for mountain biking. Rides range in difficulty from moderate to extremely challenging. You can combine a day on a mountain bike with a visit to one or more of the popular attractions here. **Bike Arenal ★** (www.bikearenal.com; ℭ **866/465-4114** in the U.S. and Canada, or 2479-9020 in Costa Rica) offers top-notch bikes and equipment and a wide range of tour possibilities.

Hardcore bikers come for the **Vuelta al Lago ★**, a 2-day race around the lake (www.vueltaallagoarenal.com; ℭ **2695-5297**).

WHITEWATER RAFTING, CANOEING, SUP & KAYAKING   For adventurous tours of the area, check out **Desafío Expeditions ★★** (www.desafiocostarica.com; ℭ **855/818-0020** in the U.S. and Canada, or 2479-0020 in Costa Rica) or **Wave Expeditions ★★** (www.waveexpeditions.com; ℭ **888/224-6105** in the U.S. and Canada, or 2479-7262 in Costa Rica). Both companies offer daily raft rides of Class I to II, III, and IV to V on different sections of the Toro, Peñas Blancas, and Sarapiquí rivers. If you want a wet and personal ride, try Desafío's tour in inflatable kayaks, or "duckies." For families, a gentle safari float on the Peñas Blancas may be the best bet. A half-day float trip on a nearby river costs around $70 per person; a full day of rafting on some rougher water costs around $99 per person, depending on what section of river you ride. Both

Whitewater kayaking on the Río Toro

Tabacón Grand Spa Thermal Resort ★★★ (www.tabacon.com; ✆ **2479-2099;** daily 10am–10pm) is the most luxurious, extensive, and expensive spot in the area to soak in hot springs. A series of variously sized pools, fed by natural springs, are spread among sumptuous gardens. One of the stronger streams flows over a sculpted waterfall, with a rock ledge underneath that provides a perfect place to sit and receive a water massage. The pools and springs closest to the volcano are the hottest. The resort also has an excellent spa, offering professional massages, mud masks, and other treatments, as well as yoga classes (appointments required). Most of the treatments are conducted in pretty, open-air gazebos. The spa here also has several sweat lodges, based on a Native American traditional design. A full-service restaurant, garden grill, and several bars round out the offerings here.

Admission is $85 for adults and $30 for children 11 and under, including lunch. A range of packages, including multiple meals, are available. The pools are busiest between 2 and 6pm. After 6pm, adults can enter for $70 and children for $25, including dinner. Management enforces a policy of limiting visitors, so reservations are recommended.

Baldi Hot Springs Hotel Resort & Spa (www.baldihotsprings.cr; ✆ **2479-2190;** $35 for adults and $17.50 for children) are the first hot springs you'll come to as you drive from La Fortuna toward Tabacón. This place has grown substantially over the years, with many different pools, slides, and bars and restaurants spread around the expansive grounds. Baldi has more of a party vibe

than other spots, with loud music blaring at some of the swim-up bars.

Just across the street from Baldi Hot Springs is the entrance of **Eco Termales** ★★★ (www.ecotermales fortuna.cr; ✆ **2479-8787;** $37 for adults and $24 for children). Smaller and more intimate than Tabacón, this series of pools amid dense forest and gardens is almost as picturesque and luxurious, though it has far fewer pools, lacks a view of the volcano, and offers much less extensive spa services. Eco Termales runs two time periods daily—10am to 4pm and 5pm to 10pm—and reservations are highly recommended, because admissions are limited to make sure the pools don't get crowded. In the same general vicinity are **Kalambu Hot Springs** (www.

---

companies also offer mountain biking, stand-up paddleboarding (SUP), and local guided trips.

A more laid-back alternative is to take a canoe tour with **Canoa Aventura** (www.canoa-aventura.com; ✆ **2479-8200**), which offers half-, full-, and multiday excursions on a variety of rivers in the region, which range from $57 to $155 per person.

DAY TRIPS

Caño Negro National Wildlife Refuge ★ is a vast network of marshes and rivers (particularly the Río Frío) 100km (62 miles) north of La Fortuna near the town of Los Chiles. The refuge is best known for its abundance of bird life, including roseate spoonbills, jabiru storks, herons, and

kalambu.com; ☏ **2479-0170**; $32 for adults and $25 for children), sort of a hot springs waterpark with slides and games; **Paradise Hot Springs** (https://paradise hotspringscr.com; ☏ **2479-1380**; $28 for adults and $16 for children), with a few pools and massage facilities; and **The Royal Corin Thermal Water Spa & Resort** (www.royalcorin.com; ☏ **2479-2201**; $49 adults and $35 children), with a small water circuit with waterfalls and pools of various temperatures.

Termales Los Laureles (www. termalesloslaureles.com; ☏ **2479-1395**) is located between Baldi and Eco Termales and Tabacón. This spot has the area's most local feel and is by far the most economical, charging just C6,000 for adults.

You can also enjoy the hot springs, pools, and facilities at the **Springs Resort & Spa** ★★ (p 359). In addition to the main pools by the hotel, it also has a few more at a beautiful riverfront area about 1km away. The Springs is open to day visitors from 8:30am to 10pm, and admission is $65 per person for a 2-day pass.

Finally, if you like your water hot, fast, and free, head to Río Chollín, a rushing river of hot water open to the public right next to Tabacón. Across from the main entrance to Tabacón, where you can park your car in its road-side spaces, walk downhill through some yellow barriers and you'll find the river.

TOP: **Taking a soothing soak in Tabacón Grand Spa Thermal Resort hot springs.**
BOTTOM: **Room at Tabacón Grand Spa Thermal Resort.**

egrets, but you can also see caimans and crocodiles. Bird-watchers should not miss this refuge, although keep in mind that the main lake dries up in the dry season (mid-Apr to Nov), which reduces the number of wading birds. Full-day tours to Caño Negro average between $65 and $80 per person. However, most of the tours run out of La Fortuna that are billed as Caño Negro never really enter the refuge but instead ply sections of the nearby Río Frío, which features similar wildlife and eco-systems. If you're interested in staying in this area and really visiting the refuge, head to **Caño Negro Natural Lodge** (p 367).

You can also visit the **Venado Caverns** ★★, a 45-minute drive away. In addition to plenty of stalactites, stalagmites, and other forma-tions, you'll see bats and unique cave fish and crabs. This tour is not for

Anhinga in Caño Negro National Wildlife Refuge

the claustrophobic, and includes wading through a river, scrambling over rocks, and sliding through some tight squeezes. This cave system is quite extensive, although tourists have access to only around 10 chambers. Still, these are quite striking, with impressive formations and ceilings more than 100 feet high in places. Tours cost between $70 and $80, including the guide and headlamps. Be prepared to get wet and muddy.

All tour agencies and hotel tour desks can arrange trips to Caño Negro and Venado Caverns.

Where to Stay in La Fortuna
MODERATE

Hotel Magic Mountain ★   You can enjoy a postcard-pretty view of Arenal Volcano's perfect cone while lying in bed in most of the rooms at Magic Mountain. But even if you can't see it from your pillow, every room comes with a private balcony or patio with a volcano view (junior suites have the view from a private Jacuzzi). Try to land a room on the second or third floor if possible, and the end units are especially well-placed. The grounds feature flowering gardens that let out onto a large free-form pool with a swim-up bar, and a couple of Jacuzzis. Magic Mountain is located at the far end of town, so a rental car comes in handy, though one could conceivably walk into town. The Lina's restaurant here is quite good, and there's a separate sports bar.

La Fortuna. www.hotelmagicmountain.com. © **2479-7246.** 42 units. $151 double; $206 suite, includes breakfast. **Amenities:** Restaurant; bar; 2 Jacuzzis; pool; spa; free Wi-Fi.

INEXPENSIVE

Right in La Fortuna, you'll find a score of budget options. One of the better choices is **Arenal Backpackers Resort** ★ (www.arenalbackpackers resort.com; © **2479-7000**), which bills itself as a "five-star hostel" for its large pool, free Wi-Fi, and volcano views. It has both shared-bathroom dorm rooms and more upscale private rooms.

A couple of places both in town and right on the outskirts of La Fortuna allow camping, with access to basic bathroom facilities, for around $5 to $10 per person per night. If you have a car, drive a bit out of town toward Tabacón and you'll find several more basic cabins and camping sites, some of which offer volcano views.

Hotel La Fortuna ★ This used to be a simple, two-story, wood-and-zinc hostel, but a fire changed all that, and now it's a modern, five-story hotel. The best rooms face west and have volcano-view balconies. Of these, the top two floors are the best, as their views aren't blocked by Hotel Las Colinas (see below) and other nearby buildings, plus are only a few dollars more a night. Inside, the rooms are fairly plain, with white tile floors and locally made furnishings that show a hint of Japanese aesthetics. The restaurant is open only for breakfast, but you're right in the heart of downtown and close to all the restaurants and shops.

1 block south of the gas station, downtown La Fortuna. www.lafortunahotel.com. © **2479-9197.** 40 units. $81–$85 double, includes buffet breakfast. **Amenities:** Restaurant; free Wi-Fi.

Hotel Las Colinas ★ This centrally located three-story hotel is a great value. The less expensive rooms here are quite plain yet all clean and cozy, while for a bit more you can upgrade and get a private volcano-view balcony and in-room Jacuzzi. Even if you don't, there's a gorgeous, open-air, second-floor terrace with perfect views of the Arenal Volcano. This common area—with its potted palms, Chinese lanterns and tables, loaner board games, and chairs and couches under atrium-style open-air roofs—really is the highlight and social center of the hotel. The service at this family-run operation is friendly, attentive, and knowledgeable.

La Fortuna. www.lascolinasarenal.com. © **2479-9305.** 21 units. $75–$103 double, includes breakfast and taxes. **Amenities:** Restaurant, free Wi-Fi.

Where to Stay near the Volcano

While La Fortuna is the major gateway town to Arenal Volcano, many of the best places to stay are on the road between La Fortuna and the national park.

EXPENSIVE

Arenal Kioro ★ You'll feel like you're right on top of the volcano here, though surrounded by superbly landscaped grounds. Rooms are very large, with extremely high ceilings and a wall of windows with a sliding-glass door that opens onto a private balcony or patio with a perfect volcano view. Sadly, they're a bit dated, with ugly floral bedspreads and a free-standing, large, in-room spa Jacuzzi, which seems to be unnecessary—the outdoor hot springs and pool are much more appealing. Guests receive free admission at the Titokú Hot Springs facility, about 6km southwest of the hotel. On the main road btw. La Fortuna and Lake Arenal, 10km (6 miles) from La Fortuna. www.hotelarenalkioro.com. ✆ **2479-1700.** 53 units. $309 double, includes breakfast and taxes. **Amenities:** 2 restaurants; 2 bars; gym; Jacuzzi; small hot-spring complex; pool; small spa; free Wi-Fi.

Nayara Resort, Spa & Gardens ★★★ Intimate, romantic, and pampering: Those are the words that come to mind when describing

Spring Villa plunge pool at Nayara Hotel, Spa & Gardens

Nayara. It's a special place, with lodgings in large and luxurious private bungalows, each with a two-person Jacuzzi, wide, volcano-facing balconies, and both an indoor and garden shower. Units 1 through 5 are closest to the restaurants and pool and thus the least private. Around the bungalows are well-tended tropical gardens (wonderful for bird-watching); trails lead through the property and down to a river. The dining options are varied and all well-executed, from the classy wine and tapas bar to a laid back Nikkei (Japanese-Peruvian) spot. The hotel does not have a natural hot springs on-site, though there is a natural spring-fed hot pool at its adjoining property, **Nayara Springs Resort** (www.nayarasprings.com). It's reached via a long and high suspension bridge, and populated with even larger villas, each with a hot, natural, spring-fed private pool.

On the main road btw. La Fortuna and Lake Arenal. www.arenalnayara.com. ✆ **888/ 332-2961** in the U.S. and Canada, or 2479-1600 in Costa Rica. 66 units. $430 double; $540 villa, includes buffet breakfast and daily yoga classes. **Amenities:** 4 restaurants; 2 bars; small spa; gym; 2 pools; 3 Jacuzzis; room service; free Wi-Fi.

The Royal Corin ★　The pool, sauna, steam, and hot-spring complex at this contemporary resort are first-rate, and include such fun touches as lounge chairs submerged in some of the pools. Around this "main attraction" are the five-story buildings that house the guestrooms, each of which has a private balcony overlooking the pools and Arenal Volcano. The rooms themselves are spacious but bland—white tile floors, white walls and ceilings, with a few splashes of color provided by artwork, patterned linens, and throw pillows. An excellent little spa is attached to the hotel, and the restaurant here is quite good.

On the main road btw. La Fortuna and Lake Arenal, 4km (2½ miles) from La Fortuna. www.royalcorin.com. ✆ **866/978-6904** in the U.S. and Canada, or 2479-2201 in Costa Rica. 54 units. $275 double; $413-$450 suites, includes breakfast. **Amenities:** Restaurant; 2 bars; babysitting; gym; 6 Jacuzzis; pools and hot springs; room service; small spa; sauna, free W-Fi.

The Springs Resort & Spa ★★★　In contrast to the intimate Nayara (see above), the Springs Resort & Spa is built on a grand scale. This massive complex features huge, comfortable rooms and great beds, but the key here is the wide range of on-site attractions and activity options, including an extensive collection of hot and temperate pools (the largest has a swim-up sushi bar), a jungle waterslide, free yoga classes, and a separate "Club Rio" adventure park (p 349) a short shuttle ride on the banks of the Arenal River. This also is the only lodge in the area with its own heliport. All rooms are oriented to offer views of the Arenal Volcano. Local cane (*caña brava*) is used extensively as paneling and wall ornamentation. This is a smart option for families, thanks to all the activities, as well as the family suites and private villas with cooking facilities. The

The Springs Resort & Spa

restaurants, spa, and overall service here are top-notch. Reality TV fans will recognize the property from appearances on The Bachelor and Keeping Up with the Kardashians.

Off the main road btw. La Fortuna and Lake Arenal, 10km (6 miles) from La Fortuna. www.thespringscostarica.com. ℂ **954/727-8333** in the U.S. or 2401-3313 in Costa Rica. 45 units. $399–$483 double. **Amenities:** 4 restaurants; 4 bars; spa, gym, pools and hot springs; room service; free Wi-Fi.

Tabacón Grand Spa Thermal Resort ★★★ You might want to stay here for the fab hot springs, even if the rooms were dark, dank and dingy—but they're not. Far from it. Guestrooms are large and well-maintained, with heavy, dark-stained wood furnishings and at least one wall of windows or sliding glass doors. Some have volcano views. Management has a deep commitment to sustainable development and environmental conservation. Plus, staying at the resort gets you unlimited access to the impressive Tabacón hot-spring complex, as well as slightly extended hours and access to a private, hotel-guests-only section of the hot springs dubbed Shangri-La. If you take into account the hefty entrance fee to the springs, this place is practically a bargain.

On the main road btw. La Fortuna and Lake Arenal. www.tabacon.com. ℂ **855/822-2266** in the U.S. and Canada, 2479-2099 for reservations in San José, or 2479-2000 at the resort. 102 units. $332–$395 double, includes breakfast. **Amenities:** 2 restaurants; 3 bars; gym; Jacuzzi; pool w/swim-up bar; room service; hot springs and spa facilities across the street; free Wi-Fi.

MODERATE

Arenal Kokoro ★★   This place arguably gets you the best bang for your buck in the area. The spacious individual "eco-cabinas" all have volcano views and small private balconies. The more economical "casona" rooms are a tad more rustic and housed in two-story blocks of four rooms. Inside you'll find a mix of locally milled wood-plank paneling and painted concrete walls—some with hand-painted murals of birds, butterflies, and fanciful trees. The hotel has a pool, a small, natural hot-springs complex and spa, and extensive and lush gardens and grounds. The staff is very friendly and helpful.

On the main road btw. La Fortuna and Lake Arenal. www.arenalkokoro.com. ✆ **2479-1222** in Costa Rica. 30 units. $120–$170 double, includes breakfast. **Amenities:** Restaurant; bar; pool; small hot springs complex and spa; free Wi-Fi.

Arenal Observatory Lodge & Spa ★★   Originally a scientific observatory associated with the Smithsonian to monitor volcanic activity, this is one of the closest hotels to the Arenal Volcano. The views from the

Guest room at Arenal Observatory Lodge

The restaurant at Arenal Observatory Lodge

rooms, restaurant, and common areas are simply spectacular. The main dining room features a massive wall of glass, with a V-shaped peak that perfectly frames the volcano. The lodge is a bit isolated from the hustle and bustle of this busy region, and is graced with a large, private reserve and an excellent network of trails bordering the national park. The best rooms and views are found in the suites and private villas below the main lodge building. Given the remote location, you'll want a rental car, ideally 4WD, if staying here.

On the flanks of Arenal Volcano. Head to the national park entrance, stay on the dirt road past the entrance, and follow the signs to the lodge. www.arenalobservatory lodge.com. ✆ **877/804-7732** in the U.S. and Canada or 2290-7011 in San José, or 2479-1070 at the lodge. 48 units. $87–$156 double; $172 suite, includes breakfast. **Amenities:** Restaurant; bar; Jacuzzi; pool; small spa; free Wi-Fi.

Hotel Silencio del Campo ★★ This friendly, family-run resort features a small collection of individual cabins oriented to take in the volcano view. All are quite spacious, with red tile floors, wooden walls, air-conditioning, TVs, and minifridges. They are a little bit too close together, but large tropical flowers and palms planted all around give them some sense of privacy. Try for one farthest from the main road and parking area. The best feature here is the lovely pool and hot-spring complex. This is by far the best hotel hot-spring complex in this price range. Service is extremely personalized and attentive.

On the main road btw. La Fortuna and Lake Arenal. www.hotelsilenciodelcampo. com. ✆ **2479-7055.** 23 units. $226 double, includes breakfast and taxes. **Amenities:** Restaurant; bar; pool and hot-spring complex; free Wi-Fi.

Volcano Lodge & Springs ★ Most of the rooms at this sprawling midsize resort offer unobstructed views of the Arenal Volcano from a private patio with locally crafted leather rocking chairs. Masonry half-walls of smooth river stones give the lodge a rustic feel, but inside you'll find flatscreen TVs and quiet air-conditioning units. Volcano Lodge has steadily grown over the years, and now features two pool areas and two separate restaurants, as well as its own little hot-springs complex, hiking trails, and children's playground. The gardens here are handsomely landscaped, and the service is very attentive, despite the fact that the lodge often caters to large tour groups.

On the main road btw. La Fortuna and Lake Arenal. www.volcanolodge.com. ✆ **800/649-5913** in the U.S. or 2479-1717. 62 units. $200–$288 double, includes breakfast and taxes. **Amenities:** Restaurant; 2 bars; 2 Jacuzzis; 2 pools; small spa; free Wi-Fi.

Lodging at Hotel Silencio del Campo

INEXPENSIVE

Although the hotels along the road between La Fortuna and the National Park tend to be geared toward higher-end travelers, more budget-conscious travelers do have a few choices, the best of which is **Cabinas Los Guayabos** (www.cabinaslosguayabos.com; © **2479-1444**), with views and a location that rival the more expensive lodgings listed above. There's also **Lomas del Volcán** (www.lomasdelvolcan.com; © **2479-9000**), with 47-rooms, a pool, and hiking trails.

Where to Eat in & Around La Fortuna

Dining in La Fortuna is nowhere near as inspiring as the area's natural attractions, but, given the town's booming tourist business, options abound. For a casual breakfast or lunch, try **Gecko Gourmet ★** (www.geckocostarica.com; © **2479-8905**), located behind the church. Other options include **Rancho La Cascada** (© **2479-8790**), **La Choza de Laurel** (www.lachozadelaurel.com; © **2479-7063**), and **Restaurante Nene's** (© **2479-9192**) for Tico fare, and **Las Brasitas** (© **2479-9819**) for Mexican. For good pizza and Italian cuisine, try either **Café Mediterranea** (© **2479-7497**), just outside town on the road to the La Fortuna Waterfall, or **Anch'io** (© **2479-7560**), just beyond Las Brasitas, on the road toward Tabacón. For fancy dining, **Los Tucanes ★** (© **2479-2020**) at the Tabacón Grand Spa resort (p 360) is a solid choice.

Don Rufino ★★ COSTA RICAN   Don Rufino is the semiofficial social center of town, with a popular open-air bar overlooking the main street. The decor has rustic touches, but the menu has gradually been moving into creative territory, sometimes using the country's biodiversity as inspiration for dishes like slow cooked lamb belly with pickled chayote. Prices are on the high end but worth it.

Main road through downtown La Fortuna, 2 blocks east of the church. www.donrufino.com. © **2479-9997.** Main courses C8.900–C13,800. Daily 11am–10:30pm. Reservations recommended during high season.

El Novillo del Arenal ★ COSTA RICAN/STEAKHOUSE   If you want local steaks or grilled chicken, but don't need the fancier ambience or accoutrements of the other places listed here, this is your spot. Portions are hearty and the price is right. The restaurant is a simple affair built on a plain concrete slab under a very high, open-air, corrugated-zinc-roof structure. When it's clear, you get an excellent view of the volcano.

On the road to Tabacón, 10km (6¼ miles) outside La Fortuna. © **2479-1910.** Main courses C4,575–C12,775. Daily noon–9pm.

Lava Lounge ★ INTERNATIONAL   California meets Costa Rica at this popular downtown restaurant. Lava Lounge's menu ranges from glorified bar food—nachos, quesadillas, wings, and wraps—to a hearty

Costa Rican *casado,* with dishes such as a thick-cut grilled pork chop or coconut shrimp with spicy mango salsa quite well done. Chef and owner Scott Bradley is often on hand, and also runs the **Tropical Cooking Class ★** (p 348) cooking school. Wooden picnic tables with bench seating fill the main dining room, so you might have to share your table.

Downtown La Fortuna, on the main road. www.lavaloungecostarica.com. © **2479-7365.** Main courses $10–$22. Daily 11am–11pm.

Soda La Hormiga ★ COSTA RICAN   Near the bus stop a block away from the main road, the open-air Soda La Hormiga serves tasty, loaded *gallos,* Costa Rica's version of the taco, as well as hearty *casados* and plates of rice and beans with a choice of protein. Pay special attention to their list of fruit drinks, including the rare *chan,* a chía like seed that turns red, Jello-like, and sweet when soaked. Service can be slow, though for the price and quality it's easy to overlook.

Calle 470 at Calle 468, Downtown La Fortuna. www.sodalahormiga.com. © **2479-9247.** Main courses C1,000–C2,500. Daily 6am–4pm

Shopping

La Fortuna is chock-full of souvenir shops selling standard tourist fare. However, the town also has an authentic craft shop, **Original Grand Gallery** (© **8946-0928**). This local artisan and his family produce sculptures in a variety of styles, specializing in faces, many of them larger than a typical home's front door. You can also find a host of animal figures, ranging in style from purely representational to rather abstract. To get there: As you leave the town of La Fortuna toward Tabacón, keep your eye on the right-hand side of the road. When you see a massive collection of wood sculptures, slow down. **Art Shop Onirica** (www.galeria oniricacr.com; © **2479-7589**), located next to La Fortuna's post office, is another good shop, featuring original oil paintings and acrylics, as well as one-off jewelry and jade pieces.

Entertainment & Nightlife

Luigi's Hotel has a midsize **casino** (© **2479-9898**) next door to its hotel and restaurant, while the open-to-the-street bar at **Don Rufino ★★** (p 364) is a popular spot for a drink. Finally, a cozy sports bar with a pool table and flatscreen TVs is on the second floor of the **Hotel Magic Mountain** (p 356).

Where to Stay & Eat Farther Afield

All the hotels listed in the following four sections are at least a half-hour drive from La Fortuna and the volcano. Most, if not all, offer both night- and day-tours to Arenal and Tabacón, but they also attract guests with their own natural charms.

EAST OF LA FORTUNA

The broad, flat San Carlos Valley spreads out to the east of La Fortuna. This is agricultural heartland, with large plantations of yuca, papaya, and other cash crops. The popular Ciudad Quesada route to or from La Fortuna will take you through this area.

In addition to the places listed below, **Leaves & Lizards** (www.leavesandlizards.com; ✆ **888/828-9245** in the U.S. and Canada, or 2478-0023 in Costa Rica), near El Muelle, wins high praise as an intimate, isolated getaway.

Termales del Bosque ★ The name translates to "Hot Springs of the Forest," and that's exactly what you'll find at this simple collection of rooms and bungalows housed in single-story concrete block buildings spread around the open grounds of a former farm. The rooms are unadorned, with plain white walls, red tile floors, and minimal furnishings, but they do have air-conditioning and TVs. The bungalows are two-bedroom units with full kitchens. The namesake hot springs are the real draw, though, with a series of pools built alongside a rushing creek amid dense rainforest. There's a natural steam room and pools in a range of temperatures. A host of tours and activities are offered.

On the road from San Carlos to Aguas Zarcas, just before El Tucano, Ciudad Quesada. www.hoteltermalesdelbosque.com. ✆ **2460-4740**. 48 units. $107 double, includes breakfast and unlimited use of hot springs. **Amenities:** 2 restaurants; bar; several hot springs pools beside a forest river; limited spa services; free Wi-Fi.

Tilajari Resort Hotel ★ A low-key small resort and nature lodge, Tilajari is on the banks of the San Carlos River, making it a wonderful place for bird-watching and wildlife viewing. The river is home to crocodiles, lizards, turtles, and a great variety of bird species. Oversized rooms with forest-green walls, tile floors, and wood ceilings are found in a row of two-story buildings that run parallel to the water, and most have a private patio or balcony with a river view. Popular with tour groups and Costa Rican families, Tilajari has extensive facilities, including tennis courts, soccer fields, game rooms, an orchid garden, a butterfly garden, and a medicinal herb garden. The hotel lies about 35 minutes from La Fortuna and the Arenal Volcano, but also provides good access to attractions in Aguas Zarcas.

Muelle, San Carlos. www.tilajari.com. ✆ **2462-1212**. 76 units. $72–$90 double; $140 suite, includes full breakfast. **Amenities:** Restaurant; bar; exercise room; Jacuzzi; pool; spa; 5 lighted tennis courts (2 indoors); free Wi-Fi.

SOUTH OF LA FORTUNA

Finca Luna Nueva Lodge ★★ (www.fincalunanuevalodge.com; ✆ **800/903-3470** in the U.S. and Canada, or 2468-4006 in Costa Rica) is a fascinating sustainable farm and tourism project, and proud advocate for the international "slow food" movement.

Chachagua Rainforest Hotel & Hacienda ★   This boutique rainforest lodge is located on 100 hectares (247 acres) of land, much of which is primary rainforest. Rooms are certainly comfortable and cozy, but consider splurging on one of the wooden bungalows, which are much roomier, have TVs and Jacuzzi tubs, and their own large, covered-deck. Throughout you'll find lots of varnished hardwood, and handsome headboards studded with sections of hardwood tree trunks. The large pool here is fed by a natural spring and kept chemical-free. The lodge has miles of excellent trails, leading through wildlife-rich rainforest, with waterfalls, rivers, and jungle lagoons to explore. It offers a host of guided adventure tours and activities. The small village of Chachagua sits 10km (6 miles) south of La Fortuna, on the road to San Ramón. The lodge itself is another 2km (1¼ miles) along a dirt road from the village.

Chachagua, Alajuela. www.chachaguarainforesthotel.com. ☏ **2468-1011.** 28 units. $149–$167 double, includes breakfast and taxes. **Amenities:** Restaurant; bar; concierge, lounge area, pool; mountain bike rental, free Wi-Fi.

Villa Blanca Cloud Forest & Spa ★★   Once the country retreat and family-run hotel of former Costa Rican President Rodrigo Carazo Odio, this beautiful mountain lodge features a series of individual little houses, or *casitas*, with clay-tile roofs, whitewashed stucco walls, rustic tile floors, and open-beam and cane ceilings. Each *casita* has a working wood-burning fireplace, which comes in handy in the cool, moist climate. The deluxe *casitas* and suites come with their own Jacuzzi tubs. The hotel's private reserve borders the Los Angeles Cloud Forest Reserve, a fascinating area and ecosystem, very similar to that found in Monteverde. In fact, some visitors have spotted the elusive resplendent quetzal here. To reach the hotel, first drive to the mountain city of San Ramón on the Inter-American Highway (CR1), northwest of San José. From here, drive north on CR142 toward Los Angeles, following signs to Villa Blanca.

San Ramón, Alajuela. www.villablanca-costarica.com. ☏ **877/288-0664** in the U.S. and Canada, or 2461-0300 in Costa Rica. 35 units. $210–$250 double, includes taxes. **Amenities:** Restaurant; bar; small spa; free Wi-Fi.

NORTH OF LA FORTUNA

Caño Negro Natural Lodge ★   Serious bird-watchers, nature lovers, and fishermen should consider this very remote lodging in the tiny lagoon-side village of Caño Negro. Bordering the Caño Negro Wildlife Refuge, this simple place offers easy access to the lakes, lagoons, and waterways of these beautiful, low-lying wetlands (one of the best places in the region to spot a jabiru stork). Dozens of tours are offered. The rooms themselves are roomy, clean, and cool, with large sliding glass doors opening on to a small patio overlooking the well-tended gardens. To get there, drive toward Los Chiles, and just before reaching the town,

follow the well-marked signs for Caño Negro Natural Lodge and the wildlife refuge. The final 18km (11 miles) is on a rugged dirt road.

Caño Negro. www.canonegrolodge.com. (✆ **2471-1426** in Costa Rica. 42 units. $130 double, includes breakfast and taxes. **Amenities:** Restaurant; bar; pool; free Wi-Fi.

REALLY REMOTE NATURE LODGES

This little-visited area along the San Carlos River near the Nicaraguan border is hard to get to, with rough and poorly maintained roads. But those who brave it will find themselves right in the heart of nature, particularly at the **Maquenque Ecolodge** ★ (www.maquenqueecolodge. com; (✆ **2479-8200**), where birders have been known to spot green macaws in the wild. To get here, head first to Pital and then continue on dirt roads to the town of Boca Tapada. It's also possible, albeit difficult, to get here on public transportation (ask your hotel for directions), or ask for the hotel to arrange transportation from San José or La Fortuna. Since anyone with four-wheel-drive can make the trip here independently, though, you're best off driving on your own.

Laguna del Lagarto Lodge ★   Although it's not exactly at the end of the road, La Laguna del Lagarto Lodge certainly feels like it. Tucked into a far northern section of Costa Rica, close to the Nicaraguan border, this rustic lodge caters primarily to bird-watchers. The bird count here tops 390 species, including the rare green macaw. Rooms are adequate and little more, with low-lying wooden bedframes sporting thin mattresses, and not much in the way of furnishings, decor, and amenities. The lodge features two man-made lakes and keeps a fleet of canoes. It also has an extensive network of hiking trails and offers a range of active adventure tours and guided hikes.

7km (3¾ miles) north of Boca Tapada. www.lagarto-lodge-costa-rica.com. (✆ **2289-8163**. 20 units. $85 double, includes breakfast and taxes. **Amenities:** Restaurant; bar; free Wi-Fi.

ALONG THE SHORES OF LAKE ARENAL ★

200km (124 miles) NW of San José; 20km (12 miles) NW of Monteverde; 70km (43 miles) SE of Liberia

Despite its many charms, this remains one of the least-developed tourism regions in Costa Rica. Lake Arenal, the largest lake in Costa Rica, is the centerpiece here. The long, beautiful lake is surrounded by rolling hills that are partly pastured and partly forested. Loads of adventures are available both on the lake and in the surrounding hills and forests. While the towns of Tilarán and Nuevo Arenal remain quiet rural communities, several excellent hotels spread out along the shores of the lake.

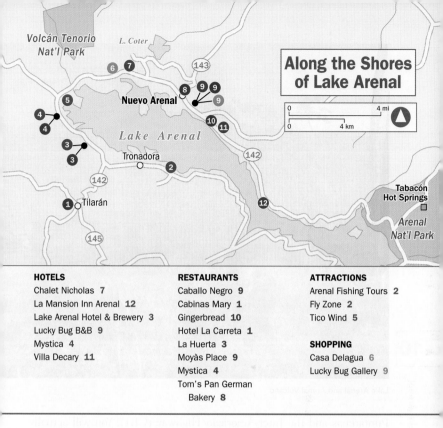

Along the Shores of Lake Arenal

| 0 | 4 mi |
| 0 | 4 km |

HOTELS
Chalet Nicholas 7
La Mansion Inn Arenal 12
Lake Arenal Hotel & Brewery 3
Lucky Bug B&B 9
Mystica 4
Villa Decary 11

RESTAURANTS
Caballo Negro 9
Cabinas Mary 1
Gingerbread 10
Hotel La Carreta 1
La Huerta 3
Moyàs Place 9
Mystica 4
Tom's Pan German
   Bakery 8

ATTRACTIONS
Arenal Fishing Tours 2
Fly Zone 2
Tico Wind 5

SHOPPING
Casa Delagua 6
Lucky Bug Gallery 9

Locals here used to curse the winds, which often come blasting across this end of the lake at 60 knots or greater. However, since the first sailboarders caught wind of Lake Arenal's combination of warm, fresh water, steady gusts, and spectacular scenery, that's changed. Even if you aren't a fanatical sailboarder, you might enjoy hanging out by the lake, hiking in the nearby forests, riding a mountain bike on dirt farm roads and one-track trails, and catching glimpses of Arenal Volcano.

The lake's other claim to fame is its rainbow-bass fishing. These fighting fish are known in Central America as *guapote* and are large members of the cichlid family. Their sharp teeth and bellicose nature make them a real challenge.

Essentials

GETTING THERE & DEPARTING By Car: From San José, you can either take the Inter-American Highway (CR1) north all the way from San José to Cañas, or first head west out of San José on the San José–Caldera Highway (CR27). When you reach Caldera, follow the signs to

Lake Arenal and Arenal Volcano

Puntarenas and the Inter-American Highway (CR1). You will actually follow signs for Liberia and San José, which are, in fact, leading you to the unmarked entrance to CR1. This road (CR23) ends when it hits the Inter-American Highway. You'll want to pass under the bridge and follow the on-ramp, which will put you on the highway heading north. This latter route is a faster and flatter drive, with no windy mountain switchbacks to contend with. In Cañas, turn east on CR142 toward Tilarán. The drive takes 3 to 4 hours. If you're continuing on to Nuevo Arenal, follow the signs in town, which will put you on the road that skirts the shore of the lake. Nuevo Arenal is about a half-hour drive from Tilarán. You can also drive here from La Fortuna, along a scenic road that winds around the lake. From La Fortuna, it's approximately 1 hour to Nuevo Arenal and 1½ hours to Tilarán.

By Bus: Transportes Tilarán buses (© **2222-3854**) leave San José for Tilarán roughly five times throughout the day between 7:30am and 6:30pm from Calle 20 and Avenida 3. The trip lasts from 4 to 5½ hours, depending on road conditions; the fare is C4,500.

Morning and afternoon buses connect **Puntarenas** to Tilarán. The ride takes about 3 hours; the fare is C1,350. (For details on getting to Puntarenas, see "Puntarenas," in chapter 9, p 292.)

The daily bus from **Monteverde** (Santa Elena) leaves at 7am. The fare for the 2½-hour trip is C1,200.

Buses from **La Fortuna** leave for Tilarán daily at 8am and 12:15 and 5:30pm, returning at 7am and 12:20 and 4:30pm. The trip takes around 2 to 3 hours; the fare is C2,350.

Direct buses to San José leave from Tilarán beginning at 5am. Buses to Puntarenas leave at 6am and 1pm daily. The bus to Santa Elena (Monteverde) leaves daily at 12:30pm. Buses also leave regularly for Cañas, and can be caught heading north or south along the Inter-American Highway.

GETTING AROUND Both Tilarán and Nuevo Arenal are very small towns, and you can easily walk most places in the compact city centers. If you need a taxi to get to a lodge on Lake Arenal, call **Taxis Unidos Tilarán** (© 2695-5324) in Tilarán, or either **Taxis Nuevo Arenal** (© 8388-3015) or **Pencho** (© 8817-6375) in Nuevo Arenal.

Exploring Along the Shores of Lake Arenal

ARTS, CRAFTS & DOWN-HOME COOKING About halfway between Nuevo Arenal and Tilarán is **Casa Delagua** ★ (© 2692-1324), the studio, gallery, and coffee shop of Costa Rican artist Juan Carlos Ruiz. There's also a good used book and DVD collection on sale here.

The **Lucky Bug Gallery** ★★ (www.luckybugcr.net; © 2695-4515) is an excellent roadside arts-and-crafts and souvenir shop, selling locally produced functional and decorative pieces. It's attached to the Lucky Bug Bed & Breakfast (p 374).

FISHING If you want to try your hand at fishing for *guapote*, call **Captain Ron** at **Arenal Fishing Tours** (www.arenalfishing.com; © 2694-4678), or just ask at your hotel. A half-day fishing trip should cost around $275 per boat, and a full day goes for around $375. The boats will usually accommodate up to three people.

HORSEBACK RIDING Any of the hotels in the area can hook you up with a horseback-riding tour for around $10 to $20 per hour.

SWIMMING You can swim in Lake Arenal, although it can get a bit rough in places, especially during peak windsurfing season. Up above Lake Arenal on the far side of the lake from Tilarán, you'll find the little heart-shaped **Lake Coter.** Surrounded by forest, the lake has good, protected swimming. (UFO watchers also claim that this is a popular pit stop for extraterrestrials.) A taxi to Lake Coter costs around C15,000.

WINDSURFING & KITEBOARDING

If you want to try windsurfing or kiteboarding, check in with **Tico Wind** ★ (www.ticowind.com; ✆ **2692-2002**), which sets up shop on the shores of the lake each year from December 1 to the end of April. Rates are $92 per day, including lunch; multiday and lesson packages also available. This is also the place to rent stand-up paddle boards and equipment.

WAKEBOARDING   Lake Arenal is a big lake with plenty of calm quiet corners to practice wakeboarding. If you're interested in lessons, or just a reliable pull on a wakeboard or water skis, contact **Fly Zone** (www.flyzone-cr.com; ✆ **8339-5876**). Simple pulls behind its specialized boat run around $135 per hour, including boards, skis, and any other necessary gear.

Windsurfing on Lake Arenal

Where to Stay

La Mansion Inn Arenal (www.lamansionarenal.com; ✆ **877/660-3830** in U.S. and Canada, or 2692-8018 in Costa Rica) is an upscale option with an excellent setting and cozy cabins.

MODERATE

Mystica ★★   This Italian-owned hilltop retreat is a primo place to unwind. It's a host to frequent yoga retreats and yoga teacher training courses. Rooms are simple but immaculate, with wood or tile floors, large windows, and a shared common lake-view veranda, with brightly varnished decking and columns made from whole tree trunks. Settle into one of the cushioned Adirondack chairs here to soak in the view or read a book. The best rooms are the private villa and the individual jungle cabins, which offer more space and a greater sense of privacy. Families or small groups can book the two-bedroom Ra Ma Da Sa house, with a full kitchen. It's on the highest spot on the property and features an outdoor bathroom with a mosaic-tiled hot tub and waterfall shower. The expansive grounds and gardens include a nice river-stone pool, as well as a massage room in a treehouse. The hotel's in-house restaurant (p 376), which utilizes a wood-burning oven, is a real plus, as well.

On the road btw. Tilarán and Nuevo Arenal. www.mysticacostarica.com. © **2692-1001**. 9 units. $130 double; $180 cabins, includes breakfast and taxes. **Amenities:** Restaurant; pool; yoga center and small spa; free Wi-Fi.

Villa Decary ★★   The original owners of Villa Decary were hardcore palm enthusiasts, so the grounds and gardens are planted with scores of unique species, including the Madagascar three-sided palm, or *Dypsis decaryi*, named for the French botanist Raymond Decary, who is also the namesake of this B&B. The grounds are beautiful, but you'll also like the cozy rooms, which are decorated with panache (bright Guatemalan bedspreads, and walls adorned with wildlife photos and primitive-style nature paintings). Rooms in the main building feature picture windows and private balconies with wonderful views of Lake Arenal; there are also three private *casitas* with full kitchens and more space.

Nuevo Arenal. www.villadecary.com. © **800/556-0505** in the U.S and Canada, or 2694-4330 in Costa Rica. 5 units, 3 casitas. $109 double; $142–$164 casita for 2, includes full breakfast. **Amenities:** Free Wi-Fi.

Lush landscape on Lake Arenal

INEXPENSIVE

Chalet Nicholas ★ You'll be made to feel right at home by John and Catherine Nicholas, who have owned this intimate, three-room bed-and-breakfast for some 25 years. The owners' Great Danes will also give you a warm welcome, which will be a plus for some visitors, a turn-off for others. All of the rooms are in the main house, feature volcano views, and are quite comfortable. The hotel has some 6 hectares (15 acres) of land, with trails and hiking opportunities right on-site along with pretty gardens with extensive orchid and heliconia collections.

2.5km (1½ miles) west of Nuevo Arenal. www.chaletnicholas.com. © **2694-4041.** 3 units. $75-$85 double, includes full breakfast. No children under 10; no credit cards.

Lake Arenal Hotel & Brewery ★ This place has changed hands a couple of times over the years. Originally it was the Greek-themed Hotel Tilawa, and its most recent incarnation was as the Volcano Brewing Company. Despite the new and more generic name, large Greek columns are still a major architectural detail here and there's a happening microbrewery and brewpub on site. Beyond those extras (and actually, the beer and pub grub is quite good), you won't find much charm in the rooms, which are adequate and clean. But the current management seems to be the most attentive in quite some time. Perched on a high hillside overlooking Lake Arenal, the hotel caters primarily to the windsurfing crowds.

On the road btw. Tilarán and Nuevo Arenal. www.lakearenalhotel.com. © **2695-5050.** 21 units. $75 double, includes breakfast. **Amenities:** Restaurant; bar; pool; Jacuzzi; tennis court; free Wi-Fi.

Lucky Bug Bed & Breakfast ★★ Set back from the road, on a small hill above a small lake, this intimate bed-and-breakfast is a swell pick. Though rooms don't have any views to speak of, they are spacious, cheery, and creative, featuring handmade furniture, hand-painted tiles, and unique artwork. All of this handiwork was done by the owner and her triplet daughters. The handcrafted iron and steel headboards are particularly captivating, and the one in the Flower room is filled in with colored stained glass. Even better are the Butterfly and Frog rooms, which have small private balconies. There's a nice restaurant attached.

Nuevo Arenal. www.luckybugcr.net. © **2694-4515.** 5 units. $89–$109 double, includes breakfast and taxes. **Amenities:** Restaurant; free Wi-Fi.

Where to Eat

Tilarán has numerous inexpensive places to eat, including the restaurant at **Hotel La Carreta** (© 2695-6593) and **Cabinas Mary** (© 2695-5479). Another couple of good options are the brewpub and **La Huerta** restaurant at the **Lake Arenal Hotel** (see above).

In Nuevo Arenal, **Tom's Pan German Bakery** (© 6694-4547) is a popular spot for breakfast, snacks, and lunch.

Caballo Negro ★ INTERNATIONAL/VEGETARIAN   This popular spot is part of the Lucky Bug Bed & Breakfast (see above) and its inventive gift shop and art gallery. The Krauskopf family bring their German heritage to the table here, offering up *jaeger schnitzel* (cutlet with cream sauce), *zigeuner schnitzel* (cutlet with tomato/paprika sauce), homemade *spätzle* (noodles), and bratwursts. The menu also has some non-German dishes and a host of vegetarian items. The eggplant parmesan is a perennial favorite.

Nuevo Arenal (about 3km/1¾ miles out of town on the road to Tilarán). © **2694-4715.** Main courses $8–$18. Daily 7am–5pm.

Mushroom antipasti at Gingerbread

Gingerbread ★★★ MEDITERRANEAN/INTERNATIONAL   Israeli-born chef Eyal Ben-Menachem is a gregarious, gracious host who keeps the needs of his guests foremost. Therefore the menu changes regularly, based on which local ingredients are at their peak, though the duck quesadillas, seared tuna salad, and shrimp risotto are a few regularly occurring specials. Portions are large, often big enough to share. In fact, depending on your group size, you may just be served a family-style meal, with no menu or selections offered—although the food will be abundant, with plenty of variety and pizzazz. If you want a touch of romance and privacy, choose patio seating. The large U-shape bar stays open long after the kitchen has closed and attracts plenty of local regulars.

On the road btw. Tilarán and Nuevo Arenal. www.gingerbreadarenal.com. © **2694-0039.** Main courses $24–$32. No credit cards. Reservations recommended. Tues–Sat 5–8pm.

Moya's Place ★ INTERNATIONAL/VEGETARIAN/PIZZA   This cozy spot is the top pick right in the town of Nuevo Arenal for its delicious wood-oven pizzas, hearty wraps, and meal-sized fresh salads. And who wouldn't like a place that's covered with kooky hand-painted murals of Mayan temples and a giant Aztec calendar? There's an on-site lending/

exchange library, and if there's any live music happening in Nuevo Arenal, it's most likely to be happening here.

Downtown Nuevo Arenal. ℓ **2694-4001.** Main courses $6–$15. Daily 6:30am–9pm.

Mystica ★ ITALIAN/PIZZA   The owners of this hotel restaurant are Italian, so they ensure the food is both authentic and excellent. The menu changes daily based on what's fresh, and many of the ingredients in the sauces, salads, and sides come straight from the hotel's organic gardens. Top picks are the brick-oven pizzas and the delicious Italian pastas and main dishes. Most also enjoy the ambience here: The chairs are painted a rainbow of bright primary colors and no two at any table match at any one time. A fireplace is lit every night, making things cozy and romantic.

Mystica hotel, on the road btw. Tilarán and Nuevo Arenal. www.mysticacostarica. com. ℓ **2692-1001.** Main courses C4,500–C9,000. Dinner by reservation only. Daily 7–9pm.

MONTEVERDE ★★★

167km (104 miles) NW of San José; 82km (51 miles) NW of Puntarenas

Monteverde, which translates to "Green Mountain," is one of the world's first and finest ecotourism destinations. The marvelous, mist-shrouded Monteverde Cloud Forest Biological Reserve and the extensive network of nearby private reserves are rich and rewarding. Bird-watchers flock here to spot the myth-inspiring resplendent quetzal, and scientists come to study the bountiful biodiversity. On top of all that, Monteverde is arguably the best place in Costa Rica for extreme adventure (rivaled perhaps by Arenal). It boasts a zipline where you can fly facedown like Superman for almost a mile, and the only bungee-jumping left in Costa Rica.

   Cloud forests are a mountaintop phenomenon. Moist, warm air sweeping in from the ocean is forced upward by mountain slopes,

Monteverde Cloud Forest Biological Reserve

Monteverde

For numbers 9-13, see Santa Elena map below

SANTA ELENA

Post Office

To San José

Santa Elena

Bus Terminal

Park Entrance

MONTEVERDE CLOUD FOREST BIOLOGICAL RESERVE

MONTEVERDE

NICARAGUA
CARIBBEAN SEA
SAN JOSÉ
PANAMA
PACIFIC OCEAN
Monteverde

Gas Station

CERRO PLANO

CASEM

Río Guacimal

Quebrada Máquina

0 1/2 mi
0 0.5 km

NIGHTLIFE
Bar Amigos **9**
La Taberna **16**
Unicornios **8**

RESTAURANTS
Café Caburé **30**
Celajes **38**
Choco Café
Don Juan **15**
Las Orquídeas
Café **14**
Morpho's Restaurant **12**
Sabor Español **21**
Sabor Tico **8**
Soa **25**
Stella's Bakery **31**
Tramonti **32**

HOTELS
Arco Iris Lodge **11**
El Establo Mountain
Hotel **28**
El Sol **20**
Hidden Canopy
Treehouses **1**
Hotel Belmar **37**
Hotel Fonda Vela **39**
Hotel Heliconia **27**
Hotel Poco a Poco **18**
Monteverde Country
Lodge **24**
Monteverde Lodge
& Gardens **19**

SHOPPING
CASEM **33**
Casa de Arte **26**

ATTRACTIONS
100% Adventura **4**
Bajo del Tigre Trail **34**
Bat Jungle **30**
Centro Panamericano de Idiomas **29**
Chocolate Tour **30**
Curicancha Reserve **35**
Don Juan Coffee Tour **3**
Ecological Sanctuary **22**
El Trapiche Tour **3**
Finca Modelo Canyoning Tour **40**
Herpetarium Adventures **17**
Monteverde Buttery Garden **23**
Monteverde Cheese Factory **36**
Monteverde Cloud Forest
Biological Reserve **41**
Monteverde Extremo **2**
Orchid Garden **13**
Original Canopy Tour **7**
Santa Elena Cloud Forest Reserve **6**
Selvatura Park **6**
Sky Trek **5**
Sky Walk **5**

Cloud forest in Monteverde National Park

and as this moist air rises, it cools, forming clouds. The mountaintops around Monteverde are blanketed almost daily in dense clouds, and as the clouds cling to the slopes, moisture condenses on forest trees. This constant level of moisture has given rise to an incredible diversity of innovative life forms and a forest in which nearly every square inch of space has some sort of plant growing. Within the cloud forest, the branches of huge trees are draped with epiphytic plants: orchids, ferns, and bromeliads. This intense botanical competition has created an almost equally diverse population of insects, birds, and other wildlife. Beyond the **resplendent quetzal,** the Monteverde area boasts more than 2,500 species of plants, 450 types of orchids, 400 species of birds, and 100 species of mammals.

Essentials

GETTING THERE & DEPARTING　**By Car:** The principal access road to Monteverde is located along the Inter-American Highway (CR1); about 20km (12 miles) north of the exit for Puntarenas is a marked turnoff for Sardinal, Santa Elena, and Monteverde. From this turnoff, the road is

The climatic conditions that make Monteverde such a biological hot spot can leave many tourists feeling chilled to the bone. More than a few visitors are unprepared for a cool, windy, and wet stay in the middle of their tropical vacation, and can find Monteverde a bit inhospitable, especially from August through November.

paved for 15km (9½ miles), to just beyond the tiny town of Guacimal. From here, it's another 20km (12 miles) to Santa Elena, the gateway town to Monteverde.

From San José, you can either take the Inter-American Highway (CR1) north all the way to the turnoff, or first head west out of San José on the San José–Caldera Highway (CR27). When you reach Caldera, follow the signs to Puntarenas and the Inter-American Highway (CR1). You will actually follow signs for Liberia and San José, which are, in fact, leading you to the unmarked entrance to CR1. This road (CR23) ends when it hits the Inter-American Highway. You'll want to pass under the bridge and follow the on-ramp, which will put you on the highway heading north. This latter route is a faster and flatter drive.

Another access road to Santa Elena is found just south of the Río Lagarto Bridge. This turnoff is the first you will come to if driving from Liberia. From the Río Lagarto turnoff, it's 38km (24 miles) to Santa Elena, and the road is unpaved the entire way.

Once you arrive, the roads in and around Santa Elena are paved, including all the way to Cerro Plano, and about halfway to the reserve.

To drive from La Fortuna to Monteverde, head past Tabacón and over the dam to Nuevo Arenal, continuing on along the well-marked, paved road that hugs the lake all the way to Tilarán. From Tilarán there is a rough dirt road that is marked at critical intersections. Keep following the signs to Santa Elena and Monterverde.

By Bus: Transportes Monteverde express buses (© **2256-7710** in San José, or 2645-7447 in Santa Elena) leave San José daily at 6:30am and 2:30pm from Calle 12 between avenidas 7 and 9. The trip takes around 4 hours; the fare is around C3,000. Buses arrive at and depart from Santa Elena. If you're staying at one of the hotels or lodges near the reserve, arrange pickup if possible, or take a taxi or local bus. Return buses for San José also depart daily at 6:30am and 2:30pm.

Three daily **Transportes Monteverde** buses depart Puntarenas for Santa Elena at 7:50am, and 1:50 and 2:15pm. The bus stop in Puntarenas is across the street from the main bus station. The fare for the 2½-hour trip is C1,600. A daily bus from Tilarán (Lake Arenal) leaves at 12:30pm. Trip duration is 2 hours (for a 40km/25-mile trip); the fare is C1,200. The express bus departs for San José daily at 6:30am and

2:30pm. The buses from Santa Elena to Puntarenas leave daily at 6:30 and 2:30pm.

Gray Line (www.graylinecostarica.com; ℗ 800/719-3105 in the U.S. and Canada, or 2220-2126 in Costa Rica) and **Interbus** (www.interbusonline.com; ℗ 4031-0888) both offer two daily buses that leave San José for Monteverde, one in the morning and one in the afternoon. The fare is around $54. Both companies will pick you up and drop you off at most San José and Monteverde area hotels. Both Gray Line and Interbus offer connections to most major destinations in Costa Rica.

To reach Liberia, take any bus down the mountain and get off as soon as you hit the Inter-American Highway. You can then flag down a bus bound for Liberia (almost any bus heading north). The Santa Elena/Tilarán bus leaves daily at 7am.

GETTING AROUND Five or so daily buses connect the town of Santa Elena and the Monteverde Cloud Forest Biological Reserve. The first bus leaves Santa Elena for the reserve at 6:15am and the last bus from the reserve leaves at 4pm. The fare is C500. Periodic van transportation also runs between the town of Santa Elena and the Santa Elena Cloud Forest Reserve. Ask around town and you should be able to find the current schedule and book a ride for around C1,000 per person. A **taxi** (℗ 2645-6969 or 2645-6666) between Santa Elena and either the Monteverde Reserve or the Santa Elena Cloud Forest Reserve costs around C5,500 for up to four people. You may have to pay about the same for a ride from Santa Elena to your lodge in Monteverde. Finally, several places around town rent **ATVs,** or all-terrain vehicles, for around $65 to $100 per day.

CITY LAYOUT The tiny town of **Santa Elena** is the gateway to the Monteverde Cloud Forest Biological Reserve, 6km (3¾ miles) outside of town along a windy road that dead-ends at the reserve entrance. As you approach Santa Elena, take the right fork in the road if you're heading directly to Monteverde. If you continue straight, you'll come into the

An ATV ride off-road

center of tiny **Santa Elena,** which has a bus stop, a health clinic, a bank, a supermarket, and a few general stores, plus a collection of simple restaurants, budget hotels, souvenir shops, and tour offices. Heading just out of town, toward Monteverde, is a small strip mall with a prominent Megasuper supermarket. **Monteverde,** on the other hand, is not a

Peace, Love, & Ecotourism

Monteverde was settled in 1951 by Quakers from the United States who wanted to leave behind the fear of war, as well as their obligation to support continued militarism through taxes and the draft. They chose Costa Rica, a country that had abolished its army in 1948. Although Monteverde's founders came here to farm, they wisely recognized the need to preserve the rare cloud forest that covered the mountain slopes above their fields, and to that end, they dedicated the largest adjacent tract of cloud forest as the Monteverde Cloud Forest Biological Reserve.

For an in-depth look into the lives and history of the local Quaker community, pick up a copy of the **"Monteverde Jubilee Family Album."** Published in 2001 by the Monteverde Association of Friends, this collection of oral histories and photographs is 260 pages of local lore and memoirs. It's very simply bound and printed but well worth the $20 price.

village in the traditional sense of the word. There's no center of town—only dirt lanes leading off from the main road to various farms. This main road has signs for all the hotels and restaurants mentioned here.

For a map of Monteverde Cloud Forest Biological Reserve, see the inside front cover of this book.

FAST FACTS   The telephone number for the **local clinic** is ☎ **2645-5076;** for the **Red Cross,** ☎ **2645-6128;** and for the **local police,** ☎ **911** or 2645-6248. The **Farmacia Monteverde** (☎ **2449-5495**) is right downtown. A **Banco Nacional** (☎ **2645-5027**) is located on a prominent corner in downtown Santa Elena, and has a 24-hour ATM.

Exploring the Monteverde Cloud Forest Biological Reserve ★★★

The **Monteverde Cloud Forest Biological Reserve** (www.reserva monteverde.com; ☎ **2645-5122**) is one of the most developed and well-maintained natural attractions in Costa Rica. The trails are clearly marked, regularly traveled, and generally gentle in terms of ascents and descents. The cloud forest here is lush and largely untouched. Still, keep

Birds at the Hummingbird Gallery

Seeing the Forest for the Trees, Bromeliads, Monkeys, Hummingbirds . . .

Because the entrance fee to Monteverde is valid for a full day, consider taking an early-morning walk with a guide and then heading off on your own either after that hike or after lunch. A guide will certainly point out and explain a lot, but there's also much to be said for walking quietly through the forest on your own or in a small group. This will also allow you to stray from the well-traveled paths in the park.

in mind that most of the birds and mammals are rare, elusive, and nocturnal. Moreover, to all but the most trained eyes, those thousands of exotic ferns, orchids, and bromeliads tend to blend into one large mass of indistinguishable green. With a guide hired through your hotel, or on one of the reserve's official guided 2- to 4 1/2-hour hikes, you can see and learn far more than you could on your own. At $19-$64 per person, the reserve's tours might seem like a splurge, especially after you pay the entrance fee, but I strongly recommend that you go with a guide.

Perhaps the most famous resident of the cloud forests of Costa Rica is the quetzal, a bird with iridescent green wings and a ruby-red breast, which has become extremely rare due to habitat destruction. The male quetzal has two long tail feathers that can reach nearly .6m (2 ft.) in length, making it one of the most spectacular birds on earth. The best time to see quetzals is early morning to midmorning, and the best months are February through April (mating season).

Other animals that have been seen in Monteverde, although sightings are extremely rare, include jaguars, ocelots, and tapirs. After the quetzal, Monteverde's most famous resident used to be the golden toad (*sapo dorado*), a rare native species. However, the golden toad has disappeared from the forest and is feared extinct. Competing theories of the toad's demise include adverse effects of a natural drought cycle, the disappearing ozone layer, pesticides, and acid rain.

ADMISSION, HOURS & TOURS The reserve is open daily from 7am to 4pm, and the entrance fee is $20 for adults and $10 for students and children. Because only 220 people are allowed into the reserve at any one time, you might be forced to wait. Most hotels can reserve a guided walk and entrance to the reserve for the following day for you, or you can get tickets in advance directly at the reserve entrance.

Some of the trails can be very muddy, depending on the season, so ask about current conditions. Before venturing into the forest, have a look around the info center. Several guidebooks are available, as well as postcards of some of the reserve's more famous animal inhabitants.

A SELF-GUIDED hike THROUGH THE RESERVE

If you're intent on exploring the reserve on your own, I suggest starting on the **Sendero El Río (River Trail)** ★★. This trail, which heads north from the reserve office, puts you immediately in the middle of dense primary cloud forest, where heavy layers of mosses, bromeliads, and epiphytes cover every branch and trunk. This very first section of trail is a prime location for spotting a resplendent quetzal.

After 15 or 20 minutes, you'll come to a little marked spur leading down to a **catarata,** or waterfall. This diminutive fall fills a small, pristine pond and is quite picturesque, but if you fail in your attempts to capture its beauty, look for its image emblazoned on postcards at souvenir stores all around the area. The entire trek to the waterfall should take you an hour or so.

From the waterfall, turn around and retrace your steps along the River Trail until you come to a fork and the **Sendero Tosi (Tosi Trail).** Follow this shortcut, which leads through varied terrain, back to the reserve entrance.

Once the River Trail and waterfall are behind you, consider a slightly more strenuous hike to a lookout atop the Continental Divide. The **Sendero Bosque Nuboso (Cloud Forest Trail)** ★ heads east from the reserve entrance. As its name implies, the trail leads through thick, virgin cloud forest. Keep your eyes open for any number of bird and mammal species, including toucans, trogons, honeycreepers, and howler monkeys. The trail has some great specimens of

massive strangler fig trees, which start as parasitic vines and eventually engulf their host tree. After 1.9km (1.2 miles), you will reach the Continental Divide. This might sound daunting, but there's a modest elevation gain of only some 65m (213 ft.).

A couple of lookout points on the divide are through clearings in the forest, but the best is **La Ventana (The Window)** ★, just beyond the end of this trail and reached via a short spur trail. Here you'll find a broad, elevated wooden deck with panoramic views. Be forewarned: It's often misty and quite windy up here.

On the way back, take the 2km (1.2-mile) **Sendero Camino (Road Trail),** much of which was once used as a rough all-terrain road. Because it is wide and open in many places, this trail is particularly good for bird-watching. About halfway along, you'll want to take a brief detour to a **suspended bridge** ★. Some 100m (330 ft.) long, this mid-forest bridge gives you a bird's-eye view of the forest canopy. The entire hike should take around 3 hours.

Night tours of the reserve leave every evening at 6:15pm. The cost is $20, including admission to the reserve, a 2-hour hike, and, most important, a guide with a high-powered searchlight. For an extra $5, round-trip transportation to and from your hotel can usually be arranged.

Exploring Outside the Reserve

In addition to everything mentioned below, all of the area hotels can arrange a wide variety of other tours and activities, including guided night tours of the cloud forest.

BIRD-WATCHING & HIKING

You'll find ample bird-watching and hiking opportunities outside the reserve boundaries. Avoid the crowds at Monteverde by heading 5km (3 miles) north from the village of Santa Elena to the **Santa Elena Cloud Forest Reserve** ★★ (www.reservasantaelena.org; © **2645-5390;** daily 7am–4pm). This 310-hectare (765-acre) reserve has a maximum elevation of 1,680m (5,510 ft.), making it the highest cloud forest in the Monteverde area. The reserve has 13km (8 miles) of hiking trails, as well as an info center. Because it borders the Monteverde reserve, a similar richness of flora and fauna is found here, although quetzals are not nearly as common. The $14 entry fee at this reserve goes directly to support a variety of good causes, including conservation and improving the local schools. Three-hour guided tours are $29 per person, not including the entrance fee. (Call the number above to make a reservation for the tour.)

Located just before the Monteverde Cloud Forest Biological Reserve, and sharing many of the same ecosystems and habitats, the **Curicancha Reserve** ★★★ (www.reservacuricancha.com; © **2645-6915;** daily 7am–3pm and 5:30–7:30pm) is an excellent alternative, especially if you're looking to avoid the crowds that can sometimes be found at the area's namesake attraction. The reserve covers 86 hectares (240 acres), of which almost half is primary cloud forest. The trails here are rich in flora and fauna, and quetzals are frequently spotted here. Entrance is $15, and a 3- to 4-hour guided hike can be arranged for an additional $20 per person.

Sky Walk ★★ (www.skyadventures.travel; © **2479-4100;** daily 7am–4pm) is a network of forest paths and suspension bridges that provides visitors with a view previously reserved for birds and monkeys. The bridges reach 39m (128 ft.) above the ground at their highest point, so acrophobia can be an issue. The Sky Walk and its sister attraction, **Sky Trek** (see "Canopy, Canyoning & Bungee," below), are about 3.5km (2¼ miles) outside of Santa Elena, on the road to the Santa Elena Cloud Forest Reserve. Admission is $39, which includes a knowledgeable guide. For $99 per person, you can do the Sky Trek canopy tour and Sky Tram, and then walk the trails and bridges of the Sky Walk. Reservations recommended; round-trip transportation from Santa Elena is $7 per person.

To learn even more about Monteverde, stop in at the **Monteverde Conservation League** (www.acmcr.org; © **2645-5003**), which administers the 22,000-hectare (54,000-acre) private reserve **Bosque Eterno de Los Niños (Children's Eternal Rain Forest)** as well as the Bajo del Tigre Trail. The Conservation League has an info center and small gift shop at the trail head of Bajo del Tigre. In addition to being a good source for information, it also sells books, T-shirts, and cards, and all proceeds go to purchase more land for the Bosque Eterno de Los Niños.

The **Bajo del Tigre Trail ★** is a 3.5km (2.3-mile) trail that's home to several different bird species not usually found within the reserve. You can take several different loops, lasting anywhere from 1 hour to several hours. The trail starts a little past the CASEM artisans' shop (see "Shopping," p 365) and is open daily from 8am to 4pm. Admission is $12 for adults and $10 for students and children under 12. These folks also do a 2-hour night hike that departs at 5:30pm, and costs $22 per adult and $19 per student. All of this is free for kids 6 and under.

Finally, you can walk the trails and grounds of the **Ecological Sanctuary ★★** (www.santuarioecologico.com. © 2645-5869; daily 7am to 5:00pm), a family-run wildlife reserve located down the Cerro Plano road. This place has four main trails through a variety of ecosystems, and wildlife viewing is often quite good. As it's a bit lower in altitude, there are a few species that can be seen here that you won't see higher up. There are a couple of pretty waterfalls off the trails. Admission is $17 for self-guided hiking on the trails; $35 adults, $31 students, and $29 children during the day for a 2-hour guided tour; and $30 adults, $25 students and $23 children for the 2-hour guided night tour at 5:30pm.

CANOPY, CANYONING & BUNGEE

100% Aventura ★★ (www.aventuracanopytour.com); © 2645-6388; daily 8am–3pm), claims to have Latin America's longest zipline, at 1,590m (64 ft. short of a mile)—a "Superman flight" in which you fly facedown between two mountains with a spectacular valley far below. If that didn't scare you enough, try the terrifying (and optional) Tarzan swing at the end of the canopy tour ($50).

Monteverde Extremo ★★★ (www.monteverdeextremo.com); © 2645-6058 or 2645-6981, offers Costa Rica's only bungee-jumping ($73)—the most extreme adventure possible in this adventure-rich place—as well as Tarzan swings, Superman flights, and ordinary ziplines. If you thrive on adrenaline, just jump off the aerial tram suspended 143m (469 feet) above the ground, attached to either a bungee cord or a Tarzan swing.

Selvatura Park ★★ (www.selvatura.com; ☎ **2645-5929;** daily 7am–4:30pm), located close to the Santa Elena Cloud Forest Reserve, is a good one-stop shop for various adventures and attractions in the area. In addition to an extensive canopy tour, with 13 cables connecting 15 platforms, it has a network of trails and suspended bridges, a huge butterfly garden, a hummingbird garden, a snake exhibit, and a wonderful insect display and museum. Prices vary depending upon how much you want to see and do. Individually, the canopy tour costs $50; the walkways and bridges $30; the snake and reptile exhibit, the butterfly garden, and the insect museum, $15 each. Packages to combine the various exhibits are available, although it's definitely confusing, and somewhat annoying, to pick the perfect package. For $132, you get the run of the entire joint, including the tours, lunch, and round-trip transportation from your Monteverde hotel.

Another popular option is offered by **Sky Adventures** ★★ (www.skyadventures.travel; ☎ **2479-4100**), which is part of a large complex of aerial adventures and hiking trails. This is one of the most extensive canopy tours in the country, and begins with a cable car ride (or **Sky Tram**) up into the cloud forest, where the zipline canopy tour features 10 cables.

Sky Adventures in Monteverde

The longest of these reaches some 770m (2,525 ft.) above the forest floor. There are no rappel descents, and you brake using the pulley system for friction. Nearby, the **Sky Walk** ★★ (p 385) is a network of forest paths and suspension bridges that can easily be combined with this adventure tour. Also here: a serpentarium and hummingbird garden. This place is about 3.5km (2¼ miles) outside the town of Santa Elena, on the road to the Santa Elena Cloud Forest Reserve. The Sky Walk is open daily from 7am to 1pm; admission is $39, which includes a knowledgeable guide. For $99 per person, you can do the Sky Trek canopy tour and Sky Tram, and then walk the trails and bridges of the Sky Walk. Reservations recommended; transportation from Santa Elena is $8-$10 per person.

Perhaps the first commercial jungle-canopy zipline in the world is run by the **Original Canopy Tour** ★ (www.canopytour.com; © 305/433-3341 in U.S or 2291-4465 in Costa Rica). Its highlight is the initial ascent, which is made by climbing up the hollowed-out interior of a giant strangler fig. The tour has 13 platforms and one rappel, and is far less terrifying than many of its competitors. The 2- to 2½-hour tours run three times daily and cost $45/adults, $35/students, and $25/children 12 and under.

Finally, if you want to add a bit more excitement to your adventure, and definitely more water, try the **Finca Modelo Canyoning Tour** ★★ (www.familiabrenestours.com; © 2645-5581). This tour involves a mix of hiking and then rappelling down the face of a series of forest waterfalls. The tallest of these waterfalls is around 40m (132 ft.). You will get wet on this tour. The cost is $70.

Anybody in average physical condition can do any of the adventure tours in Monteverde, but they're not for the faint of heart. Try to book directly with the companies listed above. Beware of touts on the streets of Monteverde, who make a small commission and frequently try to steer tourists to the operator paying the highest percentage.

HORSEBACK RIDING

Monteverde has excellent terrain for horseback riding. **Horse Trek Monteverde** ★ (www.costaricahorsebackridingvacations.com; © 866/811-0522 U.S/Canada or 2645-5874 in Costa Rica) and **Sabine's Smiling Horses** ★ (www.smilinghorses.com; © 2645-6894) are established operators, offering guided rides for $49 to $85. Horseback/boat trips link Monteverde/Santa Elena with La Fortuna (p 351).

OTHER ATTRACTIONS IN MONTEVERDE

It seems as if Monteverde has an exhibit or attraction dedicated to almost every type of tropical fauna. Butterflies abound here, and the long-established **Monteverde Butterfly Garden** ★ (www.monteverde butterflygarden.com; © 2645-5512; daily 8:30am–4pm), located near the Pensión Monteverde Inn, displays many of Costa Rica's most beautiful species. Aside from seeing the hundreds of preserved and mounted butterflies, you can watch live butterflies in the garden and greenhouse. Admission, including a guided tour, is $15/adults, $10/students, and $5 for kids ages 4 to 6. If you can, visit between 9 and 11am, when the butterflies tend to be most active.

If your taste runs toward the slithery, you can check out the informative displays at the **Herpetarium Adventures ★** (℘ 2645-6002; daily 9am–8pm), in Santa Elena on the road to the reserve. It charges $15 for adults, $12 for students and $10 for children.

Monteverde Theme Park ★ (℘ 2645-6320; daily 9:30am–8pm), a couple of hundred meters north of the Monteverde Lodge, has several attractions. A variety of amphibians populates a series of glass terrariums; nearby is a butterfly garden and canopy tour. The entrance fee ($15 for adults and $12 for students) gets you a 45-minute guided tour, and your ticket is good for 1 week, allowing for multiple visits. Stop by at least once after dark, when the tree frogs are active.

The **Bat Jungle ★★★** (www.batjungle.com; ℘ 2645-7701; daily 9am–7:30pm) provides an in-depth look into the life and habits of these odd flying mammals. A visit here includes several different types of exhibits, from skeletal remains to a large enclosure where you get to see various live species in action—the enclosure and room are kept dark, and the bats have had their biological clocks tricked into thinking that it's night. It's quite an interesting experience. The last tour starts at 6:45pm. Admission is $15 for adults and $12 for students. Children under 6 are free.

If you've had your fill of critters, you might want to stop at the **Orchid Garden ★★** (www.monteverdeorchidgarden.net; ℘ 2645-5308; daily 8am–5pm), in Santa Elena across from the Pensión El Tucano. This botanical garden has more than 425 species of orchids. The tour is fascinating, especially given the fact that you need (and are given) a magnifying glass to see some of the flowers in bloom. Admission is $12 for adults, $9 for students and free for children under 12.

AGRICULTURAL & CULINARY TOURISM

If you're looking for a glimpse into the practices and processes of daily life in this region, the **Don Juan Coffee Tour ★★** (www.donjuan coffeetour.com; ℘ 2645-7100) is a local, family-run operation that offers a 2-hour tour of its sprawling farm. Coffee is the primary crop and the focus of the tour, although there are a range of crops, including macadamia; a trapiche, or sugarcane mill; and a small, boutique chocolate-production area. As a bonus, you get a snack and coffee tasting, and you may even get to meet the farm's namesake septuagenarian, Don Juan. The tour costs $35/adults and $15/children.

A sugarcane field

El Trapiche Tour ★★ (www.eltrapichetour.com; © **2645-7780** or 2645-7650) is another family-run tour, which gives you insight into the traditional means of harvesting and processing sugarcane, as well as the general life on a farm that includes bananas, macadamia, and citrus groves. Back at the farmhouse, you get to see how the raw materials are turned into cane liquor, raw sugar, and local sweets. The 2-hour tour includes a ride in an ox-drawn cart, and a visit to the family's coffee farm and roasting facility. Depending on the season, you may even get to pick a bushel of raw coffee beans. Tours run daily at 10am and 3pm, and cost $33 for adults, and $12 for children 10 through 12, and include transportation.

Finally, if you want a detailed explanation of the processes involved in growing, harvesting, processing, and producing chocolate, be sure to stop by Café Caburé (p 396) for its **Chocolate Tour.** You'll take some chocolate beans right through the roasting, grinding, and tempering processes during the 45-minute tour. The tour is offered most days at 1:30pm, and by appointment. The cost is $15.

LEARN THE LANGUAGE

The **Centro Panamericano de Idiomas** ★ (www.cpi-edu.com; ✆ **2645-5441**) offers immersion language classes in a wonderful setting. A 1-week program with 4 hours of class per day costs $460. The center also offers language seminars on topics such as social work, medicine, and security. Be sure to check its website for seminar dates.

Where to Stay

When choosing a place to stay in Monteverde, be sure to check whether the rates include a meal plan. In the past, almost all the lodges included three meals a day in their prices, but this practice is waning.

EXPENSIVE

El Establo Mountain Hotel ★   Years ago, the Beeche family transformed its old horse stable (hence, *el establo*) into a simple roadside budget lodge. Today, that original hostel is gone, and in its place is arguably the biggest and most conventionally swank hotel in Monteverde. Large rooms are spread around sprawling grounds that rise up a steep hillside from the main road between Santa Elena and the Monteverde Cloud Forest Biological Reserve. The hotel provides a shuttle service to help you get around the hilly property, but it's not the most convenient arrangement and often makes for some unwanted waiting at times. All rooms have a private balcony or patio, and those on the upper floors of the buildings highest up the hillside have some amazing views out to the Gulf of Nicoya, which you can enjoy from the comfort of wooden rocking chairs. Rooms have a contemporary feel, with crisp coverlets, angular wooden furniture, and TVs (this is one of the few hotels in Monteverde to have any of those). There are two covered pools, two good restaurants, a small spa, an outdoor lighted tennis court, and a zipline canopy tour.

Monteverde. www.elestablo.com. ✆ **855/353-7822** in the U.S. and Canada or 2645-5110 in Costa Rica. 155 units. $157 double; $234–$287 suite, includes taxes. **Amenities:** 2 restaurants; bar; 2 covered pools; tennis; room service; spa; free Wi-Fi.

Hidden Canopy Treehouses ★★★   For an intimate, unique, in-touch-with-nature experience in the Monteverde area, you can't beat this place. Although a couple of perfectly lovely rooms are off the main lodge building, the individual "treehouses" are a much better option. Set in the forest canopy, these are all ample bungalows built on raised stilts, featuring polished hardwoods, slate bathrooms with waterfall showers, canopy beds, large picture windows, and a balcony or outdoor deck. Especially nice are the wrap-around floor-to-ceiling windows in Glade, and the private Jacuzzi nook in Eden. You can take in superb sunset views from the main lodge, where daily afternoon tea is served. Owner Jennifer King is almost always on-site and really pays attention to the fine

The lodge at Hidden Canopy Treehouses

details. This lodge has excellent in-house guides and very personalized service.

On the road to the Santa Elena Cloud Forest Reserve. www.hiddencanopy.com. ℰ **2645-5447.** 7 units. $245 double; $295–$445 double tree house, includes breakfast and afternoon happy hour. No children 14 or under; 2-night minimum. **Amenities:** Afternoon tea; free Wi-Fi.

MODERATE

Hotel Belmar ★★ One of the oldest hotels in the area, this family run lodge continues to improve and expand, with younger generations infusing much life into the property. Complete with its own organic farm and microbrewery, not to mention a bar and restaurant that hires top chefs and mixologists to update the menus, the Belmar is perhaps the area's most complete hotel. The expansive, flower filled grounds are perched on a hillside with vast views of the cloud forest canopy. Despite the building's age, the room's and their wood paneled walls, floor, and ceiling have been immaculately maintained and all have a balcony.

Monteverde. www.hotelbelmar.net. ℰ **2645-5206**. 22 units. $151–$169 double; $360–$390 suite, includes breakfast. **Amenities:** Restaurant; bar; small spa; Jacuzzi; microbrewery; free Wi-Fi.

Hotel Fonda Vela ★★ This longstanding hotel is one of the closest you'll find to the Monteverde reserve, just a 15-minute or so walk away, and it's recommendable also for its unique and pretty look. Owner Paul Smith's paintings, stained-glass works, and large sculptures are scattered throughout the hotel and grounds. Rooms, in several separate buildings, have views over the forests all the way to the Gulf of Nicoya. Locally milled wood planking is used for walls, floors, ceilings, and wainscoting. The junior suites are especially spacious. A short walk from the restaurant and rooms is a pool, a couple of Jacuzzis, pool and Ping-Pong tables, board games, and a casual bar, all housed under a high, curving atrium roof.

On the road to the Monteverde Biological Cloud Forest Reserve. www.fondavela. com. ℭ **2645-5125.** 40 units. $170 double; $227 suite, includes breakfast. **Amenities:** 2 restaurants; 2 bars; Jacuzzi; pool; free Wi-Fi.

Hotel Heliconia ★ Located at the Cerro Plano intersection along the road between Santa Elena and the Monteverde reserve, this is another local lodge that has steadily grown and expanded over the years. The largest building (on the highest part of the 6-acre property) is where you'll find the rooms with the best views. The wood-paneled walls and carpeted floors tend to give the decor a dated, motel-like feel, but it's clean and the staff is friendly. Five hot tubs and Jacuzzis are spread around the lush grounds between the hotel's several buildings. There's a large private cloud forest preserve behind the hotel, and the owners also run the Selvatura adventure center (p 387).

Monteverde. www.hotelheliconia.com. ℭ **2645-5109.** 55 units. $109–$139 double, includes breakfast. **Amenities:** Restaurant; bar; free Wi-Fi.

Hotel Poco a Poco ★★ A good choice for families with kids, the "Little by Little Hotel" is a hive of activity, with a pool, small playhouse, restaurant, heated Jacuzzi, and small spa. Located on the outskirts of Santa Elena, Poco a Poco has clean, comfortable rooms (cream tiled floors, quality beds) with modern amenities like TV/DVD systems and access to a massive DVD library. Some are a bit tight in terms of size. The restaurant is excellent and features live music nightly.

Santa Elena. www.hotelpocoapoco.com. ℭ **2645-6000** in Costa Rica. 30 units. $145–$245 double, includes breakfast. **Amenities:** Restaurant; bar; indoor pool; spa; sauna; Jacuzzi; free Wi-Fi.

Monteverde Lodge & Gardens ★★★ Some things do get better with age, and that's true of this pioneering ecolodge, which is run by Michael Kaye and Costa Rica Expeditions (p 99). Rooms are large and cozy, with hardwood floors, orthopedic beds, and a wall of windows or French doors with views of the gardens and forest. Meals are served in a large dining room with windows all around and an open fire burning under a suspended conical steel chimney. There are trails through the lush and beautiful gardens, and there's a heated outdoor pool with slate

Guest room at Monteverdge Lodge & Gardens

decking all around, as well as butterfly, orchid, and hummingbird attractions. These folks also operate one of the best guide and tour operations in the area.

Santa Elena. www.monteverdelodge.com. © **2257-0766** San José office, or 2645-5057 at the lodge. 28 units. $136–$266 double, includes breakfast and taxes. **Amenities:** Restaurant; bar; solar-heated pool; free Wi-Fi.

INEXPENSIVE

El Sol ★ (www.elsolnuestro.com; © **2645-5838**) is a unique little boutique option, on the road to the Inter-American Highway, about 10 minutes south of Santa Elena. Also worth considering is **Monteverde Country Lodge** (www.monteverdecountrylodge.com; © **888/936-5696** in U.S and Canada, or 2645-7600 in Costa Rica), a homey, simple hotel run by the folks at Hotel Poco a Poco (p 393).

For real budgeteers, there are quite a few backpacker havens in Santa Elena and spread along the road to the reserve. The best of these is the **Pensión Santa Elena** ★ (www.pensionsantaelena.com; © **2645-5051**), which also offers swankier rooms with private bathrooms in its new annex. Owned and operated by Texan Ran Smith, and right next to the popular

Taco Taco takeout counter run by his sister, this affordable hotel is centrally located in Santa Elena's triangular, three-street downtown.

Finally, it's possible to stay in a room right at the **Monteverde Cloud Forest Biological Reserve** (www.cct.or.cr; ✆ 2645-5122). There are 12 rooms here with private bathrooms that sleep anywhere from to 2 to 6. The $164 price includes three meals per day and admission to the reserve.

Arco Iris Lodge ★ This small boutique hotel is actually right in the town of Santa Elena, but you'd never know it. The expansive grounds and gardens give it a great sense of isolation and privacy (though you can still walk to shops and restaurants). The rooms come in a variety of shapes and sizes from simple standards, some with bunk beds, to individual cabins and superior rooms with a kitchenette and sleeping loft. All feature shiny varnished wood and local stonework, as well as low-lying beds with colorful Guatemalan bedspreads. German owner Susanna and her engaged staff make sure service is always top-notch.

Santa Elena. www.arcoirislodge.com. ✆ **2645-5067.** 24 units. $44–$120 double, includes breakfast and taxes. **Amenities:** Lounge; free Wi-Fi.

Relaxing by the pool at Monteverde Lodge & Gardens

Where to Eat

Because most visitors want to get an early start, they usually grab a quick breakfast at their hotel. It's also common for people to have their lodge pack them a bag lunch to take to the reserve, though there's a decent little *soda* at the reserve entrance.

You can get good pizzas and pastas at **Tramonti** ★ (www.tramonticr. com; ☎ 2645-6120), along the road to the reserve, and great paella and other Spanish specialties at **Sabor Español** ★ (☎ 2645-5387), a few miles outside of Santa Elena on the road to Tilarán. Also, the restaurant at the **Hotel Poco a Poco** (☎ 2645-6000) gets high marks for its wide range of international dishes.

A popular choice for lunch is **Stella's Bakery** (☎ 2645-5560), across from the CASEM gift shop. Bright and inviting, its selection changes regularly but might include vegetarian quiche, eggplant *parmigiana,* and salads. Stella's also features a number of decadent baked goods.

EXPENSIVE

Sofia ★ COSTA RICAN/FUSION   Here's your splurge choice, a happy change from typical Costa Rican cooking. The Nuevo Latino cuisine here is based on classic Tico dishes and local ingredients, but with intriguing twists, like tenderloin in chipotle-butter salsa or guava-glazed chicken. Owner and restaurateur Karen Nielsen has created a sophisticated and romantic ambience here, with solid wooden tables and chairs, soft lighting, and cool jazz in the background. Try to grab a seat in front of one of the large arched picture windows overlooking cloud-forest foliage.

Cerro Plano, just past the turnoff to the Butterfly Farm, on your left. ☎ **2645-7017.** Reservations recommended in high season. Main courses $12–$22. Daily 11:30am–9:30pm.

MODERATE

Café Caburé ★★ INTERNATIONAL/CHOCOLATES   Set on the second floor of a small complex also housing the Bat Jungle (p 389), with open-air seating on a broad wooden veranda, this is a good place for a decadent dessert break (though lunches and dinners here are also solid). The homemade chocolates and fancy, flavored truffles here are truly scrumptious. (And if you want to learn more about the chocolate-making and -tempering process, be sure to take the chocolate tour; see p 390). On the savory side, the main menu features a wide range of international dishes, with everything from chicken mole to shrimp curry to more straightforward but very tasty sandwiches, wraps, and fresh empanadas.

On the road btw. Santa Elena and the reserve, at the Bat Jungle. www.cabure.net. ☎ **2645-5020.** Reservations recommended in high season. Main courses C4,900–C9,900. Mon–Sat 9am–9pm.

Celajes ★★★ Spilling out on the terrace and overlooking the rainforest canopy, this restaurant inside Hotel Belmar is where locals come for a good meal. Staffed with a group of international restaurant and bar veterans and utilizing the hotel's organic farm, the menu here is Monteverde's most creative and changes often. Standbys include grilled octopus and pulled pork, while breakfast is equally as impressive, with Caribbean-style French toast and other goodies. Additionally, they have their own microbrewery, with a few beers on tap, as well as a cocktail menu that makes use of native herbs and fruits sourced from the property.

Monteverde. www.hotelbelmar.net. ⓒ **2645-5206.** Reservations recommended for dinner in high season. Main courses C2,900–C12,500. Daily 7am–9pm.

INEXPENSIVE

Morpho's Restaurant ★ COSTA RICAN/VEGETARIAN Although it's moved around over the years, Morpho's is a local institution, serving up hearty meals at reasonable prices. The large and varied *casado* (a local blue-plate special) is quite popular, as are the fresh fruit smoothies and home-baked desserts. For something a bit fancier, try the thick pork chop in a plum/cherry sauce. There are also excellent vegetarian selections. You can't miss this place, with its painted exterior covered with oversize, fluttering blue morpho butterflies. Inside, the hand-painted murals are joined by rustic furnishings including chairs made from whole tree branches and trunks.

In downtown Santa Elena, next to the Orchid Garden. www.morphosrestaurant.com. ⓒ **2645-5607.** Main courses C2,500–C9,200. Daily 11am–9pm.

Sabor Tico ★★ COSTA RICAN The name means "Tico Flavor," and that's what you get at this family-run, traditional joint. The portions are huge, and everything is extremely tasty and well prepared, although service can be slow (but friendly) when the place is busy. The *casados*, *gallos*, *arroz con pollo*, and fresh fruit juices are all excellent. These folks have opened a second location (ⓒ **2645-5968**) in the Centro Comercial Monteverde shopping plaza, but it's hard to top the more casual and authentic vibe of the original location.

> ### Take a Break
>
> If all the activities in Monteverde have worn you out, stop in at **Las Orquídeas Café** (ⓒ **2645-6850**) or the **Choco Café Don Juan** ★ (ⓒ **2645-7444**), two excellent local coffee shops just off the main drag in Santa Elena. The latter is connected to the Don Juan Coffee Farm (p 389) and has a small gift shop attached.

In downtown Santa Elena, across from the soccer field. ⓒ **2645-5827.** Main courses C2,700–C4,900. Daily 7am–9pm.

Shopping

The **Monteverde Cloud Forest Biological Reserve** has a well-stocked gift shop, just off the entrance. You'll find plenty of T-shirts, postcards, and assorted crafts here, as well as science and natural history books.

Another top shop is **CASEM COOP** ★ (www.casemcoop. blogspot.com; ✆ **2645-5190**; daily 7am–5pm), on the right side of the main road, just across from Stella's Bakery. This crafts cooperative sells embroidered clothing, T-shirts, posters, and postcards, Boruca weavings, locally grown coffee, and many other items to remind you of your visit to Monteverde. CASEM COOP is open daily 7am to 5pm.

Over the years, Monteverde has developed a nice little community of artists. Around town, you'll see paintings by artists Paul Smith and Meg Wallace, whose works are displayed at Hotel Fonda Vela and Stella's Bakery, respectively. **Casa de Arte** ★★ (www.monteverdearthouse.com; ✆ **2645-5275**) also has an interesting mix of arts and crafts.

Shopping in Monteverde

Entertainment & Nightlife

Perhaps the most popular after-dark activities in Monteverde are night hikes in one of the reserves. However, if you want a taste of the local party scene, head to **Bar Amigos** (www.baramigos.com; ✆ **2645-5071**), a large and often loud bar in the heart of Santa Elena. You'll find a bunch of flatscreen TVs showing sporting events, a couple of pool tables, and occasional live bands. There's also **Unicornio's** (✆ **5000-4210**), beside Sabor Tico, which has a similar vibe. **La Taberna** ★ (✆ **8839-5569**), on the edge of Santa Elena town, below the serpentarium is a more contemporary club vibe, this place attracts a mix of locals and tourists, cranks its music loud, and often gets people dancing.

PUERTO VIEJO DE SARAPIQUÍ ★

82km (51 miles) N of San José; 102km (63 miles) E of La Fortuna

The Sarapiquí region, named for the principal river that runs through it, lies at the foot of the Cordillera Central mountain range. To the south is the rainforest of **Braulio Carrillo National Park,** and to the east are **Tortuguero National Park ★★** and **Barra del Colorado National Wildlife Refuge ★**. In between these protected areas are thousands of acres of banana, pineapple, and palm plantations. This is an agricultural region, but there are patches of forest on private farms and reserves scattered throughout.

Within the remaining rainforest are several lodges that attract naturalists (both amateur and professional). One of these, **La Selva,** is a biological field station with a primary focus on research and education, but it welcomes ecotourists of all kinds. Bird-watching and rainforest hikes are the primary attractions in this area, but more adventure-oriented travelers will find plenty of other available activities, including ziplining and boating and rafting trips on the Sarapiquí River.

The main town in the region is Puerto Viejo de Sarapiquí—not to be confused with the south Caribbean coastal town of Puerto Viejo de Limón (sometimes called Puerto Viejo de Talamanca).

Essentials

GETTING THERE & DEPARTING By Car: The Guápiles Highway (CR32), which leads to the Caribbean coast, heads north out of downtown San José on Calle 3. Turn north before reaching Guápiles on the road to Río Frío (CR4), and continue north through Las Horquetas, passing the turn-offs for Rara Avis, La Selva, and El Gavilán lodges before reaching Puerto Viejo.

A more scenic route goes through Heredia, Barva, Varablanca, and San Miguel before reaching Puerto Viejo. This route passes very close to the Poás Volcano and directly in front of La Paz waterfall. If you want to take this route, head west out of San José, then turn north to Heredia and follow the signs for Varablanca and La Paz Waterfall Gardens.

Tip: If you plan to stop on the way to see **La Paz Waterfall Gardens ★★** or visit **Rain Forest Adventures ★** (p 402), budget at least 2 hours to visit either attraction.

> ### Getting Loopy
>
> The circular route around Braulio Carrillo National Park is what is sometimes referred to as "The Sarapiquí Loop." This loop is a pretty drive, punctuated with attractions and tour opportunities, including Poás Volcano. It also connects quite nicely with an alternative route to La Fortuna and the Arenal Volcano area (p 342).

By Bus: Empresarios Guapileños buses (© **2222-0610** in San José, or 2710-7780 in Puerto Viejo) leave San José roughly every hour between 6:30am and 6pm from **Gran Terminal del Caribe,** on Calle Central, 1 block north of Avenida 11. The trip takes 2 hours; fare is C2,650. Buses for San José leave Puerto Viejo mostly hourly from 5:30am to 5:30pm.

CITY LAYOUT   Puerto Viejo is a very small town, with a soccer field at its center. If you continue past the soccer field on the main road and stay on the paved road, then turn right at the Banco Nacional, you'll come to the Río Sarapiquí and the dock, where you can look into arranging a boat trip.

Exploring Puerto Viejo de Sarapiquí

BOAT TRIPS   The Río Sarapiquí was originally this region's, if not the country's, major transportation thoroughfare, connecting the town of Puerto Viejo with the Caribbean coast. For the adventurous, Puerto Viejo is a jumping-off point for trips down the Río Sarapiquí to Barra del Colorado National Wildlife Refuge and Tortuguero National Park on the Caribbean coast. A boat transfer for up to 10 people will cost you around $400 to $600 to Barra del Colorado or $500 to $700 to Tortuguero.

In addition to the longer trips, you can take shorter trips on the river for between $15 and $25 per person per hour. A trip down the Sarapiquí, even if it's for only an hour or two, provides opportunities to spot crocodiles, caimans, monkeys, sloths, and dozens of bird species.

If you're interested in any of the boat trips on the river, you are best off checking at your hotel, or with **Oasis Nature Tours** (www.oasis naturetours.com; © **2766-6108**). Alternatively, you can head down to the town dock on the bank of the Sarapiquí and see if you can arrange a boat trip on your own by tagging along with another group or better yet, with a bunch of locals.

CANOPY TOUR & MORE   Hacienda Pozo Azul ★ (www.pozoazul. com; © **877/810-6903** in the U.S. and Canada, or 2438-2616 in Costa Rica; daily 8am–6pm) is an extensive ecotourism operation offering a zipline tour with 13 platforms connected by nine cables. In addition, Hacienda Pozo Azul offers whitewater rafting, horseback riding, and guided hikes. It also runs a tent camp and separate rustic lodge in deep rainforest. Several differently priced combo packages are offered.

HIKING & GUIDED TOURS   Anyone can take advantage of the 56km (35 miles) of well-maintained **trails at La Selva ★★** (p 403). If you're not staying there, however, you'll have to take a guided hike, led by well-informed naturalists. Half- and full-day hikes ($35 and $45, respectively) are offered daily, but you must reserve in advance (www.threepaths. co.cr; © **2524-0607**). Tours are at 8am and 1:30pm daily.

One good hike starts at the Cantarrana ("singing frog") trail, which includes a boardwalk through a rainforest swamp. From here, you can join up with either the near or far circular loop trails—**CCC** and **CCL.**

For a more orderly introduction to the local flora, head to a botanical garden like the **Chester's Field Biological Gardens** or the nearby **Heliconia Island** (www.heliconiaisland.com; ✆ **2764-5220**), an interesting garden with more than 70 varieties of heliconia on a small island. This place is open daily from 8am to 5pm. Admission is $10 for a self-guided walk, or $18 for a guided tour.

A NATURAL HISTORY THEME PARK   The **Alma Ata Archaeological Park** is a small ongoing dig of a modest pre-Columbian gravesite that is attached to a local hotel, **Sarapiquís Rainforest Lodge** (www.sarapiquis. com; ✆ **2761-1004**). So far, 12 graves, some petroglyphs, and numerous pieces of ceramic and jewelry have been unearthed. The hotel has a small museum that displays examples of the ceramics, tools, clothing, and carvings found here, as well as other natural history exhibits. Just across the hotel's driveway, you'll find the **Chester's Field Biological Gardens,** with well-tended displays of local medicinal and ornamental plants and herbs, as well as food crops. Admission to the archaeological park and gardens costs $32, and includes lunch. If you just want to visit the museum, the cost is $18 for adults, $10 for students. Open daily, 6am to 5pm.

Just south of the SarapiquíS Rainforest Lodge is the 345-hectare (850-acre) private **Tirimbina Biological Reserve ★** (www.tirimbina. org; ✆ **2761-0333**), with a network of trails and several impressive suspension bridges, both over the river and through the forest canopy. A self-guided walk of the bridges and trails costs $17 per person, and a 2-hour guided tour costs $2 per person—definitely worth the extra few bucks. The center is open daily from 7:30am to 5pm, and from 7:30 to 9:30pm for night tours; specialized early morning bird-watching tours are also available.

RAFTING & KAYAKING   **Aguas Bravas** (www.costaricaraftingvacation. com; ✆ **2292-2072**) and **Aventuras del Sarapiquí ★** (www.sarapiqui. com; ✆ **2766-6768**) offer wet and wild rides on a variety of sections of

---

On the Boardwalk

Located about 25 minutes' drive from Puerto Viejo de Sarapiquí, **Cinco Ceibas Rainforest Reserve & Adventure Park ★★** (www.cincoceibas.com; ✆ **2476-0606**) offers up several wonderful excursions and activities in a lush rainforest setting. The main attraction here is the 1.5km elevated boardwalk through thick forest and wetlands. This boardwalk passes by several of the namesake ceiba trees, massive old-growth rainforest trees. Other activity options here include horseback riding, kayaking, and a traditional oxcart carriage ride. Several packages are offered, ranging from $40 to $125 per person, including lunch.

the Sarapiquí and Puerto Viejo rivers, ranging from Class I to Class IV. Trips cost between $56 and $95 per person. Aventuras del Sarapiquí also operates mountain-biking and horseback-riding tours in the area, and offers kayak rentals, lessons and trips for more experienced and/or daring river rats, plus innertube floats.

SNAKES UNDER GLASS Just a few blocks west of the Centro Neotrópico SarapiquíS, you'll find **Jardín de Serpientes (Snake Garden;** ℂ **2761-1059;** daily 9am–5pm), a collection of more than 50 snakes, both venomous and nonvenomous, and other reptiles and amphibians. There are also caiman and crocodiles. All are kept in clean, well-lit displays. Admission is $32 for adults and $22 for children for a guided tour. Night tours are offered with advance reservations.

Rafting on the Sarapiquí River

PINEAPPLE PRODUCTION For a peek into the world of pineapple production, visit the **Organic Paradise Tour** (ℂ **2761-0706**) in Chilamate. The farm has 33 hectares under cultivation. The 2-hour tour includes a trip through the plantation, explanations and demonstrations of the processes involved, and a sampling of the fruit. Mass pineapple production is notorious for its negative impact on the environment and workers' rights, and these folks are an important model of a sustainable alternative. The cost is $40 per person for the tour.

MAJOR ATTRACTIONS EN ROUTE If you're driving to Puerto Viejo de Sarapiquí via the Guápiles Highway, stop in at **Rain Forest Adventures ★**. You'll see the entrance just east of the bridge over the Río Sucio. For more info, see "Day Trips from San José," in chapter 6, p 163. Just up the road to the west is an entrance to Braulio Carillo National Park at Quebrada Gonzalez. Two sets of trails offer opportunities for bird-watching and introductions to the trees, orchids, and epiphytes of this very wet rainforest.

Where to Stay & Eat

All the lodges listed below arrange excursions throughout the region, including boat trips on the Sarapiquí, guided hikes in the rainforest, and horseback or mountain-bike rides.

MODERATE

Hacienda La Isla ★ (www.haciendalaisla.com; ℰ **2764-2576**) is an intimate boutique hotel near the small town of Las Horquetas.

Hotel Hacienda Sueño Azul ★ This hotel is located fairly close to Highway 32, which connects San José to the Caribbean coast, on the outskirts of the tiny village of Las Horquetas. You reach the property by crossing a couple of hammock bridges that appear too narrow for most vehicles, but seem to do the job. The rooms are large and feature rustic four-poster wooden beds and private verandas. The best of these overlook a river or lagoon. The hotel sits at the meeting point of two rivers, and water features prominently. One of the two pools is a very large, river-fed, semi-natural pool. This place often hosts yoga or wellness retreats, and horseback riding, hiking, and other active adventures are offered.

Las Horquetas de Sarapiquí. www.suenoazulresort.com. ℰ **2253-2020** reservation number in San José, 2764-1000 at the lodge. 65 units. $98–$119 double; $152 suite; includes breakfast. **Amenities:** Restaurant; bar, Jacuzzi; 2 pools; spa, free Wi-Fi.

La Quinta de Sarapiquí Country Inn ★★ Leo and Beatriz run a cozy, laid-back little lodge on the edge of the Sardinal River. Rooms feature blindingly white tile floors and painted walls, with splashes of color provided by small paintings and brightly colored bedspreads. They're kept immaculately maintained and have lots of natural light and a cheery feel. The hotel has two swimming pools, as well as a butterfly garden, poison-dart-frog garden, and a riverside trail through a reclaimed forest area.

Chilamate, Sarapiquí. www.laquintasarapiqui.com. ℰ **2222-3344** reservations office in San José, or 2761-1052 at the lodge. 40 units. $110–$140 double, includes breakfast; children under 12 stay free in parents' room. **Amenities:** Restaurant; bar; 2 pools; free Wi-Fi.

La Selva Biological Station ★ The name says it all—this is no prissy upscale ecolodge. Built primarily to accommodate biologists, researchers, and student groups, La Selva also accepts everyday tourists. Don't expect fine linens, pampering service, or memorable meals. There are very basic bunk bed and dorm-style rooms, as well as a few more plush rooms geared toward tourists more than scientists. La Selva is operated by the Organization for Tropical Studies and has more than 1,614 hectares (3,656 acres) of private reserve bordering Braulio Carrillo National Park. On-site is a very extensive well-maintained trail system

A bungalow at Selva Verde Lodge

through these forests, and the flora and fauna viewing are some of the best in Costa Rica.

Puerto Viejo. www.threepaths.co.cr. © **2524-0607** reservations office in San José, or 2766-6565 at the lodge. 24 units, 16 with shared bathroom. $90 per person based on double occupancy, includes all meals, 1 guided walk, and taxes. Rates lower for researchers and student groups. **Amenities:** Restaurant; free Wi-Fi.

Selva Verde Lodge ★★   Begun in 1982 by Giovanna Holbrook and Holbrook Travel, this was one of the first ecotourist lodges in Costa Rica and is still going strong. Set in a patch of thick forest on the banks of the Sarapiquí River, the property includes a large private reserve on the other side of the river. A series of raised wooden buildings connected by a maze of covered walkways house the main river lodge rooms, which are rather bare-bones. The decor consists of varnished wood floors, screen-and-lathe windows, beds with plain white linens, a fan, and a smallish bathroom. A few bungalows are a bit larger and have air-conditioning, but these are located across the street farther from the main lodge, restaurant, and river. A large, open-air main dining room overlooks the river. In addition to a more typical lodge menu, it also offers buffet dining (aimed primarily at tour groups), as well as pizzas from a wood-burning brick oven. There's a lovely pool area and several swimming holes along the river, plus a network of trails through the rainforest, and a zipline tour.

Chilamate, Sarapiquí. www.selvaverde.com. ✆ **800/451-7111** in the U.S. and Canada, or 2761-1800 in Costa Rica. 40 units, 8 bungalows. $118–$170 double, includes breakfast and taxes. **Amenities:** 2 restaurants; bar; pool; free Wi-Fi.

INEXPENSIVE

The **Posada Andrea Cristina** (✆ **2766-6265**), just on the outskirts of Puerto Viejo, is run by Alex Martínez, an excellent local guide and pioneering conservationist in the region. You may also consider staying at the jungle tent-camp or isolated Magsasay Lodge at **Hacienda Pozo Azul ★** (www.pozoazul.com; ✆ **877/810-6903** U.S./Canada, or 2438-2616).

Gavilán Sarapiquí River Lodge ★   This long-established local lodge is fairly basic but well-run, friendly, and relaxed. Most of the rooms are quite large, although some show their age, especially in the bathrooms, where hot water is provided by electric showerhead units affectionately known in Costa Rica as "suicide showers." The expansive grounds have beautiful gardens, as well as an unheated sunken Jacuzzi fed by a natural spring. The hotel is on a high bank of the Sarapiquí River, but on the other side of the river from town, so it's quiet and feels remote. The owners control a 49-hectare (120-acre) private reserve, and more than 450 bird species have been spotted in the area.

Puerto Viejo de Sarapiquí. www.gavilanlodge.com. ✆ **2234-9507** reservation office in San José, 2766-7131 or 8343-9480 at the lodge. 20 units. $60–$75 double, includes breakfast and taxes. **Amenities:** Restaurant; bar; Jacuzzi, free Wi-Fi.

Tirimbina Biological Reserve ★   With a nature reserve of 345 hectares (850 acres) and one of the longest suspension bridges in Costa Rica, Tirimbina offers excellent hiking trails that you can wander alone or with a guide. This center is dedicated to biological research and environmental education, and has been collecting information on local butterflies for many years. Standard rooms all have private bathrooms and air-conditioning; deluxe rooms have a semiprivate terrace. Student dorm-style rooms with shared bathrooms are also available upon request. Tirimbina Rainforest Center, as it's also known, has bird, frog, and night hikes, plus a bat program.

1km north of La Virgen, on the road to Puerto Viejo. www.tirimbina.org. ✆ **2761-1576** or 2761-0055. 29 units. $89-$110 double, includes breakfast and taxes. **Amenities:** Restaurant; gift shop; conference room; free Wi-Fi.

11

THE CENTRAL PACIFIC COAST: WHERE THE MOUNTAINS MEET THE SEA

A fter Guanacaste, the beaches of Costa Rica's central Pacific coast are the country's most popular. Options here range from the surfer and snowbird hangout of Jacó, to the ecotourist mecca of Manuel Antonio, to remote and largely undeveloped Dominical and Uvita, with their jungle-clad hillsides and rainforest waterfalls. With a dependable highway connecting San José to the coast, and improvements along the Costanera Sur highway heading south, this region has gotten even easier to visit.

Jacó and Playa Herradura are the closest major beach destinations to San José. They have historically been the first choice for young surfers and city-dwelling Costa Ricans. Just north of Playa Herradura sits **Carara National Park ★★**, one of the few places in Costa Rica where you can see the disappearing dry forest join the damp, humid forests that extend south down the coast. It's also a place to see scarlet macaws in the wild.

Just a little farther south, Manuel Antonio is one of the country's foremost ecotourist destinations, with a host of hotel and lodging options and an easily accessible national park that combines the exuberant lushness of a lowland tropical rainforest with several gorgeous beaches. **Manuel Antonio National Park ★★** is home to all four of Costa Rica's monkey species, as well as a wealth of other easily viewed flora and fauna. This is one of the country's most visited destinations, and for good reason. The wildlife is fabulous and surprisingly easy to spot, plus there is a wide range of tour and activity options open to all styles and ages of travelers.

If you're looking to get away from it all, **Dominical** and the **beaches south of Dominical ★** should be your top destination on this coast. Still a small village, the beach town of Dominical is flanked by even more remote and undeveloped beaches, including those found inside **Ballena Marine National Park ★★**.

Finally, if you can tear yourself away from the beaches and coastline here, and head slightly inland, you'll find **Chirripó National Park ★★**, a misty cloud forest that becomes a barren *páramo* (a region above 3,000m/9,840 ft.) at the peak of its namesake, Mount Chirripó—the tallest peak in Costa Rica.

The climate here is considerably more humid than that farther north in Guanacaste, but it's not nearly as hot and steamy as along the southern Pacific or Caribbean coasts.

FACING PAGE: **Private balcony at Arenas del Mar at Manuel Antonio**

THE best CENTRAL PACIFIC TRAVEL EXPERIENCES

o **Having Miles of Pacific Beach Practically to Yourself:** While Jacó, Manuel Antonio, and Dominical are all bustling tourist beaches, the rest of the long, Central Pacific coastline is almost entirely deserted. Rent a car or hire a taxi to visit any number of isolated and virtually undiscovered beaches.

o **Visiting Carara National Park:** The Tárcoles River crocodiles are best viewed from a boat, or by simply standing on the bridge just outside the park entrance. And the resident scarlet macaws can often be seen outside the park, but hiking the lush and varied trails inside Carara National Park is highly recommended. You'll be rewarded with rich foliage and some of the best bird-watching in the country. See p 416.

o **Hiking the Trails in Manuel Antonio National Park:** The trails here wind through thick tropical rainforest and periodically offer beautiful ocean views and opportunities to spot wildlife. You may not see all four species of monkeys that live here, but you are almost guaranteed to see some of these primates darting around the treetops. See p 434.

Capuchin monkeys in Manuel Antonio National Park

The Central Pacific Coast

PACIFIC OCEAN

En Route to Jacó: An Isolated Boutique Beauty

If you make a detour off the beaten path and head west via Ciudad Colón and Puriscal, consider a stop at **Ama Tierra Retreat & Wellness Center** ★ (www. amatierra.com; ✆ **866/659-3805** in the U.S. and Canada, or 2419-0110 in Costa Rica), a lovely boutique hotel and yoga retreat 50 minutes from the San José airport and about an hour from Jacó.

o **Visiting the Nauyaca Waterfalls Outside of Dominical:** Nestled in a patch of thick tropical rainforest, the Nauyaca Waterfalls are gorgeous, with an inviting pool at the base and cliff-jumping opportunities. If you want to skip the long hike, book a horseback tour and arrive in style. See p 462.

o **Climbing Mount Chirripó:** The highest mountain in Costa Rica, Mount Chirripó is a challenging but accessible peak whose summit occasionally offers simultaneous views of the Pacific Ocean and Caribbean Sea. Most visitors come to Costa Rica for the tropical climate, but the summit here is above the treeline and sometimes gets frost and even a dusting of snow. See p 472.

Manuel Antonio National Park

PLAYA HERRADURA

108km (67 miles) W of San José; 9km (6 miles) NW of Jacó

If you're coming from San José, **Playa Herradura** is the first major beach you'll hit as you head south on the coastal highway. Playa Herradura is a long stretch of brown sand that is home to the massive **Los Sueños Resort,** which is anchored by the **Los Sueños Marriott Ocean & Golf Resort ★★** (p 417) as well as a sprawling complex of condos and private homes and its attached marina. North of Herradura you'll find a few other small beaches and resorts, including the elegant **Villa Caletas ★★★** (p 417).

Essentials

GETTING THERE & DEPARTING   By Car: Head west out of San José on the San José–Caldera Highway (CR27). Just past the fourth toll booth at Pavón, follow the signs to Jacó and turn onto the Costanera Sur (CR34), the Southern Coastal Highway. From here, it's a straight shot down the coast to Playa Herradura. The trip should take a little over an hour.

   By Bus: All buses to Jacó will drop off passengers at the entrance to Playa Herradura, which is about 1km (½ mile) from the beach and Los

Los Sueños Marriott Ocean & Golf Resort

Don't Feed the Crocs

The Costanera Highway passes over the Tárcoles River just outside the entrance to **Carara National Park,** about 23km (14 miles) south of Orotina. This is a popular place to pull over and spot gargantuan crocodiles. Some can reach 3.7 to 4.6m (12–15 ft.) in length. Usually anywhere from 10 to 20 are easily visible, either swimming in the water or sunning on the banks. But be careful. First, you'll have to brave walking on a narrow sidewalk along the side of the bridge with cars and trucks speeding by. And second, car break-ins are common here, even in the seemingly safe restaurant parking lots north of the bridge. Although a police post has slightly reduced the risk, it's not a good idea to leave your car or valuables unguarded. Consider leaving someone at the car and taking turns watching the crocs.

Sueños resort complex. See "Jacó: Getting There & Departing," p 420, for bus info.

Gray Line (www.graylinecostarica.com; ✆ **800/719-3105** in the U.S. and Canada, or 2220-2126 in Costa Rica) and **Interbus** (www.interbusonline.com; ✆ **4100-0888**) both have two buses daily leaving San José for Jacó, one in the morning and one in the afternoon. The fare is $42. Both companies will pick you up at most San José–area hotels and drop you off at any hotel in or around Playa Herradura. Both also offer connections to most major tourist destinations in the country.

Buses from San José to **Quepos** and Manuel Antonio also pass by Playa Herradura and let passengers off on the highway about 1km/½ mile from town. However, during the busy months, some of these buses will refuse passengers getting off in Playa Herradura or will accept them only if they pay the full fare to Quepos or Manuel Antonio. For information and departure times of these buses, see p 438.

LAYOUT Playa Herradura is a short distance off the Southern Coastal Highway. Just before you hit the beach, you'll see the entrance to the Los Sueños resort complex and marina on your right. One dirt road runs parallel to the beach, with a few restaurants and a makeshift line of parking spaces all along its length.

FAST FACTS Playa Herradura has no real town. At the main intersection with the Southern Coastal Highway, you'll find a modern strip mall, with a large supermarket, some restaurants, shops, and a couple of ATMs.

Exploring Playa Herradura

Because they're so close, many folks staying in Playa Herradura take advantage of the tours and activities offered out of Jacó and even those offered out of Quepos and Manuel Antonio. See the respective sections below for more details.

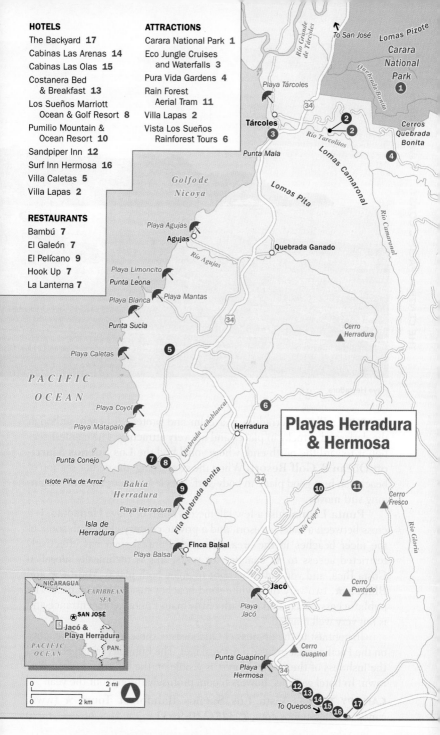

HOTELS
The Backyard **17**
Cabinas Las Arenas **14**
Cabinas Las Olas **15**
Costanera Bed
  & Breakfast **13**
Los Sueños Marriott
  Ocean & Golf Resort **8**
Pumilio Mountain &
  Ocean Resort **10**
Sandpiper Inn **12**
Surf Inn Hermosa **16**
Villa Caletas **5**
Villa Lapas **2**

RESTAURANTS
Bambú **7**
El Galeón **7**
El Pelícano **9**
Hook Up **7**
La Lanterna **7**

ATTRACTIONS
Carara National Park **1**
Eco Jungle Cruises
  and Waterfalls **3**
Pura Vida Gardens **4**
Rain Forest
  Aerial Tram **11**
Villa Lapas **2**
Vista Los Sueños
  Rainforest Tours **6**

Playas Herradura & Hermosa

Río Grande de Tárcoles
To San José
Lomas Pizote
Carara National Park
Quebrada Bonita
Playa Tárcoles
Tárcoles
Río Tarcolitos
Cerros Quebrada Bonita
Lomas Camaronal
Punta Mala
Golfo de Nicoya
Lomas Pita
Río Camaronal
Playa Agujas
Agujas
Río Agujas
Quebrada Ganado
Playa Limoncito
Punta Leona
Playa Mantas
Playa Blanca
Punta Sucia
Cerro Herradura
Playa Caletas
PACIFIC OCEAN
Playa Coyol
Playa Matapalo
Herradura
Punta Conejo
Quebrada Cañablancal
Islote Piña de Arroz
Bahía Herradura
Playa Herradura
Isla de Herradura
Fila Quebrada Bonita
Finca Balsal
Playa Balsal
Cerro Fresco
Río Copey
Cerro Puntúdo
Río Gloria
Jacó
Playa Jacó
Punta Guapinol
Playa Hermosa
Cerro Guapinol
To Quepos

NICARAGUA
CARIBBEAN SEA
SAN JOSÉ
Jacó & Playa Herradura
PACIFIC OCEAN
PAN.

0   2 mi
0   2 km

Playa Herradura

BEACHES   Playa Herradura is a calm and protected beach, although the dark sand is rocky in places and not very attractive. The calmest section is toward the north end, where you'll find the **Los Sueños Marriott Ocean & Golf Resort.** When the swell is big, the center section of beach can be a good place to body-surf, boogie-board, or try some beginning surf moves.

Punta Leona, just a few kilometers north of Playa Herradura, is a cross between a hotel, a resort, and a private country club, with some of the nicer beaches in the area. Although Punta Leona has effectively restricted access to its beaches for years, this is technically illegal in Costa Rica, and you have the right to enjoy both playas **Manta ★** and **Blanca ★,** two very nice white-sand beaches inside the complex. The public access beach road is south of the main Punta Leona entrance and is not very well marked.

In contrast to the dryness of Guanacaste, these are the first beaches on the Pacific coast to have a tropical feel. The humidity is palpable, and the lushness of the tropical forest is visible on the hillsides surrounding town. In hotel gardens, flowers bloom profusely throughout the year.

CANOPY TOURS   Vista Los Sueños Rainforest Tours ★ (www. canopyvistalossuenos.com; ✆ **321/220-9631** in the U.S. or 2637-6020 in Costa Rica; $65) is set in the hills above Playa Herradura. This tour features 12 ziplines, excellent views, and the longest cable in the area, at nearly a kilometer (almost a half-mile) in length. Round-trip transportation can be added on. They also offer jungle and river ATV tours and horseback riding to a nearby waterfall on its 80-acre property.

CROCODILE TOURS Several companies offer boat tours of the river and mangroves, and every hotel and tour agency in the area can make arrangements for you. Many operators bring along freshly killed chickens to attract the crocs, though it's irresponsible to feed any wild animals in Costa Rica. That's why I suggest going with **Eco Jungle Cruises ★** (www.ecojunglecruises.com/eng/index; ✆ **2582-0181;** 2-hr. tour $80 adults, $40 kids 4–10). Its staff doesn't believe in feeding the crocs or altering their behaviors, a policy recognized with "2 Leaves" in Costa Rica's Certification for Sustainable Tourism evaluation. There are plenty (hundreds, in fact) of crocodiles to be seen along this stretch of river and mangrove, and plenty of photo opportunities. Transportation is offered from Jacó, Playa Herradura, Manuel Antonio, or San José.

GOLF The excellent **La Iguana,** an 18-hole golf course at the Los Sueños Marriott Ocean & Golf Resort (www.golflaiguana.com; ✆ **2630-9028**), is open to non-guests. Greens fees are $175. Club and shoe rentals are available. Marriott guests pay slightly less to play here.

PURA VIDA GARDENS & WATERFALLS Just south of Carara National Park on the Costanera Sur are the **Pura Vida Gardens and Waterfalls ★** (www.puravidagarden.com; ✆ **2645-1001;** $20 adults, $10 kids over 8; daily 8am–5pm). The fee covers the gardens and trails, which lead to the waterfalls, and a new trail is being built to what's said to be the largest waterfall in Costa Rica, the 600-foot (180m) Catarata Bijagual. Pura Vida also offers **Adventure Dining** (www.adventuredining costarica.com; ✆ **8352-9419;** reservations required), with transportation, appetizers, open bar, dinner and entertainment; $110 for adults, $65 for kids under 16. Look

Pura Vida Gardens & Waterfalls

for the signs to Pura Vida Gardens and Villa Lapas (p 418). From there, it's 8km (5 miles) to the gardens.

SPORTFISHING, SCUBA DIVING & SEABORNE FUN Since the Los Sueños Marriott Resort (p 417) and its adjacent 250-slip marina opened, most local maritime activity has shifted to here. If you're interested in doing sportfishing, scuba diving, or any other waterborne activity, I recommend that you check with your hotel or at the marina. Dependable operators include **Maverick Sportfishing Tours** (www.mavericksportfish. com; ✆ **800/405-8206** in the U.S., or 8712-9683 in Costa Rica) and **Costa Rica Dreams** (www.costaricadreams.com; ✆ **337/205-0665** in the U.S., or 2637-8942 in Costa Rica). A full day of fishing runs from around $1,495 to $2,595, depending on the boat.

Carara National Park ★★

A little more than 17.5km (11 miles) north of Playa Herradura is **Carara National Park** (✆ **2637-1054;** daily 7am–4:30pm; $10/person), a nesting ground for **scarlet macaws.** It has a few kilometers of trails open to visitors. The **Sendero Acceso Universal (Universal Access Trail),** which heads out from the national park office, is broad, flat, and wheelchair-accessible. The first half of this 1km (.6-mile) stretch leads into the forest and features various informative plaques, in both English and Spanish, pointing out prominent flora. About 10 or 15 minutes into your hike, you'll see that the trail splits, forming a loop (you can go in either direction). The entire loop trail should take you about an hour. The macaws migrate daily, spending their days in the park and their nights among the coastal mangroves. It's best to view them in the early morning when they arrive, or around sunset when they head back to the coast for the evening, but a good guide can usually find them for you during the day. Whether or not you see them, you should hear their loud squawks. Among the other wildlife that you might see are caimans, coatis, armadillos, pacas, peccaries, and, of course, hundreds of species of birds. Bring along insect repellent or, better yet, wear light cotton long sleeves and pants.

Although you can certainly hike the gentle and well-marked trails of Carara independently, my advice is to take a guided tour; you'll learn a lot more about your surroundings. Most hotel desks can arrange for a guided hike to Carara National Park, or contact **Vic Tours** (www.victourscosta rica.com; ✆ **8723-3008**) for one. Also, there are almost always bilingual guides available to hire at the park entrance.

Where to Stay
EXPENSIVE
In addition to its hotel rooms, the Los Sueños resort has scores of condominium units for rent. All come with kitchens, access to swimming

pools, and the right to use the golf course here. These are excellent options for families who want to do some cooking, and for longer stays. If you want to rent a condo here, contact **Stay in Costa Rica** (www.stayincostarica.com; ✆ **866/439-5922** in the U.S. and Canada, or 2637-2661 in Costa Rica). Rates begin around $210 to $735 nightly for one- and two-bedroom units, to well over $1,000 for some of the more luxurious three-bedroom and larger units.

For something a little farther from the beach, **Pumilio Mountain & Ocean Hotel** (www.hotelpumilio.com; ✆ **800/410-8018** in U.S. and 2643-5678 in Costa Rica) is a boutique hotel and spa, located on a hillside a bit inland, between Playa Herradura and Jacó.

Los Sueños Marriott Ocean & Golf Resort ★★

This is the largest resort hotel on the Central Pacific coast, and also the best of the big ones. In fact, it revels in its size, offering up niceties that a smaller hotel can't match, like an 18-hole golf course and a massive maze of pools that are designed to bring to mind the canals of Venice. (They really are a wonder, featuring a host of small bridges connecting islands of chaise lounges and lush gardens, interspersed with secret grottoes and quiet corners.) It's a good thing the pool is so fabulous, because the beach in front of the resort is unappealing hard-packed dark sand. But the rooms are quite swank, harking back to the Spanish Colonial era with stucco walls, heavy wooden doors and furnishings, pale yellow Spanish-tile floors, and a wrought-iron railing on the (usually) tiny balcony. Buffet breakfasts are massive. And a host of good dining options are available on-site and in the nearby marina, everything from a poolside grill and traditional Costa Rican to a 1960s-style steakhouse and an elegant modern Mediterranean eatery.

Playa Herradura. www.lossuenosmarriott.com. ✆ **888/236-2427** in the U.S. and Canada, or 2630-9000 in Costa Rica; 201 units. $371–$464 double; $559–$659 suite; $800–$1,000 presidential suite. **Amenities:** 4 restaurants; bar; coffee shop; kids' activities; golf course and pro shop; mini-golf; health club and spa; pool; room service; 2 lighted tennis courts; free Wi-Fi in most public areas, paid Wi-Fi in-room.

Villa Caletas ★★★

Whimsy and luxury go hand in hand at this cliff-top hideaway, which includes the Villa Caletas Hotel and the Zephyr Palace. Villa Caletas is a tropical Victorian mansion in the rainforest overlooking the Pacific Ocean. Here you'll find an exclusive pebble beach (15-minute shuttle provided), inviting pools, a bar, and two restaurants. Guests can sip cocktails while enjoying the sunset from a recreated Greek amphitheater, and the suites and junior suites come with plunge pools or private outdoor Jacuzzis; most have great views of the Pacific Ocean.

Between Tárcoles and Playa Herradura. www.hotelvillacaletas.com. ✆ **2630-3000.** 52 units. $180–$250 double; $280 villa; $352–$700 suite; $365–$1,600 Zephyr Palace suites. Extra person $42 at Villa Caletas; $85 at Zephyr Palace. **Amenities:** 2 restaurants; 1 bar; concierge; 3 pools; Jacuzzi; spa; gym; free Wi-Fi.

Enjoying the view at Villa Caletas

Villa Lapas ★ This small, locally owned resort hotel on the banks of the Tarcolitos River provides an intriguing alternative to the beach resorts that dominate this region. The lodge is on the border of Carara National Park, which means superb bird-watching and wildlife viewing. It's not uncommon to see the namesake *lapas,* or scarlet macaws, flying overhead. The hotel has its own trails and 1.5 miles of hanging bridges, plus a recreated rural Costa Rican village, complete with a wedding chapel based on the old colonial-era church in Ujarrás (p 202). Rooms are in single-story concrete block buildings and feature red tile floors, whitewashed stucco walls, and red clay tile roofs. They are spacious but feel a bit worn. From here it's 15 to 25 minutes by car to Jacó, Playa Hermosa, and Playa Herradura.

Tárcoles. www.villalapas.com. © **2439-1816.** 70 units. $180 double w/ breakfast; $256 double all-inclusive. **Amenities:** 2 restaurants; 2 bars; pool; free Wi-Fi.

Where to Eat

At the Los Sueños Marina you'll find several options, including **Bambú,** a sushi bar and Pan-Asian restaurant; **Lanterna,** a fancy Italian restaurant; and **Hook Up,** an excellent American-style grill, serving primo lunch and light fare, with a second-floor perch and good views. You can make reservations at any of the marina restaurants by calling ℰ **2630-4050.**

EXPENSIVE

El Galeón ★★ FUSION   Although pricey, this is easily the best restaurant at the Los Sueños Marina Village. The menu is broad and creative, and the presentations are artful. Try appetizers like pulpo al olivo, which is like octopus sashimi in a purple olive sauce, or the short rib poutine. For a main dish, you can't go wrong with the Moroccan-style lamb tangine, or the whole fried red snapper with a black bean and garlic sauce. El Galeón has the best-curated wine list in the area. The setting here is lovely too: a large, open-air dining room that overlooks the marina and Herradura Bay. Whole tree trunks support a huge and soaring thatched roof, from which slow-turning ceiling fans hang.

At the Marina Village of the Los Sueños Marriott Resort (p 417). www.lsrestaurants. com. ℰ **2630-4050.** Reservations recommended. Main courses $15–$60. Daily 6–10pm.

MODERATE

El Pelícano ★ SEAFOOD/COSTA RICAN   Just across the single-lane dirt road that runs along the beach, this simple, open-air spot serves up fresh ceviche, fish, seafood, and other Tico standards. You can also get steak and pasta, but I recommend the seafood—it's caught and brought in daily. Most lunch meals (noon–4pm) come with a visit to the small salad bar. There is sometimes live music at night.

On the beach in Playa Herradura. www.elpelicanorestaurante.com. ℰ **2637-8910.** Reservations recommended in high season. Main courses C5,450–C38,000. Daily noon–10pm.

JACÓ

Jacó: 117km (73 miles) W of San José; 75km (47 miles) S of Puntarenas

Jacó is a long stretch of beach backed by a dense hodgepodge of hotels, souvenir shops, seafood restaurants, pizza joints, and rowdy bars. The main strip, running parallel to the shoreline, is a crowded and congested collection of restaurants, shops, and small strip malls, where pedestrians, bicycles, scooters, cars, and ATVs vie for right of way both day and night.

Some people love Jacó but some hate it, primarily because it is packed with tourists, especially visitors from the U.S., and because of its reputation as a party town. If you're planning a rowdy bachelor party or looking to meet young singles, this is not a bad place to go; if you're hoping to get away from it all, you've taken a wrong turn.

Jacó is popular with surfers, who are drawn by the consistent beach break. The beach itself, consisting of dark-gray sand with lots of little rocks, is not the country's most appealing, and the surf is often too rough

Playa de Jacó

for swimming. Still, given its proximity to San José, Jacó is almost always packed with a mix of foreign and Tico vacationers.

Known for its nightlife, Jacó has a raging nightlife scene that offers everything from live music venues to chill lounge environments to beachfront sports bars with pool and foosball tables (and, yes, prostitution and drugs, for which Jacó is somewhat infamous).

Essentials

GETTING THERE & DEPARTING   By Car: Head west out of San José on the San José–Caldera Highway (CR27). Just past the fourth toll booth at Pavón, follow the signs to Jacó and you'll turn onto the Costanera Sur (CR34), the Southern Coastal Highway. From here it's a straight shot down the coast to Jacó. The trip should take a little over an hour.

By Bus: Transportes Jacó express buses (www.transportes jacoruta655.com; ✆ **2290-2922**) leave San José daily every 2 hours between 7am and 7pm from the Coca-Cola bus terminal at Calle 16 between avenidas 1 and 3. The trip takes between 2½ and 3 hours; the fare is C2,395. On weekends and holidays, extra buses are sometimes added, so it's worth calling to check.

Gray Line (www.graylinecostarica.com; ☏ **800/719-3105** in the U.S. and Canada, or 2220-2126 in Costa Rica) and **Interbus** (www. interbusonline.com; ☏ **4031-0888**) have two buses daily leaving San José to Jacó, one in the morning and one in the afternoon. The fare is around $42. They will pick you up at most San José–area hotels, and both offer connections to most major tourist destinations in the country.

Buses from San José to Quepos and Manuel Antonio also pass by Jacó. (They let passengers off on the highway about 1km/½ mile from town.) However, during the busy months, some of these buses will refuse passengers getting off in Jacó or will accept them only if they pay the full fare to Quepos or Manuel Antonio. For information and departure times of these buses, see p 421.

From **Puntarenas,** you can catch daily **Transportes Quepos Puntarenas** (☏ **2777-1617**, Quepos-bound buses at 5, 7, 9, 10:30 and 11am and 1, 2:30, 4, 4:30 and 5:30pm. The buses drop you off on the highway outside town. The trip's duration is 3 hours; the fare is C2,450.

Mercado de Frutas in Jacó

The Jacó bus station is at the north end of town, at a small mall across from the Jacó Fiesta Hotel. Buses for San José leave daily every 2 hours between 5am and 5pm. Buses returning to San José from Quepos pass periodically and pick up passengers on the highway. Because schedules can change, it's best to ask at your hotel about current departure times.

CITY LAYOUT Jacó is a short distance off the southern highway. One main road runs parallel to the beach, with a host of arteries heading toward the water; you'll find most of the town's hotels and restaurants off these roads.

GETTING AROUND Almost everything is within walking distance in Jacó, but you can call **Jaco Taxi** (☏ **2643-2020** or 2643-1919) for a cab.

You can also rent a bicycle or scooter from a variety of shops and stands along the main street. A bike rental should run you around $10 to $15 per day, and a scooter should cost between $40 and $70 per day. Shop around, and make sure you get a bike that is in good condition.

For longer excursions, you can rent a car from **Budget** (www.budget. co.cr; ℂ 2643-2665), **Economy** (www.economycarrentals.com; ℂ 2643-1719), **National** (www.natcar.com; ℂ 2643-3224), or **Zuma** (www.zumarentacar.com; ℂ 2643-1528). Expect to pay about $50 to $120 for a 1-day rental. Or talk to a local taxi driver, who'd probably take you wherever you want to go for about the same price, saving you some hassle and headache.

FAST FACTS   A handful of state-run and private banks have branches in town on the main road. The **health center** (ℂ 2643-3667) and **post office** (ℂ 2643-2175) are at the Municipal Center at the south end of town. You'll find a half-dozen or so pharmacies on the town's main drag.

A gas station is on the main highway, between Playa Herradura and Jacó, and another station, **El Arroyo,** on the highway on the southern edge of Jacó. Both are open 24 hours.

A Jacó surf shop

Exploring Jacó

ATV TOURS   Several operations run ATV tours through the surrounding countryside. Tours range in length from 2 to 4 hours up to a full day, and cost between $99 and $175 per person. Contact **Adventure Tours Costa Rica** (www.adventuretourscostarica.com; ℰ **2643-5720**) or **Xploratura** (http://jaco.xploratura.com; ℰ **8695-7985**).

BEACHES   Jacó's beach has a reputation for dangerous riptides (as does most of Costa Rica's Pacific coast). Even strong swimmers have been known to drown in the powerful rips. In general, the far southern end of the beach is the calmest and safest place to swim.

As an alternative to Jacó, you may want to visit other nearby beaches, like **Playa Manta, Playa Blanca, Playa Hermosa, Esterillos,** and **Playa Bejuco.** These beaches are just south of Jacó and easily reached by car or even bicycle—if you've got a lot of energy.

CANOPY TOURS   The easiest way to get up into the canopy here is on the **Rain Forest Aerial Tram Pacific ★** (www.rfat.com; ℰ **866/759-8726** in the U.S. and Canada, or 2257-5961 in Costa Rica; see map "Playas Herradura & Hermosa"). A sister project to the original Rain Forest Aerial Tram (p 164), this attraction features modified ski-lift type gondolas that take you through and above the transitional forests bordering Carara National Park. The $60 entrance fee includes the guided 50-minute tram ride and a guided 45-minute hike on a network of trails, which feature an orchid garden and serpentarium. You can hike the company's trails for as long as you like. There are also options for a zipline canopy tour, sky bridge, and waterfall climb on the same grounds. The Aerial Tram is a few kilometers inland from an exit just north of the first entrance into Jacó.

Another notable zipline tour is available at **Chiclets Zipline ★** (http://chicletzipline.com; ℰ **2643-1880**) in nearby Playa Hermosa. This is an adventurous tour, with 16 platforms set in transitional forest, and sweeping views of the Pacific.

GOLF   The excellent **La Iguana,** an 18-hole golf course at the **Los Sueños Marriott Ocean & Golf Resort** (www.golflaiguana.com; ℰ **2630-9028**), is open to non-guests. See p 417 for details.

HORSEBACK RIDING   Horseback riding tours take travelers away from all the development in Jacó to see some nature. The best operator in the area is **Discovery Horseback** (www.horseridecostarica.com; ℰ **8838-7550**) in Playa Hermosa. It's $85 per person for a 2½-hour tour. Options range from beach riding to trails through the rainforest with stops at a jungle waterfall.

KAYAKING   **Kayak Jacó** (www.kayakjaco.com; ℰ **2643-1233**) operates several outings in either single or tandem sea kayaks, as well as eight-person outrigger canoes. Customers can admire the beautiful coastline and, when conditions permit, take a snorkel break. Kayak fishing tours and sailing trips aboard 25-foot trimarans are also available. Most tours run around 4 hours and include transportation to and from the put-in, as well as fruit and soft drinks during the trip. The tours cost $60 to $140 per person, depending on the tour and group size.

ORGANIZED TOURS FARTHER AFIELD   If you're spending your entire Costa Rican visit in Jacó but would like to see other parts of the country, you can arrange tours with **Piko Travel** (www.pikotravel.com; © **8833-1772**) or through the local offices of **Gray Line Tours** (© **2643-3231**), which operates out of the Best Western Jacó Beach Resort (p 426). Both offer a wide range of day trips, including jaunts to Arenal and Poás volcanoes; whitewater rafting trips; and cruises to Tortuga Island. Rates range from $60 to $160 for day trips. Overnight trips are also available. In addition to the above-mentioned companies, many local operators offer tour options in **Manuel Antonio,** including trips to the national park, the Rainmaker Nature Refuge, and the Damas Island estuary. See "Manuel Antonio National Park" (p 434) for more details on the types of tours and activities available there. You can reach Manuel Antonio in about an hour from Jacó.

Fishing vessels at Los Sueños Marina

SPA Acqua Spa & Salon ★ (www.acquaspajaco.com; ✆ **2643-3005**) offers massages, mud packs, face and body treatments, and mani/pedis. The spa is located across from Banco de Costa Rica.

SPORTFISHING, SCUBA DIVING & SEABORNE FUN Since the Los Sueños Marriott Resort (p 417) and its adjacent 250-slip marina opened, most local maritime activity has moved there. See p 416 for info.

SURFING The same waves that often make Playa Jacó a bit rough for swimmers make it one of the most popular beaches in the country with surfers. Nearby **Playa Hermosa, Playa Tulin,** and **Playa Escondida** are also excellent surfing beaches. Those who want to challenge the waves can rent surfboards and boogie boards for around $3 to $5 an hour or $10 to $20 per day, from any of the many surf shops along the main road. For lessons, try the **Del Mar Surf Camp ★★** (www.delmarsurf camp.com; ✆ **855/833-5627** in the U.S. or 2643-3197 in Costa Rica) or **Jacó Surf School** (www.jacosurfschool.com; ✆ **8829-4697**).

Where to Stay

Because Playa Herradura, Playa Hermosa de Jacó (not to be confused with either Playa Hermosa in Guanacaste or Playa Hermosa on the Nicoya Peninsula), Playa Esterillos, and Playa Bejuco are close, many people choose accommodations in these beach towns as well.

EXPENSIVE

Croc's Casino Resort ★★ This 17-story, 152-room behemoth, which opened in 2015, has been a game-changer in Jacó, and not just for the skyline. The luxurious rooms are decorated in a modern, not-too-splashy style, and the ocean views are awesome. You can choose from three restaurants: Adacus, with Peruvian-Mediterranean cuisine and a nice wine list; Parsley & Pepper, with Italian, Mexican, Japanese and other international foods; and El Zarpe Pool Bar and Grill for poolside snacking on wings, quesadillas, and seafood. The Liquidity Casino Bar serves up tropical cocktails to gamblers, while the Holy Moly! Disco Club lures late-night revelers. The Vegas–style casino has slots and gaming tables. A big, oceanfront pool features a waterslide and three cold-water Jacuzzis.

800m west of the Banco de Costa Rica, Jacó. www.crocscasinoresort.com. ✆ **800/ 809-5503** from U.S. and Canada; 4001-5398 in Costa Rica. 152 units. $209–$270 double; $311 suite. **Amenities:** 3 restaurants, coffee shop; 3 bars; casino; pool; spa; concierge; free Wi-Fi.

Pochote Grande ★ German owned and operated, this decades old hotel is popular among German tourists of a certain age who like to lounge around a pool in a Speedo or bikini, converse with other guests in their own language, and order *rouladen* off the menu. Rooms feature whitewashed walls and tie-dyed curtains (either groovy or weird, depending on your point of view). A wall of windows and glass doors in each room opens onto a shared veranda split by a low wall. The towels are a bit scratchy, but there's a/c in all the units and TVs in half of them. There's a nice pool, a good little restaurant, lush gardens, and a beachfront location, though it's crammed between high-rise condos and hotels.

North Jacó, near Croc's. www.hotelpochotegrande.net. *C* **2643-3236** or 2289-3204. 24 units. $230 double, includes breakfast. **Amenities:** Restaurant; bar; pool; free Wi-Fi.

MODERATE

In addition to the places listed below, the oceanfront **Apartotel Girasol** ★ (www.girasol.com; *C* **800/923-2779** in U.S. or Canada or 2643-1591 in Costa Rica), with 16 fully equipped one-bedroom apartments, is a smart option for longer stays, as is **Vacasa** (www.vacasa.com; *C* **8178-5585**), which has dozens of condo rentals spread out all over Jacó. **Hotel Poseidon** (www.hotel-poseidon.com; *C* **2643-1642**) is a pretty boutique hotel in the heart of downtown, while **Canciones del Mar** (www.cancionesdelmar.com; *C* **888/260-1523** in the U.S./Canada, or 2643-3273 in Costa Rica) and **Hotel Catalina** (www.hotelcatalinacr. com; *C* **2643-1237**) are two other good beachfront choices.

Best Western Jacó Beach Resort ★   A no-frills all-inclusive, the Best Western is popular with large charter groups but feels a bit dated. Still, room upkeep has been good over the years, and the Best Western offers decent value for those looking for an affordable all-inclusive option in Jacó. And it's in a great location, right on the beach just a short walk from all of the town's best bars, restaurants, and shops.

Jacó. www.bestwesternjacobeach.com. *C* **800/780-7234** in U.S. and Canada, or 2643-1000 in Costa Rica; 125 units. $187–$208 double, all-inclusive, covering meals, drinks, and taxes. **Amenities:** 2 restaurants; bar; kids' and adult pools; tennis and volleyball courts; free calls to U.S. and Canada; free Wi-Fi.

Club del Mar ★★   A great option on the outskirts of Jacó, Club del Mar is located at the far southern end of the beach, so it feels far removed from the crowds and craziness in the thick of town. This is also one of the safest parts of the beach for swimming, as it's somewhat protected by the rocky headlands. It's not a party hotel, but families flock here, drawn both by the calmer waters and the fact that all the comfortable, well-maintained one- and two-bedroom condos come with fully equipped kitchens, large living rooms, and washers/dryers. Standard rooms are all air-conditioned and have minifridges. All are housed in a series of two- and three-story buildings spread around gardens that are chock-full of flowering heliconia and ginger. There's also a midsize pool with a volleyball net that often attracts a pickup game, and a very good on-site restaurant, Las Sandalias.

To Playa Herradura
and San José

To Playa Hermosa &
Quepos/Manuel Antonio

PACIFIC
OCEAN

HOTELS

Apartotel Girasol **21**

Best Western Jacó
Beach Resort **4**

Canciones del Mar **6**

Club del Mar **25**

Croc's Casino Resort **1**

Hotel Catalina **23**

Hotel Nine **24**

Hotel Poseidon **7**

Monte Carlo Luxury
Condominiums **9**

Oceano Boutique Hotel **18**

Pochote Grande **3**

Room2Board **22**

RESTAURANTS

Café Bohio **8**

Caliche's Wishbone **11**

El Barco de Mariscos **15**

El Hicaco **20**

El Recreo **14**

Graffiti Restro Café & Wine Bar **26**

Green Room Café **13**

Lemon Zest **19**

Los Amigos **16**

Taco Bar **17**

Tsunami Sushi **10**

NIGHTLIFE

Clarita's Beach Bar & Grill **2**

Croc's Casino & Resort **1**

Hotel Poseidon **7**

Jacó Blu **5**

Le Loft **12**

Jacó. www.clubdelmarcostarica.com. ✆ **866/978-5669** in the U.S. and Canada, or 2643-3194 in Costa Rica. 34 units. $167 double; $246–$335 for 1- or 2-bedroom condos, taxes included. **Amenities:** Restaurant; bar; babysitting; pool; room service; small spa; bike, paddleboard and surfboard rental; free Wi-Fi.

Day Star Beachfront Condominiums ★★ Day Star offers an array of 2- to 4-bedroom luxury condo rentals with full kitchens, swimming pools, private terraces, and rooftop gardens. Most of them come with high-speed Internet, cable TV, in-room washers/dryers, a/c, telephones, and safes. Options include Bahía Azul, with two-bedroom, two-bath condos that take up the entire floor, with no shared walls ($150–$250); Bahía Encantada, a resort-like community on the north end of the beach with two- and three-bedroom units ($230–$375); and Diamante del Sol, with four-bedroom, four-and-a-half-bath condos with floor-to-ceiling windows and granite kitchen countertops ($330–$575 per night). Check website for exact property locations.

Jacó. www.daystarrentals.com. ✆ **888/760-9898** from U.S. and Canada, or 2630-9800 in Costa Rica; $150–$575. **Amenities:** Beachfront views; pools; laundry; free Wi-Fi.

Hotel Nine ★   Hotel Nine is on the serene and (usually) swimmable southern end of the beach; and the place has a happy dose of "South Beach Miami" style in the architectural details and decor. That means rooms with handsome rattan and wood furnishings and colorful throws on the beds. A small multi-tiered pool with a swim-up bar, waterfall, and Jacuzzi is at the center of the complex, and ocean views can be had from the narrow shared veranda that fronts most rooms. The on-site restaurant is terrific.

Jacó. ✆ **800/477-2486** in U.S. & Canada or 2643-5335 in Costa Rica. 14 units. $123–$148 double; $283–$408 suite, includes breakfast. No children under 6. **Amenities:** Restaurant; bar; Jacuzzi; pool; room service; surfboards; free Wi-Fi.

Monte Carlo Luxury Condominiums ★   These stylish condos with a pretty pool, located in the heart of Jacó, offer 16 luxury units for rent by the night, week, or month. All have two bedrooms, with a king-size bed in the master bedroom and a queen bed or two twin-size beds in the second room. All have two bathrooms, one with a shower and one with a bathtub, and come with fully equipped kitchens.

Jacó. www.jacomontecarlo.com. ✆ **2643-2917.** 16 units. $188 double, 2-night minimum. **Amenities:** Pool; babysitting; private driver; concierge; private chef; massage; free Wi-Fi.

Oceano Boutique Hotel and Gallery ★★   This boutique hotel is beautifully designed and has an impressive array of room choices and amenities. The six-story hotel (with a seventh-floor tanning deck) has an art gallery, a convenience store, a souvenir shop, a bistro bar/cafe, a swimming pool with hot tub and kids' pool, and even an herb garden where you can pick herbs to make your own mojitos. The standard room is a suite with a full kitchen, a bedroom with TV, a living room with a sofa bed and a second TV, and even a washer and dryer. Several units have balconies with their own little swimming pools (with mini-waterfalls). Duplex lofts are two levels, with stairs leading to a mezzanine, and sleep seven people. Four penthouses are all distinct from each other and can sleep up to 8 people, featuring very large master bedrooms with walk-in closets and marble bathrooms. The hotel is family-friendly and pet-friendly, with a $10 charge for pets and doggie beds provided.

Calle Lapas, 500m east of the POPS ice cream shop and Los Amigos restaurant, Jacó. www.oceanojaco.com. ✆ **2643-0420.** 64 units. $130-$142 double; $177-$229 suite; $406-$459 penthouse suites, includes breakfast. **Amenities:** Art gallery; convenience store; souvenir shop; bistro bar/cafe; pool; gym; free Wi-Fi.

INEXPENSIVE

There are quite a few backpacker hotels around town, so if you're looking to stay here on the cheap, walk the strip and see who's got the best room at the best price. Decent options include **Buddha House** (www.hostel buddhahouse.com; ✆ **2643-3615**), a "boutique hostel" in the heart of Jacó, and **Jacó Inn** (www.jacoinn.com; ✆ **2643-1935**), which calls itself "the perfect balance between *tranquilidad* and *fiesta.*"

Room2Board ★★ This hip hostel at the southern end of Jacó beach can make an old guy feel young again, with happy, drinking 20-somethings filling the pool and bar as if it's perpetually spring break. Despite the gaudy wave-like outcroppings on the exterior of the four-story building, the hotel has a futuristic feel thanks to its motion-sensing lights and sleek, glass-and-steel design. Room2Board has a big poolside screen showing games, events, and surfing, and an upstairs room doubles as a movie theater and yoga space, plus a communal kitchen. Call ahead if looking to save money, because the $16 shared dorms can fill up and leave you looking at a private room closer to $80. As you might guess from the double-entendre name, Room2Board has a surf school and board rentals and is a block from the ocean. Just a few rules: No pets, no prostitutes, and no children under 14.

Jacó. www.room2board.com. ℂ **2643-4949.** 21 units, with capacity for 87 people. Dorm rooms $16–$28; private room with shared bathroom $68–$79; with private bathroom $65–$79. **Amenities:** Restaurant; bar; pool; surf school; laundry service; bike rental; free Wi-Fi.

Where to Eat

Jacó has a wide range of restaurants, many catering to surfers and budget travelers. In addition to the places listed below, if you're looking for simply prepared fresh seafood, **El Barco de Mariscos** (ℂ 2643-2831) and **El Recreo** (ℂ 2643-1172) are both good bets. For traditional Costa Rican food, **Jacó Rustico** (ℂ 2643-2727) is super-popular and cheap, and for Italian food at a nice price, try **Chinita Pacific** (ℂ 8501-6651) or **Peccati Di Gola** (ℂ 2643-5867). Sushi lovers should head to **Tsunami Sushi** (ℂ 2643-3678), in the Jacó Walk Shopping Center (www.jacowalk.com), which also features restaurants and food stands selling burgers, bowls, paletas, and ceviche. For a coffee break, head to **Café Bohio** (ℂ 2643-5915) or the **Pachi's Pan** (ℂ 2643-6068).

EXPENSIVE

El Hicaco ★ COSTA RICAN/SEAFOOD This was a very humble fish shack that opened in 1978 and was later remodeled, and now it's not uncommon to see tour buses parked out front and a line of diners waiting to be seated. Prices have shot up accordingly and if you are looking for an authentic atmosphere this isn't it, but El Hicaco does serve excellent seafood, and its beachfront setting is stellar.

On the beach in downtown Jacó. www.elhicaco.com. ℂ **2643-3226.** Reservations recommended during high season. Main courses C6,500–C31,625. Daily 11am–10pm.

Graffiti Restro Café & Wine Bar ★★ FUSION It's a little hard to find Graffiti Restrsto, because it's wedged in the far back corner of a strip mall near the center of town. But it's worth the search for food that's at the apex of what you'll find in Costa Rica. Each night, a short selection of specials is written on a chalkboard, based on the chef's whims and what's fresh. The regular menu is also excellent, featuring Graffiti's signature cacao- and coffee-crusted tenderloin and Asian-spiced seared tuna. Occasionally there's live music here, and it's worth visiting the attached gift shop, which features hand-carved wooden surfboards and unique body-surfing paddles. As you might expect, it's a hip-looking place with graffiti art covering the walls. Along with the interior dining rooms, there's limited outdoor seating in the front of the restaurant.

Centro Comercial Pacific Center, downtown Jacó. www.graffiticr.com. *C* **2643-1708.** Reservations recommended in high season. Main courses C6,300–C14,300. Mon–Sat 5–10pm.

Lemon Zest ★★ SEAFOOD/FUSION   Chef/owner Richard Lemon left a teaching gig at the famed Le Cordon Bleu culinary school to open this superb eatery in 2007. His food is tasty and eclectic, ranging over a number of world influences. Among the many excellent appetizers are the buffalo lobster bites with blue cheese dipping sauce and the Korean-style beef skewers with homemade banana ketchup. Main courses are impressive, especially the green curry shrimp and the jerk pork chop with pineapple-chipotle sauce. The dining room acoustics leave something to be desired, so try to grab one of the few tables on the outdoor balcony.

Downtown Jacó. www.lemonzestjaco.com. *C* **2643-2591.** Reservations recommended in high season. Main courses C8,550–C14,300. Daily 5–10pm; closed Monday in low season. Closed mid-Sept through Oct 31.

MODERATE

Caliche's Wishbone ★ SEAFOOD/MEXICAN   This landmark was the brainchild of a local surfing legend, Caliche. It serves up hearty fare, everything from pizzas baked in a wood-fired oven, burritos, and stuffed potatoes to fresh seared tuna in a soy-wasabi sauce. Surf videos play on TVs in the main dining room, but you may prefer the tables closest to the busy sidewalk, on the covered veranda.

On the main road in Jacó. *C* **2643-3406.** Main courses C3,500–C13,000. Thurs–Tues noon–10pm.

Green Room Café ★★ BISTRO/SEAFOOD   This is yet another excellent little restaurant whipping up tasty dishes from fresh local ingredients. Green Room Cafe sources as much as it can from organic producers and local fishermen. The menu staples feature a range of breakfast and brunch items, plus sandwiches, wraps, tacos, and burgers. Nightly specials are where you'll find the most creativity, with selections like mango-shrimp tartar and thick-cut ribeye with gorgonzola butter. The atmosphere is decidedly casual and very cheery, with colored cloths draped from the ceiling and wooden chairs painted bright pastel colors. On weekend nights there's often live music or a DJ.

On the Cocal Casino road in Jacó. *C* **2643-4425.** Reservations recommended in high season. Main courses C4,750–C13,000. Sun–Thur 9am-11pm and Fri-Sat 9am–2am. No credit cards.

Los Amigos ★ INTERNATIONAL/SEAFOOD   Occupying a prime location on one of the busiest corners in downtown Jacó, this casual spot feels like a mix between a sports bar and a college-town club. The menu features a mix of American-style bar food, fresh seafood, Tex-Mex favorites, and Thai curries, rice bowls, and noodle dishes. There's outdoor seating under broad canvas umbrellas, but on hot days, you'll want to opt for the air-conditioned dining room. Live sports and surf videos are shown on 7 flatscreen TVs and broadcast onto the wall of a neighboring building.

On the main road in Jacó. www.losamigosjaco.com. ℂ **2643-2961.** Main courses C3,600–C8,600. Sun–Thurs noon–11pm.; Fri–Sat noon–1am.

INEXPENSIVE

Taco Bar ★ MEXICAN   This open-air taqueria features two long, wooden bars with seating on "swings" supported by heavy ropes (you can also choose from more traditional tables and picnic tables). It serves up a wide range of tacos, burritos, and pizzas; including seafood varieties using freshly caught fish. After choosing the main plate, you have ample choices at the well-stocked and inventive salad bar. Also open for breakfast.

½ block inland from the POPS ice cream shop, central Jacó. ℂ **2643-0222.** Main courses C2,500–C7,000. Daily 7:00am–10pm.

Shopping

Jacó has multiple shops selling T-shirts, cut-rate souvenirs, and handmade jewelry and trinkets. Most of the offerings are of pretty poor quality. At the high end **Jacó Walk Shopping Center** (www.jacowalk.com) you'll find a variety of high end shops.

Entertainment & Nightlife

Jacó is the central Pacific's party town, with tons of bars and several discos. One standout is the **Holy Moly! Disco Club** at Croc's Casino Resort, which features DJs from around the world. This place gets hopping around 11:30pm.

Other options are **Juanita's By Green Room,** a Latin bar and restaurant in Jaco Walk with daily happy hours, the **Loro Loco,** which has live music and DJs; and the **Orange Pub,** which has live music, as well as pool and foosball tables.

Jacó Blu Beach Club, located right on the beach near the center of town, is a mellow lounge with a pool, cabanas, and restaurant service by day, but at night becomes a fairly raucous bar and dance spot, especially on Wednesdays (ladies' night). **Le Loft,** on the main street near the center of town, attracts a more sophisticated and chic clubbing crowd.

Sports freaks can catch the latest games at **Clarita's Beach Bar & Grill,** on the beach toward the north end of town.

If you're into casino games, head to **Croc's Casino Resort,** which has a Las Vegas–style casino and the **Liquidity Casino Bar.**

Note: Jacó has a lot of legal prostitution, and it's not uncommon to find working women at any of the bars around town. That's not necessarily a knock against the bar.

Side Trips from Jacó: Playas Hermosa, Esterillos & Bejuco

South of Jacó, Costa Rica's coastline is a long, almost entirely straight stretch of largely undeveloped beach backed by thick forests and low-lying rice and African palm plantations.

Playa Hermosa ★, 10km (6¼ miles) southeast of Jacó, is the first beach you'll hit as you head down the Southern Coastal Highway. This is primarily a surfers' choice, but it is still a lovely spot. Aside from a small group of hotels and restaurants, most of Playa Hermosa is protected, because **olive ridley sea turtles** lay eggs here from July to December. During nesting season, all the hotel tour desks and local tour agencies can arrange a nighttime turtle nesting tour for around $45 to $60 per person.

Playa Hermosa is the only beach in this section located right along the Southern Coastal Highway; all of the rest are a kilometer or so in from the road and reached by a series of dirt access roads. If you exit the highway in Playa Hermosa, you can follow a dirt-and-sand access road that runs parallel to the shore along several miles of deserted, protected beach, as Playa Hermosa eventually becomes **Playa Tulin,** near the Tulin River mouth. This is another popular surf spot, but watch out for crocodiles.

As you continue down the coastal highway from Playa Hermosa, you will hit Esterillos. **Playa Esterillos,** 22km (14 miles) south of Jacó, is long and wide and has three separate sections, Esterillos Oeste, Centro, and Este—west, center, and east, in order as you head away from Jacó.

If you keep heading south (really southeast), you next come to **Playa Bejuco,** another long, wide, nearly deserted stretch of sand with mangroves and swampland behind it.

Safety notes: While beautiful, isolated, and expansive, the beaches of Hermosa, Esterillos, and Bejuco can be quite rough at times and dangerous for swimming. Caution is highly advised here. Also be careful on Playa Hermosa, as the fine dark sand can get extremely hot in the tropical sun; be sure to have adequate footwear and a large towel to lay out on the sand.

Playa Esterillos

WHERE TO STAY IN PLAYA HERMOSA

Moderate

Options here include the **Surf Inn Hermosa** (www.surfinnhermosa. com; ℭ **2643-7184**), which offers one-bedroom studios with kitchenettes, and two-bedroom fully equipped condo units, and the **Sandpiper Inn** (www.sandpipercostarica.com; ℭ **2643-7042**), a cozy surfer joint. Both are right on the beach.

The Backyard ★ The Backyard is run by and for surfers, though it is comfy enough to attract the casual beach goer too. Rooms are simple and unadorned, aside from framed photos of tropical beach scenes. The restaurant and bar are pretty much the only game in town, and are jam-packed most nights, with noise from the bar wafting up to the rooms. Still, right out in front is one of the best surf breaks on this coastline.

Playa Hermosa de Jacó. www.backyardhotel.com. ℭ **2643-7011.** 8 units. $130 double; $230 suite, includes breakfast. **Amenities:** Restaurant; bar; pool; free Wi-Fi.

Inexpensive

Playa Hermosa has a host of simple hotels and *cabinas* catering to surfers. Prices, conditions, and upkeep can vary greatly. If you've got the time, your best bet is to visit a few until you find the best deal on the cleanest room. **Costanera Bed & Breakfast** (www.costaneraplaya hermosa.com; ✆ **2643-7044**), **Cabinas Las Arenas** (✆ **8729-4532**), and **Cabinas Las Olas** (www.cabinaslasolas.co.cr; ✆ **2643-7021**) are good options.

WHERE TO STAY IN PLAYA ESTERILLOS

If you're looking for something remote and undeveloped, head to Playa Esterillos Este and the Hotel **Pelicano** (www.hotelpelicanocostarica. com; ✆ **2778-8105**), a homey, beachfront bed-and-breakfast.

Note: Playa Esterillos and Playa Bejuco are about midway between Jacó and Manuel Antonio, so it's very useful to have a rental car if staying here.

Expensive

Alma del Pacífico Hotel ★★   This upscale boutique hotel is a hidden gem on an undiscovered patch of sand. Originally built as a sister resort to Xandari (p 112), it now has separate owners and management. Still, the individual villas here feature the same artsy sensibility, which means they're oversized, with white tile floors, white walls, white bed linens, and loads of natural light, all accented with bold splashes of primary colors found in paintings, mosaic tile works, curtains, and more. The best villas feature ocean views and private plunge pools, and the open-air ocean-view restaurant is top-notch.

Playa Esterillos Centro. www.almadelpacifico.com. ✆ **888/960-2562** from the U.S. or Canada, 2778-7070 in Costa Rica. 20 units. $230–$280 double bungalow, $340–$505 villa, includes breakfast. **Amenities:** Restaurant; bar; concierge; Jacuzzi; 2 pools; room service; full-service spa; free Wi-Fi.

WHERE TO STAY IN PLAYA BEJUCO

Moderate

Hotel Playa Bejuco ★   This hotel is a throwback to another era. Some of the rooms look like they could have been decorated in the 1970s (although they're immaculate and quite spacious), and the area has yet to be touched by the rampant development of Jacó. If you come here, be aware that besides the on-site restaurant and bar, there's no nightlife. Though the hotel's not right on the beach, it's quite close, and you'll likely have the sand all to yourself.

Playa Bejuco. www.hotelplayabejuco.com. ✆ **2779-2000.** 20 units. $130-$167 double, includes breakfast. **Amenities:** Restaurant; bar; pool; Jacuzzi; free Wi-Fi.

MANUEL ANTONIO NATIONAL PARK ★★

140km (87 miles) SW of San José; 69km (43 miles) S of Jacó

Manuel Antonio was Costa Rica's first major ecotourism destination and remains one of its most popular. The views from the hills overlooking the

View toward Manuel Antonio National Park and Cathedral Point

park are spectacular, the beaches are idyllic, and the rainforest is crawling with howler, white-faced, spider, and squirrel monkeys, among other exotic wildlife. The downside is the abundance of the species *Homo sapiens* you'll find here. Booming tourism and development have adversely affected the natural appeal of this place, which is often criticized because it's so touristy. What was once a smattering of small hotels tucked into the forested hillside has become a string of lodges along the 7km (4⅓ miles) of road between Quepos and the national park entrance. A jumble of snack shacks, souvenir stands, and makeshift parking lots choke the beach road just outside the park, making the entrance road look more like a shantytown than a national park.

Still, this remains a beautiful destination, with a wide range of attractions and activities that make it perfect for all sorts of travelers. Gazing down on the blue Pacific from high on the hillsides of Manuel Antonio, you'll realize there's a good reason so many people come here. Offshore, rocky islands dot the vast expanse, and in the foreground, the rich, deep green of the rainforest sweeps down to the water.

One of the most popular national parks in the country, Manuel Antonio is also one of the smallest, covering fewer than 680 hectares (1,680 acres). Its several nearly perfect small beaches are connected by

435

trails that meander through the rainforest. The mountains surrounding the beaches quickly rise as you head inland from the water; however, the park was created to preserve not its beautiful beaches but its forests, home to rare squirrel monkeys, three-toed sloths, purple-and-orange crabs, and hundreds of other species. Once this entire stretch of coast was teeming with wildlife, but now only this small rocky outcrop of forest remains.

Those views that are so bewitching also have their own set of drawbacks. If you want a great view, you aren't going to be staying on the beach—in fact, you probably won't be able to walk to the beach. This means that you'll be driving back and forth, taking taxis, or riding the public bus. Also bear in mind that it's hot and humid here, and that all that lush, green rainforest means there's a lot of rain.

If you're traveling on a rock-bottom budget or are mainly interested in sportfishing, you might end up staying in the nearby town of **Quepos,** which was once a quiet banana port and now features a wide variety of restaurants, shops, and lively bars. Disease wiped out most of the banana plantations, and now the land is planted primarily with African palm trees (see "Profitable Palms," p 437).

Essentials

GETTING THERE & DEPARTING   By Plane: Both **Nature Air** (www.natureair.com; ✆ **800/235-9272** U.S./Canada, or 2299-6000) and **Sansa** (www.flysansa.com; ✆ **877/767-2672** U.S./Canada, or 2290-4100 in Costa Rica) offer daily flights to the **Quepos airport** (airport code: XQP). The flight is 30 minutes; the fare is $57 to $134 one way.

Both **Sansa** (✆ **2777-1912** in Quepos) and **Nature Air** (✆ **2777-2548** in Quepos) provide minivan airport-transfer service coordinated with their arriving and departing flights. The service costs around $8 per person each way. Taxis meet incoming flights and may be more economical. Expect to be charged between $10 and $20 per car for up to four people, depending on the distance to your hotel.

When you're ready to depart, **Sansa** (✆ **2777-1912** in Quepos) flights begin departing at 8:45am, with the final flight leaving at 4pm.

Timing Tips

Despite the above caveats, Manuel Antonio is still a fabulous destination with a wealth of activities and attractions for all types and all ages. If you steer clear of the peak months (Dec–Mar), you'll miss most of the crowds. If you must come during the peak months, try to avoid weekends, when the beach is packed with Tico families from San José. If you visit the park early in the morning, you can leave when the crowds begin to show up at midday.

Profitable Palms

On any drive to or from Quepos and Manuel Antonio, you'll pass through miles and miles of African palm plantations. Native to West Africa, *Elaeis guineensis* was planted along this stretch in the 1940s by the United Fruit Co., in response to a blight that was attacking its banana crops. The palms took hold and soon proved quite profitable, being blessed with copious bunches of plum-size nuts that are rich in oil. This oil is extracted and processed in plantations that dot the road between Jacó and Quepos. The smoke and distinct smell of this processing is easily noticed. The processed oil is eventually shipped overseas and used in a wide range of products, including soaps, cosmetics, lubricants, and food products.

These plantations are a major source of employment in the area—note the small, orderly "company towns" built for workers—but their presence is controversial. The palm trees aren't native and the farming practices are notorious for threatening biodiversity in Costa Rica and around the world.

Nature Air (© **2777-2548** in Quepos) flights leave for San José daily at 7:35am and 3:20pm.

By Car: Head west out of San José on the San José–Caldera Highway (CR27). Just past the fourth toll booth at Pavón, follow the signs to Jacó and you'll turn onto the Costanera Sur (CR34), the Southern Coastal Highway. From here it's a straight shot down the coast to Quepos and Manuel Antonio. The trip should take a little over an hour.

If you're coming from Guanacaste or any point north, take the Inter-American Highway to the Puntarenas turnoff and follow signs to the San José–Caldera Highway (CR27). Take this east toward Orotina, where it connects with the Costanera Sur (CR34). It's about a 4½-hour drive from Liberia to Quepos and Manuel Antonio.

By Bus: Tracopa buses (www.tracopacr.com; © **2221-4214**) to Manuel Antonio leave San José regularly throughout the day between 6am and 7:30pm from Calle 5 between avenidas 18 and 20. Trip duration is around 3 hours; the fare is C4,750. These buses go to the park entrance and will drop you off at any of the hotels along the way.

For your return trip, the **Quepos bus station** (© **2777-0263**) is next to the market, 3 blocks east of the water and 2 blocks north of the road to Manuel Antonio. Buses depart for San José daily between 4am and 5pm.

Gray Line (www.graylinecostarica.com; © **800/719-3105** in the U.S. and Canada, or 2220-2222 in Costa Rica) and **Interbus** (www.interbusonline.com; © **4031-0888**) both have two buses daily leaving San José for Quepos and Manuel Antonio, one in the morning and one in the afternoon. The fare is around $54. Both companies will pick up at most San José–area hotels. Both also offer connections to most major tourist destinations in the country.

Many of the buses for Quepos stop to unload and pick up passengers in **Jacó.** If you're in Jacó heading toward Manuel Antonio, you can try your luck at one of the covered bus stops on the Inter-American Highway.

In the busy winter months, tickets sell out well in advance, especially on weekends; if you can, buy your ticket several days in advance. However, you must buy your Quepos-bound tickets in San José and your San José return tickets in Quepos. If you're staying in Manuel Antonio, you can buy your return ticket for a direct bus in advance in Quepos, and then wait along the road to be picked up. There is no particular bus stop; just make sure you flag down the bus and give it time to stop—you don't want to be standing in a blind spot when the bus comes flying around a tight corner.

Buses leave **Puntarenas** for Quepos daily at 5, 8, and 11am and 12:30, 2:30, and 4:30pm. The ride takes 2 hours; the fare is C1,200. Buses for **Puntarenas** leave daily at 4:30, 7:30, and 10:30am and 12:30, 3, and 5:30pm. Any bus headed for San José or Puntarenas will let you off in Jacó.

GETTING AROUND A taxi between Quepos and Manuel Antonio (or any hotel along the road toward the park) costs between C4,000 and C5,000, depending upon the distance. At night or if the taxi must leave the main road (for hotels such as La Mariposa, Parador, Makanda, and Arenas del Mar), the charge is a little higher. If you need to call a taxi, dial ✆ **2777-0425** or 2777-1207. Taxis are supposed to use meters, although they don't always. If your taxi doesn't have a meter, or the driver won't use it, try to negotiate in advance. Ask your hotel what a taxi ride should cost.

The bus between Quepos and Manuel Antonio (✆ **2777-0318**) takes 15 minutes each way and runs roughly every half-hour from 5:30am to 9:30pm daily. The buses, which leave from the main bus terminal in Quepos, near the market, go all the way to the national park entrance before turning around and returning. You can flag down these buses from any point on the side of the road. The fare is C250.

You can also rent a car from **National/Alamo** (✆ **2777-3344**), **Economy** (✆ **2777-5260**), or **Hertz** (✆ **2777-3365**) for between $45 and $150 a day. All have offices in downtown Quepos or Manuel Antonio, but with advance notice, someone will meet you at the airport with your car for no extra charge.

If you rent a car, never leave anything of value in it. Car break-ins are common here. A couple of parking lots just outside the park entrance cost around $3 for the entire day. You should definitely keep your car in one of these while exploring the park or soaking up sun on the beach. And although these lots do offer a modicum of protection, you still should not leave anything of value exposed in the car.

CITY LAYOUT   Quepos is a small port city at the mouth of the Boca Vieja Estuary. If you're heading to Manuel Antonio National Park, or any hotel on the way to the park, after crossing the bridge into town, take the lower road (to the left of the high road). In 4 blocks, turn left, and you'll be on the road to Manuel Antonio. This road winds through town a bit before starting over the hill to all the hotels and the national park.

FAST FACTS   The telephone number of the **Quepos Hospital** is ✆ **2777-0922.** In case of emergency, you can also call the **Cruz Roja** (Red Cross; ✆ **2777-0116**). For the **local police,** call ✆ **2777-3608.** The **post office** (✆ **2777-1471**) is in downtown Quepos. Several pharmacies are in Quepos, as well as a pharmacy at the hospital, and another close to the park entrance. A half-dozen or so laundromats and laundry services are in town.

Several major Costa Rican banks have branches and ATMs in downtown Quepos, and a couple of ATMs have sprung up along the road to the national park.

Exploring the National Park

Manuel Antonio is a small park with three major trails. Most visitors come primarily to lie on a beach and check out the white-faced monkeys. Unless you're experienced in rainforest hiking, you'll see and learn a lot more if you hire a guide. You can always stay on inside the park after your guided tour is over. A 2- or 3-hour guided hike should cost between $40 and $80 per person. Almost any of the hotels in town can help you set up a tour of the park, or you can contact **Manuel Antonio Expeditions** (www.manuelantonioexpeditions.blogspot.com; ✆ **8365-1057**). Avoid hawkers dressed as guides stopping you on the street and doing a hard sell.

ENTRY POINT, FEES & REGULATIONS   The park (✆ **2777-5185**) is open Tuesday through Sunday from 7am to 4pm. The entrance fee is $16 per person. The **main park entrance** is located almost about 1.5km (almost a mile) inland, at the end of the road that leads off perpendicular to Playa Espadilla at the corner featuring the popular Marlin Restaurant.

Another ranger station and exit point is at the end of the road from Quepos. It's located across a small stream that's little more than ankle-deep at low tide but that can be knee- or even waist-deep at high tide. For years there has been talk of building a bridge over this stream; in the meantime, access to or from the park via this point is prohibited.

MINAE, the national ministry that oversees the park, has been frustratingly inconsistent about which entrance visitors may use. However, for the past several years, tickets have been sold and entry allowed only at the inland entrance. This requires about 20 to 30 minutes of hiking along an often muddy access road before you get to the beach and principal park trails. **Note:** The Parks Service allows only 800 visitors to enter each day, which could mean that you won't get in if you arrive in midafternoon during the high season. Camping is not allowed.

People feeding monkeys, and monkeys and raccoons stealing food, has become a serious problem, and the park service no longer allows visitors to bring in many types of foods.

THE BEACHES **Playa Espadilla Sur** (as opposed to Playa Espadilla, which is just outside the park; see "Hitting the Water," p 441) is the first beach within the actual park boundaries. It's usually the least crowded and one of the best places to find a quiet shade tree to plant yourself under. However, if there's any surf, this is also the roughest beach in the park. Walk along this soft-sand beach or follow a trail through the rainforest parallel to the beach to get to **Playa Manuel Antonio,** which is the most popular beach inside the park. It's a short, deep crescent of white sand backed by lush rainforest. The water here is sometimes clear enough to offer good snorkeling along the rocks at either end, and it's usually fairly calm. At low tide, Playa Manuel Antonio shows a very interesting relic: a circular stone turtle trap left by its pre-Columbian residents. From Playa Manuel Antonio, another slightly longer trail leads to **Puerto Escondido,** where a blowhole sends up plumes of spray at high tide.

THE HIKING TRAILS From either Playa Espadilla Sur or Playa Manuel Antonio, you can take a circular loop trail (1.4km/.9 mile) around a high promontory bluff. The highest point on this hike, which takes about 25 to 30 minutes round-trip, is **Punta Catedral ★★**, where the view is spectacular. The trail is a little steep in places, but anybody in average shape can do it. This is a good place to spot monkeys, as is the **trail inland** from Playa Manuel Antonio. A linear trail, it's mostly uphill, but it's not too taxing. It's great to spend hours exploring the steamy jungle and then take a refreshing dip in the ocean.

> ### Helping Out
>
> If you want to help protect the local environment and the vulnerable squirrel monkey, make a donation to the **Titi Conservation Alliance** (www.monotiti.org; © **2777-2306**), an organization supported by local businesses, or to **Kids Saving the Rainforest** (www.kidssavingtherainforest.org; © **2777-2592**), which was started in 1999 by local children.

Finally, a trail connects Puerto Escondido and **Punta Serrucho,** which has some sea caves. Be careful when hiking beyond Puerto Escondido: What seems like easy beach hiking at low tide becomes treacherous to impassable at high tide. Don't get trapped.

Hitting the Water

BEACHES OUTSIDE THE PARK **Playa Espadilla,** the gray-sand beach just outside the park boundary, is often perfect for board surfing and bodysurfing. At times it's a bit rough for swimming, but with no entrance fee, it's the most popular beach with locals and visiting Ticos. Shops by the water rent beach chairs, and umbrellas. A full-day rental of a beach umbrella and two chaise lounges costs around $10. (These are not available inside the park.) This beach is actually a great spot to learn how to surf, because several open-air shops renting surfboards and boogie boards are along the beachfront road. Rates run $5 to $10 per hour, and around $20 to $30 per day. For a lesson, check with **Manuelk Antonio Surf School** (https://manuelantoniosurfschool.com; ℭ **2777-4842**), which provides excellent attention for individuals, small groups, and families.

BOATING, KAYAKING, RAFTING & SPORTFISHING TOURS **Iguana Tours** (www.iguanatours.com; ℭ **2777-2052**) is the most established tour operator in the area, offering river rafting, sea kayaking, mangrove tours, and guided hikes.

The above company as well as **Amigos del Río** (www.amigosdelrio. net; ℭ **877/393-8332** in the U.S. or 2777-0082 in Costa Rica) offer

Whitewater rafting on the Savegre River

full-day rafting trips for around $70 to $95. Large multiperson rafts are used during the rainy season, and single-person "duckies" are broken out when the water levels drop. Both companies also offer half-day rafting adventures and sea-kayaking trips for around $69. Depending on rainfall and demand, they will run either the Naranjo or Savegre rivers. The **Savegre River ★★** is highly recommended for its stunning scenery.

Another good option in this area is the mangrove tour of the **Damas Island estuary.** These trips generally include lunch, a stop on Damas Island, and roughly 3 to 4 hours of cruising the waterways. You'll see lots of wildlife. The cost is usually $65 to $70. **Manuel Antonio Expeditions** (www.manuelantonioexpeditions.blogspot.com; ✆ 8365-1057) is a good choice for this tour.

Among the other boating options around Quepos/Manuel Antonio are excursions in search of dolphins and sunset cruises. **Iguana Tours** (p 441) and **Planet Dolphin ★** (www.planetdolphin.com; ✆ 800/943-9161 in the U.S. or 2777-1647 in Costa Rica) offer these tours for around $80 per person, depending on the size of the group and the length of the cruise. Most tours include a snorkel break, and you may see dolphins. For more of a booze cruise experience, you could try the 100-foot *Ocean King* (www.catamaranadventurescr.com; ✆ 4000-5740).

Quepos is one of Costa Rica's sportfishing centers, and sailfish, marlin, and tuna are all common in these waters. In recent years, fresh- and brackish water fishing in the mangroves and estuaries has also become popular. If you're into sportfishing, hook up with **Blue Fin Sportfishing** (www.bluefin sportfishing.com; ✆ 2777-0000) or **Luna Tours Sportfishing** (✆ 272/242-5982 in U.S. or 2777-0725 in Costa Rica). A full day of fishing should cost between $400 and $1,900, depending on the size of the boat, distance traveled, tackle provided, and amenities. With so much competition here, it pays to stop by the marina and shop around.

SCUBA DIVING & SNORKELING
Oceans Unlimited ★ (www.scuba divingcostarica.com; ✆ 401/385-6598 in the U.S. or 2777-0114 in Costa Rica) offers both scuba

A Damas Island boat tour

A Planet Dolphin sailing tour

diving and snorkel outings, as well as certification and resort courses. Because of river runoff and often less-than-stellar visibility close to Quepos, the best trips involve some travel time. Tours around Manuel Antonio run $109 per person for a two-tank scuba dive. However, **Isla del Caño** (p 491) is only about a 90-minute ride each way. This is one of the best dive sites in Costa Rica, and is highly recommended. Trips to Isla del Caño run about $125 for snorkeling and $170 for two-tank scuba dives.

Other Activities in the Area

ATV Midworld ★★ (www.midworldcostarica.com; © 2777-7181) offers a range of tours through forests and farmlands at its center on the outskirts of Quepos and Manuel Antonio.

BUTTERFLY GARDEN Greentique Wildlife Refuge ★ (www.sicomono. com/refugeatrium; © 888/742-6667 in U.S. and Canada or 2777-0850 in Costa Rica) is across from (and run by) Hotel Sí Como No (p 450). A nice bi-level **butterfly garden** ★ is the centerpiece here, but there is also a private reserve and a small network of well-groomed trails through the forest. A 1-hour guided tour of the butterfly garden costs $25 per person. This is also a good place for a night tour ($39).

A Blue Morpho butterfly

CANOPY ADVENTURES The most exciting local canopy tour is **Midworld** ★★ (www.midworldcostarica.com; ✆ **2777-7181**). Its main zipline tour features 10 cables, including the longest cables in the area. It also has a face-down "Superman" cable, as well as a ropes course. ATV tours through the surrounding rainforest stop at a waterfall pool for a dip. **Canopy Safari** ★ (www.canopysafari.com; ✆ **888/765-8475** in the U.S. and Canada, or 2777-0100 in Costa Rica) is another good option, featuring 18 treetop platforms connected by cables and suspension bridges, with a "Tarzan swing" and two rappels. The on-site butterfly garden and serpentarium are an added bonus. A canopy tour should cost around $85 per person, and up to $125 for a combo package that includes lunch.

About 20 minutes outside of Quepos is **Rainmaker Park** (www.rainmakercostarica.org; ✆ **540/349-9848** in the U.S. or 2777-3565 in Costa Rica; daily 7:30am–4:30pm). Its main attraction is a system of connected suspension bridges strung through the forest canopy, crisscrossing a deep ravine. Of the six bridges, the longest is 90m (295 ft.) across. The refuge also has a small network of trails and some great swimming holes. Entrance fee is $20, plus $15 additional for a guided tour.

FOR KIDS For a taste of local Tico rural culture, mixed in with fabulous scenery and adventure, sign up for the **Santa Juana Mountain Tour & Canopy Safari** ★★ (www.sicomono.com; ✆ **888/742-6667** in the

U.S. and Canada, or 2777-0777 in Costa Rica). This full-day tour starts off with a visit to the Canopy Safari (above) and then takes you to a local farming village in the mountains outside of Quepos. Here you can tour coffee and citrus farms, go for a horseback ride, hike trails, swim in rainforest pools, fish for tilapia, or see how sugarcane is processed. A traditional Tico lunch is included. Rates are $155 per person, depending on the size of your group, and $99 for kids under 12.

HORSEBACK RIDING Although you can sometimes find locals renting horses on the beaches outside the national park, the crowded beach is too short to enjoy a nice ride, and the horse droppings are problematic. Better yet, head back into the hills and forests. Both **Finca Valmy** (✆ **2779-1118**) and **Brisas del Nara** (www.horsebacktour.com; ✆ **2779-1235**) offer horseback excursions that pass through both primary and secondary forest and feature a swimming stop or two at a jungle waterfall. Full-day tours, including breakfast and lunch, cost between $70 and $75 per person. Finca Valmy also offers an overnight tour for serious riders, with accommodations in rustic cabins in the Santa María de Dota mountains.

PARASAILING **Aguas Azules** (www.costaricaparasailing.com; ✆ **2777-9192**) sets up shop every morning on Playa Espadilla right in front of the souvenir store Caycosta, offering parasailing rides behind a speedboat. Prices start at $75 for a single ride, which lasts around 15 minutes.

ONE-STOP ADVENTURE HOT SPOT The **ADR Adventure Park** ★★ (www.adradventurepark.com; ✆ **877/393-8332** U.S./Canada or 2777-0082 in Costa Rica) is an excellent one-stop spot for thrill seekers. Billing itself as a 10-in-1 adventure tour, ADR offers a 7-hour tour that includes a zipline, waterfall rappels, a high plunge into a jungle river pool, horseback riding, and more. The cost is $130, and includes transportation and lunch.

SOOTHE YOUR BODY & SOUL The best of the local day spas is **Raindrop Spa** (www.raindropspa.com; ✆ **800/381-3770** in the U.S. and Canada, or 2777-2880 in Costa Rica) offering a wide range of treatments, wraps, and facials. **Holis Spa** (www.spaholis.com; ✆ **2777-0939**) has open yoga classes ($15) daily at 8am in their wellness center near the entrance of Parador Hotel, and also offers private classes.

SPICE UP YOUR LIFE Located 16km (10 miles) outside of Quepos, **Villa Vanilla** ★★ (www.rainforestspices.com; ✆ **2779-1155** or 8839-2721) offers an informative and tasty tour of its open-air botanical gardens and spice farm. The commercial vanilla operation is the centerpiece, but you'll also learn about a host of other tropical spices and assorted flora, and you'll sample some sweet and savory treats and drinks. The half-day guided tour runs daily at 9am and 1pm and costs $50, including round-trip transportation from any area hotel. A small shop sells pure vanilla, cinnamon, and locally grown pepper.

Quiero Hablar Español

Academia de Español D'Amore (www. academiadamore.com; ✆ 877/434-7290 U.S./Canada, or 2777-0233 in Costa Rica) offers language-immersion programs out of a former hotel with a fabulous view on the road to Manuel Antonio. A 2-week conversational Spanish course, including a home stay and two meals daily, costs $1,100. Or you can try the **Maximo Nivel** (http://maximonivel.com; ✆ **2234-1001** or 2777-0021), which charges $1,810 for a 2-week program with a home stay.

Where to Stay

Take care when choosing your lodgings in Quepos/Manuel Antonio. You won't have much luck finding a hotel where you can walk directly out of your room and onto the beach, because Manuel Antonio has very few true beachfront hotels. In fact, most of the nicer hotels here are 1km (½ mile) or so away from the beach, high on the hill overlooking the ocean.

If you're traveling on a rock-bottom budget, you'll get more for your money by staying in Quepos and taking the bus to the beaches at Manuel Antonio. The rooms in Quepos might be small, but they're generally cleaner and more appealing than those available in the same price category closer to the park.

EXPENSIVE

Tulemar Resort ★★ (www.tulemarresort.com; ✆ 800/518-0831 in the U.S. and Canada, or 2777-0580 in Costa Rica) features a wide range of private villas and bungalows in a gated community; each unit has access to its own secluded and protected bit of beach.

If you're coming for an extended stay with the family or a large group, consider **Escape Villas** ★ (www.escapevillas.com; ✆ 888/771-2976 in the U.S., or 2203-4401 in Costa Rica) or **Manuel Antonio Rentals** ★ (www.manuelantoniovacationrentals.com; ✆ 985/247-4558 in the U.S., or 8913-9415 in Costa Rica). Both rent a broad selection of large and luxurious private villas and homes, with all the amenities and some of the best views in Manuel Antonio.

You might also check out **Byblos Resort** ★ (www.bybloshotel costarica.com; ✆ 888/929-2567 in the U.S. and Canada, or 2777-0411 in Costa Rica), which features a mix of rooms, suites, and jungle bungalows.

Arenas del Mar ★★★   This beachfront resort is in a league of its own, with handsome rooms, fabulous views, great dining, and direct access to two beaches. All rooms are wonderfully spacious, featuring pale yellow tile floors; cushy beds with leaf-print headboards; and sleek, minimalist decor. Many rooms come with a Jacuzzi tub on a private balcony. There are two main centers of operation here—one near the highest point of the property, the other down by one of the beaches—and

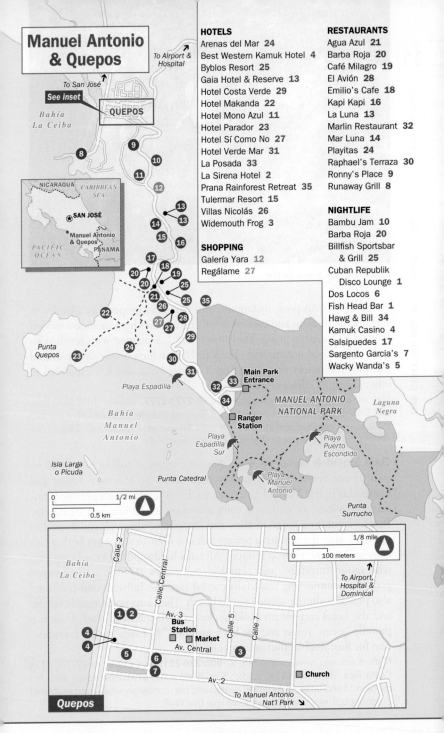

Manuel Antonio & Quepos

To Airport & Hospital

To San José

See inset

Bahía La Ceiba

QUEPOS

NICARAGUA
CARIBBEAN SEA

★ SAN JOSÉ

Manuel Antonio & Quepos

PACIFIC OCEAN

PANAMA

HOTELS
Arenas del Mar **24**
Best Western Kamuk Hotel **4**
Byblos Resort **25**
Gaia Hotel & Reserve **13**
Hotel Costa Verde **29**
Hotel Makanda **22**
Hotel Mono Azul **11**
Hotel Parador **23**
Hotel Sí Como No **27**
Hotel Verde Mar **31**
La Posada **33**
La Sirena Hotel **2**
Prana Rainforest Retreat **35**
Tulemar Resort **15**
Villas Nicolás **26**
Widemouth Frog **3**

SHOPPING
Galería Yara **12**
Regálame **27**

RESTAURANTS
Agua Azul **21**
Barba Roja **20**
Café Milagro **19**
El Avión **28**
Emilio's Cafe **18**
Kapi Kapi **16**
La Luna **13**
Marlin Restaurant **32**
Mar Luna **14**
Playitas **24**
Raphael's Terraza **30**
Ronny's Place **9**
Runaway Grill **8**

NIGHTLIFE
Bambu Jam **10**
Barba Roja **20**
Billfish Sportsbar
  & Grill **25**
Cuban Republik
  Disco Lounge **1**
Dos Locos **6**
Fish Head Bar **1**
Hawg & Bill **34**
Kamuk Casino **4**
Salsipuedes **17**
Sargento Garcia's **7**
Wacky Wanda's **5**

Punta Quepos

Main Park Entrance

Playa Espadilla

MANUEL ANTONIO NATIONAL PARK

Laguna Negra

Bahía Manuel Antonio

Ranger Station

Playa Espadilla Sur

Playa Puerto Escondido

Isla Larga o Picuda

Punta Catedral

Playa Manuel Antonio

Punta Surrucho

0   1/2 mi
0   0.5 km

Quepos

Bahía La Ceiba

Calle 2

Calle Central

Av. 3

Bus Station

Market

Av. Central

Calle 5

Calle 7

Av. 2

Church

To Airport, Hospital & Dominical

0   1/8 mile
0   100 meters

To Manuel Antonio Nat'l Park

Private hike from Arenas del Mar

each has its own pool, restaurant, and bar. This property is a leader in sustainable tourism and conservation, and all stays here include a guided tour on sustainable living. Their restaurant has aligned with revolutionary U.S. seafood organization Dock to Dish, which brings underutilized fish into the hotel's restaurants on a regular basis and has expanded to other Cayuga Collection hotels.

Manuel Antonio. www.arenasdelmar.com. © **2777-2777.** 38 units. $480-$660 double; $760–$950 suite. Additional person $70. Rates include full breakfast, a stocked minibar, and free local and international calls. **Amenities:** 2 restaurants; 2 bars; babysitting; concierge; 2 pools; room service; spa; free Wi-Fi.

Gaia Hotel & Reserve ★★ Set on a series of rolling hills amid its own private reserve, this ultra-hip hotel offers up the most luxury and pampering in the Manuel Antonio area. Every guest enjoys personal concierge services, as well as a complimentary 20-minute spa treatment. Rooms come in a range of sizes and categories, although you'll need to opt for a suite if you want a private balcony (deluxe suites get both a balcony and private rooftop terrace). All have hardwood floors, a living area with rattan furniture, and cloudlike mattresses. There's a three-tiered pool with connecting waterfalls carved into the hillside, and the hotel also provides shuttle service to the beach. The Luna restaurant is terrific and the hotel can set up cooking classes with the head chef. Gaia is a proudly "green" resort and has been awarded "4 Leaves" by the Certification for Sustainable Tourism program.

Manuel Antonio. www.gaiahr.com. © **800/226-2515** in the U.S., or 2777-9797 in Costa Rica. 20 units. $$330 studio; $385–$460 suite; $950 2-bedroom villa. No children 13 and under. **Amenities:** Restaurant; bar; concierge; small gym; multilevel outdoor pool; room service; extensive spa; free Wi-Fi.

Hotel Makanda ★★ This adults-only resort, overlooking a forested hillside sloping down to the sea, has long been one of the most scenic in the Manuel Antonio area. The lodgings, a mix of one-bedroom studio units and larger villas, are spread around the grounds (each with full kitchen or kitchenette), with hardwood walls; stone floors; and, in some, vaulted ceilings. All are large and open. In 2017, the hotel nearly doubled in size, adding a salt water infinity pool, a sushi bar, and ocean view suites. Breakfast is delivered to the villas, and the poolside restaurant is excellent.

Manuel Antonio. www.makanda.com. ✆ **888/625-2632** in the U.S., or 2777-0442 in Costa Rica. 27 units. $265–$330 studio; $400–$1500 villa, includes full breakfast. Children under 17 are not allowed, unless booking the entire resort. **Amenities:** 2 restaurants; bar; concierge; Jacuzzi; 2 pools; room service; free Wi-Fi.

Hotel Parador ★★ Located at the end of the road, with more than 4.8 hectares (12 acres) of land, and a private reserve that takes up most of a sizeable peninsula, this resort-style hotel covers some serious ground. The property is inhabited by the same animals you'll see in the national park, and it's beautifully landscaped, laced with trails and dotted with swimming pools (including a fabulous, large two-tiered family pool with a concrete crocodile in the shallow end and a central fountain and swim-up bar). The resort has four restaurants, a spa, and a wide range of lodging options. The best suites and views are found in the five-story "Las Suites" building, on a hilltop at the far side of the property. The remote

Gaia Hotel & Reserve in Manuel Antonio

Hotel Parador

and protected Biesanz beach is a short walk or shuttle ride away (the shuttle also goes to Playa Espadilla). Hotel Parador has earned "5 Leaves" in the Certification for Sustainable Tourism program.

Manuel Antonio. www.hotelparador.com. ℂ **877/506-1414** in the U.S. and Canada, or 2777-1411 in Costa Rica. 122 units. $281–$345 double; $379–$405 premium; $533 suite, includes breakfast buffet. **Amenities:** 4 restaurants; 2 bars; babysitting; concierge; health club and spa; Jacuzzi; 3 pools; room service; tennis court; free Wi-Fi.

Hotel Sí Como No ★★ This boutique resort occupies a privileged position on a high ridge about midway between Quepos and the Manuel Antonio National Park. Upon arrival you'll be drawn to the jutting triangular lookout point just off the lobby. It's all dense rainforest below, with spectacular views of the Pacific. You'll enjoy the same view from most of the rooms, almost all of which feature private balconies. Monkey sightings are quite common here. There are two restaurants, two pools (one is adults only, the other has a fun little waterslide for the kids), and an air-conditioned theater with nightly movie showings. Additionally, they operate an entire tour network and own a butterfly atrium across the street. Sí Como No's friendly and ever-present owner, Jim Damalas, was an early leader in sustainable tourism in Costa Rica and the hotel was awarded "5 Leaves" in the CST Certification for Sustainable Tourism program.

Manuel Antonio. www.sicomono.com. ℂ **888/742-6667** in the US or 2777-0777 in Costa Rica. 58 units. $287-$365 double; $419–$470 suite, includes full breakfast. Extra person $30. Children 5 and under stay free in parents' room. **Amenities:** 2 restaurants; 2 bars; babysitting; concierge; Jacuzzi; 2 pools; modest spa; free Wi-Fi.

MODERATE

Hotel Costa Verde ★ Make sure your tray table is in the upright and locked position if you stay in the converted Boeing 727 that serves as a two-bedroom suite here, with the nose appearing to be flying straight out of the rainforest. Most of the rooms in this sprawling complex are found in two tall buildings (one for families, one adults only), featuring large balconies with wonderful rainforest and ocean views. The studio and studio-plus rooms all have kitchenettes and flatscreen TVs. Not all rooms have air-conditioning or televisions, and some can be quite a hike to the main restaurant, so be sure to check before making your choice. The hotel has a series of trails, one of which leads to the beach. It's about a 10-minute walk, but because the complex is located on a steep hillside, the return trip from the beach can be strenuous. Breakfast is served at the main hotel complex, and there are three restaurants across the street. Manuel Antonio. www.costaverde.com. ⓒ **866/854-7958** in the U.S. and Canada, or 2777-0584 in Costa Rica. 70 units. $135–$245 double; $169–$375 bungalows; **Amenities:** 4 restaurants; 4 bars; 3 pools; free Wi-Fi.

Villas Nicolás ★ This collection of spacious condo units offers up the very same classic Manuel Antonio views at near-bargain prices. Virtually all of the rooms here come with large balconies, reached via arched wooden French doors. Every balcony comes equipped with a sleep-inducing rope hammock, and monkey sightings are common. Some units have full kitchens, and many can be combined to accommodate families or groups. All have different owners, so interior decor can vary from

Hotel Sí Como No

A Romantic Escape

Prana Rainforest Retreat ★★ (www.pranarainforestretreat.com; ☏ 2777-6724) caters to just one couple at a time in a cushy villa directly on the border of Manuel Antonio National Park. You'll have your own pool with a day bed suspended above one end, and can take morning yoga on a private deck beside a waterfall as monkeys and toucans frolic around you. Pick vanilla, cacao, and passionfruit right off the trees to spice up your meals. With weeklong stays starting at $1,950 per couple in the off season it's not cheap, though when else will you have an entire hotel to yourself?

tropical casual to contemporary chic. The pretty pool is surrounded by blooming gardens, and the service is friendly and personal.

Manuel Antonio. www.villasnicolas.com. ☏ **2777-0481.** 19 units. $135–$170 double; $185–$225 suite; $320–$355 upstairs-downstairs villa, includes breakfast. No children under 6. **Amenities:** Restaurant; bar; pool; free Wi-Fi.

INEXPENSIVE

The **Best Western Kamuk Hotel & Casino** (www.kamuk.co.cr; ☏ 2777-0811) and **La Sirena Hotel** (www.lasirenahotel.com; ☏ 954/493-5144 in U.S. and Canada **or 2777-0572 in Costa Rica**) are two dependable options in downtown Quepos. Both are popular with sportfishing enthusiasts, while **La Posada Private Jungle Hotel** ★ (www.laposadajungle.com; ☏ 2777-1446) is a clean option a few blocks inland from the beach, right near the main entrance to the National Park.

True budget hotels are hard to come by in and around Quepos and Manuel Antonio. Those on a tight budget should look at **Widemouth Frog** ★ (www.widemouthfrog.org; ☏ 2777-2798), a hostel in downtown Quepos, which offers everything from basic dorms with shared bathrooms to cozy double rooms with private facilities, plus a swimming pool.

Hotel Mono Azul ★   "Blue Monkey" has a hostel-like feel and very social vibe, with slightly more upscale accommodations than you'd find in a typical hostel. Husband-and-wife owners Paige Cain and John Westgard have made two rooms, a public restroom, and one swimming pool accessible to disabled travelers. The Mono Azul is the first hotel on the right on the road from Quepos to Manuel Antonio National Park, conveniently located at the bus stop. Rooms, which can be somewhat dated, vary quite a bit in size and amenities; larger and higher-priced rooms have a/c and TV. The two pool areas are quite nice, with pretty gardens and plenty of shade, and you can often spot toucans and sloths here. The busy little restaurant is a great place to meet fellow travelers.

Manuel Antonio. www.hotelmonoazul.com. ☏ **720/446-0765** from U.S. and Canada, or 2777-2572 in Costa Rica. 22 units plus a 3-bedroom villa. $70–$95 per room, which can sleep 2–5 people. **Amenities:** Restaurant; bar; lounge; 2 pools; pool table; free Wi-Fi.

Hotel Verde Mar ★ Just a short walk on a raised walkway through shady trees to Playa Espadilla, this two-story hotel has a to-die-for location, and remains the best budget beachfront hotel in Manuel Antonio. The rooms are all a good size; most come with a kitchenette; and although the flowery linens and some of the furnishings could use an update, all is kept clean. They're also prettier than they need to be, with pale yellow or green walls, and hand-carved wooden doors with local animal and nature scenes. Given that there's a small free-form pool and overall the staff is friendly and helpful, the hotel provides solid value.

Manuel Antonio. www.verdemar.com. ✆ **877/872-0459** U.S./Canada, or 2777-2122 in Costa Rica. 30 units. $55–$85 double. $105–$120 suites. **Amenities:** Pool; free Wi-Fi.

Where to Eat

Scores of dining options are available around Manuel Antonio and Quepos, and almost every hotel has some sort of restaurant. For the cheapest meals around, try a simple *soda* in Quepos, or head to one of the open-air joints on the beach road before the national park entrance. Here the standard Tico menu prevails, with prices in the C3,500-to-C6,500 range. Of these, **Marlin Restaurant** ★ (✆ **2777-1134**), right in front of Playa Espadilla, is your best bet. **Mi Lugar,** or **"Ronny's Place"** ★ (www. ronnysplace.com; ✆ **2777-5120**), on the outskirts of Quepos, is another fine option. **Mar Luna** (✆ **2777-5107**), on the main road as you climb the hill from Quepos toward Manuel Antonio, would be another choice, a Tico-owned spot specializing in seafood.

For lunch, try the beachfront **Playitas** ★★ at Arenas del Mar (p 446); in addition to its great location and secure parking, you get pool privileges for the price of an excellent meal.

For a taste of the high life, head to the **La Luna** ★ restaurant at Gaia Hotel & Reserve (p 448) for the sunset tapas menu. The views are stellar and the creative tapas very reasonably priced.

EXPENSIVE

Kapi Kapi ★★ FUSION/NUEVO LATINO Ready to propose? Kapi Kapi is the place to pick. Dim lighting; an elegant, almost Asian décor; and generous space between tables make Kapi Kapi romantic and private. And the food won't break the spell. It's very fresh, making use of local produce and seafood whenever possible, and highly inventive. Favorites on the menu include local shrimp skewered on spikes of sugarcane, grilled, and then bathed in a glaze of rum, tamarind, and coconut; and the mahi-mahi crusted in macadamia nuts and served with a sweet plum-chili sauce and Jasmine rice. The wide-ranging wine list includes selections from Italy, France, Argentina, and Chile.

On the road from Quepos to Manuel Antonio. www.restaurantekapikapi.com. ✆ **2777-5049.** Main courses C8,500–C18,500. Daily 4–10pm.

MODERATE

Agua Azul ★★ INTERNATIONAL   Sitting high above the rainforest, with sweeping views over the trees to the Pacific Ocean below, this corrugated zinc-roofed, open-air restaurant has one of the best settings in town. There's little in the way of decor, but there really doesn't need to be when the sunsets are so pretty (grab a table at the railing if you can for an unobstructed view). Agua Azul's menu seems, at first glance, to be heavy in bar-food standards, but dishes often have a creative twist (like the signature tuna margarita, seared tuna over a cucumber salad with a lime vinaigrette, all served in a salt-rimmed margarita glass). You can also get burgers, burritos, chicken fingers, and a few more substantial plates, like whole snapper in a tamarind sauce, and the chef's nightly pasta special.
Manuel Antonio, near Villas del Parque. www.cafeaguaazul.com. © **2777-5280.** Main courses C5,000–C12,500. Tues–Mon 11am–9:30pm.

Barba Roja ★ SEAFOOD/INTERNATIONAL   Open since 1975, this is a prime sunset-admiring spot, so on clear nights, you'll want to grab one of the lounge-style low tables on the broad wooden deck. Service can be slow, and the food isn't as exciting as the show in the sky, but it's usually tasty, ranging from Tex-Mex to Asian fusion. Tico standards and bar food are also served, and there's a pretty good sushi bar to boot.
Manuel Antonio. www.barbarojarestaurant.com. © **2777-0331.** Reservations recommended in high season. Main courses C4,500–C9,700. Tues–Sun 1–10pm.

Café Milagro ★★★ NUEVO LATINO/FUSION   A local institution since 1994, this offshoot of the coffee-roasting operation offers a full range of barista-brewed concoctions. But the appeal here goes well beyond java—breakfast, lunch, and dinner are served in the crayon-colored dining room and patios here, and they're all top-notch. For lunch, try Milagro's take on a traditional Cuban sandwich, replacing the pork with fresh, local mahi-mahi. The dinner menu features fusion-inspired Latin fare with everything from jerk chicken to shrimp in a coconut-rum sauce served over mango-infused rice. Creative, contemporary cocktails, as well as excellent South American wines, can be ordered at the bar or at the tables. There's live music every night of the week from 7-9pm.
On the road from Quepos to Manuel Antonio. www.cafemilagro.com. © **2777-2272.** Reservations recommended for dinner. Main courses C6,500–C15,000. Daily 7am–10pm.

El Avión ★ SEAFOOD/INTERNATIONAL   El Avión, or "the plane," is one of two former CIA C-123 supply planes used to send arms to the Contras in Nicaragua's civil war. The other one was shot down by the Sandinistas in 1986, leading to the exposure of the Iran-Contra scandal. The remaining plane was decommissioned and spent years in a hangar at the San José airport before this restaurant bought it. It now provides shade and cover for outdoor dining on this large wooden deck built under the plane's wings and an even more expansive open-air roof structure

Café Milagro

above. The food is the usual: fresh seafood, steaks, burgers, and sandwiches. But the fresh-caught seared tuna is particularly well done here, as is the *arroz con pollo* (rice with chicken). Portions are generous. The sunset view here is superb, so you should reserve in advance if you want a table with a view. The restaurant's bar is inside the old cargo plane's fuselage.

Manuel Antonio. www.elavion.net. ℂ **2777-3378.** Reservations recommended. Main courses C5,000–C12,500. Daily noon–11pm.

Emilio's Café ★★ INTERNATIONAL/BAKERY   There's no better place to start the day than Emilio's Café, a bakery with fabulous bagels and a range of pastries. But you might also want to stop here for lunch, because the salads are bursting with flavor, as are the sandwiches, made with house-baked ciabatta bread. For dinner, there's fresh fish, thick steaks, and nightly specials. You could dine here three times a day and come away satisfied—Emilio's is that good. The view is pretty swell, too, and sometimes in the evenings there's live music.

On the Mariposa road, ½ block from the intersection with the road from Quepos to Manuel Antonio. ℂ **2777-6807.** Reservations recommended. Main courses C4,500–C12,500. Wed–Mon 7am–9pm.

Raphael's Terrazas ★★ SEAFOOD/COSTA RICAN   This simple open-air restaurant has a stunning location, clinging to a steep hillside with a perfect view of the Pacific over a patch of thick rainforest. The hillside is so steep the dining rooms are terraced (hence the name) and spread over three floors connected by steep steps. The menu features a host of Tico and international classics and is heavy on fresh seafood. I recommend the excellent ceviche as a starter, followed by a *casado* of fish, chicken, or beef. More worldly options include seared tuna with a ginger, soy, and wasabi sauce, or the bacon-wrapped tenderloin in a fresh mushroom sauce.

On the road from Quepos to Manuel Antonio. © **2777-6310.** Reservations recommended. Main courses C5,300–C15,000. Tues–Sun 11am–11pm.

Runaway Grill ★★ SEAFOOD   Housed on the open second floor above and overlooking the Pez Vela Marina, Runaway Grill has kept most of the menu, vibe and management of the old El Gran Escape, including a "you hook 'em, we cook 'em" tradition. Start things off with the fresh tuna sashimi, and then go for the catch of the day, simply grilled—you won't be disappointed. Sliders, wings, and salads are also available. The attached bar is a lively place, with sports events on flatscreen TVs.

Pez Vela Marina. www.runawaygrill.com. © **2519-9095.** Reservations recommended in high season. Main courses C8,500–C22,000. Daily 11:30am–10pm.

Shopping

If you're looking for souvenirs, you'll find plenty of beach towels, beachwear, and handmade jewelry in a variety of small shops in Quepos and at the rows of open-air shops and impromptu stalls near the national park. The gift shop inside **Café Milagro** ★★★ (p 454) features a host of excellent, locally sourced craft items, as well as freshly roasted coffee. For higher-end gifts, check out Hotel Sí Como No's **Regálame** (© **2777-0777**) gift shop, which has a wide variety of craft works, clothing, and original paintings and prints, or **Galería Yara** (© **2777-4846**), a contemporary art gallery in the Plaza Yara shopping center.

Manuel Antonio Nightlife & Entertainment

The bars at the **Barba Roja** restaurant, about midway along the road between Quepos and Manuel Antonio, and the **Hotel Sí Como No** (p 450) are good places to hang out and meet people in the evenings. To shoot some pool, head to the **Billfish Sportbar & Grill** ★ at the Byblos Resort (on the main road from Quepos to the park entrance). For tapas and local *bocas,* try **Salsipuedes** (roughly midway along the same road), which translates as "get out if you can." If you want live music, **Bambu Jam** ★ (along the same road) and **Dos Locos** (in the heart of downtown), as well as **Emilio's Café** ★ (p 455), are your best bets. You might also try **The Hawg & Bill,** which fronts the beach in Playa Espadilla. In downtown Quepos, **Sargento Garcia's** and **Wacky Wanda's** are popular hangouts.

Night owls and people looking to dance can find live salsa and merengue music at **Bambu Jam,** and for real late-night action, the hottest club in town is the **Cuban Republik Disco Lounge,** in the heart of Quepos.

The **Best Western Kamuk Hotel** in Quepos and the **Byblos Resort** (p 446) both have small casinos and will even foot your cab bill if you try your luck gaming. If you want to see a movie, check what's playing at **Hotel Sí Como No**'s (p 450) little theater, although you have to eat at the restaurant or spend a minimum amount at the bar for admission.

Side Trip from Manuel Antonio: Playa Matapalo

Playa Matapalo is a long expanse of flat beach that's about midway between Quepos and Dominical. It's an easy but bumpy 26km (16 miles) south of Quepos on the Costanera Sur. It's nowhere near as developed as either of the other beaches, but that's part of its charm. The beach here seems to stretch on forever, and it's usually deserted. The surf and strong riptides frequently make Matapalo too rough for swimming, although surfing and boogie-boarding can be good. Foremost among this beach's charms are peace and quiet.

WHERE TO STAY

Matapalo is a tiny coastal village, although the actual beach is about 1km (½ mile) away. A few very small and intimate lodges are located right on the beach. One of the more unusual is **Bahari Beach Bungalows** (www.baharibeach.com; ✆ 2787-5014), which offers deluxe tents with private bathrooms, as well as more standard rooms, right on the beach. **Dreamy Contentment** (www.dreamycontentment.com; ✆ 2787-5223) is a more traditional beachfront hotel. **El Coquito del Pacifico** hotel (www.el coquito.com; ✆ 855/765-9642 in the U.S. or 2787-5031 in Costa Rica) has a restaurant popular with tourists and locals alike.

For something completely different, you can head into the hills alongside the Savegre River to **Rafiki Safari Lodge** ★ (www.rafiki safari.com; ✆ 2777-2250), which features a collection of large safari tents on elevated platforms in a rich forest setting.

DOMINICAL ★

29km (18 miles) SW of San Isidro; 42km (26 miles) S of Quepos; 160km (99 miles) S of San José

With a stunning setting and miles of beaches backed by rainforest-covered mountains, Dominical and the coastline south of it are well worth a visit. They boast spectacular views, remote jungle waterfalls, and everything from abundant budget lodgings to luxurious rainforest villas. The beach at Dominical is one of the prime surf destinations in Costa Rica, with both right and left beach breaks. When the swell is big, the wave here is a powerful and hollow tube, and the town is often packed with surfers. But be careful: It's often too rough for casual swimmers, and there have been a lot of drownings here. But you can find excellent swimming, sunbathing, and strolling beaches just a little farther south at **Dominicalito, Playa Hermosa,** and inside **Ballena Marine National Park ★★**.

Leaving Manuel Antonio, the road south to Dominical runs by mile after mile of African palm plantations. However, just before Dominical,

Dominicalito

the mountains again meet the sea. From Dominical south, the coastline is dotted with tide pools, tiny coves, and cliff-side vistas. Dominical is the largest village in the area and has several small lodges both in town and along the beach to the south. The village enjoys an enviable location on the banks of Río Barú, right where it widens considerably before emptying into the ocean. The banks of the river and throughout the surrounding forests offer good birding, with numerous shore- and sea birds, including herons, egrets, kingfishers, tanagers, toucans, and trogons.

Essentials

GETTING THERE & DEPARTING   By Plane: The nearest airport with regular service is in Quepos (p 436). From there you can hire a taxi, rent a car, or take the bus.

By Car: The traditional route from San José involves heading east out of town (toward Cartago), and then south on the Inter-American Highway (CR2) to the city of San Isidro de El General. From San Isidro, a well-marked and well-traveled route (CR243) leads to Dominical and the coast. The entire drive takes about 4 hours.

However, it's faster and easier to take the San José–Caldera Highway (CR27) west to Orotina. Just past the fourth toll booth at Pavón, this road connects with the Costanera Sur (CR34), or Southern Coastal Highway. The exit is marked for Jacó and CR34. From here, it's a straight shot down the coast. When you reach Quepos, follow the signs for Dominical. This route should take you just over 3 hours.

The Costanera Sur (CR34) heading south from Dominical to Palmar Norte, passing all the beaches mentioned below, is in excellent shape.

By Bus: To reach Dominical, you must first go to San Isidro de El General or Quepos. Buses leave San José for San Isidro roughly every hour between 4:30am and 5:30pm. See "Getting There & Departing" in "San Isidro de El General: A Base for Exploring Chirripó National Park," p 471. The trip takes 3 hours; the fare is around C3,600. The main bus stop in Dominical is near the soccer field and San Clemente restaurant.

From Quepos, **Transportes Blanco** buses (© 2771-4744) leave daily at 7, 9, and 11:30am and 3:30 and 4pm. The trip takes about 1½ hours and costs C2,600.

From San Isidro de El General, **Transportes Blanco** buses (© 2771-4744) leave for Dominical at 7, 9, and 11:30am, and 3:30pm. The bus station in San Isidro for rides to Dominical is 1 block south of the main bus station and 2 blocks west of the church. The trip duration is 1½ hours; the fare is C1,600.

When you're ready to leave, buses depart Dominical for San Isidro at 6am and 1, 2, and 4pm. Buses leave San Isidro for San José roughly every hour between 4:30am and 5:30pm. Buses to Quepos leave Dominical at 8am and 12:30 and 4:30pm.

GETTING AROUND Taxis tend to congregate in front of the soccer field. If you need a car, **Solid Rental Car** (http://solidcarrental.com; © 2787-0111) will arrange drop-off and pickup at any area hotel.

SPECIAL EVENTS Each year, this area hosts the **Envision Festival ★★★** (www.envisionfestival.com), a 3-day celebration of art, music, and dance, that's a little bit like Burning Man in the tropics. The festival usually takes place in late February or early March.

VILLAGE LAYOUT Dominical is a small village on the banks of the Río Barú. The village is to the right after you cross the bridge (heading south) and stretches out along the main road parallel to the beach. As you first come into town, you'll see the small Pueblo del Río shopping center dead ahead of you, where the road hits a "T" intersection. On your left is the soccer field and the heart of the village. To the right, a road heads to the river and up along the riverbank. If you stay on the Costanera Highway heading south, just beyond the turnoff into town is a little strip mall, **Plaza Pacífica,** with a couple of restaurants, a pharmacy, a bank, and a grocery.

FAST FACTS A branch of the **Banco de Costa Rica,** with an ATM, is located in the Plaza Pacifica.

Exploring the Beaches South of Dominical & Ballena Marine National Park

The open ocean waters just in front of town and toward the river mouth are often too rough for swimming. However, you can swim in the calm waters of the Río Barú, just in from the river mouth, or head down the beach a few kilometers to the little sheltered cove at **Roca Verde.**

If you have a car, continue driving south, exploring beaches as you go. You will first come to **Dominicalito,** a small beach and cove that

Ballena Marine National Park

shelters the local fishing fleet and that can be a decent place to swim, but continue on a bit. You'll soon hit **Playa Hermosa,** a long stretch of desolate beach with fine sand. As in Dominical, this beach is unprotected and can be rough, but it's a nicer place to sunbathe and swim than Dominical.

At the village of Uvita, 16km (10 miles) south of Dominical, you'll reach the northern end of the **Ballena Marine National Park ★★,** which protects a coral reef that stretches from Uvita south to Playa Piñuela and includes the little Isla Ballena, just offshore. To get to **Playa Uvita,** which is inside the park, turn in at the village of Bahía and continue until you hit the ocean. The beach here is actually well protected and good for swimming. At low tide, an exposed sandbar allows you to walk about and explore another tiny island. This park is named for the whales that are sometimes sighted close to shore in the winter months. If you ever fly over this area, you'll notice that this little island and the spit of land that's formed at low tide compose the perfect outline of a whale's tail. An office at the entrance here regulates the park's use and even runs a small turtle-hatching shelter and program. Entrance to the national park is $10 per person. Camping is allowed here for $2 per person per day, including access to a public restroom and shower.

Outdoor & Wellness Activities in the Area

Adventures offered in Dominical include kayak tours of the mangroves, river floats in inner tubes, and day tours to Caño Island and Corcovado National Park. To arrange any of these activities, contact **Dominical Adventures** (www.dominicalsurfadventures.com; © 2787-0431) or the staff at the **Hotel Roca Verde** (www.rocaverde.net; © 2787-0036).

DIVING For diving the rocky sites off Ballena National Park or all the way out to Isla del Caño, call **Mystic Dive Center** (www.mysticdive.com; © 2786-5217; Dec 1–Apr 15 only), which has its main office in a small strip mall down toward Playa Tortuga and Ojochal. Prices for Ballena National Park are $80 for snorkeling and $100 for a two-tank dive; rates for Isla del Caño are $130 for snorkeling and $170 for a two-tank dive.

FLYING **Fly Adventure CR** (www.flyinparadise.net; ✆ **8318-9685**) offers a variety of airborne tours of the area. Near the beach in Uvita, these folks offer everything from 30-minute introductory flights for $140 to a roughly hour-long circuit exploring the Ballena Marine National Park and neighboring mangrove forests for $250.

HIKING & HORSEBACK RIDING   Several local farms offer horseback tours through forests and orchards, and some of these farms provide overnight accommodations. **Hacienda Barú ★** (www.haciendabaru.com; ✆ **2787-0003**) offers several hikes and tours, including a walk through mangroves and along the riverbank (for some good bird-watching), a rainforest hike through 80 hectares (198 acres) of virgin jungle, an all-day trek from beach to mangrove to jungle that includes a visit to some Indian petroglyphs, an overnight camping trip, and a combination horseback-and-hiking tour. The operation, which is dedicated to conservation and reforestation, even has tree-climbing tours and a canopy platform 30m (98 ft.) above the ground, as well as a zipline canopy tour. Tour prices range from $30 for the mangrove hike to $135 for an overnight stay in the jungle. If you're traveling with a group, you'll be charged a lower per-person rate, depending on the number of people. In addition to its eco- and adventure tourism activities, Hacienda Barú also has 12 comfortable rooms at prices ranging from $85 to $95 double, including breakfast. Hacienda Barú is 3km (2 miles) north of Dominical on the road to Manuel Antonio.

    Surfing   Dominical is a major surf destination. Its long and varied beach break is justifiably popular. In general, the beach's powerful waves are best suited to experienced surfers, but beginners can check in with the instructors at the **Green Iguana Surf Camp ★** (www.greeniguana surfcamp.com; ✆ **8855-5866**), who offer lessons and surf camps. Rates

Slithery Fun

Parque Reptilandia ★★ (www.cr reptiles.com; ✆ **2787-0343;** daily 9am– 4:30pm; $12 adult, $6 children 14 and under) is among the best snake and reptile attractions in Costa Rica. With more than 70 well-designed and spacious terrariums and other enclosures, the collection includes a wide range of snakes, frogs, turtles, and lizards, as well as a crocodile. Both native and imported species are on display, including the only Komodo dragon in Central America and a huge anaconda. For those looking to spice up their visit, Fridays are feeding days. The park is a few miles outside Dominical on the road to San Isidro.

Nauyaca Waterfalls

run around $835 to $1,375 per person, based on double occupancy, for a 1-week program including accommodations at a choice of local hotels, plus lessons, unlimited surfboard use, transportation to various surf breaks, and a T-shirt.

WATERFALLS   The jungles just outside of Dominical are home to two spectacular waterfalls. The most popular and impressive is the **Santo Cristo** or **Nauyaca Waterfalls ★**, a two-tiered beauty with an excellent swimming hole and some good cliff-jumping. Most of the hotels in town can arrange for the horseback ride up here, or you can contact operator **Don Lulo** (www.cataratasnauyaca.com; ✆ **2787-0541**). A full-day tour, with both breakfast and lunch, should cost around $75 to $95 per person, including transportation to and from Dominical. The tour is a mix of hiking, horseback riding, and hanging out at the falls. It is also possible to reach these falls by horseback from an entrance near the small village of Tinamaste. (You will see signs on the road.) Similar tours are offered to the **Diamante Waterfalls,** a three-tiered set of falls with a

> ### Spanish Classes
>
> **Adventure Education Center** (www. adventurespanishschool.com; ✆ **800/237-2730** in the U.S. and Canada, or 2787-0023 in Costa Rica), right in the heart of town, offers a variety of immersion-style language programs. A standard, 1-week program—including 16 hours of class—costs $280. These folks also offer home stays, specialized family and medical language courses, and can throw some surf lessons into the package, if you're interested.

360m (1,180-ft.) drop, but a pool that's not quite as inviting as the one at Nauyaca.

YOGA Danyasa Eco-Retreat ★★ (www.danyasa.com; ✆ 2787-0229) offers a wide range of regular yoga and surf classes, as well as private instruction and longer retreats. A drop-in class costs $15, and weeklong or multi-class deals are offered.

Where to Stay

A host of beautiful private homes on the hillsides above Dominical regularly rent out rooms. Most come with several bedrooms and full kitchens, and quite a few have private pools. If you're here for an extended stay and have a four-wheel-drive vehicle (a must for most of these), check in with **Villas Alturas** ★★ (www.villasalturas.com; ✆ 760/560-3903 in the U.S. or 2200-5440 in Costa Rica).

MODERATE

Cascadas Farallas Waterfall Villas ★★ In a category all their own, these handsome villas are in the middle of thick forest and on the edge of a gorgeous stepped waterfall. The Balinese-inspired décor features four-poster beds decked out in white muslin mosquito netting. All the villas open onto patios or balconies with views of the rainforest or waterfalls. Specializing in unplugged, vegan yoga retreats and general mind-body rejuvenation, this boutique hotel and wellness retreat center is about 8km (5 miles) outside of Dominical proper. An accomplished on-site kitchen puts out predominantly vegetarian, vegan, and raw foods. Sorry, no Wi-Fi.

8km (5 miles) northeast of Dominical, on the road to San Isidro www.waterfallvillas. com. ✆ 2787-4137. 9 units. $165–$300 double; $190–$430 suites, includes breakfast. **Amenities:** Restaurant; spa.

Hotel Diuwak ★ This surfer-friendly mini-resort is just a half-block away from the waves. Rooms are basic and bland, and the service can be slack. But most folks don't seem to care, seeing that as a fair trade-off for easy access to the waves and town. The hotel has a large pool area, as well as a restaurant, bar, surf shop, and well-stocked convenience store.

Dominical. www.diuwak.com. ✆ 2787-0087. 36 units. $100–$110 double; $128 deluxe; $169–$179 suites, includes breakfast. **Amenities:** Restaurant; bar; pool, free Wi-Fi.

Hotel Roca Verde ★ Located a bit south of town, the Hotel Roca Verde has a great setting on a protected little cove with rocks and tide pools. The spacious, air-conditioned rooms are in a two-story building beside the pool and have polished cement floors and nice hand-painted murals. Each comes with one queen-size and one single bed, or two queens, and either a balcony or a patio (but you'll want to try for a second-floor unit if possible, as the balconies are a bit nicer). The big open-air restaurant and bar here are quite popular, serving up delicious thin-crust pizza, and featuring live music on Friday nights.

1km (½ mile) south of Barú River Bridge in Dominical, just off the coastal highway. ✆ **2787-0036.** 9 units. $129 double, includes breakfast. **Amenities:** Restaurant; bar; pool; pet-friendly; free Wi-Fi.

Mavi Surf Hotel ★★ Mavi, which opened in 2015, is a beautiful little hotel 300m from the beach, with eight identical, air-conditioned rooms. Stunning murals by local artist Marvin Fonseca Vargas enliven a coherent interior and exterior design, with a font that looks like green bamboo used for lettering, even the handicapped parking logo. The name "Mavi" comes from the first two letters of the Italian owners' two daughters' names, and the rooms are identified by the letters M, A, V, I, and S, U, R, F. All rooms have one king-size bed, a private patio, and a kitchenette corner with sink and fridge (no stove). The hotel serves breakfast but not lunch or dinner, though it does have a small bar for guests.

Dominical. www.mavi-surf.com. ✆ **2787-0429**. 8 units. $130, includes breakfast. **Amenities:** Pool; bar; free Wi-Fi.

Río Lindo Resort ★★ With its palm-studded courtyard, round pool, and riverfront location, you won't miss the lack of an ocean view here, and in any case, the beach is a short stroll away. Rooms have both air-conditioning and ceiling fans—a nice choice to have when one is too much or the other is too little. Private patios are decorated with big flower murals, and there's lots of distinctive art inside the rooms. Standard rooms can accommodate two or three people, and there are apartments and studios for up to four people, one of which has a kitchen. The restaurant-bar serves excellent pizza, and they hosts a pool party every Sunday with live music.

100m from the highway, Dominical. www.riolindocostarica.com. ✆ **2787-0028.** 8 units. $65 double; $125 for 4, includes breakfast. No credit cards. **Amenities:** Pool; restaurant; bar; free Wi-Fi.

INEXPENSIVE

As a popular surfer destination, Dominical has plenty of budget lodging. Some of the best choices are listed below, but if you're really counting pennies, walk around and check out what's currently available. You might find deals at the **Montañas de Agua** (www.montanasdeagua.com; ✆ **2787-0200**), about a block and a half inland from the beach, across from Domilocos. Another nearby option includes the **Antorchas Hostel** (✆ **2787-0307**), which offers basic rooms very close to the beach.

Tortilla Flats ★ If your ideal vacation is mainly about surfing on the cheap, you'll fit right in at Tortilla Flats. The unbeatable right-on-the-sand location pulls in surfers, and the *cabinas* create a cozy cabin-in-the-woods feel, though rooms are pretty bare bones (thin mattresses, and no towels are supplied). Rooms vary in size, amenities, and the number and style of beds—twin, queen, and bunk beds on offer here. All rooms have a private bathroom and fan. There's also a popular beach bar-restaurant.

Dominical. ✆ **2787-0033**. 16 units. $30 double. **Amenities:** Restaurant; bar, free Wi-Fi.

Where to Eat

On the beach, **Tortilla Flats** (see above) is the most happening spot, and its menu features decent fresh-fish dishes and a touch of fusion cuisine. Nearby, the **Surf Shak** (✆ 2787-0026) serves up hearty breakfasts, smoothies, and lunch fare. For sushi, look no further than **Dominical Sushi** (✆ 8826-7946) in the Rio Mar commercial center, while you'll find tacos and burritos at **Del Mar Taco Shop** (✆ 8428-9050), just off the beach. If you head a bit south of town, you can check out the restaurant at the **Hotel Roca Verde** (p 463), which is usually pretty good for grilled fish, steaks, and burgers.

Soda Nanyoa (✆ 2787-0164) is a basic Tico restaurant on the main road, just down a bit from the soccer field, serving local food and fresh seafood at good prices.

Fuego Brew Co. ★★ MICROBREWERY   Perched out on a jungle shrouded area near where the Rio Barú meets the Pacific, this three-level, almost giant treehouse like brewery has quietly become one of Dominical's go to hangouts. The beer, brewed in the building, is the star here, and there are a handful on tap at any given time, as well as kombucha. The menu is a little bit all over the place, though there are some standouts like the beer battered onion rings, beer mussels, and the seafood pasta (in a Pilsner beer sauce, of course).

Main street, Dominical. www.fuegobrew.com. ✆ **8992-9559.** Main courses C3,500–C11,000. Wed-Fri 11:30am–10:30pm; Sat-Sun 10:30am-10:30pm.

Maracatú ★ INTERNATIONAL/VEGETARIAN Located in the heart of Dominical, right across from the soccer field, this local hot spot specializes in healthy cuisine, particularly vegetarian and vegan fare, although you can also get fresh seafood. Choose from fajitas, veggie burgers, a range of pasta dishes, and Middle Eastern classics, like falafel and tabbouleh. The produce and seafood are locally sourced, much of it from the restaurant's organic farm in the nearby hills. Maracatú also has a vibrant lounge and bar scene and often features live music or DJs.

Across from the soccer field, Dominical. ✆ **2787-0091.** Main courses C4,000–C10,000. Daily noon–9:30pm.

Patron's Bar & Grill ★ INTERNATIONAL/STEAKHOUSE   Patron's is impossible to miss, with its full-sized Volkswagen bus mounted on a concrete pillar acting as billboard. The menu is that of a casual steakhouse, although in addition to thick cuts of beef you can get ribs, burgers, entree salads, and pastas. Patron's features a good wine list, as well as an excellent selection of local Costa Rican craft beers. A lounge area

Dominical's coastline

has live music on the weekends and a relaxed vibe, with patrons lolling on long wicker couches.

Next to the soccer field, Dominical. www.patronscostarica.com. ℂ **2787-8010.** Main courses C6,800–C11,000. Daily 6am–2am.

Dominical Nightlife & Entertainment

The big party scenes shift from night to night. **Maracatú** (p 465) hosts an open jam session every Sunday and a ladies' night every Wednesday, while **Tortilla Flats** (p 464) holds regular sunset jam sessions and a big disco night on Saturday. There's usually live music on Friday nights at **Roca Verde** (p 460). In addition, **Patron's Bar & Grill** (p 465) in the center of town is a great place to hang, with a relaxed contemporary feel and live music every Friday, Saturday, and Sunday.

South of Dominical

The beaches south of Dominical are some of the nicest and most unexplored in Costa Rica. This is a great area to roam in a rental car—it's a beautiful drive on a good highway.

Among the beaches you'll find are **Playa Ballena, Playa Uvita, Playa Piñuela, Playa Ventanas,** and **Playa Tortuga.** *Tip:* Most of

Get the Scoop

The **Uvita Tourist Information Center** (www.uvita.info; ℂ **8843-7142**) offers a wealth of knowledge, has a tour-booking and rental-car agency, and even functions as the local branch of the Costa Rican post office, DHL, and UPS. You'll find these helpful people right on the Costanera Sur, at the main intersection in Uvita.

these beaches are considered part of **Ballena Marine National Park** (p 459) and are subject to the national park entrance fee of $6 per person. If you're visiting several beaches in one day, save your ticket—it's good at all of them.

WHERE TO STAY

Just south of Dominical, on a point over Dominicalito beach, **La Parcela** (www.laparcelacr.com; ℂ **2787-0016**) rents four simple but ideally located cabins that sleep up to four people, for $75 per night, while nearby **Coconut Grove** (www.coconutgrovecr.com; ℂ **2787-0130**) offers cottages and guesthouses with direct access to Dominicalito, for between $95 and $175 double. There's also Pacific Edge (www.pacific edge.info; ℂ **2200-5428**), with 4 cabins and breathtaking views of the coast.

Expensive

Kura Design Villas ★★★   If you're looking for luxury, this all-villa, boutique hotel overlooking Ballena National Park is the best option by far. Part of the prestigious Cayuga Collection of hotels, this solar powered hotel with its striking salt water infinity pool that looks out over the vastness of the green jungle and pristine coast is beyond stunning if you can swing the price. Each of the spacious, dark-toned rooms features ocean views and a two-person hammock, while some add private plunge pools. Every detail has been considered, from the loaner iPads and Boruca tribal masks to the craft beer and locally sourced ingredients at meal time.

Bahía Ballena. www.kuracostarica.com. ℂ **8848-5744.** 6 units. $600 double; $920 suite, includes breakfast and transfers. **Amenities:** Restaurant; spa; pool; free Wi-Fi.

Moderate

Costa Paraiso Lodge ★   With lush gardens and tall palm trees, this friendly boutique hotel sits just above a series of rocky outcroppings and tide pools at the northern end of Dominicalito beach. The rooms are mostly fully equipped studio apartments. All feature cool tile floors, exposed-beam ceilings, and lots of ambient light streaming in through large windows and French doors. The Toucan Nest is the prized room here, a private bungalow in a prime location overlooking the sea. The

Pool and bar at Kura Design Villas

other units are all part of two separate duplex buildings that overlook the hotel's gardens and parking area. The lodge has a small pool. Perhaps the best feature here is the excellent **Por Que No? ★★★** restaurant (p 470). 2km (1¼ miles) south of Dominical, just off the coastal hwy., Dominicalito. www. costa-paraiso.com. ℭ **2787-0025.** 5 units. $140–$150 double. **Amenities:** Restaurant; pool; free Wi-Fi.

Cuna del Angel ★★ This boutique–cum–country club hotel has a look that's part Boruca indigenous ceremonial dwelling (love the *palapa* roof over the restaurant), but inside feels more like an Italian villa. In the airy, amenity-laden "deluxe" rooms, walls are painted a warm ochre, beds have brocaded comforters, and there are floor-to-ceiling windows and balustrade balconies. The standard "Jungle" rooms are going for a more Caribbean "shabby chic" look, with purposefully distressed armoires and a simpler, woodsy decor. The grounds are lush (you'll spot monkeys and toucans) and there's a good-size pool, a spa, and a dining room specializing in healthy cuisine. There are several vegetarian and vegan choices, and most of the produce comes from the hotel's organic farm. The hotel has earned "5 Leaves" in the Certification for Sustainable Tourism program. 9km (5½ miles) south of Dominical, just off the highway. www.cunadelangel.com. ℭ **2787-4343.** 22 units. $94–$180 double, includes buffet breakfast. **Amenities:** Restaurant; bar; Jacuzzi; pool; sauna; spa, free Wi-Fi.

Inexpensive

You'll find a campground at Playa Ballena and a couple of basic *cabinas* in Bahía and Uvita. The best of these is the **Tucan Hotel** (www.tucan hotel.com; © **2743-8140**), with a mix of private rooms and dorm accommodations and a friendly, hostel-like vibe.

If you want to be closer to the beach, check out **Canto de Ballenas** (© **2743-8085**), an interesting local cooperative with neat rooms about .7km (a little less than a half-mile) from the park entrance at Playa Uvita.

Hotel Villas Gaia ★   This quiet nature lodge offers up a handful of individual bungalows scattered through dense forests. Each of the bungalows comes with wooden walls, polished concrete floors, a private veranda, and one twin and one queen bed. All have air-conditioning. The land here heads up a modest hill from the highway. At the top of the property, you'll find the pool and pool bar, as well as bungalows with great views over rainforests to the Pacific Ocean. The rest of the bungalows are surrounded by and look out into the lush forests. Try to get one as far from the road and parking area as possible.

Playa Tortuga. www.villasgaia.com. © **2786-5044** reservations in San José, or 2786-5044 at the lodge. 14 units. $75–$90 double, includes breakfast. **Amenities:** Restaurant; bar; pool, free Wi-Fi.

La Cusinga Lodge ★★   This is a small, sustainable ecolodge set on a lovely hillside with a view of Ballena Marine National Park. Accommodations range from dorms to private cabins, all of them rustic and charming. Reforested lumber and river stones were used extensively throughout for the walls, floors, ceilings, bathrooms, walkways, and pillars. Guests gather every afternoon in the beautiful open-air common area to take in the spectacular sunsets, while a large, open-air yoga center hosts regular classes and visiting retreat groups. A trail leads down to a secluded beach, about a 10- to 15-minute walk away. The restaurant sources from local farmers and fishermen, as well as their organic garden.

Bahía Ballena. www.lacusingalodge.com. © **2770-2549.** 10 units. $95–$225 double, includes breakfast. **Amenities:** Restaurant; small spa; free Wi-Fi.

WHERE TO EAT

In addition to the places mentioned below, in Ojochal you'll find the charming **Ylang-Ylang** ★★ (© **2786-5054**), which serves Indonesian fare Wed through Sat, for dinner only to a maximum of 12 diners.

Citrus Restaurante ★★ BISTRO/FUSION   This popular local spot mixes culinary influences from far and wide. You can start things off with a Caribbean-inspired seafood soup with coconut milk and thyme, or fried calamari with a spicy Asian mayonnaise. For a main course, try the yellowfin tuna with a Panko-and-wasabi crust served over organic soba noodles. There are also daily specials and a great range of cocktails and fresh fruit drinks. Save room for their basil and orange blossom crème brûlée or the Belgian chocolate and brandy mousse. The large main dining room features a high peaked ceiling with exposed wooden beams and a massive ironwork chandelier, but the breezy seating on the open-air garden-facing patio is also nice. Weekend nights during the high season often feature live music, a DJ, or a belly dancer or fire performance troupe.

On the main road in Plaza Filibustero. ☏ **2786-5175**. restocitrus@yahoo.ca. Reservations recommended. Main courses $10–$25 Mon-Sat noon–10pm. Reduced hours in the low season.

Exotica ★★ FRENCH/INTERNATIONAL   Robert and Lucy's roadside restaurant is the grand dame of Ojochal's unexpectedly vibrant fine-dining scene. Only a handful of tables are found under the open-air thatched roof, and you'll definitely want a reservation. Although rooted in classic French cuisine, the menu shows a wide range of worldly influences from Thailand, Africa, and Costa Rica. There are daily specials, as well as longstanding favorites, like the Chicken Exotica, which comes in a red-pepper sauce and is stuffed with bacon, prunes, and blue cheese. **Note:** Exotica is the farthest of the bunch from the main road, and you may think you're lost before finding your way here.

1km (½ mile) inland from the turnoff for Ojochal. ☏ **2786-5050**. Reservations required. Main courses $10–$41. Mon–Sat 5–9pm.

Por Que No? ★★★ FUSION   This casual, open-air spot serves up some excellent grub in a striking tropical setting. The best tables have ocean and coastline views. From here it's a short walk to some ocean-fed tide pools. This is one of the best breakfast spots in the area, and as the day heats up, it fires up its outdoor wood-burning brick pizza oven and serves gourmet pizzas for lunch and dinner. Sandwiches (really full meals on buns) range from jerk chicken to a veggie burger to the house special: slow pulled pork with a pineapple barbeque sauce. You can also get a cold Asian noodle salad, or some blackened mahi-mahi with a coffee and chipotle rub.

At Costa Paraiso Lodge. 2km (1¼ miles) south of Dominical, just off the coastal hwy., Dominicalito. ☏ **2787-0025**. Main courses $7–$15; pizzas $12–$24. Tues–Sun 7am–1:30pm and 5pm–10pm.

Little Devils

If you're visiting the San Isidro area in February, head to the nearby **Rey Curré** village for the **Fiesta of the Diablitos,** where costumed Boruca Indians perform dances representative of the Spanish conquest of Central America. The 3-day event also fireworks and an Indian handicraft market—this is *the* best place in Costa Rica to buy hand-carved Boruca masks. The date varies, so it's best to contact the **Costa Rica Tourist Board** (http://visitcostarica.com) for more information.

SAN ISIDRO DE EL GENERAL: A BASE FOR EXPLORING CHIRRIPÓ NATIONAL PARK

120km (74 miles) SE of San José; 123km (76 miles) NW of Palmar Norte; 29km (18 miles) NE of Dominical

San Isidro de El General is just off the Inter-American Highway in the foothills of the Talamanca Mountains and is the largest town in this region. Although there isn't much to do right in town, this is the jumping-off point for trips to **Chirripó National Park.**

Essentials

GETTING THERE & DEPARTING   By Car: The long and winding stretch of the Inter-American Highway between San José and San Isidro is one of the most difficult sections of road in the country. Not only are there the usual car-eating potholes and periodic landslides, but you must also contend with driving over the 3,300m (10,824-ft.) **Cerro de la Muerte (Mountain of Death).** This aptly named mountain pass is legendary for its dense afternoon fogs, blinding torrential downpours, steep dropoffs, severe switchbacks, and unexpectedly breathtaking views. (Well, you wanted adventure travel, so here you go!) Drive with extreme caution, and bring a sweater or sweatshirt—it's cold up at the top. It'll take you about 3 hours to get to San Isidro.

Tip: If you want a break from the road, stop for a coffee or meal at **Mirador Valle del General** (www.valledelgeneral.com; ℰ **8384-4685** or 2200-5465; at Km 119), a rustic roadside joint with a great view, gift shop, hiking trails, and orchid collection. These folks also have a few rustic cabins, as well as a zipline canopy tour.

By Bus: Musoc buses (ℰ **2222-2422** in San José, or 2771-0414 in San Isidro) leave from their terminal at Calle Central and Avenida 22 roughly hourly between 5:30am and 6:30pm.

Tracopa (www.tracopacr.com; ℰ **2221-4214** or 2771-0468) also runs express buses between San José and San Isidro that leave at 6 and 8:30am and 12:30, 2:30, 4, and 6:30pm from Calle 5, between avenidas 18 and 20.

Whichever company you choose, the trip takes a little over 3 hours, and the fare is roughly C3,500. Return buses depart San Isidro for **San José** roughly every hour between 4:30am and 6:30pm. Buses from **Quepos** to San Isidro leave daily at 5:30 and 11:30am and 3pm. The trip duration is 3 hours; the fare is C2,500. Buses to or from **Golfito** and **Puerto Jiménez** will also drop you off in San Isidro.

CITY LAYOUT   Downtown San Isidro is just off the Inter-American Highway. A large church fronts the central park, and you'll find several

Movin' On Up

From San Gerardo de Rivas, the 14.5km (9-mile) trail to the summit lodge is well marked and maintained. The early parts of the trail are pretty steep and will take you through thick cloud forests and rainforests. After about 7.5km (4.7 miles), you reach the "Water Ridge," a flat ridge that features a small shelter and water spigot. This is roughly the midway point to the lodge and a great place to take a break.

From Water Ridge, three steep uphill sections remain: Cuesta de Agua (Water Hill), Monte Sin Fe (Mountain Without Hope), and La Cuesta de los Arrepentidos (The Hill of Regret). As you continue to climb, you will notice the flora changing. The entire elevation gain for this hike is 2,200m (7,215 ft.). La Cuesta de los Arrepentidos, your final ascent, brings you to a broad flat valley, where you'll find the summit lodge. This hike can take anywhere from 6 to 10 hours, depending on how long you linger along the way.

banks and a host of restaurants, shops, and hotels within a 2-block radius of the park. The main bus station is 2 blocks west of the north end of the central park.

Exploring Chirripó National Park ★★

At 3,819m (12,526 ft.) in elevation, Mount Chirripó is the tallest mountain in Costa Rica. If you're headed this way, come prepared for chilly weather. Actually, dress in layers and prepare for all sorts of weather: Because of the great elevations, temperatures frequently dip below freezing, especially at night. However, during the day, temperatures can soar—remember, you're still only 9 degrees from the equator. The elevation and radical temperatures have produced an environment here that's very different from the Costa Rican norm. Above 3,000m (9,840 ft.), only stunted trees and shrubs survive in a habitat known as a *páramo*. If you're driving the Inter-American Highway between San Isidro and San José, you'll pass through a páramo on the Cerro de la Muerte.

Hiking to the top of Mount Chirripó is one of Costa Rica's best adventures. On a clear day (usually in the morning), an unforgettable **view ★★★** is your reward: You can see both the Pacific Ocean and the Caribbean Sea from the summit. Although it's possible to hike from the park entrance to the summit and back down in 2 days (in fact, some daredevils even do it in 1 day), it's best to allow 3 to 4 days for the trip in order to give yourself time to enjoy your hike and spend some time on top, because that's where the glacier lakes and páramos are. For much of the way, you'll be hiking through cloud forests that are home to abundant tropical fauna, including the spectacular quetzal.

Several routes lead to the top of Mount Chirripó. The most popular, by far, leaves from **San Gerardo de Rivas.** However, it's also possible to start your hike from the nearby towns of **Herradura** or **Canaan.** All

Mount Chirripó

these places are within less than 2km (a mile) or so of each other, reached by the same major road out of San Isidro. San Gerardo is the most popular because it's the easiest route to the top and has the greatest collection of small hotels and lodges, as well as the national park office. Information on all of these routes is available at the park office.

When you're at the summit lodge, you have a number of hiking options. Just in front of the lodge are Los Crestones (the Crests), an impressive rock formation, with trails leading up and around them. The most popular, however, is to the actual summit (the lodge is a bit below the summit itself), which is about a 2-hour hike that passes through the Valle de los Conejos (Rabbit Valley) and the Valle de los Lagos (Valley of Lakes). Other hikes and trails lead off from the summit lodge, and it's easy to spend a couple of days hiking around here. A few trails will take you to the summits of several nearby peaks. Hikes should be undertaken only after carefully studying an accurate map and talking to park rangers and other hikers.

There's talk bubbling up of building a $20 million, 8 to 9 km cable car line to the summit, which would lure a significant number of tourists to the park. Though many see it as a pipe dream.

Warning: It can be dangerous for more inexperienced or out-of-shape hikers to climb Chirripó, especially by themselves. It's not very technical climbing, but it is a long, arduous hike. If you're not sure you're up for it, you can just take day hikes out of San Isidro and/or San Gerardo de Rivas, or ask at your hotel about guides.

ENTRY POINT, FEES & REGULATIONS   Although it's not that difficult to get to Chirripó National Park from nearby San Isidro, it's still rather remote. Moreover, the most difficult part of hiking Chirripo just might be the arcane reservation system. Before climbing Mount Chirripó, you must make a reservation with the local office of **SINAC,** which administers national parks (© 2742-5083). The office is officially open from 8am to noon and 1pm to 4pm, Mon through Fri for reservations, though it begins taking reservations on the first Monday of every fourth month for the subsequent next 4 months in the future. Slots sell out fast—often on the first day. In the past, walk-in hikers were allowed to climb up the next day, but this practice has ceased and advance reservations are now required.

Once you have a slot, you must then check in with **Aguas Eternas Chirripo** (www.chirripo.org; © 2742-5097) in San Gerardo de Rivas. This is a consortium of local businesses that handles the specific reservations for room and board up at the summit lodge. Without excellent Spanish skills and persistence, it's very hard to reserve a slot in advance. Many folks rely on their local hotel or an agency to do so. The park service allows a maximum of 3 nights at the lodge.

Once you have reservations all ironed out, you will need to get to the trail head. You have three choices: car, taxi, or bus. If you choose to drive, take the road out of San Isidro, heading north toward San Gerardo de Rivas, which is some 20km (12 miles) down the road. Otherwise, you can catch a bus in San Isidro that will take you directly to the trail head in San Gerardo de Rivas. Buses (© 2771-2314) leave about a half-dozen times daily from the bus station beside the central market, a block or so south of San Isidro's central park, beginning around 5:45am. It costs C1,010 one-way and takes 1½ hours. Buses return to San Isidro daily at roughly the same frequency every day. A taxi from town should cost around C15,000 to C20,000.

Alternative Booking Options

Because the reservation process is so complex and difficult for foreign tourists, your best bet is to coordinate your climb with a local hotel or tour operator. **Costa Rica Trekking Adventures** (www.chirripo.com; © 2771-4582) has some of the most extensive selections of Chirripó climbs.

Because the hike to the summit of Mount Chirripó can take between 6 and 12 hours, depending on your physical condition, consider taking a taxi so that you can start hiking when the day is still young. Better still, you should arrive the day before and spend the night in San Gerardo de Rivas (there are several inexpensive *cabinas,* a couple of mid-range options, and one very nice hotel there) before setting out early the following morning.

Note that camping is not allowed in the park. It's possible to have your gear carried up to the summit by horseback during the dry season (Dec–Apr). Independent guides and porters can always be found outside the park entrance in San Gerardo de Rivas. They charge between $30 and $40 per pack, depending on size and weight. In the rainy season, the same guides work, but they take packs up by themselves, not by horseback. The guides like to take up the packs well before dawn, so arrangements are best made the day before. The entrance fee to the national park is $18 per day.

STAYING AT THE SUMMIT LODGE   Once you get to the lodge, you'll find various rooms with bunk beds, several bathrooms and showers, and a common kitchen area, as well as a simple restaurant. It has good drinking water. *Note:* It gets cold up here at night, and the lodge seems to have been designed to be as cold, dark, and cavernous as possible. The showers are freezing. It costs around $40 per person per night to stay here, and this includes a sheet, blanket, and sleeping bag. Buffet meals at the restaurant run around $10 for breakfast and $15 for lunch or dinner.

> ### Race to the Top
>
> If simply climbing the tallest peak in Costa Rica is too mundane for you, join the annual **Carrera Campo Traviesa Al Cerro Chirripó** (www.carrerachirripo.com). Held the third or fourth Saturday of February, this is a grueling 34km (21-mile) race from the base to the summit and back. The record time, to date, is 3 hours, 15 minutes, and 3 seconds.

Other Adventures in & around San Isidro

If you want to undertake any other adventures while in San Isidro, contact **Costa Rica Trekking Adventures** (www.chirripo.com; © 2771-4582), which offers organized treks through Chirripó National Park, as well as whitewater rafting trips and other adventure tours.

Just 7km (4⅓ miles) from San Isidro is **Las Quebradas Biological Center** (© 2771-4131), a community-run private reserve with 2.7km (1.75 miles) of trails through primary rainforest. Here you can hike the trails and visit the small info center, or you can stay overnight at a rustic lodge, with an option to buy three meals a day. Camping is also permitted.

Where to Stay & Eat in San Isidro

San Isidro doesn't have much of a dining scene. Sure, the town has its fair share of local joints and simple *sodas,* but most visitors are content at their hotel restaurant. If you venture beyond your hotel, there's **Delicias Cafe ★★** (℗ **2770-2421**), a lively and inviting coffee shop and simple restaurant, just across from the central park. A good option for a coffee break or light meal is **Kafe de la Casa ★** (℗ **2770-4816**), located next to the **Thunderbird Hotel & Casino** (www.tbrcr.com; ℗ **2770-9100**).

INEXPENSIVE

Hotel Los Crestones ★ Central San Isidro doesn't have a lot of great hotel choices, but this downtown option is the best of the bunch. A complex of two- and three-story pale yellow buildings, it offers basic rooms with tile floors and bare walls. A small television is hung in the corner and there are options for air-conditioning or fans. The hotel has a swimming pool and outdoor Jacuzzi. Secure parking is provided in the central area between the buildings. Los Crestones is on the main road heading out to Dominical, on the south side of the city, across from the main soccer stadium.

San Isidro de El General (southwest side of the stadium). www.hotelloscrestones. com. ℗ **908/751-3602** in the U.S. or 2770-1200 in Costa Rica. 27 units. $50–$60 double. **Amenities:** Restaurant; pool; room service; free Wi-Fi.

Where to Stay & Eat Closer to the Trail Head

If you're climbing Mount Chirripó, you'll want to spend the night as close to the trail head as possible. Several basic *cabinas* right in San Gerardo de Rivas charge between $15 and $30 per person. The best of these are **El Descanso** (www.hoteleldescansocr.com; ℗ **2742-5061**), **Casa Mariposa** (www.hotelcasamariposa.net; ℗ **2742-5037**), and **Roca Dura** (www.hotelrocadura.com; ℗ **2742-5071;**). If you're looking for a little more comfort and a swimming pool, check out **El Pelicano** (www.hotelpelicano.net; ℗ **2742-5050**), the **Río Chirripó Lodge** (www.riochirripo.com; ℗ **2742-5109**), or the hotels listed below.

For good general information on the tiny village and its surrounding area, check out www.sangerardocostarica.com.

EXPENSIVE

Monte Azul ★★★ This boutique hotel is chic, artsy, and luxurious. Set among lush gardens, the *casitas* are spacious and brimming with contemporary art, part of the owners' collection (they have a huge studio

---

Rest Your Weary Muscles Here

If you're tired and sore from so much hiking, check out the small **Aguas Termales Gevi** (℗ **2742-5210**), located off the road between San Gerardo de Rivas and Herradura. The entrance to these humble hot springs is 1km (½ mile) beyond San Gerardo de Rivas. There are two small pools here, as well as showers and changing rooms. The entrance fee is C3,500.

A Luxury Hacienda

Set on an expansive piece of land on the outskirts of San Isidro, **Hacienda Alta Gracia** ★★ (http://altagracia.auberge resorts.com; ☏ **2105-3000**) is a collection of 50 individual *casitas* (little houses), three restaurants, a boutique spa, and an equestrian center. This very exclusive and expensive retreat features its own private airstrip accepting private flights, and offering ultralight flights around the region.

space on the grounds and often host visiting artists). All lodgings feature a queen-size bed, kitchenette, and a private garden patio. Spa treatments are offered in the comfort of your room, and meals at the hotel's Café Blue restaurant are terrific, using only organic and locally produced fruits, vegetables, coffees, and meats, as well as their own line of goat cheeses. Various arts, crafts, cooking, and mixology classes are regularly held, and the hotel has an extensive network of trails, as well as good access to Chirripó National Park.

Rivas, San Isidro. www.monteazulcr.com. ☏ **415/967-4300** in the U.S. or 2742-5222 in Costa Rica. 4 casitas. $498 double, includes 3 daily meals. **Amenities:** Restaurant; bar; concierge; free Wi-Fi.

INEXPENSIVE

Talari Mountain Lodge ★ This lodge offers more comfortable rooms and better grounds at nearly the same low price as the cluster of backpacker hotels near the Chirripó National Park entrance. It's on the banks of the Río General, some 8km (5 miles) outside of San Isidro. Rooms are housed in a simple buildings set on plain concrete blocks, with clay tile roofs, and whole tree trunks used as columns to hold up that roof. These tree trunks also come in handy for supporting the hammocks that are generously distributed. While cozy, the rooms feel as if they could use a little modernization.

Rivas, San Isidro. www.talari.co.cr. ☏ **2771-0341**. 14 units. $77 double, includes full breakfast. **Amenities:** Restaurant; bar; Jacuzzi; pool; kids' pool; indoor tennis court; free Wi-Fi in restaurant.

Where to See Quetzals in the Wild: Cerro de la Muerte & San Gerardo de Dota ★★

Between San José and San Isidro de El General, the Inter-American Highway climbs to its highest point in Costa Rica and crosses over the **Cerro de la Muerte (Mountain of Death).** About midway between San Isidro and Cartago, a deep valley descends toward the Pacific coast and the tiny town of San Gerardo de Dota. This area is one of the best places in Costa Rica to see quetzals. March through May is nesting season for these birds, and this is usually the best time to see them. However, it's possible to spot them year-round.

If you plan on spending any time in the region and want to take an organized tour, contact **Santos Tours ★** (www.santostour.net; ✆ 8855-9386), a local community tourism project that offers a range of active adventures, including waterfall hikes, coffee tours, and a canopy tour.

In addition, **Dantica Cloud Forest Lodge ★** (www.dantica.com; ✆ 2740-1067) is a small collection of lovely, private bungalows in a forested setting near San Gerardo de Dota.

WHERE TO STAY

Moderate

El Toucanet Lodge ★ This off-the-beaten-path lodge is a good place to go if you want to see quetzals, toucanets, and not a lot of people. Located in tiny Copey de Dota, El Toucanet offers eight rustic but attractive cabins with cypress interiors and nice decks, and some have a fireplace and Jacuzzi. The towels are scratchy but the water is hot, and there are plenty of blankets, which you'll need. The highlights of a stay here are the morning "quetzal quest" and the family-style evening meal. Try the house specialty, the baked trout.

Copey de Dota. www.eltoucanet.com. ✆ **2541-3045.** 8 units. $125 double; suites $174 in high season; 10% lower in low season, includes taxes and breakfast. Closed Sept–Oct. **Amenities:** Restaurant (breakfast and dinner only); free Wi-Fi.

Savegre Hotel ★★ Also known as Finca Chacón, this hotel is owned by the local Chacón family, who were pioneers in converting this remote rural farming area into a mecca for bird-watchers and ecotourists. The small resort is spread around a working apple and pear farm. These fruit trees, as well as the surrounding cloud and rainforests, attract more than 180 species of birds, including the prized resplendent quetzal. Rooms are clean and spacious, with tile floors and wood paneling on the walls. Each comes with a little space heater or fireplace, which is often necessary. The lodge is 9km (5½ miles) down a rugged dirt road off the Inter-American Highway. Four-wheel-drive is recommended, although not absolutely necessary.

Carretera Interamericana Sur Km 80, San Gerardo de Dota. www.savegre.com. ✆ **866/549-1178** in the U.S. and Canada or 2740-1028 in Costa Rica. 50 units. $134–$169 double, includes breakfast, entrance to the reserve. **Amenities:** Restaurant; bar; spa; free Wi-Fi.

Trogon Lodge ★ This is a pretty little nature lodge in a splendid setting. The rooms are in individual and duplex buildings scattered over rolling hillsides and well-tended gardens. At the center, there's a midsize pond stocked with local trout and featuring a deck out into its center, which you can use for sightseeing or a fishing perch. Even if you don't fish for the trout yourself, you'll often find it on the menu here. The varnished wood rooms are homey and enlivened by a simple photo or flower print framed and hung above the beds. All have gas heaters and plenty of room, and most have a pleasant little porch or veranda. There is also a zipline here. This is a sister lodge to **Mawamba Lodge ★** (p 545) in Tortuguero.

Carretera Interamericana Sur Km 80, San Gerardo de Dota. www.trogonlodge.com. *C* **2293-8181** in San José, or 2740-1051 at the lodge. 22 units. $136 double; $186 junior suite with Jacuzzi, includes breakfast. A full meal package runs $30–$39 per person. **Amenities:** Restaurant; bar; lounge; free Wi-Fi.

Inexpensive

El Mirador de Quetzales ★   This is one of the more rustic of the quetzal viewing lodges in this area. It's also the closest to the main highway. Also known as Finca Eddie Serrano, it is run by the friendly local Serrano family. Choose from a series of small wooden cabins and A-frame log cabins, as well as dormitory rooms in the main lodge building. Inside, you'll find low-lying beds and exposed log or varnished-wood walls. Many have low ceilings, thanks to the pitch of the A-frame roofs. Meals are served family style, and both breakfast and dinner are included in the rates, as is a 2-hour guided tour of trails through the lodge's private reserve. The quetzal viewing at this place is as good as it gets, especially between December and May.

Carretera Interamericana Sur Km 70, about 1km (½ mile) down a dirt road from the highway. www.miradorquetzalescr.com. *C* **8381-8456** or 2200-4185. 15 units. $85 per person, includes breakfast, dinner, tour, and taxes. **Amenities:** Restaurant; free Wi-Fi.

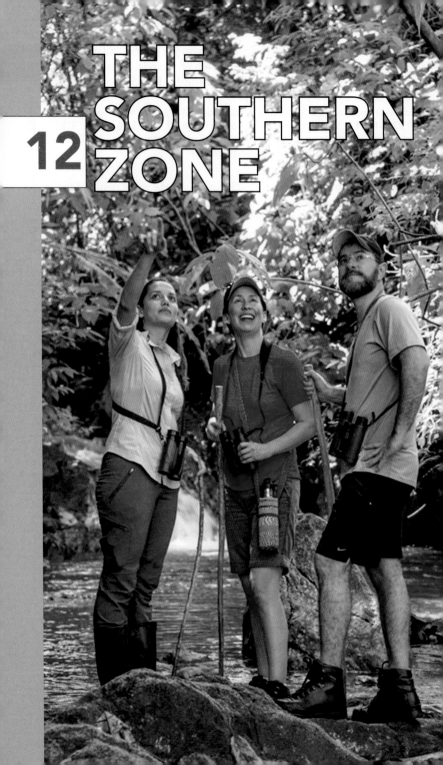

12

THE SOUTHERN ZONE

osta Rica's Southern Zone is an area of jaw-dropping beauty, with vast expanses of virgin lowland rainforest, loads of wildlife, tons of adventure opportunities, and few cities or towns. Lush, forested mountains tumble into the sea, streams run clear and clean, scarlet macaws squawk in the treetops, and dolphins and whales frolic in the Golfo Dulce. The Osa Peninsula is the most popular attraction in this region and one of the premier ecotourism destinations in the world. It's home to **Corcovado National Park ★★★**, the largest single expanse of lowland tropical rainforest in Central America, and its neighbor, **Piedras Blancas National Park ★★**, both connected by the Golfo Dulce Forestry Reserve. Scattered around the edges of these national treasures and along the shores of the Golfo Dulce are some of the country's finest nature lodges. These remote inns offer comfortable to luxurious lodgings, attentive service, informed guides, and a wide range of activities and tours, all close to the area's many natural wonders.

The Southern Zone's remoteness is often emphasized, and perhaps exaggerated. You can fly into any of four airstrips here from San José in less than an hour, or you can drive here in about six hours on good, paved roads. Beyond the population centers, though, the roads get rough and four-wheel drive is often a must. Some places can be reached only by boat, and the prime attraction, Corcovado National Park, has no roads. However, you can fly into the heart of the park, take a boat, or undertake some of the most scenic (if grueling) hiking in the country to get there. You may find that even the most luxurious lodges here are rustic and lacking in amenities like air-conditioning, TVs, and telephones, but their stunning settings more than make up for it.

In many ways, the Southern Zone is Costa Rica's final frontier, and the towns of Golfito and Puerto Jiménez remain a bit rough around the edges. (In either place, you may detect the aroma of sewage in the air while you're trying to enjoy dinner at a restaurant or drinks at a bar.) Tourism is still underdeveloped here, with no large resorts, though a

FACING PAGE: **Exploring the Osa Peninsula with a guide from Lapa Rios**

marina, a controversial Hilton hotel and condominium project are coming to Puerto Jiménez, and a big condo project is under construction in Pavones. It's best to put some planning into a vacation here, book your rooms and transport in advance, and be prepared for heat, humidity, rain, and bugs.

THE best SOUTHERN ZONE TRAVEL EXPERIENCES

o **Hiking in Corcovado National Park:** Home to one of the world's largest lowland tropical rainforests, Corcovado provides fabulous hiking and 2- to 3-day expedition prospects, with beautiful forest trails, jungle waterfalls, and a bounty of wildlife-viewing opportunities. See p 502.

o **Kayaking on the Golfo Dulce:** The calm, protected waters of the Golfo Dulce, and the rivers that flow into it through mangrove swamps, are perfect for kayaking. In addition to the gorgeous sunsets, dolphins, whales, sea turtles, and whale sharks are commonly sighted. See p 500.

o **Landing a Billfish:** The waters of southern Costa Rica are some of the country's richest fishing grounds, and in fact are said to have the world's best sailfishing. Inshore fishing in the Golfo Dulce has led to a number of world-record catches, and in the blue water outside the gulf, sailfish and blue marlin abound. See p 517.

o **Scuba Diving and Snorkeling at Caño Island:** The clear waters around this isolated Pacific island offer some of Costa Rica's best snorkeling and scuba diving, with an abundance of whitetip reef sharks. See p 491.

o **Riding a Seemingly Endless Wave in Pavones:** With the world's second-longest left break, Pavones is well-known to serious surfers, and it's the birthplace of champions. A host of other breaks around the Southern Zone are perfect for beginner, intermediate, and advanced surfers. See p 525.

DRAKE BAY ★★

145km (90 miles) S of San José; 32km (20 miles) SW of Palmar

While Drake Bay (Bahía Drake in Spanish, pronounced ba-*ee*-ah *drah*-keh) remains one of the more isolated spots in Costa Rica, the small town located at the mouth of the **Río Agujitas** has boomed over the years. Some 25 years ago there was no road, and the nearest functioning airstrip was in Palmar Sur. Today a small airstrip operates here year-round, and the gravel road connecting Drake Bay to the paved road at

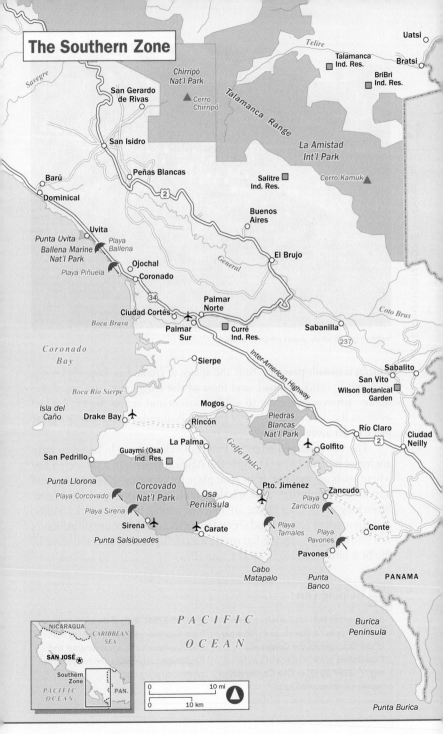

The Southern Zone

Uatsi

Telire

Talamanca
Ind. Res.

Bratsi

BriBri
Ind. Res.

Savegre

Chirripó
Nat'l Park

Cerro
Chirripó

Talamanca Range

La Amistad
Int'l Park

San Gerardo
de Rivas

San Isidro

Cerro Kamuk

Peñas Blancas

Barú

Salitre
Ind. Res.

Dominical

2

Buenos
Aires

Uvita

Punta Uvita

Playa
Ballena

General

El Brujo

Ballena Marine
Nat'l Park

Playa Piñuela

Ojochal

Coronado

34

Coto Brus

Palmar
Norte

Ciudad Cortés

Boca Brava

Palmar
Sur

Curré
Ind. Res.

Sabanilla

237

Coronado
Bay

Sierpe

Inter-American Highway

Boca Río Sierpe

Mogos

Sabalito

San Vito

Wilson Botanical
Garden

Isla del
Caño

Drake Bay

Rincón

Piedras
Blancas
Nat'l Park

Río Claro

Ciudad
Neilly

San Pedrillo

La Palma

Guaymí (Osa)
Ind. Res.

Golfo Dulce

Golfito

2

Punta Llorona

Corcovado
Nat'l Park

Osa
Peninsula

Pto. Jiménez

Zancudo

Playa
Zancudo

Playa Corcovado

Playa Sirena

Sirena

Carate

Playa Tamales

Conte

Playa
Pavones

Punta Salsipuedes

Cabo
Matapalo

Punta
Banco

Pavones

PANAMA

PACIFIC

Burica
Peninsula

OCEAN

NICARAGUA

CARIBBEAN
SEA

SAN JOSÉ

Southern
Zone

PAN.

PACIFIC
OCEAN

0   10 mi

0   10 km

Punta Burica

Swimming with whale sharks off Osa Peninsula

Rincón is usually passable. Still, the village of Drake Bay, formally known as Agujitas, remains small, and most of the lodges here are quiet and remote getaways catering to wildlife lovers and scuba divers. Tucked away on the northwest corner of the Osa Peninsula, Drake Bay is a great place to get away from it all.

The bay is named after Sir Francis Drake, who is believed to have anchored here in 1579. The tiny Río Agujitas flows into a protected bay where boats are moored. It's a great place for canoeing or swimming, and a number of **dolphin- and whale-watching tours** depart from here. Stretching south from Drake are miles of remote beaches, rocky points, and stretches of primary and secondary rainforest. Adventurous explorers will find tide pools, spring-fed rivers, waterfalls, forest trails, and some of the best bird-watching in all of Costa Rica.

Helping Out

If you want to help local efforts to protect the fragile rainforests and wild areas of the Osa, contact the **Corcovado Foundation** (www.corcovadofoundation. org; ✆ **2297-3013**) or **Osa Conservation** (www.osaconservation.org; ✆ **2735-5756**). Both of these groups have volunteer programs, ranging from trail maintenance to environmental and English-language education to sea-turtle protection programs.

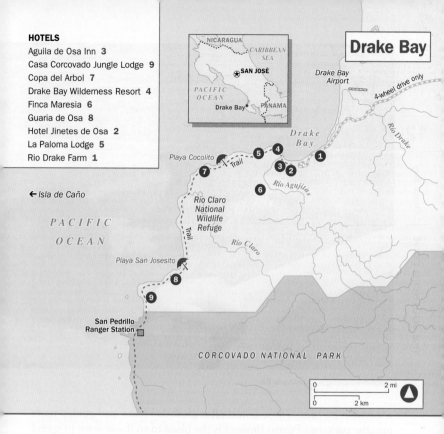

HOTELS

Aguila de Osa Inn **3**
Casa Corcovado Jungle Lodge **9**
Copa del Arbol **7**
Drake Bay Wilderness Resort **4**
Finca Maresia **6**
Guaria de Osa **8**
Hotel Jinetes de Osa **2**
La Paloma Lodge **5**
Rio Drake Farm **1**

If you want to go to Drake Bay, be advised that almost all the visitors here have advance bookings at an all-inclusive resort. This is not the place to come if you like to "wing it," traveling first and seeking lodging later, nor will you find a lively community here where you'll run into other backpackers bumming around. The tourism model here is almost exclusively pre-booked with all-inclusive packages.

South of Drake Bay are the wilds of the **Osa Peninsula,** including **Corcovado National Park,** which is often described as the crown jewel of Costa Rican parks. It covers about a third of the Osa Peninsula and contains the largest single expanse of virgin lowland rainforest in Central America. For this reason, Corcovado is well known among researchers studying rainforest ecology. If you come here, you'll learn firsthand why they're called rainforests: Some parts of the peninsula receive up to 700cm (23 ft.) of rain per year—that's more than three Shaquille O'Neals.

Puerto Jiménez (p 496) is the best jumping-off place if you want to spend time hiking and camping in Corcovado National Park. Drake Bay is primarily a collection of high-end hotels, very isolated and mostly

Dolphin-watching tour in Drake Bay

accessible by boat. These hotels offer great day hikes and guided tours into the park, but Puerto Jiménez is the place to go if you want to spend more time in the park. (It has hotels for all budgets, the parks office, and land transportation to Carate and Los Patos, from which visitors can hike into the various stations.) From the Drake Bay side, you're more dependent on a boat ride/organized tour from one of the lodges to explore the park, but these lodges offer other guided outings in addition to visits to the park.

Essentials

Because Drake Bay is so remote, I recommend that you have a room reservation and transportation (often arranged with your hotel) before you arrive. Most of the lodges are spread along several kilometers of coastline, and it is impossible to wander from one to another looking for a room.

Tip: A flashlight and rain gear are always useful in Costa Rica, and during the rainy season in Drake Bay, they're absolutely essential.

GETTING THERE   By Plane: Most visitors fly directly into the little airstrip at Drake Bay (airport code: DRK), although the more adventurous can fly to Palmar Sur (p 490) and then boat down the Sierpe River through the Térraba-Sierpe wetlands, the largest mangrove swamp in the Northern Hemisphere. All lodges will either arrange transportation for you or include it in their packages. Both **Nature Air** (www.natureair. com; ✆ **800/235-9272** in the U.S. and Canada, or 2299-6000 in Costa Rica) and **Sansa** (www.flysansa.com; ✆ **877/767-2672** in the U.S. and Canada, or 2290-4100 in Costa Rica) fly directly to Drake Bay from San José's Juan Santamaría International Airport. Flights also depart San José daily from the same airport for Palmar Sur. Fares range from $84 to $144 each way by air; a taxi to Sierpe runs about $30 and a boat ride to Drake $20.

If your travels take you to Drake Bay via Palmar Sur, you must then take a 15-minute bus or taxi ride over dirt roads to the small town of **Sierpe.** This bumpy route runs through several **banana plantations** and past an important archaeological site featuring the stone spheres of the Diquís indigenous group. In Sierpe, you board a small boat for a 40km (25-mile) ride to Drake Bay; see "By Taxi & Boat from Sierpe," below. The first half of this trip snakes through a maze of mangrove canals and the main river channel before negotiating the mouth of the

Kayaking through the mangroves

Sierpe River and heading out to sea for the final leg to the bay. **Warning:** Entering and exiting the Sierpe River mouth is often a very rough ride.

By Bus: Tracopa buses (www. tracopacr.com; ✆ **2221-4214** or 2290-1308) leave San José daily for the Southern Zone throughout the day, between 5am and 6:30pm from Calle 9 and Avenida 18. Almost all stop in Palmar Norte, but make sure to ask. The ride takes around 6 hours; fares are around C7,800. Once in Palmar Norte, ask for the next bus for Sierpe. If it doesn't leave for a while (buses aren't frequent), consider taking a taxi.

By Taxi & Boat from Sierpe: When you arrive at either the Palmar Norte bus station or the Palmar Sur airstrip (airport code: PMZ), you'll most likely first need to take a taxi to the village of Sierpe. The fare should be around $35. If you're booked with one of the main lodges, chances are your transportation is included. Even if you're not booked with one of the lodges, a host of taxi and minibus drivers offer the trip. When you get to Sierpe, head to the river dock at either the Las Vegas Restaurant or the Hotel Oleaje Sereno to book passage on the collective water taxis. This will cost you an additional $20, or you can charter a private boat for your party for $200 or so. Collective water taxis are timed to coincide with the twice-daily Sansa flights from San José.

By Car: Driving to Drake Bay is not for the faint of car. Four-wheel drive is essential on the sometimes steep gravel road, and you have to cross three streams and one fair-sized river, plus there's a scary little bridge with two planks for your tires and no rails. If you do drive here from the capital, take the San José–Caldera Highway (CR27) to the first exit after the fourth toll booth and follow the signs to Jacó, where you will pick up the Southern Highway, or Costanera Sur (CR34). Take this south past Jacó, Quepos, Dominical, and Uvita, and turn right onto the Inter-American Highway (CR2) at Palmar Norte. Take this road south to the junction at Chacarita, where you can gas up before turning right toward the Osa Peninsula, following the signs for Puerto Jiménez and Corcovado. Just before the Rincón River bridge, turn right to follow the signs to Drake. About 5km from Drake, there's one fairly wide river that can become impassable in the rainy season, but you can leave your car at the Drake Bay Backpackers Hostel and catch a ride the rest of the way for $20 or so. The road ends in the town of Drake Bay, formally known as Agujitas, so from there you must take a boat to reach destinations to the south. The only hotels that you can actually drive up to are very basic cabins in town.

DEPARTING If you're not flying directly out of Drake Bay, have your lodge arrange a boat trip back to Sierpe for you. Be sure that the lodge also arranges for a taxi to meet you in Sierpe for the trip to Palmar Sur or Palmar Norte. (If you're on a tight budget, you can ask around to see whether a late-morning public bus is still running from Sierpe to Palmar Norte.) In Palmar Sur you can catch your round-trip return flight, and from Palmar Norte you can catch north- and southbound buses along the Inter-American and Costanera highways.

Exploring Drake Bay

Beaches, forests, wildlife, and solitude are the main reasons to visit Drake Bay. Although Corcovado National Park (see "Puerto Jiménez: Gateway to Corcovado National Park," p 496) is the area's star attraction, there are plenty of other nearby options. The Osa Peninsula is home to an unbelievable variety of plants and animals: more than 140 species of mammals, 400 species of birds, and 130 species of amphibians and reptiles. You can expect to see coatimundis, scarlet macaws, parrots,

Flock of wild Scarlet Macaws flying near Drake Bay, Corcovado National Park

hummingbirds, and as many as four species of monkeys. Other inhabitants include jaguars, tapirs, peccaries, sloths, anteaters, and crocodiles.

Around Drake Bay and within the park are miles of trails through rainforests and swamps, down beaches, and around rocky headlands. All of the lodges listed offer guided excursions into the park, but since the park service closed the trail between the San Pedrillo and Sirena ranger stations, it is no longer possible to hike around the peninsula from Drake Bay.

All lodges in the area have their own in-house tour operations and offer a host of half- and full-day tours and activities, including hikes in Corcovado, snorkeling trips to Caño Island, horseback rides, and wildlife-viewing treks. In some cases, tours are included in your room rate or package; in others, they must be bought *a la carte.* Other options include mountain biking and sea kayaking. Most of these tours run between $65 and $120; scuba diving costs about $150 for a two-tank dive with equipment, and sportfishing runs $900 to $2,000, depending on the size of the boat and other amenities.

CANOPY TOUR If you want to try a zipline canopy adventure, the **Drake Bay Canopy Tour** (www.canopytour.com/drakebay.html; © 8314-5454 or 2231-5806) has six cable runs, several "Tarzan swings," and a

THOSE mysterious stone spheres

Although Costa Rica lacks the great cities, giant temples, and bas-relief carvings of the Maya, Aztec, and Olmec civilizations of northern Mesoamerica, its pre-Columbian inhabitants left a unique legacy that has archaeologists and anthropologists still scratching their heads. Over a period of several centuries, hundreds of painstakingly carved and carefully positioned stone spheres were left by the peoples who lived throughout the Diquís Delta, which flanks the Térraba River in southern Costa Rica. The orbs, which range from grapefruit size to more than 2m (6½ ft.) in diameter, can weigh up to 15 tons, and all are nearly perfect spheres.

Archaeologists believe that the spheres were created during two defined cultural periods. The first, called the Aguas Buenas period, dates from around A.D. 100 to 500. Few spheres survive from this time. The second phase, during which spheres were created in apparently greater numbers, is called the Chiriquí period and lasted from approximately A.D. 800 to 1500. The "balls" believed to have been carved during this time frame are widely dispersed along the entire length of the lower section of the Térraba River. To date, only one known quarry for the spheres has been discovered, in the mountains above the Diquís Delta, which points to a difficult and lengthy transportation process.

Some archaeologists believe the spheres were hand-carved in a very time-consuming process, using stone tools. Another theory holds that granite blocks were placed at the base of powerful waterfalls, and the hydraulic beating of the water eventually turned and carved the rock into these near-perfect spheres. And more than a few theories have credited extraterrestrial intervention for the creation of the spheres.

Most of the stone balls have been found at the archaeological remains of defined settlements and are associated with either central plazas or known burial sites. Their size and placement have been interpreted to have both social and celestial importance, although their exact significance remains a mystery. Unfortunately, many of the stone balls have been plundered and are currently used as lawn ornaments in the fancier neighborhoods of San José. Some have even been shipped out of the country. The **Museo**

Nacional de Costa Rica (p 131) has a nice collection, including one massive sphere in its center courtyard. It's a never-fail photo op. You can also see the stone balls near the small **airports in Palmar Sur** and **Drake Bay,** and on **Isla del Caño** (which is 19km/12 miles off the Pacific Coast near Drake Bay).

The best place to see the spheres is the **Finca 6 Archaeological Museum** ★★ (*ⓒ* **2100-6000;** daily 8am–4pm; $6), located between Palmar Sur and Sierpe. (The blue sign saying "Finca 6," right next to a one-lane bridge, is easy to miss.) It's estimated that nearly 10% of all stone spheres produced in Costa Rica can be found on the 10 or so acres that comprise Finca 6. A small museum provides background and displays of some smaller spheres and other artifacts. From here, trails lead out to several excavations of archaeological finds where a range of large stone spheres and other relics are displayed in their original positioning. Finca 6 is located 6km south of Palmar Sur. This unique archaeological site is easily visited by anyone arriving or departing Drake Bay via Sierpe.

Toucan feeding on fruit

hanging bridge, all set in lush forests just outside Drake Bay. The 2-hour tour costs $55.

ISLA DEL CAÑO   One of the most popular excursions from Drake Bay is a trip to **Isla del Caño** and the **Caño Island Biological Reserve** ★★ for snorkeling or scuba diving or hiking on the island. Caño Island, about 19km (12 miles) off the Drake shore, was once home to a pre-Columbian culture about which little is known. Few animals or birds live on the island, but the coral reefs that ring the island teem with life, making this one of Costa Rica's prime **scuba diving sites** ★★. Visibility is often very good, especially during the dry season, and the beach has easily accessible snorkeling. All the lodges listed below offer trips to Isla del Caño. The Costa Rican National Park service severely restricts access to the island, and visiting groups are not allowed to picnic there. Typically, tours arrive in the morning, conduct their snorkel and scuba excursions, and then head back to the mainland for a picnic lunch and some beach time.

NIGHT TOUR   One of the most compelling tour options in Drake Bay is a 2-hour **night tour** ★★★ (www.thenighttour.com; ✆ **8701-7356** or 8701-7462; $40 per person) offered by Tracie Stice, the "Bug Lady," and her partner Gianfranco Gómez. Equipped with headlamps, participants get a bug's-eye view of the forest at night. You might see some larger forest dwellers, but most of the tour is a fascinating exploration of the nocturnal world of insects, arachnids, frogs, toads, and snakes. Among the highlights is watching Tracie pry open the portal of a trapdoor spider, and you might see an orange-kneed tarantula.

WHALE-WATCHING   Drake Bay is one of the best places in Costa Rica for **whale-watching;** Northern Pacific humpback whales are commonly spotted in the area from March through April, and Southern Pacific populations September through October. All the hotels listed below can arrange whale-watching and dolphin-spotting trips. Two resident marine biologists, Shawn Larkin and Roy Sancho, are often hired by the better hotels, but depending on demand and availability, the hotels may send

Drake Bay Beach

you out with one of their own captains.

If you want more information on the local whale-watching scene, or to contact Shawn Larkin directly, go to **www.costacetacea.com**. They offer deep-water free diving and snorkel tours aimed at providing the chance to swim in close proximity to large pelagic fish, mammals, and reptiles.

Where to Stay & Eat

Given the remote location and logistics of reaching Drake Bay, as well as the individual isolation of each hotel, nearly all the hotels listed below deal almost exclusively in package trips that include transportation, meals, tours, and taxes. I list the most common packages, although all the lodges will work with you to accommodate longer or shorter stays. Nightly room rates are listed only where they're available and practical, generally at the more moderately priced hotels.

In addition to the places listed below, **Guaria de Osa** ★ (www. guariadeosa.com; ℂ **510/235-4313** in the U.S.) is a lovely lodge near the Río Claro, specializing in yoga, spiritual, and educational retreats.

EXPENSIVE

In addition to the lodges reviewed below, **Copa del Arbol** ★★ (www. copadearbol.com; ℂ **831/246-4265** in the U.S., or 8935-1212 in Costa Rica) is another intimate jungle lodge located on the water's edge about midway between the village of Drake Bay and the San Pedrillo ranger station at the entrance to Corcovado National Park.

Aguila de Osa Inn ★   Set on a steep hillside that borders the Agujitas River right near the point where it empties out into Drake Bay, this is an

---

Where's the Beach?

While the beach at Drake Bay itself is acceptable and calm for swimming, it's far from spectacular. If you're staying at La Paloma Lodge, there's a popular patch of sand known as Cocalito beach, about a 10-minute hike away. The nicest beaches around involve taking a day trip to Isla del Caño or San Josesito. The latter is a stunning beach farther south on the peninsula with excellent snorkeling possibilities.

Casa Corcovado Jungle Lodge

expertly operated jungle lodge, with much of the credit going to owner Bradd Johnson, who is very much a hands-on proprietor. This is one of the only high-end lodges in the area without a swimming pool and the rooms are a bit of an uphill hike from the main lodge, but the rooms are airy and comfortable; the service is attentive; and the food is downright fabulous, much of it grown on the property. The lodge has especially good scuba diving and sport fishing operations, with its own modern boats, top-notch equipment, and knowledgeable skippers and divemasters.

Drake Bay. www.aguiladeosa.com. *©* **866/924-8452** in the U.S. and Canada, 2296-2190 in San José, or 8840-2929 at the lodge. 11 deluxe rooms and 2 suites. $505–$665 for 3 days/2 nights; $715-$955 for 4 days/3 nights in high season. Rates are per person based on double occupancy and include round-trip transportation from Palmar Sur or Drake Bay airports, welcome cocktail, and all meals. Closed Oct. **Amenities:** Restaurant; bar; free kayaks; free Wi-Fi.

Casa Corcovado Jungle Lodge ★ The closest of all the jungle lodges on the Drake Bay side of Corcovado National Park, Casa Corcovado has a collection of well-appointed individual and duplex bungalows built on the site of a former cacao plantation. Most of the former farmland has been reclaimed, and the whole operation is surrounded by dense primary forest. The property has two pretty swimming pools and a semi-private beach that is sometimes swimmable. Every afternoon, guests gather at "Margarita Sunset Point," a grassy bluff on a high point overlooking the Pacific Ocean, for cocktails, snacks, and the sunset. Owner Stephen Lill is a dedicated environmentalist involved in numerous local conservation and sustainable-development projects.

Osa Peninsula. www.casacorcovado.com. (**C**) **888/896-6097** in the U.S. and Canada, **2256-3181.** 14 units. $855–$1,165 per person for 3 days/2 nights; $1,150–$1,465 for 4 days/3 nights. Rates are based on double occupancy and include round-trip transportation from San José, all meals, daily tours, park fees, and taxes. Closed Sept 1–Nov 14. **Amenities:** Restaurant; 2 bars; 2 pools; free Wi-Fi.

La Paloma Lodge ★★★   This is one of the top nature lodges in Costa Rica—the views are superb, the setting sublime, and the wildlife viewing and adventure opportunities are as good as it gets. Rooms are beautiful, with gleaming hardwood decks and interiors, and most are two-story, with a bedroom and bathroom upstairs and down connected by a spiral staircase. The best are the large Sunset Ranchos, which sit on a prominent high point with a panoramic view of the sea, with massive master bedrooms featuring nothing but windows on three sides. Even the slightly more humble standard rooms are large and plush, with private balconies and mesmerizing views. The food and service are top-notch,

Guest room at La Paloma Lodge

with guests seated together at long tables, swapping tales over four-course dinners. A small pool sits on the edge of a jungle-clad hillside, and Cocalito Beach is a short hike down a winding trail through the rainforest. Packages include two tours, usually a boat ride into Corcovado National Park and a snorkeling trip to El Caño Island. The lodge takes conservation seriously, and is actively involved in protecting the region.

Drake Bay. www.lapalomalodge.com. © **2293-7502.** 11 units. $1,085–$1,385 per person for 4 days/3 nights with 2 tours; $1,350–$1,730 per person for 5 days/4 nights with 2 tours. Rates are based on double occupancy and include all meals, park fees, and indicated tours. Lower rates in off-season. Closed around Sept 15–Nov 1. **Amenities:** Restaurant; bar; pool; free use of kayaks; free Wi-Fi.

MODERATE

In addition to the spot listed below, you might check out **Finca Maresia** ★ (www.fincamaresia.com; © **2775-0279**), a pretty boutique property located between Drake Bay and the national park.

Drake Bay Wilderness Resort ★★ This has one of the best locations of all the lodges in Drake Bay, on a large chunk of land with the Agujitas River and Drake Bay on one side and the open Pacific Ocean on the other. Rooms feature hand-painted murals on concrete walls, and comfortable beds. A couple of budget rooms share bathrooms and shower

Drake Bay Wilderness Resort

facilities. The shoreline right at the lodge is a bit too rocky for swimming, but there's a nice pool naturally fed and filled with seawater. Owner Marleny's chocolate-chip cookies are regionally renowned.

Drake Bay. www.drakebay.com. © **2775-1716** or 2775-1715. 20 units. $865 per person for 4 days/3 nights with 2 tours, includes all meals and taxes. **Amenities:** Restaurant; bar; saltwater pool; free use of canoes and kayaks; free Wi-Fi.

INEXPENSIVE

Rio Drake Farm ★   For a DIY Drake Bay experience on a tight budget, Rio Drake Farm is your best option. Owned by a Swiss biologist and her Costa Rican naturalist guide husband, the small guesthouse and horse ranch has just a few basic rooms with private bathrooms, electric fans, and paintings of local wildlife decorating the walls. Each is fronted by a small patio with a hammock. There's free use of canoes and use of the kitchen, plus low priced options for nearly any type of tour in the area.

Drake Bay. www.riodrakefarm.com. © **8830-9911**. 4 units. $54 double, includes taxes and breakfast. **Amenities:** Shared kitchen; free Wi-Fi (5-9pm).

Hotel Jinetes de Osa ★★   Just off the water at the far southern end of the Drake Bay shore, this is an excellent budget to mid-priced option. Many of the rooms have splendid ocean views, all have hot water, and some are air-conditioned. However, be prepared for a bit of a climb. The hotel specializes in dive trips and is recognized as a full-service PADI (Professional Association of Diving Instructors) resort.

Drake Bay. www.jinetesdeosa.com. © **866/553-7073** in the U.S. and Canada, or 2231-5806 in Costa Rica. 13 units. $100–$165 double, includes breakfast. **Amenities:** Restaurant; bar; free Wi-Fi.

PUERTO JIMÉNEZ: GATEWAY TO CORCOVADO NATIONAL PARK

35km (22 miles) W of Golfito by water (90km/56 miles by road); 85km (53 miles) S of Palmar Norte

Don't let its small size and languid pace fool you. **Puerto Jiménez** ★ is a bustling little burg, where rough jungle gold-panners mix with wealthy ecotourists, budget backpackers, serious surfers, and the occasional celebrity seeking anonymity and escape. Located on the Golfo Dulce shoreline in the eastern Osa Peninsula, the town is just a few streets wide in any direction, with a soccer field, a few general stores, budget hotels, tourism offices, an airstrip, some inexpensive *sodas*, and several bars. Scarlet macaws fly overhead, and mealy parrots provide wake-up calls.

   Corcovado National Park has its park service headquarters here, and the town makes an excellent base for exploring this vast wilderness area. Signs in English on walls around town advertise a variety of tours,

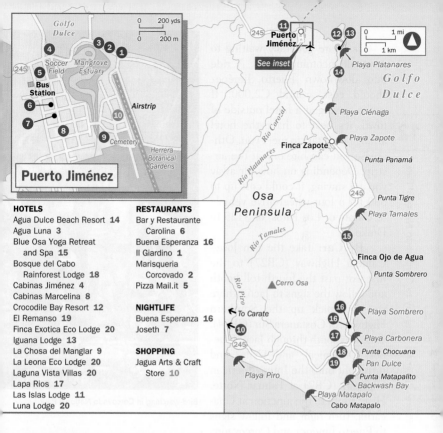

HOTELS

Agua Dulce Beach Resort 14
Agua Luna 3
Blue Osa Yoga Retreat
   and Spa 15
Bosque del Cabo
   Rainforest Lodge 18
Cabinas Jiménez 4
Cabinas Marcelina 8
Crocodile Bay Resort 12
El Remanso 19
Finca Exotica Eco Lodge 20
Iguana Lodge 13
La Chosa del Manglar 9
La Leona Eco Lodge 20
Laguna Vista Villas 20
Lapa Rios 17
Las Islas Lodge 11
Luna Lodge 20

RESTAURANTS

Bar y Restaurante
   Carolina 6
Buena Esperanza 16
Il Giardino 1
Marisqueria
   Corcovado 2
Pizza Mail.it 5

NIGHTLIFE

Buena Esperanza 16
Joseth 7

SHOPPING

Jagua Arts & Craft
   Store 10

including a host of activities outside the park. If the in-town accommodations are too basic, you'll find several far more luxurious places farther south on the Osa Peninsula.

Cabo Matapalo (the southern tip of the peninsula) is a prime surf spot, home to several dependable right point breaks. Sometimes the waves at Pan Dulce and Backwash actually connect, and can provide rides almost as long as those to be had in the more famous Pavones (see "Playa Pavones: A Surfer's Mecca," p 525).

Essentials

GETTING THERE & DEPARTING   By Plane: Both **Nature Air** (www.natureair.com; ✆ **800/235-9272** in the U.S. and Canada, or 2299-6000 in Costa Rica) and **Sansa** (www.flysansa.com; ✆ **877/767-2672** in the U.S. and Canada, or 2290-4100 in Costa Rica) have daily direct flights to Puerto Jiménez from San José. The flight duration is around 55 minutes, although this flight often includes brief stops in Golfito or Drake Bay. Fares range from $84 to $144, one-way. Because of the remoteness of this area and the unpredictable flux of traffic, both Sansa and Nature Air sometimes improvise on scheduling, so it's always best to confirm.

Taxis are generally waiting to meet all incoming flights. A ride into downtown Puerto Jiménez should cost around C2,000. If you're staying at a hotel outside of town, it's best to have the hotel arrange for a taxi to meet you. Otherwise you can hire one at the airstrip. Depending on how far away you are staying, it could cost up to $80 for a four-wheel-drive vehicle to Carate or Los Patos, or $125 to Drake.

By Car: Take the San José–Caldera Highway (CR27) to the first exit past the fourth toll booth and follow the signs to Jacó, where you will pick up the Southern Highway, or Costanera Sur (CR34). Take this south through Jacó, Quepos, Dominical, and Uvita, and turn right onto the Inter-American Highway (CR2) at Palmar Norte. Head south to the junction at Chacarita, turn right and follow signs to Puerto Jiménez and Corcovado.

Bird-watching in Corcovado National Park

By Bus: Transportes Blanco-Lobo express buses (© **2257-4121** in San José, or 2771-4744 in Puerto Jiménez) leave San José daily at 8am and noon from Calle 12, between avenidas 7 and 9. The trip takes 7 to 8 hours; the fare is C7,500. Buses depart Puerto Jiménez for San José daily at 5am and 9am.

By Boat: A passenger ferry that seats about 20 makes several runs a day between Golfito and Puerto Jiménez. The fare is C3,000, and the ride takes a half-hour. The ferry operates between the *muellecito* (little dock) in Golfito and the *muelle* (public dock) in Puerto Jiménez. You can also charter a boat taxi between the two places.

VISITOR INFORMATION Puerto Jiménez is an interesting town on the southeast coast of the Osa Peninsula where raucous scarlet macaws are so numerous they're practically pests. The public pier is over a bridge past the north end of the soccer field, and the bus stop is a block west of the center of town. You'll find a couple of Internet cafes in town; the best is **CafeNet El Sol** (www.soldeosa.com; © **8632-8150**), which is a great place to book tours and get information, and is also a Wi-Fi hot spot.

FAST FACTS Four-wheel-drive taxis are plentiful in Puerto Jiménez. You'll find them cruising or parked along the main street of town, or have your hotel call one. You can rent a car here from **Solid Car Rental** (www.solidcarrental.com; 🕾 **800/390-7065** in U.S. and Canada, or 2442-6000 in Costa Rica), or from **Alamo** (www.alamocostarica.com; 🕾 **2735-5175** in Costa Rica).

Exploring Puerto Jiménez

While Puerto Jiménez has typically been a staging ground for adventures farther out toward Carate and Corcovado, quite a few activities and tours can be undertaken closer to town.

If you're looking to spend some time on the beach, head south of town on the airstrip road for a long, pretty stretch of sand called **Playa Platanares.** Here there are a couple of nice hotels, the **Iguana Lodge** and the **Agua Dulce Lodge.** Swimmers beware: The surf can be very powerful. If you head farther south on the peninsula, you'll come to the beaches of **Pan Dulce, Backwash,** and **Matapalo,** all major surf spots with consistently well-formed right point breaks and wave size depending on the swells coming in from the South Pacific. Backwash has a spectacular long wave for intermediate and advanced surfers and an internal wave that is optimal for learners. **Pollo Surf School** (http://pollosurf school.com) offers year-round surf lessons ($55).

Osa Aventura (www.osaaventura.com; 🕾 **2735-5758** or 8372-6135) is a local tour company that offers a host of guided tours and wildlife-watching expeditions around the Osa Peninsula and into Corcovado National Park. Rates run between $80 and $300 per person, depending upon group size and the tour.

Osa Corcovado Tour and Travel (www.soldeosa.com); 🕾 **8632-8150**) also arranges Corcovado tours, guides, transportation, lodging, and—if you're looking for your own slice of paradise—real estate, through its affiliate Osa Pen Realty.

SOME EXTREME ADVENTURE If you want to get your adrenaline flowing, check in with **Everyday Adventures,** also known as **Psycho Tours** ★★★ (www.psychotours.com; 🕾 **8353-8619**). Andy Pruter and his guides specialize in two adventure tours in Matapalo, waterfall rappelling and tree climbing. The latter features a free climb (with safety rope) up a 60m (200-ft.) strangler fig, where you reach a natural platform at around 18m (60 ft.), ring a cowbell, and then take a deep breath for the Tarzan swing, belayed down by your guide. This is accompanied by an informative hike through primary rainforest and can be paired with a couple of rappels down jungle waterfalls, the highest of which is around 30m (100 ft.)—and is scary good fun. You can do either one of the above adventures separately, but I recommend the 5- to 6-hour combo tour, which costs $130.

OSA WILDLIFE SANCTUARY Reachable only by boat, the **Osa Wildlife Sanctuary** ★★★ (www.osawildlife.org; ✆ **8348-0499**) is a delightful animal rescue center on the shore of the northern Golfo Dulce, completely surrounded by Piedras Blancas National Park. Here you can see an ocelot, kinkajous, sloths, tayra, peccary, scarlet macaws, a porcupine, and capuchin and squirrel monkeys, most of them rescued from the pet trade or from crippling accidents. Daily tours are offered by volunteers or founder Carol Patrick, who is as charming as her wards. A donation of $25 per person is requested for the tour. To arrange transportation by boat, check with your hotel, any tour office, or captains on the public pier.

CHOCOLATE TOUR **Finca Kobo** ★ (www.fincakobo.com; ✆ **8398-7604**), near La Palma, 17km (11 miles) northwest of Puerto Jiménez, offers an informative tour of this organic cacao plantation. You'll see all the stages involved in growing cacao and transforming these precious beans (used as currency by pre-Columbian cultures) into chocolate. At the end of the tour, you'll get to sample some of the handiwork, dipping local fruit into fresh chocolate fondue. The tour costs $32; children 8 and under are half-price. Finca Kobo also has a few rooms and bungalows for rent.

KAYAKING Kayaking trips around the estuary, up into the mangroves, and out into the gulf are very popular. **Aventuras Tropicales**

A kayak tour near Puerto Jiménez

Cycling on the beach in Puerto Jiménez

(www.aventurastropicales.com; © **2735-5195**) offers daily paddles through the mangroves, as well as sunset trips where you can sometimes see dolphins. More adventurous multiday kayak and camping trips are also available, in price and comfort ranges from budget to luxury (staying at various lodges around the Golfo Dulce). You can also book with **Osa Tourz** (www.osatourz.com; © **8632-8150**).

SPORTFISHING   If you'd like to do some inshore (inside the gulf) or off-shore (deep-sea) fishing, look up **Crocodile Bay Resort** (www.crocodile bay.com; © **800/733-1115** in the U.S. and Canada, or 2735-5631 in Costa Rica). This upscale fishing lodge, one of the largest fishing outfit-ters in Central America, is close to the Puerto Jiménez airstrip. The own-ers have added a 28-room hotel and have plans to build a full service marina and a controversial Curio Collection by Hilton hotel and condo-minium project, starting in 2018. Three-day fishing packages start at $1,985 per person based on double occupancy.

Another top outfitter is **Las Islas Lodge** (www.lasislaslodge.com; © **2735-5510**), 1km west of downtown Puerto Jiménez, which offers half- and full-day inshore and offshore fishing trips for $1,200 to $1,600 for up to six anglers, or surf fishing (from the shore) for $135 to $185 per person with two to four people.

SURF & SUP   Pollo's Surf School ★ (www.pollosurfschool.com; © **8366-6559**) is located near some excellent learning waves on Pan Dulce Beach. Pollo's is also the place to try stand-up paddling (SUP). A 2-hour surfing lesson costs $55.

Exploring Corcovado National Park ★★★

Exploring Corcovado National Park is not something to be undertaken lightly, but neither is it the challenge that some people make it out to be. The weather is the biggest obstacle to overnight backpacking trips through the park. The heat and humidity are often extreme, and frequent rainstorms can make trails fairly muddy. Within a couple of hours of Puerto Jiménez (by 4WD vehicle) are two entrances to the park, at La Leona and Los Patos; however, the park has no roads, so before you reach the entrances, you'll have to start hiking. All Corcovado visitors must be accompanied by licensed, professional guides.

The park is amazingly rich in biodiversity. It is one of the only places in Costa Rica that is home to all four of the country's monkey species—howler, white-faced, squirrel, and spider. Its large size makes it an ideal habitat for wild cats, including the endangered jaguar, as well as other large mammals, like the Baird's tapir. Apart from the jaguar, other cat species found here include the ocelot, margay, jaguarundi, and puma.

Monkeys in Osa Wildlife Sanctuary

Nearly 400 species of birds have been recorded inside the park. Scarlet macaws are commonly sighted here. Other common bird species include antbirds, manakins, toucans, tanagers, hummingbirds, and puffbirds. Once thought extinct in Costa Rica, the harpy eagle has been spotted here as well in recent years. Most rivers in Corcovado are home to crocodiles and at high tide are frequented by bull sharks. For this reason, river crossings must be coordinated with low tide. Your guide will know the ropes.

Because of its size and remoteness, Corcovado National Park is best explored over 2 to 3 days; no more than 5 days are permitted at one time. Still, it is possible to enter and hike the park on a day trip. The best way to do this is to book a tour with your lodge on the Osa Peninsula, from a tour company in Puerto Jiménez, or through a lodge in Drake Bay (see "Where to Stay & Eat," p 492).

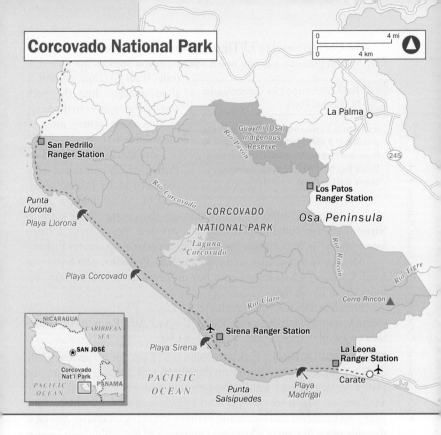

Corcovado National Park

GETTING THERE & ENTRY POINTS   The park has four primary ranger stations, two of which serve as entry and exit points for multiday expeditions. You can drive all the way to Los Patos Ranger Station, but La Leona is still a 3km hike past the end of the road. Perhaps the easiest way to reach the **La Leona Ranger Station** from Puerto Jiménez is a 3km (1.75-mile) hike, which should take about 20-minutes, from Carate, which is accessible by car, taxi, or the twice-daily *colectivo* truck. A new visitor center is under construction there.

To travel there by "public transportation" from Puerto Jiménez, pick up one of the collective buses (actually, a 4WD pickup truck with a tarpaulin cover and slat seats in the back) that leave Puerto Jiménez for Carate daily at 6am and 1:30pm, returning at 8am and 4pm. The one-way fare is about $10. A small fleet of these trucks leaves one block south of the bus terminal, and will stop to pick up anyone who flags them down along the way. Your other option is to hire a taxi, which will charge about $80 to or from Carate.

En route to Carate, you will pass several campgrounds and small lodges. If you are unable to get a spot at one of the campsites in the park, you can stay at one of these and hike the park during the day.

You can also travel to **El Tigre,** about 14km (8¾ miles) by dirt road from Puerto Jiménez, site of a newly opened ranger station. But note that trails from El Tigre go only a short distance into the park and do not connect to the heart of Corcovado, where most of the wildlife is.

Trail Distances in Corcovado National Park

It's 14km (8.7 miles) from La Leona to Sirena, and 3km (1.9 miles) farther from Carate. From San Pedrillo, it's 20km (13 miles) to Drake Bay. It's 19km (12 miles) between Sirena and Los Patos.

Another entrance is in **Los Patos,** which is reached from the town of La Palma, northwest of Puerto Jiménez. From here, a 19km (12-mile) trail runs through the center of the park to **Sirena,** a ranger station and research facility (see "Beach Treks & Rainforest Hikes," p 505). Sirena has a landing strip used by charter flights.

The northern entrance to the park is **San Pedrillo,** which you can reach by taking a boat from Drake Bay or Sierpe (p 487). It's 14km (8¼ miles) from Drake Bay.

For an aerial view you can charter a plane in Puerto Jiménez to take you to Carate ($180) or Sirena ($360). Contact **Alfa Romeo Air Charters** (www.alfaromeoair.com; ☏ 8632-8150).

FEES & REGULATIONS   Park admission is $15 per person per day. Only the Sirena station is equipped with dormitory-style lodgings and camping platforms (see below) with bathrooms and showers and cafeteria-style meal service. Meals are costly ($20–$25), so you might consider packing your own breakfast and lunch and perhaps splurging on dinner. Sirena is the only place in Corcovado where camping and overnight dorm lodging is allowed. All must be reserved in advance by contacting the **ACOSA** (Area de Conservacion de Osa) in Puerto Jiménez (☏ 2735-5036; pncorcovado@gmail.com). However, its offices, adjacent to the airstrip, are notoriously poor at answering e-mails and attending to reservations. Only a limited number of people are allowed to camp or to enter on day trips and all must be accompanied by a certified guide, so make your reservations well in advance. Your best bet is to go with a lodge or to contact full-service outfitters **Osa Corcovado Tour & Travel** (www.corcovado guide.com; ☏ 8632-8150) or **Osa Aventura** (www.osaaventura.com; ☏ 2735-5758 or 8372-6135).

Important Corcovado Tips

If you plan to hike the beach trail from La Leona, pick up a tide table at the park headquarters office in Puerto Jiménez, or check with your guide. At high tide, the trails and river crossings can be dangerous or impassable.

If you plan to spend a night or more in the park, you'll want to stock up on food, water, and other essentials in Puerto Jiménez, or else pre-arrange food service at Sirena for $20 to $25 per meal.

BEACH TREKS & RAINFOREST HIKES   Corcovado has some of the best hiking trails in the world, with animals so acclimated to humans that they barely glance at you, much less run away (most aren't a threat to humans, but keep your distance from the peccaries). The most popular trail starts at La Leona, near Carate, and leads to Sirena. Between any two ranger stations, the hiking is arduous and takes all or most of a day. In 2006, the environment minister of Costa Rica was lost in Corcovado for three days after a mother tapir attacked him. Today, nobody is allowed into the park without a licensed guide, and for good reason. This is a wild place without neat trails or clear signage. At times you have to cross rivers inhabited by crocodiles, with bull sharks drifting in at high tide looking for dinner.

The **Sirena** ranger station is a fascinating destination. As a research facility, it attracts scientists studying the rainforest, but most visitors are hardcore ecotourists and backpackers, who can be a surprisingly cheerless lot. If you're looking for a big party, you've come to the wrong place. But for a wild, buggy, snaky, hot, wet adventure, Corcovado is unsurpassable.

WHERE TO STAY & EAT IN THE PARK   Reservations are essential at the various ranger stations if you plan to eat or sleep inside the park (p 492). **Sirena** has dorm-style accommodations for 28 people, as well as a campground, cafeteria and landing strip for charter flights. Camping inside Corcovado is currently available only at **Sirena.** Every ranger station has potable water, but it's advisable to pack in your own. You should never drink from a river. Campsites in the park are $5 per person per night. A dorm bed at the Sirena station runs $12, but you must bring your own sheets, and a mosquito net is also a good idea. Meals here are $20 for breakfast and $25 for lunch and dinner. Everything must be reserved in advance.

Where to Stay in Puerto Jiménez
EXPENSIVE
Crocodile Bay Resort ★   This high-end sportfishing resort features a fleet of top-notch boats, quality gear, and excellent captains. Set on a large piece of land on the outskirts of town, this sprawling resort has its own 750-foot pier jutting out into the Golfo Dulce. Rooms are fishy fun, too, with carved wooden marlin, tuna, and wahoo adorning doors and cabinets. Food is good, service is attentive, and in addition to fishing, a wide range of adventure tours is also offered. There's also a well-equipped spa. Rooms are air-conditioned but a bit dated, with glass doors that tend to rattle when neighbors walk around. This place gets bustling early as anglers head out, so it's not a great place to sleep in, but there's a convivial scene in the bar later on as they return to swap tales. Crocodile Bay is

building a state-of-the-art marina (over the opposition of many locals) and a brand-new Curio Collection by Hilton hotel set to open in 2018. Puerto Jiménez. www.crocodilebay.com. ℭ **800/733-1115** in the U.S. and Canada, or 2559-7990 in Costa Rica. 40 units. $299 per person based on double occupancy, includes all meals and non-alcoholic beverages. A wide range of fishing and adventure tour packages is available. **Amenities:** Restaurant; bar; pool; large modern spa; watersports equipment rental; free Wi-Fi.

Iguana Lodge ★★   Located on the outskirts of Puerto Jiménez, this beachfront mini-resort has rooms in a wide range of prices. The second-floor units of the two-story casitas are best, although the "club rooms" are less expensive. All feature wood floors, bamboo and wicker furnishings, and a hammock. With a massive second-story open-air, wood-floor studio, yoga is a big attraction here, and there are often classes, or a visiting group conducting a retreat. The gardens are sumptuous, with a pool and plenty of open-air covered areas to chill, plus Playa Platanares is just steps away.

Playa Platanares. www.iguanalodge.com. ℭ **800/259-9123** in the U.S. and Canada, or 8848-0752 in Costa Rica. 19 units. $188 club room; $229 per person casita; $679 3-bedroom beach house. Club rooms include breakfast. Casitas include breakfast and dinner; villas do not include any meals. All rates include taxes. **Amenities:** 2 restaurants; bar; hot tub; pool; spa; watersports equipment rental; free Wi-Fi.

MODERATE

Agua Dulce Beach Resort ★   About 3km (almost 2 miles) south of the Puerto Jiménez airstrip, you'll find this pretty hotel, just across a sandy track from a beautiful beach (Playa Preciosa, also known as Platanares) with some powerful surf. Unless you're Michael Phelps, you might enjoy swimming in the cool blue pool here more than braving the pounding waves. These are classy accommodations with a big restaurant and an upstairs bar with a great view.

Playa Preciosa. www.aguadulceresort.com. ℭ **8310-6304.** 40 units. $74–$139 per night, includes breakfast. **Amenities:** Restaurant; bar; pool; free Wi-Fi.

Las Islas Lodge ★   About 1km west of town, this Costa Rican–owned fishing lodge provides excellent accommodations and a first-class fishing experience. Owner and fishing captain Oscar Villalobos and his wife, María Fernanda, oversee the bilingual, expert service, whether you're lazing in a hammock at the hotel or fighting a sailfish in blue water.

Puerto Jiménez. www.lasislaslodge.com. ℭ **2735-5510.** 10 units. $69–$99 per night, includes breakfast in high season. **Amenities:** Pool; laundry service; free Wi-Fi.

INEXPENSIVE

In addition to the places listed below, **Cabinas Marcelina** (www.cabinas marcelina.com; ℭ **2735-5007**) is a clean, dependable budget option right in the heart of town. **Agua Luna** (ℭ **2735-5204**) is conveniently located, with rooms right at the foot of the town's public pier and close to a mangrove forest.

Cabinas Jiménez ★ On the waterfront 2 blocks from town, this hotel offers 15 air-conditioned rooms with fridges and a deck with hammocks. Some cabins have kitchens and private decks overlooking the water, and there's a private waterfront 2-bedroom, 2-bath house with kitchen and deck. Rooms and common areas are enlivened by hand-painted murals, carved animal sculptures, and complex ironworks on the windows. The large, wood-and-bamboo rancho located just off the small kidney-shaped pool has a commanding view of the Puerto Jiménez harbor. The hotel offers guests free use of kayaks and bicycles. The owner offers excellent boat tours of the Golfo Dulce and the nearby mangroves.

Puerto Jiménez, 50m (165 ft.) north of the soccer field. www.cabinasjimenez.com. ✆ **2735-5090.** 18 units. $60-$120 double. **Amenities:** Pool; free Wi-Fi.

La Chosa del Manglar ★ With 4-acres of gardens and trees beside the mangroves, this hotel offers up rich wildlife viewing right on-site. The communal kitchen and lounge are popular gathering places, and there's a Ping-Pong table. The rooms come in a wide range of shapes and sizes, and are clean if somewhat bare-bones (colorful hand-painted details adorn the walls, and there's wooden furniture in some, giving them a bit more personality). The town and waterfront are each about 3 or 4 blocks away, in opposite directions. All rooms have hot water, a/c, and private baths.

125m (410 ft.) west of the airstrip, Puerto Jiménez. www.lachosa.com. ✆ **2735-5002.** 18 units. $29-$89 double; $229 for a 4-bedroom house for 8. **Amenities:** Free Wi-Fi.

Where to Stay & Eat Around the Osa Peninsula

As with most of the lodges in Drake Bay, the accommodations listed in this section include three meals a day in their rates and do a large share of their bookings in package trips. Per-night rates are listed, but the price categories have been adjusted to take into account the fact that all meals are included. Ask about package rates if you plan to take several tours and stay awhile: They could save you money.

In addition to the lodges listed below, options range from small B&Bs to fully equipped home rentals. Surfers, in particular, might want to inquire into one of several rental houses located close to the beach at Matapalo.

You can look into **Finca Exótica Eco-Lodge** ★ (www.fincaexotica.com; ✆ **4070-0054**), a delightful oceanview lodge, and **La Leona Eco-Lodge** ★ (www.laleonaecolodge.com; ✆ **2735-5705**), a rustic lodge and tent-camp option on the outskirts of the park.

This is a very isolated area, with just one gravel road connecting all the lodges, nature reserves, and parks. Almost all visitors here take all their meals at their lodge. If you want to venture away for some good simple home cooking, head to Martina Hoffman's **Buena Esperanza,** on the main road at Carbonera, near Matapalo.

The listings below are some of the best ecolodges Costa Rica has to offer, and most are pretty pricey. Bear in mind that the rooms have no TVs, telephones, or air-conditioning, the roads are not paved, and there are no towns to speak of. Consequently, there are also no crowds and few modern distractions. The lodges listed below are 40 minutes to 2 hours outside Puerto Jimenez, along a rough dirt road, with several river crossings.

EXPENSIVE

Blue Osa Yoga Retreat & Spa ★   What better place to practice yoga or attain your teacher training than steps from the beach in the middle of the rainforest? The solar powered Blue Osa is a new age paradise where farm to table, mostly plant-based meals are served at communal tables and the eco-spa comes with a Zen garden. The cozy yet simple rooms, offered shared or private, come with wood floors and colorful bedspreads. The hotel offers specialized, weeklong yoga retreats throughout the year.
Playa Sombrero. www.blueosa.com. ✆ **844/628-4982** in the U.S. and Canada, 12 units. $298 double, includes all meals, yoga, and transportation from Puerto Jimenez. **Amenities:** Restaurant; bar; spa; pool; free Wi-Fi.

Bosque del Cabo Rainforest Lodge ★★★   Among the most spectacular of the Matapalo ecolodges, Bosque del Cabo is perched some 152m (500 ft.) above the water on more than 303 hectares (750 acres), with neatly manicured grounds, multiple nature trails, a cool hanging bridge, and access to both the Pacific Ocean and the Golfo Dulce. Thirteen elegant bungalows and three fully equipped houses have great ocean views, and others are surrounded by tropical gardens. All are classily done up in hardwoods, cane, and tile, and some of the bungalows have thatched roofs. There are two nice pools (one is an adult quiet pool) and many miles of wildlife trails, but also a thrillingly high zipline and tree platform set in a Manu tree, a tree-climbing tour inside a hollowed-out tree, waterfall-rappelling courses, massage and reflexology treatments, and more. Owners Phil and Kim Spier are often on hand to make sure things run smoothly; it's thanks to their efforts that the resort has earned "5 Leaves" multiple times in the CST Certification for Sustainable Tourism evaluation.
Matapalo, Osa Peninsula. www.bosquedelcabo.com. ✆ **2735-5206** or 8389-2846. 18 units. $200–$295 per person cabins, includes all meals and taxes. $595 per day houses. Round-trip transportation from Puerto Jiménez airport, $30 per person. **Amenities:** Restaurant; bar; 2 pools; surfboard rental; onsite guide; free Wi-Fi.

El Remanso ★★   This magnificent collection of rooms, private cabins, and duplexes is just past Cabo Matapalo, 22km (14 miles) from Puerto Jiménez. It features a large main lodge and bamboo restaurant structure with a Pacific Ocean view, surrounded by towering rainforest trees. Rooms are spread around the sprawling gardens and grounds, and a few have ocean views. The lodge offers a variety of internal tours, including guided walks, waterfall rappelling, and a canopy tour with five cables and four platforms, plus a new 300-foot suspension bridge. El Remanso uses only renewable energy, and has earned "5 Leaves" in the CST Certification for Sustainable Tourism program.

Matapalo, Osa Peninsula. www.elremanso.com. ℂ **2735-5569** or 8814-5775. 14 units. $180–$270 per person, includes all 3 meals and taxes. **Amenities:** Restaurant; bar; pool; free Wi-Fi.

Laguna Vista Villas ★★ This "Rainforest Beach Lagoon" has a dazzling infinity pool surrounded by rich green rainforest on a peninsula overlooking a freshwater lagoon and Playa Carate, the southern gateway to Corcovado National Park. Managed by the attentive and trilingual Martine Racette of Ottawa, this sustainable property has eight villas, two of which are honeymoon suites with their own private pools. All rooms have king-size beds, fans, and large bathrooms with hot showers.

Carate, Osa Peninsula. www.lagunavistavillas.com. ℂ **+39 333-632-2113** in Europe (best to book online). 8 villas. $195 per person, double occupancy, includes all meals and taxes. **Amenities:** Pool; restaurant; kayaks; free Wi-Fi.

Lapa Ríos ★★★ Luxury in the jungle doesn't get much better than this. Built by owners John and Karen Lewis and now managed by the Cayuga chain of ecolodges, this trailblazing hotel was one of the first to put ecotourism on the Osa Peninsula map. Rooms are spacious, private, and oriented toward the ocean, with high-peaked thatched roofs and

A bungalow at Lapa Ríos

open screen walls (no glass). A small tropical garden and large deck, complete with outdoor shower and hammock, more than double the living space. (There's also an indoor shower open to the elements except for a screen, with vegetation for privacy.) Rooms are housed in a series of units stretching in a line down the spine of a mountain ridge. If you get one of the lower units, be prepared for a bit of a hike to and from the main lodge, restaurant, and pool area. As is common in the area, the main lodge and restaurant feature a high thatched roof overhead. There's a large spiral staircase leading up to a great lookout, and even if you can't afford to stay here, it's a great place to stop for a cocktail. Lapa Ríos sits on a 400-hectare (988-acre) private rainforest reserve, with a well-maintained trail system and an abundance of flora and fauna. Activities included with lodging include birding tours, jungle and waterfall hikes, night walks, and tours of a local school. Note that there's Wi-Fi here only in one common area.

Matapalo, Osa Peninsula. www.laparios.com. ✆ **2735-5130.** 17 bungalows. $360–$480 per person based on double occupancy, includes all meals, unlimited tours and onsite activities, and round-trip transportation from Puerto Jiménez. Discounts for kids aged 6 and 11; no children under 6. **Amenities:** Restaurant; bar; pool; spa; free Wi-Fi.

MODERATE

Luna Lodge ★ Among the most remote ecolodges reachable by road in the Osa, Luna Lodge is located up a rugged dirt track in dense rainforest above the tiny village of Carate, where the road ends 3km before Corcovado National Park begins. The nicest accommodations here are large bungalows with conical thatched roofs, four-poster beds with mosquito netting, and showers open to the outdoors surrounded by head-high rock walls (and no doors on the bathrooms). One of these bungalows and its bathroom is completely wheelchair-accessible. Lower in price are the newer hacienda–style rooms adjacent to the main lodge, while surprisingly comfortable platform tents, with bathrooms inside, are more economical. The hydro-electric-powered Luna Lodge is spread over a steep hillside, so

Bungalows at Luna Lodge

you'll get some exercise climbing the stone steps to the upper units. If you tend to run warm, be advised that not only is there no air-conditioning, there are no fans, although there are plans to install the latter. Yoga with a view is offered each morning on a large outdoor platform, there are three nice waterfalls on the property, and the birding is world-class. If headed here with a group, consider chartering a flight into the Carate airstrip with Aero Caribe, or prepare for a long drive.

Carate, Osa Peninsula. www.lunalodge.com. © **888/760-0760** in the U.S. and Canada, or 4070-0010 in Costa Rica. 17 units. $133 for a tent; $170 for a hacienda room; $216 for a private bungalow. Rates are double occupancy, and include all meals and taxes. A range of package tours, spa treatments, and yoga classes are available, as well as round-trip transportation from Puerto Jiménez for a fee, or free transport from the Carate airstrip. **Amenities:** Restaurant; bar; massage; pool; yoga; free Wi-Fi from 2–6pm.

Where to Eat in Puerto Jiménez

In addition to the places listed below, you might head to the waterfront **Marisquería Corcovado** (© **2735-5659**), a lively local joint serving up excellent seafood and local specialties. They'll even cook up your fresh catch for you if you've been fishing.

Bar y Restaurante Carolina ★ COSTA RICAN   This simple Costa Rican diner is the social and tourist hub of Puerto Jiménez. Bright rainforest scenes are painted on the interior walls, while the open-air front opens to the city's main street. You can get filling *casados,* fresh grilled fish, a hamburger, BLT, spaghetti, or a number of local dishes here.

On the main street. © **2735-5185.** Main courses C3,300–C8,600. Daily 6am–10pm.

Il Giardino ★★ ITALIAN/INTERNATIONAL/SEAFOOD   This is the best fine-dining experience available in Puerto Jimenez, although this place is far from fancy. (Think: lots of open-air seating, from tables under shade umbrellas to the open-air interior dining room.) The pastas and ravioli are all homemade and delicious, and the seafood is freshly caught and perfectly prepared. It's an odd combination, but these folks also frequently do sushi nights, and are even open for breakfast. Everything is made fresh to order, so the kitchen can be a bit slow at times.

On the beachfront, just down from the public pier, Puerto Jiménez. www.ilgiardino italianrestaurant.com. © **2735-5129.** Main courses C4,200–C14,000. Daily 7am–10pm.

Pizza Mail.it ★ ITALIAN   Nadia Zollia of Trieste, Italy, opened this great restaurant with the strange name in 2008, and it soon became the most popular pizza in town. It serves roughly 20 types of pizza, the most popular being the Pizza Tica, with ground beef among several other ingredients. Pasta bolognese is a great choice among the heaping plates of pasta. As for the name Pizza Mail.it, there's a myth that it comes from the fact that the post office is next door. It actually comes from Zollia's original intention of opening a small takeout place, with ".it" being the Italian suffix for e-mail addresses.

Across from the soccer field in Puerto Jiménez. ✆ **2735-5483.** Main courses C3,500–C9,000. Daily 3:30–10:30pm in high season.

Shopping

Jagua Arts & Craft Store ★★★ (✆ **2735-5267**) stocks excellent local and regional art and craft works, including fine jewelry and blown glass. *Tip:* Many folks head to this store while waiting for their departing flight out of Puerto Jiménez, because it's near the airstrip. Be sure to give yourself enough time to explore the collection here. Jagua also has a nice open-air lounge with locally made ice cream for sale and free coffee. It's a great place to wait for a flight or a transfer to your remote lodge.

Entertainment & Nightlife

The waterfront **Agua Luna** bar (which is close to but separated from the Agua Luna Hotel) can be a lively scene at night, with a dance floor, pool table and karaoke. And there are no fewer than three bars in one block on the main street in the heart of town; the most inviting of these is **Joseth,** also spelled Josseth, where you can get your karaoke on.

If you're staying in the Matapalo area farther out on the Osa and want to hang with locals, head to **Buena Esperanza.** This place can get pretty lively on a Friday or Saturday night. It's the only game in town, but it's got good game.

GOLFITO: GATEWAY TO THE GOLFO DULCE

87km (54 miles) S of Palmar Norte; 337km (209 miles) S of San José

Despite being the largest and most important city in Costa Rica's Southern Zone, Golfito itself is not a popular tourist destination. In its prime, this was a major banana port, but following years of rising taxes, falling prices, and labor disputes, United Fruit pulled out in 1985. Things may change in the future, as rumors perennially abound about the construction of an international airport, major marina, or big tuna farm. For the moment, none of these megaprojects has gotten off the drawing board. Golfito is home to a unique sort of megamall (the "Depósito Libre") where goods can be bought at greatly reduced duties, making it one of the cheapest places in Costa Rica to buy TVs, refrigerators, tires, or just about anything else.

Golfito is a major sportfishing center and a popular gateway to a slew of nature lodges spread along the quiet waters, isolated bays, and lush rainforests of the Golfo Dulce. In 1998, much of the rainforest bordering the Golfo Dulce was officially declared the **Piedras Blancas National Park ★★**, which includes 12,000 hectares (29,640 acres) of primary forests, as well as protected secondary forests and pasturelands.

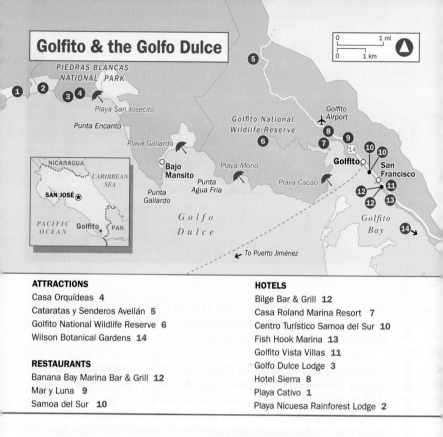

Golfito & the Golfo Dulce

PIEDRAS BLANCAS
NATIONAL PARK

Playa San Josecito

Punta Encanto

Playa Gallardo

Bajo
Mansito

Punta
Agua Fria

Punta
Gallardo

Playa Mono

Golfo
Dulce

NICARAGUA

CARIBBEAN
SEA

SAN JOSÉ

PACIFIC
OCEAN   Golfito   PAN.

Golfito National
Wildlife Reserve

Golfito
Airport

Golfito

San
Francisco

Playa Cacao

Golfito
Bay

To Puerto Jiménez

0   1 mi
0   1 km

ATTRACTIONS
Casa Orquídeas 4
Cataratas y Senderos Avellán 5
Golfito National Wildlife Reserve 6
Wilson Botanical Gardens 14

RESTAURANTS
Banana Bay Marina Bar & Grill 12
Mar y Luna 9
Samoa del Sur 10

HOTELS
Bilge Bar & Grill 12
Casa Roland Marina Resort 7
Centro Turístico Samoa del Sur 10
Fish Hook Marina 13
Golfito Vista Villas 11
Golfo Dulce Lodge 3
Hotel Sierra 8
Playa Cativo 1
Playa Nicuesa Rainforest Lodge 2

Golfito is located on the eastern side of the Golfo Dulce, at the foot of lush green mountains. The setting alone gives it the potential to be one of the most attractive cities in the country. However, the areas around the municipal park and public dock are somewhat seedy, and the downtown is run-down and overpopulated with bars. Still, if you go a bit farther along the bay, you come to the old United Fruit Company housing. Here you'll find well-maintained wooden houses painted bright colors and surrounded by neatly manicured gardens. Toucans are commonly sighted. It's all very lush and green and clean—an altogether different picture from that painted by most port towns in this country. When a duty-free zone was opened here, these old homes experienced a minor renaissance and several were converted into small hotels. Ticos come here in droves on weekends to take advantage of cheap prices on name-brand goods and clothing at the duty-free zone; sometimes all these shoppers make finding a room difficult.

Essentials

GETTING THERE & DEPARTING   By Plane: Both **Nature Air** (www.natureair.com; ℂ **800/235-9272** in the U.S. and Canada, or 2299-6000 in Costa Rica) and **Sansa** (www.flysansa.com; ℂ **877/767-2672**

The Golfito shoreline

in the U.S. and Canada, or 2290-4100 in Costa Rica) have a couple of direct flights daily to the Golfito airstrip (airport code: GLF). The trip duration is around 1 hour; the fares run $94 to $149 each way.

By Car: Take the San José–Caldera Highway (CR27) to the first exit past the fourth toll booth, where you will pick up the Southern Highway, or Costanera Sur (CR34). Take this south through Jacó, Quepos, and Dominical to Palmar Norte, where you'll meet up with the Inter-American Highway (CR2). Take this south. When you get to Río Claro, you'll notice a gas station and quite a bit of activity. Turn right here and follow the signs to Golfito. The drive takes about 6 hours.

By Bus: Tracopa buses (www.tracopacr.com; 🕿 **2221-4214** or 2290-1308) leave San José daily for the Southern Zone throughout the day, between 5am and 6:30pm from Calle 9 and avenida 18. Almost all stop in Palmar Norte, but be sure to ask. The ride takes around 6 hours, with fares in the C8,000 range. Buses depart Golfito for San José daily at 5am and 1:30pm from the bus station near the municipal dock. Another option is to catch a bus headed for the Panama border town of Paso Canoas and get off in Río Claro, where you can catch a bus or taxi for Golfito.

By Boat: A passenger ferry that seats about 20 makes several runs a day between Golfito and Puerto Jiménez. The fare is C3,000, and the ride takes a half-hour. The ferry operates between the *muellecito* (little dock) in Golfito and the *muelle* (public dock) in Puerto Jiménez. You can also charter a boat taxi between the two places.

GETTING AROUND Taxis are plentiful in Golfito, and are constantly cruising the main road from the outskirts of town to the duty-free port, often at alarming speeds. A taxi ride anywhere in town should cost under C1,000. Local buses also ply this loop. The fare for the bus is about C400.

If you drive down here and head out to one of the remote lodges on the gulf, you can leave your car at Samoa del Sur (see "Where to Stay," p 517) for around $12 per day.

If you need to rent a car in Golfito, check in with **Solid Car Rental** (www.solidcarrental.com; ✆ **800/390-7065** in U.S. and Canada; 2442-6000 in Costa Rica).

If you can't get to your next destination by boat, bus, commuter airline, or car, **Alfa Romeo Air Charters** (www.alfaromeoair.com; ✆ **8632-8150**) runs charters to most of the nearby destinations, including Carate, Drake Bay, Sirena, and Puerto Jiménez. A five-passenger plane costs around $200 to $450 one-way, depending on your destination.

Exploring Golfito & Surroundings

Golfito is not known for good swimming beaches, but a short boat ride away is the lovely **Playa Puntarenitas,** a sandy spit at the entrance to Golfito Bay (not to be confused with Punta Arenitas on the western side of the Golfo Dulce near Puerto Jiménez). This is a primitive but quaint area with beach shacks that sell beer, seafood, lobster, pork, chicken, and other delicacies, cooked the old-fashioned way on wood-burning stoves. You may feel a bit lost in time, as if you're visiting Costa Rica in the 1970s. Before you ask for the Wi-Fi password, notice there is no electricity. Here you'll find calm waters and soft sand that make for perfect swimming. You can get to Puntarenitas in a taxi boat for C1,000 per person with four people, or you can even take a kayak.

Another option is **Playa Cacao,** where the beach is rocky but the seafood is good at two old-fashioned and charming restaurants on the beach, Lola's and Siete Mares. A taxi boat to Playa Cacao can run C3,500 per person, and it's always good to settle the price in advance.

BOTANICAL GARDENS   About 30 minutes by boat out of Golfito, you'll find **Casa Orquídeas** ★★ (✆ **8829-1247;** Sat–Thurs 8am–4pm), a private botanical garden lovingly built and maintained by Ron and Trudy MacAllister, who settled this remote piece of land in the 1970s. Most hotels in the area offer trips here, including transportation and a 2-hour tour of the gardens. You can also book your own trip out of Golfito with Golfito Monkey Tours (http://golfitomonkey.com; ✆ **8665-5705**). During the tour, you'll sample fresh fruits picked right off the trees. The entrance and guided tour is $10 per person, but it'll cost you between $80 and $100 to hire a boat for the round-trip ride. Regularly scheduled tours are on Thursdays and Sundays at 8:30am (three-person minimum).

If you have a serious interest in botanical gardens or bird-watching, consider an excursion to **Wilson Botanical Gardens** ★★★ at the **Las Cruces Biological Station** (www.threepaths.co.cr; ✆ **2524-0607** in San José or 2773-4004 at the gardens), just outside the town of San Vito, about 65km (40 miles) to the northeast. The gardens are owned and maintained by the Organization for Tropical Studies and include more

Golfito Bay

than 7,000 species of tropical plants from around the world. Among the plants grown here are many endangered species, which make the gardens of interest to botanical researchers. With so many beautiful and unusual flowers amid the manicured grounds, even a neophyte can't help but be astounded. All this luscious flora has attracted at least 360 species of birds. A 4-hour guided walk costs $40; a shorter, 2-hour hike will run you $30. If you'd like to spend the night here, 12 well-appointed rooms are available. Rates include one guided walk, three meals, and taxes, and run $90 per person, based on double occupancy. Reservations are essential if you want to spend the night, and it's usually a good idea to make a reservation for a simple day visit and hike. The gardens are about 6km (3¾ miles) before San Vito. To get here from Golfito, drive out to the Inter-American Highway and continue south toward Panama. In Ciudad Neily, turn north. A taxi from Golfito should cost around $40 to $50 each way.

HIKING   With a trail head located just on the outskirts of town, the **Golfito National Wildlife Reserve ★** (daily 8am–4pm; $10 admission) is the closest place to Golfito for a hike in the area's typical local lowland rainforests. The reserve is home to much of the same wildlife and flora you'll find in more famous national parks in the region. A well-marked trail begins near the ranger station. You can hike it yourself or go as part of an organized tour with Costa Rica Trips (✆ **8665-5705**). Sometimes admission isn't charged, and often the hours aren't enforced.

About a 20-minute drive over a rough dirt road from Golfito will bring you to the **Cataratas y Senderos Avellán** (✆ **8633-4768**; $5). Entry includes a 2-hour guided hike through the forests and a visit to a beautiful forest waterfall, with several refreshing pools perfect for swimming. A taxi should cost around $25 one-way. Horseback riding ($30) is available, camping is allowed, and meals are served by the friendly owners, the Gamba family. For most people, the best way to visit this site is to go as part of an organized trip with Golfito Monkey Tours (© **8665-5705**).

SPORTFISHING The waters off Golfito offer some of the best **sportfishing** in Costa Rica. Most game-fish species can be caught here year-round, including tuna, dorado, blue and black marlin, sailfish, and roosterfish. Nov through May is the peak period for sailfish and blue marlin. If you'd like to try hooking a big one, contact **Banana Bay Marina** (www.bananabaymarinagolfito.com; © **2775-0255**) or **Fish Hook Marina** (www.fish-hook-marina.com; © **2775-1624**). Both operations boast a full-service marina, waterside rooms for guests, and a fleet of sportfishing boats and captains. A full-day trip costs between $1,000 and $1,800. You can also try the **Zancudo Lodge** (www.the zancudolodge.com; © **800/854-8791** U.S./Canada, or 2776-0008 in Costa Rica), based out of the Zancudo Lodge (p 523) in nearby Playa Zancudo. The lodge can arrange pickup in Golfito.

ZIPLINING ★ High above Golfito in the rainforest reserve is a thrilling canopy zipline tour run by the adventure pioneers of this area, Bosque Mar (© **8846-6673**), who have built 13 platforms with 3,000m of descent and a 75m waterfall along the way. Cost is $75 per person with free transportation from your hotel. Contact Osa Tropical (www.osa-tropical. com; © **2735-5062**) for more information.

Where to Stay

IN GOLFITO

Moderate

Casa Roland Marina Resort ★ This is easily the most modern and luxurious option available in Golfito, although that's not a high bar to clear. The hotel is located in the old United Fruit Company compound near the popular duty-free zone, and not on the water. Rooms are comfortable and attractive, with heavy wooden beds, wicker chairs, and paintings of rural Costa Rican scenes. Best rooms and suites are on the main floor, as those on the lower level have much less natural light. The main restaurant and bar area feature beautiful stained-glass works. A lovely, large, free-form pool is in a recreation area across the street from the main hotel.

Near the duty-free zone, Golfito. www.casarolandgolfito.com. © **888/398-6435** in the U.S. and Canada, or 2775-0180 in Costa Rica. 53 units. $109-$144 double; $169 junior suite; $207 master suite, includes breakfast and taxes. **Amenities:** Restaurant; bar; pool; gym; sauna; billiards; room service; free Wi-Fi.

Hotel Sierra ★ Set right between the airstrip and duty-free zone, and within easy walking distance of each, this large resort-style hotel is one of the more popular options for Tico shoppers coming to Golfito to hunt for bargains. Covered walkways connect a series of two-story, pale-yellow buildings with red zinc roofs. The rooms are spacious and feature clean tile floors and large windows letting in lots of light. All rooms have two queen-size beds, and prices are the same year-round, based on the number of guests per room. The large outdoor pool is ringed with lounge chairs and shade umbrellas. There's also a small children's pool.

Near the duty-free zone, Golfito. www.hotelsierra.com. ℂ **2775-0666.** 72 units. $70 for 1; $90 for 2; $105 for 3; $125 for 4, includes breakfast and taxes. **Amenities:** Restaurant; bar; pool; free Wi-Fi.

Inexpensive

Centro Turístico Samoa del Sur ★   This longstanding waterfront hotel is a good option if you want to be right on the water in Golfito proper. The rooms are comfortable, if a bit worn, with red tile floors, hardwood furniture, and a long shared veranda. The hotel features a popular bar and French restaurant, small marina, pool, and playground, which are open to the public for a fee. There's also a unique seashell museum, with pretty shells from around the world. Samoa del Sur runs one of the more dependable parking lots for travelers with rental cars heading by boat to farther-flung Golfo Dulce nature lodges.

100m (328 ft.) north of the public dock, Golfito. http://samoadelsur.com. ℂ **2775-0233.** 19 units. $96 double, includes breakfast and taxes. **Amenities:** Restaurant; bar; pool; room service; kayak rentals; free Wi-Fi.

Golfito Vista Villas ★★   This small complex of fully furnished apartments on a beautifully landscaped hillside, with a forest reserve in back and Golfito Bay in front, is a great option if you like to have your own kitchen and all the comforts of home. The complex has four fully furnished 1- and 2-bedroom apartments, plus a studio with kitchenette, all with a/c, cable TV, Wi-Fi, telephone, and hot showers. All units have balconies facing the bay, and the gorgeous sunsets are included.

On Golfito's main waterfront road, across from the Banana Bay Marina. www.golfito-costarica.com. ℂ **2775-1614** or 8886-9360. 5 units. $38–$98 double, with discounts for longer stays. No credit cards (PayPal accepted). **Amenities:** Free Wi-Fi.

Where to Eat

Bilge Bar & Grill ★★   INTERNATIONAL/SEAFOOD   Painted a bright yellow, and overlooking the Banana Bay Marina, this simple, open-air joint serves up fresh seafood and typical bar food. The Bilge burger is popular because it's large and well-prepared, but those in the know opt for the fresh mahi-mahi burger, which comes either fried or grilled.

At the Banana Bay Marina, on the waterfront in downtown Golfito. www.bananabaymarinagolfito.com. ℂ **2775-0383.** Main courses C4,000–C13,600. Daily 6am–10pm.

Mar y Luna ★   COSTA RICAN/SEAFOOD   This friendly bayfront restaurant serves up Tico fare, fresh seafood, and a mix of international dishes and bar food. The whole fried fish is the house specialty. The sunsets are lovely, and are made better with fresh ceviche and a cool drink on the main dining deck facing the water, under a plain zinc roof held up by rough-hewn tree trunks. Inside, fishing buoys and mounted stuffed fish are hung on the walls and from the rafters. Some nights there's live music.

Km 3, on the waterfront, by INVU building. www.marylunagolfito.com. ℂ **2775-0192.** Main courses C4,600–C12,800. Daily 7am–10pm.

Entertainment & Nightlife

Golfito is a rough-and-tumble port town, and it pays to be careful here after dark. Most folks stick close to their hotel bar and restaurant. Of these, the bar/restaurants at **Samoa del Sur, Mar y Luna,** and the **Bilge Bar & Grill** ★ are the liveliest. Another popular, if somewhat oddly located, spot is the bar **La Pista** (ℂ **2775-9015**), near the airstrip.

ALONG THE SHORES OF THE GOLFO DULCE

The lodges listed here are on the shores of the Golfo Dulce. This area has no roads, so you must get to the lodges by boat. I recommend that you have firm reservations when visiting this area, so your transportation can be prearranged. If worse comes to worst, you can hire a boat taxi at the *muellecito* (little dock), just beyond the gas station, or La Bomba, in Golfito, for between $50 and $100, depending on your destination. If driving a rental vehicle, arrange for secure parking. See "Park It," p 522.

Playa Cativo Lodge ★★   Reached only by boat, this isolated property that has gone through changes of name and ownership finally seems to be stable. The chic rooms, all with ocean views, feature wrap around windows, reclaimed hardwood floors, and handicrafts from local artisans. The private reserve is intersected with self-guided walking tours past waterfalls, while free to use kayaks and stand up paddleboards allow you to explore the waterfront. The lodge prides itself on its three daily multi-course meals, which are made with produce from the property's own farm and local producers. Tours for an additional fee include kayaking on the Rio Esquinas, night hikes, and whale and dolphin watching.

Golfo Dulce. www.playacativo.com. ℂ **2200-3131.** 8 units. $310-$490 per person, double, includes all meals, transfers, some tours, and taxes. **Amenities:** Restaurant; bar; spa; pool; library; free Wi-Fi.

Playa Nicuesa Rainforest Lodge ★★★   This exquisite lodge is one of the most remote ecolodges in the Southern Zone, accessible only by boat, about a 30-minute ride from Golfito deep inside the Golfo Dulce. The wildlife and nature viewing here is fabulous (it's a good place to find the endemic Golfo Dulce frog), as are the hikes through primary forest on the lodge's own 66-hectare (163-acre) private reserve adjoining the much larger Piedras Blancas National Park. From here you can go kayaking or snorkeling in the Golfo Dulce, where dolphins are common and whale sharks are occasionally spotted. Rooms are rich in local hardwoods, and each has an element that makes guests feel like they're one with nature. Tasty family-style meals are served in the large main lodge building, which soars over two floors featuring sitting areas, a library, and reception, all entirely open to the surrounding forest. The lodge does not have Wi-Fi.

Golfo Dulce. www.nicuesalodge.com. ☏ **866/504-8116** in the U.S., or 2258-8250 in Costa Rica. 9 units. $245–$425 per person per night, double occupancy; $145 children 6–12; not recommended for children under 6. Rates include all meals, taxes, and transfers to and from either Golfito or Puerto Jiménez. 2-night minimum stay required except Dec 22–Jan 1, when a 4-night stay is required. Closed Oct 1–Nov 16. **Amenities:** Restaurant; bar; free kayaks, snorkeling gear, and fishing equipment; no Wi-Fi.

PLAYA ZANCUDO ★

19km (12 miles) S of Golfito by boat; 35km (22 miles) S of Golfito by road

Playa Zancudo is one of Costa Rica's most undeveloped beach destinations. If you're looking for a remote and low-key beach getaway, it's hard to beat Zancudo. It's pretty far from just about everything, and with relatively few places to stay, it's virtually never crowded. However, the small number of hotel rooms means the better ones, such as those listed here, can fill up fast in the high season. The beach itself is long and flat, and because it's protected from the full force of Pacific waves, it's one of the calmest beaches on this coast and relatively good for swimming, especially toward the northern end. The beach has a splendid view across the Golfo Dulce, and the sunsets are exquisite.

Essentials

GETTING THERE   By Plane: The nearest airport is in Golfito. See "Golfito: Gateway to the Golfo Dulce," p 512, for details. To get from the airport to Playa Zancudo, your best bets are by boat or taxi.

A fishing vessel off Playa Zancudo

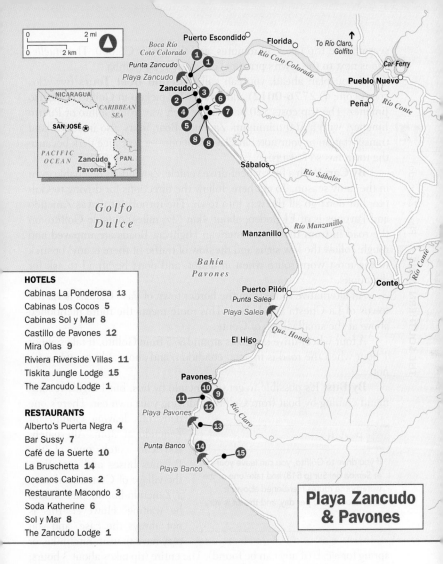

HOTELS

Cabinas La Ponderosa **13**
Cabinas Los Cocos **5**
Cabinas Sol y Mar **8**
Castillo de Pavones **12**
Mira Olas **9**
Riviera Riverside Villas **11**
Tiskita Jungle Lodge **15**
The Zancudo Lodge **1**

RESTAURANTS

Alberto's Puerta Negra **4**
Bar Sussy **7**
Café de la Suerte **10**
La Bruschetta **14**
Oceanos Cabinas **2**
Restaurante Macondo **3**
Soda Katherine **6**
Sol y Mar **8**
The Zancudo Lodge **1**

Playa Zancudo & Pavones

By Boat: Water taxis can be hired in Golfito to make the trip out to Playa Zancudo. When the tide is high, the boats take a route through the mangroves. This is by far the calmest and most scenic way to get to Zancudo. When the tide is low, boats must stay out in the gulf, which can get choppy at times. It costs around $20 to $25 per person for a water taxi, with a $40 minimum. If you can round up any sort of group, be sure to negotiate. The ride takes about 30 minutes.

Also, a passenger launch from the *muellecito* (little dock) in Golfito normally leaves at noon daily or every other day, depending on the season. The trip takes 30 minutes, and the fare is C6,000. The *muelle-cito* is next to the town's principal gas station, La Bomba.

If you plan ahead, you can call **Zancudo Boat Tours** (www.los cocos.com; © **2776-0012**) and arrange for pickup in Golfito or Puerto Jiménez. The trip costs $20 per person each way from Golfito or Puerto Jiménez, with a $60 minimum. Zancudo Boat Tours also includes land transportation to your hotel in Playa Zancudo—a very nice perk because the town has so few taxis.

By Car: With a four-wheel-drive vehicle, Zancudo is reachable even in the rainy season. To get here, follow the directions for driving to Golfito, but don't go all the way into town. The turnoff for playas Zancudo and Pavones is at El Rodeo, about 4km (2½ miles) outside Golfito, on the road in from the Inter-American Highway. Roads are unpaved and rough; follow the few signs and the flow of traffic (if there is any) or stick to the most worn route when in doubt, and don't be afraid to ask for directions.

An alternative route from the border town of Paso Canoas is via the towns of La Cuesta and Laurel. This route meets the route mentioned above at the small village of Conte.

A four-wheel-drive taxi costs around $75 from Golfito. It takes about 1 hour when the road is in good condition, and about 2 hours when it's not.

By Bus: It's possible to get to Zancudo by bus, but I highly recommend coming by boat from Golfito or driving your own car. There's one daily bus leaving Golfito for Zancudo at 3pm. Alternately, you can catch one of the Pavones buses and get off in the village of Conte. In theory, a Zancudo-bound bus should be waiting. However, this is not always the case, and you may have to wait, hitchhike, or spring for a cab (if any can be found). The entire trip takes about 3 hours; the fare is around $3.50.

> **Park It**
>
> If you drive to Golfito, you can leave your car at Samoa del Sur (p 518) and take one of the waterborne routes mentioned above. It costs around $10 per day, and the lot is very secure.

DEPARTING   The public launch to Golfito leaves daily at 7am from the dock near the school, in the center of Zancudo. You can also arrange a water taxi back to Golfito, but it's best to work with your hotel owner and make a reservation at least a day in advance. **Zancudo Boat Tours** will take you for $20 per person, with a $60 minimum. Zancudo will also take you to the **Osa Peninsula** for the same $20 per person, with a $60 minimum. The bus to Golfito leaves Zancudo each morning at 5:30am. You can catch the bus anywhere along the main road.

ORIENTATION   Zancudo is a long, narrow peninsula (sometimes only 90m/295 ft. or so wide) at the mouth of the Río Colorado. On one side is the beach, on the other a mangrove swamp. One road runs the length of the beach, and along this road, spread out over several kilometers of long, flat beach, you'll find the hotels mentioned below.

Exploring Playa Zancudo

The main activity at Zancudo is relaxing, and people take it seriously. Every lodge has hammocks, and if you bring a good book, you can spend hours swinging slowly in the tropical breezes. The beach along Zancudo is great for swimming. It's generally a little calmer on the northern end and gets rougher (good for bodysurfing) as you head south. There are a couple of bars and even a disco, but visitors are most likely to spend their time just hanging at their hotel or in restaurants meeting like-minded folks or playing board games. If you want to take a horseback ride on the beach, your hotel can arrange it.

Susan England, who runs Cabinas Los Cocos, also operates **Zancudo Boat Tours** (www.loscocos.com; © **2776-0012**), which offers kayaking tours, trips to the Casa Orquídeas Botanical Garden, hikes on the Osa Peninsula, a trip up the Río Coto to watch birds and wildlife, and more. A boat trip through the Río Coto mangroves will turn up a remarkable number of sea- and shorebirds, as well as the chance to see a crocodile resting on a riverbank, or a white-faced monkey leaping overhead. Tour prices are $50 to $75 per person, with discounts available for larger groups.

For fishing, ask at your hotel, or contact the **Zancudo Lodge** (see below). A full day of fishing with lunch and beer should cost between $950 and $1,600 per boat.

Because a mangrove swamp is directly behind the beach, mosquitoes and sand flies can be a problem when the winds die down, so be sure to bring insect repellent. Just FYI, *zancudo* means "mosquito."

Where to Stay

Quite a few fully equipped beach houses are for rent here for long stays. Once again, Susan England at **Los Cocos** (www.loscocos.com; © **2776-0012**) is your best bet for lining up one of these houses, which rent for $600 to $1,000 per week.

EXPENSIVE

The Zancudo Lodge ★★★ The only upscale lodging in Playa Zancudo, this beachfront lodge is located toward the far northern tip of the peninsula and caters predominantly to anglers—more than 70 IGFA records have been set here. All of the rooms have air-conditioning, flatscreen TVs, hardwood floors, and handsome contemporary decor. The Internet is superfast, and the TV is high-definition. The resort also offers a saltwater swimming pool. Its restaurant, the Game Fisher, serves sophisticated cuisine, usually featuring at least some of the daily catch, as well as the organic vegetables that are grown on-site. On the lagoon side of the peninsula, the lodge maintains a marina, with a fleet of well-equipped open-cockpit fishing boats. All-inclusive fishing packages are also available.

Playa Zancudo. www.zancudolodge.com. © **800/854-8791** in the U.S. or Canada, or 2776-0008 in Costa Rica. 15 units. $275 double; $340–$575 bungalow or suite. **Amenities:** Restaurant; bar; pool; free Wi-Fi.

MODERATE

Cabinas Los Cocos ★ The late Andrew Robertson and his wife Susan England homesteaded this lovely collection of four private cabins, set under tall trees and thick foliage, just steps from the beach. Two of the houses are reclaimed homes from the former United Fruit Company plantation in nearby Golfito. All feature thatched roofs and a private veranda, and offer a kitchen or kitchenette, encouraging longer stays. Susan continues to run Zancudo Boat Tours, a top-notch operation providing waterborne transportation and tour activities around the region.

Playa Zancudo. www.loscocos.com. © **2776-0012.** 4 units. $75 double. Weekly discounts available. No credit cards. **Amenities:** Free bikes and boogie boards; rental kayaks and stand-up paddle boards; free Wi-Fi.

INEXPENSIVE

Cabinas Sol y Mar ★ This place offers cozy and functional ocean-facing rooms with screened windows whose heavy wooden shutters swing open wide to let in light and the breeze. It also has one of Zancudo's best restaurants (see below) and fair pricing, and you can expect a warm welcome from owners Rick and Lori. They're always on hand and have a knack for making guests feel like family. On-site camping is also allowed here and they also have a three-level house for rent by the month.

Playa Zancudo. www.zancudo.com. © **2776-0014.** 6 units. $33–$50 double. Open all year, with lower prices Sept–Nov. **Amenities:** Restaurant; bar; free Wi-Fi.

Where to Eat

In addition to the place listed below, you might try the tasty Italian meals at **Restaurante Macondo** (© 2776-0157) or **Alberto's Puerta Negra** ★ (© 2776-0181). If you want basic Tico fare and some local company, head to **Bar Sussy** (© 2776-0107) or **Soda Katherine** (© 2776-0124). For a good breakfast, lunch, or dinner, or perhaps just a midday ice-cream treat, check out the open-air restaurant **Playa Cacao** ★ (© 8886-8362), which serves excellent freshly caught seafood and also runs kayak tours.

Finally, for some refined dining or a special occasion, head to the **Zancudo Lodge** (see above).

Sol y Mar ★ INTERNATIONAL/SEAFOOD This friendly, open-air restaurant and bar is undeniably the social (and culinary) center of this tiny beach town. The menu is long and varied, ranging from the fresh daily catch in a Thai coconut-curry sauce to dry-rubbed beef served with basil butter. There are also plenty of bar food staples, as well as twice-weekly barbeque nights. If there's live music in town, it's likely to be here, and the Sunday horseshoe tournament is a beloved tradition.

At Cabinas Sol y Mar. ✆ **2776-0014.** Main courses C3,900–C7,600. Daily 8am–9pm.

PLAYA PAVONES: A SURFER'S MECCA ★

40km (25 miles) S of Golfito

Hailed as the world's second-longest left break, Pavones is a legendary surfing destination. It takes around 1.8m (6 ft.) of swell to get this wave cranking, but when the surf's up, you're in for a long ride—so long, in fact, that it's much easier to walk back through town to where the wave is breaking than to paddle back. The swells are most consistent during the rainy season, but you'll find surfers here year-round. Locals tend to be pretty possessive of their turf, so don't be surprised if you receive a cool welcome in the water.

Other than surfing, nothing much goes on here; however, the surrounding rainforests are quite nice, and the beaches feature some rocky coves and points that give Pavones a bit more visual appeal than Zancudo. If you're feeling energetic, you can go for a horseback ride or hike into the rainforests that back up the town, or stroll south on the beaches that stretch toward Punta Banco and beyond, all the way to the Panamanian border. This is an isolated destination catering almost exclusively to

The legendary left at Pavones

A WILD ride

Surfers first discovered the amazing wave off Pavones in the late 1970s. When conditions are right, this wave peels off in one continuous ribbon for over 2km (1¼ miles). Your skills better be up to snuff, and your legs better be in good shape if you want to ride this wave.

Pavones got some good press in Allan Weisbecker's 2001 novel "In Search of Captain Zero: A Surfer's Road Trip Beyond the End of the Road." The word was out, and surfers began flocking to Pavones from all over. On any given day—when the wave is working—you are likely to find surfers from the United States, Brazil, Argentina, Israel, Australia, Peru, and any number of other countries.

However, the town and wave are not without controversy. Aside from the typical territorial spats that erupt over most popular waves, Pavones has been the site of a series of prominent squabbles that include land disputes, drug busts, fist fights, and even murders. For a unique and in-depth account of the town, its wave, and some of these controversies, check out Weisbecker's "Can't You Get Along with Anyone?: A Writer's Memoir and a Tale of a Lost Surfer's Paradise."

backpackers. Be prepared—Pavones is a tiny village with few amenities (and no ATMs, so bring cash), and most of the accommodations are quite basic.

Essentials

GETTING THERE & DEPARTING **By Plane:** The nearest airport with regularly scheduled flights is in Golfito (p 512). Tiskita Jungle Lodge (p 527) has a private airstrip. Depending on space, you might be able to arrange transportation to Pavones on one of its charter flights even if you are not staying there.

By Car: If you have a four-wheel-drive vehicle, you can reach Pavones even in the rainy season. Follow the directions for driving to Golfito (p 513), but don't go all the way into town. The turnoff for playas Zancudo and Pavones is at El Rodeo, about 4km (2½ miles) outside of Golfito, on the road in from the Inter-American Highway. It's mostly rough gravel and dirt roads. Follow the few signs and the flow of traffic (if there is any) or stick to the most worn route when in doubt.

An alternative route from Paso Canoas (at the border) goes via the towns of La Cuesta and Laurel. This route meets the route mentioned above at the small village of Conte.

Be sure to fill up your tank in Golfito, Rio Claro, or the small town of Laurel, because Pavones has no gas station.

By Bus: Two daily buses (no phone) go to Pavones from Golfito at 10am and 3pm. Trip duration is 2½ hours; the fare is C1750. Buses to Golfito depart Pavones daily at 5:30am and 12:30pm. This is a very remote destination, and the bus schedule is subject to change, so it always pays to check in advance.

Exploring Pavones

Surfing is the big draw in Pavones. For board rentals, head to **Sea Kings Surf Shop** (www.surfpavones.com [click "Surf Shop"]; © **2776-2015**). If there are no waves, or you want some other form of exercise, check in with **Shooting Star Yoga** (www.yogapavones.com; © **2776-2107**).

If you're interested in a guided tour, call **Pavones Tours** (www.pavonestours.com; © **2776-2119**), which offers a wide range of adventure outings, including horseback rides on the beach and whale- and dolphin-watching cruises in small boats, as well as kitesurfing, sportfishing, scuba diving, and kayak trips.

Alternately, you can do a day tour and guided hike at **Tiskita Jungle Lodge** (see below), for $25 per person, with advance reservation.

Where to Stay & Eat

In addition to the remote nature lodge listed below, **Riviera Riverside Villas** (www.pavonesriviera.com; © **2776-2396**) offers modern, plush, individual cabins (as well as fully equipped house rentals) a block or so inland from the water, right alongside the Río Claro. **Cabinas La Ponderosa** ★ (www.laponderosapavones.com; © **2776-2076**) is a small, beachfront collection of cabins and private, rustic villas, a bit outside of town, on the way to Punta Banco.

Right in Pavones, several basic lodges cater to itinerant surfers, with rooms for between $10 and $20 per night for a double. Most welcome walk-ins. For cheap in-town lodgings, there's **Mira Olas** (www.miraolas.com; © **2776-2006**), 2 blocks up from the soccer field.

For dining, opt for **Café de la Suerte** ★ (© **2776-2388**), a lively little joint fronting the village soccer field that serves breakfast and lunch and specializes in vegetarian items, freshly baked goods, and fruit smoothies. This cafe serves dinner during the high season and rents out cute, cozy, A/C-equipped rooms. Heading out toward Punta Banco, **La Bruschetta** ★ (© **2776-2174**) is another good option, with chef and owner Lela serving up excellent pizzas, pastas, and other Italian-based fare.

EXPENSIVE

Tiskita Jungle Lodge ★★ This impressive ecolodge is the loving (and intense) handiwork of Peter and Lisbeth Aspinall. Carved into a rainforest-covered hillside with panoramic views of the Pacific Ocean, the lodge features nine bungalows with a total of 17 rooms. The bungalows are wood, wood, and more glowing wood, with dozens of windows letting the views in. Trails on the private reserve lead to jungle waterfalls and idyllic swimming holes. The dark black volcanic sand beach is a relatively short hike downhill, but a good workout on the way back. Between

Suite at Castillo de Pavones

the lodge and the shore lies a private airstrip with a grassy runway kept cut short by grazing cattle. A charter flight in is the quickest and most common means of reaching Tiskita, though it can be reached by road with patience and a 4x4. Peter is a pioneer in conservation and ecotourism in Costa Rica. He is also an avid farmer with an impressive and extensive collection of tropical flora, including a wide range of exotic fruits, vegetables and nuts from around the globe. The lodge closes to all but groups in the off-season.

6km (3¾ miles) southeast of Pavones. www.tiskita.com. ℂ **2296-8125** reservation office in San José, or 2776-2194 at the lodge. 17 units. $285 per person double; $342 per person family room; $380 per person suite, includes all meals, 2 daily guided hikes, and taxes. 3-night minimum required. Discounts for children 12 and under. **Amenities:** Restaurant; bar; small pool, outdoor yoga deck; free Wi-Fi.

MODERATE

Castillo de Pavones ★   Set on a hillside just above the town and the famous break of Pavones, this is your best option for easy access to the waves and a bit more in the way of creature comforts than you'll find at most other in-town options. There are only a few rooms here, but all are large, airy, and feature plenty of windows. Some have private balconies with hand-fashioned driftwood railings, and all feature 2-person Jacuzzi tubs and a mix of peculiar furnishings and quirky stone- and tilework. Still, the hotel's friendly staff, excellent restaurant, and rooftop bar and lookout more than make up for any design flaws. The rooftop bar is the highlight of the building, completely open on three sides and featuring seating at a long plank hewn from a giant tree.

4 blocks uphill from the center of town, Pavones. www.castillodepavones.com. ℂ **2776-2191.** 5 units. $125–$150 double; $400 villa, includes breakfast. **Amenities:** Restaurant; bar; free surfboard usage; free Wi-Fi.

THE CARIBBEAN COAST

13

Costa Rica's Caribbean coast feels like another country. The pace is slower, the food is spicier, the tropical heat is more palpable, and the rhythmic lilt of patois and reggae music fills the air. This remains one of Costa Rica's least explored regions, with more than half the coastline still inaccessible except by boat or small plane. This isolation has helped preserve large tracts of virgin lowland rainforest, which are now set aside as **Tortuguero National Park ★★** and **Barra del Colorado National Wildlife Refuge ★**. These two parks, on the coast's northern reaches, are among Costa Rica's most popular destinations for adventurers and ecotourists. Of particular interest are the sea turtles that nest here. Farther south, **Cahuita National Park ★★** is another popular park, located just off its namesake beach village. It was set up to preserve 200 hectares (494 acres) of coral reef, but its palm tree–lined white-sand beaches and gentle trails are stunning. When you're ready for nice lodging, fine dining, and a hearty party, the village of **Puerto Viejo ★★** is hard to top anywhere in Costa Rica.

So remote was the Caribbean coast from Costa Rica's population centers in the Central Valley that it developed a culture all its own. The original inhabitants of the area included people of the Bribri and Cabécar tribes, which proudly maintain their cultures on indigenous reserves in the Talamanca Mountains. In fact, until the 1870s, this area had few non-Indians. However, when Minor Keith (p 25) built a railroad from San José to Limón and began planting bananas, he brought in black laborers from Jamaica and other Caribbean islands to lay the track and work the plantations. These workers and their descendants established fishing and farming communities up and down the coast. Today dreadlocked Rastafarians, reggae music, Creole cooking, and the English-based patois of this Afro-Caribbean culture give the region a quasi-Jamaican flavor, a striking contrast with Latino Costa Rican culture.

PREVIOUS PAGE: **Bird-watching while kayaking through Tortuguero National Park**

Caribbean Weather

The Caribbean coast has a unique weather pattern. It's said that there are two seasons: the rainy season and the very rainy season. Whereas you'll almost never get even a drop of rain in Guanacaste during Costa Rica's typical dry season (mid-Nov to Apr), on the Caribbean coast it can rain almost any day of the year. The months of September and October, when torrential rains pound most of the rest of the country, are two of the drier and more dependably sunny months here. Visit during these months and you'll find lower prices and fewer tourists.

The Caribbean coast has only one big city, **Limón,** a major commercial port and popular cruise ship port of call. However, the city itself is of little interest to most visitors, who often head south to the coast's spectacular beaches, or north to the jungle canals of Tortuguero.

Over the years, the Caribbean coast has garnered a reputation as being a dangerous, drug-infested zone, rife with crime. And though there have been several high-profile crimes in the area and petty theft can be an issue, this reputation is exaggerated. The same crime and drug problems found here exist in San José and most of the popular beach destinations on the Pacific coast. Use common sense and take normal precautions and you should have no problems on the Caribbean coast.

THE best CARIBBEAN COAST TRAVEL EXPERIENCES

- **Landing a Tarpon off Barra del Colorado:** Reaching lengths of between 1.8 and 2.8m (6–8 ft.), and often weighing in at well over 200 pounds, tarpon are a hard-fighting and high-jumping game fish. Barra del Colorado is a prime fishing ground. See p 534.

- **Cruising the Rainforest Canals of Tortuguero:** Lined by thick tropical rainforest and rich in wildlife, the canals surrounding Tortuguero are home to manatees, caimans, green macaws, and several monkey species. See p 535.

- **Tasting Chocolate at the Source:** Taking you "from bean to bar," **Caribeans Chocolate Tour** starts with a walk in an organic cacao farm and ends with a tasting of freshly made, organic chocolate. See p 583.

- **Watching Surfers Challenge Salsa Brava:** Sometimes called "Little Pipeline," Puerto Viejo's Salsa Brava is a fast, steep wave that breaks over sharp, shallow coral, and is most definitely *not* for beginners. The wave is pretty close to shore, making this a good place to watch some world-class surfing. See p 573.

- **Snorkeling Off Manzanillo:** One of Costa Rica's most bountiful and beautiful coral reefs lies just off the coast of the small village of

Manzanillo. In addition to coral, sponges, and reef fish, you may also catch a glimpse of a dolphin or sea turtle. See p 582.

BARRA DEL COLORADO ★

115km (71 miles) NE of San José

Most visitors to Barra del Colorado come for the fishing. Tarpon and snook fishing are world-class, or you can head farther offshore for deep-sea action. Barra del Colorado is part of the same ecosystem as Tortuguero National Park (p 535); as in Tortuguero, an abundance of wildlife and rainforest fauna lives in the rivers and canals.

Named for its location at the mouth of the Río Colorado near the Costa Rica–Nicaragua border, Barra del Colorado can be reached only by boat or small plane. The town is a small, rickety collection of raised stilt houses, and it supports a diverse population of Afro-Caribbean and Miskito Indian residents, Nicaraguan migrants, and transient commercial fishermen.

It's hot and humid here most of the year, and it rains a lot, so although some of the lodges have at times offered a "tarpon guarantee," there are no guarantees about the weather.

A Tortuguero National Park boat tour

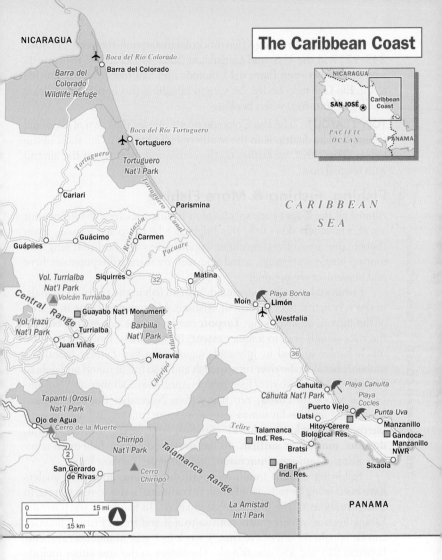

The Caribbean Coast

NICARAGUA

Boca del Río Colorado
Barra del Colorado

Barra del Colorado Wildlife Refuge

NICARAGUA

SAN JOSÉ — Caribbean Coast

PACIFIC OCEAN

PANAMA

Boca del Río Tortuguero
Tortuguero

Tortuguero Nat'l Park

Cariari

Parismina

CARIBBEAN SEA

Guácimo

Carmen

Guápiles

Vol. Turrialba Nat'l Park

Siquirres

Matina

32

Volcán Turrialba

Moín

Playa Bonita

Limón

Guayabo Nat'l Monument

Vol. Irazú Nat'l Park

Turrialba

Juan Viñas

Barbilla Nat'l Park

Westfalia

Moravia

36

Cahuita

Playa Cahuita

Cahuita Nat'l Park

Playa Cocles

Tapanti (Orosi) Nat'l Park

Puerto Viejo

Ojo de Agua

Cerro de la Muerte

Uatsi

Punta Uva

Manzanillo

Telire

Hitoy-Cerere Biological Res.

Chirripó Nat'l Park

Talamanca Ind. Res.

Gandoca-Manzanillo NWR

San Gerardo de Rivas

Bratsi

2

Cerro Chirripó

BriBri Ind. Res.

Sixaola

Talamanca Range

0   15 mi
0   15 km

La Amistad Int'l Park

PANAMA

Essentials

GETTING THERE & DEPARTING   By Plane: Most visitors come here on multiday fishing packages, and most of the area's lodges include charter flights as part of their package trips, or will book you a flight.

By Boat: It is also possible to travel to Barra del Colorado by boat from **Puerto Viejo de Sarapiquí** (see chapter 10). Expect to pay $400 to $600 each way for a boat that holds up to 10 people. Check at the public dock in Puerto Viejo de Sarapiquí or call **Oasis Nature Tours** (www.oasisnaturetours.com; ⌀ **2766-6108**).

Río Colorado Lodge (www.riocoloradotarponfishing.com; © **800/ 243-9777** in the U.S. and Canada, or 2232-4063/2232-8610) runs its own launch between Barra del Colorado and San José. If you're staying at the Río Colorado Lodge, be sure to ask about this option (for at least one leg of your trip) when booking.

TOWN LAYOUT The Río Colorado neatly divides the town of Barra del Colorado. The airstrip is in the southern half of town, as are most of the lodges. Those that are farther up the canals will meet you at the airstrip with a small boat.

Fishing, Fishing & More Fishing

Almost all the lodges here specialize in fishing packages. If you (or your significant other) don't fish, this might not be the place for you. Even though the area offers excellent opportunities for bird-watching and touring jungle waterways, a rod and reel are standard equipment here and binoculars are optional.

Fishing takes place year-round. You can fish in the rivers and canals, in the very active river mouth, or offshore. Most anglers come in search of the tarpon, or silver king. **Tarpon** can be caught year-round, both in the river mouth and, to a lesser extent, in the canals; however, they are much harder to land in July and August—the two rainiest months— probably because the river runs so high and is so full of runoff and debris. **Snook,** an aggressive river fish, peak in April, May, October, and November; fat snook, or *calba,* run heavy from November through January. Depending on how far out to sea you venture, you might hook up with **barracuda, jack, mackerel** (Spanish and king), **wahoo, tuna, dorado, marlin,** or **sailfish.** In the rivers and canals, fishermen regularly bring in *mojarra, machaca,* and *guapote* (rainbow bass).

Following current trends in sportfishing, more and more anglers have been using fly rods, in addition to traditional rod-and-reel setups, to land just about all the fish mentioned above. To fish here, you'll need a fishing license, which covers both saltwater and fresh. Fishing licenses can be bought for anywhere from 1 week to 1 year in duration and cost between $15 and $50 accordingly. The lodges in the area either include these in their packages or can readily provide them for you.

If you don't fish, ask whether your lodge has a good naturalist guide or canoes or kayaks for rent.

Where to Stay & Eat

Almost all the hotels here specialize in package tours, including all meals, fishing and tackle, taxes, and usually transportation and liquor too, so rates are high. With no dependable budget hotels, Barra remains a remote and difficult destination for those looking to save.

Río Colorado Lodge ★   Founded in 1972 by the legendary fisherman and conservation activist Archie Fields, this lodge has been catering to discerning anglers for more than 4 decades. The property is a rambling complex of wooden structures with spotless, if dated, rooms connected by a network of raised walkways. The lodge has distinct bar, lounge, and dining areas, where folks gather to tell tall fishing tales. The food and the fishing guides are top-notch. Current owner Dan Wise took over from Archie and is often on hand.

Barra del Colorado. www.riocoloradotarponfishing.com. *©* **800/243-9777** in U.S. and Canada, or 2232-4063 or 2232-8610 in Costa Rica. 18 units. $2,248–$4,211 per person for 5–7 nights, meals included; some packages include lodging in San José, fishing license, lures, and beverages. Non-fishing guests $245 per person per day, meals included. **Amenities:** Restaurant; bar; Jacuzzi; free Wi-Fi.

Silver King Lodge ★★   For more comfort and pampering during the hours when you're not stalking massive tarpon, this dedicated fishing lodge is the first choice. The large complex of rooms and common areas is built on pilings above the river and flood levels, and is connected by a network of covered wooden walkways. Room quality, food, and service are miles above anything else in the area. The whole place is awash in varnished hardwoods. In fact, the varnish is so well maintained you might reach for your sunglasses inside the rooms or bar and dining areas. The rooms themselves feel massive, and all come with two queen beds and built-in racks for all your fishing gear. The lodge has a lovely outdoor pool and covered Jacuzzi. Abundant and varied buffet meals are served. You might not find better coconut-battered snook anywhere.

Barra del Colorado. www.silverkinglodge.com. *©* **877/335-0755** in the U.S. 10 units. Call for precise pricing; approx. $2,750–$3,960 per person, double occupancy, for 3 days of fishing, air transfer to/from San José, all meals, liquor, and taxes; $545 per person per extra day, including all fishing, meals, liquor, and taxes. Closed June–Aug and Nov–Jan. **Amenities:** Restaurant; bar; Jacuzzi; pool; small spa; free Wi-Fi.

TORTUGUERO NATIONAL PARK ★★

250km (155 miles) NE of San José; 79km (49 miles) N of Limón

Tortuguero is a tiny fishing village connected to the rest of mainland Costa Rica by a series of rivers and canals. This aquatic highway is lined with a mix of farmland and dense tropical rainforest that is home to howler and spider monkeys, three-toed sloths, toucans, and green macaws. A trip through the canals surrounding Tortuguero is a lot like cruising the Amazon basin, though on a much smaller scale.

"Tortuguero" comes from the Spanish name for the giant sea turtles (*tortugas*) that nest on the beaches of this region every year from early March to mid-October (prime season is July–Oct, and peak months are Aug–Sept). The chance to see this nesting attracts many people to this remote region, but just as many come to explore the intricate network of jungle canals that serve as the region's main transportation arteries.

Independent travel is not the norm here, although it's possible. Most travelers rely on their lodge for boat transportation through the canals and into town. At most of the lodges around Tortuguero, almost everything is done in groups, including the bus rides to and fro, boat trips through the canals, and family-style meals.

Important: More than 508cm (200 in.) of rain fall here annually, so you can expect a downpour at any time of the year. Most of the lodges will provide you with rain gear (including ponchos and rubber boots), but it can't hurt to carry your own.

An angler pulling in a tarpon in Barra del Colorado

Essentials

GETTING THERE & DEPARTING

By Plane: Nature Air (www.nature air.com; © **800/235-9272** in the U.S. and Canada, or 2299-6000 in Costa Rica) has one daily flight at 6am to **Tortuguero** airstrip from Juan Santamaría International Airport in San José. The flight takes about 30 minutes; the fare is $69 to $109 each way. The return flight leaves daily at 6:30am for San José. Extra flights are often added in high season, and departure times vary according to weather conditions. Many local lodges also run charter flights as part of their package trips. Arrange with your hotel to pick you up at the airstrip. Otherwise you'll have to ask one of the other hotels' boat captains to give you a lift, which they'll usually do for a few dollars.

By Car: It's not possible to drive to Tortuguero. If you have a car, your best bet is either to leave it in San José and take an organized tour, or drive it to Limón or Moín, find a secure hotel or public parking lot, and then follow the directions for arriving by boat below. La Pavona has a secure parking lot useful for those meeting the boats plying the Cariari and La Pavona route outlined below.

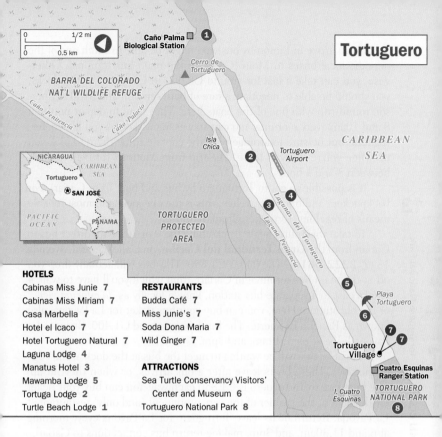

Tortuguero

0 — 1/2 mi
0 — 0.5 km

Caño Palma □ **1**
Biological Station

Cerro de Tortuguero ▲

BARRA DEL COLORADO NAT'L WILDLIFE REFUGE

Caño Penitencia

Caño Palacio

NICARAGUA
CARIBBEAN SEA
Tortuguero
⊛ SAN JOSÉ
PACIFIC OCEAN
PANAMA

Isla Chica

TORTUGUERO PROTECTED AREA

2

Tortuguero Airport

4

3

Lagunas del Tortuguero

Laguna Penitencia

CARIBBEAN SEA

5

Playa Tortuguero

6

7 **7**

Tortuguero Village ●

□ Cuatro Esquinas Ranger Station

I. Cuatro Esquinas

TORTUGUERO NATIONAL PARK

8

HOTELS

Cabinas Miss Junie **7**
Cabinas Miss Miriam **7**
Casa Marbella **7**
Hotel el Icaco **7**
Hotel Tortuguero Natural **7**
Laguna Lodge **4**
Manatus Hotel **3**
Mawamba Lodge **5**
Tortuga Lodge **2**
Turtle Beach Lodge **1**

RESTAURANTS

Budda Café **7**
Miss Junie's **7**
Soda Dona Maria **7**
Wild Ginger **7**

ATTRACTIONS

Sea Turtle Conservancy Visitors' Center and Museum **6**
Tortuguero National Park **8**

By Boat: Flying to Tortuguero is convenient if you don't have much time, but a boat trip through the canals and rivers of this region is often the highlight of any visit. You'll first have to ride by bus or minivan from San José to Moín, Caño Blanco, or one of the other embarkation points; then it's 2 to 3 hours on a boat, usually with hard wooden benches or plastic seats. All of the more expensive lodges listed offer their own bus and boat transportation packages, which include the boat ride through the canals. However, if you're coming here on the cheap and plan to stay at one of the less expensive lodges or at a budget *cabina* in Tortuguero, you will have to arrange your own transportation. In this case, you have a few options.

One option is to get yourself to Limón and then to the public docks in **Moín,** just to the north, and try to find a boat on your own. You can reach Limón easily by public bus from San José (see p 549). If you're coming by car, make sure you drive all the way to Limón or Moín, unless you have prior arrangements out of Cariari or Caño Blanco Marina.

If you arrive in Limón by bus, you might be able to catch one of the periodic local buses to Moín (C350) at the main bus terminal. Otherwise, you can take a taxi for around C8,000 to C10,000. At the docks, you should be able to negotiate a fare of between $65 and $100 per person round-trip with one of the boats here. They tend to depart between 8 and 10am every morning. You can stay as many days as you like in Tortuguero, but be sure to arrange with the captain to be there to pick you up when you're ready to leave. The trip from Moín to Tortuguero takes between 3 and 4 hours.

It is possible to get to Tortuguero by bus and boat from Cariari. For backpackers and budget travelers, this is the cheapest and most reliable means of reaching Tortuguero from San José.

To take this route, begin by catching the 9 or 10:30am direct bus to Cariari from the **Gran Terminal del Caribe,** on Calle Central, Avenida 13 (🕿 **2222-0610**). The fare is C1,850. This bus will actually drop you off at the main bus terminal in Cariari, from which you'll have to walk 4 blocks east to a separate bus station, known locally as *"la estación vieja,"* or the old station. Here, you can buy your bus ticket for La Pavona, also known as Rancho El Suerte. The bus fare is around C1,400. Buses to La Pavona leave at 6am, 11am, and 3pm.

A boat or two will be waiting to meet the bus at the dock at the edge of the river. These boats leave after a bus arrives, or when they fill up. The boat fare to Tortuguero is C1,850 each way. You can buy your ticket for the boat at the cashier of the very prominent (and only) restaurant at La Pavona. Return boats leave Tortuguero for La Pavona every morning at 6 and 11:30am, and 3pm, making return bus connections to Cariari.

Warning: Beware of unscrupulous operators providing misinformation by offering to sell you "packaged transportation" to Tortuguero, when all they are doing is charging you extra to buy the tickets described above. Be especially careful if people selling you boat transportation aggressively steer you to a specific hotel, claim that your first choice is full, or insist that you must buy a package with them that includes the transportation, lodging, and guide services. If you have doubts or want to check on the current state of this route, check out **www.tortuguerovillage. com**, which has detailed directions to Tortuguero by a variety of routes.

Finally, it's also possible, albeit expensive, to travel to Tortuguero by boat from **Puerto Viejo de Sarapiquí** (see chapter 10). Expect to pay $400 to $600 each way for a boat that holds up to 10 people. Check at the public dock in Puerto Viejo de Sarapiquí if you're interested. The ride usually takes about 3 to 4 hours, and the boats tend to leave in the morning.

VILLAGE LAYOUT Tortuguero is one of the most remote locations in Costa Rica. With no roads into this area and no cars in the village, all

A stilt house in Tortuguero

transportation is by boat, foot, or bicycle. Most of the lodges are spread out over several kilometers to the north of Tortuguero Village on either side of the main canal; the small airstrip is at the north end of the beach-side spit of land. At the far northern end of the main canal, you'll see the **Cerro de Tortuguero (Tortuguero Hill),** which, at some 119m (390 ft.), towers over the area. The hike to the top is a popular half-day tour and offers some good views of the Tortuguero canal and village, as well as the sea.

The village of Tortuguero is a small collection of houses and shops connected by footpaths. It's spread out on a thin spit of land, bordered on one side by the Caribbean Sea and on the other by the main canal. At most points, it's less than 300m (984 ft.) wide. In the center of the village, you'll find a small playground, the town's health clinic, and a soccer field.

If you stay at a hotel on the ocean side of the canal, you'll be able to walk into and explore the village; if you're across the canal, you'll be dependent on the lodge's boat transportation. Some of the lodges across the canal have their own jungle trails that might appeal to naturalists.

FAST FACTS Tortuguero has no banks, or currency-exchange houses, but it does have a Banco de Costa Rica ATM on the main drag. Regardless, be sure to bring enough cash in colones to cover any expenses and incidental charges, as it's often out of cash. The local hotels and shops generally charge a commission to exchange dollars.

Exploring the National Park

According to existing records, sea turtles have frequented Tortuguero National Park since at least 1592, largely due to its extreme isolation. Over the years, turtles were captured and their eggs were harvested by local settlers; by the 1950s, this practice became so widespread that turtles faced extinction. Regulations controlling this mini-industry were passed in 1963, and in 1970 Tortuguero National Park was established.

Today, four species of sea turtles nest here: the green turtle, the hawksbill, the loggerhead, and the giant leatherback. The park's beaches are excellent places to watch sea turtles nest, especially at night. However, the beaches are not appropriate for swimming. The surf is usually very rough, and the river mouths attract sharks that feed on the turtle hatchlings and the many fish that live here.

Green turtles are the most common turtle found in Tortuguero, so you're more likely to see one of them than any other species if you visit during the prime nesting season from **July to mid-October** (Aug–Sept are peak months). **Loggerheads** are very rare, so don't be disappointed if you don't see one. The **giant leatherback** is perhaps the most spectacular sea turtle to watch laying eggs. The largest of all turtle species, the leatherback can grow to 2m (6½ ft.) long and weigh well over 1,000 pounds. They nest from late February to June, predominantly in the southern part of the park. See the "In Search of Turtles" box on p 113.

You can explore the park's rainforest, either by foot or by boat,

A turtle hatchling heading to sea

Turtle Tips

- Visitors to the beach at night must be accompanied by a licensed guide. Tours generally last between 2 and 4 hours.

- Sometimes you must walk quite a bit to encounter a nesting turtle. Wear sneakers or walking shoes rather than sandals. The beach is very dark at night, and it's easy to trip or step on driftwood or other detritus.

- Wear dark clothes. White T-shirts are not permitted.

- Flashlights, camera flashes, and lighted video cameras are prohibited on turtle tours.

- Smoking is prohibited on the beach at night.

and look for some of the incredible varieties of wildlife that live here: jaguars, anteaters, howler monkeys, collared and white-lipped peccaries, some 350 species of birds, and countless butterflies, among others. Some of the more colorful and common bird species you might see include the rufescent tiger heron, keel-billed toucan, northern jacana, red-lored parrot, and ringed kingfisher. Boat tours are far and away the most popular way to visit this park. One frequently very muddy trail starts at the park entrance and runs for about 2km (1.25 miles) through the rainforest and along the beach.

Although it's a perfect habitat, West Indian manatees (*Trichechus manatus*) are rare and threatened in the canals, rivers, and lagoons of Costa Rica's Caribbean coast. Hunting and propeller injuries are the prime culprits. Your chances of seeing one of these gentle aquatic mammals are extremely remote.

ENTRY POINT, FEES & REGULATIONS The Tortuguero National Park entrance and ranger station are at the south end of Tortuguero Village. The ranger station is inside a landlocked old patrol boat, and a small, informative open-air kiosk explains a bit about the park and its environs. Admission to the park is $17. However, most people visit Tortuguero as part of a package tour. Be sure to confirm whether the park entrance is included in the price. Moreover, only certain canals and trails leaving from the park station are actually within the park. Many hotels and private guides take their tours to a series of canals that border the park and are very similar in terms of flora and fauna but don't require park entrance. When the turtles are nesting, arrange a night tour in advance with either your hotel or one of the private guides working in town. These guided tours generally run between $15 and $25. Flashlights and flash cameras are not permitted on the beach at night because the lights discourage the turtles from nesting.

ORGANIZED TOURS All of the lodges listed below, with the exception of the most inexpensive accommodations in Tortuguero Village, offer package tours that include various hikes and river tours; this is generally the best way to visit the area.

In addition, several San José–based tour companies offer budget 2-day/1-night excursions to Tortuguero, including transportation, all meals, and limited tours around the region. Prices range between $200 and $350 per person, and guests are lodged in one of the basic hotels in Tortuguero Village or in one of the nicer lodges listed below. Reputable companies include **Exploradores Outdoors ★** (www.exploradores outdoors.com; ✆ **646/205-0828** U.S./Canada, or 2222-6262 in Costa Rica), **Jungle Tom Safaris** (www.jungletomsafaris.com; ✆ **2221-7878**), and **Iguana Verde Tours** (www.iguanaverdetours.com; ✆ **2231-6803**). Some operators offer 1-day trips in which tourists spend almost all their time coming and going, with a quick tour of the canals and lunch in Tortuguero. These trips generally run $125 to $150 per person, but if you really want to experience Tortuguero, I recommend staying for at least 2 nights.

Alternatively, you could go with **Riverboat Francesca ★** (www. tortuguerocanals.com; ✆ **2226-0986**), run by two pioneering guides in this region who operate a fleet of their own boats. The couple offers a range of overnight and multiday packages to Tortuguero, with lodging options at most of the major lodges here.

BOAT CANAL TOURS Aside from watching turtles nest, the unique thing to do in Tortuguero is tour the canals by boat, spying tropical birds and native wildlife. Most lodges can arrange a canal tour, but you can also arrange a tour through one of the independent operators in the village of Tortuguero, such as Riverboat Francesca (see above), **Victor Barrantes** at the Tortuguero Info Center (✆ 8928-1169; tortuguero_info@racsa.co.cr), or **Daryl Loth** (http://casamarbella.tripod.com; ✆ **8833-0827**), who runs Casa Marbella (p 548) in town center. Additionally, you can ask for a recommendation at the **Sea Turtle Conservancy Visitors' Center and Museum** (✆ **2767-1576**). Most guides charge $20 to $25 per person for a tour of the canals. If you travel through the park, you'll also have to pay the park entrance fee of $15 per person.

Exploring Tortuguero Village

The most popular attraction in town is the small **Sea Turtle Conservancy Visitors' Center and Museum ★** (www.conserveturtles.org; ✆ **2767-1576**). The museum has info and exhibits on a whole range of native flora and fauna, but its primary focus is on the life and natural history of the sea turtles. Most visits to the museum include a short,

Tortuguero

informative video on the turtles. All the proceeds from the gift shop go toward conservation and turtle protection. The museum is open daily from 10am to noon and 2 to 5pm. Admission is $2, but more generous donations are encouraged.

In the village, you can also rent dugout canoes, known in Costa Rica as *cayucos* or *pangas*. Be careful before renting and taking off in one of these; they tend to be heavy, slow, and hard to maneuver.

You'll find a handful of souvenir shops spread around the center of the village. The **Paraíso Tropical Gift Shop** has the largest selection of gifts and souvenirs, while the **Jungle Shop** has a higher-end selection of wares and donates 10% of its profits to local schools.

Where to Stay

Although the room rates below may appear high, keep in mind that they usually include round-trip transportation from San José (which amounts to about $100 per person), plus all meals, taxes, and usually some tours. When broken down into nightly room rates, most of the lodges are really charging only $60 to $150 for a double room. *Note:* Package rates below are for the least expensive travel option, which is a bus and boat

Boat rides through Tortuguero National Park

combination in and out. All lodges also offer packages with a plane flight, either one or both ways.

EXPENSIVE

Manatus Hotel ★★   If air-conditioning and TV are important to you, this is the place to stay, because Manatus is the only hotel to offer those niceties. Other creature comforts include pretty rooms with hand-painted sinks and comfy four-poster beds bedecked in white muslin mosquito netting. The netting is actually mostly for show, oddly enough, as the net is entirely open at the top and the rooms are well sealed off from bugs. The hotel also has a well-run little spa and a restaurant with Afro-Caribbean dishes, plus an exercise room and art gallery featuring local and regional artists. Manatus is one of the smaller lodges in the area, allowing for a more intimate experience and more personalized service.

Tortuguero. www.manatushotel.com. ✆ **2239-4854** reservations in San José, or 2709-8197 at the hotel. 12 units. $297 per person for 2 days/1 night; $422 per person for 3 days/2 nights, double occupancy, includes all meals, taxes, and daily tours. No children under 3 years. **Amenities:** Restaurant; bar; pool; small spa and gym; free Wi-Fi.

Mawamba Lodge ★ Mawamba is a collection of raised wooden buildings amid lush gardens on the ocean side of the main canal. This is the closest of the main nature lodges to the town, which is convenient for those looking to spend a bit more time soaking up the village's local flavor. The rooms are simple and tidy, with walls and floors of dark varnished hardwoods. All come with some sort of shared or private veranda, and most of these are equipped with hammocks or rocking chairs. The four "superior" rooms are individual bungalows, featuring more space, king beds, large bathrooms with deep soaking tubs, and river views. The lodge has a large pool and several bar and restaurant venues, including a restaurant built on an old barge and moored just off the lodge's river bank. Butterfly, frog, and iguana breeding projects ensure great wildlife viewing. Some tours offered, such as kayaking and night tours, cost extra. Tortuguero. www.grupomawamba.com. ⓒ **2293-8181.** 54 units. $230–$299 per person for 2 days/1 night; $321–$406 per person for 3 days/2 nights, double occupancy, includes round-trip transfer from San José, all meals, taxes, and some tours. Discounts for children 5–11; kids 4 and under free. **Amenities:** Restaurant; bar; pool; free Wi-Fi.

Tortuga Lodge & Gardens ★★★ This was one of the first upscale resorts to set up shop here, and it has been immaculately maintained.

River view suite at Tortuga Lodge

Tortuga Lodge restaurant on the Tortuguero River

Like other lodges in its class, it has amenities like ceiling fans, solar powered hot water, and landscaped gardens—plus a snazzy stone-lined pool,
a waterfront dining room with some of the better local cuisine, and 20
hectares (50 acres) of grounds and jungle. The paths snaking through the
property offer superb hiking. The bamboo-furnished rooms are class
acts, the best ones being on the upper floor, with sleek varnished wood,
verandas, and hammocks. The large, canal-front deck is built on several
levels stepping up from the water and joining with the large dining room
and bar, and it serves as the social hub for the lodge. Service is
impeccable.

Tortuguero. www.tortugalodge.com. © **2257-0766** for reservations in San José, or
2709-8136 at the lodge. 27 units. $212 double, tax included; more for packages
including meals, tours, and transportation. **Amenities:** Restaurant; bar; pool; free
Wi-Fi.

Turtle Beach Lodge ★   Tucked away down a narrow canal on a thin
strip of sand and jungle with a turtle-shaped pool fronting the sea, this is
the most isolated of the main Tortuguero nature lodges (it's about 5 miles
from the village). It sits on 175 acres of private reserve with miles of

The beach at Turtle Beach Lodge

private trails and deserted beachfront. During turtle nesting season, it offers superb night tours, as guests have this section of beach all to themselves. The rooms are rustic affairs set on simple concrete foundations, with walls that are mostly fine-mesh screening.

Caño Palma, Tortuguero. www.turtlebeachlodge.com. © **2248-0707** in San José, or 2206-4020 at the lodge. 53 units. $260 per person for 2 days/1 night; $350 per person for 3 days/2 nights. Double occupancy, includes round-trip transfer from San José, all meals, taxes, and tours. **Amenities:** Restaurant; bar; pool; free Wi-Fi.

MODERATE

Laguna Lodge ★   Think of this as summer camp for adults. Rooms are adequate but basic, with screened rather than glass windows (which means that they can get noisy, as all the guestrooms are in a series of one-story buildings with shared verandas). It's also double the size of the other lodges in the area, so it can feel a bit too bustling. But does that really matter when you're surrounded by all this glorious nature? Laguna Lodge sits on the ocean side of the main canal, about a 20- to 30-minute walk north of Tortuguero Village. It boasts splendid gardens, including a butterfly and a frog garden, and two resort-style pools; the beach is just a couple hundred yards away. Meals are served buffet-style in a large, covered, open-air dining room overlooking Tortuguero's main canal.

Tortuguero. www.lagunatortuguero.com. © **888/259-5615** in U.S. and Canada, or 2272-4943 in Costa Rica. 100 units. $251 per person for 2 days/1 night; $319 per person for 3 days/2 nights. Double occupancy, includes round-trip transfer from San José, tours, taxes, and all meals. Children 5–11 half-price; children under 5 free. **Amenities:** Restaurant; 2 bars; 2 pools; free Wi-Fi.

INEXPENSIVE

Several basic *cabinas* in the village of Tortuguero offer budget lodgings for $30 to $60 per person. **Cabinas Miss Junie** (© **2709-8102**) and **Cabinas Miss Miriam** (© **2709-8002**) are the traditional favorites, though you may prefer Casa Marbella (below). The other choices are **Hotel El Icaco** (www.hotelelicaco.com; © **2709-8044**), and **Hotel Tortuguero Natural** (www.hoteltortugueronatural.com; © **2767-0466**).

Casa Marbella ★ Owned by Daryl Loth, one of the most respected local guides around, and his wife Luz, this B&B occupies a clapboard home right on the canal in the heart of the village. All rooms come with one or two low-lying wooden beds, large windows, hardwood floors, and hot water showers. The best have views of the water. There's a small covered canal-front patio where breakfast is served, and which also serves as a nice spot to relax, read, or watch birds. Beyond leading tours, Daryl can also help arrange a wide variety of activities in the area.

Tortuguero. http://casamarbella.tripod.com. © **2709-8011** or 8833-0827. 11 units. $40–$45 double; $55–$65 superior, includes breakfast. No credit cards. **Amenities:** Small communal kitchen, free Wi-Fi.

Where to Eat

Most visitors take all their meals as part of a package at their hotel. The town has a couple of simple sodas and restaurants. The best of these are **Miss Junie's** (© **2709-8102**) and **Soda Dona Maria** (© **8870-8634**).

Budda Café ★ INTERNATIONAL With an appropriately Zen atmosphere of canal-front outdoor seating—try and grab one of the tables on the over-the-water deck—this happy cafe has been in business for years, drawing locals, volunteers, and tourists who aren't eating all three meals at their lodge. The food is rather standard, consisting of ceviche, pizzas, pastas, crepes, and a range of main dishes (plus excellent desserts).

On the main canal, next to the ICE building, Tortuguero. www.buddacafe.com. © **2709-8084.** Main courses C4,500–C13,000. Daily noon–9pm.

Wild Ginger ★★ INTERNATIONAL Welcome to Tortuguero's one real upscale option. Here that means a "California meets Costa Rica" menu that features everything from seasonal lobster and mango ceviche to beef tenderloin in a coffee rub. Ginger-marinated chicken with passion-fruit sauce is a highlight. Wild Ginger also creates a number of options for vegetarians and vegans. The setting is nice, too: polished concrete floors, hand-painted murals, and lots of open air. Service is stellar, and you may feel like the owners are old friends by the time you pay the check.

On the ocean-side path, north end of Tortuguero. www.wildgingercr.com. © **2709-8240.** Main courses C6,000–C10,000. Wed-Mon 6–9pm.

LIMÓN: GATEWAY TO TORTUGUERO NATIONAL PARK & SOUTHERN COASTAL BEACHES

160km (99 miles) E of San José; 55km (34 miles) N of Puerto Viejo

It was just offshore from present-day Limón, in the lee of Isla Uvita, that Christopher Columbus is said to have anchored in 1502, on his fourth and final voyage to the New World. Believing that this was potentially a very rich land, he christened it Costa Rica ("Rich Coast"). Although this land never supplied the Spanish crown with much in the way of gold or jewels, the spot where Columbus anchored has proved over the centuries to be the best port on Costa Rica's Caribbean coast. Today, Limón is a hardscrabble port city that ships millions of pounds of bananas northward every year. It also receives a fair share of the country's ocean-borne imports and a modest number of cruise-ship callings. On days when a cruise ship is in port, you'll find the city bustling far beyond the norm.

Limón is not generally considered a tourist destination, and few tourists take the time to tour the city, except those stopping here on cruise ships. Very few choose to stay here, though it's worth a visit during Carnaval.

If you want to get in some beach time while you're in Limón, hop in a taxi or a local bus and head north a few kilometers to **Playa Bonita,** a small public beach. Although the water isn't very clean and is usually too rough for swimming, the setting is much more attractive than downtown. This beach is popular with surfers.

A Fall Festival

Limón's biggest yearly event, and one of the liveliest festivals in Costa Rica, is **Carnaval,** around Columbus Day (Oct 12). For a week, languid Limón shifts into high gear for a nonstop bacchanal orchestrated to the beat of reggae, soca, and calypso music. During the revelries,

residents don costumes and take to the streets in a dazzling parade of color. Festivities include marching bands, dancers, and parade floats. If you want to experience Carnaval, make your reservations early because hotels fill up fast.

Essentials

GETTING THERE & DEPARTING   By Plane: Sansa (www.flysansa.com; *©* **877/767-2672** in the U.S. and Canada, or 2290-4100 in Costa Rica) began daily flights into Limón's small seaside airstrip in 2015. They offer afternoon flights from San José to Limón to Tortuguero and back to San José. Fares run between $65 and $90, one-way. The airport is located a few miles south of the city, on the coastal road to Cahuita and Puerto Viejo.

Local taxis are usually waiting for arriving flights. However, if you're looking to head down the coast to Cahuita or Puerto Viejo and beyond, it's recommend to arrange a transfer beforehand either with your hotel, or **Gecko Trail Adventures** (www.geckotrail.com; *©* **2756-8412**), a Puerto Viejo–based tour agency and transfer company.

By Car: The Guápiles Highway (CR32) heads north out of San José on Calle 3 before turning east and passing close to Barva Volcano and through the rainforests of Braulio Carrillo National Park en route to Limón. The route, lined with stands selling sweet loaves of pan bon, takes about 2½ hours and is spectacularly beautiful, especially when it's not raining or misty. Alternately, you can take the old highway, which is also scenic but slower. It heads east out of San José on Avenida Central and passes through San Pedro and then Curridabat before reaching Cartago. From Cartago on, the narrow and winding road passes through Turrialba before descending out of the mountains to Siquirres, where the old highway meets the new. This route takes around 4 hours to get to Limón.

By Bus: Transportes Caribeños buses (*©* **2222-0610** in San José, or 2758-2575 in Limón) leave San José every hour daily between 5am and 7pm from the Caribbean bus terminal (Gran Terminal del Caribe) on Calle Central, Avenida 13. Friday and Sunday, the last bus leaves at 8pm. The trip duration is around 3 hours. The buses are either direct or local (*corriente*), and they don't alternate in any particularly predictable fashion. Local buses are generally older and less comfortable and stop en route to pick up passengers from the roadside. The fare is around C3,500 one-way.

> ## Along the Way
>
> If you're driving to the Caribbean coast, consider combining the trip with a stop at the Rain Forest Aerial Tram (p 164), or the Puerto Viejo de Sarapiquí area (p 399).

Buses leave Limón for San José every hour between 5am and 7pm, and similarly alternate between local and direct, with the last bus leaving 1 hour later on Sundays. The Limón bus terminal is on the main road into town, several blocks west of the downtown area and Parque Vargas.

Buses (*©* **2758-1572** for the terminal) to **Cahuita** and **Puerto Viejo** leave from here roughly every hour from 7:30am to 4:30pm daily.

Buses to **Punta Uva** and **Manzanillo,** both of which are south of Puerto Viejo, leave Limón daily at 5:30 6:30, 8:30, 10:30am, and 12:30, 3:30, 5:30, and 6:30pm from the same station.

CITY LAYOUT   Nearly all addresses in Limón are measured from the central market, which is aptly located smack-dab in the center of town, or from Parque Vargas, which is at the east end of town fronting the sea. The cruise-ship dock is just south of Parque Vargas. A pedestrian mall runs from Parque Vargas to the west for several blocks.

FAST FACTS   A host of private and national banks are in the small downtown area. You can reach the **local police** at ℂ **2758-1148** and the **Red Cross** at ℂ **2758-0125.** The **Tony Facio Hospital** (ℂ **2758-2222**) is just outside of downtown on the road to Playa Bonita.

Exploring Limón

Limón has little for tourists to do or see. The closest true attraction, **Veragua Rainforest Park** (p 553), is about a 40-minute drive. If you do end up spending any time in Limón, be sure to take a seat in **Parque Vargas** along the seawall and watch the citizens go about their business. Occupying a city block on the waterfront, this is a quiet oasis in the heart

Outdoor market in Limón

Veragua Rainforest Park

of downtown. You may even spot some sloths living in the trees here. If you want to shop for souvenirs, head to the **cruise ship terminal** whenever a ship is in port, and you'll find more than your fair share of vendors.

Finally, if you're interested in architecture, take a walk around town. When banana shipments built this port, local merchants erected elaborately decorated buildings, several of which have survived the city's many earthquakes, humid weather, and salty sea air. There's a certain charm in the town's fallen grace, drooping balconies, rotting woodwork, and chipped paint. One of the city's most famous buildings was known locally as the **Black Star Line**, located on Avenida 5 and Calle 5. Built in 1922, as the headquarters for Marcus Garvey's United Negro Improvement Association, it was restored and was the setting of a popular restaurant, but it burned down in 2016 and has yet to be rebuilt.

Just be careful: Despite being an increasingly popular cruise port, Limón is a rough and impoverished port town. Street crime and violence are problems. Tourists should stick to the very well-worn city center and spots mentioned here. Avoid walking anywhere at night, and even in the daytime, it's best to travel with someone else.

A ONE-STOP SHOP RAINFOREST TOURISM SPOT

Located outside of Limón in a patch of thick rainforest south of the banana town of Liverpool, **Veragua Rainforest Park** ★ (www.veragua rainforest.com; ✆ **4000-0949**) is a popular destination for cruise-ship excursions, but it's a worthy stop for anyone visiting the area. Attractions include a serpentarium, butterfly garden, entomology lab, hummingbird garden, insect exhibit, frog room, zipline canopy tour, and a short tram ride to a rainforest trail system. Along the trails, you'll find a beautiful little waterfall. A half-day tour runs $66, or $55 for children 4 to 12; a full day with canopy tour is $99, or $75 for children over 5. The park is open Tues to Sun from 8am to 3pm; closed Mon except when cruise ships are in town. Overnight options with simple quarters can be arranged.

Where to Stay

Hotel Maribu Caribe ★　About 2 miles north of Limón proper near Playa Bonita, Hotel Maribu Caribe's oceanfront setting more than compensates for its distance from town. The bungalows are forgettable but clean and kept cool with strong air-conditioners. Each has a patio a short walk from the central pool area. The coast is rocky directly in front of the property, but there's sand a short walk away.

Playa Bonita. www.maribu-caribe.com. ✆ **2795-4010**. 56 units. $70–$80 double, includes breakfast and taxes. **Amenities:** Restaurant; pool; free Wi-Fi (public areas).

Park Hotel ★　If spending a night in downtown Limón, this should be your first (and only) choice. The longstanding Park Hotel sits facing the water in the heart of downtown; a break wall and pedestrian promenade front the hotel. The exterior has been repainted from a gaudy pink to a mellow yellow, and let's hope it stays that way. Rooms are nothing to write home about, but spotless and blessed with a/c and small, outdated TVs. A popular restaurant here serves local Caribbean fare, Tico standards, and some Chinese dishes, perfectly reflecting the cultural mix of Limón.

Limón, Av. 3, btw. calles 1 and 3. www.parkhotellimon.com. ✆ **2758-4364**. 32 units. $74–$125 double, includes taxes and breakfast. **Amenities:** Restaurant; free Wi-Fi.

Where to Eat

Dining options are pretty limited in Limón. The restaurant at the **Park Hotel** (above) is reliable, but try to sample the local staple *pati*, a fried-dough concoction that is stuffed with a slightly spicy ground meat filling. You'll find *pati* vendors all over downtown Limón, including at the iconic **Soda El Patty** (✆ 2798-3407), on the corner of Avenida 5 and Calle 7.

If you're looking for a panoramic view, head to **Bar & Restaurante El Faro** (✆ **2758-4020**) or the **Red Snapper** (✆ **2758-7613**), which are located near each other up on El Resbalón, the highest point in town, near all the city's cellphone towers. Both serve traditional local fare and fresh seafood, and occasionally offer live music on weekend nights.

En Route South

Staying at the lodge listed below is a great way to enhance your Caribbean beach time with a wildlife-rich adventure deep in the jungle.

Selva Bananito Lodge ★★★   This remote ecolodge at the foot of Cerro Muchilla is as "eco" as they come, with its own private nature preserve and owners who are committed to conservation. The 1,275-hectare property was purchased in 1974 for farming and logging, but a decade later Jürgen Stein and his sisters persuaded their father to stop cutting down trees and start saving them. The lodge opened in 1995 as an alternate source of income, in hopes of promoting conservation through tourism. The bird-watching here is fabulous, and video cameras in the preserve routinely capture jaguars, ocelots, and pumas on the prowl. The gorgeous superior rooms on stilts offer two queen-size beds and louvered windows, and open onto broad verandas with pristine rainforest views.

Solar power provides electric light, hot showers, and a ceiling fan, though there are no power outlets in the rooms, and Internet and cellphone service are unreliable. This is a great place to unplug and commune with nature, and to go horseback riding, hiking, tree-climbing and waterfall rappelling. Meals are served family-style in the *rancho*, which has ceiling fans but no lighting except candles. To get here, cross the wide Bananito River in your own 4WD vehicle if you dare, or arrange for the staff to pick you up on the other side of the river or in the town of Bananito.

Near Bananito, southwest of Limón. www.selvabananito.com. ✆ **2253-8118.** 11 units. $100–$120 per person per day, double occupancy, all meals and taxes included; $160–$180 per person per day with meals, a tour, transfer from Bananito, and taxes included. **Amenities:** Restaurant with gluten-free and vegetarian options; wide range of tours.

A hungry monkey in Cahuita

CAHUITA ★

200km (124 miles) E of San José; 42km (26 miles) S of Limón; 13km (8 miles) N of Puerto Viejo

Cahuita is a small beach village and the first major tourist destination south of Limón. Nevertheless, the tourism boom in Puerto Viejo and the beaches to the south have in many ways passed Cahuita by. Depending on your point of view, that can be a reason to stay or to decide to head farther south. Any way you slice it, Cahuita is one of the more laid-back villages in Costa Rica. The few dirt and gravel streets here are host to a languid parade of pedestrian traffic, parted occasionally by a bicycle, car, or bus. After a short time, you'll find yourself slipping into the heat-induced torpor that affects anyone who ends up here.

The village traces its roots to Afro-Caribbean fishermen and laborers who settled in this region in the mid-1800s, and today the population is still mainly English-speaking black Costa Ricans whose culture and language set them apart from most of the country.

People come to Cahuita for its miles of pristine beaches, which stretch both north and south from town. The southern beaches, the forest behind them, and the coral reef offshore are all part of **Cahuita National Park ★★**. Silt and pesticides washing down from nearby banana plantations have taken a heavy toll on the reefs, so don't expect the snorkeling to be world-class. But on a calm day, it can be pretty good, and the beaches are idyllic every day. It can rain almost any time of year here, but the most dependably dry months are September and October.

Essentials

GETTING THERE & DEPARTING   By Plane: See p 550 for Limón info. *Note:* While taxis do meet all incoming flights, I highly recommend you arrange a specific private transfer with your hotel if possible.

By Car: Follow the directions on p 550 for getting to Limón. As you enter Limón, about 5 blocks before the busiest section of downtown, watch for a paved road to the right, just before the railroad tracks. Take this road (CR36) south to Cahuita, passing the airstrip and the beach on your left as you leave Limón. Alternatively, a turnoff with signs for Sixaola and La Bomba is several miles before Limón. This winding shortcut skirts the city and puts you on the coastal road (CR36) several miles south of Limón.

By Bus: Mepe express buses (www.mepecr.com; © **2257-8129**) leave San José daily at 6 and 10am, noon, and 2 and 4pm from the Caribbean bus terminal (Gran Terminal del Caribe) on Calle Central, Avenida 13. The trip's duration is 4 hours; the fare is C4,800. During peak periods, extra buses are often added. However, it's wise to check because this bus line (Mepe) is one of the most fickle.

You can also catch a bus to **Limón** (see p 550) and then transfer to a Cahuita- or Puerto Viejo–bound bus (℃ **2758-1572**) in Limón. These buses leave roughly every 2 hours between 7:30am and 4:30pm from the main Terminal Talamanca in Limón. Buses from Limón to Manzanillo also stop in Cahuita and leave from the same spot roughly every 2 hours between 6:30am and 6:30pm. The trip takes 1 hour; the fare is C2,5000.

Interbus (www.interbusonline.com; ℃ **4100-0888**) has a daily bus that leaves San José for Cahuita at 7:20am. The fare is $54. Interbus buses leave Cahuita daily at both 6am and 1:30pm. Interbus will pick you up at most area hotels in both San José and Cahuita, and offers connections to various other destinations around Costa Rica.

Buses departing **Puerto Viejo** and Sixaola (on the Panama border) stop in Cahuita roughly every 2 hours between 7am and 7pm en route to San José. However, the schedule is far from precise, so it's always best to check with your hotel. Moreover, these buses are often full, particularly on weekends and in the high season. To avoid standing in the aisle all the way to San José, it is sometimes better to take a bus first to Limón and then catch one of the frequent Limón–San José buses. Buses to Limón pass through Cahuita regularly throughout the day.

VILLAGE LAYOUT   Cahuita has about eight dirt streets. The highway runs parallel to the coast, with three main access roads running perpendicular. The northernmost of these bypasses town and brings you to the northern end of Playa Negra. It's marked with signs for the Magellan Inn and other hotels. The second road takes you to the southern end of Playa Negra, about 1km (a half-mile) closer to town. The third road is the principal entrance into town. The village's main street, parallel to the highway, dead-ends at the national park entrance (a footbridge over a small stream).

Buses drop passengers off at a terminal at the back of a small strip mall on the main entrance road into town. Cabs will be waiting to take you to the lodges on Playa Negra. Or you can walk north on the street that runs between Coco's Bar and the small park. This road curves to the left and continues 1.6km (1 mile) or so out to Playa Negra.

FAST FACTS   The police station (℃ **2755-0217**) is located where the road from Playa Negra turns into town. You'll find the post office (℃ **2755-0096**) as well as a well-equipped pharmacy, **Farmacia Cahuita** (℃ **2755-0505**), and a bank with an ATM in the small strip mall in front of the bus station. If you can't find a cab, ask your hotel to call you one.

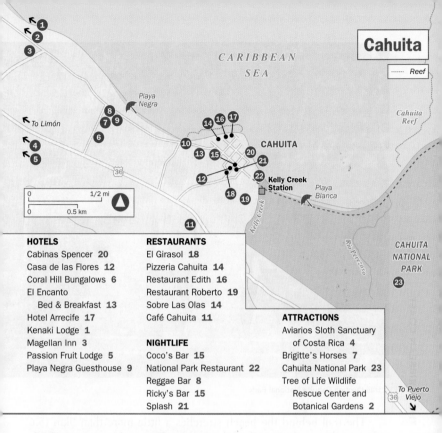

Cahuita

CARIBBEAN SEA

------- Reef

Cahuita Reef

Playa Negra

To Limón

Playa Negra

CAHUITA

Kelly Creek Station

Playa Blanca

Kelly Creek

Río Perezoso

CAHUITA NATIONAL PARK

0 ____ 1/2 mi
0 ____ 0.5 km

36

To Puerto Viejo

36

HOTELS

Cabinas Spencer **20**
Casa de las Flores **12**
Coral Hill Bungalows **6**
El Encanto
   Bed & Breakfast **13**
Hotel Arrecife **17**
Kenaki Lodge **1**
Magellan Inn **3**
Passion Fruit Lodge **5**
Playa Negra Guesthouse **9**

RESTAURANTS

El Girasol **18**
Pizzeria Cahuita **14**
Restaurant Edith **16**
Restaurant Roberto **19**
Sobre Las Olas **14**
Café Cahuita **11**

NIGHTLIFE

Coco's Bar **15**
National Park Restaurant **22**
Reggae Bar **8**
Ricky's Bar **15**
Splash **21**

ATTRACTIONS

Aviarios Sloth Sanctuary
   of Costa Rica **4**
Brigitte's Horses **7**
Cahuita National Park **23**
Tree of Life Wildlife
   Rescue Center and
   Botanical Gardens **2**

Exploring Cahuita National Park ★★

This little gem of a national park sits at the southern edge of Cahuita. Although the pristine white-sand beach, with its picture-perfect coconut palms and lush coastal forest backing it, is the main draw here, the park was actually created to preserve the 240-hectare (787-acre) **coral reef** just offshore. The reef contains 35 species of coral and provides a haven for hundreds of brightly colored tropical fish. You can walk on the beach itself or follow the trail that runs through the forest just behind the beach.

One of the best places to swim is just before or beyond the **Río Perezoso** (Lazy River), several hundred meters inside Cahuita National Park. The trail behind the beach is great for bird-watching, and you might see a sloth or some howler or white-faced monkeys. Nearer at hand, you're likely to hear crabs and lizards scuttling in the dry leaves on the forest floor. A half-dozen or so species of land crabs live in this region, including some that are a beautiful bright orange and purple.

A trail through Cahuita National Park

The trail behind the beach stretches a little more than 9km (5.6 miles) to the southern end of the park at **Puerto Vargas** (© **2755-0302**), where you'll find a lovely white-sand beach. The best section of reef is off the point at Punta Cahuita, and you can snorkel here if accompanied by a local guide. If you don't dawdle, the 3.8km (2.4-mile) hike to Punta Cahuita should take a little over an hour each way—although I'd allow plenty of extra time to enjoy the flora and fauna, and take a dip or two in the sea.

Although you can snorkel from the shore at Punta Cahuita, it's best to have a boat take you out to the nicest coral heads just offshore. A 3-hour **snorkel trip** costs between $20 and $35 per person, with equipment. You can arrange one with any of the local tour companies listed below. **Note:** These trips are best taken when the seas are calm—for safety's sake, visibility, and comfort.

ENTRY POINTS, FEES & REGULATIONS The **in-town park entrance** is just over a footbridge at the end of the village's main street. It has restroom facilities, changing rooms, and storage lockers. This is the best place to enter for a day hike and some beach time.

The alternate park entrance is at the southern end of the park in **Puerto Vargas.** This is where you should come if you don't feel up to

Exploring the Park

One great way to explore Cahuita National Park is to pack a picnic lunch and snorkel gear and hire a guide in the town of Cahuita. You're not supposed to snorkel here without a local guide, and you'll see a lot more animals with a guide's expert eye. You can then hike the rainforest trail to Punta Cahuita, where you can snorkel the reef, swim in the tide pools, and have lunch. (But don't ever leave valuables unattended on the beach—any beach.) After that you can return the way you came, if you have a car in Cahuita, or even better, continue on to Puerto Vargas and catch a bus or taxi from there. For most of this hike, you can choose between the shaded jungle trail or the sunny beach, stopping for a cooling dip when the mood strikes.

hiking a couple of hours to reach the good snorkeling spots. The road to Puerto Vargas is approximately 5km (3 miles) south of Cahuita.

There's no **admission** fee to enter the park, but donations are suggested. The park is open from dawn to dusk for day visitors.

GETTING THERE   By Car: The turnoff for the Puerto Vargas entrance is clearly marked 5km (3 miles) south of Cahuita.

By Bus: Your best bet is to get off a Puerto Viejo– or Sixaola-bound bus at the turnoff for the Puerto Vargas entrance (well-marked, but tell

Playa Vargas in Cahuita National Park

the bus driver in advance). The guard station/entrance is about 500m (1,640 ft.) down this road. The beach and trails are several kilometers farther.

Beaches & Activities Outside the Park

Outside the park, the best place for swimming is **Playa Negra,** especially the stretch right in front of the Playa Negra Guesthouse (p 563). The waves here are often good for bodysurfing, boogie-boarding, or surfing. If you want to rent a board or try a surf lesson, check in with Rennie at **Willie's Tours** (see below) or **Brigitte** (see below).

Cahuita has plenty of options for organized adventure trips or tours. I recommend **Cahuita Tours** (www.cahuitatours.com; ✆ 2755-0101) and **Willie's Tours ★** (www.williestourscostarica.com; ✆ 2755-1024 or 8917-6982). Both are located along Cahuita's main road, and offer a wide range of tours, from snorkeling to rainforest hikes to visits to nearby indigenous reserves. They also offer multiday trips to Tortuguero, as well as to Bocas del Toro, Panama.

HORSEBACK RIDING **Brigitte** (www.brigittecahuita.com; ✆ 2755-0053) offers guided horseback tours for $35 to $85. She also rents mountain bikes and surfboards and has a few cabins available on the ranch.

WILDLIFE VIEWING Bird-watchers and sloth lovers should head north 11km (7 miles) to **Aviarios Sloth Sanctuary of Costa Rica ★★** (www.slothsanctuary.com; ✆ 2750-0775). Its signature tour features an informative visit to a sloth rehabilitation project and learning center, as well as a 1-hour canoe tour through the surrounding estuary and river system ($30 for adults, $15 for kids 5–12; kids under 5 free). More than 330 species of birds have been spotted here. You'll get an up-close look at a range of rescued wild sloths, both adults and babies, as well as several bred in captivity. After that, you can hike the trail system and look for sloths in the wild. Tours start every hour, from 8am to 2pm. Make reservations in advance. The sanctuary (closed on Mondays) also offers a few cozy and quaint rooms if you want to spend more time exploring the bird-watching and wildlife options, as well as the sloth rescue project.

A sloth at the Aviarios Sloth Sanctuary of Costa Rica

Toward the northern end of the dirt road leading out beyond Playa Negra is the **Tree of Life Wildlife Rescue Center and Botanical Gardens** ★ (www.treeoflifecostarica.com; © **2755-0014**). Stroll through extensive, well-maintained gardens, where large cages house a range of rescued and recovering local fauna, including toucans, monkeys, coatimundi, deer, and peccaries. It's open Tuesday through Sunday, with a daily guided tour at 11am, though it closes in September and October. Admission is $15.

Where to Stay

In addition to the places listed below, **Coral Hill Bungalows** ★★ (www.coralhillbungalows.com; © **2755-0479**) has three individual bungalows with free breakfast and Wi-Fi in a garden setting, about a block or so inland from the beach at Playa Negra.

Casa de las Flores (www.lacasadelasfloreshotel.com; © **2755-0326**) has neat and cheery rooms and is on the main road in the center of town, close to the national park entrance. Also, five kilometers north of town on the opposite side of the highway, is **Passion Fruit Lodge** (© **8939-9823**; http://passionfruitlodge.com), with five standalone cabins on a sprawling, jungle clad property with an outdoor pool.

INEXPENSIVE

El Encanto Bed & Breakfast ★★   A short stroll from the beaches and main drag, the popular El Encanto does seem to have a touch of enchantment to it. A tranquil compound that's dominated by a white-washed, colonial-style guesthouse, it's an exotic mix of the tropical (bromeliads, heliconias, and orchids all over) and the indigenous Central American (seven guestrooms with arched doorways and windows, lively artwork on the walls, and varnished wood or red terra cotta floors). Modern conveniences aren't ignored: There's a small pool and gazebos that house a two-person Jacuzzi, and a pair of hanging chairs meant to lull you into a midafternoon siesta. Service is extremely friendly and accommodating.

Just outside Cahuita on the road to Playa Negra. ⓒ **2755-0113.** www.elencanto cahuita.com. 7 units. $95 double; $115 studio, $210 studio suite, includes breakfast. Lower rates in off season; higher during peak weeks. **Amenities:** Restaurant, pool; Jacuzzi, small spa and Wi-Fi.

Hotel Arrecife ★   A seafront location and small pool give this very inexpensive backpacker haunt some appeal. Set facing the sea, this spartan place features a row of rooms in a low concrete building. The rooms are kept acceptably tidy and come with one twin and one double bed, as well as TVs, hot showers, and fans. Next door is Restaurant Edith (see p 564).

Cahuita (about 100m/328 ft. east of the police station). www.cabinasarrecife.com. ⓒ **2755-0081** or 8835-2940. 11 units. $34 double; $44 double with A/C, includes taxes. **Amenities:** Pool; free Wi-Fi.

Kenaki Lodge ★   This small, family-run operation several miles north of town is just across the road from the beach. The Balinese-style lodge has a few rooms and private one- and two-bedroom bungalows with kitchens. The wood floor rooms are not luxurious by any means, but are cozy and get good air flow. Discounts are offered for long term stays.

Playa Grande, Cahuita. www.kenakilodge.com. ⓒ **2755-0485.** 6 units. $100 double; $120-220 bungalows, includes breakfast (not for bungalows). No credit cards. **Amenities:** Free Wi-Fi, dojo, bicycle rentals.

Magellan Inn ★★   Canadian Terry Newton is the second-generation owner/manager of this quaint boutique hotel, and she's kept the balance of elements that makes this place special. Service is friendly but not intrusive; rooms are spacious, clean and decorated with tropical touches like wildlife paintings and the grounds are beautiful, with abundant flowers and a lovely saltwater pool built into the local coral.

At the far end of Playa Negra, about 2km/1¼ miles north of Cahuita. www.magellan boutiquehotel.com. ⓒ **2755-0035.** 6 units. $98 double, includes breakfast. **Amenities:** Bar; lounge; pool; yoga/meditation/massage center; horseback riding; free Wi-Fi.

Playa Negra Guesthouse ★★★ The best beachfront hotel in Cahuita by a long shot, Playa Negra Guesthouse is set just across a dirt-and-sand lane from a quiet and palm-lined stretch of beach. The hotel has well-tended, exuberant gardens, rooms with lots of personality, and plantation-style cottages (love the art on the walls and the unusual bed-spreads). A couple of these cottages—painted in Crayola colors and adorned with intricate gingerbread trim—come with full kitchens, making them ideal for families or those planning on an extended stay. Owners Pierre and Marise are always present to give advice and help in any way. No meals are served here, but several restaurants are within an easy walk, and the center of Cahuita is about 1.6km (1 mile) away.

On Playa Negra, about 1.5km/1 mile north of Cahuita. www.playanegra.cr. ☏ **2755-0127.** 7 units. $59–$107 double; cottages for 2–3, $134–$165, plus tax. **Amenities:** Pool; laundry service; free Wi-Fi.

Where to Eat

Coconut figures into a lot of the regional cuisine here. Most nights, local women cook up pots of various local specialties and sell them from the front porches of the two discos or from streetside stands around town; a full meal will cost you around $5.

Playa Negra Guesthouse

In addition to the places listed below, for good, fresh Italian fare, try **El Girasol** (© **2755-1164**), a small, elegant family-run joint on the main road into town. Another popular Italian option is **Pizzeria Cahuita** (© **2755-0179**), located between the police station and Restaurant Edith.

Café Cahuita ★ COFFEEHOUSE   The town's best breakfast spot features good coffee drinks of all types, made-to-order eggs, smoothies, and crepes. You'll dine on these and more (it's also open for lunch) in an airy, slightly rickety old wooden raised-stilt building on the main street near the center of the village.

On the main road in Cahuita, near the entrance to the national park. No phone. Main courses C2,000–C7,000. No credit cards. Daily 6:30am–4pm.

Restaurant Edith ★ CREOLE/COSTA RICAN   When tourists were just starting to discover Cahuita, a well-known local lady named Miss Edith Brown started serving them down-home Caribbean cooking from her front porch. Now she and her daughters (and other family members) run Restaurant Edith, which may not be long on decor but delivers the goods, made to order. Dig in to flavorful local specialties like *rondon* (see "That Run-Down Feeling" box, p 577) and jerk chicken, served with typical sides like breadfruit and coconut rice and beans. Keep in mind that service is Caribbean slow, and during high season you may have to share a table.

By the police station, Cahuita. © **2755-0248.** Main courses C5,000–C20,000. No credit cards. Tues–Sun 7:30am–10pm.

Restaurante Roberto ★ SEAFOOD   Run by a fifth generation Cahuita fishermen, lobster is the specialty at this thatched roof restaurant in the center of town. There are a few tanks inside the dining area, ensuring that the crustaceans are as fresh as possible. Skip the nachos and other international dishes. Service can be painfully slow.

On the main road in Cahuita, 2 blocks north of National Park entrance. © **2755-0177.** Main courses C2,500–C12,000. No credit cards. Daily noon–10pm.

Sobre Las Olas ★★ SEAFOOD/ITALIAN   Both locals and visitors love this place (including a sloth that often travels through the trees right outside around dinnertime, much to the delight of diners). Not only does this small, oceanfront restaurant have one of the best settings in the region (if not the country), with the sea just steps away, and a stunning view down the coastline, but the food is excellent. The Italian owners prepare the freshest local seafood in a variety of ways, touching on their home-country heritage and Caribbean cuisine in equal measure. You might choose between a ceviche or a carpaccio of fresh snapper to start, followed by Sicilian-style pasta with locally caught shrimp, or a filet of mahi-mahi in a coconut cream sauce. After eating, you can saunter onto

| Cahuita's Calypso Legend |

Walter "Gavitt" Ferguson, who turned 98 in 2017, is a musical legend. For decades, Ferguson labored and sang in obscurity. Occasionally he would record a personalized cassette tape of original tunes for an interested tourist willing to part with $5. Finally, in 2002, Ferguson was recorded by the local label Papaya Music (www.papayamusic.com). Today, he has two CDs of original songs, "Babylon" and "Dr. Bombodee." Ask around town and you should be able to find a copy.

the beach and commandeer one of the hammocks strung between the trees.

Just north of Cahuita on the road to Playa Negra. © **2755-0109.** Main courses C6,000–C12,000. Wed–Mon noon–10pm.

Shopping

For a wide selection of beachwear, local crafts, cheesy souvenirs, and batik clothing, try **CoCo Boutique,** on the main road near the entrance to the park. Folks also come here to have their hair wrapped in colorful threads and strung with beads. Heading north out of town, similar wares are offered at the **Cahuita Tours** gift shop. Also, local and itinerant artisans in makeshift stands near the park entrance sell handmade jewelry and crafts.

If you're interested in the region, pick up a copy of Paula Palmer's book "What Happen: A Folk-History of Costa Rica's Talamanca Coast," based on interviews with many of the area's oldest residents. It's a fun and interesting read, and you just might meet someone mentioned in the book.

Nightlife & Entertainment

Coco's Bar ★, a classic Rasta painted Caribbean watering hole and restaurant at the main crossroads in town, has traditionally been the place to while away the nights (and days, for that matter). Cold beer and very loud reggae and soca music are the lures. Just across the street, the two-story **Ricky's Bar** tries to give Coco's a run for its money, and many people ping-pong between the two. Toward the park entrance, the **National Park Restaurant** has a popular bar, with loud music and dancing on most nights during the high season and on weekends during the off-season. Out toward Playa Negra, the **Reggae Bar ★** has a convivial vibe, with thumping tropical tunes blasting most nights. For gamesters, there's **Splash** (© **8889-9668**), a restaurant and sports bar in the center of the village. Splash has billiard and foosball tables, as well as regular movie and karaoke nights, live bands, and DJs. It also has a small

Cahuita locals playing a friendly game of dominoes

swimming pool open to restaurant guests, and is especially refreshing on hot afternoons, although it's often tempting to late-night revelers as well.

PUERTO VIEJO ★★

200km (124 miles) E of San José; 55km (34 miles) S of Limón

Puerto Viejo is the Caribbean coast's top destination, and deservedly so. Not to be confused with the landlocked Puerto Viejo de Sarapiquí in the north, this beach town is sometimes called Puerto Viejo de Limón or Puerto Viejo de Talamanca. Hotels, restaurants, bars, and shops abound, and the streets teem with bicycles, cars, trucks, tourists, expats, and locals. Here you can feel perfectly normal strolling the main street in a bikini, and don't be surprised if someone offers you something to smoke. The town is popular with surfers who come to ride its famous and fearsome Salsa Brava wave, and the only slightly mellower Playa Cocles (p 580) beach break. Non-surfers can enjoy other primo swimming beaches, plenty of active adventure options, nearby rainforest trails, and a slew of restaurants.

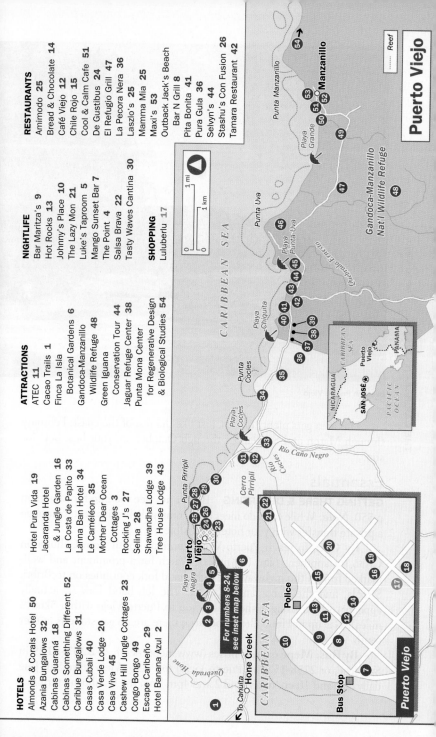

HOTELS

Almonds & Corals Hotel **50**
Azania Bungalows **32**
Cabinas Guaraná **18**
Cabinas Something Different **52**
Caribe Bungalows **31**
Casas Cubaií **40**
Casa Verde Lodge **20**
Casa Viva **45**
Cashew Hill Jungle Cottages **23**
Congo Bongo **49**
Escape Caribeño **29**
Hotel Banana Azul **2**

Hotel Pura Vida **19**
Jacaranda Hotel
  & Jungle Garden **16**
La Costa de Papito **33**
Lanna Ban Hotel **34**
Le Caméléon **35**
Mother Dear Ocean
  Cottages **3**
Rocking J's **27**
Selina **28**
Shawandha Lodge **39**
Tree House Lodge **43**

ATTRACTIONS

ATEC **11**
Cacao Trails **1**
Finca La Isla
  Botanical Gardens **6**
Gandoca-Manzanillo
  Wildlife Refuge **48**
Green Iguana
  Conservation Tour **44**
Jaguar Refuge Center **38**
Punta Mona Center
  for Regenerative Design
  & Biological Studies **54**

NIGHTLIFE

Bar Maritza's **9**
Hot Rocks **13**
Johnny's Place **10**
The Lazy Mon **21**
Luke's Taproom **5**
Mango Sunset Bar **7**
The Point **4**
Salsa Brava **22**
Tasty Waves Cantina **30**

SHOPPING

Luluberlu **17**

RESTAURANTS

Amimodo **25**
Bread & Chocolate **14**
Café Viejo **12**
Chile Rojo **15**
Cool & Calm Cafe **51**
De Gustibus **24**
El Refugio Grill **47**
La Pecora Nera **36**
Laszlo's **25**
Mamma Mia **25**
Maxi's **53**
Outback Jack's Beach
  Bar N Grill **8**
Pita Bonita **41**
Pura Gula **36**
Selvyn's **44**
Stashu's Con Fusion **26**
Tamara Restaurant **42**

Puerto Viejo

567

Beach in Puerto Viejo

This area gets plenty of rain, just like the rest of the coast; February through March and September through October are your best bets for sun.

Essentials

GETTING THERE & DEPARTING   By Plane: See the info for Limón on p 550. *Note:* While taxis do meet all incoming flights, it's best to arrange a private transfer with your hotel if possible.

By Car: To reach Puerto Viejo, continue south from Cahuita on CR36 for another 16km (10 miles). Watch for a prominent and well-marked fork in the highway. The right-hand fork continues on to Bribri, Sixaola, and the Panamanian border. The left-hand fork (it actually appears to be a straight shot) takes you to Puerto Viejo within 5km (3 miles). Gas up in Hone Creek, because there are no gas stations farther south.

By Bus: Mepe express buses (www.mepecr.com; ✆ **2257-8129** in San José, or 2758-1572 in Puerto Viejo) to Puerto Viejo leave San José daily at 6 and 10am, noon, and 2 and 4pm from the Caribbean terminal

(Gran Terminal del Caribe) on Calle Central, Avenida 13. The trip's duration is 4½ to 5 hours; the fare is C6,000. During peak periods, extra buses are sometimes added. Always ask if the bus is continuing on to **Manzanillo** (helpful if you're staying in a hotel south of town).

Interbus (www.interbusonline.com; ℂ **4100-0888**) has daily buses that leave San José for Puerto Viejo at 7:20am and 2:30pm. The fare is $54. Interbus buses leave Puerto Viejo daily at 6am and 1:30pm. Interbus will pick you up at most hotels in both San José and Puerto Viejo, and offers connections to various other destinations around Costa Rica.

Or you can catch a bus to **Limón** (p 550) and then transfer to a Puerto Viejo–bound bus in Limón. These latter buses (ℂ **2758-1572**) leave roughly every hour between 7:30am and 4:30pm from the main terminal in Limón. Buses from Limón to Manzanillo stop in Puerto Viejo and leave daily about every 2 hours between 5:50am and 6:30pm. The trip is 1½ hours; the fare is C2,000 to Puerto Viejo, and C2,550 to Manzanillo.

If you arrive in Puerto Viejo by bus, be leery of street salesmen offering hotel rooms. In most cases, they work on a small commission from

A beached barge at Puerto Viejo

whatever hotel or *cabina* is hiring, and, in some cases, they'll steer you away from a better hotel or falsely claim that it's full.

Express buses leave Puerto Viejo for San José daily at 9 and 11am and 4pm. Buses for Limón leave daily roughly every 2 hours between 9:30am and 6:30pm. However, schedules are subject to change, so it's best to check with your hotel. Buses to **Punta Uva** and **Manzanillo** leave Puerto Viejo about a half-dozen times throughout the day.

GETTING AROUND Taxis are fairly easy to come by around Puerto Viejo. You'll either find them hanging around the *parquecito* (little park), or you can call **Taxi PV** (📞 **2750-0439**). You can rent scooters and bicycles from a handful of roadside operators around town. If you need to rent a car, head to **Adobe Rent A Car** (www.adobecar.com; 📞 **2750-0290**).

TOWN LAYOUT The road in from the highway runs parallel to Playa Negra, or Black Sand Beach (not the beach in Cahuita), for a few hundred meters before entering the village of Puerto Viejo. The sea is on your left and forested hills on your right as you come into town. It's another 15km (9⅓ miles) south to Manzanillo. This road is paved all the way to Manzanillo, although many sections are marked with enormous potholes.

FAST FACTS You'll find a couple of banks and ATMs, as well as the **post office** (📞 2750-0404), near the entrance to town. A **police office** (📞 **2750-0230**) is on the beach, near Johnny's Place (p 580).

There are several self- and full-service laundry facilities around town. The one at **Café Rico** (📞 **2750-0510**) will give you a free cup of coffee, cappuccino, or espresso while you wait.

Exploring Puerto Viejo

CULTURAL & ADVENTURE TOURS The **Asociación Talamanqueña de Ecoturismo y Conservación** ★★★ (**ATEC;** Talamancan Association of Ecotourism and Conservation; www.ateccr.org; 📞 **2750-0398**), across the street from the Soda Tamara, is a local organization dedicated to preserving the environment and cultural heritage of this area and promoting ecologically sound development. If you plan to stay in Puerto Viejo for an extended period of time and would like to contribute to the community, ask about volunteering. In addition to functioning as the local info center, Internet cafe, and traveler's hub, ATEC runs a little shop that sells T-shirts, maps, posters, and books.

ATEC also offers quite a few tours, including **half-day walks** that focus on nature and either the local Afro-Caribbean culture or the indigenous Bribri culture. These walks pass through farms and forests; along the way you'll learn about local history, customs, medicinal plants, and indigenous mythology, and have an opportunity to see sloths, monkeys, iguanas, keel-billed toucans, and other wildlife. A range of different walks lead through the nearby **Bribri Indians' Kékölди Reserve,** as well as more strenuous hikes through the primary rainforest. **Bird walks** and **night walks** will help you spot more of the area wildlife; there are even overnight treks. The local guides have a wealth of information and make a hike through the forest a truly educational experience. ATEC can arrange snorkeling and fishing trips in dugout canoes, and everything from surf lessons to dance classes. ATEC can also help you arrange overnight and multiday **camping trips** into the Talamanca Mountains and through neighboring indigenous reserves, as well as trips to Tortuguero and even a 7- to 10-day transcontinental trek to the Pacific coast. Half-day tours and night walks range from $32 to $65, while full-day to overnight tours run between $75 and $129. Some tours require a minimum of three or four people and several days' advance notice. The ATEC office is open Mon through Sat from 8am to 8pm and Sun from 11am to 7pm.

Local tour operators **Exploradores Outdoors ★★** (www. exploradoresoutdoors.com; ✆ **2750-2020**), **Gecko Trail Adventures ★★** (www.geckotrail.com; ✆ **2756-8412**), and **Terraventuras ★** (www.terraventuras.com; ✆ **2750-0750**) all offer a host of half- and full-day adventure tours into the jungle or sea for between $40 and $280 per person. One especially popular tour is Terraventuras's zipline canopy tour, which features 22 treetop platforms, a large harnessed swing, and a rappel.

SCUBA DIVING   Scuba divers can check in with **Reef Runners Dive Shop** (www.reefrunnerdivers.com; ✆ **2750-0480**) or **Punta Uva Dive Center** (www.puntauvadivecenter.com; ✆ **2759-9191**). Both of these operations frequent a variety of dive sites between Puerto Viejo and Punta Mona, and if you're lucky the seas will be calm and visibility good—although throughout most of the year, it can be a bit rough and murky here. Reef Runners has an office in downtown Puerto Viejo, while Punta Uva Dive Center has its operations center right off the beach in Punta Uva. Rates run between $80 and $120 for a two-tank boat dive.

A LITTLE MIND & BODY REVITALIZATION   Indulgence **Spa & Beauty Salon ★★** (www.indulgencespa-salon.com; ✆ **2750-0536**), located at La Costa de Papito (p 589), has a wide range of massage, beauty, and body treatment options at reasonable rates.

Pure Jungle Spa ★★ (www.purejunglespa.com; ✆ **2756-8413**) offers a similar menu of treatment options in a lovely space close to downtown, just across from Rocking J's (p 576). The spa makes many of its own oils, masks, wraps, and exfoliants.

Better suited to a longer stay or organized retreat, **Samasati** (www. samasati.com; ✆ **800/563-9643** in the U.S., or 2737-3418 in Costa

13

THE CARIBBEAN COAST

Puerto Viejo

Rica) is a lovely jungle yoga retreat and spa, with spectacular hillside views of the Caribbean Sea and surrounding forests. Rates run between $190 and $260 per person per day, depending on occupancy and room type, and include two vegetarian meals per day. A wide range of tour, massage, and yoga packages are available. If you're staying elsewhere in Puerto Viejo or Cahuita, you can come up for yoga classes ($15), meditation ($15), or private massages ($95–$145) with advance notice. Samasati is located a few of kilometers before Puerto Viejo (near the turnoff for Bribri) and roughly 1.6km (1 mile) up into the jungle.

NOT YOUR EVERYDAY GARDENS
One of the nicest ways to spend a day in Puerto Viejo is to visit the **Finca La Isla Botanical Gardens ★★ (⌀ 8886-8530;** www.costaricaorganicsfarm.com; Fri–Mon 10am–4pm), inland from the Black Sand Beach on a side road just north of El Pizote lodge. Peter Kring and his late wife Lindy poured time and love into the creation of this collection of native and imported tropical flora. Here you'll see medicinal, commercial, and just plain wild flowering plants, fruits, herbs, trees, and bushes, plus gorge on whatever is ripe at the moment. A rigorous rainforest loop trail leaves from the grounds. Entry to the garden is $6 per person for a self-guided tour (you can buy a trail map for an extra $1), or $30 for a 2½-hour guided tour (minimum of three people).

ABOVE: **A spa treatment at Pure Jungle Spa**
BELOW: **Cacao fruit**

Cacao Trails ★ (© 756-8186; www.cacaotrails.com), also called the Museo Nacional de Cacao, is near Hone Creek between Cahuita and Puerto Viejo. It's a one-stop attraction featuring botanical gardens; an open-air museum, demonstrating cacao cultivation and processing; a series of trails; a large open-air restaurant; and a swimming pool. You can take canoe rides on the bordering Carbon River, and even watch leatherback sea turtles lay their eggs during the nesting season (p 113). Admission is $25, including a guided tour. A full day of activities, including lunch and a canoe trip as well as the guided tour, costs $47. During turtle nesting season, night tours are offered in Cahuita National Park.

Cacao beans drying in the sun

SUNNING & SURFING **Surfing** has historically been the main draw here, but increasing numbers of visitors are coming for the miles of beautiful and uncrowded **beaches** ★★, acres of lush rainforests, and laidback atmosphere. For swimming and sunbathing, locals like to hang out on the small patches of sand in front of Lazy Mon and Johnny's Place. Small, protected tide pools are in front of each of these bars for cooling off. Lazy Mon has several hammocks; you're likely to stumble upon a pickup beach volleyball match or soccer game here.

If you want a more open patch of sand and sea, head north to **Playa Negra,** along the road into town, or, better yet, to the beaches south of town around Punta Uva and all the way down to Manzanillo, where the coral reefs keep the surf much more manageable (p 582).

Just offshore of Puerto Viejo is a shallow reef where powerful storm-generated waves sometimes reach 6m (20 ft.). **Salsa Brava** ★★★, as it's known, is the prime surf break on the Caribbean coast. Even when the waves are small, this spot is recommended only for very experienced surfers because of the danger of the reef. Other popular beach breaks are south of town on Playa Cocles.

Several operators and makeshift roadside stands offer bicycles, scooters, boogie boards, surfboards, and snorkel gear for rent. Compare prices and the quality of the equipment before handing over money.

The beach in front of Lazy Mon

ANOTHER WAY TO GET WET & WILD **Exploradores Outdoors** ★★
(www.exploradoresoutdoors.com; © **646/205-0828** U.S., 2222-6262
in San José, or 2750-2020 in Puerto Viejo) runs daily whitewater rafting
trips on the Pacuare and Reventazón rivers. The full-day trip, including
transportation, breakfast, and lunch, is $99. If you want to combine
whitewater rafting with your transportation to or from the Caribbean
coast, the company can pick you up in San José or La Fortuna with all
your luggage, take you for a day of rafting, and drop you off at day's end
at your hotel anywhere on the Caribbean coast from Cahuita to Manzanillo. You can use this option in the other direction, as well. Exploradores
Outdoors also offers a combination kayaking and hiking tour to Punta
Uva, as well as overnight tours to Tortuguero.

Where to Stay

For a longer stay, close to town, you might want to check out **Cashew
Hill Jungle Cottages** (www.cashewhilllodge.co.cr; © **2750-0001**).
On a hill just on the outskirts of town, Cashew Hill offers simple
but immaculate individual one- and two-bedroom bungalows, with
kitchenettes.

Also consider **Mother Dear Ocean Cottages** ★ (www.mother dearcr.com), which offers two fully equipped cottages on the beach in Playa Negra, though there is a 3-night minimum.

MODERATE

Hotel Banana Azul ★★★   Colin Brownlee of Canada says he's not renting rooms, he's selling experiences, and it seems to be a winning formula at this popular beachfront hotel. It's located on the far northern end of Playa Negra, a vast stretch of beach backed by thick forest that stretches north from here all the way to Cahuita National Park. The decor features such fabulous touches as koi ponds with turtles in the middle of the ceramic-tiled common lounge. One of the top draws here is the Azul Beach Club, which serves food and drinks on the beach, with shaded lounge chairs and a great ocean view. Banana Azul calls itself "straight-friendly," with a clientele that's 20% gay, and caters mostly to couples. Four snazzy two-story condo-style units, called Villas Banana Verde ★★★ have full kitchens and private plunge pools. Additionally, they have another four rooms in an annex next door, called Casa Las Brisas.

Playa Negra. www.bananaazul.com. ✆ **2750-2035.** 14 units. $109 double; $159 suites, includes breakfast. No children under 16. **Amenities:** Restaurant; bar; bike rental; Jacuzzi; pool; free Wi-Fi.

INEXPENSIVE

True budget hounds will find an abundance of basic hotels and *cabinas* in downtown Puerto Viejo in addition to those listed below. Of these, the 10-room **Hotel Pura Vida** (www.hotel-puravida.com; ✆ **2750-0002**) is worth a look.

Cabinas Guaraná ★   Clean, safe, and friendly—so what if the sheets are getting a bit worn here? Most visitors are so pleased with the prices, the friendly reception, and the cheery decor (yellow walls with windows trimmed in bold purples and blues, louvered windows, low beds with slatted wooden headboards) that they forget to complain. The hotel is set a block inland from the town's main street, and has a quieter feel than you'd expect for such a centrally located lodging.

1½ blocks inland from Café Viejo, Puerto Viejo. www.hotelguarana.com. ✆ **2750-0244.** 12 units. $45 double. Rates slightly lower in off-season. **Amenities:** Lounge; communal kitchen; free Wi-Fi.

Casa Verde Lodge ★★   Casa Verde is an eye-pleasing, tranquil place with spa services and a lovely, landscaped pool area. Budget travelers are catered to in the Heliconia and Bromelia rooms, which come with shared bathroom facilities and are somewhat spartan. Larger cabins and rooms with private baths are available for those who want more privacy. All have dark, well-worn wooden floors, and most have a private balcony or patio. The flowering gardens are nice, and the rooms, grounds, and even shared bathrooms and showers are immaculately maintained. In the town center.

Puerto Viejo. www.casaverdelodge.com. © **2750-0015.** 17 units, 9 with private bathroom. $55 double with shared bathroom; $69-85 double with private bathroom. **Amenities:** Outdoor pool; massage hut; free Wi-Fi.

Escape Caribeño ★★

Owned by a very friendly Italian couple, Gloria Gavioli and Mauro Marchiori, these pretty bungalows are just on the outskirts of Puerto Viejo, a 7-minute walk from downtown. Ten units are on the inland side of the road, surrounded by well-tended tropical gardens; and four are on the ocean side, steps from the beach. Gloria loves her flowers and keeps her gardens spick-and-span. All rooms have air-conditioning, private bath with hot water, safe, minibar and refrigerator.

On the southeast edge of Puerto Viejo on the main road. www.escapecaribeno.com. © **2750-0103.** 14 units. $75–$95 double. **Amenities:** Ocean views; gated parking; night security; laundry service; free Wi-Fi.

Jacaranda Hotel & Jungle Garden ★

Within walking distance of the center of town, this is a serene, gated lodge where rooms face inward toward the lush garden area. Rooms have painted murals and handsome rattan beds but tend to be a bit small. Only two come with air-conditioning; the rest have fans and all have mosquito netting. There's also near daily yoga offered on-site, plus a small spa with a range of massage treatments. The friendly Trinidadian owner, Vera, is a wealth of local knowledge.

1½ blocks inland from Café Viejo, Puerto Viejo. www.cabinasjacaranda.net. © **2750-0069.** 14 units. $60 double. No credit cards. **Amenities:** Communal kitchen; small spa; free Wi-Fi.

Rocking J's ★

If the countercultural party scene in Puerto Viejo has a headquarters, it's Rocking J's, kinda like an artsily done-up summer camp for recent college grads or a hippy commune–cum–beach resort for the backpacker set. Lodging options range from an open-air thatched-roof communal hammock area to a second-floor camping platform where you can pop up your own tent or rent one of theirs. With each of these options you get a small locker area to store your gear. There are also private rooms, but the fun here is the communal living—bonfire parties on the beach out back; whipping up grub in the kitchen; downing pretty good (and cheap) burritos in the restaurant; playing Ping-Pong in the rec room. Fun!

Just southeast of downtown Puerto Viejo. www.rockingjs.com. © **2750-0665** or 2750-0657. 35 units, 3 with private bathroom. $7–$8 per person in a tent or hammock; $15 dorm room; $26–$55 double with shared bathroom; $60–$70 double with private bathroom. **Amenities:** Restaurant; bar; free Wi-Fi.

Selina ★   Just down the road from Rocking J's towards Playa Cocles is this inexpensive hotel and hostel, part of an international chain with more locations in Panama and Colombia. The property is set back in the trees from a rocky beach with rooms and dorms spread out between a beautiful wooden and a more non-descript building beside it. There's also an outdoor pool and thatched roof palapa that serves as the bar and restaurant, as well as board rentals, transfer service, and a tour desk.

Just southeast of downtown Puerto Viejo. www.selina.com/puerto-viejo. © **2750-0690.** 26 units. $14-18 dorm bed; $35–$50 double with shared bathroom; $75–$150 double with private bathroom. Pet-friendly. **Amenities:** Restaurant; bar; pool; shared kitchen; board rentals; transfers; free Wi-Fi.

Where to Eat

To really sample the local cuisine, you need to look up a few local women. Ask around for **Miss Dolly, Miss Sam, Miss Isma, Miss Irma,** and **Ghetto Girl** who all dish out sit-down meals in their modest little *sodas*. In addition to locally seasoned fish and chicken served with rice and beans, these joints are usually a great place to find *pan bon* (a local sweet, dark bread), ginger cakes, *pati* (meat-filled turnovers), and *rondon*. Just ask around for these ladies, and someone will direct you to them.

> ### That Run-Down Feeling
>
> *Rondon* soup is a spicy coconut milk–based soup or stew made with anything the cook can "run down"—it usually includes a mix of local tubers (potato, sweet potato, or yucca), other vegetables (carrots or corn), and often some seafood. Be sure to try this authentic taste of the Caribbean.

Puerto Viejo has a glut of excellent Italian restaurants; in addition to the places listed below, **Amimodo** ★ (© **2750-0257**) serves an excellent lobster ravioli, as well as a *carpaccio* of home-smoked shark. **Mamma Mia** ★ (© **8547-5878**), meanwhile, has the best pizza in town. Right next door to Mamma Mia, but inexplicably lacking a sign, is **Laszlo's** (© **8730-6185**), where the tuna and seabass are divine.

EXPENSIVE

Café Viejo Lounge Restaurant ★★ ITALIAN   Opened in 2003 by three brothers from Rimini, Italy, this local hotspot sits right on the main drag in the center of town. It's easy to spot, with white muslin drapes hanging from wooden posts and separating the open-air dining room from the busy streets beyond the veils. Wood-oven pizzas and a wide range of homemade pastas form the backbone of the extensive menu. But you can also order up fresh whole fish, and an assortment of chicken and beef main dishes emphasizing the cuisine of northern Italy. Fresh lobster ravioli are a house specialty. After the kitchen closes, this place transforms nightly into a hip European-style club. Final perk: an impressive wine list.

Avenida 71 at Calle 215. © **2750-0817.** www.cafeviejo.com. Main courses C8500–C19,000. Wed–Mon 6–11:30pm.

MODERATE

Stashu's Con Fusion ★★ INTERNATIONAL   A native of Guyana who has also lived in Trinidad and Toronto, Stash Golas is a local legend, and his cooking and restaurant have been Puerto Viejo mainstays for years, albeit with a couple different locations and names. The current incarnation serves up his classic mix of world fusion cuisines, with fish, seafood, beef, chicken, and vegetables featured in curries or with Thai-, Jamaican- or Mexican-tinged sauces. The tandoori chicken is excellent, with a homemade spicy sauce consisting of 18 ingredients. Thanks to the painted paper lanterns and creative artwork, Stashu's is a good place for a romantic dinner. There's occasionally live reggae or jazz music.

On the main road just southeast of downtown Puerto Viejo. © **2750-0530.** Main courses C3,500–C8,900. Thurs–Tues 5–10pm.

INEXPENSIVE

Bread & Chocolate ★★ BREAKFAST/AMERICAN   Take your menu guidance from the name: The bread (biscuits, bagels, and such) is top-notch and baked here; and the chocolate can't be beat, whether you have it as a drink, in a range of truffles, or flavoring brownies. But this eatery also offers a range of tasty breakfast plates, as well as sandwiches (jerk chicken, roast beef, etc) and salads. The open-air dining room is small, with just a handful of wooden tables and chairs, and it fills up fast. It's not uncommon to have to wait a little on weekends and during high season. If you don't want to wait, you can always get an order to go.

½ block south of Café Viejo, downtown Puerto Viejo. © **2750-0723.** Main courses C3,200–C4,700. No credit cards. Tues–Sat 6:30am–6:30pm; Sun 6:30am–2:30pm.

Chile Rojo ★ PAN-ASIAN/MEDITERRANEAN   This downtown favorite on the main drag, across from where boats are anchored, offers excellent Thai and Indian food, curries, sushi, and Middle Eastern classics like hummus, falafel, and tabbouleh (vegetarians have many options here). Monday nights feature a sushi buffet.

Downtown Puerto Viejo. © **2750-0025.** Main courses C3,000–C7,000. Wed–Mon 11:30am–10:30pm.

De Gustibus ★★ CAFÉ/BAKERY   Start your day with a donut or Puerto Viejo's best breakfast sandwich at this wildly popular, wood fronted and lined bakery on the main road on the eastern side of town.

There is a range of inexpensive baked goods, including pizza, focaccia, and apple strudel, as well as juices and coffee drinks.

On the main road. ℂ **2756-8397.** Main courses C600–C5,000. Daily 6:45am–6pm.

Outback Jack's Beach Bar N Grill ★ INTERNATIONAL/ BARBECUE This boisterous, Australian-themed beach bar and grill is gaudy and whimsical, and looks like it was created by a team of painters and interior designers high on acid and working during a tornado. The menu features typical bar-food appetizers, barbeque ribs, spicy chicken wings and "shrimp on the Barbie." You can also get whole fried red snapper and a range of grilled meats, including a large, juicy T-bone steak. The mixed grill platter is ideal for sharing.

½ block south of the Puerto Viejo bus stop. ℂ **8471-2622.** Main courses C5,000–C15,000. Open daily except Wed; 2pm–midnight.

Tamara Restaurant ★ COSTA RICAN/CARIBBEAN A handful of humble little restaurants around town serve local food made fresh by their namesake owner and chef, though none is as popular as Tamara. Occupying a prized spot near the water yet still on the town's main road, this open-air spot specializes in rice and beans (made with coconut milk) served with Caribbean-style chicken, fish, or meat dishes. The low, wooden picket fence that separates this place from the street is painted in the bold red, green, yellow, and black colors emblematic of the strong Jamaican influence and heritage of this coastline.

On the main road. ℂ **2750-0148.** Main courses C2,500–C30,000. Daily 11:30am–10pm.

Shopping

Puerto Viejo attracts a lot of local and international bohemians, who seem to survive solely on the sale of handmade jewelry, painted ceramic trinkets (mainly pipes), and imported Indonesian textiles. You'll find them at makeshift stands set up by the town's *parquecito* (little park), which comprises a few wooden benches in front of the sea beside Soda Tamara.

In addition to the makeshift outdoor stands, a host of well-stocked gift and crafts shops are spread around town. **Luluberlu ★** (ℂ **2750-0394**), located inland across from Cabinas Guaraná, features locally produced craftwork, including shell mobiles and mirrors with mosaic-inlaid frames, as well as imports from Thailand and India.

Tip: Locally produced chocolate, made by several local chocolatiers, can be found for sale at many gift shops and restaurants around town.

Nightlife & Entertainment

Puerto Viejo's classic night spot is **Hot Rocks** ★★ (© 8708-3183), with its big stage, live music, karaoke, packed bar, and pool and foosball tables, handily set in the center of town, where the main road meets the harbor.

A bit farther southeast is **Lazy Mon** ★ (www.thelazymon.com), with pool and Ping-Pong tables and regular live bands or DJs. Also popular is the nearby oceanfront **Salsa Brava** ★ (© 2750-0241). At all three of these, you can kick off your shoes and stand in the warm Caribbean waves while sipping a beer and chatting with other visitors.

There's also **Luke's Taproom** at Kaya's Place (© 2750-0690) 200 meters west of town, which offers 17 taps of craft beer from the hotel's own microbrewery, BriBri Springs.

Johnny's Place ★ (© 2750-2000) next to the police station, and **Mango Sunset Bar** ★ near the water, beside the bus station, featuring either live music or a DJ most nights.

For a laid-back beachfront sports bar, head to **The Point** ★ (© 2756-8491; www.thepointcostarica.com), which is located right where the road to Puerto Viejo hits Playa Negra. This convivial, open-air joint features six screens, and offers up three different Costa Rican microbrews on tap.

Rocking J's (p 576) sometimes features live music. For a more local scene, check out **Bar Maritza's** (© 2750-0443), in the center of town, across from the basketball court and especially popular on Sunday nights.

Finally, heading south of town, at the start of Playa Cocles, **Tasty Waves Cantina** (© 2750-0507) has a very lively scene, with live bands, karaoke, trivia nights, and open jam sessions.

PLAYAS COCLES, CHIQUITA, MANZANILLO & SOUTH OF PUERTO VIEJO ★★★

200km (124 miles) E of San José; 55km (34 miles) S of Limón

On the coastal road south of Puerto Viejo are several of Costa Rica's best beaches. Soft white sands are fronted by the Caribbean Sea and backed by thick rainforest. **Playa Cocles** is a popular surf spot, with a powerful and dependable beach break. South of here, the isolated **Playa Chiquita** is characterized by small pocket coves and calm pools formed by dead coral reefs raised slightly above sea level by the 1991 earthquake. Beyond this lies **Punta Uva**, a long, curving swath of beach punctuated by its namesake point (or *punta*), a rainforest-clad mound of land that

The Punta Uva shoreline

looks vaguely like a bunch of grapes from a distance. If you come here, be sure to hike the short loop trail up and around the point. From Punta Uva, the coastline stretches to the large and popular **Playa Manzanillo.** Along the way, the white sands are fronted by a living coral reef, which breaks up the waves and keeps the swimming here generally calm and protected. When it's calm (Aug–Oct), the waters here are some of the clearest anywhere in the country, with good snorkeling. The tiny village of Manzanillo is literally the end of the road. The shoreline heading south from Manzanillo, located inside the **Gandoca-Manzanillo Wildlife Refuge,** is especially beautiful, with a series of pocket coves and small beaches, featuring small islands and rocky outcroppings offshore, and backed by thick rainforest. This park stretches all the way to the Panamanian border.

Essentials

GETTING THERE & DEPARTING   By Car: A single two-lane road runs south out of Puerto Viejo and ends in Manzanillo. A few dirt roads lead off this paved road, both toward the beach and into the mountains.

By Bus: Follow the directions above for getting to Puerto Viejo. Local buses to Punta Uva and Manzanillo leave Puerto Viejo about a half-dozen times throughout the day.

GETTING AROUND A taxi from Puerto Viejo should cost $8-$10 to Punta Uva or $12-$14 to Manzanillo. Alternatively, it's about 1½ hours each way by bike, with only two small hills to contend with. Most of the hotels in this area either offer free bicycles or will help arrange a rental.

It's also possible to walk along the beach all the way from Puerto Viejo to Manzanillo, with just a couple of short detours inland around rocky points. However, I recommend you catch a ride down to Manzanillo and save your walking energies for the trails and beaches inside the refuge.

AREA LAYOUT As you drive south, the first beach you will hit is **Playa Cocles** ★, which is 2km (1¼ miles) from Puerto Viejo. A little farther, you'll find **Playa Chiquita** ★, which is 5km (3 miles) from Puerto Viejo, followed by **Punta Uva** ★★ at 8.4km (5¼ miles) away, and **Manzanillo** ★★, some 13km (8 miles) away.

FAST FACTS Manzanillo is the only thing that resembles a town in this area, but there are small markets mixed in with a string of hotels, restaurants, and private homes that line the main road.

Exploring Playas Cocles, Chiquita, Manzanillo & South of Puerto Viejo

For all intents and purposes, this string of beaches is an extension of Puerto Viejo, and all the tours, activities, and attractions mentioned above can be enjoyed by those staying here. For scuba diving, snorkeling, sportfishing excursions, or dolphin tours around Manzanillo and the beaches south of Puerto Viejo, check at any of the agencies in Manzanillo or Puerto Viejo.

MANZANILLO & THE GANDOCA–MANZANILLO WILD-LIFE REFUGE ★★

13km (8 miles) south of Puerto Viejo

The **Gandoca–Manzanillo Wildlife Refuge** ★★ encompasses the small village and extends all the way to the Panamanian border. Manatees, crocodiles, and more than 350 species of birds live within the boundaries of the reserve. The reserve also includes the coral reef offshore—when the seas are calm, this is the best **snorkeling** and **diving** spot on this entire coast. Four species of **sea turtles** nest on one 8.9km (5½-mile) stretch of beach within the reserve between March and July. Three species of dolphins (Atlantic spotted, bottlenose, and the rare tucuxi) also frolic in the waters just off Manzanillo. This tucuxi species

Wild and unspoiled coastline in Gandoca–Manzanillo Wildlife Refuge

favors the brackish estuary waters, but has actually been observed mating with local bottlenose dolphins. Many tour guides and operators offer boat trips out to spot them.

If you want to explore the refuge, you can easily find the single, well-maintained trail by walking along the beach just south of town until you have to wade across a small river. On the other side, you'll pick up the trail. This is a wild and remote area, and it's best to do this hike with a guide.

SWEET STUFF ★★ **Caribeans Chocolate Tour** (www.caribeans chocolate.com; ℂ **8836-8930** or 8341-2034; Mon 10am, Tues and Thurs 10am and 2pm, Fri and Sat 2pm; $28) explores a working organic cacao plantation and chocolate production facility. The tour illustrates the entire process of growing, harvesting, and processing cacao, and of course there's a tasting at the end. When you get around to the tasting, organic wine pairings are also available.

(ORGANIC) PEAS & LOVE ★ The **Punta Mona Center For Regenerative Design & Botanical Studies** (inside the Gandoca–Manzanillo

You'll spot many iguanas on the Green Iguana Conservation Tour.

refuge; www.puntamona.org) offers day visits to its fascinating organic permaculture gardens.

HORSEBACK RIDING ★★ Caribe Horse Riding Club (located between Punta Uva and Manzanillo; www.caribehorse.com; ⓒ **8705-4250;** $50–$165/person) runs one of the better and more interesting horseback riding operations in the country. It offers a range of rides, from short 90-minute beach jaunts to full-day excursions into the mountains and nearby reserves, and even night rides. The half-day, Hippo Camp Tour features human and equine wading in the warm waters of the Caribbean Sea.

ESPECIALLY FOR KIDS

Several wildlife rescue centers and animal preservation centers operate in the area. The **Jaguar Rescue Center ★★** (www.jaguarrescue.com; ⓒ **2750-0710;** guided tours Mon–Sat 9:30 and 11:30am; $20 adults, free for kids under 11) is the most extensive of the batch. Located in Playa Chiquita, it features a range of local animals, including monkeys, sloths, snakes, caimans, turtles, birds, and more. Just don't expect to see

On to Panama

Costa Rica's southeast coast, particularly Puerto Viejo, is a popular jumping-off point for trips into Panama. The nearest and most popular destination is the island retreat of Bocas del Toro. Most tour agencies and hotel desks can arrange tours to Panama. The most reliable and easiest way to get to Bocas del Toro is to take the daily **Caribe Shuttle** (www.caribeshuttle.com; 🅲 **2750-0626**), which will take you via land and boat for $33 each way; check the website or call for departure times.

a jaguar; the center was named after an orphaned jaguar that died years ago.

Also in Playa Chiquita, at the Tree House Lodge (see p 588), is the **Green Iguana Conservation Tour ★** (www.iguanaverde.com; 🅲 **2750-0706;** Tues and Thurs at 8:30am; $15/person). This educational tour focuses on the life cycle and habits of this reptile, which is a threatened species. The tour features a walk around a massive natural enclosure, as well as a video presentation. Other tours may be arranged by appointment.

Playa Manzanillo

Where to Stay Between Puerto Viejo & Manzanillo

You might want to rent a car if you plan to stay at one of these hotels, because public transportation is sporadic and taxis aren't always available. If you arrive by bus, however, a rented bicycle or scooter might be all you need to get around once you are settled.

EXPENSIVE

Le Caméléon ★   Contemporary comforts and style are the lure at Le Caméléon, by which I mean this is the place where you'll find rooms with air-conditioning, flatscreen TVs, and chic, contemporary design. The latter consists of minimalist, all-white rooms livened up by unusual lighting accents. On-site is a beach club with attentive waiter service, a small pool and Jacuzzi, plus beachfront lounging options, set on the far southern end of Playa Cocles. The entire mini-resort is connected by a network of wooden walkways and surrounded by thick forest. *Tip:* You may prefer the second floor "superior" rooms over the slightly larger first-floor junior suites. The superior rooms have higher ceilings, larger balconies, and ceiling fans (in addition to air-conditioning).

Playa Cocles, Puerto Viejo. www.lecameleonhotel.com. © **2750-0501.** 23 units. $199 double; deluxe $249 double; junior suite $299; suite $509, includes breakfast. **Amenities:** Restaurant; bar; beach club; Jacuzzi; pool; laundry service; free Wi-Fi.

MODERATE

In addition to the places listed below, **Casa Viva** (www.puntauva.net; © **2750-0089**) offers beautiful, fully equipped one- and two-bedroom houses just steps from the sand on Punta Uva.

Almonds & Corals Hotel ★   Don't let the word "hotel" fool you. At Almonds & Corals you'll be staying inside a 3-hectare wildlife reserve in tent-cabin hybrids on stilts. Yup, this is "glamping" (glamorous camping, or some would say glorified camping), so your digs are tents with benefits like electric lamps, four-poster beds, private baths with hot water, private Jacuzzis, fridges, safes, and fans. One drawback here, aside from the price and how worn some of the units are getting, is the fact that the units are very close to each other, and with no solid walls, there's not a lot of privacy or sound insulation. The lodge is set in a patch of dense forest on the northern end of Playa Manzanillo. A maze of low wooden walkways connects the rooms to the main dining area and beach, although an on-site zipline canopy tour is another popular way to reach the sand.

Manzanillo. www.almondsandcorals.com. © **888/373-9042** U.S./Canada, or 2271-3000 in San José, or 2759-9056 at the hotel. 24 units. Triple suite $145 for up to 3; quadruple suite $195; master suite $245, includes breakfast and taxes. **Amenities:** Restaurant; bar; spa; bike and watersports equipment rental; free Wi-Fi.

Cariblue Bungalows ★★ A posh mid-range option, Cariblue Bungalows has the feel of a tropical country club. The pool is the biggest in the region, with a swim-up bar; cobblestone walkways cut through manicured grounds and gardens; and amenities ranging from the SoleLuna restaurant to a tropical bar, lounge area, and game room. You'll find a range of rooms, from budget options with no air-conditioning to deluxe rooms, individual bungalows, and large suites. The superior bungalows, which are wooden cabins raised off the ground, and featuring spacious private balconies, are perhaps the best value. Cariblue is located directly in front of Playa Cocles, about 1.6km (1 mile) south of Puerto Viejo.

Playa Cocles. www.cariblue.com. ⓒ **2750-0518.** 45 units. $128-$180double; $145–$220 bungalows and suites, includes taxes and breakfast. **Amenities:** 2 restaurants; bar/lounge; pool bar; 2 Jacuzzis; 2 pools; spa; gift shop; surf school; free Wi-Fi.

Lanna Ban Hotel ★★ A relative newcomer to the area, Lanna Ban has a unique, Zen-like design meant to resemble a 12th-century Thai village, with Buddha statues, lotus flowers imported from Thailand blooming in the fish pond, and high peaked roofs topped with golden decorations that symbolize protection. Rooms come with one queen bed or two and are beautifully designed with Eastern wood carvings, while bathrooms are done in marble imported from India. Elaborate wooden window shutters can be opened wide like doors or propped open vertically for more privacy, and cable TV and ceiling fans add to the creature comforts. Costa Rican owner Ignacio Gil, an importer of clothing who travels widely in Asia, has done an impressive job of reproducing an architectural style from the other side of the world in a pleasantly coherent design. The hotel serves a continental breakfast but has no restaurant for lunch or dinner, though there are plenty of good ones nearby.

Playa Cocles. www.lannaban.com. ⓒ **2750-3053.** 18 units. $100-$120 bungalow, includes continental breakfast. **Amenities:** Bike rental; free Wi-Fi.

Shawandha Lodge ★★ Located in a patch of thick forest across the road from the lovely Playa Chiquita, this was one of the first boutique lodges in the area and it's still going strong. The individual wooden bungalows are beautiful, and they spread out among the trees and gardens, giving each a sense of privacy and seclusion. They all feature high-pitched thatched roofs, private verandas, and mosaic-tile creations in the bathrooms and showers. A short path leads to a pretty beach with tide pools and little coves stretching. There's a midsize pool just off the main lodge, with a stone waterfall in a garden setting. The restaurant, Wandha,

The Tree House Lodge

serves a blend of French, Dutch, and tropical fare, though it's pricey for the area.

Playa Chiquita. www.shawandha.com. ℂ **2750-0018** or 2750-0701. 14 units. $145 double, includes breakfast. Extra bed $30. **Amenities:** Restaurant; bar; pool; free Wi-Fi.

Tree House Lodge ★★★ Everything has a funky, fun, Gilligan's Island feel to it here, and artistic touches and distinct architectural feats make each unit memorable. The namesake Tree House is built on high stilts, reached via a suspension bridge, and features a toilet in the middle of a hollowed-out tree. The three-bedroom Beach Suite features a massive, domed bathroom lit by fanciful portholes and skylights of multicolored glass. Each of the units has a full kitchen, and two are air-conditioned. The whole compound is surrounded by tall rainforest trees, and anyone with a decent eye should be able to spot monkeys, and perhaps even a three-toed sloth. There's no pool, but right in front of the lodge lies a highly coveted section of white sand beach leading down to Punta Uva. The owners also run an iguana conservation project (p 585) and follow an impressive list of sustainable practices, ranging from solar heated water and producing their own organic fertilizer to wastewater cleaned by water lillies.

Punta Uva. www.costaricatreehouse.com. (C) **2750-0706.** 5 units. $200–$390 double, taxes included. **Amenities:** Free Wi-Fi.

INEXPENSIVE

In Manzanillo, the simple **Cabinas Something Different** ((C) **2759-9014**) are a good option, while **Congo Bongo** (www.congo-bongo.com; (C) **2759-9016**) offers fully equipped houses in a forest setting.

Azania Bungalows ★ This Argentine-owned lodge sits across from the beach, snuggled amid forest and densely planted gardens. It has 10 identical wooden cabins with high roofs, lots of space and rooms with either one queen-size or two twin beds, one of which is located in a small loft accessed by a steep ladder. Lattice over the windows lets in mottled light, and is especially pleasing in the showers, where you feel connected to the surrounding forest while still maintaining a sense of privacy. Each cabin comes with a front porch hung with a cozy hammock. The restaurant serves a mix of local fare, seafood, and Argentine specialties.

Playa Cocles. www.azania-costarica.com. (C) **2750-0540.** 10 bungalows. $100 double, includes full breakfast. **Amenities:** Restaurant; bar; bike rental; laundry service; pool; free Wi-Fi.

Casas Cubali ★ These four typical Caribbean stilted, wooden houses painted in pastel colors are spread out on the oceanfront at Playa Chiquita. Each house has a unique layout and a large patio area, though all are quite simple, with no A/C or TVs, just good ventilation and mosquito nets. The houses are mostly self-service, with kitchenettes and a cleaning crew that stops by every other day.

Playa Chiquita (Km 4.5 on the road to Manzaillo). www.cubalihouses.com. (C) **8313-6275.** 4 units. $68–$108, includes breakfast. Pet-friendly. **Amenities:** Free Wi-Fi.

La Costa de Papito ★★ This string of stylish bungalows is right in the Goldilocks zone—close to Puerto Viejo but not too close, inexpensive but not too cheap, surrounded by jungle but right across from the beach. Built by New York transplant Eddie Ryan in the mid-1990s in a style he calls "rustic elegance," the hotel has 12 stilt-raised bungalows and one budget cabin where arches and curves are favored over 90-degree angles. Furniture is handmade from local lumber, often using whole tree limbs, roots, and trunk sections. Each room has its own porch with hammocks, and sightings of monkeys, sloths, anteaters, and toucans are not uncommon. Rooms are equipped with ceiling fans and stand-up fans and have hot water and safes, and some have delightfully whimsical Flintstones-style bathrooms. The hotel welcomes pets, with three rules: No barking, no biting, and no sleeping in the bed. The **Qué Rico**

Papito restaurant is excellent and features live music twice a week. Eddie's wife, Auxi, runs the on-site **Indulgence Spa & Beauty Salon,** where you can get a massage, facial, waxing, mani/pedi, body treatment, or haircut.

Playa Cocles. www.lacostadepapito.com. ℂ **2750-0704** or 2750-0080. 13 units. $99–$107 double, includes breakfast. $17 per extra person; $7 for children. **Amenities:** Restaurant; bar; bike and boogie board rentals; spa and beauty salon; surf lessons; free Wi-Fi.

Where to Eat Between Puerto Viejo & Manzanillo

In addition to the restaurants listed below, **Tasty Waves ★** (ℂ **2750-0507**) is a California style cantina with burgers and burritos, plus a lively bar with cocktails, craft beer, and live music on some nights.. Down the road, in Punta Uva, **Selvyn's** (ℂ **2750-0664**; www.selvinpuntauva.com) is an excellent option for local cuisine and fresh seafood, with amiable hosts Selvyn and Blanca Brown. **Pita Bonita** (ℂ **2756-8173**) serves up wonderful vegetarian Middle Eastern cuisine at an open-air spot between Playa Chiquita and Punta Uva.

Farther south still, the **El Refugio Grill ★** (ℂ **2759-9007**) is an Argentine-owned restaurant featuring perfectly grilled steaks, sausages, and fresh tuna steaks and other seafood in a romantic rainforest setting.

Finally, near the end of the line, where the road first hits the beach at Manzanillo, **Cool & Calm Café** (ℂ **2750-3151**) is winning faithful fans with its local cuisine and friendly atmosphere.

La Pecora Nera ★★★ ITALIAN   This is among the very best restaurants not only on the Caribbean coast but in all of Costa Rica. Chef/owner Ilario Gionnoni is a master and a marvel of perpetual motion. He is constantly innovating; raises his own chickens and pigs; and grows as much of his own fresh fruits, vegetables, and herbs as he can. The menu is long and varied, but if you simply ask Ilario what's best that day—he won't steer you wrong. Among the memorable dishes here are shrimp cocktail with a beet-based spicy dipping sauce; and rooster ragù over homemade gnocchi. The large, multilevel, open-air dining room is dimly lit and romantic, with heavy wooden tables spread widely for privacy.

50m (164 ft.) inland from a well-marked turnoff on the main road south just beyond the soccer field in Playa Cocles. ℂ **2750-0490.** Reservations recommended. Main courses C6,000–C19,500. Tues–Sun 5:30–10pm.

Maxi's ★ COSTA RICAN/CARIBBEAN   This ramshackle, two-story beachfront restaurant and bar is a local landmark. Generous portions of rice and beans are served with freshly caught seafood and large, fried plantain chips, or *patacones*. Guests come mainly for the social scene and fabulous view of the beach and sea just steps away.

On the beach, Manzanillo. ℂ **2759-9073.** Main courses C4,200–C17,500; lobster C1,000–C40,000. Daily noon–10pm.

Pura Gula ★★ COSTA RICAN/CARIBBEAN   Follow the ethos of Slow food, this chilled-out open-air place in Playa Chiquita focuses on organic, mostly local produce and making everything from scratch. The menu is fresh and varied, with everything from gazpacho and Pad Thai to steaks and house made gnocchi with a toasted macadamia nut pesto. Follow up with a spicy cacao tart or one of their house flan. Three course set menus with a glass of wine are often offered for C30,000.

Playa Chiquita. © **8634-6404.** Main courses C6,600–C10,000. Daily noon–10pm.

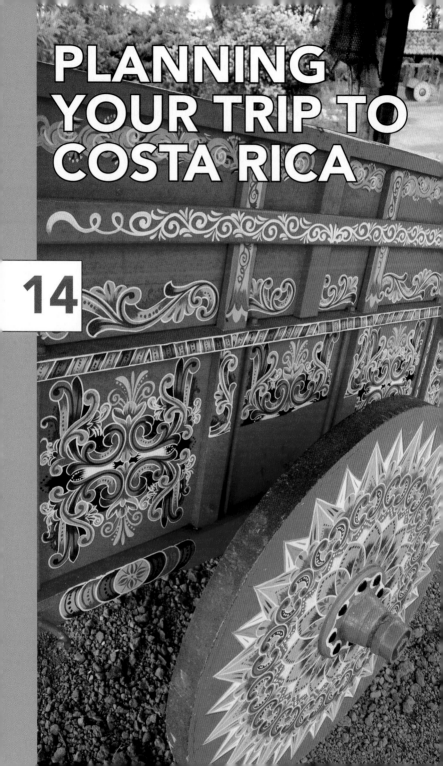

PLANNING YOUR TRIP TO COSTA RICA

14

C osta Rica is no longer the next new thing. Neither is it old hat. As Costa Rica has matured into a major tourist destination, things have gotten easier and easier for international travelers. That said, most travelers—even experienced travelers and repeat visitors—will want to do some serious pre-trip planning. This chapter provides a variety of planning tools, including information on how to get there, tips on accommodations, and quick, on-the-ground resources.

GETTING THERE
By Plane

It takes between 3 and 7 hours to fly to Costa Rica from most U.S. cities, the origin of most direct and connecting flights. Most international flights still land in San José's **Juan Santamaría International Airport** (www.fly2sanjose.com; © **2437-2626** for 24-hr. airport information; airport code SJO). Some regional flights, such as to Managua, Nicaragua or Bocas del Toro, Panama, use the smaller **Pavas International Airport** (airport code SYQ), also known as Tobias Bolaños International Airport, closer to downtown San José. More and more direct international flights are touching down in Liberia's **Daniel Oduber International Airport** (www.liberiacostaricaairport.net; © **2668-1010;** airport code LIR).

Liberia is the gateway to the beaches of the Guanacaste region and the Nicoya Peninsula, and a direct flight here eliminates the need for a separate commuter flight in a small aircraft or roughly 5 hours in a car or bus. If you're planning to spend most or all of your vacation in Guanacaste, you'll want to fly in and out of Liberia. However, San José is a much more convenient gateway if you're planning to head to the Central Pacific coast, the Caribbean coast, or the Southern Zone.

Numerous airlines fly into Costa Rica. Be warned that the smaller Latin American carriers may make several stops en route to San José, thus increasing flying time.

By Bus

Bus service runs regularly from Panama City, Panama, and Managua, Nicaragua. If at all possible, it's worth the splurge for a deluxe or express

FACING PAGE: **A Costa Rican oxcart**

bus. In terms of travel time and convenience, it's always better to get a direct bus rather than one that stops along the way—and you've got a better chance of getting a working restroom in a direct/express or deluxe bus. Some even have television sets showing movies.

Several bus lines with regular daily departures connect the major capital cities of Central America. Call **Transnica** (www.transnica.com; © 2223-4242), or **Tica Bus Company** (www.ticabus.com; © 2296-9788) for further information. These lines service Costa Rica directly from Managua, with connections to the other principal cities of Central America. Tica Bus also has service between Costa Rica and Panama. None of them will reserve a seat by telephone, and schedules change frequently according to season and demand, so buy your ticket in advance—several days in advance, if you plan to travel on weekends or holidays. From Managua, it's 11 hours and 450km (279 miles) to San José, and the one-way fare is around $30 to $45. From Panama City, it's a 20-hour, 900km (558-mile) trip. The one-way fare is around $40 to $55.

Whenever you're traveling by bus through Central America, keep an eye on your belongings, especially at rest and border stops, whether they're in an overhead bin or stored below decks in a luggage compartment.

By Car

Driving to Costa Rica from North America is no light undertaking, but it can be done. The best reason to drive to Costa Rica is because you have a car you want to keep. Border crossings are always stressful, but especially when you're driving your own vehicle, for which you are constantly required to produce a lot of paperwork. The El Salvador–Honduras and Nicaragua–Costa Rica borders can be especially arduous. In some countries, including Mexico, you have to buy temporary auto insurance to enter the country. Border fixers are ubiquitous—guys who will swarm your car offering to walk you through the process of crossing the border, for whatever tip you care to pay (maybe $20 for an easy crossing, $50 for one where some guard is being difficult). Many find that it is best to hire one, if only to keep the others at bay, and to walk you through the mystifying process. All in all, driving to Costa Rica is doable and generally safe, though best undertaken by at least two people, including one who speaks Spanish. From the central and eastern United States, the quickest route is through Brownsville, along the Gulf of Mexico, and then on through Guatemala, El Salvador, Honduras, and Nicaragua (you can skip El Salvador if you choose, though it has the best highways in the region).

The Best Websites About Costa Rica

o **The Tico Times** (www.ticotimes.net): Established in 1956, the Tico Times is the oldest and most trusted English-language news source in Central America. It went online-only in 2014, but it continues to be a robust source of news, sports, business, travel, and real-estate coverage.

o **Costa Rica Maps** (www.mapcr.com): In addition to selling a wonderful waterproof map of the country, this site features several excellent downloadable national, regional, and city maps, and a host of other useful information.

o **The U.S. Embassy in Costa Rica** (http://costarica.usembassy.gov): The official site of the U.S. Embassy in Costa Rica has good info and regular updates of concern to U.S. citizens abroad, as well as about Costa Rica in general.

o **Facebook** (www.facebook.com): There are several Facebook groups in which expats share tips on living in Costa Rica living. Search for "Gringo Expats in Costa Rica," "Expatriates in Costa Rica," "Buy Sell Costa Rica Expats," or "Costa Rica Uncensored."

o **La Nación Digital** (www.nacion.com): If you can read Spanish, this is an excellent site to visit regularly. The entire content of the country's paper of record is placed online daily, and there's an extensive searchable archive.

CAR DOCUMENTS   You will need a current driver's license, a passport, the original title for your vehicle, proof of registration, and possibly proof of insurance to enter this country or others. Your first task upon crossing most borders, the fixers will tell you, is to go to a shop to get a photocopy of all these documents. You can make multiple copies of most documents in advance and bring them with you, but you'll still need to get a copy of your passport with recent entry stamps after you cross a border.

CENTRAL AMERICAN AUTO INSURANCE   Contact **Sanborn's Insurance Company** (www.sanbornsinsurance.com; © **800/222-0158**), which has agents at various border towns in the United States. Sanborn's has been in this business over 50 years and can supply you with trip insurance for Mexico and Central America as well as driving tips and an itinerary.

CAR SAFETY   Be sure your car is in excellent working order. Find hotels with gated parking, and leave nothing of value in your car. Avoid driving at night. Bring enough cash, in pesos, so you don't have to go looking for an ATM. For information on car rentals and gasoline in Costa Rica, see "Getting Around: By Car," later in this section.

By Boat

Some 350 cruise ships stop each year in Costa Rica, calling at Limón on the Caribbean coast, and at Puerto Caldera and Puntarenas on the Pacific coast. Many are part of routes that cruise through the Panama Canal.

GETTING AROUND
By Plane

Flying is one of the best ways to get around Costa Rica. Because the country is quite small, flights are short and not too expensive. Sansa and Nature Air are the country's domestic airlines. In the high season (late Nov to late Apr), be sure to book reservations well in advance. Both companies have online booking systems (see websites, below).

Sansa (www.flysansa.com; ℂ 877/767-2672 in the U.S. and Canada, or 2290-4100 in Costa Rica) operates from a private terminal at San José's **Juan Santamaría International Airport** (see p 593).

Nature Air (www.natureair.com; ℂ 800/235-9272 in the U.S. and Canada, or 2299-6000 in Costa Rica) operates from the main terminal at San José's **Juan Santamaría International Airport** (see p 593), as well as the smaller Pavas International Airport.

By Car

Renting a car is perhaps the best way to see Costa Rica on your own terms, so long as you're prepared for narrow roads riddled with potholes, one-lane bridges, muddy backroads, and sometimes frustrating behavior by other drivers. Be advised that driving in the Central Valley urban area can be a white-knuckle experience, with baffling street layouts, lanes that end without warning, two-way streets that become one-way, harrowing roundabouts, and lots of tight squeezes between cars jostling for position. But once you get out of the big city, you'll find that driving is much easier.

Be forewarned, however: Although rental cars no longer bear special license plates, they are still readily identifiable to thieves and are frequently targeted. (Nothing is ever safe in a car in Costa Rica, although parking in guarded lots helps.) Transit Police also sometimes target tourists; never pay money directly to an officer who stops you for any traffic violation.

Before driving off with a rental car, be sure that you inspect the exterior and point out to the rental company representative every scratch, dent, tear, or any other damage. It's a common practice with many Costa Rican car-rental companies to claim that you owe payment for minor dings and dents that the company finds when you return the car. Also, if you get into an accident, be sure that the rental company doesn't try to bill you for a higher amount than the deductible on your rental contract.

These caveats aren't meant to scare you off from driving in Costa Rica. Thousands of tourists rent cars here every year, and the large majority of them encounter no problems. Just keep your wits about you and guard against car break-ins. Also, keep in mind that four-wheel-drive vehicles are particularly useful in the rainy season (May to mid-Nov) and for navigating the bumpy, poorly paved roads year-round.

Among the major international agencies operating in Costa Rica are **Alamo, Avis, Budget, Hertz, National, Payless,** and **Thrifty.** For a complete list of car-rental agencies and their contact information, see the "Getting Around" sections of major tourist destinations in this book.

GASOLINE (PETROL)   Gasoline is sold as "regular" and "super." Both are unleaded; super is higher octane. Diesel is available at almost every gas station as well. Most rental cars run on super, but always ask your rental agent what type of gas your car takes. When going off to remote places, try to leave with a full tank of gas, because gas stations can be hard to find. If you need to gas up in a small town, you can sometimes get gasoline from enterprising families who sell it by the liter from their houses.

ROAD CONDITIONS   The awful road conditions throughout Costa Rica are legendary. The hot sun and hard rain take a hard toll on the roads. Even paved roads are often badly potholed, so stay alert. Conditions get especially tricky during the rainy season, when heavy rains and runoff can quickly destroy a stretch of pavement.

Note: Estimated driving times are listed throughout this book, but bear in mind that it might take longer than estimated to reach your destination during the rainy season, if roads have deteriorated or are being repaired, or when there is a sudden surge of traffic, which seems to happen often.

Route numbers are somewhat sporadically and arbitrarily used. You'll also find frequent signs listing the number of kilometers to various towns or cities, but turnoffs are not always marked. The Waze app is incredibly useful for finding your way around, provided you have a data plan on your phone that you can use outside your home country.

Most car rental agencies offer the opportunity to rent out GPS units along with your car rental. Rates run between $8 and $15 per day. If you have your own GPS unit, several maps of Costa Rica are available. Although you still can't simply enter a street address, most commercial GPS maps of Costa Rica feature hundreds of prominent points of interest (POI), and you should be able to plug in a POI close to your destination.

RENTER'S INSURANCE Third Party Waiver, or Supplemental Liability Insurance (SLI) is mandatory in Costa Rica, regardless of your home policy or credit card coverage.

Even if you hold **your own car-insurance policy** at home or use a credit card that provides coverage, this coverage doesn't always extend abroad. Be sure to find out whether you'll be covered in Costa Rica, whether your policy extends to all persons who will be driving the rental car, how much liability is covered in case an outside party is injured in an accident, and whether the *type* of vehicle you are renting is included under your contract.

DRIVING RULES To drive in Costa Rica, you must carry a valid driver's license from your home country, and you must have your passport. Seat belts are required for the driver and front-seat passengers. Motorcyclists must wear helmets. Police sometimes turn on their emergency lights for no apparent reason, so if there's a police car behind you with its lights on, that doesn't necessarily mean you're being pulled over. Speed enforcement is lax, but sometimes police pull over every vehicle on a highway to check their papers. If you do get a speeding ticket, it can be charged to your credit card up to a year later if you leave the country without paying it.

To reduce congestion and fuel consumption, a rotating ban on traffic takes place in the central core of San José Monday through Friday from 6am to 7pm. The ban affects cars with licenses ending in the digits 1 or 2 on Monday; 3 or 4 on Tuesday; 5 or 6 on Wednesday; 7 or 8 on Thursday; and 9 or 0 on Friday. If you are caught driving a car with the banned license plate during these hours on a specified day, you will be ticketed.

BREAKDOWNS Be warned that emergency services, both vehicular and medical, are extremely limited outside San José, and their availability is directly related to the remoteness of your location at the time of breakdown. You'll find service stations spread over the entire length of the Inter-American Highway, and most of these have tow trucks and mechanics. The major towns of Puntarenas, Liberia, Quepos, San Isidro, Palmar, and Golfito all have hospitals, and most moderately sized cities and tourist destinations have some sort of clinic or healthcare provider.

If you're involved in an accident, contact the **National Insurance Institute (INS)** at ✆ **800/800-8000,** and the **Transit Police** (✆ **2222-9330**). You can also call ✆ **911,** where operators should be able to redirect your call to the appropriate agency.

Note that if you're involved in a collision, drivers are not supposed to move their vehicles, even if they're drivable and blocking the road, until Transit Police arrive to examine the scene. This rule was recently changed to make an exception for minor fender-benders where the two drivers agree to a resolution.

If you don't speak Spanish, expect added difficulty in any emergency or stressful situation. Don't expect that police officers, hospital personnel, service station personnel, or mechanics will speak English.

If your car breaks down and you're unable to get well off the road, check your trunk for reflecting triangles. If you find some, place them as a warning for approaching traffic, arranged in a wedge that starts at the shoulder about 30m (98 ft.) back and nudges gradually toward your car.

People have been robbed by seemingly friendly Ticos who stop to give assistance, and there are reports of organized gangs who puncture tires of rental cars at rest stops or busy intersections, only to follow them, offer assistance, and make off with valuables. If you find yourself with a flat tire, try to ride it to a safe place. If that's not possible, try to pull over into a well-lit public spot. Keep the doors of the car locked and an eye on your belongings while changing the tire.

By Bus

This is by far the most economical way to get around Costa Rica. Buses are inexpensive and relatively well maintained, and they go nearly everywhere. **Local buses,** the cheapest and slowest, stop frequently and are generally a bit dilapidated. **Express buses** run between San José and most beach towns and major cities; these tend to be newer units and more comfortable, although very few are so new or modern as to have restroom facilities, and they sometimes operate only on weekends and holidays.

Two companies run regular, fixed-schedule departures in passenger vans and small buses to most of the major tourist destinations in the country. **Gray Line** (www.graylinecostarica.com; © **800/719-3105** in the U.S. and Canada, or 2220-2126 in Costa Rica) has about 10 departures leaving San José each morning and heading or connecting to Jacó, Manuel Antonio, Liberia, Playa Hermosa, La Fortuna, Tamarindo, and playas Conchal and Flamingo. Return trips to San José are daily from these destinations and a variety of interconnecting routes. **Interbus** (www.interbusonline.com; © **4100-0888**) has a similar route map and connections. Fares run between $44 and $84, depending on the destination.

Beware: Both of these companies offer pickup and drop-off at a wide range of hotels. This means that if you are the first picked up or last dropped off, you might have to sit through a long period of subsequent stops before finally hitting the road or reaching your destination. For details on how to get to various destinations from San José, see the "Getting There" sections in the preceding chapters.

By Taxi

Taxis are readily available in San José and most popular destinations. In San José, your best bet is usually to hail one in the street. However, during rush hour and rainstorms, and in more remote destinations, it is probably best to call a cab. Throughout this book, numbers for local taxi companies are listed in the "Getting Around" sections. If no number is listed, ask at your hotel, or, if you're out and about, at the nearest restaurant or shop.

All city taxis, and even some rural cabs, have meters (*marías*), although drivers sometimes refuse to use them, particularly with foreigners. If this is the case, be sure to negotiate the price up front. Always try to get drivers to use the meter first (say, *"Ponga la maría, por favor"*). The official rate at this writing is C630 per kilometer (½ mile). If you have a rough idea of how far it is to your destination, you can estimate how much it should cost from these figures, or you can ask at your hotel how much your ride should cost. After 10pm, taxis are legally allowed to add a 20% surcharge. Some of the meters are programmed to include the extra charge, but be careful: Some drivers will use the evening setting during the daytime or (at night) to charge an extra 20% on top of the higher meter setting. The Uber smart phone app, while still in a legal gray area, tends to be cheaper.

By Thumb

Although buses serve most towns in Costa Rica, service can be infrequent in the remote regions, so local people often hitchhike to get to their destinations sooner. If you're driving a car, people will frequently ask you for a ride. Hitchhiking is not recommended on major roadways or in urban areas. In rural areas, it's usually pretty safe. (However, women should be extremely cautious about hitchhiking anywhere in Costa Rica.) If you choose to thumb it, keep in mind that if a bus doesn't go to your destination, there probably aren't too many cars going there, either. Good luck.

TIPS ON WHERE TO STAY

When the Costa Rican tourist boom began in the late 1980s, hotels popped up like mushrooms in a crowded cow pasture. By the 1990s, the country's first true megaresorts opened, and then more followed, and now still more are under construction or in the planning phase. Except during the few busiest weeks of the year, there's a relative glut of rooms in Costa Rica. That said, most hotels are small to midsize, and the best ones fill up fast throughout much of the year. You'll generally have to reserve well in advance if you want to land a room at any of the more popular or highly rated hotels. Still, in broader terms, the glut of rooms is good news for travelers and bargain hunters. Less popular hotels that want to survive are being forced to reduce their rates and provide better service.

Be aware that almost all hotel prices in Costa Rica—and the rest of the world, for that matter—are not truly fixed. Rates go up and down by season and by the volume of bookings. That's why you will often see one rate on a hotel's website, another rate on a discounter site (such as **Agoda. com**) and still another rate on another booking site (perhaps **Expedia. com**). We've tried to present realistic rate ranges for all the hotels listed. We've done so by searching online travel agencies like **booking.com** and hotel search sites like **hotelscombined.com**, to find prices for a room for two, taxes included, on both Feb. 15 (high season) and Oct. 15 (low season). In most cases, we used the range of prices obtained in this manner, though in the few cases with complicating factors, we used the hotels' stated prices, either from their websites or from interviews with their management.

Hotel listings in this book are separated into three categories: expensive, $200 and up; moderate, $100 to $200; and inexpensive, under $100 for a room for two people. Though we've tried to specify if rates include the 13% tax imposed on all hotels, be sure to confirm this when booking. This tax is often not included in listed rates on hotel websites.

Hotel Options

Costa Rica has hotels to suit every budget and travel style. In addition to the Four Seasons, Andaz Papagayo, and JW Marriott, a host of luxury boutique hotels around the country will satisfy the high-end traveler.

Still, the country's strong suit is its **moderately priced hotels.** In the $100-to-$200 price range, you'll find comfortable and sometimes outstanding accommodations almost anywhere in the country. However, room size and quality vary quite a bit within this price range, so don't expect the kind of uniformity that you may find at home.

If you're even more budget- or bohemian-minded, you can find quite a few good deals for less than $100 for two. You can occasionally find private rooms with shared baths and dorm rooms that are perfectly comfortable for under $20, though they are becoming rarer. Be aware that budget lodging often means either cold-water showers or showers heated by electrical heat-coil units mounted at the shower head, affectionately known as "suicide showers." If your hotel has one, do not adjust it while the water is running, and avoid touching it accidentally while showering. Except where noted, all rooms listed in this guide have private bathrooms.

Note: Air-conditioning is not a given in many midrange hotels and even in some of the more upscale. Depending on the temperature of your locale and your tolerance for warm places, this may or may not be a problem for you. In most places, cooler nights and well-placed ceiling fans are often more than enough to keep things pleasant.

Bed-and-breakfasts are also abundant. Although most are in the San José area, you'll also find B&Bs (often owned and operated by expats) throughout the country.

Costa Rica has many small, nature-oriented **ecolodges.** These offer opportunities to see wildlife (including sloths, monkeys, and hundreds of species of birds) and learn about tropical forests. They range from spartan facilities catering primarily to scientific researchers to luxury lodgings that are among the finest in the country. Although the nightly rates at these lodges are often quite moderate, prices start to climb when you throw in transportation (often on chartered planes), guided excursions, and meals. Also, many of these lodges are quite remote, so be sure you know how to get there and which tours and services are included in your stay.

A couple of uniquely Costa Rican accommodations types that you might encounter are the **apartotel** and the **cabina.** An apartotel is just what it sounds like: an apartment hotel where you'll get a full kitchen and one or two bedrooms, along with daily maid service. _Cabinas_ are Costa Rica's version of cheap vacation lodging. They're very basic and inexpensive—often just cinder-block buildings divided into small rooms. Occasionally, you'll find a _cabina_ in which the units are actually cabins, but these are a rarity. _Cabinas_ often have clothes-washing sinks (_pilas_), and some have kitchenettes. They cater primarily to Tico families on vacation.

STAYING HEALTHY

Staying healthy on a trip to Costa Rica is predominantly a matter of being a little cautious about what you eat and drink, and using common sense. Know your physical limits and don't overexert yourself in the ocean, on hikes, or during athletic activities. Many beaches have dangerous riptides, and drownings are sadly common. As you climb above 3,000m (10,000 ft.), you may feel the effects of altitude sickness. Be sure to drink plenty of water and not overexert yourself. Limit your exposure to the sun, especially during the first few days of your trip and, thereafter, from 11am to 2pm. Use sunscreen with a high protection factor, and apply it liberally. Remember that children need more protection than adults. The water in San José and most of the country's heavily visited spots is generally safe to drink, but if you want to take no chances, stick to bottled water.

General Availability of Healthcare

In general, Costa Rica has a high level of medical care and services for a developing nation. The better private hospitals and doctors in San José are very good. In fact, given the relatively low-cost nature of care and treatment, a sizable number of foreigners come to Costa Rica each year for elective surgery and other care.

Pharmacies are widely available, and generally well stocked. In most cases, you will not need a doctor's script to fill or refill a prescription.

If You Get Sick

Your hotel front desk should be your best source of information and assistance if you get sick while in Costa Rica. In addition, your local consulate in Costa Rica can provide a list of area doctors who speak English. I list the best hospitals in San José in "Fast Facts: San José," in chapter 6 (p 128); these have the most modern facilities in the country. Most state-run hospitals and walk-in clinics around the country have emergency rooms that can treat most conditions, although you're better off going to a private hospital in San José if that's an option.

Regional Health Concerns

TROPICAL ILLNESSES Your chance of contracting any serious tropical disease in Costa Rica is slim, especially if you stick to the beaches or traditional spots for visitors. However, malaria, dengue fever, leptospirosis, and zika all exist in Costa Rica, so it's a good idea to know what they are.

Malaria is found in the lowlands on both coasts and in the Northern Zone. Although it's rarely found in urban areas, it's still a problem in remote wooded regions and along the Caribbean coast. Malaria prophylaxes are available, but several have side effects, and others are of questionable effectiveness. Consult your doctor regarding what is currently considered the best preventive treatment for malaria. Be sure to ask whether a recommended drug will cause you to be hypersensitive to the sun; it would be a shame to come down here for the beaches and then

red TIDES

Also known as harmful algal blooms (HAB), red tides are a phenomenon occurring in oceans worldwide. Red tides can arise from natural or man-made causes. Some are seasonal, while others may be provoked by pollution or chemical waste. Some are toxic and others are benign. Harmful algal blooms are often accompanied by dead fish and sea life. Rising sea temperatures have been cited as one cause of an increase in HAB occurrences, although they have been recorded in frigid arctic waters. Some can turn ocean waters a deep red, while color changes from deep green to murky brown have also been documented. Some, in fact, do not affect the water color at all. Tidal changes have no causal link to red tides, so the name is a bit of a misnomer.

All red tides are characterized by rapid and massive reproduction of algae or phytoplankton. Pacific-coast beaches have been hardest hit, especially those along the Nicoya Peninsula. Still, red tides have been recorded all along both of the country's coastlines. In Costa Rica, red tides tend to be more common near the start of the rainy season. Most only last a day or so, although some have lasted as long as a couple of weeks. It's extremely hard to tell for certain if a red tide is a dangerous algal bloom or not. If you notice a deep red or unnatural brown tint to the water, it is best to refrain from swimming. Due to dark sands and benign river runoff, many of Costa Rica's beaches often appear to have brownish water that is perfectly safe for swimming. Ask around locally to find out the current water conditions.

have to hide under an umbrella the whole time. Because malaria-carrying mosquitoes usually come out at night, you should do as much as possible to avoid being bitten after dark. If you are in a malaria-prone area, wear long pants and long sleeves, use insect repellent, and either sleep under a mosquito net or burn mosquito coils.

Of greater concern is **dengue fever,** which has had periodic outbreaks in Latin America since the mid-1990s. Dengue fever is similar to malaria and is spread by an aggressive daytime mosquito. This mosquito seems to be most common in lowland urban areas, and Puntarenas, Liberia, and Limón have been the worst-hit cities in Costa Rica. Dengue is also known as "bone-break fever" because it is usually accompanied by severe body aches. The first infection with dengue fever will make you very sick but should cause no serious damage. However, a second infection with a different strain of the dengue virus can lead to internal hemorrhaging and could be life-threatening.

One tropical fever you should know about is **leptospirosis.** There are more than 200 strains of leptospires, animal-borne bacteria transmitted to humans via contact with drinking, swimming, or bathing water. This bacterial infection is easily treated with antibiotics; however, it can quickly cause very high fever and chills, and should be treated promptly.

If you develop a high fever accompanied by severe body aches, nausea, diarrhea, or vomiting during or shortly after a visit to Costa Rica, consult a physician as soon as possible.

Costa Rica has historically had very few outbreaks of cholera. This is largely due to an extensive public-awareness campaign that has promoted good hygiene and increased sanitation. Your chances of contracting cholera while you're here are very slight.

The **zika virus** became a major concern throughout tropical areas of Latin America in 2016. The tropical mosquito borne virus is spread by day flying mosquitoes (including Ae. aegypti and Ae. albopictus) and is generally so mild that 80% of people who contract it never know they have it. Symptoms are similar to dengue fever, normally lasting for two days to six days, however, zika is particularly dangerous for women who are pregnant or planning to become pregnant as the virus poses a serious health problem for fetuses, especially in the first trimester. Before traveling to affected areas, it is best to consult your family's physician and other doctors if you are pregnant or planning to become pregnant.

DIETARY RED FLAGS Even though the water in San José and most popular destinations in Costa Rica is generally safe, and even if you're careful to buy bottled water, order *frescos en leche* (fruit shakes made with milk rather than water), and drink your soft drink without ice cubes, you still might encounter some intestinal difficulties. Most of this is just due to tender stomachs coming into contact with slightly more aggressive Latin American intestinal flora. In extreme cases of diarrhea or intestinal discomfort, it's worth taking a stool sample to a lab for analysis. The results will usually pinpoint the amoebic or parasitic culprit, which can then be readily treated with available over-the-counter medicines.

Except in the most established and hygienic of restaurants, it's also advisable to avoid *ceviche,* a raw seafood salad, especially if it has any shellfish in it. It could be home to any number of bacterial critters.

BUGS, BITES & OTHER WILDLIFE CONCERNS Although Costa Rica has Africanized bees (the notorious "killer bees" of fact and fable) and several species of venomous snakes, your chances of being bitten are minimal, especially if you refrain from sticking your hands into hives or under rocks in the forest. If you know that you're allergic to bee stings, consult your doctor before traveling.

At the beaches, you'll probably be bitten by *purrujas* (sand fleas), especially on the lower part of your legs. These nearly invisible insects leave an itchy welt. Try not to scratch because this can lead to open sores and infections. *Purrujas* are most active at sunrise and sunset, so you might want to cover up or avoid the beaches at these times.

Snakebites are rare, and the majority of snakes in Costa Rica are nonvenomous. If you do encounter a snake, keep your distance. Avoid sticking your hands under rocks, branches, and fallen trees, and avoid brushing up against vegetation.

Scorpions, black widow spiders, tarantulas, bullet ants, and biting insects of many types can all be found in Costa Rica. In general, they are not nearly the danger or nuisance most visitors fear. Watch where you stick your hands; in addition, you might want to shake out your clothes and shoes before putting them on to avoid any painful surprises.

RIPTIDES   Many of Costa Rica's beaches have riptides: strong currents that can drag swimmers out to sea. A riptide occurs when water that has been dumped on the shore by strong waves forms a channel back out to open water. If you get caught in a riptide, you can't escape the current by swimming toward shore; it's like trying to swim upstream in a river. To break free of the current, swim parallel to shore and use the energy of the waves to help you get back to the beach.

[Fast FACTS] COSTA RICA

Area Codes   Costa Rica doesn't have area codes. All phone numbers are eight-digits numbers.

Business Hours

Banks are usually open Monday through Friday from 9am to 4pm, though many have begun to offer extended hours. Post offices are usually open Monday through Friday from 8am to 5:30pm, and Saturday from 7:30am to noon. (In small towns, post offices may close on Sat.) Stores are generally open Monday through Saturday from 9am to 6pm (many close for 1 hr. at lunch), but stores in modern malls generally stay open until 8 or 9pm and don't close for lunch. Most bars are open until 1 or 2am, although some go later.

Customs   Visitors to Costa Rica are permitted to bring in all manner of items for personal use, including cameras, video cameras tape recorders, personal computers, and music players. Customs officials in Costa Rica seldom check tourists' luggage.

Doctors   Your hotel front desk will be your best source of info on what to do if you get sick and where to go for treatment. Most have the number of a trusted doctor on hand. Your local consulate in Costa Rica can also provide a list of area doctors who speak English. Also see "Staying Healthy," p 602.

Drinking Laws   Alcoholic beverages are sold every day of the week throughout the year, although some cantons ban

the sale of alcohol in the days before Easter. The legal drinking age is 18, though it's sporadically enforced. Liquor, beer, and wine is sold in liquor stores called *licoreras,* and in most supermarkets and convenience stores.

Electricity   The standard in Costa Rica is the same as in the United States and Canada: 110 volts AC (60 cycles). However, three-pronged outlets can be scarce, so it's helpful to bring along an adapter.

Embassies & Consulates   The following are located in San José: **United States Embassy,** Calle 98 and Avenida Central, Pavas (© **2519-2000;** https://cr.usembassy.gov); **Canadian Embassy,** Oficentro Ejecutivo La Sabana,

Edificio 5 (www.costarica.
gc.ca; ✆ **2242-4400**); and
British Embassy, Edificio
Colón, 11th Floor, Paseo
Colón between calles 38
and 40 (www.gov.uk/
government/world/
costa-rica; ✆ **2258-2025**).
San José does not have an
Australian, Irish, or New
Zealand embassy.

Emergencies   For any
emergency, dial ✆ **911**
(which should have an
English-speaking operator);
for an ambulance, call
✆ **1028;** and to report a
fire, call ✆ **1118.** If 911
doesn't work, contact the
police at ✆ **2222-1365** or
2221-5337, and hopefully
they can find someone who
speaks English.

Family Travel   Hotels
in Costa Rica often give
discounts for children, and
allow children to stay for
free in a parent's room. Still,
these discounts and the
cutoff ages vary according
to the hotel; in general,
don't assume that your kids
can stay in your room for
free.

Some hotels, villas, and
cabinas come equipped
with kitchenettes or full
kitchen facilities. These can
be a real money-saver for
those traveling with
children.

Hotels offering regular,
dependable babysitting
service are few and far
between. If you will need
babysitting, make sure that
your hotel offers it, and be
sure to ask if the sitters are
bilingual. In many cases,

they are not. This is usually
not a problem with infants
and toddlers, but it can be
for older children.

Insurance   For informa-
tion on traveler's insurance,
trip-cancellation insurance,
and medical insurance
while traveling, visit www.
frommers.com/tips/
health-and-travel-insurance.

Internet & Wi-Fi
Internet cafes were once
ubiquitous but are increasingly rare, as most hotels
and restaurants offer high-
speed Wi-Fi access, usually
for free.

Language   Spanish is
the official language of
Costa Rica. However, in
most tourist areas, you'll be
surprised by how well Costa
Ricans speak English. Additionally, English is widely
spoken along the Carib-
bean coast. See chapter 15
for some key Spanish terms
and phrases.

Legal Aid   If you need
legal help, your best bet is
to first contact your local
embassy or consulate. See
"Embassies & Consulates,"
above, for contact details.

LGBT Travelers
Costa Rica is a Catholic,
conservative, macho coun-
try where public displays of
same-sex affection are rare
and considered somewhat
shocking. However, gay and
lesbian tourism to Costa
Rica is quite robust, and
LGBT travelers are generally
treated with respect and
should not experience any
harassment.

Mail   At press time, it
cost C600 to mail a letter to
the United States, and C650
to Europe. You can get
stamps at post offices and
at some gift shops in large
hotels. Given the Costa
Rican postal service's track
record, I recommend pay-
ing an extra C850 to have
anything of any value certified. Better yet, use an
international courier service
or wait until you get home
to post it. Contact **DHL,** on
Paseo Colón between calles
30 and 32 (www.dhl.com;
✆ **2209-6000**); **EMS Courier,** with desks at most post
offices (www.correos.go.cr;
✆ **2223-9766**); **FedEx** is
based in Heredia but will
arrange pickup anywhere in
the metropolitan area (www.
fedex.com; ✆ **2239-0576**);
or **United Parcel Service,**
in Pavas (www.ups.com;
✆ **2290-2828**).

Medical Require-
ments   No shots or inoc-
ulations are required to
enter Costa Rica. The
exception to this is for those
who have recently been
traveling in a country or
region known to have yel-
low fever. In this case, proof
of a yellow fever vaccination
is required. Also see "Staying Healthy," p 602 in this
chapter.

Mobile Phones
Costa Rica uses **GSM**
(Global System for Mobile
Communications) networks.
If your cellphone is on a
GSM system, and you have
a world-capable multiband
phone, you should be able

to make and receive calls in Costa Rica. Just call your wireless provider and ask for "international roaming" to be activated on your account. Per-minute charges can be high, though—up to $5 in Costa Rica, depending upon your plan.

Costa Rica has three main cellphone companies and a couple of smaller outfits. The main providers are the government-run ICE/Kolbi and the international giants Claro and Movistar. All offer a range of prepaid and traditional plans.

You can purchase a **prepaid SIM card for an unlocked GSM phone** at the airport and at shops all around the country. A prepaid SIM card costs around $2 to $4. Cards usually come loaded with some minutes, and you can buy additional minutes separately either online or at cellphone stores and ICE offices around the country.

If you don't have your own unlocked GSM phone, you might consider buying one here. Shops around the country offer basic, functional phones with a local line, beginning at around $35.

In addition, most of the major car-rental agencies offer cellphone rentals. Rates run around $5 to $7 per day or $25 to $50 per week for the rental, with charges of 50¢ to $1.50 per minute for local calls and $1 to $3 per minute for international calls.

Money & Costs The unit of currency in Costa Rica is the **colón.** In this book, prices are listed in the currency you are most likely to see quoted. Hence, nearly all hotel prices and most tour and transportation prices are listed in dollars, since the hotels, airlines, tour agencies, and transport companies quote their prices in dollars. Many restaurants do, as well. Still, a good many restaurants, as well as taxis and other local goods and services, are advertised and quoted in colones. In those cases, prices listed are in colones (C).

The colón is divided into 100 **céntimos.** The smallest coins are white 5- and 10-colon coins, followed by gold-hued 25-, 50-, 100-, and 500-colón coins.

Paper notes come in denominations of 1,000, 2,000, 5,000, 10,000 and 20,000 colones. You might hear people refer to a "rojo" or "tucán," which are slang terms for the red 1,000- and yellow 5,000-colón bills, respectively. One-hundred-colón denominations are called "tejas," so "cinco tejas" is 500 colones.

Forged bills are not entirely uncommon. When receiving change in colones, it's a good idea to check the larger bills, which should have protective bands or hidden images that appear when held up to the light.

You can change money at all banks in Costa Rica, though you must produce your passport to do so. Because banks handle money exchanges, Costa Rica has very few exchange houses. One major exception to this is the **Global Exchange** (www.global exchange.co.cr; ☎ 2431-0686) offices at the international airports. Be forewarned that they change money at more than 10% below the official exchange rate. Airport taxis accept U.S. dollars, so there isn't necessarily any great need to exchange money the moment you arrive.

THE VALUE OF THE COLÓN VS. OTHER POPULAR CURRENCIES

Colones	Aus$	Can$	Euro (€)	NZ$	UK £	US$
570	A$1.30	C$1.34	€.90	NZ$1.45	77p	$1.00

WHAT THINGS COST IN COSTA RICA	US$	COSTA RICAN COLONES
Taxi from the airport to downtown San José	25.00–40.00	C10,000–C22,000
Double room, moderate	120.00	C68,550
Double room, inexpensive	70.00	C40,000
Three-course dinner for one without wine, moderate	20.00–30.00	C11,400–C17,000
Bottle of beer	1.50–3.00	C860–C1,700
Cup of coffee	1.00–1.50	C570–C860
1 gallon/1 liter of premium gas	3.78 per gallon; 1.13 per liter	C2,160 per gallon; C645 per liter
Admission to most museums	2.00–5.00	C1,100–C2,900
Admission to most national parks	15.00	C8,570

Hotels will often exchange money as well, but they might shave a few colones off the exchange rate.

If you plan on carrying around dollars to pay for goods and services, be aware that most Costa Rican businesses, be they restaurants, convenience stores, or gas stations, will give a very unfavorable exchange rate.

Your best bet for getting colones is usually by direct withdrawal from your home account via a bank card or debit card, although check in advance if you will be assessed any fees or charges by your home bank. In general, ATMs in Costa Rica still don't add on service fees. Paying with a credit card will also get you the going bank exchange rate. But again, try to get a credit card with no foreign transaction fees.

It's extremely risky to exchange money on the streets. In addition to forged bills and short counts, street money-changers often work in teams that can leave you holding neither colones nor dollars. Also be very careful when leaving a bank. Criminals are often looking for foreigners who have just withdrawn or exchanged cash.

The currency conversions provided in the "Value of the Colón vs. Other Popular Currencies" box were correct at press time. However, rates fluctuate, so before departing, consult a currency exchange website such as **www.oanda.com/ currency/converter** to check up-to-the-minute rates.

MasterCard and **Visa** are the most widely accepted credit cards in

Costa Rica, followed by **American Express**. Most hotels and restaurants accept them, especially in touristy areas. Discover and Diners Club are far less widely accepted.

Beware of hidden credit card fees while traveling. Check with your credit or debit card issuer to see what fees, if any, will be charged for overseas transactions. Fees for credit and debit cards while out of the country—even if those charges were made in U.S. dollars—can amount to 3% or more of the purchase price. Check with your bank before departing to avoid any surprise charges on your statement.

Costa Rica has a modern and widespread network of ATMs. You should find ATMs in all but the most remote tourist destinations and isolated nature lodges. In response to several "express kidnappings" in San José, in which people were taken at gunpoint to an ATM to clean out their bank accounts, some banks shut down ATM service between 10pm and 5am. Others dispense money 24 hours a day.

It's probably a good idea to change your PIN to a four-digit PIN. While many ATMs in Costa Rica will accept five- and six-digit PINs, some will only accept four-digit PINs.

Newspapers & Magazines

Costa Rica has a half-dozen or so Spanish-language dailies, and you can get *Time* magazine and several U.S. newspapers at some hotel gift shops and a few of the bookstores in San José. If you read Spanish, *La Nación* is the paper you'll want. Its "Viva" and "Tiempo Libre" sections list what's going on in the world of music, theater, dance, and more.

Packing

Be sure to pack the essentials: sunscreen, insect repellent, camera, swimsuit, a wide-brimmed hat, all prescription medications, and so forth. You'll want good hiking shoes and/or beach footwear, depending upon your itinerary. It's also a good idea to bring a waterproof headlamp or flashlight and refillable water bottle. Lightweight, long-sleeved shirts and long pants are good protection from both the sun and insects. Surfers use "rash guards," quick-drying Lycra or polyester shirts, which provide great protection from the sun while swimming.

If you're just heading to Guanacaste between December and March, you won't need anything for the rain. Otherwise, bring an umbrella and rain gear. Most high-end hotels provide umbrellas. If you plan to do any wildlife-viewing, bringing your own binoculars is a good idea, as is a field guide (p 31).

Passports

Citizens of the United States, Canada, Great Britain, and most European nations may visit Costa Rica for a maximum of 90 days. No visa is necessary, but you must have a valid passport. Citizens of Australia, Ireland, and New Zealand can enter the country without a visa and stay for 30 days, although once in the country, visitors can apply for an extension.

It is advised to always have at least one or two consecutive blank pages in your passport to allow space for visas and stamps that need to appear together. It is also important to note when your passport expires. Many countries require your passport to have at least 6 months left before its expiration in order to allow you in.

Police

In most cases, dial ☎ **911** for the police, and you should be able to get someone who speaks English on the line. Other numbers for the **Judicial Police** are ☎ **2222-1365** and 2221-5337. The numbers for the **Traffic Police (Policía de Tránsito)** are ☎ **800/8726-7486** toll-free nationwide, or 2222-9245.

Safety

Although most of Costa Rica is safe, petty crime and robberies committed against tourists are endemic. San José, in particular, is known for its pickpockets. A woman should keep a tight grip on her purse (keep it tucked under your arm). Thieves also target gold chains, cameras and video cameras, prominent jewelry, and nice sunglasses. Be sure not to leave valuables unsecured in your hotel room, or unattended—even for a moment—on the beach. Given the high rate of stolen passports in Costa Rica, mostly as collateral damage in a typical pickpocketing or room robbery, it is recommended that, whenever possible, you leave your passport in a hotel safe, and travel with a photocopy of the pertinent pages. Avoid parking a car on the street in Costa Rica, especially in San José; plenty of public parking lots are around the city.

Rental cars generally stand out and are easily spotted by thieves. Don't leave anything of value in a car parked on the street, not even for a moment. Be wary of solicitous strangers who stop to help you change a tire or take you to a service station. Although most are truly good Samaritans, there are bandits who prey on roadside breakdowns. See "Getting Around: By Car," p 596, for more info.

Inter-city buses are also frequent targets of stealthy thieves. Try not to check your bags into the hold of a bus if they will fit in the rack above your seat. If it can't be avoided, keep your eye on what leaves the hold. If you put your bags in an overhead rack, keep an eye on them.

Single women should use common sense and take precaution, especially after dark. Men and women should avoid walking alone at night, especially on deserted beaches or dark streets.

Senior Travelers
Be sure to mention that you're a senior when you make your travel reservations. Although it's not common policy in Costa Rica to offer senior discounts, don't be shy about asking for one anyway. You never know. Always carry some kind of identification, such as a driver's license, that shows your date of birth, especially if you've kept your youthful glow.

Many reliable agencies and organizations serve the 50-plus market. **Road Scholar,** formerly known as Elderhostel

(www.roadscholar.org; ☎ **800/454-5768** in the U.S. and Canada), arranges Costa Rica study programs for those ages 55 and older, as well as intergenerational trips good for families. **ElderTreks** (www.eldertreks. com; ☎ **800/741-7956** in the U.S. and Canada; 0808-234-1714 in the UK) offers small-group tours to Costa Rica for travelers 50 and older.

Smoking
Though many Costa Ricans smoke, smoking is prohibited in all public spaces, including restaurants, bars, offices, and such outdoor areas as public parks and bus stops.

Student Travelers
Although you won't find any discounts at the national parks, most museums and other attractions around Costa Rica do offer discounts for students. It can't hurt to ask.

Taxes
The national 13% value added tax (often written IVA in Costa Rica) is added to all goods and services. This includes hotel and restaurant bills. Restaurants also add a 10% service charge, for a total of 23% more on your bill. Some hotels add a 10% "resort fee."

The airport departure tax is $29, and must be paid prior to check-in. This is almost always incorporated into most airline ticket prices at time of purchase. If not, you will be able to pay it at check-in.

Telephones
Costa Rica has an excellent and widespread phone system. A phone call within the country costs around C15 per minute. Pay phones are relatively scarce. If you do find one, it might take a calling card or coins. Calling cards are much more practical. You can purchase calling cards in a host of gift shops and pharmacies. However, there are several competing calling-card companies, and certain cards work only with certain phones. **CHIP** calling cards work with a computer chip and just slide into specific phones, although these phones aren't widely available. Better bets are the **197** and **199** calling cards, which are sold in varying denominations. These have a scratch-off PIN and can be used from any phone in the country. Generally, the 197 cards are sold in smaller denominations and are used for local calling, while the 199 cards are deemed international and are easier to find in larger denominations. Either card can be used to make any call, provided the card can cover the cost. Another perk of the 199 cards is the fact that you can get the instructions in English. For local calls, it is often easiest to call from your hotel, although you may be charged around C150 to C300 per call.

You might also see about getting yourself a

local mobile phone; for information on this, see "Mobile Phones" (p 607).

To call Costa Rica from abroad:

1. Dial the international access code: 011 from the U.S. and Canada; 00 from the UK, Ireland, or New Zealand; or 0011 from Australia.

2. Dial the country code 506.

3. Dial the eight-digit number.

To make international calls from Costa Rica: First dial 00 and then the country code (U.S. or Canada 1, UK 44, Ireland 353, Australia 61, New Zealand 64). Next dial the area code and number. For example, if you want to call the British Embassy in Washington, D.C., you would dial 00-1-202-588-7800.

For directory assistance: Dial 1113 if you're looking for a number inside Costa Rica; dial 1024 for numbers to all other countries.

For operator assistance: If you need operator assistance in making a call, dial 1116 if you're trying to make an international call, and 0 if you want to call a number in Costa Rica.

Toll-free numbers: Numbers beginning with 0800 or 800 within Costa Rica are toll-free, but calling a 1-800 number in the States from Costa Rica is not toll-free. In fact, it costs

the same as an overseas call.

Time   Costa Rica is on Central Standard Time (same as Chicago and St. Louis), 6 hours behind Greenwich Mean Time. Costa Rica does not use daylight-saving time, so the time difference is an additional hour from early March through early November.

Tipping   Tipping is not necessary in restaurants, where a 10% service charge is always added to your bill (along with a 13% tax). If service was particularly good, you can leave a little at your own discretion, but it's not mandatory. Porters and bellhops get around C500 to C1,000 per bag. You don't need to tip a taxi driver unless the service has been superior; a tip is not usually expected.

Toilets   To find a bathroom, ask for the "baño" or the "servicio." They are marked damas (women) and hombres or caballeros (men). Public restrooms are hard to come by. You will almost never find a public restroom in a city park or downtown area. Public restrooms are usually at most national park entrances, and much less frequently inside the national park. In towns and cities, it gets much trickier, and sometimes you have to count on a hotel or restaurant. The same goes for most beaches. Bus and gas stations often have

restrooms, but many of these are pretty grim. In some restrooms around the country, especially more remote and natural areas, it's common practice not to flush any foreign matter, aside from your business, down the toilet. This includes toilet paper, sanitary napkins, cigarette butts, and so forth. You will usually find a little sign advising you of this practice in the restroom.

Travelers with Disabilities   Although Costa Rica does have a law mandating Equality of Opportunities for People with Disabilities, and some facilities have been adapted, in general, there are relatively few buildings, bathrooms, public buses, or taxis specifically designed for travelers with disabilities in the country. In San José, sidewalks are particularly crowded and uneven, and they are nonexistent in most of the rest of the country. Few hotels offer wheelchair-accessible accommodations, though this is gradually changing.

Many travel agencies offer customized tours and itineraries for travelers with disabilities. Among them are **Eco Adventure International** (www.eaiadventure. com; ☏ **888/710-9453** in the U.S. and Canada); **Flying Wheels Travel** (www. flyingwheelstravel.com; ☏ **612/381-1622**); and **Accessible Journeys** (www.

disabilitytravel.com; © **800/846-4537** or 610/521-0339).

Access-Able Travel Source (www.access-able.com; © **303/232-2979**) has a comprehensive database of travel agents around the world with experience in accessible travel; destination-specific access information; and links to such resources as service animals, equipment rentals, and access guides.

Another great organization that offers a vast range of resources and assistance to travelers with disabilities is **SATH** (Society for Accessible Travel & Hospitality; www.sath.org; © **212/447-7284**).

Visitor Information

In the United States or Canada, you can get basic info on Costa Rica through the **Costa Rican Tourism Board** www.visitcostarica.com; © **866/267-8274** in the U.S. and Canada, or 2299-5827 in Costa Rica). Travelers from the United Kingdom, Australia, and New Zealand will have to rely primarily on this website, or call direct to Costa Rica, because the ICT does not have toll-free access in these countries.

You can pick up a map at the ICT's information desk at the airport when you arrive, or at its downtown San José offices (although the destination maps that come with this book are sufficient for most purposes). Perhaps the best map to have is the water-proof country map of Costa Rica put out by **Toucan Maps** (www.mapcr.com), which can be ordered directly from its website or any major online bookseller, like Amazon.com.

Water

Although the water in San José is generally safe to drink, water quality varies outside the city. Because many travelers have tender digestive tracts, you might want to play it safe: Stick to bottled drinks and avoid ice.

Women Travelers

For lack of better phrasing, Costa Rica is a typically "macho" Latin American nation. Single women can expect catcalls, hisses, whistles, and honking horns, especially in San José. In most cases, while annoying, this is harmless and intended by Tico men as a compliment. Nonetheless, women should be careful walking alone at night throughout the country. Also, see "Safety," earlier in this section.

SPANISH TERMS & PHRASES

15

T icos are pretty *tranquilo* about most things, and they tend to speak at a relaxed speed and enunciate clearly, especially when addressing a foreigner. Costa Ricans are known for saying "*Mae*," which means "Dude," but has become a form of verbal punctuation used in some circles in almost every sentence. A notable idiosyncrasy here is creating diminutives with "ico" instead of "ito" ("un poquitico")—hence the words "Tico" and "Tica" to describe Costa Rican men and women. Ticos are said to have an odd way of pronouncing the "R" at the beginning of a word, as in "Rica"—the "R" is never rolled or trilled. All in all, rest assured that if your *español* is not *buenísimo*, most Costa Ricans will speak slow, proper Spanish to you.

BASIC WORDS & PHRASES

English	Spanish	Pronunciation
Hello	Hola	**oh-lah**
Good morning	Buenos días	**bweh-nohs dee-ahs**
Good afternoon	Buenas tardes	**bweh-nas tahr-dehs**
Good night	Buenas noches	**bweh-nas noh-ches**
Hi	Buenas	**bweh-nas**
How are you?	¿Cómo está usted?	**koh-moh ehs-tah oo-sted**

English	Spanish	Pronunciation
Just fine	Muy bien	**mwee byen**
Thank you	Gracias	*grah*-**syas**
Goodbye	Adiós	**ah**-*dios*
Please	Por favor	**por fa**-*vor*
Yes	Sí	**see**
No	No	**no**
Excuse me (to get by someone)	Con permiso	**con per**-*mee*-**so**
Excuse me (to ask a question)	Disculpe	**dees**-*kool*-**peh**
Give me	Deme	*deh*-**meh**
Where is . . . ?	¿Dónde está . . . ?	*dohn*-**deh ehs**-*tah*
the station	la estación	**la ehs-tah**-*syohn*
the bus stop	la parada	**la pah**-*rah*-**dah**
the toilet	el servicio	**el ser**-*vee*-**see-oh**
Where is there . . . ?	Dónde hay . . . ?	*dohn*-**deh ai**
a hotel	un hotel	**oon oh**-*tehl*
a restaurant	un restaurante	**oon res-tau**-*rahn*-**teh**
To the right	A la derecha	**ah lah deh**-*reh*-**chah**
To the left	A la izquierda	**ah lah ees**-*kyehr*-**dah**
Straight ahead	Adelante	**ah-deh**-*lahn*-**teh**
I would like . . .	Quiero . . .	*kyeh*-**roh**
to eat	comer	**ko**-*mehr*
a room	una habitación	*oo*-**nah ah-bee-tah**-*syohn*
How much is it?	¿Cuánto es?	*kwahn*-**toh es**
When?	¿Cuándo?	*kwan*-**doh**
What?	¿Qué?	**keh**
Yesterday	Ayer	**ah**-*yehr*
Today	Hoy	**oy**
Tomorrow	Mañana	**mah**-*nyah*-**nah**
Breakfast	Desayuno	**deh-sah**-*yoo*-**noh**
Lunch	Almuerzo	**ahl**-*mwehr*-**soh**
Dinner	Cena	*seh*-**nah**
Do you speak English?	¿Habla inglés?	**ah**-blah **een**-*glehss*
I don't speak Spanish.	No hablo español.	**noh** *ahb*-**lo ehss-pah**-*nyohl*

NUMBERS

English	Spanish	Pronunciation
zero	cero	**ser-oh**
one	uno	**oo-noh**
two	dos	**dohss**
three	tres	**trehss**
four	cuatro	**kwah-troh**
five	cinco	**seen-koh**
six	seis	**sayss**
seven	siete	**syeh-teh**
eight	ocho	**oh-choh**
nine	nueve	**nweh-beh**
ten	diez	**dyehss**
eleven	once	**ohn-seh**
twelve	doce	**doh-seh**
thirteen	trece	**treh-seh**
fourteen	catorce	**kah-tohr-seh**
fifteen	quince	**keen-seh**
sixteen	dieciséis	**dyeh-see-sayss**
seventeen	diecisiete	**dyeh-see-syeh-teh**
eighteen	dieciocho	**dyeh-see-oh-choh**
nineteen	diecinueve	**dyeh-see-nweh-beh**
twenty	veinte	**bayn-teh**
thirty	treinta	**trayn-tah**
forty	cuarenta	**kwah-rehn-tah**
fifty	cincuenta	**seen-kwehn-tah**
sixty	sesenta	**seh-sehn-tah**
seventy	setenta	**seh-tehn-tah**
eighty	ochenta	**oh-chehn-tah**
ninety	noventa	**noh-behn-tah**
one hundred	cien	**syehn**
one thousand	mil	**meel**

Basic Words & Phrases

SPANISH TERMS & PHRASES

DAYS OF THE WEEK

English	Spanish	Pronunciation
Monday	lunes	*loo*-nehs
Tuesday	martes	*mahr*-tehs
Wednesday	miércoles	*myehr*-koh-lehs
Thursday	jueves	*wheh*-behs
Friday	viernes	*byehr*-nehs
Saturday	sábado	*sah*-bah-doh
Sunday	domingo	doh-*meen*-go

COSTA RICAN WORDS & PHRASES

Birra Beer

Boca Appetizer (literally "mouth")

Bomba Gas station (literally "pump")

Brete Job

Buena nota Right on

Casado Traditional lunch with meat, rice, beans, salad (literally "married," suggesting this is the kind of lunch a married man brings to work)

Chapa Stupid, clumsy

Chepe Nickname for San José

Choza House, home; also called *chante*

Chunche Knickknack; thing; "whatchamacallit"

Cien metros 100 meters, or one block

Con gusto, con mucho gusto You're welcome

De hoy en ocho A week from now

Diay Common linguistic punctuation, can mean "Gosh," "Well," or "Wow"

Estar de chicha To be angry

Fría A cold beer—una fría, por favor (literally "cold")

Fut Short for *fútbol*, or soccer

Goma Hangover

Harina Money (literally "flour")

La sele   La *Selección*, the Costa Rican national soccer team

Limpio   Broke; out of money (literally "clean")

Macha or **machita**   A blond woman

Mae   "Man" or "Dude"

Mala nota   Bummer

Mejenga   Pickup soccer game

Ponga la maría, por favor   This is how you ask a taxi driver to turn on the meter

Pulpería   A small market or convenience store

Pura paja   Pure nonsense

Pura vida   Literally, "pure life"; translates as "everything's great"

Qué torta   What a mess; what a screw-up

Si Dios quiere   God willing

Soda   A casual diner-style restaurant serving cheap food

Tica, Tico   Costa Rican

Tiquicia   Costa Rica

Tuanis   Most excellent, cool, great

Una teja   100 colones

Un rojo   1,000 colones

Un tucán   5,000 colones

Upe!   Often shouted outside a door to see if anyone is home instead of knocking

Zarpe   Last drink of the night; "one for the road"

MENU TERMS
SEAFOOD

Almejas Clams	**Lenguado** Sole
Atún Tuna	**Mejillones** Mussels
Bacalao Cod	**Ostras** Oysters
Calamares Squid	**Pargo** Snapper
Camarones Shrimp	**Pulpo** Octopus
Cangrejo Crab	**Trucha** Trout
Ceviche Marinated seafood salad	
Dorado Dolphin, mahi mahi	
Langosta Lobster	

Menu Terms

SPANISH TERMS & PHRASES

MEATS

Albóndigas Meatballs

Bistec Beefsteak

Cerdo Pork

Chicharrones Fried pork rinds

Chorizo Sausage

Chuleta Pork chop

Cordero Lamb

Costillas Ribs

Delmonico Ribeye

Jamón Ham

Lengua Tongue

Lomo Sirloin

Lomito Tenderloin

Pato Duck

Pavo Turkey

Pincho Shish-kebab

Pollo Chicken

Salchicha Sausage, hot dog

VEGETABLES

Aceitunas Olives

Alcachofa Artichoke

Berenjena Eggplant

Cebolla Onion

Elote Corn on the cob

Ensalada Salad

Espinacas Spinach

Frijoles Beans

Lechuga Lettuce

Maíz Corn

Palmito Heart of palm

Papa Potato

Pepino Cucumber

Tomate Tomato

Yuca Yucca, cassava, or manioc

Zanahoria Carrot

FRUITS

Aguacate Avocado

Banano Banana

Carambola Star fruit

Cereza Cherry

Ciruela Plum

Durazno Peach

Frambuesa Raspberry

Fresa Strawberry

Granadilla Sweet passion fruit

Limón Lemon or lime

Mango Mango

Manzana Apple

Maracuya Tart passion fruit

Melón Melon

Mora Blackberry

Naranja Orange

Papaya Papaya

Piña Pineapple

Plátano Plantain

Sandía Watermelon

Toronja Grapefruit

BASICS

Aceite Oil

Ajo Garlic

Arreglado Small meat sandwich

Azúcar Sugar

Casado Plate of the day

Gallo Corn tortilla topped with meat or chicken

Gallo pinto Rice and beans

Hielo Ice

Mantequilla Butter

Miel Honey

Mostaza Mustard

Natilla Sour cream

Olla de carne Meat and vegetable soup

Pan Bread

Patacones Fried plantain chips

Picadillo Chopped vegetable side dish

Pimienta Pepper

Queso Cheese

Sal Salt

Tamal Filled cornmeal pastry

Tortilla Flat corn pancake

DRINKS

Agua purificada Purified water

Agua con gas Sparkling water

Agua sin gas Plain water

Bebida Drink

Café Coffee

Café con leche Coffee with milk

Cerveza Beer

Chocolate caliente Hot chocolate

Jugo Juice

Leche Milk

Natural Fruit juice

Natural con leche Milkshake

Refresco Soft drink

Ron Rum

Té Tea

Trago Alcoholic drink

OTHER RESTAURANT TERMS

Al grill Grilled

Al horno Oven-baked

Al vapor Steamed

Asado Roasted

Caliente Hot

Cambio or **vuelto** Change

Cocido Cooked

Comida Food

Congelado Frozen

Crudo Raw

El baño Toilet

Frío Cold

Frito Fried

Grande Big or large

La cuenta The check

Medio Medium

Medio rojo Medium rare

Muy cocido Well-done

Pequeño Small

Poco cocido or **rojo** Rare

Tres cuartos Medium-well-done

OTHER USEFUL TERMS

HOTEL TERMS

Abanico Fan

Aire acondicionado Air-conditioning

Almohada Pillow

Baño Bathroom

Baño privado Private bathroom

Caja de seguridad Safe

Calefacción Heating

Cama Bed

Cobija Blanket

Colchón Mattress

Cuarto or **Habitación** Room

Escritorio Desk

Habitación simple/sencilla Single room

Habitación doble Double room

Habitación triple Triple room

Llave Key

Mosquitero Mosquito net

Sábanas Sheets

Seguro de puerta Door lock

Silla Chair

Telecable Cable TV

Ventilador Fan

TRAVEL TERMS

Aduana Customs

Aeropuerto Airport

Avenida Avenue

Avión Airplane

Aviso Warning

Bote Boat

Bus Bus

Cajero ATM

Calle Street

Cheques viajeros Traveler's checks

Correo Mail, or post office

Cuadra City block

Dinero Money

Embajada Embassy

Embarque Boarding

Entrada Entrance

Equipaje Luggage

Este East

Frontera Border

Lancha Boat

Norte North

Occidente West

Oeste West

Oriente East

Pasaporte Passport

Plata Money

Puerta de salida or **puerta de embarque** Boarding gate

Salida Exit

Sur South

Tarjeta de embarque Boarding pass

Vuelo Flight

SPANISH TERMS & PHRASES | Other Useful Terms

EMERGENCY TERMS

Ambulancia Ambulance

¡Auxilio! Help!

Bomberos Firefighters

Clínica Clinic or hospital

Déjame en paz Leave me alone

Doctor or **médico** Doctor

Emergencia Emergency

Enfermera Nurse

Enfermo/enferma Sick

Farmacia Pharmacy

Fuego or **incendio** Fire

Hospital Hospital

Ladrón Thief

Peligroso Dangerous

Policía Police

¡Váyase! Go away!

Index

623

Restaurants